# GREAT ATHLETES

## RACING & INDIVIDUAL SPORTS

# GREAT ATHLETES

## RACING & INDIVIDUAL SPORTS

*Edited by*
**The Editors of Salem Press**

*Special Consultant*
**Rafer Johnson**

SALEM PRESS
Pasadena, California   Hackensack, New Jersey

*Editor in Chief:* Dawn P. Dawson

| | |
|---|---|
| *Editorial Director:* Christina J. Moose | *Photo Editor:* Cynthia Breslin Beres |
| *Managing Editor:* R. Kent Rasmussen | *Acquisitions Editor:* Mark Rehn |
| *Manuscript Editor:* Christopher Rager | *Page Design and Layout:* James Hutson |
| *Research Supervisor:* Jeffry Jensen | *Additional Layout:* Frank Montaño and Mary Overell |
| *Production Editor:* Andrea Miller | *Editorial Assistant:* Brett Weisberg |

*Cover photo:* David Davies/PA Photos/Landov

**Library of Congress Cataloging-in-Publication Data**

Great athletes / edited by The Editors of Salem Press ; special consultant Rafer Johnson.
 p.  cm.
Includes bibliographical references and index.
 ISBN 978-1-58765-473-2 (set : alk. paper) — ISBN 978-1-58765-482-4 (games, races, etc. : alk. paper)
1. Athletes—Biography—Dictionaries. I. Johnson, Rafer, 1935- II. Salem Press.
 GV697.A1G68 2009
 796.0922—dc22

 [B]

2009021905

First Printing

PRINTED IN THE UNITED STATES OF AMERICA

# *Contents*

# Publisher's Note

*Great Athletes: Racing and Individual Sports* is part of Salem Press's greatly expanded and redesigned *Great Athletes* series, which also includes self-contained volumes on baseball, basketball, boxing and soccer, football, golf and tennis, and Olympic sports. The full 13-volume series presents articles on the lives, sports careers, and unique achievements of 1,470 outstanding competitors and champions in the world of sports. These athletes—many of whom have achieved world renown—represent more than 75 different nations and territories and more than 80 different sports. Their stories are told in succinct, 1,000-word-long profiles accessible in tone and style to readers in grades 7 and up.

The 13 *Great Athletes* volumes, which include a cumulative index volume, are built on the work of three earlier Salem Press publications designed for middle and high school readers—the 20 slender volumes of *The Twentieth Century: Great Athletes* (1992), their 3-volume supplement (1994), and the 8 stouter volumes of *Great Athletes, Revised* (2002). This new 13-volume edition retains articles on every athlete covered in those earlier editions and adds more than 415 entirely new articles—a 40 percent increase—to bring the overall total to 1,470 articles.

The present volume adds 42 new articles to the 95 in the previous edition to cover a total of 137 athletes—an increase of 44 percent over the previous edition. The content of other articles has been reviewed and updated as necessary, with many articles substantially revised, expanded, or replaced, and the bibliographical citations for virtually all articles have been updated. Information in every article is current up to the beginning of Spring, 2009.

## Criteria for Inclusion

*Great Athletes: Racing and Individual Sports* is a composite volume that brings together athletes from a wide variety of sports. With the exception of various forms of auto and horse racing, most of these sports lack the large audiences and extensive media coverage of the sports featured in other *Great Athletes* volumes. The lesser-known racing sports include bicycle and powerboat racing, non-Olympic

yachting, and even dog-sledding. Individual sports include billiards, bodybuilding, bowling, chess, mountaineering, rodeo, sumo wresting, triathlon, and waterskiing.

This is an especially interesting volume. In addition to covering a wide diversity of sports, it presents stories that are often even more compelling than those of elite athletes in better-known sports because many of its athletes are driven by goals other than the promise of great financial rewards or fame. Moreover, because many of these athletes are not well known, readers will find here a great deal of information not readily available elsewhere.

In selecting new names to add to *Great Athletes: Racing and Individual Sports*, first consideration was given to athletes whose extraordinary achievements have made their names household words in North America, such as race car drivers Jeff Burton and Dale Earnhardt, Jr. Consideration was next given to less established current athletes who appear destined for future greatness, such as race car drivers Lewis Hamilton and Danica Patrick and surfer Kelly Slater. Adding new sports was also a goal, and this edition of *Great Athletes* is the first with articles on angling (Roland Martin), BMX racing (Dave Mirra), and skateboarding (Tony Hawk).

## Organization

Each article covers the life and career of a single athlete, all of whose names are arranged in one alphabetical stream. All articles are accompanied by statistical tables, and most are accompanied by photographs of their subjects. Every article also lists up-to-date bibliographical notes under the heading "Additional Sources." These sections list from three to five readily available books and articles containing information pertinent to the athlete and sport covered in the article. Appendixes at the end of the volume contain additional sources in published books and Web sites.

Averaging three pages in length, each article is written in clear language and presented in a uniform, easily readable format. All articles are divided into four subheaded sections that cover the athlete's life and achievements chronologically.

- *Early Life* presents such basic biographical information as vital dates, parentage, siblings, and early education. It also sketches the social milieu in which the athlete grew up and discusses other formative experiences.

- *The Road to Excellence* picks up where the athlete's earliest serious involvement in sports began. This section describes experiences and influences that shaped the subject's athletic prowess and propelled the athlete toward greatness. These sections also often discuss obstacles—such as poverty, discrimination, and physical disabilities—that many great athletes have had to overcome.

- *The Emerging Champion* traces the subject's advance from the threshold of sports stardom to higher levels of achievement. This section explains the characteristics and circumstances that combined to make the athlete among the best in the world in his or her sport.

- *Continuing the Story* tracks the athlete's subsequent career, examining how the athlete may have set new goals and had achievements that inspired others. This section also offers insights into the athlete's life away from sports. Readers will also learn about the innovations and contributions that athletes have made to their sports and, in many cases, to society at large.

- *Summary* recapitulates the subject's story, paying special attention to honors that the subject has won and to the human qualities that have made the athlete special in the world of sports.

## Appendixes

At the back of this volume, readers will find 14 appendixes, most of which are entirely new to this edition. The appendixes are arranged under these two broad headings:

- *Resources* contains a bibliography of recently published books on sports covered in this volume, a categorized listing of sites on the World Wide Web relevant to these sports, a Glossary defining most of the specialized terms used in essays, and a Time Line that lists names of all the athletes covered in essays in order of their birth dates.

- *All-Time Great Athletes* includes lists of hall of fame members for 5 different sports and 5 lists of all-time greats and racing champions.

The *Cumulative Indexes* volume, which accompanies the full *Great Athletes* series, includes every appendix found in this and other volumes on specific sports, *plus* additional appendixes containing information that pertains to all sports. These appendixes include a general bibliography, a comprehensive Web site list, a Time Line integrating the names of all 1,470 athletes in *Great Athletes*, 2 lists of the greatest athletes of the twentieth century, 3 multisport halls of fame, and 10 different athlete-of-the-year awards.

## Indexes

Following the Appendixes in *Great Athletes: Racing and Individual Sports*, readers will find three indexes listing athletes by their names, countries, and sports. Because some athletes have competed in more than one sport, readers may wish also to consult the *Cumulative Indexes* volume. Its sport, country, and name indexes list all the athletes covered in the full *Great Athletes* series.

## Acknowledgments

Once again, Salem Press takes great pleasure in thanking the 383 scholars and experts who wrote and updated the articles making *Great Athletes* possible. Their names can be found at the ends of the articles they have written and in the list of contributors that follows the "Introduction." We also take immense pleasure in again thanking our special consultant, Rafer Johnson, for bringing his unique insights to this project. As an Olympic champion and world record-holder in track and field's demanding decathlon, he has experienced an extraordinarily broad range of physical and mental challenges at the highest levels of competition. Moreover, he has a lifetime of experience working with, and closely observing, athletes at every level—from five-year-old soccer players to Olympic and professional champions. He truly understands what constitutes athletic greatness and what is required to achieve it. For this reason, readers will not want to overlook his "Introduction."

## Acronyms Used in Articles

Salem's general practice is to use acronyms only after they have been explained within each essay. Because of the frequency with which many terms appear in *Great Athletes: Racing and Individual Sports*, that practice is partly suspended for the acronyms listed here:

CART  Championship Auto Racing Teams

ESPN  Entertainment and Sports Programming Network

NASCAR  National Association for Stock Car Auto Racing

PBA  Professional Bowlers Association

WPBA  Women's Professional Bowling Association

# Introduction

Five decades after reaching my own pinnacle of success in sports, I still get a thrill watching other athletes perform. I have competed with and against some of the greatest athletes in the world, watched others up close and from a distance, and read about still others. I admire the accomplishments of all of them, for I know something of what it takes to achieve greatness in sports, and I especially admire those who inspire others.

This revised edition of *Great Athletes* provides a wonderful opportunity for young readers to learn about the finest athletes of the modern era of sports. Reading the stories of the men and women in these pages carries me back to my own youth, when I first began playing games and became interested in sports heroes. Almost all sports interested me, but I gravitated to baseball, basketball, football, and track and field. Eventually, I dedicated most of my young adult years to track and field's decathlon, which I loved because its ten events allowed me to use many different skills.

Throughout those years, one thing remained constant: I wanted to *win*. To do that meant being the best that I could be. I wondered what I could learn from the lives of great athletes. From an early age I enjoyed reading about sports champions and wondered how they did as well as they did. What traits and talents did the greatest of them have? I gradually came to understand that the essence of greatness in sports lies in competition. In fact, the very word *athlete* itself goes back to a Greek word for "competitor." Being competitive is the single most important attribute any athlete can have, but other traits are important, too. Readers may gain insights into the athletes covered in these volumes by considering the ten events of the decathlon as symbols of ten traits that contribute to athletic greatness. All champions have at least a few of these traits; truly great champions have most of them.

## Speed and Quickness

Decathlon events are spread over two days, with five events staged on each day. The first event is always the 100-meter dash—one of the most glamor-

ous events in track and field. Men and women—such as Usain Bolt and Florence Griffith-Joyner—who capture its world records are considered the fastest humans on earth. In a race that lasts only a few seconds, speed is everything, and there is no room for mistakes.

Appropriately, speed is the first of the three standards of athletic excellence expressed in the Olympic motto, *Citius, altius, fortius* (faster, higher, stronger). Its importance in racing sports such as cycling, rowing, running, speed skating, swimming, and the triathlon is obvious: Athletes who reach the finish line soonest win; those who arrive later lose. Speed is also important in every sport that requires moving around a lot, such as baseball, basketball, boxing, football, handball, soccer, tennis, volleyball, water polo, and virtually all the events of track and field. The best athletes in these sports are usually fast.

Athletes who lack speed generally make up for it in other kinds of quickness. For example, while running speed has helped make some football quarterbacks—such as Vince Young—great, some quarterbacks who are slow afoot have achieved greatness with other forms of quickness. Joe Namath is an example. Although he was embarrassingly slow on his feet, he read opposing teams' defenses so fast that he could make lightning-quick decisions and release his passes faster than almost any other quarterback who played the game.

As important as speed is, there are a few sports in which it means little. Billiards, bowling, and golf, for example, all permit competitors to take considerable time responding to opponents' moves. Even so, speed can be important where one may least expect it. For example, major chess competitions are clocked, and making moves too slowly can cost players games.

## Courage

The decathlon's second event, the long jump, represents one of the purest contests in sports: Competitors simply run up to a mark and jump as far as they can. Each jumper gets several tries, and only the best marks matter. While it sounds simple, it involves critical little things that can go wrong and ruin one's chance of winning. When the great Jesse Owens jumped in the 1936 Olympics in Berlin, for example, he missed his takeoff mark so many times that he risked disqualification. What saved him was the encouragement of a rival German jumper, who advised him to start his jump from well behind the regular takeoff mark. It takes courage to overcome the fear of making mistakes and concentrate on jumping. It also takes courage to overcome the fear of injury.

A great athlete may have abundant courage but rarely need to call upon it. However, most truly great athletes eventually face moments when they would fail if their courage abandoned them. In fact, courage is often what separates being good from being great. True courage should not be confused with the absence of fear, for it is the ability to overcome fear, including the very natural fears of injury and pain. A wonderful example is gymnast Kerri Strug's amazing spirit in the 1996 Olympics. Ignoring the pain of torn ligaments and a serious ankle sprain, she helped the U.S. women win a team gold medal by performing her final vault at great personal risk.

Some sports challenge athletes with real and persistent threats of serious injuries and even death. Among the most dangerous are alpine skiing, auto racing, boxing, football, horse racing, mountaineering, and rodeo—all of which have killed and disabled many fine athletes. No one can achieve greatness in such sports without exceptional courage.

Consider also the courage required to step up to bat against a baseball pitcher who throws hardballs mere inches away from your head at speeds of more than ninety miles an hour. Or, imagine preparing to dive from atop a 10-meter platform, resting only on your toes, with your heels projecting over the edge, knowing that your head will pass within inches of the rock-hard edge of the platform. Greg Louganis once cut his head open on such a dive. After he had his scalp stitched up, he returned to continue diving into a pool of water colored pink by his own blood. He won the competition.

Another kind of courage is needed to perform in the face of adversity that may have nothing to do with sport itself. The best known example of that kind of courage is the immortal Jackie Robinson, who broke the color line in baseball in 1947. As the first African American player in the modern major leagues, Jackie faced criticism, verbal harassment, and even physical abuse almost everywhere he played. He not only persevered but also had a career that would have been regarded as exceptional even if his color had never been an issue.

## Strength

The shot put, the decathlon's third event, requires many special traits, but the most obvious is strength. The metal ball male shot putters heave weighs 16 pounds—more than an average bowling ball. Agility, balance, and speed are all important to the event, but together they can accomplish nothing without great strength. Strength is also the third standard expressed in the Olympic motto, *Citius, altius, fortius.*

Strength is especially valuable in sports that put competitors in direct physical contact with each other—sports such as basketball, boxing, football, and wrestling. Whenever athletes push and pull against each other, the stronger generally prevail. Strength is also crucial in sports requiring lifting, pulling, pushing, paddling, or propelling objects, or controlling vehicles or animals. Such sports include auto racing, baseball and softball, bodybuilding and weightlifting, canoeing and kayaking, golf, horse racing, rowing, and all track and field throwing events.

One sport in which the role of strength has never been underestimated is wrestling. One of the most impressive demonstrations of strength in the sport occurred at the 2000 Olympic Games at Sydney when Rulon Gardner, in a performance of a lifetime, defeated former Olympic champion Aleksandr Karelin in the super-heavyweight class of Greco-Roman wrestling.

## Visualization

Visualization is the ability to see what one needs to do before actually doing it. Perhaps no sport better exemplifies its importance than the high jump—the decathlon's fourth event. In contrast to the long jump and throwing events—in which competitors strive to maximize distance in every effort, the high jump (like the pole vault) sets a bar at a fixed height that competitors must clear. Before jumping, they take time to study the bar and visualize what they must do to clear it. If the bar is set at 7 feet, a jump of 6 feet 11¾ inches fails; a jump of 8 feet succeeds, but counts only for 7 feet. To conserve strength for later jumps, jumpers must carefully calculate how much effort to exert at each height, and to do this, they must be able to visualize.

Great baseball and softball batters also visualize well. Before pitches even reach the plate, batters see the balls coming and visualize their bats hitting them. Likewise, great golfers see their balls landing on the greens before they even swing. Soccer players, such as Ronaldo, see the balls going into the goal before they even kick them. Billiard players, such as Jeanette Lee, see all the balls moving on the table before they even touch the cue balls. Bowlers, like Lisa Wagner, see the pins tumbling down before they release their balls.

Visualization is especially important to shooters, such as Lones Wigger, and archers, such as Denise Parker and Jay Barrs, who know exactly what their targets look like, as well as the spots from where they will fire, before they even take aim. In contrast to most other sports, they can practice in conditions almost identical to those in which they compete. However, the athletes against whom they compete have the same advantage, so the edge usually goes to those who visualize better.

Players in games such as basketball, hockey, soccer, and water polo fire upon fixed targets from constantly changing positions—often in the face of opponents doing everything they can to make them miss. Nevertheless, visualization is important to them as well. In basketball, players are said to be in a "groove," or a "zone," when they visualize shots so well they seem unable to miss. Kobe Bryant and Lisa Leslie are among the greatest visualizers in their sport, just as Babe Ruth, Hank Aaron, and Albert Pujols have been great at visualizing home runs in baseball. In tennis, I always admired Arthur Ashe's knack for planning matches in his mind, then systematically dismantling his opponents.

At another level, boxer Muhammad Ali was great at visualizing his entire future. Big, strong, and quick and able to move with the best of them, he had it all. I had the great pleasure of touring college campuses with him after we both won gold medals at the Rome Olympics in 1960. Muhammad (then known as Cassius Clay) had visualized his Olympic victory before it happened, and when I first knew him he was already reciting poetry and predicting what the future held for him. He saw it all in advance and called every move—something he became famous for later, when he taunted opponents by predicting the rounds in which he would knock them out.

## Determination and Resilience

The final event of the first day of decathlon competition is the 400-meter run. Almost exactly a quarter mile, this race stands at the point that divides sprints from middle-distances. Should runners go all out, as in a sprint, or pace themselves, as middle-distance runners do? Coming as it does, as the last event of the exhausting first day of decathlon competition, the 400-meter race tests the mettle of decathletes by extracting one last great effort from them before they can rest up for the next day's grueling events. How they choose to run the race has to do with how determined they are to win the entire decathlon.

Every great athlete who wants to be a champion must have the determination to do whatever it takes to achieve that goal. Even so, determination alone is not enough. This was proven dramatically when basketball's Michael Jordan—whom journalists later voted the greatest athlete of the twentieth century—quit basketball in 1994 to fulfill his lifelong dream to play professional baseball. Despite working hard, he spent a frustrating season and a half in the minor leagues and merely proved two things: that determination alone cannot guarantee success, and that baseball is a more difficult sport than many people had realized.

Resilience, an extension of determination, is the ability to overcome adversity, or apparently hopeless situations, and to bounce back from outright defeat. Some might argue that no one can be greater than an athlete who never loses; however, athletes who continually win are never required to change what they do or do any soul searching. By contrast, athletes who lose must examine themselves closely and consider making changes. I have always felt that true greatness in sports is exemplified by the ability to come back from defeat, as heavyweight boxer Floyd Patterson did after losing his world title to Ingemar Johansson in a humiliating 3-round knockout in 1959. Only those athletes who face adversity and defeat can prove they have resilience.

Among athletes who have impressed me the most with their determination and resilience is speed skater Eric Heiden, who was not only the first American to win world speed-skating championships, but the first speed skater ever to win all five events in the Winter Olympics. Another amazingly determined athlete is Jim Abbott, who refused to allow the fact that he was born with only one hand stop him from becoming a Major League Baseball pitcher—one who even pitched a no-hit game. Who could not admire Bo Jackson? An all-star in both professional football and Major League Baseball, he suffered what appeared to be a career-ending football injury. After undergoing hip-joint replacement surgery, he defied all logic by returning to play several more seasons of baseball. Cyclist Lance Armstrong also falls into this category. He won multiple Tour de France championships after recovering from cancer.

## Execution

Day two of the decathlon opens with the technically challenging 110-meter high hurdles. A brutally demanding event, it requires speed, leaping ability, and perfect timing. In short, it is an event that requires careful execution—the ability to perform precisely when it matters. Sports differ greatly in the precision of execution they demand. Getting off great throws in the discus, shot put, and javelin, for example, requires superb execution, but the direction in which the objects go is not critical. By contrast, archers, shooters, and golfers must hit precise targets. Some sports not only demand that execution be precise but also that it be repeated. A baseball pitcher who throws two perfect strikes fails if the opposing batter hits the third pitch over the fence. Likewise, a quarterback who leads his team down the field with five consecutive perfect passes fails if his next pass is intercepted.

Consider the differences between the kind of execution demanded by diving and pole vaulting. Divers lose points if their toes are not straight the moment they enter the water. By contrast, pole vaulters can land any way they want, so long as they clear the bar. Moreover, a diver gets only one chance on each dive, while pole vaulters get three chances at each height they attempt—and they can even skip certain heights to save energy for later jumps at greater heights. On the other hand, a diver who executes a dive badly will merely get a poor score, while a pole vaulter who misses too many jumps will get no score at all—which is exactly what hap-

pened to decathlete Dan O'Brien in the 1992 U.S. Olympic Trials. Although Dan was the world's top decathlete at that time, his failure to clear a height in the pole vault kept him off the Olympic team. (To his credit, he came back to win a gold medal in 1996.)

Figure skating and gymnastics are other sports that measure execution with a microscope. In gymnastics, the standard of perfection is a score of ten—which was first achieved in the Olympics by Nadia Comăneci in 1976. However, scores in those sports are not based on objective measures but on the evaluations of judges, whose own standards can and do change. By contrast, archery, shooting, and bowling are unusual in being sports that offer objective standards of perfection. In bowling, that standard is the 300 points awarded to players who bowl all strikes.

Among all athletes noted for their execution, one in particular stands out in my estimation: golf's Tiger Woods. After Tiger had played professionally for only a few years, he established himself as one of the greatest golfers ever. He has beaten the best that golf has had to offer by record margins in major competitions, and wherever he plays, he is the favorite to win. Most impressive is his seeming ability to do whatever he needs to win, regardless of the situation. Few athletes in any sport, or in any era, have come close to matching Tiger's versatile and consistent execution.

## Focus

After the high hurdles, the decathlon's discus event is a comparative relief. Nevertheless, it presents its own special demands, one of which is focus—the ability to maintain uninterrupted concentration. Like shot putters, discus throwers work within a tiny circle, within which they must concentrate all their attention and all their energy into throwing the heavy disk as far as they can.

Not surprisingly, one of the greatest discus throwers in history, Al Oerter, was also one of the greatest examples of focus in sports. His four gold medals between 1956 and 1968 made him the first track and field athlete in Olympic history to win any event four times in a row. In addition to beating out the best discus throwers in the world four consecutive times, he improved his own performance at each Olympiad and even won with a serious rib injury in 1964. Eight years after retiring from competition, he returned at age forty to throw the discus farther than ever and earn a spot as an alternate on the 1980 U.S. Olympic team.

Important in all sports, focus is especially important in those in which a single lapse in concentration may result in instant defeat. In boxing, a knockout can suddenly end a bout. Focus may be even more crucial in wrestling. Wrestlers grapple each other continuously, probing for openings that will allow them to pin their opponents. Few sports match wrestling in nonstop intensity; a single split-second lapse on the part of a wrestler can spell disaster. Great wrestlers, such as Cael Sanderson and Aleksandr Karelin, must therefore rank among the most focused athletes in history.

## Balance and Coordination

Of all the decathlon events, the most difficult to perform is the pole vault. Think of what it entails: Holding long skinny poles, vaulters run at full speed down a narrow path toward a pit; then, without breaking stride, push the tips of their poles into a tiny slot, propel their bodies upward, and use the poles to flip themselves over bars more than two or three times their height above the ground, finally to drop down on the opposite side. Success in the pole vault demands many traits, but the most important arc balance and coordination. Vaulters use their hands, feet, and bodies, all at the same time, and do everything at breakneck speed, with almost no margin for error. There are no uncoordinated champion pole vaulters.

Despite its difficulty, pole vaulting is an event in which some decathletes have performed especially well—perhaps because they, as a group, have versatile skills. I have long taken pride in the fact that my close friend, college teammate, and Olympic rival, C. K. Yang, once set a world record in the pole vault during a decathlon. C. K.'s record was all the more impressive because he achieved it midway through the second day of an intense competition. Imagine what balance and coordination he must have had to propel his body over the record-breaking height after having subjected it to the wear and tear of seven other events.

I cannot think of any athlete, in any sport, who demonstrated more versatility in coordination and balance than Michael Jordan, who could seemingly score from any spot on the floor, at any time, and under any conditions. Not only did he always have his offensive game together, he was also one of the greatest defensive players in the game. Moreover, his mere presence brought balance to his entire team.

## Preparation

The ninth event of the decathlon is the javelin— a throwing event that goes back to ancient times. A more difficult event than it may appear to be, it requires more than its share of special preparation. This may be why we rarely see athletes who compete in both the javelin and other events, though the versatile Babe Didrikson Zaharias was an exception.

Along with determination—to which it is closely allied—preparation is a vital trait of great athletes, especially in modern competition. It is no longer possible for even the greatest natural athletes to win against top competition without extensive preparation, which means practice, training for strength and stamina, proper diet and rest, and studying opponents diligently. Football players, especially quarterbacks and defensive backs, spend hours before every game studying films of opponents.

I was fortunate to grow up with an athlete who exemplifies preparation: my younger brother, Jimmy Johnson, who would become defensive back for the San Francisco 49ers for seventeen years and later be elected to the Pro Football Hall of Fame. Every week, Jimmy had to face a completely different set of pass receivers, but he was always ready because he studied their moves and trained himself to run backward fast enough to keep offenses in front of him so he could see every move they made. Coach Tom Landry of the Dallas Cowboys once told me that he always had the Cowboys attack on the side opposite from Jimmy.

Another exceptionally well prepared athlete was Magic Johnson, the great Lakers basketball guard, who played every position on the floor in more than one game. During his rookie season he had one of the greatest performances in playoff history during the NBA Finals. When a health problem prevented the Lakers' great center, Kareem Abdul-Jabbar, from playing in the sixth game against Philadelphia, Magic stunned everyone by filling in for him at center and scoring 44 points. He went on to become one of the great point guards in basketball history because he always knew where every player on the court should be at every moment.

## Stamina

If there is one event that most decathletes dread, it is the grueling 1,500-meter race that concludes the two-day competition. While C. K. Yang once set a world-record in the pole vault during a decathlon, no decathlete has ever come close to anything even resembling a world-class mark in the 1,500 meters. On the other hand, it is probable that no world-class middle-distance runner has ever run a 1,500-meter race immediately after competing in nine other events. To win a decathlon, the trick is not to come in first in this final race, but simply to survive it. For decathletes, it is not so much a race as a test of stamina.

When I competed in the decathlon in the Rome Olympics of 1960, I had to go head-to-head against my friend C. K. Yang through nine events, all the while knowing that the gold medal would be decided in the last event—the 1,500 meters. C. K. was one of the toughest and most durable athletes I have ever known, and I realized I could not beat him in that race. However, after the javelin, I led by enough points so that all I had to do was stay close to him. I managed to do it and win the gold medal, but running that race was not an experience I would care to repeat.

Stamina is not really a skill, but a measure of the strength to withstand or overcome exhaustion. Rare is the sport that does not demand some stamina. Stamina can be measured in a single performance— such as a long-distance race—in a tournament, or in the course of a long season.

The classic models of stamina are marathon runners, whose 26-plus-mile race keeps them moving continuously for more than two hours. Soccer is one of the most demanding of stamina among team sports. Its players move almost constantly and may run as far as 5 miles in a 90-minute game that allows few substitutions. Basketball players run nearly as much as soccer players, but their games are shorter and allow more substitutions and rest periods. However, the sport can be even more tiring than soccer because its teams play more frequently and play more games overall. Baseball players provide yet another contrast. They spend a great deal of time during their games sitting on the bench, and when they are on the field, players other than the pitcher and catcher rarely need to exert themselves more than a few seconds at a time. However, their season has the most games of all, and their constant travel is draining. All these sports and others demand great stamina from their players, and their greatest players are usually those who hold up the best.

To most people, chess seems like a physically undemanding game. However, its greatest players must be in top physical condition to withstand the unrelenting mental pressure of tournament and match competitions, which can last for weeks. Bobby Fisher, one of the game's greatest—and most eccentric—champions, exercised heavily when he competed in order to stay in shape. Even sprinters who spend only 10 or 11 seconds on the track in each race, need stamina. In order to reach the finals of major competitions, they must endure the physical and mental strains of several days of preliminary heats.

In reducing what makes athletes great to just ten traits, I realize that I have oversimplified things, but that matters little, as my purpose here is merely to introduce readers to what makes the athletes in these volumes great. Within these pages you will find stories exemplifying many other traits, and that is good, as among the things that make athletes endlessly fascinating are their diversity and complexity.

*Rafer Johnson*

# Contributors

Randy L. Abbott
*University of Evansville*

Tony Abbott
*Trumbull, Connecticut*

Michael Adams
*City College of New York
Graduate Center*

Patrick Adcock
*Henderson State University*

Amy Adelstein
*Toluca Lake, California*

Richard Adler
*University of Michigan, Dearborn*

Paul C. Alexander II
*Southern Illinois University*

Elizabeth Jeanne Alford
*Southern Illinois University,
Carbondale*

Eleanor B. Amico
*Whitewater, Wisconsin*

Ronald L. Ammons
*University of Findlay*

Earl Andresen
*University of Texas, Arlington*

David L. Andrews
*University of Illinois, Urbana-
Champaign*

Frank Ardolino
*University of Hawaii*

Vikki M. Armstrong
*Fayetteville State University*

Bryan Aubrey
*Maharishi International University*

Patti Auer
*United States Gymnastics Federation*

Philip Bader
*Pasadena, California*

Sylvia P. Baeza
*Applied Ballet Theater*

Amanda J. Bahr-Evola
*Southern Illinois University,
Edwardsville*

Alan Bairner
*Loughborough University*

JoAnn Balingit
*University of Delaware*

Susan J. Bandy
*United States International University*

Jessie F. Banks
*University of Southern Colorado*

Linda Bannister
*Loyola Marymount University*

C. Robert Barnett
*Marshall University*

David Barratt
*Montreat College*

Maryanne Barsotti
*Warren, Michigan*

Bijan Bayne
*Association for Professional Basketball
Research*

Barbara C. Beattie
*Sarasota, Florida*

Suzanne M. Beaudet
*University of Maine, Presque Isle*

Joseph Beerman
*Borough of Manhattan Community
College, CUNY*

Keith J. Bell
*Western Carolina University*

Stephen T. Bell
*Independent Scholar*

Alvin K. Benson
*Utah Valley University*

Chuck Berg
*University of Kansas*

S. Carol Berg
*College of St. Benedict*

Milton Berman
*University of Rochester*

Terry D. Bilhartz
*Sam Houston State University*

Cynthia A. Bily
*Adrian College*

Nicholas Birns
*New School University*

Joe Blankenbaker
*Georgia Southern University*

Carol Blassingame
*Texas A&M University*

Elaine M. Blinde
*Southern Illinois University,
Carbondale*

Harold R. Blythe, Jr.
*Eastern Kentucky University*

Jo-Ellen Lipman Boon
*Independent Scholar*

Trevor D. Bopp
*Texas A&M University*

Stephen Borelli
*USA Today*

John Boyd
*Appalachian State University*

Marlene Bradford
*Texas A&M University*

Michael R. Bradley
*Motlow College*

Carmi Brandis
*Fort Collins, Colorado*

Kevin L. Brennan
*Ouachita Baptist University*

Matt Brillinger
*Carleton University*

John A. Britton
*Francis Marion University*

Norbert Brockman
*St. Mary's University of San Antonio*

Howard Bromberg
*University of Michigan Law School*

Valerie Brooke
*Riverside Community College*

Dana D. Brooks
*West Virginia University*

Alan Brown
*Livingston University*

Valerie Brown
*Northwest Kansas Educational Service Center*

Thomas W. Buchanan
*Ancilla Domini College*

Fred Buchstein
*John Carroll University*

David Buehrer
*Valdosta State University*

Cathy M. Buell
*San Jose State University*

Michael H. Burchett
*Limestone College*

Edmund J. Campion
*University of Tennessee, Knoxville*

Peter Carino
*Indiana State University*

Lewis H. Carlson
*Western Michigan University*

Russell N. Carney
*Missouri State University*

Bob Carroll
*Professional Football Researchers Association*

Culley C. Carson
*University of North Carolina*

Craig Causer
*Pompton Lakes, New Jersey*

David Chapman
*North American Society of Sports Historians*

Paul J. Chara, Jr.
*Northwestern College*

Frederick B. Chary
*Indiana University Northwest*

Jerry E. Clark
*Creighton University*

Rhonda L. Clements
*Hofstra University*

Douglas Clouatre
*MidPlains Community College*

Kathryn A. Cochran
*University of Kansas*

Susan Coleman
*West Texas A&M University*

Caroline Collins
*Quincy University*

Brett Conway
*Namseoul University*

Carol Cooper
*University of Northern Iowa*

Richard Hauer Costa
*Texas A&M University*

Michael Coulter
*Grove City College*

David A. Crain
*South Dakota State University*

Louise Crain
*South Dakota State University*

Scott A. G. M. Crawford
*Eastern Illinois University*

Lee B. Croft
*Arizona State University*

Ronald L. Crosbie
*Marshall University*

Thomas S. Cross
*Texas A&M University*

Brian Culp
*Indiana University*

Michael D. Cummings, Jr.
*Madonna University*

Joanna Davenport
*Auburn University*

Kathy Davis
*North Carolina State University*

Mary Virginia Davis
*California State University, Sacramento*

Buck Dawson
*International Swimming Hall of Fame*

Dawn P. Dawson
*Pasadena, California*

Margaret Debicki
*Los Angeles, California*

Bill Delaney
*San Diego, California*

Paul Dellinger
*Wytheville, Virginia*

Andy DeRoche
*Front Range Community College*

James I. Deutsch
*Smithsonian Institution*

# Contributors

Joseph Dewey
*University of Pittsburgh, Johnstown*

M. Casey Diana
*Arizona State University*

Randy J. Dietz
*South Carolina State University*

Jonathan E. Dinneen
*VeriSign, Inc.*

Marcia B. Dinneen
*Bridgewater State College*

Dennis M. Docheff
*Whitworth College*

Cecilia Donohue
*Madonna University*

Pamela D. Doughty
*Texas A&M University*

Thomas Drucker
*University of Wisconsin, Whitewater*

Jill Dupont
*University of Chicago*

William G. Durick
*Blue Valley School District*

W. P. Edelstein
*Los Angeles, California*

Bruce L. Edwards
*Bowling Green State University*

William U. Eiland
*University of Georgia*

Henry A. Eisenhart
*University of Oklahoma*

Kenneth Ellingwood
*Los Angeles, California*

Julie Elliott
*Indiana University South Bend*

Mark R. Ellis
*University of Nebraska, Kearney*

Robert P. Ellis
*Northboro, Massachusetts*

Don Emmons
*Glendale News-Press*

Robert T. Epling
*North American Society of
Sports Historians*

Thomas L. Erskine
*Salisbury University*

Steven G. Estes
*California State University, Fullerton*

Don Evans
*The College of New Jersey*

Jack Ewing
*Boise, Idaho*

Kevin Eyster
*Madonna University*

Norman B. Ferris
*Middle Tennessee State University*

John W. Fiero
*University of Southwestern Louisiana*

Paul Finkelman
*Brooklyn Law School*

Paul Finnicum
*Arkansas State University*

Jane Brodsky Fitzpatrick
*Graduate Center, City University
of New York*

Michael J. Fratzke
*Indiana Wesleyan University*

Tom Frazier
*Cumberland College*

A. Bruce Frederick
*International Gymnastics Hall of Fame
and Museum*

Daniel J. Fuller
*Kent State University*

Jean C. Fulton
*Maharishi International University*

Carter Gaddis
*Tampa Tribune*

Thomas R. Garrett
*Society for American Baseball Research*

Jan Giel
*Drexel University*

Daniel R. Gilbert
*Moravian College*

Duane A. Gill
*Mississippi State University*

Vincent F. A. Golphin
*The Writing Company*

Bruce Gordon
*Auburn University, Montgomery*

Margaret Bozenna Goscilo
*University of Pittsburgh*

John Gould
*Independent Scholar*

Karen Gould
*Austin, Texas*

Lewis L. Gould
*University of Texas, Austin*

Larry Gragg
*University of Missouri, Rolla*

Lloyd J. Graybar
*Eastern Kentucky University*

Wanda Green
*University of Northern Iowa*

William C. Griffin
*Appalachian State University*

Irwin Halfond
*McKendree College*

Jan Hall
*Columbus, Ohio*

Roger D. Hardaway
*Northwestern Oklahoma State
University*

William Harper
*Purdue University*

Robert Harrison
*University of Arkansas Community College*

P. Graham Hatcher
*Shelton State Community College*

Karen Hayslett-McCall
*University of Texas, Dallas*

Leslie Heaphy
*Kent State University, Stark*

Bernadette Zbicki Heiney
*Lock Haven University of Pennsylvania*

Timothy C. Hemmis
*Edinboro University of Pennsylvania*

Steve Hewitt
*University of Birmingham*

Carol L. Higy
*Methodist College*

Randall W. Hines
*Susquehanna University*

Joseph W. Hinton
*Portland, Oregon*

Arthur D. Hlavaty
*Yonkers, New York*

Carl W. Hoagstrom
*Ohio Northern University*

William H. Hoffman
*Fort Meyers, Florida*

Kimberley M. Holloway
*King College*

John R. Holmes
*Franciscan University of Steubenville*

Joseph Horrigan
*Pro Football Hall of Fame*

William L. Howard
*Chicago State University*

Shane L. Hudson
*Texas A&M University*

Mary Hurd
*East Tennessee State University*

Raymond Pierre Hylton
*Virginia Union University*

Shirley Ito
*Amateur Athletic Foundation of Los Angeles*

Frederick Ivor-Campbell
*North American Society of Sports Historians*

Shakuntala Jayaswal
*University of New Haven*

Doresa A. Jennings
*Shorter College*

Albert C. Jensen
*Central Florida Community College*

Jeffry Jensen
*Altadena, California*

Bruce E. Johansen
*University of Nebraska, Omaha*

Lloyd Johnson
*Campbell University*

Mary Johnson
*University of South Florida*

Alexander Jordan
*Boston University*

David Kasserman
*Rowan University*

Robert B. Kebric
*University of Louisville*

Rodney D. Keller
*Ricks College*

Barbara J. Kelly
*University of Delaware*

Kimberley H. Kidd
*East Tennessee State University King College*

Leigh Husband Kimmel
*Indianapolis, Indiana*

Tom Kinder
*Bridgewater College*

Joe King
*Alameda Journal*

Jane Kirkpatrick
*Auburn University, Montgomery*

Paul M. Klenowski
*Thiel College*

Darlene A. Kluka
*University of Alabama, Birmingham*

Lynne Klyse
*California State University, Sacramento*

Bill Knight
*Western Illinois University*

Francis M. Kozub
*College at Brockport, State University of New York*

Lynn C. Kronzek
*University of Judaism*

Shawn Ladda
*Manhattan College*

P. Huston Ladner
*University of Mississippi*

Philip E. Lampe
*University of the Incarnate Word*

Tom Lansford
*University of Southern Mississippi*

Eugene Larson
*Los Angeles Pierce College*

Rustin Larson
*Maharishi International University*

Kevin R. Lasley
*Eastern Illinois University*

Mary Lou LeCompte
*University of Texas, Austin*

Denyse Lemaire
*Rowan University*

# Contributors

Victor Lindsey
*East Central University*

Alar Lipping
*Northern Kentucky University*

Janet Long
*Pasadena, California*

M. Philip Lucas
*Cornell College*

Leonard K. Lucenko
*Montclair State College*

R. C. Lutz
*Madison Advisors*

Robert McClenaghan
*Pasadena, California*

Arthur F. McClure
*Central Missouri State University*

Roxanne McDonald
*New London, New Hampshire*

Alan McDougall
*University of Guelph*

Mary McElroy
*Kansas State University*

Thomas D. McGrath
*Baylor University*

Marcia J. Mackey
*Central Michigan University*

Michelle C. K. McKowen
*New York, New York*

John McNamara
*Beltsville, Maryland*

Joe McPherson
*East Tennessee State University*

Paul Madden
*Hardin Simmons University*

Mark J. Madigan
*University of Vermont*

Philip Magnier
*Maharishi International University*

H. R. Mahood
*Memphis State University*

Barry Mann
*Atlanta, Georgia*

Nancy Farm Mannikko
*Centers for Disease Control & Prevention*

Robert R. Mathisen
*Western Baptist College*

Russell Medbery
*Colby-Sawyer College*

Joella H. Mehrhof
*Emporia State University*

Julia M. Meyers
*Duquesne University*

Ken Millen-Penn
*Fairmont State College*

Glenn A. Miller
*Texas A&M University*

Lauren Mitchell
*St. Louis, Missouri*

Christian H. Moe
*Southern Illinois University, Carbondale*

Mario Morelli
*Western Illinois University*

Caitlin Moriarity
*Brisbane, California*

Elizabeth C. E. Morrish
*State University of New York, Oneonta*

Todd Moye
*Atlanta, Georgia*

Tinker D. Murray
*Southwest Texas State University*

Alex Mwakikoti
*University of Texas, Arlington*

Alice Myers
*Bard College at Simon's Rock*

Michael V. Namorato
*University of Mississippi*

Jerome L. Neapolitan
*Tennessee Technological University*

Alicia Neumann
*San Francisco, California*

Caryn E. Neumann
*Miami University of Ohio, Middletown*

Mark A. Newman
*University of Virginia*

Betsy L. Nichols
*Reynoldsburg, Ohio*

James W. Oberly
*University of Wisconsin, Eau Claire*

George O'Brien
*Georgetown University*

Wendy Cobb Orrison
*Washington and Lee University*

Sheril A. Palermo
*Cupertino, California*

R. K. L. Panjabi
*Memorial University of Newfoundland*

Robert J. Paradowski
*Rochester Institute of Technology*

Thomas R. Park
*Florida State University*

Robert Passaro
*Tucson, Arizona*

Cheryl Pawlowski
*University of Northern Colorado*

Leslie A. Pearl
*San Diego, California*

Judy C. Peel
*University of North Carolina, Wilmington*

Martha E. Pemberton
*Galesville, Wisconsin*

William E. Pemberton
*University of Wisconsin, La Crosse*

Lori A. Petersen
*Minot, North Dakota*

Nis Petersen
*Jersey City State College*

Douglas A. Phillips
*Sierra Vista, Arizona*

Debra L. Picker
*Long Beach, California*

Betty L. Plummer
*Dillard University*

Bill Plummer III
*Amateur Softball Association
    of America*

Michael Polley
*Columbia College*

Francis Poole
*University of Delaware*

Jon R. Poole
*Virginia Polytechnic Institute and State
    University*

David L. Porter
*William Penn University*

John G. Powell
*Greenville, South Carolina*

Victoria Price
*Lamar University*

Maureen J. Puffer-Rothenberg
*Valdosta State University*

Christopher Rager
*San Dimas, California*

Steven J. Ramold
*Eastern Michigan University*

C. Mervyn Rasmussen
*Renton, Washington*

John David Rausch, Jr.
*West Texas A&M University*

Abe C. Ravitz
*California State University,
    Dominguez Hills*

Nancy Raymond
*International Gymnast Magazine*

Shirley H. M. Reekie
*San Jose State University*

Christel Reges
*Grand Valley State University*

Victoria Reynolds
*Mandeville High School*

Betty Richardson
*Southern Illinois University,
    Edwardsville*

Alice C. Richer
*Spaulding Rehabilitation Center*

David R. Rider
*Bloomsburg University*

Robert B. Ridinger
*Northern Illinois University*

Edward A. Riedinger
*Ohio State University Libraries*

Edward J. Rielly
*Saint Joseph's College of Maine*

Jan Rintala
*Northern Illinois University*

Thurman W. Robins
*Texas Southern University*

Vicki K. Robinson
*State University of New York,
    Farmingdale*

Mark Rogers
*University of Chicago*

Wynn Rogers
*San Dimas, California*

Carl F. Rothfuss
*Central Michigan University*

William B. Roy
*United States Air Force Academy*

A. K. Ruffin
*George Washington University*

Todd Runestad
*American Ski Association*

J. Edmund Rush
*Boise, Idaho*

Michael Salmon
*Amateur Athletic Foundation of
    Los Angeles*

Rebecca J. Sankner
*Southern Illinois University,
    Carbondale*

Timothy M. Sawicki
*Canisius College*

Ronald C. Sawyer
*State University of New York,
    Binghamton*

Ann M. Scanlon
*State University of New York, College at
    Cortland*

Daniel C. Scavone
*University of Southern Indiana*

Elizabeth D. Schafer
*Loachapoka, Alabama*

Lamia Nuseibeh Scherzinger
*Indiana University*

Walter R. Schneider
*Central Michigan University*

J. Christopher Schnell
*Southeast Missouri State University*

Kathleen Schongar
*The May School*

Stephen Schwartz
*Buffalo State College*

Deborah Service
*Los Angeles, California*

Chrissa Shamberger
*Ohio State University*

# Contributors

Tom Shieber
*Mt. Wilson, California*

Theodore Shields
*Surfside Beach, South Carolina*

Peter W. Shoun
*East Tennessee State University*

R. Baird Shuman
*University of Illinois, Urbana-Champaign*

Thomas J. Sienkewicz
*Monmouth College*

Richard Slapsys
*University of Massachusetts, Lowell*

Elizabeth Ferry Slocum
*Pasadena, California*

John Slocum
*Pasadena, California*

Gary Scott Smith
*Grove City College*

Harold L. Smith
*University of Houston, Victoria*

Ira Smolensky
*Monmouth College*

A. J. Sobczak
*Santa Barbara, California*

Ray Sobczak
*Salem, Wisconsin*

Mark Stanbrough
*Emporia State University*

Alison Stankrauff
*Indiana University South Bend*

Michael Stellefson
*Texas A&M University*

Glenn Ellen Starr Stilling
*Appalachian State University*

Gerald H. Strauss
*Bloomsburg University*

Deborah Stroman
*University of North Carolina*

James Sullivan
*California State University, Los Angeles*

Cynthia J. W. Svoboda
*Bridgewater State College*

William R. Swanson
*South Carolina State College*

J. K. Sweeney
*South Dakota State University*

Charles A. Sweet, Jr.
*Eastern Kentucky University*

Glenn L. Swygart
*Tennessee Temple University*

James Tackach
*Roger Williams University*

Felicia Friendly Thomas
*California State Polytechnic University, Pomona*

Jennifer L. Titanski
*Lock Haven University of Pennsylvania*

Evelyn Toft
*Fort Hays State University*

Alecia C. Townsend Beckie
*New York, New York*

Anh Tran
*Wichita State University*

Marcella Bush Trevino
*Texas A&M University, Kingsville*

Kathleen Tritschler
*Guilford College*

Brad Tufts
*Bucknell University*

Karen M. Turner
*Temple University*

Sara Vidar
*Los Angeles, California*

Hal J. Walker
*University of Connecticut*

Spencer Weber Waller
*Loyola University Chicago*

Annita Marie Ward
*Salem-Teikyo University*

Shawncey Webb
*Taylor University*

Chuck Weis
*American Canoe Association*

Michael J. Welch
*Guilford College*

Paula D. Welch
*University of Florida*

Allen Wells
*Bowdoin College*

Winifred Whelan
*St. Bonaventure University*

Nan White
*Maharishi International University*

Nicholas White
*Maharishi International University*

Rita S. Wiggs
*Methodist College*

Ryan K. Williams
*University of Illinois, Springfield*

Brook Wilson
*Independent Scholar*

John Wilson
*Wheaton, Illinois*

Rusty Wilson
*Ohio State University*

Wayne Wilson
*Amateur Athletic Foundation of Los Angeles*

John D. Windhausen
*St. Anselm College*

Michael Witkoski
*University of South Carolina*

Sheri Woodburn
*Cupertino, California*

Lisa A. Wroble
*Redford Township District Library*

Philip Wong
*Pasadena, California*

Jerry Jaye Wright
*Pennsylvania State University, Altoona*

Frank Wu
*University of Wisconsin, Madison*

Greg Woo
*Independent Scholar*

Scott Wright
*University of St. Thomas*

Brooke K. Zibel
*University of North Texas*

# GREAT ATHLETES

## RACING & INDIVIDUAL SPORTS

# *Akebono*

**Born:** May 8, 1969
Waimanalo, Hawaii
**Also known as:** Chad George Haaheo Rowan
(birth name); Akebono Taro

### Early Life
The man who wrestled under the name of Akebono was born Chad George Haaheo Rowan on May 8, 1969. His parents were Randolph Rowan, a taxi and tour-bus driver, and Janice Rowan, a counselor for troubled children. Chad grew up in Waimanalo, a small town east of Honolulu, Hawaii. His father, who coached baseball and basketball in his spare time, encouraged Chad and his two younger brothers to participate in sports.

At Kaiser High School in neighboring Hawaii Kai, Chad played basketball and became an all-star center. After graduation, he attended Hawaii Pacific University on a basketball scholarship. However, he sat out his freshman season. He had no interest in studies and was dissatisfied with his situation. Early in the school year, he had met former Hawaii resident Jesse Kuhaulua, a retired sumo wrestler who owned the Azumazeki sumo training school in Tokyo, Japan. Kuhaulua suggested that Chad train as a wrestler. After his disappointing year at Hawaii Pacific University, Chad decided to try sumo.

### The Road to Excellence
During his first six months in Japan, Chad was lonely and frustrated. Learning to speak Japanese and adjusting to the sumo way of life were difficult. Sumo is organized into six divisions that are further divided into levels. *Sumotori*, those who practice sumo, advance based on success in the ring. Competitors in the top two divisions receive official salaries, plus endorsements and private rooms. The other *sumotori* live in communal rooms and receive only expense money and bonuses. Low-ranking wrestlers do menial chores and wait on seniors.

Like the other *sumotori*, Chad rose early and stretched, lifted weights, ran, and wrestled. He ate meals of rice and vegetables and took naps afterward to put on weight. However, Chad was slow to learn sumo techniques. Successful *sumotori* must be mentally focused and physically strong enough to push an opponent out of the ring or down to the mat quickly. Because Chad was clumsy, Kuhaulua had misgivings about his ability. Smaller wrestlers were easily throwing him. Chad, though, was unwilling to return home a failure. He determined to make sumo an integral part of his physical and mental makeup.

*Akebono (left) defeating Tamakasuga by pushing him out of the ring during a 2000 sumo tournament.* (AFP/Getty Images)

1

Beginning with his debut in 1988, Akebono, which means "Dawn," moved steadily up the ranks. For two years, he wrestled in seven bouts in each of the fifteen-day tournaments held six times a year. In January, 1990, after twelve tournaments, he was promoted to *juryo*, the second-highest division. Along with the awards that belong to those of this class, Akebono earned the respect of fans and fellow *sumotori*; relatively few wrestlers attain either of the two highest divisions.

## The Emerging Champion

*Sumotori* in the upper two divisions are required to participate in fifteen bouts in each tournament. Akebono handled the challenge with ease. In November of 1990, he was promoted to the *makuuchi* division, which consists of five levels—*maegashira, komusubi, sekiwake, ozeki,* and *yokozuna,* or grand champion. The top level represents the highest achievement in sumo; to many fans, it is an almost godlike status.

Akebono continued to rise through the levels of *makuuchi*. In May of 1991, he set a record by winning eighteen consecutive tournaments and was promoted to *sekiwake*; in 1992, he was promoted to *ozeki*. Akebono was determined to attain the highest rank in sumo, though it was unknown whether or not the Japan Sumo Association would allow a foreigner to do so in Japan's national sport. By the end of the 1993 Summer Grand Sumo Tournament, Akebono's impressive record and his dignified character persuaded the Japan Sumo Association that Akebono was worthy of the promotion. At the age of twenty-three, the 6-foot 8-inch, 466-pound Akebono became the sixty-fourth *yokozuna* since the seventeenth century. He was also the first non-Japanese wrestler to achieve this status.

Rituals are an important part of sumo and reflect the sport's mythical background and religious associations. The first match was supposedly fought by gods; however, the sport's origin, which goes back more than fifteen hundred years, is unknown. At his three-and-one-half-hour initiation held at the Meiji Shrine, Akebono performed his first public ring-entering ceremony as *yokozuna*. Wearing a white cotton belt representing purity and strength, Akebono held up his hands and stomped on the ground, a symbolic action meant to get the gods' attention so that they will drive away evil spirits and bless the harvest. The rice-straw bales that demarcate the ring are also suggestive of bountiful harvests. An earthenware pot with offerings for a safe and prosperous tournament is buried in the mound on which the ring is located, and *sumotori* toss salt to purify the ring and ward off accidents. The roof that is suspended over the ring resembles that of a Shinto shrine.

## Continuing the Story

When a *yokozuna* stomps his feet in the ring during ritual ceremony, fans chant "*Nippon ichi,*" meaning "the best man in Japan." Understandably, Akebono felt a great deal of pressure to win his first tournament as *yokozuna*. Victory, however, eluded him in the tournaments held in March and May, 1993. Although *yokozuna* cannot be demoted to lower-ranked *sumotori* after losing two consecutive tournaments, they can be asked to retire when they are deemed unable to fulfill expectations. In the Grand Sumo Tournament in July, however, Akebono triumphed over a field of especially strong competitors. After his first victory as *yokozuna*, he hoped to maintain a high level of wrestling for many years and to carry out his duties as a trustee and a representative of the Japan Sumo Association.

By 1994, Akebono had won seven competitions—called *yusho*—which is more than many wrestlers win during an entire career. However, knee injuries and a weight problem forced him to miss numerous competitions. Between 1994 and 1998, Akebono won only two *yusho*. Returning to form in 1999, Akebono won the Nagoya Basho, his first *makkuchi* division championship since 1997. In November of 2000, he won the Emperor's Cup, his eleventh career victory. In 2001, with age and weight contributing to his continued health problems, Akebono retired. After his sumo career ended, Akebono became a coach for the Japan Sumo Association. In 2003, he joined K-1, a type of mixed martial art, but, because of his weight, did not successfully make the transition from one form of fighting to another.

## Summary

Sumo was completely foreign to Chad Rowan when he went to Japan, but he was determined to train hard and to learn its ritual and cultural requirements. Within five years, under the ring name of Akebono, he rose from the lowest rank to the grand champion.

*Frank Ardolino*

## Additional Sources

Gin, Willie. "Akebono." *Current Biography* 60, no. 8 (1999).

Hall Mina. *The Big Book of Sumo.* Berkeley, Calif.: Stone Bridge, 1997.

Panek, Mark. *Gaijin Yokozuna: A Biography of Chad Rowan.* Honolulu: University of Hawaii Press, 2006.

# Mark Allen

**Born:** January 12, 1958
      Glendale, California
**Also known as:** The Grip

## Early Life

Mark Allen was born in Glendale, California, in 1958. When his father began medical school, his family moved to St. Louis, Missouri. After his father finished medical school, Mark and his family relocated to Palo Alto, California. As a child, Mark believed that everyone had a special talent. He felt that if he could find his, he would be unbeatable at something.

Mark began swimming in the fifth grade and continued through junior high school. He started competing on swim teams when he was ten. Because of his swimming schedule, he did not have much time to hang out at the mall or go to the movies. Mark swam with his team for about an hour a day before school.

Though Mark felt that his entire life revolved around swimming and school, he did not mind the workouts because he enjoyed spending time with his teammates. The training also helped him to become such a good swimmer that after high school he competed on his college team. In 1980, he graduated with a degree in biology from the University of California at San Diego. He was accepted into medical school, but he decided against attending.

## The Road to Excellence

Two years after Mark graduated from college, while working as a lifeguard, he saw the Ironman Triathlon on television. Every year, the Ironman is held in Hawaii. Competitors must swim 2.4 miles, bike 112 miles, and run a 26.2-mile marathon. Mark was intrigued by the sport and especially inspired as he watched triathlete Julie Moss collapse yards from the finish line and crawl her way to second place.

Mark thought the sport was crazy but wanted to try it. He bought running shoes and a racing bike and started training. He found that he was even better at running and cycling than he was at swimming. A few months later, Mark entered his first triathlon. He finished in fourth place. Later that

same year, he won the 1982 Horny Toad Triathlon in San Diego, California.

Mark continued competing in triathlons of various distances. He trained about five hours a day, seven days a week, from January through October. Each year, he ran about 2,500 miles, swam about 450 miles, and biked about 15,000 miles.

Mark also took care of his body. He ate six meals a day. He stopped training in November and December so that his body could rest. He slept almost as hard as he competed—nine or ten hours a night. He even took a nap in the afternoon.

## The Emerging Champion

Every time Mark practiced, he tried to reach the speeds he wanted during a race. If he wanted to run five-minute miles in a race, he trained at five miles a minute. Using this training method, he competed in and lost six times the Hawaii Ironman Triathlon Championships—the most prestigious triathlon event in the world.

Then, Dr. Phil Maffetone recommended that Mark train within a certain heart range. Maffetone told Mark that this would cause him to burn fat as the major fuel supply instead of carbohydrates. To get his heart rate low enough he had to slow down.

However, as Mark trained for four months at a lower heart rate, his times kept dropping. When he ran more intensely and got to his previous heart rates, his times were much faster. In 1989, after following this training regimen, he won the Hawaii Ironman Triathlon.

## Continuing the Story

Mark won the Ironman in Hawaii five consecutive times and six times in all. He also excelled at the Olympic Triathlon distance: a 1.5-kilometer swim, a 40-kilometer bike ride, and a 10-kilometer run. In 1989, in Avignon, France, he won the inaugural Triathlon World Championships by more than a minute. He was undefeated ten times in the Nice International Championships, one of the most important triathlons in the world. He won twenty consecutive races from 1988 to 1991. He ran a 2-hour 40-minute marathon in the third stage of the 1989

Hawaii Ironman. During his racing career, he finished in the top three in 90 percent of the competitions he entered. In 1995, he won his last Ironman Triathlon; at the age of thirty-seven, he was the oldest champion ever.

Mark chose to end his racing career in 1996. However, in May, 1998, he became the first 40-year-old triathlete to win an Ironman qualifier. He loved triathlons. He enjoyed the challenge of attaining something that appeared unattainable. He loved the training, the travel, and the racing. He believed that success came because he greatly enjoyed the sport.

*Triathlete* magazine named Mark the triathlete of the year six times. In 1997, *Outside* magazine selected him as the world's fittest man. In 2002, he was inducted into the Ironman Hall of Fame.

After retiring from competition, Mark worked as a sports commentator for the Hawaii Ironman and for ESPN race events. He also provided commentary at the 2000 Sydney Olympics, which was the first time that the triathlon was included in the Olympic Games.

Mark also became an athletic trainer for triathletes and a motivational speaker. He authored *Total Triathlete* and *Workouts for Working People*, a book about how to exercise and be fit throughout one's life. In 1989, Mark married triathlete Julie Moss.

## Summary

Though Mark Allen lost the Hawaii Ironman six times, he did not give up. He trained within a certain heart range and then won the Ironman in Hawaii five consecutive times and six times altogether. He had found his special talent. Success came as he focused his efforts on something he enjoyed.

*Chrissa Shamberger*

## Additional Sources

Allen, Mark, and Bob Babbitt. *Mark Allen's Total Triathlete*. Chicago: Contemporary Books, 1988.

Allen, Mark, Julie Moss, and Bob Babbitt. *Workouts for Working People: How You Can Get in Great Shape While Staying Employed*. New York: Villard, 2000.

Gibbs, Peter. "Building up a Solid Foundation for Fitness." *The Nelson Mail*, August 3, 2007.

Smith, Pohla. "Mark Allen." *Sports Illustrated for Kids* 6, no. 3, p. 44.

Walters, John. "Fast Afoot or Fast Asleep." *Sports Illustrated* 78, no. 21 (May 31, 1993).

### Ironman World Championships

| Year | Location | Place | Time |
|------|----------|-------|---------|
| 1989 | Kona, Hawaii | 1st | 8:09:15 |
| 1990 | Kona, Hawaii | 1st | 8:28:17 |
| 1991 | Kona, Hawaii | 1st | 8:18:32 |
| 1992 | Kona, Hawaii | 1st | 8:09:08 |
| 1993 | Kona, Hawaii | 1st | 8:07:45 |
| 1995 | Kona, Hawaii | 1st | 8:20:34 |

# *Bobby Allison*

**Born:** December 3, 1937
     Miami, Florida
**Also known as:** Robert Arthur Allison (full name)

## Early Life

Robert Arthur Allison was born on December 3, 1937, in Miami, Florida, the fourth child in a family of thirteen children. His mother Katherine stayed at home while his father Edmond sold automobile parts. Bobby's family remained in Miami while Bobby grew up and attended school. Because of his father's involvement with automobiles, Bobby was around cars from an early age. Gradually, he and his younger brother Donnie became interested in stock-car racing. While still in high school, Bobby

*Bobby Allison made his NASCAR debut at the Daytona 500 in 1961 and earned the last of his eighty-four victories at the 1988 version of the race.* (Courtesy of Daytona International Speedway)

raced his street car at Hialeah Speedway. After his first crash, his father stepped in and briefly ended Bobby's career.

## The Road to Excellence

Bobby was determined to drive a race car and, because there were only a few tracks in the south Florida area, he began looking for a place with greater opportunities to race. In 1959, Bobby and Donnie drove their pickup truck from Miami to Alabama. They had no particular destination in mind, and, after stopping at a gas station to ask where the nearest short track was, they headed to Montgomery. At first, the brothers lived in their truck and in $1.50-per-night boarding houses. Because of numerous racetracks close to Montgomery, Bobbie and Donnie were able to race almost every night of the week. As a result, Bobby gained valuable racing experience in a very short time.

In the 1960's, Bobby and Donnie made Hueytown, Alabama, their home. They put together a racing team that was to become known as the Alabama Gang. Soon Bobby was running races on short tracks all over the United States. In both 1962 and 1963, Bobby won the National Association for Stock Car Auto Racing (NASCAR) Modified-Special Championship. Competing in more than one hundred races a year, he won the NASCAR Modified Championship in 1964 and 1965. During the following years, Bobby's racing career continued to develop, and he established one of the most impressive racing records in motor-sports history.

## The Emerging Champion

Bobby's success on shorter racetracks led him to the longer superspeedways, and in 1965, he joined the Grand National Winston Cup Division of NASCAR. Soon he was racing at Atlanta, Georgia; Talladega, Alabama; Darlington, South Carolina; and Daytona Beach, Florida, in longer, 400-, 500-, and 600-mile races. In 1972, he was named Martini & Rossi driver of the year. Other honors followed as his fame and popularity grew. He was voted most popular driver in the Motor Racing Network poll six times in twelve years.

## NASCAR Circuit Victories

|  |  |
|---|---|
| 1962-63 | NASCAR Modified-Special |
| 1964-65 | NASCAR Modified |
| 1967, 1972 | American 500 |
| 1969 | Staley 400 |
| 1969, 1972 | Southeastern 500 |
| 1969, 1979-80 | Capital City 400 |
| 1970, 1972 | Atlanta Journal 500 |
|  | Volunteer 500 |
| 1971 | Talladega 500 |
|  | Champion Spark Plug 400 |
| 1971-72, 1975, 1983 | Heinz Southern 500 |
| 1971-72, 1978 | National 500 |
| 1971-72, 1980 | Mason-Dixon 500 |
| 1971, 1973, 1979 | Riverside 400 |
| 1971, 1981 | World 500 |
|  | Gabriel 400 |
| 1971, 1981, 1984 | Coca-Cola 500 |
| 1972 | Nashville 400 |
| 1973 | Wilkes 400 |
| 1974 | Richmond 500 |
| 1975 | CRC Chemicals Rebel 500 |
| 1975, 1981 | Winston Western 500 |
| 1978 | Delaware 500 |
| 1978, 1982, 1988 | Daytona 500 |
| 1979 | Carolina 500 |
|  | Northwestern Bank 400 |
| 1979, 1981, 1986 | Winston 500 |
| 1980 | Firecracker 400 |
|  | Holly Farms 400 |
| 1983 | NASCAR Winston Cup Championship |

By the 1980's, Bobby emerged as one of the most skilled competitors on the superspeedways, but he continued to drive in races at shorter tracks whenever his busy schedule permitted. Bobby's great skill and sheer love of racing paid off in a string of Grand National victories in the 1970's and 1980's, including three wins of the Daytona 500. He was the NASCAR Winston Cup champion in 1983.

### Continuing the Story

Although off the track Bobby was as a deeply religious, gentle, warm, and patient man, he possessed a no-nonsense approach on the track. One of the longest rivalries in stock-car-racing history was between Bobby and Richard "The King" Petty. For five years, the two champions rubbed fenders on superspeedways as well as short tracks until finally they decided to meet and reconcile their differences.

Bobby's career had its ups and downs. In 1976 and 1977, he was involved in two spectacular crashes and was seriously injured. Although in one crash he suffered eleven broken bones and spent several days in intensive care, Bobby still managed to qualify for the next big race. These setbacks kept him out of the winner's circle until 1978, when he won the Daytona 500.

In June, 1988, Bobby suffered the worst injuries of his professional career in a devastating pileup at Pocono Raceway in Pennsylvania. As a result of multiple injuries and a severe skull fracture, Bobby was left in a coma. There were fears that he might never recover. A priest was flown to his bedside. Months in the hospital were followed by more months of therapy. With the support of his family and friends, he made remarkable progress. After eighteen months of healing and rehabilitation, he was able to participate again in motor racing. This time, however, he was not driving.

After Bobby had his near-fatal crash, Mike Alexander, an up-and-coming young driver, took over and drove the Allison Buick in the remaining races that season. As soon as Bobby was on his feet again, he put together a new racing team that included Alexander as driver. While still undergoing therapy, Bobby spent his time at the racetracks, offering advice on racing strategy, but he never raced again.

Tragically, in the early 1990's, Bobby lost two sons to the world of racing. Clifford, his youngest

## Honors and Awards

|  |  |
|---|---|
| 1965 | NASCAR Modified Most Popular Driver |
| 1965, 1974 | NASCAR Late Model Sportsman Most Popular Driver |
| 1968-69, 1972, 1975 | Union 76-Darlington Record Club Award |
| 1971-73, 1981-83 | NASCAR Most Popular Driver |
| 1972 | Martini & Rossi Driver of the Year |
| 1972, 1983 | Olsonite Driver of the Year |
| 1980 | IROC Series Champion |
| 1984 | Inducted into Alabama Sports Hall of Fame |
| 1986 | Inducted into Florida Sports Hall of Fame |
| 1991 | Inducted into American Auto Racing Writers and Broadcasters Association Hall of Fame |
| 1992 | Inducted into Motorsports Hall of Fame of America |
| 1993 | Inducted into International Motorsports Hall of Fame |
| 1998 | Named one of NASCAR's fifty greatest drivers |
| 2006 | Inducted into Michigan International Speedway and Jackson Hall of Fame "Victory Lane" |

son, died in a practice run at the Michigan International Speedway, and Davey died at the Talladega Superspeedway. Nevertheless, though all his trials, Bobby still participated in the sport he loved.

## Summary

The qualities that make a race-car driver a champion are similar to those needed to excel in other sports: intensity, courage, endurance, great skill, and the will to win. These Bobby Allison had in abundance during those years when he was logging more than 150,000 racing miles on the way to more than 500 career victories. As Bobby struggled with a different set of challenges following his accident and loss of his sons, he showed his fans that he still had what it took to be a winner.

*Francis Poole*

## Additional Sources

Allison, Bobby. *Bobby Allison: A Racer's Racer.* Champaign, Ill.: Sports, 2003.

Gillispie, Tom. *Racing Families: A Tribute to Racing's Fastest Dynasties.* Dallas, Tex.: Beckett, 2000.

Golenbock, Peter. *Miracle: Bobby Allison and the Saga of the Alabama Gang.* New York: St. Martin's Press, 2006.

White, Ben. *The Bobby Allison Story: Circle of Triumph.* Osceola, Wis.: Motorbooks International, 1998.

# *Viswanathan Anand*

**Born:** December 11, 1969
Madras (now Chennai), Tamil Nadu, India
**Also known as:** Anand (birth name); Vishy;
Lightning Kid; the Tiger from Madras

## Early Life

Viswanathan Anand was born on December 11, 1969, in Madras (now Chennai), in the state of Tamil Nadu, India, to Viswanathan and Susheela. Following Indian tradition, he took his father's name, Viswanathan, and was given the name Anand. His father worked as general manager for Southern Railways, while his mother stayed at home. Anand was born the youngest of three children. He has an older brother, Shivakumar, and an older sister, Anuradha. After watching his siblings playing chess, he became curious about the game. From an early age, Anand exhibited a photographic memory. When Anand was six, his mother began teaching him how to play chess. He also began attending the Tal Chess Club in Madras in order to take lessons from chess master Manuel Aaron.

*Viswanathan Anand during a championship held at the top of the World Trade Center on September 11, 1995.* (AP/Wide World Photos)

## The Road to Excellence

In 1983, Anand won the Indian sub-junior chess championship. To capture this title, he won all nine games in which he competed. This was a remarkable achievement: For a competitor to earn a perfect score in a championship is rare. In the next year, Anand became the youngest Indian to capture the International Master Championship. Those close to Anand realized he was making extraordinary progress as a chess competitor. At the age of sixteen, he became the Indian national chess champion. When Anand was young, his father taught him the value of doing things in a disciplined manner. The self-control Anand learned as a child served him well in his future as a chess champion.

In 1987, Anand once again showed how much progress he had made as a chess player by winning the World Junior Chess Championship. At merely sixteen years old, he had captured a title that no other Indian ever had. Anand's meteoric rise in the world of chess seemed to be without limit. In 1988, he became a grand master. He was the first Indian to achieve such a honored level in the game. In addition to his focus on chess, he received a degree in commerce from Loyola College in Madras.

## The Emerging Champion

By the early 1990's, Anand had established himself as one of the best chess players in the world. During the decade, he won several important chess titles. Anand soon became a contender for the World Chess Championship. Chess has a long and illustrious history. Its origins are traced to the Gupta Empire of ancient India. During the sixth century C.E., the game of *chaturanga* originated. Eventually, the game came to Europe and, over the centuries, transformed into chess. By the mid-fifteenth century, the modern game of chess had taken root. While the first world champion in chess was determined in 1886, the championship was not administered by the International Chess Federation (FIDE) until 1948. FIDE was the only official governing body of world chess compe-

## Milestones

|  |  |
|------|-------------|
| 1983 | Indian junior champion |
| 1984 | International master |
| 1985 | Indian campion |
| 1987 | World junior champion |
| 1988 | Became Grandmaster |
| 2000 | World Chess Federation world champion |
|      | World Chess Federation world blitz champion |
| 2003 | World Chess Federation world rapid champion |
| 2007-08 | World Chess Champion |

## Summary

By becoming World Chess Champion, Viswanathan Anand became a national hero in his native India. At a young age, Anand was considered the first chess prodigy since the great American chess player Bobby Fischer. Although Anand appreciated the adulation, he came to realize that he had much expected of him. Over the years, he received several awards, including the 1985 Arjuna Award for outstanding Indian sportsman in chess, the 1987 Padma Shri Award, and the 1991-1992 Rajiv Gandhi Khel Ratna Award. He also won several Chess Oscars—in 1997, 1998, 2003, 2004, and 2007—the Sportstar Millennium Award in 1998, and the Padma Vibhushan Award in 2007. In modern chess history, Anand is one of the few chess champions from a country other than the old Soviet Union or Russia. With his brilliant mastery of the game and his disciplined approach to competition, he became recognized not only as a great champion but also as an inspiration to a whole generation of young Indian chess players.

*Jeffry Jensen*

tition until 1993, when the world champion, Garry Kasparov, severed his ties with the organization. In 1993, Kasparov and Nigel Short established the Professional Chess Association (PCA). This organization was short-lived, though, and folded in 1996.

From 1993 to 2006, there existed the championship sanctioned by the FIDE and the Classical World Championship. Kasparov remained the Classical World Champion from 1993 until 2000. In 2000, Vladimir Kramnik became champion of this rival world chess championship. He remained Classical World Champion until 2006. Anand became the FIDE world champion in 2000. With his victory, he became the first Indian to win the World Chess Championship. He held the title until 2002. The two rival championships did not resolve their differences and unify the title until 2006.

### Continuing the Story

While Anand's 2000 World Championship was a significant event, his 2007 World Chess Championship was a major event. The 2007 FIDE World Chess Championship was held in Mexico City, Mexico. Anand finished the double round-robin tournament with nine points out of a possible fourteen. Kramnik and Boris Gelfand tied for second place. With this victory, Anand had established himself as the undisputed champion. For the 2008 World Chess Championship, Anand had to defend his title against Kramnik. The championship was held in Bonn, Germany, from October 14 to November 2, 2008. Anand and Kramnik were to play a twelve-game match in which one of the two players had to score 6½ points in order to claim victory. After playing eleven games, Anand retained his title by scoring the 6½ points necessary to win. Over the course of the championship, he had three wins, seven draws, and one loss.

### Additional Sources

Anand, Viswanathan, with John Nunn. *Vishy Anand: My Best Games of Chess.* Rev. ed. London: Gambit, 2001.

Karmarkar, Amit. "Teammate Reveals the Process Behind Anand's Success." *The Times of India*, October 31, 2008.

Keene, Raymond D. *World Chess Championship: Kasparov Versus Anand.* New York: Henry Holt, 1995.

Keene, Raymond D., with Julian Simpole. *Vishy's Victory: The Undisputed 2007 World Chess Championship in Mexico City.* London: Impala Press Film Division, 2007.

McClain, Dylan Loeb. "With Draw, Anand Keeps World Chess Title." *The New York Times*, October 30, 2008.

Norwood, David. *Vishy Anand: Chess Super-Talent.* New York: Henry Holt, 1995.

## Honors and Awards

|  |  |
|------|-------|
| 1985 | Outstanding Indian chess sportsman |
| 1987 | Padma Shri award |
| 1991-92 | Rajiv Gandhi Khel Ratna sports award |
| 1997-98, 2003-04, 2007 | Chess Oscar |
| 2000 | Padma Bhushan award |
| 2007 | Padma Vibhushan award |

# Mario Andretti

**Born:** February 28, 1940
      Montona, Italy (now Motovun, Croatia)
**Also known as:** Mario Gabriele Andretti (full
   name)

### Early Life

Mario Gabriele Andretti and his identical twin brother Aldo were born to Alvise, a farmer, and Rina Andretti on February 28, 1940, in Montona, Italy (now Motovun, Croatia), near Trieste. The twins were born six years after their sister, Anna Maria. Times were hard in Italy after World War II, and the family spent seven years in a displaced persons' camp in Lucca, near Florence, Italy.

Not long after World War II, the twins became involved with automobiles. Their first job was parking cars, even though, at age thirteen, neither boy could drive. Other than a cultural inclination toward automobile racing, Mario recalled two major influences on his decision to become a career racer. First was uncle Bruno Benvegnu, a member of the Italian air force, who sparked Mario's interest in daring activities, and second was the thrill Mario got when he saw Alberto Ascari win the 1954 Monza Grand Prix. Barely into their teens, Mario and Aldo took advantage of an Italian government program designed to develop a new breed of Italian drivers. They found a sponsor for a three-hundred-dollar car and built up a local following as they won twenty or so motor races.

### The Road to Excellence

Alvise and Rina Andretti decided to move the family to the United States, where the future would be brighter. In 1955, sponsored by a relative in Nazareth, Pennsylvania, the Andretti family left Italy for good. Life in the New World was indeed far brighter for the Andrettis. Within two years, they had achieved the American dream of home and car ownership. The twins started working in a gas station, where they further refined their mechanical skills as well as their grasp of the English language.

Both Mario and Aldo got involved in the local dirt-track racing scene, and both had their share of mishaps. In 1957, Mario had his most serious racing-related injury ever when he broke his nose in a crash. Fate was not so kind to Aldo when, in 1958, he smashed against a fence and was in a coma for weeks. Aldo never fully recovered from this injury, but Mario continued to race.

In 1961, Mario married Dee Ann Hoch, who had been his tutor for correspondence courses he needed to earn his high school diploma. The couple had three children: two boys, Michael and Jeffrey, who shared their father's enthusiasm for racing, and one daughter, Barbra Dee. Mario worked his way up to the top ranks of sprint-car drivers. By 1964, the same year he became a naturalized American citizen, Mario was third in the national standings.

*Mario Andretti posing after winning the 1967 Daytona 500.* (RacingOne/Getty Images)

## The Emerging Champion

Mario's big break came in 1965. He was scouted by master mechanic Clint Brawner, who recognized Mario's potential and was impressed by his extensive mechanical knowledge and ability to work with his crew. With Brawner's recommendation, Mario joined a professional racing team and, that year, won the United States Auto Club national championship. Also in 1965, twenty-five-year-old Mario competed in the Indianapolis 500 for the first time. He placed third and was named rookie of the year. Four years later, and still a member of the same team, Mario won the 1969 Indianapolis 500.

At only 5 feet 6 inches tall and 134 pounds, Mario was considered by many to be too small for racing. However, his powerful wrists, hands, and shoulders, his mechanical expertise, and his extraordinary stamina and determination proved to be more important than sheer size. Mario also has a

### Record

Most pole positions won on the CART circuit, 64

### Honors and Awards

1965  Indianapolis 500 Rookie of the Year
1982  CART Goodwill Ambassador
1986  Inducted into Indianapolis Motor Speedway Hall of Fame
1990  Inducted into Motorsports Hall of Fame of America
1992  Driver of the Quarter Century
      Associated Press Driver of the Century
1995  Awarded honorary Doctor of Science degree, New England Institute of Technology
1996  Inducted into National Sprint Car Hall of Fame, Knoxville, Iowa
1999  Received Lifetime Achievement in Sports award, Coalition of Italo-American Association
2000  Chosen Associated Press Driver of the Century
      Inducted into International Motorsports Hall of Fame, Talladega, Alabama
2004  Inducted into Sebring International Raceway Hall of Fame, Sebring, Florida
2005  Inducted into Automotive Hall of Fame, Dearborn, Michigan
      Selected to the International Race of Champions (IROC) All-Time Legends Team
2006  Awarded Commendatore dell'Ordine al Merito della Repubblica Italian
2007  Received the Vince Lombardi Award of Excellence

### CART, Grand Prix, and Other Victories

| | |
|---|---|
| 1965-66 | Hoosier Grand Prix |
| | USAC National Champion |
| 1966 | Milwaukee 100 |
| | Atlanta 300 |
| 1966-67 | Hoosier 100 |
| 1966-67, 1985 | Milwaukee 200 |
| 1966-67, 1988, 1993 | Phoenix 200 |
| 1966, 1968 | Trenton 200 |
| 1967 | Daytona 500 |
| 1967, 1973, 1978 | Trenton 150 |
| 1968, 1973-74 | DuQuoin 100 |
| 1969 | Indianapolis 500 |
| | Pike's Peak Hill Climb |
| | Riverside 300 |
| | Trenton 300 |
| | Hanford 200 |
| 1969, 1973-74 | Tony Bettenhausen 100 |
| 1971 | South African Grand Prix |
| | Ontario, California, Grand Prix |
| 1974 | Valvoline/USAC Silver Crown Champion |
| 1977 | Italian Grand Prix |
| | United States Grand Prix West |
| 1977-78 | French Grand Prix |
| | Spanish Grand Prix |
| 1978 | Argentine Grand Prix |
| | Belgian Grand Prix |
| | German Grand Prix |
| | Netherlands Grand Prix |
| | World Championship of Drivers |
| 1980 | Michigan 150 |
| 1983-84, 1987 | Road America 200 |
| 1984 | Meadowlands Grand Prix |
| | Michigan 500 |
| | Michigan 200 |
| | Mid-Ohio 200 |
| | PPG Indy Car World Series Championship |
| 1984-85, 1987 | Long Beach Grand Prix |
| 1985-86 | Portland 200 |
| 1986 | Pocono 500 |
| 1988 | Cleveland Grand Prix |

reputation for staying cool under pressure, which helped him in the racing cockpit where temperatures can reach 140 degrees.

Having met the biggest challenge the oval track had to offer, Mario began to compete in Formula One racing. Known for its treacherous winding roads and varied courses in countries throughout the world, this was an entirely different type of racing. In 1971, with wins at Kyalami, South Africa's Grand Prix, and in Ontario, California, Mario began to develop his reputation as the man who could win any kind of auto race.

## Continuing the Story

In 1978, victory and tragedy came together for Mario, when he won the international racing world's most coveted prize, the Formula One world championship. Mario's teammate and good friend Swedish driver Ronnie Peterson also was Mario's primary rival for the championship. However, auto racing is a dangerous, and sometimes lethal, sport. Before the end of the season, when Ronnie was competing in an important race, he got into a fiery ten-car crash that cost him his life. Mario's Formula One world championship win was tainted by the loss of a great friend.

During Mario's third decade of racing professionally, he joined the glamorous Newman-Haas team, partially named after racing enthusiast and well-known film star Paul Newman. In 1984, Mario won driver of the year, becoming the first individual to win this award in each of three consecutive decades. Mario won the Phoenix 200 in April of 1993, his final race and his 109th major career victory. He retired from active racing in 1994.

Mario's sons, Michael and Jeffrey, inherited their father's love for the dangerous sport. In 1990, all three made racing history when they competed against each other during an Indianapolis car race. In 2006, Mario's grandson and Michael's son Marco began racing in the Indy Racing League (IRL). He finished second in the Indianapolis 500 and was awarded rookie of the year, joining his father and grandfather as a recipient of the award. In 2000, Mario's legendary status was solidified when he was voted driver of the century by the Associated Press and inducted into the International Motorsports Hall of Fame.

## Summary

Arriving in the United States at age fifteen with only a rudimentary understanding of English did not stop Mario Andretti from developing his love for cars and auto racing. Mario soon rose to be the premier auto racer in America, and later, in the world. As the first driver in motor-racing history to win both the Indianapolis and Formula One titles, Mario proved to be not only a skilled driver, but also a flexible one, winning on more than one hundred different types of tracks and courses.

*Leslie A. Pearl*

## Additional Sources

Andretti, Mario. *Andretti*. San Francisco, Calif.: Collins, 1994.

Daly, Derek, and Mario Andretti. *Race to Win: How to Become a Complete Champion Driver*. St. Paul, Minn.: Motorbooks International, 2008.

Kirby, Gordon. *Mario Andretti: A Driving Passion*. Phoenix, Ariz.: David Bull, 2001.

Nygaard, Peter. *Mario Andretti Photo Album: World Champion Driver Series*. Hudson, Wis.: Iconografix, 1999.

O'Leary, Mike. *Mario Andretti*. St. Paul, Minn.: Motorbooks International, 2002.

# Earl Anthony

**Born:** April 27, 1938
Tacoma, Washington
**Died:** August 14, 2001
New Berlin, Wisconsin
**Also known as:** Earl Roderick Anthony (full name)

### Early Life

Earl Roderick Anthony was born in Tacoma, Washington, on April 27, 1938. He was the youngest of three children of Earl Roderick, a career Army man, and Laura Ellen Anthony. Earl's father was often away because of his military duties, and Earl learned early to like independence.

The first sport in which Earl excelled was baseball. He especially enjoyed pitching, the most solitary position in the game. In tenth grade, he asked the high school coach if he could try out for the varsity team. When told to wait one more year until he was stronger, the stubborn young man decided not to play for the high school team at all. Instead, he pitched for an adult city league until he graduated from high school.

### The Road to Excellence

Earl joined the United States Air Force and continued to pitch for its baseball team. Although he was good enough to be scouted by the Dodgers in 1959, he knew that his future was not in professional baseball. When his four-year military commitment ended, Earl, already married to his high school sweetheart, Marylou, needed a job to provide for his wife, mortgage, and soon-to-arrive child. He took a job at a wholesale grocery company on the graveyard shift.

At this point in his life, Earl gave up baseball. However, his competitiveness and desire to win that he

had felt since childhood remained. At the age of twenty-one, Earl Anthony discovered his new sport. He joined the grocery company's league and bowled seriously for the first time. There are connections between pitching a baseball and bowling. The distance from a pitching mound to home plate is 60 feet 6 inches while a bowling alley is 60 feet in length. Like pitching a baseball, bowling is an individual act that requires similar body movement. Not surprisingly, Earl felt attracted to bowling.

During his first bowling season, the left-handed Earl lost a considerable amount of money in "pot games," in which each player bets an equal amount of money and the winner takes all, with his 165 average. He practiced early in the morning, after working all night, often setting pins in return for

*Earl Anthony in 1974.* (AP/Wide World Photos)

## PBA Tour Victories

| | |
|---|---|
| 1970 | Seattle |
| 1971 | New York City |
| 1972 | Portland; Redwood City; St. Louis |
| 1973 | Seattle; National Championship at Oklahoma City |
| 1974 | Firestone Tournament of Champions; National Championship at Downey; Davenport; Jackson; Waukegan; Battle Creek |
| 1975 | Arcadia; Garden City; National Championship at Downey; Davenport; Jackson; Waukegan; Battle Creek |
| 1976 | Hartford; Miami; Fresno; Norwalk; Waukegan; Battle Creek |
| 1977 | Torrance; Waukegan |
| 1978 | Kissimmee; Firestone Tournament of Champions |
| 1979-80 | Garden City |
| 1982 | St. Louis; Peoria; National Championship at Toledo; Milwaukee |
| 1983 | National Championship at Toledo; Peoria |
| 1988 | Senior Championship at Canton |
| 1990 | Houston; Senior Invitational at Las Vegas; Senior Championship at Canton |

## Other Major Victories

| | |
|---|---|
| 1976 | AMF Grand Prix |
| 1977, 1984 | ABC Masters |

the use of a lane. Another way in which he kept down the costs of bowling was to "shadow bowl," or throw the ball down a lane at imaginary pins. He never used an instructor. All of his hard work was rewarded when, after only one year, Earl's average soared into the low 200's. Earl began to win many of the "pot games" and found that he bowled well under pressure. He began to think of bowling professionally.

### The Emerging Champion

Earl was confident in his ability to be a success in professional bowling, but he was also aware that travel and tournament entrance expenses quickly add up to about fifteen thousand dollars a year. That was out of reach for the grocer and father of three. Earl's friend David Tuell, Jr., attorney and fellow bowler, agreed to sponsor him in return for a portion of his winnings.

In 1970, at thirty-one years of age, Earl joined the Professional Bowlers Association (PBA) and became a full-time professional bowler. For the next thirteen years, he spent about thirty weeks a year on the road, almost always leaving Marylou at home with the couple's three children. Only Puff, the family dog, and four bowling balls accompanied him regularly as he traveled across the country to the various tournaments.

When it was Earl's turn to bowl, one could see the intense concentration on his face. The only thought on his mind was how to throw a 16-pound plastic ball down a 60-foot maple lane in order to knock down ten plastic-coated maple pins. He was able to ignore everything else around him, fans and television cameras included.

This concentration paid off. Earl was voted the male bowler of the decade for the 1970's by the Bowling Writers Association of America and given a place in the PBA's Hall of Fame in 1981. In 1982, he became the first bowler in history to earn more than one million dollars in prize money after winning his fifth national championship in Toledo, Ohio. As his popularity grew, he also earned money endorsing bowling balls, wrist supports, and clothing.

### Continuing the Story

In June, 1978, Earl, a 6-foot 1-inch, 195-pound smoker, suffered a heart attack. Just two months later, however, he was back on tour at his usual grueling pace, winning tournaments and titles in bowling alleys across the country.

In 1983, only thirteen years after his first professional victory in the 1970 Seattle Open, Earl retired from professional bowling as the most successful

## PBA Records

41 titles
145 top-five finishes
Highest eighteen-game score, 4,515 (1977)
Highest twenty-four-game score, 5,825 (1970)

## Honors and Awards

| | |
|---|---|
| 1972-75 | *Bowlers Journal* All-American Team |
| 1973-75, 1980, 1983 | George Young High Average Award |
| 1974-76, 1981-83 | BWAA Bowler of the Year |
| | PBA Player of the Year |
| 1981 | Male Bowler of the Decade |
| | Inducted into PBA Hall of Fame |
| 1986 | Inducted into ABC Hall of Fame |

bowler in the history of the sport. He had compiled an unmatched record that included six national championship victories. The graceful left-hander won the PBA player of the year award six times.

In 1984, Earl joined the NBC television network sportscasting team as a bowling expert and analyst for PBA coverage. In his retirement, Earl also managed two bowling centers, authored a second book, *Championship Bowling* (1983), and campaigned to raise the level of prize money in professional bowling to become equal with professional golf winnings.

## Summary

Although Earl Anthony was very successful, he always maintained an unassuming lifestyle. A quiet and unathletic-looking man with a 1940's crew cut and horn-rimmed glasses, Earl always appeared unremarkable until he began his five-step approach. As he threw the ball with his famous, pronounced right hook, the look of concentration on his face portrayed his champion status. Earl used a winning mixture of concentration and determination to be the best at what he did.

*Leslie A. Pearl*

## Additional Sources

Anthony, Earl, and Dawson Taylor. *Winning Bowling*. Chicago: Contemporary Books, 1994.

Ballantini, Brett. "Earl Anthony: His Influence Resonates." *Bowling Digest*, December, 2001.

Herbst, Dan. *Bowling Three Hundred: Top Pros Share Their Secrets to Rolling the Perfect Game*. Chicago: Contemporary Books, 1993.

Pezzano, Chuck. "International Hall Right Up Bowlers' Alley." *The Record*, April 22, 2007, p. S10.

Zielinski, Graeme. "Bowling's High Roller: Champion Earl Anthony Had Confidence to Spare." *The Washington Post*, August 17, 2001, p. C1.

# *Eddie Arcaro*

**Born:** February 19, 1916
    Cincinnati, Ohio
**Died:** November 14, 1997
    Miami, Florida
**Also known as:** George Edward Arcaro (full
    name); the Master

### Early Life

George Edward Arcaro was born on February 19, 1916, in Cincinnati, Ohio. He weighed only 3 pounds at birth and was called the "shoebox baby." His father had several small businesses, but his income was modest.

Eddie wanted to play team sports in school but was too small; even as an adult he was only 5 feet 2 inches and weighed about 114 pounds. At the age of eleven, he and his family moved to the horse-racing state of Kentucky. He realized that his small size was an advantage as a jockey. He quit school when he was thirteen and began to exercise horses at Latonia, a local track. Eddie was strong, graceful,

and tough. A sledding accident crippled him in 1928, but, contrary to his doctor's prediction, he quickly walked again. This accident revealed that Eddie had the determination that a great jockey needed.

### The Road to Excellence

Eddie's father wanted him to finish school but gave him one year to prove himself. Although his first two employers said that he would never be a good jockey, Eddie persevered. Horseman Clarence Davison was impressed by Eddie's willingness to perform all the hard and dirty chores around the stable and his love for horses. Davison put Eddie through years of rigorous schooling. He taught Eddie jockeying techniques: pacing the horse to leave speed at the end of the race, balancing his weight to avoid interfering with his mount's movements, understanding a horse's mannerisms, whipping right- or left-handed, and picking the best footing around a track. Horse racing was a rough sport when Eddie started riding. Davison helped Eddie become a scrappy rider who knew every illegal trick in the book, a requirement for a jockey to survive at that time.

Although he started out as a hard rider in a rough sport, intelligence became the hallmark of Eddie's riding. Furthermore, his hard work began to pay off. At the age of sixteen, Eddie won fourteen races in one week. Observers realized that he had valuable potential. In 1934, Eddie jumped to the big time when he was hired by Calumet Farms. He made $350 a month plus 10 percent of the winnings. From this time on, he worked for the best trainers and racing farms, including Calumet Farms and Greentree Stables.

### The Emerging Champion

Eddie's career was an illustration of the importance of perseverance and determination in achieving success. His early teachers did not consider him a talented

*Eddie Arcaro, who twice won horse racing's triple crown, holding the Belmont trophy in 1954. (AP/Wide World Photos)*

## Major Championship Victories

| Year | Race | Horse |
|------|------|-------|
| 1938 | Kentucky Derby | Lawrin |
| 1941 | Belmont Stakes | Whirlaway |
| | Kentucky Derby | Whirlaway |
| | Preakness Stakes | Whirlaway |
| 1942 | Belmont Stakes | Shut Out |
| 1945 | Belmont Stakes | Pavot |
| | Kentucky Derby | Hoop Jr. |
| 1948 | Belmont Stakes | Citation |
| | Kentucky Derby | Citation |
| | Preakness Stakes | Citation |
| 1950 | Preakness Stakes | Hill Prince |
| 1951 | Preakness Stakes | Bold |
| 1952 | Kentucky Derby | Hill Gail |
| 1955 | Belmont Stakes | Nashua |
| | Preakness Stakes | Nashua |
| 1957 | Preakness Stakes | Bold Ruler |

natural jockey, but he became great through hard work and intelligence. He proved that what many people consider to be a physical handicap—small size—could be an advantage. His greatest personal victory came in achieving self-control. When Eddie began racing, he had a fierce temper and received many suspensions. In 1942, he was banned for a year from all tracks after a dangerous clash with another jockey during a race. This suspension brought him to his senses. Control of himself and his mount became one of his major strengths as a jockey.

In a short space of ten years, Eddie moved to the top of his sport. His public recognition began on May 7, 1938, when he won his first Kentucky Derby on Lawrin. Year after year, he rode the most famous horses of his day. In 1941, he won horse racing's greatest prize, the triple crown, by winning the Kentucky Derby, the Belmont Stakes, and the Preakness Stakes. He won on Whirlaway, which he called the most exciting horse he ever rode. By 1944, he was regarded as the nation's top jockey and one of the greatest in history. During this period, Eddie won more than $1 million a year five times. In 1948, he set a record by winning $1,686,330. He won his second Triple Crown in 1948, on Citation, which he said was the greatest horse he ever rode.

Victory after victory followed. He continued to win throughout the 1950's. Eddie was one of only

two jockeys to win the Kentucky Derby five times. In 1955, Eddie and Nashua won the Belmont and Preakness. In 1957, Eddie finished first in the Preakness on Bold Ruler. Eddie Arcaro was horse racing's top money winner for six years. His purse money totaled $30,039,543.

### Continuing the Story

After Eddie achieved control over his temper, he became one of the best-loved figures in racing. He lived quietly and enjoyed his fame and money. Eddie became a multimillionaire and owned three expensive homes. He made investments in oil, had a wholesale saddlery business, and owned a West Coast chain of restaurants. Despite his competitiveness, Eddie became very popular with other jockeys. Some people said that he was self-centered, but the widow of Albert Snider saw another side. Her husband had been chosen to ride Citation in the 1948 Kentucky Derby, but he died in an accident. Eddie rode Citation in his place and won. He split his share of the purse with Mrs. Snider.

Eddie rode in his last race at Pimlico racetrack in Baltimore, Maryland, on November 16, 1961. After retiring, he worked as a television commentator on racing events and wrote a book, *I Ride to Win!* (1951). During his leisure time, Eddie golfed. He brought to that sport all of the energy and intelligence that he displayed in horse racing.

### Summary

Eddie Arcaro turned his small size into an asset and became one of the great sportsmen of his time. He combined intelligence, strength, and courage with a special ability to understand horses. Although some believed his natural talent was limited, hard

### Records and Milestones

Annual money leader (1940, 1942, 1948, 1950, 1952, 1955)
Triple Crown winner aboard Whirlaway (1941)
Triple Crown winner aboard Citation (1948)
First jockey to ride two Triple Crown winners
24,092 mounts
4,779 victories

### Honors and Awards

| | |
|------|------|
| 1955 | Inducted into Pimlico Jockeys Hall of Fame |
| 1958 | Inducted into Jockeys' Hall of Fame |

work made him a master of his profession. He started as a scrappy, competitive rider but became known as the "gentleman jockey." Eddie was called the most famous man to ride a horse in the United States since Paul Revere.

*Martha E. Pemberton*

## Additional Sources

Arcaro, Eddie. *I Ride to Win!* New York: Greenberg, 1951.

Cannon, Jimmy. "Arcaro a Gentleman Horseman." *New York Post*, September 8, 2002, p. 111.

Chew, Peter. *The Kentucky Derby: The First One Hundred Years.* Boston: Houghton Mifflin, 1974.

Claypool, Jim. "Eddie Arcaro Rode Hard, Fast, to Win." *Cincinnati Post*, May 1, 2006, p. B3.

Kindred, Dave. "Horse Racing's Little Big Man." *Sporting News* 221, no. 47 (November 24, 1997): 7.

Nack, William. "The Headiest Horseman." *Sports Illustrated* 87, no. 21 (November 24, 1997): 21-22.

Platt, Jim, and James Buckley. *Sports Immortals: Stories of Inspiration and Achievement.* Chicago: Triumph Books, 2002.

# *Lance Armstrong*

**Born:** September 18, 1971
    Plano, Texas
**Also known as:** Lance Edward Gunderson (birth
    name); Lance Edward Armstrong (full name);
    Mellow Johnny

### Early Life
On September 18, 1971, Lance Edward Gunderson was born to seventeen-year-old Linda Gayle Mooneyham and Eddie Charles Gunderson. Lance's parents divorced before he was two years old. When Lance was three, his mother married Terry Armstrong, who adopted Lance. The couple divorced, and Lance's mother raised him by herself.

*Lance Armstrong racing in 2002.* (AP/Wide World Photos)

By fifth grade, Lance was already a great endurance athlete. His mother encouraged him in sports, and Lance credits her for his work ethic and ability to persevere. He excelled in the triathlon, a challenging event consisting of swimming, bicycling, and running. At the age of thirteen, he won his first IronKids Triathlon and was a professional triathlete at sixteen years old. He also competed in local bike races. In 1988, *Triathlete* magazine named him rookie of the year. Lance was the National Sprint Triathlon Champion in 1989 and 1990.

### The Road to Excellence
Lance's favorite event was bicycle racing. He left high school during his senior year to train with the U.S. Olympic cycling development team in Colorado Springs, Colorado. He later attended private classes in order to receive his high school diploma. Meanwhile, the U.S. Cycling Federation had recruited him for its junior national team, and in 1989, Lance competed in the Junior World Championships in Moscow, Soviet Union (now Russia).

After high school, Lance had success on the amateur cycling circuit. In 1990 and 1991, he rode with the Subaru-Montgomery team and joined the U.S. National Cycling Team in 1991. At the 1990 World Championship Road Race, he placed eleventh, posting the fastest time of any American since 1976. In 1991, he became the national amateur road race champion, and he defeated the world's best professional cyclists at a difficult multiple-stage race, the Settimana Bergamasca (later known as Settimana Ciclistica Lombarda) (Lombardic cycling week), in Italy. At the U.S. Olympic time trials, Lance finished second. He was favored to win the road race at the 1992 Olympics in Barcelona, but he finished fourteenth. After the Olympics, he became a professional cyclist with the Motorola team based in the United States.

### The Emerging Champion
Lance finished last in his first professional race, the 1992 San Sebastián Classic in Spain. He refused to quit and became a cycling superstar within the next

few years. In 1993, he won the Union Cycliste Internationale Road World Championship and the CoreStates United States Professional Racing Organization National Road Championship. He won the Tour of America, the Thrift Drug Classic, the Trofeo Laigueglia, and the Kmart West Virginia Classic. In 1994, he won the Thrift Drug Classic again.

In 1993 and 1995, he won stages in the Tour de France, the world's most prestigious cycling race. Started in 1903, the event is a twenty-three-day, twenty-one-stage road race over more than 2,000 miles in France and nearby countries. Lance became the first American to win a European one-day classic when he won the 1995 San Sebastián Classic. In 1995 and 1996, he won the prestigious Tour Du Pont, which covered several Mid-Atlantic states.

By 1996, Lance was ranked the number-one cyclist in the world. He competed at the 1996 Summer Olympics in Atlanta, Georgia, and signed a lucrative contract with the French team Cofidis. However, in October, Lance was diagnosed with malignant testicular cancer, which had spread to his brain and lungs. He was given only a 50 percent chance of living. In 1997, before he knew if he would recover, he established the Lance Armstrong Foundation (LAF) to help the cancer community through advocacy, education, and research. After undergoing surgeries and aggressive chemotherapy, he recovered and returned to cycling in 1998.

### Continuing the Story

In the summer of 1999, as the lead rider of the newly formed U.S. Postal Service Pro Cycling Team, Lance became the second American to win the Tour de France and the first riding with an American team. Lance and the team won the Tour de France every year from 1999 to 2004. With his sixth consecutive win in 2004, he broke the record set by Miguel Indurain, who was the first to win five in a row, from 1991 to 1995.

| Honors and Awards | |
|---|---|
| 1992, 1996, 2000 | U.S. Olympic team |
| 1993, 1995-96, 1998-99, 2002, 2005 | Selected *VeloNews* magazine's North American Male Cyclist of the Year |
| 1999 | Received Mendrisio d'Or Award in Switzerland |
| | Selected ABC's Wide World of Sports Athlete of the Year |
| 1999-2001, 2003-04 | Received Velo d'Or Award by *Velo* Magazine, France |
| 1999, 2001-03 | Selected United States Olympic Committee (USOC) SportsMan of the Year |
| 2000 | Bronze medal, Olympic Games |
| | *VeloNews*, Male Cyclist of the Year |
| | World's Most Outstanding Athlete Award, Jesse Owens International Trophy |
| | Laureus World Comeback of the Year |
| 2000-01, 2003-04 | Selected *VeloNews* magazine's International Cyclist of the Year |
| 2002 | Selected *Sports Illustrated* Sportsman of the Year |
| 2002-05 | Selected Associated Press Male Athlete of the Year |
| 2003 | Laureus World Sportsman of the Year |
| | Selected Reuters Sportsman of the Year |
| | Received BBC Sports Personality of the Year Overseas Personality Award |
| 2003-06 | Received ESPY Award for Best Male Athlete |
| 2004 | Awarded Trophee de L'Academie des Sport, France |

In the 2005 Tour de France, Lance rode for the Discovery Channel Pro Cycling Team, formerly the U.S. Postal Service Pro Cycling Team. He retired from competitive racing after winning his seventh and final Tour de France; he set the record for the most wins ever.

After retiring in 2005, Lance devoted more time to his cancer foundation and other projects. In 2006, a group of sports celebrities including Lance, Andre Agassi, Muhammad Ali, Mia Hamm, Jackie Joyner-Kersee, and Cal Ripken, Jr., established Athletes for Hope to help other athletes become involved in sports philanthropy. Lance won the best athlete award at the Kids' Choice Awards in 2006 and was named male athlete of the year at the 2006 ESPY Awards show. He ran in the 2006 New York City Marathon and raised more than $600,000 for LiveStrong/LAF. In December, 2007, Lance was part of the seven-country United Service Organizations holiday tour for U.S. troops.

## Major Championships

| | |
|---|---|
| 1991 | U.S. National Amateur Champion |
| 1992 | First Union Grand Prix |
| | Thrift Drug Classic |
| 1993 | $1 million Thrift Drug Triple Crown |
| | U.S. National Road Race Championship |
| | World Championship |
| 1994 | Thrift Drug Classic |
| 1995 | Classico San Sebastian |
| 1995-96 | Tour DuPont |
| 1996 | Fleche Wallone |
| 1998 | Cascade Classic |
| | Rheinland Pfalz Rundfahrt |
| | Sprint 56K Criterium |
| | Tour of Luxembourg |
| 1999 | Boxmeer Criterium |
| 1999, 2000-05 | Tour de France |

## Summary

The legendary Lance Armstrong is considered one of the greatest and most inspirational athletes ever. From 1999 to 2005, he set a world record with seven consecutive Tour de France victories. Even more awe inspiring was that he won these races after a near-death battle with cancer. He became a world representative for the cancer community. By December, 2007, his LAF had provided more than $20.3 million for research and more than $6.1 million in grants to community organizations. Lance's memoir, *It's Not About the Bike: My Journey Back to Life* became a *New York Times* bestseller.

In September, 2008, Lance shocked the world by announcing his intention to return to competitive racing. Moreover, he stated his intention of winning the Tour de France in 2009.

*Alice Myers*

## Additional Sources

Armstrong, Lance. *It's Not About the Bike: My Journey Back to Life.* New York: Berkley Books, 2001.

Armstrong, Lance, and Sally Jenkins. *Every Second Counts.* New York: Broadway Books, 2003.

Coyle, Daniel. *Lance Armstrong's War.* New York: HarperCollins, 2005.

Kearns, Brad. *How Lance Does It.* New York: McGraw-Hill, 2007.

# *Bob Askin*

**Born:** May 9, 1900
Rochester, New York
**Died:** October 8, 1973
Miles City, Montana

### Early Life

Bob Askin was born on May 9, 1900, in Rochester, New York, where his father was a railroad engineer. When Bob was five years old, his family moved to South Dakota, where he saw the famous Buffalo Bill's Wild West show. That exciting performance by cowboys, cowgirls, American Indians, and sharpshooters thrilled Bob and made him want to become a cowboy.

Bob got his wish in 1909, when the family moved to a government homestead near Ismay, in southeastern Montana. Ismay was in the heart of ranching country, and Bob and his eight siblings were soon spending most of their time on horseback. They rode to and from their one-room school, which was open about three months a year. They also helped with the ranch chores, and like all youngsters in the West, played many games on horseback.

### The Road to Excellence

Bob had a natural talent with animals and was an outstanding roper and rider by his early teens. Besides working for the family, he was hired by the biggest ranchers in the area to break and tame horses. Bob was so talented that he went from ranch to ranch, breaking horses no one else could handle, and earning higher wages than regular cowboys.

Bob's success in riding wild broncs led people to hold special contests where he matched his skills against older cowboys. Long before organized rodeos came to rural communities like Ismay, the local people gathered around, making a circle with their horses and wagons to form a little arena where the cowboys could ride. The only prizes were usually pride and "bragging rights." Bob entered his first real rodeo when he was fifteen at the 1915 Fourth of July celebration in Miles City, Montana. Most Western cattle towns had big celebrations on Independence Day, and Miles City was no exception. People came from all over the area to join the fes-

tivities and watch the contests. Bob won the bronc riding, the first of his many rodeo championships.

Before World War I, rodeo was not a very big sport. Most rodeos were held in the far West during the summer months. Bob entered and won many of those local rodeos and continued working on ranches the rest of the year.

### The Emerging Champion

In 1917, Bob joined the United States Army and was sent to Camp Lewis, Washington. There, the seventeen-year-old soldier stayed aboard several notorious bucking horses that no cowboy had ever ridden. He became more famous than ever. After the war, Bob came home to find that a terrible winter and a

*Bob Askin.* (Courtesy of ProRodeo Hall of Fame and Museum of the American Cowboy)

23

depression had about ruined the big cattle ranches. Needing to earn a living, he decided to try a rodeo career. He soon became the toughest bronc rider in the business and was seldom bucked off.

Bob's first big break came in 1924, when he was among the top cowboys and cowgirls invited to compete at the first international rodeo, in London, England. There, Bob won the bronc riding and was named the world's champion. After the rodeo, many of the participants stayed in Europe to compete and give exhibitions. Touring Europe was quite an experience for a young man like Bob, who had spent most of his life in the far western United States.

Also in 1924, Bob married Helen Fulton, who was from Ismay. During the next seven years, Bob won almost every important bronc riding championship in the United States. It is impossible to know all of them because there are no official records from those years. The Professional Rodeo Cowboys Association (PRCA) was not formed until 1936. The National Finals Rodeo (NFR) did not start until 1959.

Bob won at some very big rodeos in the 1920's and early 1930's. He won the bronc riding title at the famous Pendleton Roundup in 1925. In 1927 and 1928, he was named the world's champion of bronc riding at Madison Square Garden, the site of the most important rodeo in the country at the time. At these and other rodeos in the United States and Canada, he also won money in bull riding and calf roping. Today, few cowboys win money in three such different events.

In Canada in 1926, Bob caused a bucking horse named Midnight to become famous. Bob rode Midnight to the championship at Montreal, but the next week at Toronto, Midnight was the winner. By bucking off Bob Askin, the number-one bronc rider in the world, Midnight became a legend and is still remembered today.

### Continuing the Story

By that time, Bob was known far and wide as "The Man from Ismay," the most famous citizen of his tiny Montana hometown. In winning his many championships, he also changed his sport. Many cowboys copied Bob's style of spurring broncs from front to back. He was also one of the first successful rodeo cowboys to use small spurs instead of the big Mexican-style spurs that had been used since the 1800's.

## Championship Victories

| | |
|---|---|
| 1915 | Saddle Bronc Riding, Miles City, Mont. |
| 1924 | Saddle Bronc Riding, Wembley Stadium Rodeo |
| 1924, 1927 | Saddle Bronc Riding, Los Angeles Rodeo |
| 1925 | Saddle Bronc Riding, Pendleton Roundup |
| | Saddle Bronc Riding, Kansas City, Kans. |
| 1926 | Saddle Bronc Riding, Montreal, Quebec |
| 1927 | Saddle Bronc Riding, Vancouver, British Columbia |
| 1927-28 | Saddle Bronc Riding, Madison Square Garden Rodeo |
| | Saddle Bronc Riding, Chicago Stadium Rodeo |

## Honors and Awards

| | |
|---|---|
| 1978 | Inducted into Rodeo Hall of Fame |

Although he was only thirty-four at the time, Bob retired from rodeo in 1934, having ridden bucking broncs for twenty-five years. He and Helen remained at Ismay, where they raised three sons and two daughters and later enjoyed thirteen grandchildren. Bob never lost interest in rodeo, and from 1968 until his death in 1973, he attended every NFR. There he got to know the contestants and thrilled a whole new generation of cowboys with his tales of the olden days.

### Summary

Bob Askin was one of the most famous rodeo cowboys of his era, and the winner of almost every important rodeo championship of the 1920's. His success changed the style of bronc riding. He was so beloved that the National Cowboy Hall of Fame at Oklahoma City, Oklahoma, issued a special bulletin announcing his 1973 death in Miles City, Montana. Sadly, he did not live to enjoy his greatest honor. In 1978, he was elected to the Rodeo Hall of Fame as the greatest bronc rider of his day.

*Mary Lou LeCompte*

### Additional Sources

Allen, Michael. *Rodeo Cowboys in the North American Imagination.* Reno: University of Nevada Press, 1998.

Fredriksson, Kristine. *American Rodeo from Buffalo Bill to Big Business.* College Station: Texas A&M Press, 1985.

Wooden, Wayne S., and Gavin Ehringer. *Rodeo in America: Wranglers, Roughstock, and Paydirt.* Lawrence: University Press of Kansas, 1996.

# *Kenny Bartram*

**Born:** August 23, 1978
     Stillwater Oklahoma
**Also known as:** Kenny Lee Bartram (full name);
    Cowboy; K-Style; Hazard

## Early Life

Kenny Lee Bartram was born August 23, 1978, in Stillwater, Oklahoma. He gained a love for motorcycles and racing motocross from his uncle, Guy "Coop" Cooper, who was the 125cc national champion in 1990. Kenny watched his uncle compete and knew he was destined to emulate him. He won his first championship after finishing high school. In 1997 and 1999, he was the Oklahoma state pro-class champion in 125cc and 250cc divisions. In 1999, Kenny entered the Gravity Games national competition and took home a gold medal in doubles competition.

## The Road to Excellence

After winning several motocross championships, Kenny found freestyle riding to be a more creative way to compete. Many motorcyclists were experimenting with freestyle riding in their backyards, but the event was not included in extreme-sports competitions. In 1999, that changed when freestyle became a part of the X Games.

Freestyle motocross (FMX) is divided into two competitions. The first is the "big air" competition, in which opponents compete on a dirt track with 60-foot gaps—the space between two points over which a freestyler will jump—and take three jumps, trying to perform the most complicated and stylish trick they can while in the air. The second portion of FMX competition is the Freestyle Motocross, in which riders have 90 seconds to perform as many jumps and tricks as they can around a track with various jumps and ramps. A ten-person panel judges both of these events and awards up to one hundred points. The total number of points for the two events determines the winner.

During Kenny's first few professional years of freestyle riding, he broke many bones and had difficulty against the other competitors. However, he later emerged as one of the greatest freestyle motocross riders of all time.

## The Emerging Champion

Kenny rarely missed a competition. For the first four years of his FMX tenure he competed constantly and won often. In 2000, he won a bronze medal in the Gravity Games and became an International Freestyle Motocross Association (IFMA) champion. In 2001, he won a gold medal in the big air event at the summer X Games, with a trick called the Shaolin Sterilizer, and a silver medal at the extreme X Games. In 2002, he continued to win, becoming the IFMA and Van's triple crown overall freestyle champion. In 2003, he finished second in the Van's triple crown championship and won a Red Bull X Fighters championship. Also in 2003, he was the World Freeride Association's big-air and freestyle champion.

*Kenny Bartram at the 2004 X Games.* (AP/Wide World Photos)

## X-Games Results

| | |
|---|---|
| 2001 | Gold medal (big air) |
| 2002 | Silver medal (freestyle) |
| 2003 | Gold medal (freestyle) |
| | Bronze medal (big air) |
| 2005 | Silver medal (freestyle) |

Furthermore, Kenny became the 2003 X Games global champion in freestyle and received a bronze medal in big air. In 2005, he won a freestyle gold medal at the Gravity Games and a silver medal for freestyle at the X Games. At these X Games, he performed one of his best aerial stunts but received only fourth place in the best-trick category.

### Continuing the Story

As of 2008, Kenny had won a total of fifty-seven career IFMA awards, more than any other rider in the sport. However, he paid a physical price for these victories. He lost seven teeth, had seventeen broken bones, and had one broken blood vessel in his brain. These and other injuries partially contributed to Kenny's decision to change his focus from freestyle riding to rally-car racing. In 2006, he stopped freestyle racing, except for endorsements or other demonstrations. Though he continued to participate, he shifted to rally-car racing and other adventures, such as bull riding for a Country Music Channel reality television show and playing a character in the video game *Crusty Demons*.

Though Kenny halted his freestyle motocross career, he did not lose his determination. In 2006, Rally America welcomed Kenny, and he began competing. Rally racing is a grueling sport. The only contact the riders are allowed is with their "codrivers": teammates looking at a computerized image of the course who alert the driver about what to expect around the next corner. The drivers rely on these codrivers to direct them away from cliffs, ravines, and ditches. This sort of extreme racing was the next level for Kenny. Though a champion rarely quits at the apex of his reign, those who knew Kenny were not surprised he began rally-car racing. In 2006, he was named Rally America's rookie of the year and production-class and two-wheel-drive overall national champion.

### Summary

Kenny Bartram altered the face of extreme sports but stayed unaltered by his celebrity. He continued to live in Stillwater, Oklahoma, and drove a pickup truck. Though he compiled more wins than any other freestyle rider and hoped to do the same in rally racing, he remembered when he was a boy, watching his uncle Coop ride dirt tracks in rural Oklahoma.

*Pamela D. Doughty*

### Additional Sources

Milan, Garth. *Freestyle Motocross: Jump Tricks from the Pros.* Osceola, Wis.: Motorbooks, 2000.

Rohrer, Russ. *Ten Days in the Dirt: The Spectacle of Off-Road Motorcycling.* Osceola, Wis.: Motorbooks, 2004.

Scott, Michael. *Motocourse 2007-2008: The World's Leading MotoGP and Superbike Annual.* Silverstone, England: Crash Media Group, 2008.

## Honors and Awards

| | |
|---|---|
| 1997, 1999 | Oklahoma state motocross champion |
| 2002 | International Freestyle Motocross Association champion |
| 2003 | World Freeride Association Series champion (freestyle; big air) |
| 2005 | Freestyle gold medal (Gravity Games) |
| 2006 | Rally America rookie of the year |
| | Rally America national champion (two-wheel drive; production class) |

# Earl W. Bascom

**Born:** June 19, 1906
Vernal, Utah
**Died:** August 28, 1995
Victorville, California
**Also known as:** Cowboy of Cowboy Artists

## Early Life

Earl Bascom was born in a log cabin on a ranch in Vernal, Utah. His family eventually included six brothers, four sisters, and a stepbrother, all of whom developed riding talents. Earl's father, John W. Bascom, once served as a deputy sheriff; Earl's mother died when he was six. The family moved to a ranch in Canada, where Earl grew up. He later worked on some of the biggest horse and cattle ranches in the United States and Canada, breaking wild horses in Canada, Utah, Colorado, Montana, and Wyoming. He also punched cattle and went on trail drives, the largest of which involved rounding up approximately 7,000 horses. At times, he worked as a stagecoach driver, miner, blacksmith, and rancher.

## The Road to Excellence

Earl began his rodeo career in 1916, the early days of rodeo competition. He and three of his brothers—Raymond, Melvin, and Weldon—all became rodeo pioneers and were known as the "Bronc-Bustin' Bascom Boys." In 1916, at their ranch in Canada, the brothers designed and constructed the first side-delivery chute ever used by rodeo riders and animals. Three years later, Earl and his father designed and built the first reverse-opening chute. In 1922, Earl invented a hornless bronco saddle and, in 1924, a one-hand bareback rigging to which riders hang on. Both devises have continued to be used in professional rodeos. Earl also designed the first high-cut riding chaps, used regularly by subsequent rodeo riders.

In 1935, in Columbia, Mississippi, using electric lights, Earl and his brother Weldon produced the first outdoor night rodeo. Earl designed and constructed Mississippi's first permanent rodeo arena a year later. He con-

tinued working in rodeos for one-quarter of a century in practically all aspects of the sport, including bareback riding, saddle-bronc riding, bull riding, steer riding, steer wrestling, and wild-horse racing. He also worked outside the performance arena at such jobs as rodeo producer and announcer. During the rodeos in Mississippi, Earl met and married Nadine Diffey. He was declared "Rodeo's First Collegiate Cowboy" because he used his rodeo earnings between 1933 and 1940 to attend and graduate from college.

## The Emerging Champion

Besides helping to develop rodeo as a sport and designing some of its basic equipment, Earl competed in every area of the sport during a career that lasted from 1916 to 1940. Besides excelling in his own competitive events, he worked as a pickup man, for riders who were thrown from their animals, and as a rodeo clown, a job which often involved diverting a wild animal from injuring a grounded rider. For his role in the development of rodeo as a sport, he was given honorary memberships in the Cowboys' Turtle Association (later known as the Professional Rodeo Cowboys Association) and the Canadian Pro Rodeo Association.

Earl was also an entertainer, sometimes anonymously. One famous example involved the "Ladies' Wild Mule Ride," which began when a Mississippi farmer brought a cantankerous mule to the rodeo and asked if the rodeo people might tame it. Instead, the rodeo personnel invented the mule ride

## Rodeo Championships

| | |
|---|---|
| 1930 | All-around champion (Three-Bar Ranch Stampede) (Saskatchewan) |
| 1933 | North American championship (Calgary Stampede) (Calgary, Alberta) |
| 1934 | All-around champion (Lethbridge Stampede) (Lethbridge, Alberta) |
| 1935 | All-around champion (Raymond Stampede) (Raymond, Alberta) |
| 1936 | All-around champion (Nephi Stampede) (Nephi, Utah) |
| 1937 | All-around champion (Pocatello Rodeo) (Pocatello, Idaho) |
| 1938 | All-around champion (Rigby Rodeo) (Rigby, Idaho) |
| 1939 | All-around champion (Portland Rodeo) (Portland, Oregon) |
| 1940 | All-around champion (Raymond Stampede) (Raymond, Alberta) |

on the spot for that evening's rodeo and asked the audience if any women would volunteer to ride the mule. Earl put on a long dress and bonnet to disguise himself and sat in the stands when the announcement was made. He raised his hand to "volunteer," walked with a dainty step over to the mule, climbed aboard, and rode the animal to a standstill. Then he got off and went behind the chutes to change back to his regular clothing. For years, residents talked about the unidentified girl who rode a wild mule at a rodeo and then disappeared.

## Continuing the Story

Earl garnered many of his top rodeo awards in the 1930's. He was the all-around champion in the 1930 Three-Bar Ranch Stampede, in Saskatchewan, Canada; the bareback and all-around champion in Lethbridge, Alberta, Canada, in 1934; the saddle-bronc, steer-decorating, and all-around champion in Raymond, Alberta, in 1935; the all-around champion in Nephi, Utah, in 1936; the saddle-bronc, bareback, bull-riding, and all-around champion in Pocatello, Idaho, in 1937; the bareback and all-around champion in Rigby, Idaho, in 1938; the bareback, bull-riding, and all-around champion in Portland, Oregon, in 1939; and the saddle-bronc, bareback, and all-around champion in Raymond, in 1940. However, arguably his best year was 1933, when he placed second in the North American Championship Rodeo and third in the Championship of the World and set a new world-championship-rodeo record.

Earl gained international fame in the rodeo world and was inducted into four rodeo halls of fame. He was inducted into the Canadian Rodeo Hall of Fame in 1984. A year later, he became the first rodeo athlete to be inducted into the Utah Sports Hall of Fame. In 1987, he became the first rodeo cowboy to be elected to the Raymond Sports Hall of Fame in Alberta. Rodeos in Utah, California, and Alberta all designated him as "Legendary Cowboy" in 1989. He was granted honorary membership into the National Police Rodeo Association in 1995. In the same year, he was recognized at a rodeo reunion in Colorado Springs, Colorado, as the world's oldest living rodeo clown and bullfighter. Rodeo championships bearing his name have been established in three states and in Canada, and the National High School Rodeo Association established an award in his honor. A summary of his life and career has been written into the *Congressional Record.*

## Summary

Earl Bascom was born and grew up in the open ranges of the American and Canadian West. He witnessed and helped the development of the region. He became acquainted with cowboy movie star Roy Rogers and worked on a few movies in Hollywood himself. Rogers dubbed Earl the "Cowboy of Cowboy Artists." Earl became well-known as a Western artist and sculptor. He was the first cowboy to be named a Fellow of the Royal Society of Arts in London, England, and the oldest cowboy elected to the Professional Rodeo Cowboy Artists Association.

*Paul Dellinger*

## Additional Sources

Bernstein, Joel. *Wild Ride: The History and Lore of Rodeo.* Layton, Utah: Gibbs Smith, 2007.

Campion, Lynn. *Rodeo: Behind the Scenes at America's Most Exciting Sport.* Guilford, Conn.: Lyons Press, 2004.

Jordan, Bob. *Rodeo History and Legends.* Montrose, Colo.: Rodeo Stuff, 1993.

Porter, Willard H. *Who's Who in Rodeo.* Oklahoma City, Okla.: National Cowboy Hall of Fame, 1982.

Woerner, Gail Hughbanks. *Fearless Funnymen: The History of the Rodeo Clown.* Austin, Tex.: Eakin Press, 1993.

# *Russell Baze*

**Born:** August 7, 1958
      Vancouver, British Columbia, Canada

## Early Life

Russell Baze was born on August 7, 1958, in Vancouver, British Columbia, where his father Joe raced horses at Exhibition Park. Russell grew up in Washington State. He came from a family involved in every aspect of horse racing. Before becoming a trainer, his father was a successful rider at Bay Meadows, Golden Gate Fields, and Longacres. His younger brother, Dale, was an exercise rider. Many of his uncles and cousins became involved in the sport as trainers, jockeys, grooms, or farriers.

In 1974, just before his sixteenth birthday, Russell rode aboard an Appaloosa in his first race. On October 18 of that same year, his racing career began officially. He rode Captain Thunder at Yakima Meadows and finished fourth. On October 28, 1974, at Yakima Meadows, he won his first race, on

*Russell Baze at Santa Anita in Arcadia, California.*
(Patty Yount/Ai Wire/Landov)

a horse named Oregon Warrior, trained by his father. By the end of the year, Russell had ridden twenty mounts and had two first-, three second- and four third-place finishes.

## The Road to Excellence

By the early 1980's, Russell had already made a reputation for himself as a jockey at Northern California tracks. Although he continued to ride in claiming races, he also began to win handicap and invitational races. Starting with wins in the 1981 Silky Sullivan Handicap and the California Derby, he won a total of eight major races during the 1980's. In 1982, he won the Golden Gate Fields Handicap and the Bay Meadows Handicap. In 1984, he finished first in the Oak Tree Invitational Stakes and the El Camino Real Derby. In 1986, he added the Del Mar Debutante Stakes to his list of wins. In 1988, he won the Longacres Mile Handicap; in 1989, he once again won the Oak Tree Invitational Stakes. On October 14, 1989, aboard the three-year-old colt Hawkster, he set the Santa Anita Park record for a one and one-half mile race on turf.

## The Emerging Champion

In the 1990's, Russell continued riding in all classes of races and always had a full card of mounts. On April 16, 1992, at Golden Gate Fields, he set a Northern California record for the most victories in a single day of racing. He rode nine horses and won with seven of them. From 1992 to 1996, he won more than four hundred races each year. This exceptional record earned him an Eclipse Special Award in 1995. He was the first jockey to ever win more than four hundred races in a year for four consecutive years.

In 1995, the National Turf Writers Association presented its first Isaac Murphy Award in honor of hall-of-fame jockey Isaac Murphy, a nineteenth-century rider who won with 44 percent of his mounts. The award honors the jockey with the highest winning percentage who has competed in at least five hundred races during the year. Russell won the award that year and won it every subsequent year to 2007 with the exception of 2004, when he was sidelined with injuries. In 1999, he was inducted into the Jockeys' Hall of Fame.

On November 14, 2004, at Golden Gate Fields, Russell rode Lost in the Fog in his maiden race and finished first. This was the beginning of a jockey and thoroughbred association that lasted throughout Lost in the Fog's career. With the exception of the Riva Ridge Breeders' Cup Stakes at Belmont Park, Russell rode Lost in the Fog in all of his fourteen starts. Russell was aboard Lost in the Fog for nine of his ten consecutive victories, which earned the horse the 2005 Eclipse Award for outstanding sprint horse. A seventh-place finish in the 2005 Breeders' Cup Sprint eliminated Lost in the Fog from contention for the Eclipse Award for horse of the year. However, in 2006, Russell and Lost in the Fog were back and started the season with a second-place finish in the Oakland Tribune race and a first place in the Aristides Breeders' Cup Stake at Churchill Downs, setting a new stakes record. Then, on July 15, Lost in the Fog finished ninth in the Smile Sprint Handicap at Calder Race Course. A thorough veterinarian examination revealed that Lost in the Fog had inoperable cancer. On September 17, the horse was euthanized.

### Continuing the Story

In January, 2005, Russell won his 8,834th race, placing him in second position to Laffit Pincay, Jr., among jockeys with the most caeer victories. Pincay had 9,530 career wins. On November 30, 2006, Russell tied Pincay's record with a win aboard Christie's Fame at Bay Meadows. Russell had been asked to ride Christie's Fame just shortly before the race when jockey Ricky Frazier had to withdraw because of illness.

The next day, December 1, 2006, Russell won his 9,531st race aboard Butterfly Belle in a $12,500 claiming race. With this victory, he became the winningest jockey in the world. Then, on February 1, 2008, he won his 10,000th race, riding Two Step Cat at Golden Gate Fields.

### Summary

Though Russell Baze rode in only two Kentucky Derbies and did not win any of the major, world-famous thoroughbred races, he contributed significantly to the sport. He spent the greater part of his career riding in the San Francisco Bay Area, where he became the foremost jockey in the region, and was an example of an everyday, hardworking jockey who rode a full program of horses each race day. Through 2008, he compiled a total of thirty-six riding championships at Bay Meadows and twenty-nine riding titles at Golden Gate Fields. He was the nation's winningest jockey nine years and ranked twenty-seventh in the nation for purses won with a total approaching $7 million.

*Shawncey Webb*

### Additional Sources

Gruender, Scott A. *Jockey: The Rider's Life in American Thoroughbred Racing.* Jefferson, N.C.: McFarland, 2006.

Mooney, Nan. *My Racing Heart: The Passionate World of Thoroughbreds and the Track.* New York: Harper Paperbacks, 2003.

Simon, Mary, and Mark Simon. *Racing Through the Century: The Story of Thoroughbred Racing in America.* Irvine, Calif.: BowTie Press, 2002.

## Major Victories

| Year | Race |
|---|---|
| 1981 | California Derby |
| 1981, 1988 | Silky Sullivan Handicap |
| 1982, 1995, 2005 | Bay Meadows Handicap |
| 1982, 2000 | Golden Gate Fields Handicap |
| 1984, 1989 | Oak Tree Invitational Stakes |
| 1984, 1998, 2005-07 | El Camino Real Derby |
| 1986 | Del Mar Debutante Stakes |
| 1988, 2003, 2004 | Longacres Mile Handicap |
| 1990 | San Carlos Handicap |
| | San Gorgonio Handicap |
| | Oak Leaf Stakes |
| 1991 | Bed o' Roses Breeders' Cup Handicap |
| 1996 | Oklahoma Derby |
| 2002 | Bay Meadows Breeders' Cup Sprint Handicap |
| 2005 | Bay Shore Stakes |
| 2006 | Churchill Downs Handicap |
| | Aristides Breeders' Cup Stakes |
| 2008 | Azalea Breeders' Cup Stakes |

## Honors, Awards, and Milestones

|  |  |
|---|---|
| 1992-96, 2000, 2002, 2005, 2007 | Led the United States in victories nine years |
| 1995 | Eclipse Special Award |
| 1995-2003, 2005-07 | Isaac Murphy Award |
| 1999 | Inducted into Jockeys' Hall of Fame |
| 2002 | George Woolf Memorial Jockey Award |
| 2006 | Set record for most career wins with 9,531 |
| 2008 | Recorded 10,000th victory |

# *Layne Beachley*

**Born:** May 24, 1972
Sydney, Australia
**Also known as:** Layne Collette Beachley (full name); Tania Maris Gardner (birth name); Gidget; Beach

## Early Life

Layne Collette Beachley was born Tania Maris Gardner in Sydney, Australia, on May 24, 1972. She was premature and spent weeks in an incubator before she was given up for adoption by her seventeen-year-old, unwed mother. Valerie and Neil Beachley adopted the baby and renamed her. Her father was a lifeguard and taught Layne to surf at the age of four. She was an athletic youth and also played soccer and tennis. When Layne was six years old, her adoptive mother died. Layne increasingly found solace in surfing. She had to overcome the stereotype that female surfers were more passive. Surrounded in the water by males, she developed an aggressive style and a fierce competitiveness.

## The Road to Excellence

Layne entered her first surfing contest at the age of fourteen and traveled around Australia competing

*Seven-time world surfing champion Layne Beachley in 2008.* (Getty Images)

in contests. At sixteen years old, Layne became a professional surfer, riding in contests sponsored by the Association of Surfing Professionals (ASP). Her first few years on the tour were difficult, and she initially failed to fulfill her potential. Unlike many of her contemporary female surfers at the time, Layne engaged in a strict and vigorous cross-training program. Eventually, her strength-building program was emulated by other women surfers. In 1990, Layne was ranked seventeenth in the world. She attracted the attention of the ASP women's world champion and fellow Australian Pam Burridge, who became a close friend and mentor.

In 1993, Layne won her first contest on the world tour and ended the year ranked sixth by the ASP. She was widely regarded as one of the best young female surfers on the world tour. However, that year, she also developed chronic fatigue syndrome, an illness which threatened to end her career. She recovered and finished fourth in the world in 1995; she was ranked second the next year. The syndrome, likely the result of overtraining, affected her again in 1996. She also suffered from a bout of depression caused by both the chronic fatigue syndrome and anxiety about her future in the sport. Nonetheless, that year, she finished third on the world tour after a strong performance at a contest at Sunset Beach in Hawaii.

## The Emerging Champion

Although Layne had enormous potential, her first years on the ASP Tour were plagued by inconsistency. She gained some notable victories, but these were often followed by poor performances in subsequent events. The unevenness of her performances was generally blamed on overtraining and overexertion. Nonetheless, she was accepted as one of best women big-wave riders and performed well in

**31**

## Honors and Awards

| | |
|---|---|
| 1999-2003 | *Surfing Life* surfer of the year |
| 1999-2003, 2006 | Women's Association of Surfing Professionals world champion |
| 2000, 2002-03 | New South Wales sportsperson of the year |
| 2001 | ESPN surfer of the year |
| 2003 | Australian female athlete of the year |
| 2003-04 | *Surfer* female surfer of the year |
| 2004 | Laureus World Alternative Sportsperson of the Year |
| 2005 | Teen Choice Awards: extreme female athlete of the year |
| 2006 | Inducted into Surfers' Hall of Fame |
| | Inducted into Surfers' Walk of Fame |
| 2007 | Surf Industry Manufacturers Association special achievement award |

larger surf, wave faces of twelve feet or more, especially on the Hawaiian portions of the ASP Tour.

After 1996, Layne settled into an appropriate training regime that balanced exercise and performance. She became involved romantically with Hawaiian big-wave surfer Ken Bradshaw. Despite his expertise in larger surf, Bradshaw helped Layne improve her consistency on smaller waves. Layne was second in the world in 1997. In 1998, Layne dominated the women's world tour. In addition to a series of surf contest victories, she won her first world tour and did so with the largest margin of points in ASP history. She declared her goal was to beat Lisa Andersen's record of four consecutive tour victories from 1994 to 1997.

### Continuing the Story

From 1999 through 2003, Layne won six straight world titles, more than any other female surfer in ASP history. Her victories, along with her ability to master big waves, earned women's surfing new measures of respect and attention. Layne emerged as a tireless proponent of women's surfing; she endeavored consistently to secure more media and public attention for the sport. She often provided commentary and interviews, especially in Australia, where she was a national celebrity. In 2003, she founded the Aim for the Stars Foundation to provide financial support for girls and young women to pursue academic and sporting opportunities.

Layne did not win world titles in 2004 or 2005. A serious neck injury, a herniated disc, led her to consider retirement in 2005. However, following therapy and rehabilitation, she decided to compete for another year. In 2006, defying predictions

that age and injury had reduced her competitiveness, Layne won the ASP Tour again. In addition, in 2006, Layne rode the largest wave ever ridden by a female surfer. In Oahu, Hawaii, she dropped in on a fifty-foot wave while "tow-in" surfing. Tow-in surfing involves using a Jet Ski to provide the surfer with enough speed to ride extremely large waves. Traditionally, tow-in surfing was considered the domain of male surfers, but Layne's performance broke the stereotype.

Layne was the recipient of a number of awards and honors. In 2006, while still competing on the ASP Tour, she was inducted into the Australian Surfing Hall of Fame and the U.S. Surfers' Hall of Fame. She was also named ESPN surfer of the year in 2001 and the Australian female athlete of the year in 2003. She even sponsored her own surf contest, the Havaianas Layne Classic at Manly Beach, Sydney, Australia, in 2006. As a result of her fame, Layne appeared in a number of films, including *Blue Crush* (2002). In 2007, in her seventeenth year on the ASP Tour, Layne finished fourth in the overall standings. By the end of that year, she had won twenty-nine career ASP world championship contests.

### Summary

Layne Beachley was the greatest female performer in competitive surfing. Her succession of world championships, in combination with her other accomplishments, helped to increase the legitimacy and popularity of female surfing. Her willingness and ability to ride big surf set the precedent for a new generation of women surfers who increasingly surfed waves that had once been the domain of their male counterparts.

*Tom Lansford*

### Additional Sources

Chase, Linda, and Elizabeth Pepin. *Surfing: Women of the Waves*. Layton, Utah: Gibbs Smith, 2007.

Gabbard, Andrea. *Girl in the Curl: A Century of Women in Surfing*. Berkeley, Calif.: Seal Press, 2000.

Southerden, Louise, and Layne Beachley. *Surf's Up: The Girl's Guide to Surfing*. New York: Ballantine Books, 2005.

# *Kenny Bernstein*

**Born:** September 6, 1944
Clovis, New Mexico
**Also known as:** King of Speed

## Early Life

Kenny Bernstein was born in Clovis, New Mexico, to a working-class family. In Kenny's early childhood, his family moved to Lubbock, Texas. By age nine, Kenny's father, Bert Bernstein, gave Kenny his first job. Bert was the store manager for Levine's department store in Lubbock and charged Kenny with the small task of selling socks, which introduced the future businessman and drag racer to the principles of good business practice. With his earned cash, Kenny quickly developed a love for hot rods. In high school, he began building and racing them. Making money was Kenny's love; therefore, after high school, he attended Arlington State College (now the University of Texas at Arlington) and studied business administration.

## The Road to Excellence

Kenny's love for racing cars endured. In 1966, he dropped out of Arlington State in order to pursue drag racing. However, he had to pay for his hobby alone and sold high-end women's clothing while traveling to races. Kenny was victorious in many of his races on the Texas Pro Fuel Circuit but suspended his drag racing in 1970 to spend time with his family. Even though Kenny was not making money racing, he was still an entrepreneur: He opened the Dallas Wrecker Service in 1971. Kenny wanted to continue racing and did so part time in both Top Fuel and Funny Cars.

However, part-time racing was not enough for Kenny. He sold Dallas Wrecker Service and divorced his wife to be able to race full time again. He participated in some National Hot Rod Association (NHRA) races for Ray Allen, and his best finish was second at the 1973 Winternationals at Pomona, California. Despite becoming successful, in 1974, Kenny again devoted himself to business, opening the Chelsea Street Pub restaurant chain in Lubbock. He returned to drag racing in 1978. In 1979, he won his first professional event at the NHRA Cajun Nationals in Baton Rouge, Louisiana. Kenny also won two races in the International Hot Rod Association (IHRA) and won the IHRA Winston Championship.

*Kenny Bernstein.* (AP/Wide World Photos)

## The Emerging Champion

Kenny garnered numerous sponsorship offers because of his success. In 1980, Anheuser-Busch became Kenny's full sponsor. However, many media outlets did not condone alcohol promotions. Therefore, Kenny, as a savvy businessman, named his Funny Car the Budweiser King to help with media coverage. In 1981, Kenny became the first drag racer to win events and set records in all three major drag-racing circuits: the NHRA, the IHRA, and the American Hot Rod Association. On March 18, 1984, at the Gatornationals in Gainesville, Florida, Kenny became the first Funny Car driver to break the 260 miles-per-hour barrier.

In 1985, Kenny founded King Racing, his first racing team that was not drag-racing affiliated. King Racing enjoyed success in the National Association for Stock Car Auto Racing (NASCAR) Winston Cup division. The team had three victories in Winston Cup between 1985 and 1990. Also in 1985, Kenny won his first of four consecutive NHRA Winston Championships racing Funny Cars by reaching nine of twelve final rounds. Kenny's four championships tied him with Don Prudhomme for the most consecutive championships in the NHRA. During his stretch of dominance in Funny Cars, between 1985 and 1988, Kenny broke numerous time and speed records. In 1987, he created the King Protofab Indy Car team, which raced in the Championship Auto Racing Teams (CART) series.

In 1989, after years of dominating Funny Car races, Kenny moved to the Top Fuel division. Thus, _Car Craft_ magazine named Kenny its 1990 person of the year, as the individual with the greatest impact on drag racing.

### Honors and Awards

| | |
|---|---|
| 1981 | _Drag Racing_ magazine's "Real World Champion" |
| 1985-87 | _Car Craft_ Funny Car all-star driver |
| 1985-88, 1992 | American Auto Racing Writers and Broadcasters Association all-American |
| 1988 | _Motorweek Illustrated_ driver of the year |
| 1990, 1992 | _Car Craft_ person of the year |
| 1992 | _Car Craft_ Top Fuel all-star driver |
| 2006 | Inducted into Texas Motor Sports Hall of Fame |
| 2007 | Inducted into Don Garlits International Drag Racing Hall of Fame |

### Milestone Victories

| | |
|---|---|
| 1979 | First professional victory—National Hot Rod Association (NHRA) |
| | International Hot Rod Association (IHRA) Winston championship |
| 1981 | First driver to win races in one season in NHRA, IHRA, and American Hot Rod Association |
| 1985-88, 1996, 2001 | NHRA Winston Championship (latter two victories in "Top Fuel") |
| 1987 | Big Bud Shootout winner |

### Continuing the Story

Adjusting to Top Fuel did not take long for Kenny. In 1991, he tied the single-season record for Top Fuel wins with six victories. In 1992, he earned the title the "King of Speed." He eclipsed the 300 miles-per-hour mark at the Gatornationals. In 1994, Kenny broke the 310 miles-per-hour barrier twice at the season-ending Winston Select Finals in Pomona. Kenny's highest speed was 314.46 miles per hour en route to winning the event. In addition, Scott Goodyear's victory for King Racing at the Michigan International Speedway made Kenny the first owner to win events in CART, NASCAR, and NHRA.

In 1996, Kenny won the NHRA Top Fuel Championship, making him the first driver to win both Top Fuel and Funny Car Championships. By 1999, Kenny's sponsorship with Anheuser-Busch had become the second longest in motorsports history. In 2001, Kenny experienced his greatest success. He not only won the Top Fuel Championship but also set the NHRA world records for elapsed time and speed. In June, Kenny set an elapsed-time run of 4.477 seconds at Route 66 Speedway in Chicago, Illinois. In October, at Maple Grove Raceway in Reading, Pennsylvania, he set the speed record at 332.18 miles per hour. Because of his stellar career, Kenny was voted the sixth greatest NHRA driver ever. He retired after the 2002 season. His son

### Records

| | |
|---|---|
| 1986 | First driver to break 5.50-second barrier |
| | First Funny Car driver to break 270-MPH barrier |
| 1987 | First driver to break 5.40-second barrier |
| 1992 | First Funny Car driver to break the 300-MPH barrier |

Brandon took over the Budweiser King but was injured in May, 2003, which forced Kenny to race once again. He won four more events and retired a second time in 2004. In 2007, Kenny abandoned retirement once again, racing Funny Cars for one season.

## Summary

Kenny Bernstein pursued a dream without help from anyone and became one of the best drag racers ever. He earned numerous accolades and money. His father gave him business lessons, which helped him become a focused businessperson. However, apart from his successful business ventures, Kenny is remembered as the King of Speed.

*Paul C. Alexander II*

## Additional Sources

Bernstein, Kenny, and Bill Stephens. *Kenny Bernstein: Living Legend.* Champaign, Ill.: Sports, 2004.

McGee, David M., and Kenny Bernstein. *Bristol Dragway.* Charleston, S.C.: Arcadia, 2007.

Sakkis, Tony. *Drag Racing Legends.* Minneapolis: Motorbooks International, 1996.

# Bill Bowness

**Born:** October 1, 1958
    Arcadia, California
**Also known as:** William McLean Bowness (full
    name)

## Early Life

Born on October 1, 1958, in Arcadia, California, William McLean Bowness lived with his two sisters and his parents. His father was a project manager for a company that manufactured galvanized steel, and his mother worked as a service manager for Pacific Telephone. For many years, Bill attended a parochial school in nearby Temple City. He liked school but did not like studying. What he did like was sports. He started playing ice hockey when he was seven years old, and he also enjoyed softball, football, and basketball. In high school, he joined the tennis and water-polo teams, becoming a well-rounded athlete.

When he was old enough, Bill got a part-time job and saved money to buy an old boat. He taught himself how to water-ski, but he did not ski competitively. For him, skiing was just a way to have fun. However, his life was forever altered when he was eighteen years old. While he was driving in Idaho, his car's trailer hitch broke, causing an accident that left Bill paralyzed from the hips down.

## The Road to Excellence

Although the automobile accident made Bill a paraplegic, he still loved sports. During the 1980's, Royce Andes, a former member of the U.S. barefoot ski team, contacted Bill while he was attending college at Chico State University to see if he would be interested in testing a new kind of water ski. Andes had become a quadriplegic, and he wanted to make an effective sit-ski for disabled water skiers. Bill agreed to help.

After learning to use the sit-ski, Bill became an accomplished water skier. He entered and won several small competitions. Then, in 1986, he traveled to Norway to compete in an international disabled waterskiing tournament. Bill skied so well that he won the competition easily. In fact, his skill level was so great that officials decided to raise the maximum speed for future tournaments.

When Bill returned from Norway, he felt confident about his ability to sit-ski. He began to pursue the sport in earnest, looking for coaches to help him become better. After much practice, he became a member of the U.S. disabled waterskiing team. Some of the athletes were blind, some were amputees, and some were sit-skiers like Bill.

## The Emerging Champion

Because disabled waterskiing was a relatively new sport, not many competitions existed. In 1987, the U.S. team entered the first World Disabled Water Ski Championships in London. Bill performed exceptionally in the slalom event. His boat went 36 miles per hour, and his towrope was shortened four times, which made the course more difficult. Bill's performance earned him a gold medal.

Bill realized how valuable Andes's wide, fiberglass, 10-inch-wide and 6-foot-long sit-ski was. A canvas sling seat kept the skier positioned about 8 inches above the water. The equipment was not cumbersome, and Bill was able to maneuver easily on the slalom course.

To keep in shape for waterskiing, Bill practiced intensively. He also believed in cross training. He played tennis twice a week, hit racquetballs, shot basketballs, and became interested in marathons, training 70 to 80 miles per week in a special track chair. All this physical exercise helped Bill become a strong and coordinated competitor. He also trained regularly with both disabled and able-bodied water-skiers.

After competitors from more countries began joining disabled waterskiing, the International Water Skiing Federation decided to allow world records to be set. In 1989, Bill traveled to Perth, Australia, to compete in the second World Disabled Water Ski Championships. Here Bill set a world record. He earned a gold medal for both the slalom and the jump events. Additionally, he took the gold medal for the overall best in the competition.

When Bill returned from Australia, he had a dislocated disc in his neck. He had surgery in the

## *Major Championships*

| Year | Competition | Event | Place |
|------|-------------|-------|-------|
| 1986 | International invitational tournament, Norway | Slalom | 1st |
| 1987 | First World Disabled Water Ski Championships, London | Slalom | 1st |
| 1989 | Second World Disabled Water Ski Championships, Perth, Australia | Slalom | 1st |
|      |  | Jump | 1st |
|      |  | Overall sit-ski | 1st |
| 1990 | Short Line Open | Slalom | 1st |
| 1993 | World Disabled Water Ski Championships | Slalom | 1st |
|      |  | Trick | 1st |
|      |  | Jump | 1st |
|      |  | Individual overall | 1st |
|      |  | Team overall | 1st |
| 1995 | World Disabled Water Ski Championships, New South Wales, Australia | Slalom | 2d |
|      |  | Trick | 2d |
|      |  | Individual overall | 2d |
|      |  | Jump | 3d |
|      |  | Team overall | 1st |
| 1997 | World Disabled Water Ski Championships, Florida | Slalom | 3d |
|      |  | Jump | 3d |
|      |  | Team overall | 2d |
|      |  | Individual overall | 1st |
| 2001 | Disabled National Water Ski Championships, Altamonte Springs, Florida | Individual overall | 1st |
| 2002 | Disabled National Water Ski Championships, Altamonte Springs, Florida | Individual overall | 1st |
| 2003 | Disabled National Water Ski Championships, Altamonte Springs, Florida | Individual overall | 1st |
|      |  | Jump | 1st |
|      | World Disabled Water Ski Championships, Altamonte Springs, Florida | Individual overall | 2d |
|      |  | Jump | 2d |
|      |  | Team overall | 1st |
|      |  | Trick | 3d |

spring of 1990. In September, he set a new world record for the slalom in a competition at Shortline Lake, near Sacramento, California.

## Continuing the Story

Bill's drive for excellence and his natural athletic ability were part of what helped him succeed. He believed in setting challenging goals. He did not believe a label like "disabled" should automatically limit a person's experiences. He tried to convey this positive attitude to physically challenged people whom he taught in both water-skiing and snow-skiing classes.

Bill became a popular speaker at schools and with civic groups. He raised money for disabled sports programs and wrote a handbook about disabled waterskiing. A neck injury prevented Bill from competing in the 1991 World Disabled Water Ski Championships, but he returned in 1993 to sweep the competition with first-place finishes in the slalom, trick, jump, individual overall, and team overall categories. In 1995 and 1997, he fin-ished first again in the team and individual overall categories.

Beginning in 1987, Bill skied in every World Disabled Water Ski event except the 2001 championship. During that time, he skied all over the world. He also skied on snow, competed in the Paralympics, and won many medals in that sport as well. Bill set three world records in the slalom and three world records in the jump. He was overall national champion seven times, from 1993 to 1995 and from 2001 to 2004, at the U.S. Disabled Water Ski Championships and was a nine-time individual world champion in slalom, trick, and jump skiing.

Bill and his wife taught adaptive snow and water skiing. They divided their time between homes in Brandon, Mississippi, and Truckee, California. Bill became a member of the board of directors of the Water Skiers with Disabilities Association. He became coach for the 2008-2012 Professional Ski Instructors of America-American Association of Snowboard Instructors national teams. Bill also coached the 2009 U.S. disabled water ski team.

## Summary

Determination and confidence were always parts of Bill Bowness's personality. His positive attitude helped him recuperate quickly and influenced his outlook about his future following a disabling accident. For him, life was a series of competitions in which he was determined to do well. One of the pioneers of skiing with a disability, Bill broke world records in slalom and jumping events and was a nine-time disabled world champion. He and his wife continued to give back to their sport as instructors and coaches of disabled skiers both on water and on snow.

*Lynne Klyse, updated by Jack Ewing*

## Additional Sources

Batcheller, Lori J. *Alpine Achievement: A Chronicle of the United States Disabled Ski Team.* Bloomington, Ind.: 1st Books, 2002.

Dobbs, Jean, and Barry Corbet, eds. *Spinal Network: The Total Wheelchair Resource Book.* Horsham, Pa.: Nine Lives Press, 2002.

Klein, Stanley D., and Gary Karp, eds. *From There to Here: Stories of Adjustment to Spinal Cord Injury.* Shanghai, China: No Limits Communications, 2004.

Leitner, Michael J., and Sara F. Leitner. *Leisure Enhancement.* New York: Haworth Press, 2004.

# *Trevor Brazile*

**Born:** November 16, 1976
     Amarillo, Texas
**Also known as:** King of Rodeo

## Early Life

Trevor Brazile was born in Amarillo, Texas, on November 16, 1976. His parents were both rodeo competitors. His father, Jimmy, qualified four times for the Professional Rodeo Cowboys Association (PRCA) National Finals Steer Roping. His mother, Glenda, competed in women's rodeo. Trevor's father wanted him to be a cowboy, and the entire family encouraged Trevor to develop roping skills at an early age. He was riding horses by the time he was two years old. At four, he was tracking cattle, and at five, he was practicing breakaway roping. By age twelve, he was earning money roping. Trevor was dedicated to roping, which made practice and hard work the center of his life.

When Trevor was eighteen years old, he qualified for the world rodeo show and was recognized by Wrangler as a serious competitor. He also received a rodeo scholarship to Vernon Regional Ju-nior College, where he completed an associate's degree in arts and sciences. Upon receiving another rodeo scholarship, he enrolled at West Texas A&M University. In 1996, he joined the PRCA. During the 1997-1998 season, he won the title of tie-down roping champion in the Amateur Intercollegiate Rodeo Southwest Region. During his junior year, the success he was experiencing as a rodeo cowboy persuaded him to pursue rodeo roping as a career. He left college to rodeo full time.

## The Road to Excellence

Trevor continued to improve his skill in roping. In 1998, he became the Texas Circuit Steer Roping Champion and the Timed-Event Champion of the World. He had been runner-up in this event in 1997. Partnering with J. P. Wickett, he won the team roping title at the San Antonio Stock Show and Rodeo. In 1999 and 2000, Trevor continued to win titles. In 1999, he won tie-down-roping titles at the Grand National Rodeo in San Francisco, California, and the Pendleton, Oregon, Round-Up and was the cochampion tie-down roper at the American Royal Rodeo in Kansas City, Missouri. In 2000, he won four more tie-down-roping titles. In 2001, he was the runner-up in tie-down roping in the Copenhagen Cup Finale in Las Vegas, Nevada, and earned tie-down-roping wins at Rodeo Houston and the Puyallup Fair Rodeo. He also won the all-around title at the Guymon Pioneer Days Rodeo.

In 2002, he won his first PRCA World All-Around Cowboy title and nine other titles, including two tie-down titles, one team-roping title, and one steer-roping title. He finished the season with winnings of $79,157 in tie-down roping and took third place in tie-down roping at the Wrangler National Finals Rodeo. He also earned $15,446 and a fourth-place finish in steer roping at the PRCA National Finals Steer Roping. His horse Tinys

*Trevor Brazile competes at the National Finals Rodeo in 1999.* (John Gurzinski/Getty Images)

Clipso, nicknamed Tweeter, was voted American Quarter Horse Association tie-down-roping horse of the year.

## The Emerging Champion

Having won the 2002 PRCA World All-Around title, Trevor began the 2003 season with a goal of winning the title again. His 2002 title was secured on the last day of competition. The race between he and Jesse Bail had gone down to the final rounds. In order to secure a greater margin of victory, Trevor decided he needed to qualify in four events—tie-down roping, steer roping, team-roping header and team-roping heeler—at the Wrangler National Finals Rodeo. Trevor already had several good horses but needed a heading horse, so he purchased Calhoun, who had twice earned honors as heading horse of the year. Trevor became the first cowboy to qualify in four events. In fact, he not only qualified in his four chosen events but also earned the 2003 PRCA World All-Around title and became the first cowboy to win consecutive PRCA World All-Around titles since Joe Beaver in 1995 and 1996.

---

### Honors and Awards

| | |
|---|---|
| 1997-98 | Tie-down roping champion: National Intercollegiate Rodeo Association (Southwest Region) |
| 1998, 2000 | Steer roping champion (Texas Circuit) |
| 1998, 2003-04 | World champion: timed-event |
| | Inducted into Rodeo Hall of Fame |
| 2002-04 | World Champion (all-around) |
| 2003 | Qualified for the Wrangler National Finals Rodeo in four events (record) |
| 2005 | Sundowner Stampede PRCA Rodeo (Coleman, Oklahoma) (all-around champion) |
| | Dodge City, Kansas, Roundup Rodeo (all-around champion) |
| | PRCA Pro Rodeo (Window Rock, Arizona) (all-around champion) |
| | Will Rogers Stampede (Claremore, Oklahoma) (all-around champion) |
| 2006 | First place: Dodge National Circuit Final Rodeo Qualifications |
| | Laughlin, Nevada, River Stampede (all-around champion) |
| | Clark County Fair and Rodeo (Logandale, Nevada) (all-around champion) |

---

## Continuing the Story

In 2004, Trevor had even more success, winning his third consecutive all-around title. He performed so well that he guaranteed the title for himself in the first rounds. This win placed him in a select group of exceptional cowboys. He was the first to win the title for three consecutive years since Ty Murray accomplished the feat from 1989 to 1991. In 2007, Trevor further demonstrated his extraordinary talent as a rodeo cowboy. He won the PRCA's triple crown, an award that had not been won since his father-in-law Roy Cooper won it in 1983. Trevor won the award by gaining three world titles in the same year of competition: steer roping, all-around, and tie-down roping.

Although Trevor remained an active contender in rodeo events, he began to contemplate postretirement plans. Given his fondness for horses, he wanted to remain involved with the horse industry. Trevor has proven his ability as a horse trainer. His roping horse, Real Cool Dual—nicknamed Texaco—an American quarter horse, who was given to Trevor after the horse refused to perform in a cutting-horse competition, was named horse of the finals in the Amarillo, Texas, rodeo. When Trevor received Texaco, the horse trusted no one and was frightened of calves. After four years of patience and work, Trevor turned him into a champion roping horse.

## Summary

Trevor Brazile is aptly called the "King of Rodeo." His career earnings totaled nearly $3 million. He holds eight rodeo titles, including five PRCA World All-Around Cowboy titles and a PRCA triple crown. He qualified for the Wrangler National Rodeo Finals fourteen times, PRCA National Finals Steer Roping eleven times, and Dodge National Circuit Final Rodeo once.

*Shawncey Webb*

## Additional Sources

Campion, Lynn. *Rodeo: Behind the Scenes at America's Most Exciting Sport.* Guilford, Conn.: Lyons Press, 2004.

Woerner, Gail Hughbanks. *Rope to Win: The History of Steer, Calf, and Team Roping.* Austin, Tex.: Eakin, 2007.

Wooden, Wayne S., and Gavin Ehringer. *Rodeo in America: Wranglers, Roughstock, and Paydirt.* Lawrence: University Press of Kansas, 1999.

# Jeff Burton

**Born:** June 29, 1967
South Boston, Virginia
**Also known as:** Jeffrey Brian Burton (full name);
JB

## Early Life

Jeffrey Brian Burton was born into a racing family. His brother, Ward, was a NASCAR Cup driver, and his father, John, was a Busch Car team owner. With the influence of his family, Jeff started racing go-karts at the age of seven. By the time he was ten, he had won two state championships in go-karts. At that point, he began the switch to cars. In 1986, he won six Late Model Series events at his home track in South Boston. In 1988, he won another seven races and was named South Boston Speedway's most popular driver.

## The Road to Excellence

In 1988, the twenty-one-year-old Jeff made a big move in his racing career, as he advanced to the Busch (later known as Nationwide) Series. The Nationwide Series is, in essence, the NASCAR Cup minor leagues, and Jeff started his first race, driving for his father in the Miller Classic at Martinsville Speedway in Virginia. He finished twenty-eighth.

The following year, Jeff drove John Burton's #12 Pontiac again and had much better results, although he couldn't claim his first victory. In 1990, when he switched to driving for Sam Ard, he won his first race, the Zerex 150 at Martinsville. That year was the first that he raced full time in the Busch Series.

In 1991, Jeff switched teams again, driving for owner Bill Papke. He finished twelfth in the overall standings. He also collected his second win. In 1992, Jeff signed to race with Filbert Martocci and Filmar Racing and finished in ninth place, a career high at the time, in the final standings. In addition, he won another race that year.

## The Emerging Champion

Jeff's move to Filmar Racing was a good one. The team helped to place him in his first Winston Cup, (later known as Nextel Cup) race. He participated in only one Cup race that year, in the Slick 50 300 at New Hampshire. Though Jeff raced only once and finished thirty-seventh, Stavola Brothers Racing hired him to drive a full schedule in 1994. That year, he finished in the top five twice, in the top ten three times, and top fifteen six times. With those kinds of credentials, Jeff was named the rookie of the year.

While 1994 was the kind of year of which a driver dreams to start his Cup career, the following year was a step backward. Jeff finished the year in thirty-second place and had only three top-fifteen finishes. Nevertheless, one of the most important and well-funded owners in NASCAR, Jack Roush, saw Jeff's potential and signed him for the 1996 season. From this point, Jeff's career flourished. He finished in the top five six times and in the top ten twelve times; he ended the season thirteenth in overall points. However, his first Cup victory remained elusive. Finally, on April 6, 1997, at Texas Motor Speedway's inaugural race, the Interstate Batteries 500, Jeff won. He had finally arrived.

## Continuing the Story

Jeff continued to have success driving for Roush Racing, including one of the most dominating driving performances in twenty-two years. At the Jiffy Lube 300, at the New Hampshire International Speedway, Jeff won the race, leading it from start to finish. He became the first driver since Cale Yarborough in 1978 to accomplish the feat.

Over the next few years, Jeff's relationship with Roush Racing began to disintegrate. Roush's desire to develop younger drivers on his team, coupled with the inability to secure the proper funding for Jeff's team, led Jeff to switch to Richard Childress Racing (RCR) midway through the 2004 season. The move proved to be a wise one, as Jeff's statistics and average finishing position improved. His first victory with RCR came at Dover, Delaware, on September 24, 2006. The win ended a streak of 175 races without a victory.

In his fourth year with RCR, Jeff solidified his status as the leader of the team. In 2006 and 2007, he made NASCAR's Chase for the Cup Championship, which is the sport's version of a playoff. Aside

## Sprint Cup Series Victories

| Date | Race | Location |
|------|------|----------|
| Apr. 6, 1997 | Interstate Batteries 500 | Texas Motor Speedway |
| July 13, 1997 | Jiffy Lube 300 | New Hampshire International Speedway |
| Sept. 28, 1997 | Hanes 500 | Martinsville Speedway |
| July 12, 1998 | Jiffy Lube 300 | New Hampshire International Speedway |
| Sept. 12, 1998 | Exide NASCAR Select Batteries 400 | Richmond International Raceway |
| Mar. 7, 1999 | Las Vegas 400 | Las Vegas Motor Speedway |
| Mar. 21, 1999 | TranSouth Financial 400 | Darlington Raceway |
| May 30, 1999 | Coca-Cola 600 | Lowe's Motor Speedway |
| July 11, 1999 | Jiffy Lube 300 | New Hampshire International Speedway |
| Sept. 5, 1999 | Pepsi Southern 500 | Darlington Raceway |
| Oct. 24, 1999 | Pop Secret Microwave Popcorn 400 | North Carolina Speedway |
| Mar. 5, 2000 | CarsDirect.com 400 | Las Vegas Motor Speedway |
| July 1, 2000 | Pepsi 400 | Daytona International Speedway |
| Sept. 17, 2000 | Dura Lube 300 | New Hampshire International Speedway |
| Nov. 5, 2000 | Checker Auto Parts/Dura Lube 500 | Phoenix International Raceway |
| May 27, 2001 | Coca-Cola 600 | Lowe's Motor Speedway |
| Oct. 28, 2001 | Checker Auto Parts 500 | Phoenix International Raceway |
| Sept. 24, 2006 | Dover 400 | Dover International Speedway |
| Apr. 15, 2007 | Samsung 500 | Texas Motor Speedway |
| Mar. 16, 2008 | Food City 500 | Bristol Motor Speedway |

from racing, Jeff spent time with his two children, Paige and Harrison. His wife, Kim, who was his high school sweetheart, was a regular at the track when Jeff was racing. She also served on the board of directors for the Duke University Children's Hospital, an organization to which the Burtons regularly donated. Part of the second floor was named the "Jeff Burton Racing Zone."

## Summary

Because of his calm demeanor and his tendency to speak out on issues in NASCAR, Jeff is often called "The Governor" in the garage. As of 2008, he had 20 wins over his Cup career and wanted to continue racing for as long as possible. He was one of several racers who helped raise the profile of NASCAR, making stud-car racing one of the most popular sports in the United States.

*P. Huston Ladner*

## Additional Sources

Dayton, Connor. *Jeff Burton.* New York: PowerKids Press, 2008.

Miller, Timothy, and Steve Milton. *NASCAR Now!* 3d ed. Richmond Hill, Ont.: Firefly Books, 2008.

White, Ben, and Nigel Kinrade. *The Drivers of NASCAR.* Rev. ed. St. Paul, Minn.: Crestline, 2006.

# Susan Butcher

**Born:** December 26, 1954
       Cambridge, Massachusetts
**Died:** August 5, 2006
       Seattle, Washington
**Also known as:** Susan Howlett Butcher (full name)

### Early Life

Susan Howlett Butcher was born in Cambridge, Massachusetts, on December 26, 1954. Susan spent her childhood in Cambridge with her sister, Kate, and her parents, Charles and Agnes Butcher. Her early yearning for outdoor adventure was satisfied by spending summers on the Maine seashore. She enjoyed woodworking, dreamed of building a boat to sail around the world, and had a great fondness for animals. After her cherished Labrador retriever, Calev, died when Susan was fifteen, she was delighted to receive a Siberian husky from her aunt, soon joined by another Susan purchased herself. Given the choice by her parents of giving up one of her dogs or moving out, she opted to live with her grandmother in Maine.

By the age of seventeen, Susan wanted to live in the wilderness with many pet dogs. In 1973, she relocated to Boulder, Colorado, and shared a house with a woman who owned fifty huskies. This enabled her, over the next three years, to race a husky team on weekends, in addition to working as a veterinary technician. These experiences increased her knowledge of dog breeding and training and of racing techniques. In the same year, Susan read about the first running of the Iditarod, the race that came to be associated with her career as a musher.

### The Road to Excellence

In 1975, Susan moved to Fairbanks, Alaska, hired by the University of Alaska to work on an environmental project involving the endangered musk oxen. She settled into a bush cabin in the Wrangell Mountains with her dogs and concentrated on developing a team of Alaskan huskies bred to travel more than one hundred miles a day while enduring snow-covered terrains, frozen rivers, and frigid temperatures dropping to fifty degrees below zero Fahrenheit. During the summers, Susan traveled to Fairbanks to work on a musk-oxen farm as a midwife. She developed the philosophy that high-performance dogs must be treated with respect and affection. Susan instilled loyalty, self-confidence, and trust into her eighteen dogs, gave them names associated with storybook characters, and permitted them to enter her home. This display of kindness and adoration for the dog as an athlete was unlike the behavior of other racers, who instilled fear in the animal.

*Susan Butcher, who won four Iditarod races.* (AP/Wide World Photos)

## Major Championships

| Year | Competition | Place |
|------|-------------|-------|
| 1978 | Iditarod Trail Sled Dog Race | 19th |
| 1979 | Iditarod Trail Sled Dog Race | 9th |
| 1980 | Iditarod Trail Sled Dog Race | 5th |
| 1981 | Iditarod Trail Sled Dog Race | 5th |
| 1982 | Iditarod Trail Sled Dog Race | 2d |
| 1983 | Iditarod Trail Sled Dog Race | 9th |
| 1984 | Iditarod Trail Sled Dog Race | 2d |
| 1986 | Iditarod Trail Sled Dog Race (11 days, 15 hours, 6 minutes) | 1st |
|      | John Beargrease Sled Dog Marathon | 2d |
| 1987 | Iditarod Trail Sled Dog Race (11 days, 2 hours, 5 minutes, 13 seconds) | 1st |
| 1988 | Iditarod Trail Sled Dog Race (11 days, 11 hours, 41 minutes, 40 seconds) | 1st |
| 1989 | Iditarod Trail Sled Dog Race | 2d |
| 1990 | Iditarod Trail Sled Dog Race (11 days, 1 hour, 53 minutes, 23 seconds) | 1st |
|      | John Beargrease Sled Dog Marathon (87 hours, 15 minutes) | 1st |
| 1991 | Iditarod Trail Sled Dog Race | 3d |
|      | John Beargrease Sled Dog Marathon | 2d |

Creating a winning sled-dog team demanded daily self-sacrifice. Rising at 5:30 A.M., Susan fed the dogs a breakfast of vitamins and meat broth before their practice runs. Winter runs could be as long as sixty miles, although a typical run was twenty miles, five days a week. The lack of snow in the summer required Susan to use a different practice strategy. Hitching a team of dogs to a terrain vehicle, she had them pull against the drag of the engine set in low gear. It took twelve to sixteen hours a day to train several teams of dogs, and several additional hours to massage the dogs' sore muscles. Susan knew the importance of logging seven thousand miles yearly before attempting the treacherous Iditarod Trail Sled Dog Race. She also realized the need to maintain a high level of physical fitness, because the role of a musher required her to run behind the sled, pushing and pumping with one foot or the other.

### The Emerging Champion

In 1977, the musk oxen project moved to Unalakleet, Alaska, where Butcher was introduced to Joe Reddington, Sr., the organizer of the Iditarod. He encouraged her and helped her find a sponsor for her first Iditarod Race in 1978, in which she placed nineteenth. Her three previous years of living in an area that was accessible only by plane and was twenty-five miles to the nearest village had prepared her for the twelve to thirty days of isolation sometimes required to complete the race. Susan

had become accustomed to the lack of running water and electricity, and she seldom used a clock or calendar. She was familiar with the race's 1,158-mile course that began in Anchorage, Alaska. She knew that blizzards often erase any signs of the trail that crosses the Alaska mountain range, veers west along the winding Yukon River, and twists north up the Bering Sea coast to Nome, Alaska. Susan's determination to face the hairpin turns reflected the 1925 heroic efforts used to deliver lifesaving serum to eliminate a diphtheria epidemic in the gold mining town of Iditarod. From 1978 to 1982, Susan rose in rank to become one of the top ten competitors.

A tragedy occurred in the 1985 race. When Susan's team was ahead of the sixty-one other mushers, a rogue moose attacked her sled, killing two dogs and injuring thirteen others before another contestant killed the animal. This forced Susan to drop out of the race and gave a competitor, Libby Riddles, the honor of becoming the first woman to win the Iditarod.

### Continuing the Story

Over the next three years, Susan realized her dreams. With greater fortitude, she won the 1986 Iditarod in slightly less than twelve days, breaking all previous records. In 1987, she set a new course record of just over eleven days. She attributed her record times to her philosophy that participants do not win because they do one or two things well during the course of a race. Instead, competitors win because they correctly and consistently perform a

## Honors, Awards, and Records

| | |
|------|------|
| 1987-88 | Women's Sports Foundation Sportswoman of the Year |
| 1988 | First sled dog racer to capture three consecutive Iditarod Trail Sled Dog Race victories |
| 1989 | Tangueray Amateur Athlete Achievement Award |
| 1997 | Inducted into Iditarod Hall of Fame |
| 2008 | March 1st declared Susan Butcher Day in Anchorage, Alaska |

thousand little tasks throughout the year, like training the dogs to peak at race time; feeding them a healthy diet of measured fish, beaver, and cream cheese; upgrading sleds with plastic runner materials and custom-fitted harnesses; and preparing for the subzero temperatures and sleeplessness. Mushers frequently receive only two hours of sleep nightly, although each participant is required to take a twenty-four-hour rest stop at one of the twenty-four checkpoints along the trail, where the dogs are examined for injuries and dehydration.

In 1988, Susan encountered two violent storms and snow-packed hills before crossing the finish line fourteen hours ahead of the nearest challenger. This victory earned Susan the distinction as the first sled-dog racer to win three consecutive Iditarod races. Adding to this honor, Susan's world-record time and victory in 1990 matched the record of Rick Swenson, the only other racer to win four Iditarod races up to that time. Swenson won his fifth in 1991. In 1995, after many years of mushing as a competitor, Susan retired.

In 1997, Susan was inducted into the Iditarod Hall of Fame and remained close to sled-dog racing as a trainer. With her husband, David Monson, she founded Trail Breaker Kennel one hundred miles south of the Arctic Circle on the Chena River in Eureka, Alaska, where she trained more than 150 dogs year-round. In 2002, she was diagnosed with polycythemia vera, a blood disorder later seen to be a manifestation of acute myelogenous leukemia. Susan received chemotherapy at the University of Washington and a bone marrow transplant in May, 2006, after the cancer went into remission.

With the resurgence of the cancer and the development of graft-versus-host disease associated with the transplant, she died on August 5, 2006.

## Summary

As a woman pioneer in a traditionally male-dominated sport, Susan Butcher proved that personal sacrifice and perseverance were essential elements of a winning strategy. Her focused approach to training her dogs for speed and stamina, to cope with the challenging terrain of the Alaskan bush country, helped her become one of the greatest long-distance sled-dog racers of the Iditarod race. At the time of her death, she remained the only person to have won the Iditarod in three successive years. In an interview with *Women's Sport and Fitness* in 1987, she stated that her goal had never been to be the first woman or the best woman, but to be the best sled-dog racer.

*Rhonda L. Clements, updated by Robert B. Ridinger*

## Additional Sources

Bechtel, Mark. "Four-Time Iditarod Champion Susan Butcher." *Sports Illustrated* 105, no. 6 (August 14, 2006): 17-18.

Duncan, Joyce. *Ahead of Their Time: A Biographical Dictionary of Risk-Taking Women.* Westport, Conn.: Greenwood Press, 2002.

Harmon, Melissa Burdick. "Alone Against the Arctic." *Biography* 3, no. 3 (March, 1999): 96-102.

"Whoa, Doggie!" *National Geographic Traveler* 20, no. 7 (October, 2003): 65.

*Women in World History: A Biographical Encyclopedia.* Waterford, Conn.: Yorkin Publications, 1999.

# *Connie Carpenter*

**Born:** February 26, 1957
     Madison, Wisconsin
**Also known as:** Connie Carpenter-Phinney (full
    name)
**Other major sport:** Speed skating

## Early Life

Born and raised in a cold region of the United States, Connie Carpenter became a prodigy in speed skating. In Wisconsin, first she learned to walk; then she learned to skate. The only daughter in a family that included three sons, Connie developed her competitive edge early in life. She learned that doing well was important to her. Though her brothers were also competitive, her parents were not. They created a home that was supportive and comfortable.

## The Road to Excellence

Beginning in kindergarten, Connie participated in skating championships in Madison. She won in her age group every year. By the seventh grade, she became serious about skating and began training more intensely by running and biking. In 1972, she went to Norway to train with Finn Halvorsen, a Norwegian speed-skating coach. After training daily for eight months by running, sprinting, lifting weights, and taking vitamins, Connie qualified for the U.S. Olympic speed-skating team when she was fourteen years old. In the Winter Games in Sapporo, Japan, Connie earned a seventh-place finish in the 1,500-meter speed-skating race.

After the Olympics, Connie continued to compete, but she suffered from anemia, a back problem, and, finally, a stress fracture in her foot. In 1976, she won the overall title at the U.S. Speed Skating Championships. However, because of an ankle injury exacerbated by the stress fracture, she could not compete at the 1976 Winter Olympics. As part of her rehabilitation,

Connie cross-trained by cycling. She had turned to this sport in the past during the nonwinter months and once again used cycling to strengthen her legs.

## The Emerging Champion

As a speed skater, Connie had developed strong upper-leg muscles, which are also needed to excel in cycling. As she trained in cycling, she found that her passion for it surpassed her interest in speed skating. She began competing in regional races and in 1976, 1977, and 1979 won the U.S. Road & Pursuit Championship.

*Connie Carpenter.* (Peter Brouillet/Getty Images)

## Major Championships

| Year | Competition | Place |
|------|-------------|-------|
| 1976 | U.S. Outdoor Speed Skating Championships | Overall Title |
| 1976-77, 1979 | U.S. Road & Pursuit Championships (Cycling) | 1st |
| 1980 | NCAA Crew Championship | 1st |
| 1981 | National Road Race (Cycling) | 1st |
| 1982-83 | National Criterium (Cycling) | 1st |
| 1983 | World Pursuit Cycling | 1st |
| 1984 | Olympic Games, Road Race | Gold |

Connie moved to Northern California to live in a climate more conducive to biking, then entered the University of California at Berkeley and competed in a new sport, rowing, because her brother had rowed on his college team. After six months of rowing, she qualified for the crew team. In 1980, Connie was part of the team that won the National Collegiate Athletic Association (NCAA) championship four-oared shell-with-coxswain event. Connie was an expert rower as well as an accomplished speed skater and cyclist.

Once again, however, Connie switched sports. An announcement was made that the 1984 Los Angeles Summer Olympic Games would include the women's individual road race. In 1981, Connie went back to cycling and won the National Road Championship. She continued to compete and was the 1982 and 1983 National Criterium champion. Also in 1983, Connie set a world record in the World Pursuit Championship.

After marrying fellow cyclist Davis Phinney, Connie returned to the Olympics in 1984, this time on the U.S. cycling team during the Summer Games. On a hot race day and on a difficult course, she knew she had to give a final push to win. In the final moments of the women's road race, Connie inched ahead of her U.S. teammate, Rebecca Twigg, by throwing her bike forward and crossing the finish line less than a half wheel ahead of her. The two teammates' finishing times were identical: two hours, eleven minutes, and fourteen seconds. However, Connie won the Olympic gold medal. She was the first American in seventy-two years to win an Olympic cycling medal. The U.S. cycling team earned four medals; Connie's husband, Davis, finished fifth in the men's road race.

### Continuing the Story

After her Olympic victory, Connie continued to receive honors. She was inducted into the International Women's Sports Hall of Fame in 1990 and the U.S. Olympics Hall of Fame in 1992. In June, 2000, *Bicycling* magazine named the 1984 U.S. Olympic team's accomplishments, in which they won more medals than any other cycling team in history, one of the "Fifteen Greatest Moments in U.S. Cycling." Connie and her husband settled in Copper Mountain, Colorado, to run a cycling camp.

### Summary

Connie Carpenter was a natural athlete who excelled in several sports—speed skating, crew, and cycling. She has won awards and honors for all of these sports. Despite her injuries, Connie's continuous participation in sports, and in particular, competitions, made her one of the most honored female athletes in U.S. history.

*Betsy L. Nichols*

### Additional Sources

"Connie Carpenter Phinney." *Physician and Sports-Medicine* 24, no. 7 (July, 1996): 112.

Layden, Joseph. *Women in Sports: The Complete Book on the World's Greatest Female Athletes.* Los Angeles: General, 1997.

Martin, Scott. "The Heroes of 1984: U.S. Olympic Cyclists." *Bicycling* 37 (January, 1996): 36-41.

Phinney, Davis, and Connie Carpenter. *Training for Cycling: The Ultimate Guide to Improved Performance.* New York: Putnam, 1992.

## Honors and Awards

| | |
|------|------|
| 1990 | Inducted into International Women's Sports Hall of Fame |
| 1992 | Inducted into U.S. Olympic Hall of Fame |

# Corky Carroll

**Born:** September 9, 1947
Alhambra, California
**Also known as:** Charles Curtis Carroll (full name)

## Early Life

Charles Curtis "Corky" Carroll was born on September 9, 1947, in Alhambra, California, and grew up in Surfside Colony, about nine miles north of Huntington Beach, California. He was the only child born to a father who worked as an electrician and a mother who had formerly worked as a radio singer in the era when radio was performed live. Against the objections of his mother, Corky spent all of his spare time in the ocean, surfing and paddleboarding from sunrise until sunset.

The home in which Corky was raised was located on the beach, so the ocean always played a major role in Corky's life. He learned to swim at about the same age most children learn to walk. Soon after, he and his friends began searching for anything that floated on which to ride the waves. Around the age of five or six, Corky managed to stand upright on a borrowed surfboard and ride his first wave.

## The Road to Excellence

During the 1950's "long boards," made of wood and standing 9 to 10 feet in length, were the standard. Their weight made surfing a sport that required not only the coordination and stamina necessary to maneuver in the surf but also sheer strength. Corky, an athlete dedicated to his sport, kept in top physical condition by paddleboarding and surfing daily. Because of his intensely competitive nature, he usually met the challenge to be the

### Honors, Awards, and Milestones

| | |
|---|---|
| 1963 | U.S. Junior Champion |
| 1966-70 | Overall U.S. Surfing Champion |
| 1967 | *Surfer* magazine Most Popular Surfer |
| | International Pro-Am Champion |
| 1967-69 | World International Surfing Champion |
| 1996 | Inducted into Huntington Beach Surfing Walk of Fame |
| 2002 | Inducted into Surfers' Hall of Fame |

best. This went beyond competitive surfing into all aspects of his life. When Corky was about sixteen years of age, he was known as one of the world's fastest paddleboarders, a further example of his need to excel.

Excellence, however, does have its price. Daily exposure to the intense sunlight caused Corky to develop an eye disease called pterygium, which was diagnosed in 1960. It caused a natural growth to form over the eye to protect it from the harsh glare of the sun's reflection on the water. He underwent surgery but only two weeks later was once again where he felt most at home, in the surf. The only difference in his appearance after surgery was that he began wearing sunglasses.

Corky's determination and his strong, brash, humorous personality emerged at an early age. A surfer who did more than merely ride waves, Corky made 8mm films, one of which was entitled *Surf Savages*, and showed them to local surfers at club meetings. He later formed musical groups that released a number of albums. His reputation as a personality, as well as a "hotdogger" performance surfer, was established early in the close-knit Southern California surfing community.

## The Emerging Champion

In the 1960's, surfing enjoyed enormous popularity as a sport and as a lifestyle. Surfing in Southern California centered in Huntington Beach, where Corky attended high school. In 1962, at the age of fifteen, he won his first surfing contest. The following year, he was named junior champion. His fame began to grow beyond the scope of the local folklore, and Corky became the man to beat in international surfing circles.

Corky married for the first time when he was still in his teens. He fathered a son, Clint, when he was only nineteen years of age and about to become famous across the country and around the world.

Corky was the first professional surfer. In addition to winning prize money from surfing contests and championships worldwide, he was the first surfer to be paid to do nothing but surf and endorse products related to swimwear and surfboards.

Corky also designed surfboards, worked as advertising director at *Surfer* magazine, judged contests, and participated in other activities related to the sport in which he excelled.

Corky was the overall U.S. surfing champion for five years in a row, spanning 1966 through 1970. He complemented that achievement with the title of international surfing champion for three of those years, 1967, 1968, and 1969. In 1967, in a readers' poll, Corky Carroll was voted *Surfer* magazine's most popular surfer. That same year, only days before the international championship off Lima, Peru, Corky swallowed some contaminated ocean water and fell ill. Stubborn and determined, Corky ignored his doctor's orders, sneaked out of the Peruvian hospital, and went to the beach, where he surfed his way to another title in spite of his illness.

## Continuing the Story

Corky won surfing contests based on his skill as a performance rider, or trick rider, rather than as a big-wave rider, although competition in the 1960's differed from the contests that took place decades later. Corky commented on the fact that surfing contests were far less organized when he competed than they later became. Complete objectivity in scoring this sport will always prove difficult because no two waves are exactly the same, but the professional surfing associations made great strides in standardizing contest scoring. Whereas only two surfers compete at the same time in later eras, as many as six or seven competed simultaneously in the earlier period of surfing.

Corky continued to surf near his home in San Clemente, California. His son, Clint, also surfed in local pro-am contests. Corky also played and taught tennis. He wrote a book and a television script and made celebrity appearances in television commercials. He enjoyed performing as a comedian, a talent that was evident in his competitive surfing days.

In the years following his retirement from professional competition, Corky opened a surf school in Huntington Beach, launched a career in music, and created his own line of sportswear. He remained an icon among younger generations of surfing professionals and enthusiasts.

## Summary

When he was between seven and nineteen years of age, Corky Carroll won fifty-two major surfing contests and was the first surfer who made his living from the sport. Whether using long or short boards, Corky was able to master the waves.

*Leslie A. Pearl*

## Additional Sources

Carroll, Corky, and Joel Engel. *Surf-Dog Days and Bitchin' Nights.* Chicago: Contemporary Books, 1989.

Hicks, Jerry. "Surfer Corky Carroll Catches Wave of Fame." *Los Angeles Times* (Orange County edition), July 25, 1996, p. 1.

Kampion, Drew. *Stoked! A History of Surf Culture.* Salt Lake City, Utah: G. Smith, 2003.

Klein, Debra. "Be True to Your Surf School." *Newsweek* 139, no. 23 (June 10, 2002): 57.

# Don Carter

**Born:** July 29, 1926
    St. Louis, Missouri
**Also known as:** Donald James Carter (full name);
  Mr. Bowling

## Early Life

Donald James Carter was born on July 29, 1926, in St. Louis, Missouri. The younger of two sons, he was raised by his mother, Gladys Carter, after his father deserted the family while Don was still an infant.

As a boy, Don worked as a pinsetter for a local bowling alley in St. Louis. He first bowled at the age of thirteen, and later, while still in high school, built a lane in the basement of his house so that he could practice. Other sports held an interest for Don as well. During his years at Wellston High School, he earned four varsity letters in baseball and three in football before graduating in 1944.

Following graduation, Don joined the U.S. Navy and served as a ship radarman in the South Pacific for two years. He was discharged in June, 1946, with the rank of third-class petty officer.

## The Road to Excellence

After leaving the Navy, Don was signed to play professional baseball by Bill Beckman of the Philadelphia Athletics. Don spent the 1947 season playing infielder and pitching for a minor-league team in Red Springs, North Carolina. However, Don felt he was not a major-league prospect and returned home to St. Louis at the end of the 1947 season.

Don was soon bowling in rec-

reational leagues while holding various jobs. His work as a janitor, bartender, and plant worker left him little time for competitive tournament bowling. Don's mother was a source of encouragement during these difficult years, allowing Don to live at home and save money for bowling.

Eventually, Don's perseverance began to pay off.

*Don Carter, who was a founder and the first president of the Professional Bowlers Association.* (Courtesy of Amateur Athletic Foundation of Los Angeles)

He became a bowling instructor at Silver Shield Lanes in St. Louis, then later at Floriss Lanes; both jobs gave him the opportunity to earn money and hone his bowling skills. These developing skills caught the attention of the Pfeiffer bowling team of Detroit, which invited Don to join its ranks in 1951, offering him no salary but a chance to refine his skills in competition. Don accepted the invitation and took a job in the Detroit recreation department, making sixty dollars a week to help cover his expenses.

Don received other recognition for his bowling ability in 1952; the *Bowlers Journal* named him to its all-American team. This was the first major award for Don, but it certainly was not the last. In 1953, Don married LaVerne Haverly, a bowling champion from Los Angeles, California. Don and LaVerne eventually had two children, Cathy and Jimmy.

## The Emerging Champion

Don went on to dominate bowling through the 1950's and early 1960's. He won more tournaments and money than any other bowler. His accomplishments earned him the nickname "Mr. Bowling." The 1952 all-star championship became Don's first major title. He won the same tournament in 1953, as well as two team tournaments as a member of the Pfeiffer squad. For his efforts, the Bowling Writers Association of America honored him as the bowler of the year.

Meanwhile, the Pfeiffer bowling team continued to be successful, due in large part to Don, and other teams recognized this fact. In 1953, a newly formed team in St. Louis, sponsored by the Anheuser-Busch company, persuaded Don to join them. The team was molded around Don, and the

---

### PBA Tour Victories

| | |
|---|---|
| 1960 | Paramus; National Championship at Memphis |
| 1962 | Houston; Seattle; Tucson; Rochester |

### Other Major Victories

| | |
|---|---|
| 1953-54, 1957-58 | U.S. Open |
| 1957, 1959-62 | World's Invitational |
| 1961 | ABC Masters |

---

team proceeded to win six national team titles between 1955 and 1962.

Don also continued his individual excellence during this period. By 1964, Don had won five World's Invitational titles and six bowler of the year awards and had been named an all-American an amazing ten times. In addition to his prowess on the lanes, Don influenced bowling in other ways. He was a driving force in the development of the Professional Bowlers Association (PBA) in 1958, and when a rival association formed in 1961, featuring many top bowlers, Don stuck by the PBA. The rival group folded in less than a year.

### Continuing the Story

Such achievements mark the long career of the man voted "Greatest Bowler of All Time" in 1970. Don continued to bowl until 1973, when he retired from competition. He eventually moved to Miami, Florida, with his second wife, Paula, whom he had married in 1976.

The ability to concentrate was often cited as something that separated Don from other bowlers. He rarely spoke during his matches, and his steely nerves allowed him to remain focused even when under great pressure. The pressure was so intense that Don often lost up to 8 pounds during a single match. This intense temperament might be attributed to the criticism Don had to overcome early in his career because of his unusual bowling technique. Bowling purists believed the correct form was to crouch only slightly when bowling and release the ball with an extended arm. Don, however, crouched very low on his approach, and when he released the ball, his arm was bent at the elbow. Criticism did not affect Don; he simply laughed and said, "I guess I just learned to bowl wrong."

---

### Records

Most top-five finishes in a year, 18 (1962)
Most consecutive top-five finishes, 7 (1962)

### Honors and Awards

| | |
|---|---|
| 1952-54, 1957-63 | *Bowlers Journal* All-American Team |
| 1953-54, 1957-58, 1960, 1962 | BWAA Bowler of the Year |
| 1958-59, 1961-62 | President of PBA |
| 1970 | Voted "Greatest Bowler of All Time" |
| | Inducted into ABC Hall of Fame |
| 1975 | Inducted into PBA Hall of Fame |

A winning personality, combined with his concentration, made Don a bowling favorite. He was popular among his peers, as was evident when Don was named the first president of the PBA. Don was also popular among fans. They cheered his every strike at tournaments and groaned when things did not go so well. Perhaps they could identify with Don because of his background and his awkward bowling style.

## Summary

From a humble beginning in the sport, Don Carter rose to be the best bowler of his time. Although his style was dubbed unothodox, Don became a bowling legend. In 1970, he was elected to the American Bowling Congress (ABC) Hall of Fame, and in 1975, Don became a charter member of the PBA Hall of Fame.

*Robert T. Epling*

## Additional Sources

Carter, Don. *Bowling the Pro Way.* New York: Viking Press, 1975.

Hickok, Ralph. *A Who's Who of Sports Champions.* Boston: Houghton Mifflin, 1995.

Jowdy, John. *Bowling Execution.* Champaign, Ill.: Human Kinetics, 2002.

Porter, David L., ed. *Biographical Dictionary of American Sports: Basketball and Other Indoor Sports.* Westport, Conn.: Greenwood Press, 1989.

# Jim Clark

**Born:** March 4, 1936
Kilmany, Scotland
**Died:** April 7, 1968
Hockenheim, West Germany (now in Germany)
**Also known as:** James Clark, Jr. (full name)

## Early Life

James Clark, Jr., was born into a wealthy farming family on March 4, 1936, in Kilmany, Scotland. The youngest and only boy in a family of seven, Jim was always interested in farming, and on his holidays from boarding school, he became involved in the running of his father's farm. Jim's earliest experience of driving was on the farm's tractors. Jim's father always encouraged his Jim's interest in driving, and, by the age of ten, Jim had his own car to drive around the farm.

## The Road to Excellence

Jim's first contact with motorsports came in 1948, when his eldest sister married a local farmer whose hobby was car racing. Watching his brother-in-law race made Jim determined to be on the track. At seventeen, Jim passed his driving test and, as a reward, was given the family Sunbeam. He entered the car in a precision driving contest, which he won. Jim gained more driving experience by entering driving competitions and minor rallies in the Scottish border country.

In June, 1956, Jim took part in his first proper race. Driving a Dampf Kraft Wagen (DKW) in Aberdeen, he finished last. Jim's initial failure did not deter him or the growing number of local backers who saw in him enough promise to sponsor his career. Later in the same month, Jim was on the winner's rostrum, having driven the family Sunbeam to victory in a local race.

Over the next few years, Jim won numerous races, but, more inportant, involvement in the sport gained him invaluable experience. By 1958, he had been successful enough for his backers to form the Border Reivers team, which provided the cars for Jim's developing career.

Jim's sponsors were pressuring him to turn pro-fessional so he could make the break into big-time motor racing. However, because he was the only son in a farming family, his parents wanted him to give up racing and devote his time to the farm. Jim was torn between these two options. In the end, he decided to pursue his dreams in motor racing.

## The Emerging Champion

Jim drove his first professional race in a single-seater car in December, 1959, at Brands Hatch in England. News traveled fast about this talented young Scot, and he was signed by Team Lotus to drive in Formula Two and Formula Junior competitions.

Under the guidance of team manager Colin Chapman, Jim drove his Lotus to nine victories in the 1960 season, becoming Formula Junior World cochampion. Jim impressed Chapman sufficiently for the Lotus head to offer him a drive in the Formula One Dutch Grand Prix. At the age of twenty-four, Jim was driving in the highest level of motor racing. His fifth-place finish gave observers notice of the greatness that was to come.

Jim's first full season as a Formula One driver was 1961. Throughout this first year, Jim was criticized as too young and inexperienced. Although his results were not outstanding, Jim practiced hard to develop his driving skills.

---

### CART, Grand Prix, and Other Victories

| | |
|---|---|
| 1960 | Formula Junior World Cochampion |
| 1961, 1963, 1965, 1968 | South African Grand Prix |
| 1962 | Aintree 200 |
| 1962-65 | Belgian Grand Prix |
| 1962-65, 1967 | British Grand Prix |
| 1962, 1966-67 | United States Grand Prix |
| 1963 | Milwaukee 200 |
| | Italian Grand Prix |
| 1963-65, 1967 | Dutch Grand Prix |
| | Netherlands Grand Prix |
| 1963, 1965 | French Grand Prix |
| | World Championship of Drivers |
| 1963, 1967 | Mexican Grand Prix |
| 1965 | Indianapolis 500 |
| | German Grand Prix |
| 1965, 1967-68 | Tasman Cup Series Championship |

In 1962, Jim's efforts began to pay off. He won his first Grand Prix, in Belgium, and two other victories led to the runner-up spot in the drivers' championship. Jim's critics were silenced. For such a young driver, he showed an incredible ability to concentrate, which, in conjunction with his great enthusiasm and natural ability, made him a formidable competitor.

Everything came together for Jim in 1963. He had done his apprenticeship in Formula One, and, driving a powerful Lotus, he earned the World Championship of Drivers. During the course of the season, he won six Grand Prix championships, four in succession. Still only twenty-seven, Jim had reached the pinnacle of his sport.

### Continuing the Story

Although Jim had reached the top in Formula One, he still was inquisitive and eager to learn everything about driving. As a result, Jim often experimented and explored other types of motor racing. Jim's most famous venture into an unfamiliar form of racing came at the Indianapolis 500. He had finished second in his first race in 1963. Driving an Indy version of a Formula One race car, Jim dominated the race in 1965 and beat the second-place finisher by more than a lap.

Having barely failed to retain the Formula One drivers' championship in 1964, Jim was not denied in 1965. His precision and superb reflexes were evident on all types of road surface. He won five consecutive Grand Prix and took the championship despite a series of mechanical failures toward the end of the season.

Jim had frustrating seasons in 1966 and 1967, plagued by more car troubles. By 1968, Jim and his Lotus car were back with a vengeance. In the opening South African Grand Prix, he thrilled the crowd with a stunning display that left the rest of the field trailing behind. This victory was Jim's twenty-fifth in the Formula One championship, and with it, he broke the record number of victories set by the legendary Juan Manuel Fangio.

Jim was the driver to beat in the 1968 Formula One championship. He was at his peak, driving a fast car with supreme confidence. Because Jim was

---

### Records

Most Tasman Cup Series Championships, 3
Most Tasman Cup Series victories, 14
Most Tasman Cup Series victories in a season, 5 (1967)

### Honors and Awards

| | |
|---|---|
| 1963 | Indianapolis 500 Rookie of the Year |
| 1964 | Order of the British Empire |
| 1988 | Inducted into Indianapolis Motor Speedway Hall of Fame |
| 1990 | Inducted into International Motor Sports Hall of Fame |
| | Inducted into Motorsports Hall of Fame of America |

---

still thirsty for knowledge about driving, he frequently entered Formula Two races. On April 7, 1968, he was competing in such a race at Hockenheim in West Germany (now in Germany). Light rain was falling when his Lotus went out of control at 175 miles per hour and crashed into trees. Jim's neck was broken, and he died instantly. The reason for Jim's fatal accident has never been conclusively established.

### Summary

Jim Clark was one of the greatest racing drivers of all time. The shy Scot possessed immense natural talent and felt most comfortable when behind the wheel. The greatest irony in Jim's life was that he died during a race that he had little chance of winning and which was of little importance to his career. However, this was simply a reflection of Jim's dedication to his sport. Racing dominated Jim's life, and his insatiable passion for cars and driving made him the great driver that he was.

*David L. Andrews*

### Additional Sources

Darley, Peter. *Jim Clark: Life at Team Lotus.* Littleton, Colo.: Coterie Press, 2007.

Dymock, Eric. *Jim Clark: First of the Greats.* St. Paul, Minn.: Motorbooks International, 2003.

Young, Eoin S. *Jim Clark and His Most Successful Lotus: The Twin Biographies of a Legendary Racing Driver and His 1963 World Championship Winning Lotus 25 R4.* Newbury Park, Calif.: Haynes, 2004.

# Ronnie Coleman

**Born:** May 13, 1964
  Monroe, Louisiana
**Also known as:** Ronald Dean Coleman (full name)

## Early Life

Ronald Dean Coleman was born May 13, 1964, in Monroe, Louisiana, to a single mother, Jessie Benton, and grew up in nearby Bastrop with three younger siblings—one brother and two sisters. Ronnie divided his time among school, sports, and part-time jobs to help support his family. He excelled at football and was recognized as one of the hardest working and most dedicated athletes on the team. He worked out and lifted weights during

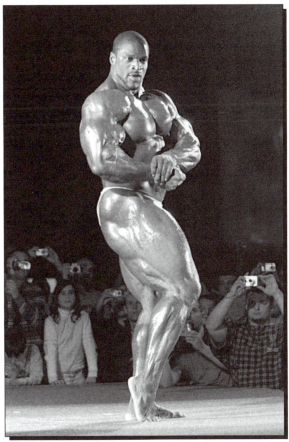

*Ronnie Coleman posing at the Euroshow Nutrend in 2006.* (Getty Images)

the summer months to prepare for the football season.

Ronnie played football for Grambling State University and graduated cum laude in 1989 with an accounting degree. In order to pursue a career in accounting, Ronnie moved to Dallas, Texas. While delivering pizzas to support himself, Ronnie noticed that the Arlington, Texas, Police Department was hiring. He joined the department and lifted weights when not on duty.

## The Road to Excellence

Ronnie was noticed by fellow officers who referred him to Metroflex Gym, an institution quickly becoming known as a training facility for powerlifters and bodybuilders. Brian Dobson, the owner of the gym, persuaded Ronnie to become his workout partner, offering a free membership and the chance to eventually compete professionally. Within the first year of training with Dobson, Ronnie had gained 15 pounds of muscle, could bench press 500 pounds, and could deadlift more than 700 pounds.

In 1990, after training for only four months, Ronnie competed in and won his first bodybuilding contest. That same year, he also won the heavyweight and overall titles at the National Physique Committee (NPC) Texas Championships and placed third among heavyweights at the NPC National Bodybuilding and Fitness Championships, his first professional qualifier. The following year, Ronnie placed fourth in the NPC National Bodybuilding and Fitness Championships. He was first at the International Federation of Body Builders (now International Federation of Bodybuilding and Fitness) (IFBB) World Amateur Championships (previously known as the Mr. Universe contest), which earned him his IFBB professional card.

On May 9, 1992, in Chicago, Illinois, Ronnie made his professional debut and placed eleventh. Two weeks later, he placed fourteenth at the IFBB Night of Champions. Since he had won at the IFBB World Amateur Championships, Ronnie qualified for Mr. Olympia, the so-called Super Bowl of bodybuilding. Ronnie entered the Mr. Olympia contest

## Titles and Championships

| | |
|---|---|
| 1990 | Mr. Texas |
| 1991 | World Amateur Championships |
| 1995-96 | Canada Pro Cup |
| 1997, 2003-04 | Grand Prix (Russia) |
| 1998 | Toronto Pro Invitational |
| | Grand Prix (Finland, Germany) |
| 1998-2005 | Mr. Olympia |
| 1999-2000 | World Pro Championships |
| 1999-2000, 2004 | Grand Prix (England) |
| 2001 | Arnold Schwarzenegger Classic |
| | Grand Prix (New Zealand) |
| 2002, 2004 | Grand Prix (Holland) |

weighing approximately 215 pounds; he finished the competition tied for last place. The following year, he failed to qualify for Mr. Olympia; the year after, he qualified but placed only fifteenth. In 1995, although he placed only eleventh at the Mr. Olympia competition, he won his first professional contest, the IFBB Canada Pro Cup, gaining him a contract with Met-Rx, a nutritional product company.

### The Emerging Champion

Finally, in 1996 and 1997, Ronnie broke into the top ten at Mr. Olympia with sixth-and ninth-place finishes, respectively. On October 10, 1998, at the age of thirty-four, Ronnie competed in the Mr. Olympia contest in New York. That year, he had began working with nutritionist Chad Nicholls. Ronnie came into the contest weighing 250 pounds and won by three points.

Because the 1998 Mt. Olympia contest had been so close, many experts believed that Ronnie would not be able to defend the title. However, Ronnie chose not to compete before the Mr. Olympia contest; instead, he concentrated solely on training and preparing for the competition. As a result, Ronnie won his second title with a perfect score. The win was controversial: After the scores were announced, second-place finisher Flex Wheeler turned his back to the judges, removed his medals from his neck, and raised his hand in the "number-one" sign to show his disagreement with the placing.

### Continuing the Story

In 2000, Ronnie tallied back-to-back perfect scores, winning the Mr. Olympia competition for a third consecutive year. However, in 2001, up-and-coming competitor Jay Cutler finished a close second to Ronnie. The first two rounds of posing went to Jay, but the last two went to Ronnie, which enabled him to win by six points. Ronnie won another close contest the following year but silenced his critics in 2003 with a perfect score. He had won his sixth title. In 2004, Ronnie entered Mr. Olympia at forty years old. Once again, Ronnie came into the contest at almost 300 pounds and won with a perfect score. He ended the year with a total of twenty-five first-place IFBB finishes. In 2005, Ronnie won his eighth Mr. Olympia title, tying the all-time record set by Lee Haney from 1984 to 1991.

In 2006, Ronnie tried to break Haney's record by going for his ninth-straight win but finished second to Jay Cutler (not the football player). After finishing fourth in the 2007 Mr. Olympia competition, Ronnie announced his retirement.

### Summary

The sport of bodybuilding entails year-round competition. The participating athletes must be in the best shape of their lives at each event. The sport takes dedication, hard work, genetic predisposition, and a love for competition. Ronnie Coleman had these traits long before he began training professionally. His tenacious mentality helped earn him a record-tying eight Mr. Olympia titles and a record twenty-five IFBB wins.

*Lamia Nuseibeh Scherzinger*

### Additional Sources

Kruh, Nancy. "Ronnie Coleman: Nobody Messes with This Arlington Cop, A.K.A. Mr. Olympia." *Dallas Morning News*, October, 1999.

Torres, John Albert. *Legends of Health and Fitness: Fitness Stars of Bodybuilding*. Hockessin, Del.: Mitchell Lane, 2000.

# Dennis Conner

**Born:** September 16, 1943
San Diego, California
**Also known as:** Dennis Walter Conner (full name)

### Early Life

Dennis Conner was born on September 16, 1943, in San Diego, California. He grew up in the Point Loma district, half a block from the prestigious San Diego Yacht Club. Dennis's father was a jet engineer who also fished commercially. The family was not poor, but Dennis did not have as much money as his yacht-club friends, and this gave him something of an inferiority complex.

Dennis first sailed at the age of seven, and he began to spend so much time hanging around the San Diego Yacht Club that he was considered a bit of a pest. Eventually, at the age of twelve, Dennis was admitted to junior membership in the club, but, because of his lack of money, he crewed for other people rather than owning his own boat.

Dennis was an awkward, chubby child who nevertheless lettered in track, cross country, and basketball in high school. He was not outstanding in these sports, but in sailing, he realized that his physique was no handicap.

### The Road to Excellence

While in high school, Dennis had a small Penguin sailboat and crewed in 18-foot Starlet keelboats. He also began crewing on many different larger boats. At first, he thought that not having his own big boat was a disadvantage. Later, he realized that this gave him the chance to learn from all the other crews what worked best. He saw that thorough preparation of the boat and the crew were the keys to success.

After high school, Dennis attended San Diego State University and majored in business. Most summers he worked in sail lofts. He began to crew regularly for a man who owned a carpet business. Later, Dennis went to work for him and eventually became his business partner.

In 1970, Dennis bought his first big boat, acquiring a seventeen-hundred-dollar half share in a 33-foot boat. In 1971, he bought a secondhand Star-class boat (23-foot keelboat) and won the world championship.

In the early 1970's, Dennis built a big boat reputation with wins both in fleet racing, between multi-

*Dennis Conner celebrating a victory in 2002.* (Nigel Marple/Reuters/Landov)

ple competitors, and in match racing, between two boats only, racing head-to-head. The latter requires especially fine skills, as the boats are rarely far apart. Dennis won the Congressional Cup for the top U.S. sailors in round-robin match racing in 1973 and 1975, and the Southern Offshore Racing Conference (SORC), a series of offshore fleet races, in 1975. He helped the U.S. team to third place in the 1975 Admiral's Cup in Britain.

## The Emerging Champion

In 1974, Dennis first sailed in the races that made him famous: the America's Cup series. He was the helmsman of the U.S. defender, *Courageous*, during the starting procedures—considered the most crucial part of match racing—and then acted as tactician during the race. *Courageous* won the series 4-0 against the Australians.

At the Olympic Games in 1976, Dennis won a bronze medal in the Tempest class, a two-person 22-foot keelboat, and in 1977, he won the world Star Championship again with five straight first-place finishes against eighty-nine boats, the feat of which Dennis was most proud. When the America's Cup was held in 1980, Dennis was skipper of the U.S. defender, *Freedom*, winning the series 4-1.

The 1983 America's Cup was between the U.S. defender, *Liberty*, and the challenger, *Australia II*. At the time, the United States had held the America's Cup for 132 years, the longest winning streak in any sports event. Public attention was on *Australia II* because she had a revolutionary wing-shaped keel. This gave the boat superior performance. The American boat, by contrast, was badly designed. The stage was set for the fight of Dennis's life.

In the best-of-seven series, *Liberty* won the first two races, and *Australia II* won the third. *Liberty* won the fourth race but suffered gear failure in the fifth. The Australian boat then won the sixth race

---

### Major Championship Victories

| | |
|---|---|
| 1971, 1977 | World Championship (Star class) |
| 1974 | America's Cup (as helmsman) |
| 1976 | U.S. Olympic bronze medalist (Tempest class) |
| 1980, 1987-88 | America's Cup (as skipper) |
| 1991, 1994 | World Championship (Etchells class) |
| 1993 | National Championship (Australia Etchells class) |

---

### Honors and Awards

| | |
|---|---|
| 1975, 1980, 1987 | U.S. Yachtsman of the Year |
| 1993 | America's Cup Hall of Fame |

---

to level the series 3-3. The final race was held in light winds, and Dennis Conner in *Liberty* led for much of the race. On the next-to-last leg, however, the Australian crew chose the breezier side of the course and won by 41 seconds, clinching the America's Cup.

## Continuing the Story

Dennis did not want to be remembered as the man who lost the America's Cup, so his preparations for the next series, in 1987, were incredibly detailed. Unlike many helmsmen, Dennis did much of his own fund-raising; it takes millions of dollars to mount a successful America's Cup campaign. He enjoyed the power of talking to the wealthiest people in the U.S. business world on equal terms.

Dennis demanded total dedication from all members of his organization. He once said in an interview that he did not even particularly like sailing, but that it was the competition, drive, and winning that excited him. Many people in sailing thought this attitude took the fun out of the sport.

In the 1987 races, Dennis sailed to victory over the Australians. He won in four straight races, and thus the first man to lose the America's Cup was also the first to regain the trophy. He was declared U.S. yachtsman of the year.

In 1988, a New Zealand crew challenged for the Cup in a huge 90-foot boat. At first, Dennis and his group tried to have the large boat declared illegal in court, but this failed. Dennis built a fast 60-foot catamaran in response. At this, the New Zealanders went to court to get Dennis's boat declared illegal. The races were a hopeless mismatch. Dennis won the best-of-three series in two.

Though Dennis was well-known for his victories at the America's Cup, he also had great success in other national and international events. In 1993, Dennis set a transatlantic record of eleven days and eight hours in the Gold Cup race; the old record had stood since 1905. He also won the New Zealand Etchells National Championship in 1997, and the Etchells World Championship in 1991 and 1994.

In 1992, 1995, 2000, and 2003, Dennis skippered the *Stars and Stripes* without bringing home the Cup. Despite these overall losses, Dennis won more than one hundred America's Cup races.

## Summary

The 6-foot 1-inch, 200-pound Dennis Conner did not look like a sportsman, and ironically, he was a virtual nonswimmer. With grit and determination in place of money, the carpet salesman from San Diego made himself into a top ocean sailor. He became perhaps the most hard-driven, single-minded sailor of all time in his relentless pursuit of victory.

*Shirley H. M. Reekie*

## Additional Sources

Conner, Dennis. *Stars and Stripes: Official Record, 2003.* San Diego, Calif.: Dennis Conner Sports, 2003.

Conner, Dennis, and Michael Levitt. *The America's Cup: The History of Sailing's Greatest Competition in the Twentieth Century.* New York: St. Martin's Press, 1998.

Hoffer, Richard. "Ships of Fools." *Sports Illustrated* 97, no. 23 (December 9, 2002): 68-72.

Lassa, Todd. "Conner's Fortunes Suffer Amid Waning Interest in Yachting." *San Diego Business Journal* 11, no. 4 (January 22, 1990): 1-2.

# Ángel Cordero, Jr.

**Born:** November 8, 1942
      Santurce, San Juan, Puerto Rico
**Also known as:** Ángel Tomás Cordero, Jr. (full
    name)

### Early Life

Ángel Tomás Cordero, Jr., was born on November 8, 1942, in San Juan, Puerto Rico. According to his father, Ángel was born to race. The Puerto Rico racing encyclopedia includes an entire page of jockeys with the surname Cordero, and there is an equally long list of riders with the surname Hernandez, which was Ángel's mother's maiden name.

From the time he could walk, Ángel wanted to race horses. His father and grandfather, both fa-

*Ángel Cordero, Jr., covered in mud after a race in the 1970's. (Robert Riger/Getty Images)*

mous jockeys in Puerto Rico, helped foster this desire. Ángel did not even know that a world existed outside racing until he went to school at the age of five. Ángel's father wanted him to be a doctor because of the danger in horse racing but eventually accepted his son's desire to be a jockey. Ángel went to the track to work and learn about racing before and after school. After graduation, however, Ángel pursued racing and nothing else.

### The Road to Excellence

Ángel began to race at a local track in San Juan. Six months before his eighteenth birthday, he took a terrible fall in a race: Five jockeys went down and were injured. Although he was only slightly injured, Ángel was shaken and decided to quit racing. However, five days later he returned to the track, ready to resume riding.

Ángel was a determined, almost obsessive, jockey and rode wildly. He was considered dangerous because of his desire to win. Another hard fall resulted in two broken ribs, but he was riding again as soon as he was healthy.

The next year at the El Comandante racetrack Ángel was extremely successful. After his place as the leading apprentice rider, he became the top journeyman rider in Puerto Rico with 124 wins. This record number of wins was amazing because, first, the track was open only three days a week and, second, Ángel had been suspended from racing for five months for dangerous tactics.

### The Emerging Champion

In 1962, Ángel arrived in New York, to try his hand at American horse racing. He had no friends or family and could not speak English. After several months of disappointment—riding forty-one times and winning only once—he returned to Puerto Rico totally disheartened. He got married, regained his confidence and drive, and returned with his wife to New York in 1965.

At first Ángel's races were peppered with successes, but he still felt like quitting. Ángel knew a lot about racing—he knew how to give orders but did not like taking them. Even though he had more

## Major Championship Victories

| Year | Race | Horse |
|------|------|-------|
| 1974 | Kentucky Derby | Cannonade |
| 1976 | Belmont Stakes | Bold Force |
|      | Kentucky Derby | Bold Force |
| 1980 | Preakness Stakes | Codex |
| 1984 | Preakness Stakes | Gate Dancer |
| 1985 | Kentucky Derby | Spend a Buck |
|      | Breeders' Cup Distaff | Life's Magic |
| 1988 | Breeders' Cup Juvenile Fillies | Open Mind |
|      | Breeders' Cup Sprint | Gulch |
| 1989 | Breeders' Cup Sprint | Dancing Spree |

talent than anyone else, he was treated by other jockeys as though he were not good enough to clean stables. Once Ángel learned to channel his anger and intensity into racing, however, he began to win more races.

In the United States, as in Puerto Rico, Ángel became known for his aggressive and daring riding style. He also became famous for his style of dismount. Once, at Belmont, before the race, the horse bucked and Ángel was hurled through the air. Somehow he managed to land on his feet, smiling. After that he dismounted by leaping off the horse as if it was a trampoline and landing with both feet on the ground.

In 1974, Ángel rode a spectacular race in the Kentucky Derby. Many jockeys decided to take the outside rail, but Ángel was aggressive and went for the inside rail. He was on a horse that was not given much of a chance, but Ángel survived two bumpings and won from fourteen lengths back.

### Continuing the Story

Ángel was a fixture in the New York Racing Association for more than twenty years. He was the leading rider in New York six times during his career. Several times, he was the nation's wins and money leader. His mounts earned more than $150 million, including a North American record of more than $10 million in 1983. In the same year, he was honored with his second consecutive Eclipse Award, the most respected award in horse racing. Over the span of his career, Ángel won the Kentucky Derby three times, the Preakness Stakes twice, and the Belmont Stakes once.

Through the years, Ángel's drive to win only became stronger. He gave something back to horse racing. Talented and successful, Ángel shared his skills with many young jockeys from his homeland. He retired from racing in 1992.

### Summary

Ángel Cordero, Jr., finished his racing career with 7,057 wins in 38,646 starts, including three Kentucky Derby victories. Upon his retirement in 1992, he ranked sixth all-time in career winnings, with $164.5 million. Ángel was one of the most dominant jockeys in horse racing.

*Brooke K. Zibel*

### Additional Sources

Platt, Jim, and James Buckley. *Sports Immortals: Stories of Inspiration and Achievement.* Chicago: Triumph Books, 2002.

Sugar, Bert Randolph, and Cornell Richardson. *Horse Sense: An Inside Look at the Sport of Kings.* Hoboken, N.J.: John Wiley & Sons, 2003.

## Milestones

Annual money leader in 1976
His 7,057 victories rank sixth all-time

## Honors and Awards

| 1982-83 | Eclipse Award, Outstanding Jockey |
| 1988 | Inducted into Jockeys' Hall of Fame |

# *Russell Coutts*

**Born:** March 1, 1962
　　　　Wellington, New Zealand

### Early Life

Russell Coutts was born in Wellington, New Zealand, to Alan Coutts, a construction supervisor, and Beverly Johnson Coutts. Sailing was in Russell's background. His grandmother, Priscilla Johnson, won yacht races during the 1920's and 1930's, and his grandfather sailed as well. His parents met at the Napier Sailing Club. Russell started going to regattas when he was five to watch his older brothers race P-class dinghies. At home he played with model boats, contemplating racing strategies. By age nine he had learned to sail on protected Paremata Harbor, north of Wellington. The sandbars and wind shifts provided different challenges to the neophyte sailor. His first boat was the seven-foot P-class, a great training boat. At the age of nine, he won his first race and thought he knew everything about sailing. However, not knowing the starboard/port rule resulted in many collisions and his nickname "Crash Coutts." Subsequently, Russell became a student of the rules of sailing and learned about tactics, improving boat speed, and other skills.

When Russell was eleven, the family moved to Dunedin, in New Zealand's South Island. They had a boat shed close to the water, enabling Russell to sail whenever he wished. That year, he won the Wellington P-Class Freshwater Championships. His life was focused on sailing. When a high school teacher asked him what he wanted to do, Russell replied that he wanted to win the America's Cup, the oldest trophy in international sports and the crown of sailing accomplishment.

### The Road to Excellence

Following high school, in 1979, Russell enrolled in the school of engineering at the University of Auckland. He took seven years to finish his degree because of the time off he took for sailing competitions. Russell had his ups and downs and, at one point, considered retiring from sailing after a disappointing showing in the Texas world championships. He raced in two world championships before winning, in 1981, the International Sailing Federation (ISAF) World Youth Sailing Championship, held in Portugal. Encouraged by his father, Russell

*Russell Coutts admiring the America's Cup.* (Jeff Haynes/Getty Images)

decided to try for an Olympic medal. He chose to race in the Finn class. Finns are 16-foot dinghies. Despite painful boils on his backside, Russell won the Olympic gold medal at the 1984 Los Angeles Games.

## The Emerging Champion

As an Olympic champion, Russell became a high-profile sailor. However, to pursue his dream of winning the America's Cup, he had to become an expert in match racing. Heretofore, his experience was racing against a fleet of boats, not against only one other boat. The boats used for match racing also had crews; Russell was used to single-handed racing. Optimistic, Russell entered the 1985 Citizen Cup match-racing regatta in Auckland. He hit a bridge and then slammed into the race committee boat, reviving his old name, "Crash Coutts." Defeated, Russell returned to school, completed his degree, and married in 1986. He and his wife later divorced. In 1989, after working as an engineer, Russell decided to learn as much as possible about match racing and try again. By the end of 1990, he was ranked number two in world match racing and won the ISAF World Match Racing Championship in 1992 and 1993.

Russell skippered in more match-racing events than any other sailor and was selected by a New Zealand racing syndicate, Team New Zealand, to campaign for the 1995 America's Cup in San Diego, California. Skippering *Black Magic*, Russell and his team began the series of round-robin races to see which boat would be the America's Cup challenger. After winning thirty-seven races and losing only one, Russell won the Louis Vuitton Cup and the right to challenge America's Cup defender

---

**Victories and Championships**

| | |
|---|---|
| 1981 | ISAF World Youth Sailing Championship |
| 1984 | Olympic Games, gold medal, Finn class |
| 1992-93, 1996, 2001, 2006-07 | ISAF World Championship |
| 1993 | Admiral's Cup |
| 1995, 2000, 2003 | America's Cup |

---

*Young America*, skippered by Dennis Conner, a four-time winner of the America's Cup. In competition for the America's Cup, Russell bested Conner by winning 5 to 0, the greatest margin of victory in the 144-year history of the event. The cup victory was the first for New Zealand. In 2000, Russell defended the America's Cup in Auckland, sweeping *Luna Rossa*, the Italian challenger, sponsored by Prada, 5-0. With this victory New Zealand became the first country other than the United States to successfully defend the America's Cup. Some time after winning the cup for New Zealand, Russell was recruited by Team Alingh, a Swiss conglomerate. Much to the dismay of New Zealanders, who considered him to be a traitor, Russell sailed the Swiss boat to victory in 2003, bringing the America's Cup to landlocked Switzerland.

## Continuing the Story

Following his victory, Russell had an unpleasant falling out with Ernesto Bertarelli, the owner of the Swiss syndicate, who fired Russell in April, 2004, and then won a court case, prohibiting Russell from racing for a competitor in the 2007 America's Cup. Russell continued to sail and win in other championship races and returned to the cup campaign in 2007 as skipper for BMW Oracle Racing, an American syndicate. In addition to sailing, Russell, using his engineering background, designed a new RC44, an all-carbon-fiber boat. In 2007, he and sailing competitor Paul Cayard launched the World Sailing League. Using high-performance, one-design boats designed by Russell, the league consisted of twelve teams that raced in an international grand prix series. Russell and his second wife, Jennifer Little Coutts, whom he married in 1999, had three children. Russell also had one child from his first marriage.

---

**Honors and Awards**

| | |
|---|---|
| 1984 | New Zealand yachtsman of the year |
| 1994 | Silberne Lorbeerblatt Award (German) |
| 1995 | Honored as Commander of the British Empire (CBE) |
| | Sperry world sailor of the year |
| | Halberg Award |
| 1995, 2003 | International Sailing Federation world sailor of the year |
| 1996 | World Trophy for Oceania |
| | Inducted into America's Cup Hall of Fame |
| 2000 | Honored with New Zealand Order of Merit (Distinguished Companion) |

## Summary

Russell Coutts, one of the most successful helmsmen in America's Cup history, was inducted in the America's Cup Hall of Fame in 1996. He was the first to win fourteen consecutive America's Cup races. In addition, he won many international championships and was awarded several honors, including Commander of the British Empire and the Distinguished Companion of the New Zealand Order of Merit.

*Marcia B. Dinneen*

## Additional Sources

Coutts, Russell, and Paul Larsen. *Challenge 2000: The Race to Win the America's Cup.* Alexandria, Va.: Time-Life Books, 1999.

_____. *Course to Victory.* Auckland, New Zealand: Hodder Moa Beckett, 1996.

Rubinstein, Julian. "This Kiwi Is One Sly Skipper." *Sports Illustrated* 28 (July, 1997): 6-7.

Wise, Mike, and Warren St. John. "New Zealand Cries Betrayal as Skipper Races for Swiss." *The New York Times*, January 10, 2003, p. A1.

# *Tom Curren*

**Born:** July 3, 1964
 Santa Barbara, California

## Early Life

Tom Curren was born on July 3, 1964, in Santa Barbara, a coastal city north of Los Angeles, California. Tom's parents intentionally chose to live in a place that was near some of the best surfing spots in the United States. Tom's father, Pat Curren, was an avid surfer, surfboard designer, and skin diver. He loved the ocean and the life that went with riding waves.

Tom's father had dropped out of high school at the age of sixteen to pursue surfing. He met Tom's mother, Jeanine Curren, while watching a surfing film in La Jolla, California, and soon after, they were married in Hawaii. On the North Shore of Oahu, Pat rode the biggest waves, often as big as 30 feet. Every ride was a gamble, with the possibility of serious injury or even death.

Tom's family moved back to back to California, and Tom grew up in Santa Barbara. He often

Tom Curren, who was a three-time world champion in surfing. (Sergio Moraes/Reuters/Landov)

pushed a skiff out into the surf of the Pacific Ocean and watched his father dive for abalone. However, Tom did not get his first surfboard until a family vacation in Hawaii. His father bought six-year-old Tom a surfboard and began getting him involved in the sport. Later, back in California, Tom surfed after school at a place called Hammond's Reef. He also loved to play the drums: When he was not surfing, he could often be heard pounding out rock rhythms in his room.

## The Road to Excellence

As Tom grew up, he and his father spent hours surfing together. Although Pat Curren was a legend as a big-wave rider, he never pushed Tom to surf competitively. However, from an early age, Tom displayed better than average surfing talent.

As a young teenager, Tom spent time with some negative influences. He got involved with drinking and smoking marijuana. As a result, his mother began taking him to church with her and encouraging him to channel his energy into surfing. She took him to whatever local surfing contests he entered, stayed until the contest was over, and drove him home.

Gradually, the attentiveness and understanding Tom's mother gave Tom paid off. In 1978, at the age of fourteen, Tom won the boys fourteen-and-under Western Surfing Association title. He won the 1978 and 1979 United States National Junior Surfing Championship, and in 1980, at sixteen, he won the World Junior Surfing Championship.

## The Emerging Champion

In 1981, Pat Curren left his family, an event that cast a shadow on Tom's life. Even before Pat moved away, communication between father and son had become strained. Leaving his problems on the beach, however, Tom continued to perfect his wave-riding skills. In 1982, he won the World Amateur

Surfing Championship. He also entered his first contests on the professional tour.

In his first year surfing as a professional, he won the Marui Pro in Japan and was ranked eighteenth overall in the world. In 1983, Tom married Marie, an avid surfer and a Frenchwoman whom he had met in a surf shop in Santa Barbara.

During the early 1980's, Tom's quiet determination and competitiveness, as well as his ability to flow with the wave's energy and perform amazing maneuvers, led Tom to additional victories against the dominant Australian surfers. Competitors and friends alike attributed much of his success to the stabilizing effects of his marriage and religious beliefs.

However, Tom had to overcome more difficulties. Although he won four major events in 1983 and three in 1984, his overall world ranking was only ninth. The pressures of the tour included long stretches away from home, frequent travel to distant countries, and an increasingly competitive atmosphere as contest prize money grew.

In 1985, the promise Tom showed in his first seasons as a professional was finally realized. Surfing against the best in the world, he began the year by winning several major events, including the Stubbies Classic and the Fosters Surfmasters. He ended the season by winning the Association of Surfing Professionals (ASP) World Tour Championship, becoming the first American to do so. To solidify himself as one of the best surfers, he returned to win a second ASP World Tour Championship in 1986.

### Continuing the Story

Tom was on his way to becoming a surfing legend. After a string of victories and two world titles during the mid-1980's, he had become a major influence on young surfers. Suddenly, parents and their children began showing up for surf contests. Tom's image as a clean-living, focused athlete had changed the attitudes of many people who considered surfing part of a marginal lifestyle.

One of the high points in Tom's surfing career came in 1985, when he traveled to Costa Rica to star in a surfing film. During his two-week stay, he was reunited with his father, who was living there on a banana and cacao farm. After years of separation and noncommunication, father and son surfed together as they had years before.

In 1989, Tom decided to take a rest from the pressures of touring. He and his wife spent the year at their home in southern France with Lee Ann, their newborn daughter. During his time off, Tom played music and surfed avocationally, as he had done when he first started surfing.

### Notable Victories

| Year | Competition |
| --- | --- |
| 1978 | Western Surfing Association Championship, Boys 14 and under |
| 1978-79 | U.S. National Junior Championship |
| 1980 | World Junior Championship |
| 1982 | World Amateur Championship |
| 1982-83, 1990 | Marui Pro |
| 1983 | Straight Talk Tyre |
| | Hang Ten California |
| 1983-84, 1988 | Op Pro |
| 1984 | Rip Curl Bell's Classic |
| 1984-85 | Stubbies Classic |
| 1985 | Philishave Tracer |
| | BHP Steel International |
| 1985-86 | Fosters Surfmasters |
| 1985-86, 1990 | ASP World Tour Championship |
| 1986 | Gotcha Pro |
| | Lacanau Pro |
| 1986-88 | Marui Japan Open |
| | Stubbies Pro |
| 1989 | Rip Curl Pro Landes |
| 1990 | O'Neill/Pepsi Cold Water Classic |
| | Bundaberg Rum Masters |
| | Rip Curl Coca-Cola Classic |
| | Quiksilver Lacanau Pro |
| | Arena Surfmasters |
| | Buondi Pro |
| 1992 | Wyland Galleries Pro |
| 1997 | The Surfer's Card Pro |
| | Body Glove Surfbout X |
| 1998 | East Coast Surf Champs/Clarion |
| 1999 | T & C Lacanau Pro |
| | Body Glove Surfbout XII |
| 2001 | Billabong Panama Pro |
| | Quiksilver Pro |
| 2002 | O'Neill Deep Blue Open |

When Tom returned to the contest circuit in 1990, he was ranked fifty-fifth and had to qualify for each event by going through trials, or "heats." He put on a tremendous display of surfing skill and won seven events. In doing so, he broke several ASP records and regained his ASP World Tour title, his third overall.

In 1994, Tom was featured in Dana Brown's *Endless Summer II*. The film was the follow-up to the 1966 classic. In the film, surfing is shown throughout the world, and Tom was part of the segment on surfing in France. Aside from the time on screen, the film helped introduce the world to Tom's other passion: music.

Following a victory at the Wyland Galleries Pro in Hawaii, Tom's interest in professional competition waned again. His sponsor, Rip Curl, launched a promotional video series called *The Search*, which featured Tom and a crew of other surfers traveling across the globe in search of the perfect wave.

In 1999, Tom returned to the professional circuit and demonstrated that he remained among the world's best surfers. He placed third in the 2000 Biarritz Surf Trophée in France.

Afterward, Tom moved back to California with his second wife, Maki, and their two sons. He shifted much of his energy into music and played concerts at various surf competitions. He released a number of albums and toured to support them. Though surfing was not his main focus, he continued to compete in occasional contests with Rip Curl as a sponsor.

## ASP World Tour Records

Second most events won, 33

Most events won in a season, 7, 1990 (record shared)

Most money won in a season (1985, 1986, 1990)

Most consecutive seasons winning ASP WCT event, 10, 1982-1991 (record shared)

First trialist to capture the ASP World Tour Championship

First surfer to recapture the ASP World Tour Championship

At 26 years, 5 months of age, the oldest ASP World Tour title holder (record broken)

## Summary

Tom Curren won his first major contest at the age of fourteen. Some years later, he captured a world championship. Afterward, he showed the same quiet grace and fearless enthusiasm for his sport that he did as a young man. To Tom, surfing was more than simply a form of recreation. His goal was to a search for the perfect relationship between surfer and wave.

*Francis Poole, updated by P. Huston Ladner*

## Additional Sources

Barilotti, S. "Tom Curren: The Surfer's Surfer." *Boy's Life* 82, no. 2 (1992).

Nunn, K. "Surfing Champion." *Rolling Stone*, July 16, 1987.

Warshaw, Matt. *The Encyclopedia of Surfing*. Orlando, Fla.: Harcourt, 2005.

# *Pat Day*

**Born:** October 13, 1953
      Brush, Colorado
**Also known as:** Patrick Alan Day (full name)

## Early Life

Patrick Alan "Pat" Day was born October 13, 1953, in the small town of Brush, in northeastern Colorado. He grew up in the even smaller ranching town of Eagle, west of Denver, in the heart of the Rocky Mountains and the White River National Forest. Pat's father was an avid horseman who taught him basic horsemanship. As a youth, Pat excelled in sports, particularly wrestling and rodeo, despite his diminutive stature. In summers, he performed in the Little Britches Rodeo and was a member of his high school rodeo team during the school year. His dream of becoming a professional rodeo cowboy briefly became a reality after he graduated from high school in 1971. Though

*Pat Day at Hollywood Park in 1987.* (Mike Powell/Getty Images)

skilled on horseback, bull riding left the 4-foot 11-inch, 100-pound Pat bruised and battered. In January, 1973, he abandoned rodeo riding for horse racing. He moved to Riverside Thoroughbred Farm in Southern California to train as a jockey.

## The Road to Excellence

In July of 1973, at Prescott Downs, Arizona, nineteen-year-old Pat first tasted victory, in a 7-furlong claiming race atop a colt named Forblunged. Pat was a natural jockey. During his first few years, he won numerous races on tracks in Illinois, Louisiana, and Massachusetts. Early success went to his head, and he was considered arrogant both on and off the track.

In the mid-1970's he married Deborah Bailey. Her father, a former jockey, persuaded Pat to try his skill at the top-ranked New York tracks; Pat tried but failed. The temptation of the big city proved overwhelming, and he turned to alcohol and drugs. By the late 1970's, he had ruined his marriage and all but destroyed his career. He left New York for Miami, but nothing changed. Substance abuse eventually caused him to stop riding altogether for a time.

Then, Pat turned around his personal and professional life. In 1979, he remarried, to Sheila Ann Johnson, who vehemently opposed his drug use. A friend persuaded him to return to the track. He did, and in 1982, he won more races than any rider in the United States: 399. He repeated as the top rider in 1983. In early 1984, Pat's transformation was completed when he became a born-again Christian. His new disciplined life had a positive and significant influence on his racing career. In 1984, he not only won his third consecutive victories title, with 399, but also won his first big race, the $3 million Breeders' Cup Classic, aboard Wild Again. For the first time, he won the Eclipse Award as the country's outstanding jockey of the year.

## The Emerging Champion

In the 1980's, Pat emerged as one of horse racing's premier jockeys. In 1985, he captured his first triple-crown victory riding Tank's Prospect in the

## Major Championship Victories

| Year | Race | Horse |
|------|------|-------|
| 1984 | Breeders' Cup Classic | Wild Again |
| 1985 | Preakness Stakes | Tank's Prospect |
| 1986 | Breeders' Cup Distaff | Lady's Secret |
| 1987 | Breeders' Cup Juvenile Fillies | Epitome |
|      | Breeders' Cup Turf | Theatrical |
| 1989 | Belmont Stakes | Easy Goer |
| 1990 | Breeders' Cup Classic | Unbridled |
|      | Preakness Stakes | Summer Squall |
| 1991 | Breeders' Cup Distaff | Dance Smartly |
|      | Canadian Triple Crown | Dance Smartly |
| 1992 | Kentucky Derby | Lil E. Tee |
| 1994 | Breeders' Cup Juvenile Fillies | Flanders |
|      | Breeders' Cup Juvenile | Timber Country |
|      | Preakness Stakes | Tabasco Cat |
|      | Belmont Stakes | Tabasco Cat |
| 1995 | Preakness Stakes | Timber Country |
| 1996 | Preakness Stakes | Louis Quatorze |
| 1997 | Breeders' Cup Juvenile | Favorite Trick |
| 1998 | Breeders' Cup Classic | Awesome Again |
| 1999 | Breeders' Cup Classic | Cat Thief |
| 2000 | Kentucky Oaks | Secret Status |
|      | Belmont Stakes | Commendable |
| 2001 | Breeders' Cup Distaff | Unbridled Elaine |
| 2002 | United Nations Stakes | With Anticipation |
| 2003 | Hawthorne Gold Cup Handicap | Perfect Drift |
|      | Raven Run Stakes | Yell |

Preakness, which is the second leg of the triple crown. That year, Pat was also honored with the George Woolf Memorial Jockey Award, bestowed annually upon the North American jockey demonstrating the highest standards of professional and personal conduct.

The following year was one of Pat's best: He won his second Eclipse Award; led the nation in victories for the fourth time, with 429 first-place finishes; and rode the Breeders' Cup Distaff winner and horse of the year, Lady's Secret. In 1987, Pat won his third Eclipse Award.

Pat had another stellar year in 1989. His favorite mount that year was Easy Goer, a horse often compared to the great triple-crown winner Secretariat. Though favored to win the triple crown, Easy Goer lost in the first two legs to Sunday Silence. However, in the Belmont Stakes, Pat and Easy Goer prevailed, beating Sunday Silence by eight lengths. Pat, who rode Easy Goer in all twenty of the horse's career starts, considered this champion thoroughbred the best horse he had

ever ridden. In that same year, Pat became the only jockey to ever win eight out of nine races in one day. When the decade ended, Pat had won 3,270 races, more than any other jockey during that time. In 1989, Lucien Laurin, the trainer of Secretariat, stated that he considered Pat "the greatest rider today, bar none."

In 1990, Pat won his second Breeders' Cup Classic, with Unbridled; won his second Preakness Stakes, astride Summer Squall; and again led the country in wins, with 364. Perhaps his greatest year as a jockey was 1991. Although he did not win any legs of the American triple crown, he did win the Canadian triple crown aboard Dance Smartly, a future hall-of-fame filly. In that year, Pat set a record for most stakes won in a single season, won his fourth Eclipse Award, and led the nation in victories for the sixth time in his career. This amazing year was topped off by Pat's induction into the National Museum of Racing's Jockeys' Hall of Fame in Saratoga Springs, New York.

### Continuing the Story

In 1992, Pat had one of his most emotional wins. Prior to 1992, he had lost in each of the nine Kentucky Derbies in which he raced. That year, he rode the 17-1 long shot, Lil E. Tee. He visited a children's hospital the day before the Derby, met a young boy recovering from a bone-marrow transplant, and promised him he would win the Kentucky Derby and would wear a hat in the winner's circle displaying the hospital's name. Lil E. Tee won, and Pat kept his promise to the boy.

Following Pat's 1992 victory at the Kentucky Derby—his first and only win at that event—Pat continued winning triple-crown races and piling up horse-racing honors: He received the New York

## Honors, Awards, and Records

| | |
|---|---|
| 1982-84, 1986, 1990-91 | Nation's winningest jockey |
| 1984, 1986-87, 1991 | Eclipse Award as Outstanding Jockey |
| 1985 | George Woolf Memorial Jockey Award |
| 1991 | Set record for most Stakes won in a single season |
| | Canadian Triple Crown Winner |
| | Inducted into Jockeys' Hall of Fame |
| 1995 | Mike Venezia Award |
| 2000 | All-time winningest rider: Keeneland Race Track |
| | 2,000 wins at Churchill Downs |
| 2005 | Received Big Sport of Turfdom Award |

Racing Association's 1995 Mike Venezia Award for extraordinary sportsmanship and citizenship. In 1994, 1995, and 1996, Pat won the Preakness Stakes, becoming the first jockey to win this race three consecutive times. In 1994, he won his second Belmont Stakes aboard Preakness winner Tabasco Cat. His third Belmont win came in 2000 on the long shot Commendable. Pat set the record for most victories ever at Churchill Downs.

On May 31, 2001, Pat rode to victory aboard Camden Park at Churchill Downs to score his eight thousandth career win, joining an elite group of jockeys to achieve that distinction. In August, 2005, following hip surgery that caused him to miss the Kentucky Derby for the first time in more than two decades, Pat announced his retirement at Churchill Downs. After thirty-two years, during which time he rode in more than 40,000 races, he recorded 8,804 wins and a 21.8 percent winning average. The top money-winning jockey in Breeders' Cup history, with nearly $23 million in prize money, Pat also retired as the top money-winner in racing history—almost $300 million.

Pat had a daughter, Irene Elizabeth, and settled with his wife Sheila in Crestwood, a suburb of Louisville, Kentucky. He planned to devote the remainder of his life to spreading the Gospel through the Race Track Chaplaincy of America, the organization with which he became involved after his conversion to Christianity in 1984.

## Summary

From a childhood dream of becoming a rodeo champion, Pat Day emerged as one of America's greatest professional thoroughbred-racing jockeys. By his own account, his religious conversion in the 1980's was greatly responsible for his success. With perseverance, he became the third rider in racing history to break the eight-thousand-win barrier and retired as the leading money-winner in history, earning nearly $300 million throughout his thirty-two-year career.

*Ken Millen-Penn, updated by Jack Ewing*

## Additional Sources

Drager, Marvin. *The Most Glorious Crown: The Story of America's Triple Crown Thoroughbreds from Sir Barton to Affirmed.* Chicago: Triumph Books, 2005.

Duke, Jacqueline. "A Long Journey into the Light for Day." *The Racing Times*, October 11, 1991, p. 3.

Gruender, Scott A. *Jockey: The Rider's Life in American Thoroughbred Racing.* Jefferson, N.C.: McFarland, 2006.

Nack, William. "Great Day." *Sports Illustrated* 76, no. 18 (May 11, 1992): 16.

Reed, William F. "Night and Day." *Sports Illustrated* 84, no. 21 (May 27, 1996): 56.

Shulman, Lenny. *Ride of Their Lives: The Triumphs and Turmoil of Today's Top Jockeys.* Lexington, Ky.: Eclipse Press, 2002.

# *Eddie Delahoussaye*

**Born:** September 21, 1951
New Iberia, Louisiana
**Also known as:** Edward J. Delahoussaye (full name); Eddie D.

## Early Life
Edward J. Delahoussaye was born on September 21, 1951, in New Iberia, Louisiana. His father owned racehorses, and his uncles were horse trainers. Growing up in a family involved in horse racing, Eddie began riding horses at an early age. By the time he was ten years old, he was riding in match races at the nonparimutuel, or "bush" tracks, of Louisiana. Throughout his early teens, he was a quarter-horse jockey and rode mixed breeds. In 1967, he rode in his first recognized race at the fairgrounds in New Orleans, Louisiana. The following year he began riding thoroughbreds at Evangeline Downs in Carencro, Louisiana. On June 29, 1968, riding Brown Shill, he won his first officially sanctioned race.

## The Road to Excellence
During the 1970's, Eddie became one of the best-known riders in New Orleans. He was soon riding successfully throughout the Midwest and enjoyed wins at Arlington Park in Arlington Heights, Illinois; Churchill Downs in Louisville, Kentucky; and Keeneland in Lexington, Kentucky. He was recognized as the circuit's premier jockey. In 1978, he won the prestigious All-Star Jockeys competition at the Hollywood Park track in Inglewood, California. This brought his total for the year to 384 wins and earned him recognition as the United States Champion Jockey.

In 1979, Eddie decided to move to Southern California. He rode at the major California tracks: Hollywood Park, Del Mar, and Santa Anita. In 1980 and 1981, Eddie continued to win significant races, including the Kentucky Oaks, the Eddie Read Handicap, the Palomar Handicap, the Bing Crosby Handicap, and the Del Mar Futurity. In 1981, he finished second at the Kentucky Derby aboard Woodchopper.

That same year, he was awarded the George Woolf Memorial Jockey Award. Established in honor of hall-of-fame jockey George Woolf, who met an untimely death at the age of thirty-five, the award is presented only once to any one jockey. The award recipient is chosen by members of the Jockey Guild and is presented at Santa Anita. To be chosen for the award, a jockey must ride thoroughbred horses in North America and display high professional and personal standards of conduct.

## The Emerging Champion
Eddie's accomplishments during the following two decades established him as a first-rate jockey and

*Eddie Delahoussaye celebrating after winning the 1983 Kentucky Derby aboard Sunny's Halo.* (AP/Wide World Photos)

champion. In 1982, he won the Kentucky Derby riding Gato Del Sol. In this race, he brought the horse from the back of the field to win. Almost from the start of the one-mile-and-one-quarter race, Gato Del Sol trailed the nineteen-horse field. At the half-mile marker, Eddie and Gato Del Sol began to move up in the field. At the mile marker, Gato Del Sol was fifth; he continued to gain ground and won by two and one-half lengths. In 1983, Eddie again rode to victory in the Kentucky Derby. This time he was aboard Sonny's Halo and won the race by two lengths. In 1988, aboard Risen Sun, he won both the Preakness and the Belmont Stakes. In 1992, he won his second Belmont Stakes riding A. P. Indy.

During this time, Eddie won many other important races, including seven Breeders' Cups, two Del Mar Futurities, the Jockey Gold Cup, and two Pacific Classics. He was particularly successful as a Breeders' Cup jockey. In 1992, he won the Breeders' Cup Classic, with I. P. Indy, and the Breeders' Cup Sprint, with Thirty Slews. In 1993, he won the Breeders' Cup Distaff with Hollywood Wildcat and the Breeders' Cup Sprint with Cardmania. The same year, he was inducted into the National Museum of Racing's Jockeys' Hall of Fame. On February 7, 1999, he became the fourteenth jockey to win 6,000 races. This win came at Santa Anita aboard Sweecakesandshakes.

## Continuing the Story

Eddie continued riding, winning major races and increasing his lifetime winnings through 2002. He won his third and fourth Palomar Handicaps in 2000 and 2001, respectively. His two previous had

| Major Wins | | | |
|---|---|---|---|
| 1982 | Kentucky Derby | 1991 | Breeders' Cup Juvenile Fillies |
| 1983 | Kentucky Derby | 1992 | Breeders' Cup Classic |
| 1984 | Breeders' Cup Distaff | | Belmont Stakes |
| 1988 | Preakness Stakes | | Breeders' Cup Sprint |
| | Belmont Stakes | 1993 | Breeders' Cup Distaff |
| 1989 | Breeders' Cup Turf | | Breeders' Cup Sprint |

been in 1980 and 1988. In 2000, he won the Del Mar Derby for the fourth time. In March, 2002, the Louisiana Sports Writers Association elected him to the Louisiana Sports Hall of Fame. Eddie was chosen for the honor in his first year of eligibility.

On August 30, 2002, at Del Mar, Eddie's mount fell; he suffered serious head and neck injuries. Eddie endured several months of therapy and, in January, 2003, upon the advice of his doctors, he announced his retirement from racing.

## Summary

Eddie Delahoussaye's career as a thoroughbred jockey spanned thirty-four years. Although he did not become a triple-crown-winning jockey—which entails winning the Kentucky Derby, the Preakness, and the Belmont in the same season—he won five triple-crown races. In addition, he won seven Breeders' Cup races and many other major stakes and futurity races. During his career, he rode 39,213 mounts. He retired with 6,384 wins and earnings of $195,881,170. He ranked twelfth all time in wins and sixth in money earned.

*Shawncey Webb*

## Additional Sources

Bowen, Edward. *At the Wire: Horse Racing's Greatest Moments.* Forestville, Calif.: Eclipse Press, 2001.

Privman, Jay. *Breeders' Cup: Thoroughbred Racing's Championship Day.* Liguori, Mo.: Triumph Books, 2001.

Shulman, Larry. *Ride of Their Lives: The Triumph of Today's Top Jockeys.* Forestville, Calif.: Eclipse Press, 2002.

| Honors and Awards | |
|---|---|
| 1978 | United States Champion Jockey Eclipse Award |
| 1981 | George Woolf Memorial Jockey Award |
| 1993 | Inducted into Jockeys' Hall of Fame |
| 2002 | Inducted into Louisiana Sports Hall of Fame |

# *Raimondo D'Inezeo*

**Born:** February 8, 1925
Poggio Mirteto, Italy

## Early Life

Raimondo D'Inezeo was born on February 8, 1925, in Rome, Italy, with two assets: a talented and helpful older brother, Piero, who became his riding companion, and a father, Sergeant-Major Carlo Constante D'Inezeo, who had a riding school near Rome and was known as one of the best horse trainers and teachers of riding and show jumping in Italy. A third advantage was that Raimondo's father taught the new Caprilli method of show jumping. Named for the Italian cavalry officer Federico Caprilli, it was a change of position for the rider. Instead of leaning back into the saddle during the jump and letting the weight of the rider interfere with the natural movement of the horse, Caprilli shortened the stirrups so the rider could rise up out of the saddle, lean forward, raise the seat, and thus conform to rather than work against the horse's natural jumping arc. Another gift Raimondo's father passed on to his sons was his understanding of horses—how to make them obedient, cooperative, and balanced. Even as a boy, Raimondo had developed an understanding of horses, an asset that made him a world-class champion.

Raimondo at first felt he could not compete with his talented older brother and decided to go to the University of Rome. The brothers were different: Piero was open and confident; Raimondo was quieter and less confident. However, riding and show jumping were in Raimondo's blood. After two years, Raimondo left the university and joined the Italian cavalry, which had adopted the Caprilli method, so that he could continue his father's teaching.

Raimondo left the cavalry to be part of the Italian jumping team at the 1948 London Olympics. The Italian team did not win any medals, but the contest was valuable experience.

## The Road to Excellence

In 1950, Raimondo joined the *carabinieri*, or Italian mounted police, where, as in the cavalry, he could train with excellent horses and equipment. The Italian government supported the purchase of the best jumping horses, most of which came from Ireland. Raimondo practiced every spare moment he could find, and in 1952, together with his brother Piero, was part of the Italian jumping team at the Helsinki Olympics. Although the Italian team was ahead, Piero missed his turn in the jumping and the team was eliminated.

Raimondo and his brother did better at the 1956 Stockholm Olympics. Although the Germans, under Hans Günter Winkler, placed first in both individual and team jumping, Raimondo, on his horse Merano, was second in individual jumping, winning the silver medal. His brother Piero, on Uruguay, was third, winning the bronze medal. Both brothers were part of the Italian jumping team that won another silver medal. Raimondo won the title of world show jumping champion at Aachen, Germany, that same year.

## The Emerging Champion

Although Raimondo never had the style of his older brother, he had a better understanding of horses, giving them every form of assistance possible. In the end, he became the better jumper. This was obvious at the 1960 Rome Olympics, where the Italians, because of Raimondo, swept the field. Against a background of his wildly cheering countrymen, Rai-

## Major Championships

| Year | Competition | Event | Place |
|---|---|---|---|
| 1956 | World Championship | Show jumping | 1st |
| | Olympic Games | Individual jumping | Silver |
| | | Team jumping | Silver |
| 1960 | Olympic Games | Individual jumping | Gold |
| | | Team jumping | Bronze |
| 1964, 1972 | Olympic Games | Team jumping | Bronze |
| 1974 | Dublin Horse Show, Guiness Gold Cup | — | Winner |

mondo, on Posillipo, won the gold medal in individual jumping. His brother Piero, on The Rock, was second, winning the silver. The Italian jumping team, with both Raimondo and Piero as members, won the bronze medal.

## Continuing the Story

Raimondo's young daughter was killed in a tragic skiing accident, and for a while he thought he would never jump again. In his daughter's memory, however, Raimondo became more determined than ever to win. He took part in the equestrian event in the next four Olympics, winning in two. In 1964, at the Tokyo Olympics, the Italian jumping team, with Raimondo as captain on Posillipo, placed third, winning the bronze medal. In 1968, at the Mexico City Olympics, the Italian jumping team, with Raimondo as captain on Bellevue, failed to win a medal, placing fifth. The team made a comeback at the Munich Olympics in 1972, placing third and winning a bronze medal. Raimondo's horse this time was Fiorello. Although he won no medals in 1968, Raimondo set a record by participating in eight consecutive Olympic Games, from 1948 to 1976.

## Summary

Although Raimondo D'Inezeo had advantages, he also faced handicaps such as a talented older brother and the loss of a child. Through constant practice, the adoption of new methods, and the utilization of natural talents, Raimondo became one of the greatest show jumpers of the twentieth century.

*Nis Petersen*

## Additional Sources

Wallechinsky, David, and Jaime Loucky. *The Complete Book of the Olympics: 2008 Edition.* London: Aurum Press, 2008.

Wathen, Guy. *Great Horsemen of the World.* North Pomfret, Vt.: Trafalgar Square, 1991.

Wise, Michael T., Christina Bankes, and Jane Laing, eds. *Chronicle of the Olympics, 1896-1996.* New York: Dorling Kindersley, 1996.

# *Mark Donohue*

**Born:** March 18, 1937
Summit, New Jersey
**Died:** August 19, 1975
Graz, Austria
**Also known as:** Mark Neary Donohue, Jr. (full
name); Captain Nice

## Early Life

Mark Neary Donohue, Jr., born on March 18, 1937, grew up in Summit, New Jersey. Before the age of ten, he was able to drive the family car along the awkward and difficult driveway into the garage. The family barn became his auto shop. Once when the barn caught fire, Mark ran for help, then rushed back into the barn to put out the fire. This act was not sheer recklessness: He knew exactly the location of the fire extinguisher, the path the burning gasoline would take, and how to escape if he could not douse the fire. The flames were extinguished before the fire department arrived.

Mark was also a survivor; he was not stopped by scarlet fever, a tonsillectomy, vein cauterizations, an appendectomy, or even polio. These early traumas taught him to adopt a stoic attitude, which freed him to think rationally and sensibly even in the midst of pain and confusion.

## The Road to Excellence

In 1959, Mark graduated with a degree in mechanical engineering from Brown University. Soon after, Mark sold his souped-up Corvette and, with this money, bought an Elva Courier with an Morris Garages (MG) engine. While working as a mechanical engineer, he entered the Elva in various regional amateur races. By 1961, he was racing all over the country and winning frequently. He won three national amateur sports car championships before turning professional in 1966.

Mark joined the team headed by Roger Penske, a former amateur driving champion. Mark began by test-driving cars for Penske but soon was racing for him. In 1967 and 1968, Mark won the United States Road Racing Championship. When that series of races was discontinued, Mark successfully raced a modified Chevrolet Camaro in the Trans-American Sedan Series for small, sporty cars. He also competed successfully in a different arena: the Canadian-American Challenge Series (Can-Am). The Formula Seven cars in these races were "technically unlimited": virtually no rules governed the engine or bodywork, allowing creativity in the design.

## The Emerging Champion

By 1969, Penske had convinced Mark that the new goal was the Indianapolis 500. Indy-type cars, unlike Can-Am cars, have defined maximum engine sizes and other technical restrictions and run on a mixture of methanol and nitromethane. The Indianapolis 500 is the biggest event in American auto racing and one of the most widely attended annual events in the country. At Indianapolis, Mark's quiet disposition earned him a new nickname:

*Mark Donohue at the Ontario Speedway in 1971.* (AP/Wide World Photos)

## Sports Cars and Other Victories

| | |
|---|---|
| 1966 | Can-Am Challenge Cup Race (Mosport Park) |
| 1967-68 | U.S. Road Racing Overall Driving Champion |
| 1968 | Can-Am Challenge Cup Race (Bridgehampton Race circuit) |
| | Trans-Am Race (Sebring Road Course) |
| 1968-69, 1971 | Trans-Am Overall Driving Champion |
| 1968-71 | Trans-Am Race (Mont-Treblant circuit) |
| 1969 | The 24 Hours of Daytona |
| | Trans-Am Race (Laguna Seca Raceway) |
| | Trans-Am Race (Riverside International Raceway) |
| 1969, 1971 | Watkins Glen Grand Prix |
| 1970-71 | Trans-Am Race (Road America) |
| 1971 | USAC 200-Mile |
| | Trans-Am Race (Edmonton International Speedway) |
| | Michigan 200 |
| 1971-72 | USAC 500-Mile |
| 1972 | Indianapolis 500 |
| 1972-73 | Can-Am Challenge Cup Race (Edmonton International Speedway) |
| 1973 | Winston Western 500 |
| | Watkins Glen Grand Prix Champion |
| | Can-Am Challenge Cup Race (Laguna Seca Raceway) |
| | Can-Am Challenge Cup Race (Riverside International Raceway) |
| | Can-Am Challenge Cup Race (Road America) |
| | Can-Am Challenge Cup Series Championship |
| 1974 | International Race of Champions Champion Driver |

Captain Nice. Mark finished seventh and was voted rookie of the year.

Mark and Penske concentrated their efforts on the Indianapolis 500 the next year, but a disappointed Mark finished a distant second, behind Al Unser, who had led nearly the entire race. By this time, however, the long hours Mark spent preparing for races had taken a toll on his personal life. He separated from his wife and two children.

Mark set his sights on the Indianapolis 500 for 1971. During a practice run, he broke the track record by going 177 miles per hour, and, about a week later, he ran 180 miles per hour. Winning the Indianapolis 500, however, did not depend solely on speed; it also entailed completing the race. Mark had built up an almost unbeatable lead when a gearbox broke and he had to drop out of the race. Worse yet, his car, a McLaren M16, was soon destroyed in a freak accident. Later that year, Mark won the first Schaefer 500-mile race, and the experience of winning a long, Indy-type race helped him the following year.

In 1972, Mark and Penske were ready. Their plan was to race with an "underpowered" car that

would give them good speed but, more important, was reliable enough to endure the grueling 500 miles. Mark finally succeeded in winning the Indianapolis 500, setting a new Indy record at more than 163 miles per hour.

A few weeks later, Mark was testing a new Porsche prototype at Road Atlanta when the steering disintegrated on the track. He badly injured his left knee. While he recuperated, he kept thinking of racing. In particular, he wanted to challenge Team McLaren, which had dominated the past five or six years of the Can-Am series. The next season, Mark returned to racing and won most of the Can-Am races and the overall championship, then abruptly retired. As far as American auto racing was concerned, Mark had done it all.

**Continuing the Story**

In February, 1974, Mark briefly emerged from retirement for the International Race of Champions designed to determine who was the greatest of the great drivers. The competitors in this race were each given a Porsche Carrera to drive. Mark won it easily, beating Bobby Unser, A. J. Foyt, Peter Revson, David Pearson, and George Follmer.

Mark retired from driving again to engineer a Grand Prix—Formula One—car for young driver Peter Revson. Engines of Grand Prix cars are smaller than those of Indy-type cars, run on ordinary gasoline, and are rear-mounted in cigar-shaped cars. When Revson was killed in a crash, Mark came out of retirement and began racing the Formula One car that he had helped design. Grand Prix racing—dominated by Europeans such

## Record

Most victories on the Trans-Am circuit, 29

## Honors and Awards

| | |
|---|---|
| 1968 | Driver of the Year |
| 1969 | Indianapolis 500 Rookie of the Year |
| 1990 | Inducted into International Motor Sports Hall of Fame |
| | Inducted into Motorsports Hall of Fame of America |

as Jackie Stewart—was the "missing link," the racing category that Mark had yet to master. Mark's best Grand Prix showing with this new car was fifth, but he was looking forward to a better season the following year.

While he was doing 160-mile-per-hour practice laps for the Austrian Grand Prix, his left front tire lost air and his Penske March 751 crashed. Mark died in a hospital two days later, on August 19, 1975. At his bedside were his father, Mark, Sr.; Penske; and his second wife of eight months, Eden. Mark was a champion to the end—two weeks before his death, he had set a world speed record on a closed track in a turbocharged Porsche, driving at more than 221 miles per hour.

## Summary

Some race-car drivers, many of whom never finished high school, complained that Mark Donohue had an unfair advantage because he was trained in engineering. Despite his technical expertise, he showed that champions win because of careful planning, precise execution, cool nerves, and, above all, driving instinct. Mark was the consummate race-car driver and a champion in all racing categories.

*Frank Wu*

## Additional Sources

Arron, Simon, and Mark Hughes. *The Complete Book of Formula One*. St. Paul, Minn.: Motorbooks International, 2003.

Reed, Terry. *Indy: The Race and Ritual of the Indianapolis 500*. Washington, D.C.: Potomac Books, 2005.

Rusz, Joe. "Mark Donohue." *Road and Track* 51, no. 11 (July, 2000): 103-104.

Smith, Steven Cole. "A Trip Down Memory Lane at 198 MPH." *Motor Trend* 57, no. 12 (December, 2005): 138-142.

# Dale Earnhardt

**Born:** April 29, 1951
     Kannapolis, North Carolina
**Died:** February 18, 2001
     Daytona Beach, Florida
**Also known as:** Ralph Dale Earnhardt (full
     name); the Intimidator

## Early Life

Ralph Dale Earnhardt was born on April 29, 1951, in Kannapolis, North Carolina. His father, Ralph Earnhardt, raced stock cars. From early childhood, Dale was often at the track with his mother, Martha, and his brothers and sisters, Randy, Danny, Kay, and Cathy, to watch his father—dubbed "Ironheart"—race. Sometimes, as many as three races a week were run. Dale's father was not a superstar, but his hard work supported the family. In 1972, he was killed in a racing accident at the age of forty-four. Dale grew up as much in the garage as he did in the house; he was knowledgeable about auto mechanics as a young boy. He always remembered his father's advice to "stay cool on the racetrack."

## The Road to Excellence

Dale was so interested in racing stock cars that he quit school in the ninth grade. This later concerned him because he was often in situations where, as he would say, "I miss an education." His father strongly opposed Dale's decision to quit school, which adversely affected their relationship for a time.

Dale was a good mechanic and pit crew member, and his father began to teach him about driving. By age nineteen, Dale had his own racer and was gaining experience on the dirt tracks of the South. Dale's driving style was much like his father's: fiercely aggressive and competitive. In fact, Dale soon earned the nickname "Ironfoot." Dirt track racing, however, is not a lucrative sport, so Dale worked as a welder and a mechanic to support his family. Just when it appeared Dale would have to give up racing to work at another job full time, he was hired by Rod Osterlund to drive for the 1979 season. Dale took advantage of this opportunity and, at the end of 1979, the National Association

for Stock Car Auto Racing (NASCAR) named him rookie of the year. In 1980, Dale won the NASCAR Winston Cup Championship.

## The Emerging Champion

This championship was far from an easy victory. Going into the final race of the year, Dale led Cale Yarborough by only 29 points out of a possible 4,000. For the last several races, Yarborough had been steadily closing the gap, which had been as wide as 230 points. Also, Dale's pit crew chief had quit in the middle of the season, and Dale's young, inexperienced crew was not thought to be good enough to carry him through to victory.

For the first 365 miles of the 500-mile race, Dale fought high winds and hard luck. He had to finish fifth to win the championship. One by one, other

*Dale Earnhardt had seventy-six wins on the NASCAR circuit before his untimely death in 2001.* (Courtesy of Daytona International Speedway)

cars broke down or dropped out until Yarborough and Dale were left to duel. Then, on a pit stop, Dale seemed to run out of luck. He sideswiped the pit wall, scattering his pit crew and, before his tires were changed, he roared out of the pit with his car still on the jack. By the time all this was straightened out, Dale was in fifth place again, but Yarborough had also lost ground and was third. That is where the race ended, with Dale earning the title narrowly.

### Continuing the Story

Aggressive drivers win races, but they also are often involved in controversies. In 1983 and 1984, Dale won the Talladega 500, and both times his strong driving helped him take the lead at the end of the race. He was the first driver ever to win this race consecutively. Dale won 12 of 19 events, then a NASCAR record. In 1986, Dale was fined five thousand dollars for reckless driving during a race and was briefly placed on probation. In a race at Richmond, Virginia, Dale collided with Darrell Waltrip when Waltrip tried to pass near the end of the race. During the 1987 season, Dale won nine races, but in three of them he bumped the leaders and then passed. At the 1987 Winston Invitational—an all-star race at Charlotte, North Carolina—Dale was involved in five bumping incidents. Regardless of these controversies, he won the NASCAR Winston Cup Championship again in 1986, 1987, and 1990 and collected more than one million dollars in winnings.

Dale did not think he was a careless driver or that he took advantage of anybody. He saw stock car racing as a tough sport that called for physically and mentally tough drivers. Off the track, Dale was an easy person to know. He preferred to deal truthfully with every person.

As a result of his competitiveness, Dale had sev-

| NASCAR Circuit Victories | |
|---|---|
| 1979-80 | Southeastern 500 |
| 1979-80, 1985, 1987 | Valleydale 500 |
| 1980 | Coca-Cola 500 Champion |
| | Old Dominion 500 |
| | National 500 |
| | Nashville 420 |
| 1980, 1986 | Mello Yello 500 |
| 1980, 1986-87, 1990-91, 1993-94 | NASCAR Winston Cup Champion |
| 1982, 1986-87, 1990 | Transouth 500 |
| 1983, 1986, 1990 | Daytona 500 Twin 125 Qualifying Race |
| 1983-84, 1999 | Talladega 500 |
| 1984, 1986, 1989 | Atlanta Journal 500 |
| 1985 | Goody's 500 |
| 1985, 1987 | Miller High Life 400 |
| 1985, 1987-88 | Busch 500 |
| 1986 | Coca-Cola 600 |
| 1986-87, 1989 | First Union 400 |
| 1987 | Virginia National Bank 500 |
| | Goodwrench 500 |
| | Summer 500 |
| | Miller American 400 |
| | Wrangler Jeans Indigo 400 |
| 1987, 1989-90 | Heinz Southern 500 |
| 1988, 1990 | Motorcraft 500 |
| | Sovran Bank 500 |
| 1989 | Budweiser 500 |
| | Peak Performance 500 |
| 1990 | Motorcraft 500 |
| | Miller Genuine Draft 400 |
| | Pepsi 400 |
| | Busch Pole Award |
| | Checker 500 |
| 1990-91 | Die Hard 500 |
| 1990, 1995, 1999 | International Race of Champions |
| 1990, 2000 | Winston 500 Champion |
| 1991 | Champion Spark Plug 300 |
| | Tyson 400 |
| 1998 | Daytona 500 |
| 1999 | Bristol 5000 |
| 2000 | Cracker Barrel Old Country Store 500 |

| Honors and Awards | |
|---|---|
| 1979 | NASCAR Rookie of the Year |
| 1998 | Fifty Greatest Drivers in NASCAR History |
| 2001 | NASCAR Most Popular Driver Award |
| 2002 | Inducted into Motorsports Hall of Fame |
| 2006 | Inducted into International Motorsports Hall of Fame |

eral excellent seasons. After successful seasons in 1988 and 1989, Dale won eleven races in 1990, including the International Race of Champions (IROC) title. In 1990 and again in 1991, he came close to winning the prestigious Daytona 500, but each year, his goal was deterred by an accident. In 1991, he was charging from second place when a multicar crash took him out of the race with only three laps to go.

Dale won back-to-back Winston Cup Championships in 1990-1991 and 1993-1994; this brought his total to seven and secured a place in stock-car-racing history. In 1995, Dale ended the season with five first-place finishes and more than $3 million in earnings. Dale struggled in 1997, with no wins and only seven finishes in the top five. Although he won only one event in 1998, it was a big one—the Daytona 500. In 1999, he improved even more, winning three NASCAR events, plus the IROC. In 2000, he finished the season in second place with 4,690 points, just 265 shy of winning his eighth Winston Cup Championship.

Dale was killed on February 18, 2001, in a high-speed crash that occurred in the final lap of his twenty-third Daytona 500. Fans mourned his death at the age of forty-nine, and NASCAR was forced to reconsider issues concerning driver protection.

A husband and father of four, Dale ended his career with seventy-six wins and seven Winston Cup championships. In 1998, the man nicknamed "The Intimidator" was honored as one of the fifty greatest drivers in NASCAR history—an honor he shared with his father. Dale's son, Dale Earnhart, Jr., was left to continue the family legacy.

## Summary

A hard competitor, Dale Earnhardt liked winning and was not afraid of hard work. While he competed fiercely on the track, he was friendly off it. Dale liked to work on a farm he bought in North Carolina, where he enjoyed raising cattle. How- ever, to Dale, racing was as natural as breathing. In 2002 and 2006, he was elected posthumously into the Motorsports Hall of Fame of America and into the International Motorsports Hall of Fame, respectively.

*Michael R. Bradley*

## Additional Sources

Cothren, Larry. *Earnhardt: A Racing Family Legacy.* St. Paul, Minn.: Crestline, 2003.

*The Earnhardt Collection: The Most Comprehensive Archive Ever Assembled.* Chicago: Triumph Books, 2003.

*The Earnhardts: Racing's First Family.* New York: Sports Illustrated, 2004.

Garfield, Ken. *Dale Earnhardt: The Intimidator.* Champaign, Ill.: Sports, 2000.

Garner, Joe. *Speed, Guts, and Glory: One Hundred Unforgettable Moments in NASCAR History.* New York: Warner Books, 2006.

McGee, Ryan. *Ultimate NASCAR: One Hundred Defining Moments in Stock Car Racing History.* New York: ESPN Books, 2007.

Mayne, Kevin. *Three: The Dale Earnhardt Story.* New York: Hyperion, 2004.

Moore, Bob. *Dale Earnhardt: A Legend for the Ages.* Chicago: Triumph Books, 2002.

# *Dale Earnhardt, Jr.*

**Born:** October 10, 1974
     Kannapolis, North Carolina
**Also known as:** Ralph Dale Earnhardt, Jr. (full
    name); Junior; Little E; Junebug

## Early Life

Ralph Dale Earnhardt, Jr., was born on October 10, 1974, the son of Ralph Dale Earnhardt, Sr., and Brenda Lorraine Gee Earnhardt. He came from a family of auto racers: His grandfather, Ralph Earnhardt, who, in 1998, was named one of National Association for Stock Car Auto Racing's (NASCAR's) Fifty Greatest Drivers, was well known for racing on the dirt track. In addition, Dale, Jr.'s, maternal grandfather, Robert Gee, worked in NASCAR for Hendrick Motorsports' All-Star Racing team.

Although born in Kannapolis, Dale, Jr., grew up in poverty in Mooresville, the third of four children. Dale, Sr., worked as a welder for the Great Dane Trucking Company and a mechanic for Punch Whitaker's auto repair shop but dreamed of becoming a champion race-car driver. On weekends, he drove his used car locally in NASCAR Sportsman Division races, which were later renamed the Busch Series races and the Nationwide Series races.

## The Road to Excellence

When Dale, Sr., founded Dale Earnhardt, Inc. (DEI) in 1980, he imagined a racing company that he could pass on to his sons Kerry and Dale, Jr. Inspired by his father, Dale, Jr., started racing at seventeen years old. He competed at the Concord Motorsport Park in Concord, North Carolina, in the Street Stock Division. His first race car was a "junker," a 1979 Monte Carlo he acquired with the help of his half brother Kerry.

Dale, Jr., graduated from Mooresville High School and attended Mitchell Com-

munity College in Statesville, North Carolina, acquiring an associate's degree in automotive technology. In 1991, he went to work at Dale Earnhardt Chevrolet as a mechanic and gained a reputation as the fastest oil-changer on the premises. Meanwhile, he continued to race and entered NASCAR's Late Model Stock Division. In 1998, he became a full-time driver for DEI and immediately found

*Dale Earnhardt, Jr., celebrating after winning a race in 2008.* (John Harrelson/Getty Images)

success on the track. In DEI's #3 A.C. Delco Chevrolet, he won consecutive NASCAR Busch Series Championships in 1998 and 1999.

The year 2000 proved to be particularly enterprising for Dale. He won at the Texas Motor Speedway, the Richmond International Raceway, and an all-star exhibition. At the Pepsi 400, the Earnhardt family made news when Dale, Sr., competed against his sons, representing only the second time that a father had competed against two of his sons on the racetrack.

## The Emerging Champion

Dale, Jr., hoped the year 2001 would be equally successful, but it turned out to be one of his worst. During the final lap of the Daytona 500, Dale, Sr., crashed at turn four and was fatally injured. Dale, Jr., took second place, finishing behind Michael Waltrip, but could not forget seeing his father's crushed car in his rearview mirror. Struggling to compose himself, he rebounded with wins at Dover, Talladega, and Daytona to finish eighth in points.

From 2003 to 2006, Dale, Jr., proved to be a driver fully the equal of his famous father. In 2003, he won at Talladega, breaking records for consecutive wins. From 2003 to 2007, he was awarded the NASCAR National Motorsports Press Association Chex most popular driver award every year. In 2004, he won the Daytona 500 and, in the fall, both the Busch Series Winston Cup races at Bristol.

Despite his racing success, Dale, Jr., did not forget his roots. In 2006, he drove a vintage Budweiser car at Michigan International Speedway on Father's Day in memory of his grandfather and father. All three men had driven a #8 car at one time in their respective careers. Fittingly, Dale, Jr., commemorated both his father and his grandfather by driving in a vintage #8 vehicle.

In 2007, Dale, suffered disappointment. Not only did he finish thirty-second at Daytona and seventh at Bristol, but also he was docked one hun-

| Notable Victories | | |
|---|---|---|
| Year | Track | Location |
| 2000 | Texas Motor Speedway | Fort Worth, Texas |
| | Richmond International Raceway | Richmond, Virginia |
| 2001 | Dover International Speedway | Dover, Delaware |
| | Talladega Superspeedway | Talladega, Alabama |
| | Daytona International Speedway | Daytona Beach, Florida |
| 2002 | Talladega Superspeedway | Talladega, Alabama |
| 2003 | Talladega Superspeedway | Talladega, Alabama |
| | Phoenix International Raceway | Avondale, Arizona |
| 2004 | Daytona International Speedway | Daytona Beach, Florida |
| | Atlanta Motor Speedway | Hampton, Georgia |
| | Richmond International Raceway | Richmond, Virginia |
| | Bristol Motor Speedway | Bristol, Tennessee |
| | Talladega Superspeedway | Talladega, Alabama |
| | Phoenix International Raceway | Avondale, Arizona |
| 2005 | Chicagoland Speedway | Joliet, Illinois |
| 2006 | Richmond International Raceway | Richmond, Virginia |
| 2008 | Michigan International Speedway | Brooklyn, Michigan |

dred driver-championship points for his use of illegal mounting brackets on May 14. On August 5, 2007, Dale ended his slump when he took second place at Pocono Raceway.

## Continuing the Story

On May 10, 2007, after much speculation, Dale announced he was leaving DEI and signing a five-year contract to drive for Hendrick Motorsports, replacing Kyle Busch. His decision, based solely on his goal of winning the Sprint Cup Championship, was pragmatic. Dale believed that as long as he remained a driver for DEI he would not be able to achieve his goal. He claimed the organization, headed by his stepmother Teresa, was not inclined to provide him with the cutting-edge tools and parts that he needed to win.

Dale's decision caused a certain amount of friction in DEI. On July 13, 2007, Budweiser pulled its sponsorship of Dale because of contractual conflicts. On August 15, 2007, a public announcement stated that Dale would not be taking his usual car number with him to Hendrick Motorsports in 2008. His late grandfather Ralph had used both #8 and #88, but Dale was more sentimental about #8 because his father had also used that number. Just as he blamed his stepmother for preventing him

## Honors and Awards

| | |
|---|---|
| 1998-99 | NASCAR Busch Series Championship |
| 2000 | Winston XVI winner |
| 2003-07 | NASCAR most popular driver |
| 2004 | Daytona 500 winner |

from having majority ownership in DEI, Dale, Jr., criticized Teresa for withholding the "traditional" Earnhardt number.

## Summary

Beginning as a regional sport in the south, by the start of the twenty-first century, NASCAR ranked behind only professional football in popularity in the United States. Much of the credit for the sport's rise goes to the racers who devoted their lives to NASCAR and encouraged the tradition of family participation. In the 2000's, Dale Earnhardt, Jr., dominated NASCAR. He loves the racing environ-ment and often joked that, upon retirement, he still wanted to spend his time at the track.

*Julia M. Meyers*

## Additional Sources

Cothren, Larry. *Dale Earnhardt, Jr.: Making a Legend of His Own.* Osceola, Wis.: Motorbook International, 2005.

Poole, David. *Dale, Jr., Takes Charge: The Life and Legacy of Nascar's Superstar.* Chicago: Triumph Books, 2004.

Savage, Jeff. *Dale Earnhardt, Jr.* Minneapolis: Lerner, 2005.

# *Paul Elvstrøm*

**Born:** February 25, 1928
      Hellerup, Denmark
**Also known as:** Paul Bert Elvstrøm

## Early Life

Paul Elvstrøm was born on February 25, 1928, in Hellerup, Denmark, just a few miles north of the capital, Copenhagen. Hellerup is on the coast, and Paul's family had a history of seafaring. His father was a captain who had sailed around Cape Horn. Paul was the youngest of four children, but the second was drowned while a toddler. One might have thought this would turn the family away from the sea, but Paul was rowing at the age of five, then sailing a small homemade boat soon after. He learned to sail largely by teaching himself, with great perseverance.

## The Road to Excellence

Paul was racing at ten and won his first race two years later. With his older brother as his crew, Paul beat twenty adults by a wide margin. In 1940, he joined the local Hellerup Sailing Club. Just as Paul was getting serious about sailing, Germany occupied Denmark during World War II, and all sailing on the sea was forbidden. Paul did not give up sailing, however, because he bicycled to a nearby lake and continued to practice there. When he left school, he was apprenticed as a stone mason; later he became a building contractor. He did not enjoy these jobs; he preferred to be sailing.

In 1948, at the age of nineteen, Paul was narrowly selected for the Danish Olympic sailing team. The Firefly dinghy, a 12-foot, two-sailed boat, was the class chosen for the single-handed racing series. The selectors were not sure of Paul because he had never even seen a Firefly dinghy, let alone sailed one. In his first Olympic race, the shy Paul retired from the race. A competitor bluffed Paul into thinking that he had broken a rule when he had not. In the races following, however, Paul finished sixth, third, twelfth, and fifth, and ended the series with two first places to give him the gold medal. Paul was always a sporting competitor, and while he took the rules to their limits, he always sailed fairly.

## The Emerging Champion

For the 1952 Olympics, the Firefly class was replaced by the Finn class, a one-person, one-sailed boat of 14¾ feet. Finn boats require great strength to sail well,

*Paul Elvstrøm.* (AP/Wide World Photos)

## Major Championship Victories

| | |
|---|---|
| 1948 | Olympic gold medalist (Firefly class) |
| 1952, 1956, 1960 | Olympic gold medalist (Finn class) |
| 1957-58 | World Championship (5-0-5 class) |
| 1958-59 | World Championship (Finn class) |
| 1959 | World Championship (Snipe class) |
| 1962 | World Championship (Flying Dutchman class) (as crew) |
| 1966 | World Championship (5.5-meter class) |
| 1966-67 | World Championship (Star class) |
| 1969, 1974 | World Championship (Soling class) |
| 1974, 1981 | World Championship (½-ton class) |

because they have a large sail area. Paul was one of the first sailors to work out to build up muscle strength specifically for sailing. He built a mock-up boat in his basement so that he could practice hanging over the edge to keep the boat upright. In his second Olympics, Paul won another gold medal in a fleet of twenty-eight competitors. In fact, his points lead was so great after the sixth race that he did not even need to compete in the seventh, but he did anyway, and won it, too.

The 1956 Olympics was held in very windy conditions, but Paul won his third consecutive gold medal, again in a Finn dinghy. Between his third and fourth Olympics, Paul won five world championships in three different boat classes: 5-0-5's (16-foot dinghies), Finns, and Snipes (15½-foot dinghies). He was the top small-boat sailor in the world.

Over the years, Paul had suffered from painful headaches, and this problem was worsening. He was gripped by extreme nervous tension before and during races, and in 1959, he passed out in a race for the Snipe class world championship. He won the championship but told the Danish Sports Federation that he was giving up international competition because he found the pressure too great. He was talked into competing in the 1960 Olympics but was barely able to sleep. He arrived at the start almost at breaking point.

In addition to this pressure, in 1960, Paul was competing for a possible fourth consecutive gold medal. No one had ever achieved this feat in the Olympics in any sport. When a much larger fleet of thirty-five Finn boats took part in the 1960 Games, even more pressure was on Paul. Despite

collapsing the night before the sixth race, he won it and clinched his fourth gold medal. He was physically unable to compete in the seventh race because of his lack of sleep.

### Continuing the Story

For five years, Paul gave up international competition. As an observer at the 1964 Olympics, he saw that sailing could be fun if one was not too intensely involved. With new emphasis on enjoyment, Paul reentered top-level sailing and won three more world championships in the 5.5-meter (35-foot keelboat), Star (22-foot keelboat), and Soling (26¾-foot keelboat) classes.

In the 1968 Olympics, Paul entered in the Star class and finished a much happier fourth. In 1972, Paul also failed to win a medal, finishing thirteenth in the Soling class, and it looked as though his Olympic career was over. He concentrated more on his successful sailmaking and boat equipment businesses, and on writing sailing books. His most famous book was a simplified version of the sailing rules, together with little plastic boat models to recreate racing incidents.

In 1982, Paul was awarded the Olympic Order in Bronze for his extraordinary volunteer effort as an Olympic amateur athlete. By 1984, Paul was married, with four adult daughters, but amazingly, he was chosen for the Danish team again. His youngest daughter, Trine, crewed for him in the Tornado catamaran class, one of the world's fastest, most demanding boats to sail. Paul narrowly missed the bronze medal. Clearly having fun now, Paul qualified for the 1988 Olympics, his eighth Games, in the Tornado class, again with his daughter. He thus completed a forty-year span of Olympic competition in his sixtieth year.

In 1990, Paul was awarded the Beppe Croce Trophy of the International Yacht Racing Union, sailing's governing body, for lifetime dedication to yachting. In 1996, he was named the Danish Sports-

## Honors and Awards

| | |
|---|---|
| 1982 | Olympic Order in Bronze |
| 1990 | International Yacht Racing Union Beppe Croce Trophy |
| 1996 | Selected Danish Sportsman of the Century |
| 2007 | Inducted into International Sailing Federation Sailing Hall of Fame |

man of the Century. In 2007, he was one of six inductees in the inaugural class of the International Sailing Federation Sailing Hall of Fame.

## Summary

Paul Elvstrøm's ability to overcome physical and mental problems and return to top-level sailing, his long time-span of successful international competition, and his sportsmanship made him a legend in small-boat racing. He was devoted to his sport, and to helping newcomers find the same fulfillment he had. He was known worldwide through his sailmaking, racing equipment, and publications.

*Shirley H. M. Reekie*

## Additional Sources

Deaves, Robert. *Finnatics: The History and Techniques of Finn Sailing.* Newport, Isle of Wight, England: The International Finn Association, 1999.

Elvstrøm Paul, and Søren Krause. *Paul Elvstrøm Explains the Racing Rules of Sailing, 2005-2008 Rules.* Camden, Maine: International Marine/McGraw-Hill, 2005.

Greenberg, Stan. *Whitaker's Olympic Almanack: An Encyclopaedia of the Olympic Games.* Chicago: Fitzroy Dearborn, 2000.

Wallechinsky, David, and Jaime Loucky. *The Complete Book of the Olympics: 2008 Edition.* London: Aurum Press, 2008.

# Juan Manuel Fangio

**Born:** June 24, 1911
      Balcarce, Argentina
**Died:** July 17, 1995
      Buenos Aires, Argentina
**Also known as:** El Maestro

## Early Life

Juan Manuel Fangio was born on June 24, 1911, in Balcarce, Argentina. He was the youngest of four children, two boys and two girls. Juan's parents were Italian immigrants. Because of the family's poverty, Juan went to work at the age of ten, when he became an apprentice mechanic at a local garage. This job inspired his love of automobiles. Many of the cars in which Juan first raced, he built almost from scratch. Juan's career as a driver had a late start, partly as a result of illness as a teenager. Success did not come overnight; he was in his late twenties before he began to win races regularly.

## The Road to Excellence

In the years leading up to World War II, motor racing grew rapidly as a spectator sport. As a result, competition grew more intense, and the sport be-

*Juan Manuel Fangio preparing for the 1953 Grand Prix of Modena, Italy. (AP/Wide World Photos)*

came highly organized. The number of cars with different engine capacities and body types grew, so that competition had to be strictly regulated. Technical improvements also meant longer races, making endurance an additional feature of competition.

Juan's first important win came in 1940, in a race that placed almost impossible demands of endurance on both car and driver. This was the Gran Premio Internacional del Norte, a race from Buenos Aires to Lima, Peru, and back—a distance of approximately six thousand miles. Not even the rough roads on which Juan learned competitive driving prepared him for the race's forbidding terrain and challenging variations of climate. In 1942, Juan repeated his success in this race; both times, he drove a Chevrolet.

In the period between his two Gran Premio victories, Juan won almost every Grand Prix race in Argentina—including four in 1942—and other endurance races. Beginning in 1942, war interrupted motorsports in Argentina for five years. When racing resumed, the dictator Juan Perón was in power. A reluctant Juan was recruited to be his country's representative in international Grand Prix racing. At the age of thirty-six, and lacking high-level Formula One racing experience, Juan began to prepare for his greatest professional challenge. In 1949, he raced his sponsors' Maserati against Europe's top drivers.

## The Emerging Champion

At that time, the world of Formula One racing consisted of a large number of races; of these, only a few awarded points toward the world championship. Largely centered on European tracks and drivers, the Formula One circuit was a test of Juan's character and skill. In addition, he was more than just a participant in the sport. He was also an ambassador for his country.

Juan's first season competing for the Formula One World Championship was successful. He had six victories in races that counted for the championship. The next year, 1950, he was invited to drive for the official Alfa Romeo team, and he was equally impressive. In both years, and for the rest of his career, Juan was also phenomenally successful in non-championship Grand Prix and endurance races, such as the Twenty-Four Hours of Le Mans, the Pan-American Road Race, and the Mille Miglia. In 1951, Juan won his first world championship in an Alfa Romeo. A brilliant beginning to the next season came to nothing after he suffered a serious accident, but he returned to place second in the world championship in 1953. In 1954, his skill and nerve began to raise his performances to legendary status, when he won the first of his four consecutive world championships. The Mercedes automobiles in which he won the 1954 and 1955 championships were, he said, his favorites. When Mercedes withdrew from Grand Prix competition, Juan became the number-one driver for Ferrari.

In 1957, his final world championship year, he returned to the Maserati team. He clinched the championship that year by placing first in twelve of the fourteen points-awarding races, and second in the other two. The high point of Juan's 1957 season, and perhaps his most remarkable single achievement in Grand Prix racing, was in the German Grand Prix at the daunting Nürburgring. His ability to make the most of his car and deal with pressure produced a come-from-behind win. This race was the ultimate reward for all the hard work he had put in over the years. His days of apprenticeship gave Juan a remarkable sensitivity to the power and potential of his car, enabling him to win races when the competition seemed to have superior vehicles. His early experience in endurance races also trained him to respond quickly and decisively to the unexpected. The combination of knowledge, temperament, and skill made Juan a model of consistency and smoothness in one of the most dangerous sports.

## Continuing the Story

Juan retired in 1958. He had won twenty-four Grand Prix races, at that time a remarkable achievement, particularly in view of the intense competition between manufacturers, the number of great young drivers in the early postwar period, and the promotion of Formula One racing as an international glamour sport. In terms of overall achievement, Juan's career is more impressive than any of his competitors'. His number of total victories exceeds anyone else's, as does his percentage of victories in races started.

### Grand Prix Victories

| | |
|---|---|
| 1950, 1954-55 | Belgian Grand Prix |
| 1950, 1957 | Monaco Grand Prix |
| 1950-51, 1954, 1957 | French Grand Prix |
| 1951 | Spanish Grand Prix |
| 1951, 1954 | Swiss Grand Prix |
| 1953-55 | Italian Grand Prix |
| 1954-57 | Argentinean Grand Prix |
| 1954, 1956-57 | German Grand Prix |
| 1955 | Dutch Grand Prix |
| 1956 | British Grand Prix |

Although Juan traveled and raced in some of the most fashionable and famous places in the world, he remained attached to his native Balcarce—and to Argentina. His achievements made him a national hero and brought international respect to his country. After his retirement, he returned home and established a racetrack at Balcarce. Later, he became president of the Argentina division of Mercedes-Benz. When Juan first came to Europe to race, he was not taken seriously because of his short stature and unathletic appearance. Like many other champions, Juan made his response at the proper time and place—in his car, taking the checkered flag.

## Summary

Juan Manuel Fangio combined a finely tuned temperament with the courage and determination essential to effective competition at the highest level. His career illustrated how a blend of personality and skill can make an athlete resemble an artist.

*George O'Brien*

## Additional Sources

Donaldson, Gerald. *Juan Manuel Fangio: The Life Behind the Legend.* London: Virgin, 2003.

Ludvigsen, Karl E., and Rodolfo Mailander. *Juan Manuel Fangio: Motor Racing's Grand Master.* Newbury Park, Calif.: Haynes North America, 1999.

Nygaard, Peter. *Juan Manuel Fangio: Photo Album.* Hudson, Wis.: Iconografix, 1999.

Walker, Rob. "Nürburgring 1957." *Road and Track* 53, no. 3 (November, 2001): 156-157.

### Honors and Awards

| | |
|---|---|
| 1951, 1954-57 | World Championship of Drivers |
| 1990 | Inducted into International Motorsports Hall of Fame |

# Tom Ferguson

**Born:** December 20, 1950
      Tahlequah, Oklahoma
**Also known as:** Thomas R. Ferguson (full name);
    the Bionic Cowboy

## Early Life

Tom Ferguson was born on December 20, 1950, in Tahlequah, Oklahoma, and, as a baby, he and his family moved to San Jose, California. They stayed there until 1973, when they moved back to Oklahoma and opened a western shop in Miami, Oklahoma. Tom was exposed to rodeo at an early age. His father, Ira, was a carpenter who had worked at different rodeo events. He encouraged Tom and his older brother, Larry, to join him in the practice pen while they were living on a five-acre ranch in San Martin. At an early age, the boys learned steer wrestling from their father and his ranch hands, two of whom were former world champions. Tom and Larry listened carefully to the secrets that the older cowboys shared with them. They had a pet burro, which they used to practice roping and bulldogging. The boys accepted criticism from their elders and tried to apply the principles that they had learned.

## The Road to Excellence

By the time Tom was in his teens, he had chosen rodeo as his primary sport. He had tried all of the major sports but was either too small or too slow for most of them. His winner's mentality did not permit him to stay very long with a sport in which he could not excel. Like many rodeo cowboys, Tom began his career by entering junior rodeos and amateur contests while he was still in high school. Tom was different, however, in that he did not go into professional rodeo straight out of high school. Instead, he joined the rodeo team at California Polytechnic and State University at San Luis Obispo, where he majored in agriculture business management. Although he eventually planned to become a professional rodeo cowboy, Tom went to college so that he had another career in case he could not make a living at rodeo. He was concerned that he might be too short to be a good steer wrestler. Tom's apprehension about his potential as a rodeo star soon proved to be unfounded. When he was just a freshman, Tom was second in the nation in intercollegiate steer wrestling competition. In his junior year, he missed the title in calf roping by only three points. When he entered his senior year in college in the fall of 1972, Tom joined the Professional Rodeo Cowboys Association (PRCA) so that he could work the Cow Palace Rodeo in San Francisco.

## The Emerging Champion

Tom decided to take a break from college in January, 1973, so that he could enter the big indoor rodeos. Tom was in fifth place in all-around competition at the end of January and in third place when the rodeos ended in the middle of March. Tom did well considering that he was competing against such standout performers as Bob Ragsdale and Larry Mahan. He also had earned $10,500 for his efforts. A soon as the rodeos ended, Tom had to de-

*Tom Ferguson who won six consecutive World All-Around Championships in the 1970's.* (ProRodeo Hall of Fame and Museum of the American Cowboy)

## Milestones

| | |
|---|---|
| 1974 | PRCA Calf Roping Champion |
| | Inducted into Rodeo Hall of Fame |
| 1974, 1975-79 | PRCA World Champion All-Around Cowboy |
| 1976 | PRCA Steer Wrestling Champion |
| | Prairie Circuit Steer Wrestling Champion |
| 1976-78 | National Finals Rodeo (NFR) World Champion All-Around Cowboy |
| 1977-78 | NFR Steer Wrestling Champion |
| 1977-78, 1981 | NFR Steer Wrestling Average Winner |
| 1978 | Prairie Circuit Calf Roping Champion |
| 1984 | Texas Circuit Champion All-Around Cowboy |
| 1986-87 | Southeastern Circuit Champion All-Around Cowboy |

## Records

Six PRCA World Champion All-Around Cowboy titles (record shared with Larry Mahan)
First rodeo cowboy to win $100,000 in a season, 1978
First rodeo cowboy to win $1,000,000 in a lifetime

cide whether to turn professional or resume his college career. Tom returned to college at the end of March but dropped out just a few weeks later. He did not want to be a student or a member of the school's rodeo team if he did not have the time to put forth his best effort.

The honors that Tom had collected by the end of 1973 showed that he had made the right choice. He finished the season as runner-up to PRCA All-Around Cowboy champion Larry Mahan. He was also runner-up to the national intercollegiate all-around champion. Tom realized that he probably would have won championship honors in professional and college rodeo competitions if he had devoted himself full time to one or the other. In 1974, the year that Tom became a professional rodeo cowboy, he set a pattern that he followed for the remainder of the decade. By the end of the year, he was the top money winner, amassing $66,929, and had won the PRCA Calf Roping Championship. Between 1974 and 1979, he won six consecutive All-Around Cowboy championships, an honor that he shares with Larry Mahan. In addition, in 1978, he became the first cowboy to win more than $100,000 in a single season. With typical modesty, he gave most of the credit for his wins to his horse. Still, his almost superhuman feats earned him the nickname "The Bionic Cowboy."

### Continuing the Story

During the 1980's, the prospects of gold and glory inspired Tom to push his aging body to the limit.

At a Houston rodeo in 1982, he won $17,225, which was the most that a cowboy had ever won at a regular season rodeo. As important as his previous wins were, they were dwarfed by the milestone that he attained in 1986. In that year, Tom became the first cowboy to earn $1 million in a career on the PRCA circuit.

In large part, Tom's success was the result of his tenacious attitude. If he did not do well in one rodeo, he concentrated on doing his best at the next. Unlike many cowboys, he focused on his own performance instead of worrying about the competition. Characteristic of a champion, he possessed a fierce desire to win. Tom's ruthless approach to rodeo, and to winning in particular, tarnished his reputation somewhat. Tom, however, was always keenly aware that rodeo cowboys are different from professional athletes who are guaranteed enormous salaries and huge bonuses. Consequently, he tried to make as much as he could before his body wore out. Tom's "bad-boy" image was attributable to a refusal to worry about what others said or thought about him. Tom always measured his achievements by his own standards.

### Summary

Tom Ferguson may never be known as the best calf roper or the best steer wrestler in the world. On the other hand, he was undoubtedly the best two-event man in rodeo. While Tom's detractors credit his success to greed, those who know him best say that it was his positive mental attitude that enabled him to break as many records as he did.

*Alan Brown*

### Additional Sources

Allen, Michael. *Rodeo Cowboys in the North American Imagination.* Reno: University of Nevada Press, 1998.

Ehringer, Gavin, and Gary Vorhes. *Rodeo Legends: Twenty Extraordinary Athletes of America's Sport.* 2d ed. Colorado Springs, Colo.: Western Horseman Magazine, 2003.

Wooden, Wayne S., and Gavin Ehringer. *Rodeo in America: Wranglers, Roughstock, and Paydirt.* Lawrence: University Press of Kansas, 1996.

# Bobby Fischer

**Born:** March 9, 1943
     Chicago, Illinois
**Died:** January 17, 2008
     Reykjavik, Iceland
**Also known as:** Robert James Fischer (full name)

## Early Life

Robert James Fischer was born to Gerard and Regina Fischer in Chicago on March 9, 1943. His father, a biophysicist, and his mother, fluent in six languages, divorced when Bobby was two and his sister Joan was seven. To support her family, Regina worked as an elementary school teacher and a registered nurse in California and Arizona, finally settling in Brooklyn, New York. While her mother was

*Bobby Fischer, who became the first American-born chess grand master.* (Library of Congress)

at work, Joan brought home games, including chess, to keep her six-year-old brother amused. Bobby figured out the chess moves from the enclosed directions, and he quickly outmatched his sister. With his mother's help, in 1951, Bobby participated in a chess exhibition at the Grand Army Plaza Library and joined the Brooklyn Chess Club. The club's president, Carmine Nigro, was an early mentor to Bobby.

## The Road to Excellence

At the age of twelve Bobby competed in his first United States Junior Championship, finishing twentieth out of twenty-six competitors. He joined the Manhattan Chess Club, which became the springboard for his meteoric rise. He scored his first success in 1956, in Philadelphia, where he became the youngest player, at thirteen years old, to win the U.S. Junior Chess Championship. A few months later, he gained national recognition by playing the so-called "game of the century" at the 1956 Rosenwald Tournament against Donald Byrne, who had won the 1953 U.S. Open. Bobby's winning moves, which involved sacrificing his queen and a rook in a mating attack, were praised as the most insightful ever created by a young player. He finished fourth in the U.S. Open. After a setback early in 1957, when he failed to qualify for the Manhattan Chess Club Championship, Bobby achieved an unparalleled series of victories. He repeated his previous success in the U.S. Junior Chess Championships and also won the U.S. Speed Chess Championships and the New Jersey State Open. His crowning achievement came at the end of 1957, when, playing in his first U.S. Chess Championship, he overtook international grand master Samuel Reshevsky to win first prize. At fourteen, Bobby had become the youngest American champion ever.

## The Emerging Champion

After achieving national prominence, Bobby wanted to become the strongest player in the world. He realized that this would not be easy because no American had ever won the World Chess

Championship, but he felt that he had the required winning spirit. His first international recognition came in 1958, when he placed fifth in the Interzonal Tournament against a field of strong competitors. As a result, he was named an international grand master, the youngest in the history of chess.

In 1959, he dropped out of school to devote himself completely to chess. His professional career met with both failures—he played unevenly in some South American tournaments—and successes—he placed third at a 1959 international tournament in Zurich, Switzerland. He also began to exhibit the eccentric behavior—complaining about match conditions and prize money and disappearing from public view—that characterized his later career. The opinions he expressed in interviews also generated controversy. For example, he claimed that such great world champions as Mikhail Botvinnik and Mikhail Tal were "Russian potzers" whom he would crush, and that female chess champions were much inferior to men. A month after this interview, Tal gave Bobby his comeuppance when he beat Bobby in the 1961 international chess tournament held in Bled, Yugoslavia (now in Slovenia).

### Continuing the Story

In 1962, at the International Interzonal Tournament in Stockholm, Sweden, Bobby placed first in what *Chess Life* described as "the finest performance by an American in the history of chess." However, he came in a disappointing fourth in the Candidates Tournament in Curaçao in the Netherlands Antilles. Commentators attributed his poor showing to his waste of mental energy in trying to win drawn positions, but Bobby, in an article in *Sports Illustrated*, attributed his failure to cheating by the Soviets. He accused them of prearranging draws to guarantee that Soviet players would win against non-Soviet opponents.

During the middle and late 1960's, Bobby had numerous disagreements with officials over rules, conditions, and prizes, which led to his refusal to play in several tournaments and his partial withdrawal from international chess. On the national scene, however, he continued to dominate the American championships, including an 11-0 triumph over all competitors in 1963-1964, the first time that had ever been done.

Bobby's return to international competition in

---

### Records and Milestones

| | |
|---|---|
| 1957 | At 14, youngest person to become U.S. Chess Champion |

### Honors and Awards

| | |
|---|---|
| 1957 | United States Chess Champion |
| 1958 | International grand master |
| 1970-72 | Chess Oscar |
| 1972 | Achieved Federation Internationale des Échecs (FIDE) Arpad Elo International Rating of 2,785—highest to date |
| 1987 | U.S. House of Representatives passes resolution recognizing Bobby Fischer as World Chess Champion |

---

the early 1970's was spectacular. In March, 1970, he played in the so-called "match of the century," a contest between the Soviet Union and the rest of the world held in Belgrade, Yugoslavia (now in Serbia). Although the Soviets won narrowly, 20½-19½, Bobby's defeat of Tigran Petrosian was memorable. From December 2, 1970, to September 30, 1971, Bobby won twenty consecutive games by overpowering three top grand masters: Soviet Mark Taimanov, 6-0; Denmark's Bent Larsen, 6-0; and Soviet Petrosian, 6½-2½. In this way, he qualified to become world champion in 1972.

Bobby's complaints about location and prize money complicated his match for the world championship with Boris Spassky. Bobby did not show up in Reykjavik, Iceland, for the opening ceremony, and he agreed to participate only after a British financier doubled the prize money to $250,000. During the match, controversies about Bobby made it the most publicized chess event of all time. After losing the first two games, the second by forfeit, Bobby overwhelmed Spassky in the first half of the contest to build up a lead that his opponent was unable to overcome. Bobby eventually won 12½ to 8½, thus becoming the first world chess champion from the United States. He had become an American hero, albeit an eccentric one. He accepted the City of New York Gold Medal but refused the mayor's offer of a ticker-tape parade, since he did not "believe in hero worship."

Then, something strange happened. After appearing on television talk shows and receiving numerous offers for product endorsements, book contracts, and other commercial deals, Bobby abruptly abandoned the world stage. He could have become the first "chess millionaire," but he decided to live out of the public eye in California. He never played in an officially sanctioned chess tournament again.

In 1975, when Bobby failed to agree to terms for a defense of his title against Anatoly Karpov, the International Chess Federation stripped him of his world championship. Karpov defended his title against Victor Korchnoi but eventually lost it to Garry Kasparov. Meanwhile, Bobby lived in seclusion, though his friends claimed that he followed what happened in the chess world. He lived frugally and was able to make money from telephone consultations and meetings with wealthy chess fanatics.

In September, 1992, Bobby emerged from seclusion to play a privately organized match against Boris Spassky in Montenegro and Yugoslavia. After this rematch, which Bobby won, he remained abroad. Because he violated an American law by participating in this match, the U.S. government considered him a fugitive from indictment; he faced arrest and a possible ten-year jail sentence if he returned to the United States. In 2003, his U.S. passport was revoked. He was later arrested at Narita International Airport in Japan for attempting to use the passport.

Bobby's career and disappearances became a pivotal theme in the critically acclaimed film *Searching for Bobby Fischer* (1993). During the 1990's the impression created by him in interviews and by reports in magazine articles was of a chess monomaniac who had become increasingly eccentric and possibly mentally unbalanced. For example, though he was half Jewish, Bobby asked that his name be deleted from the *Encyclopedia Judaica*. In a 1999 interview broadcast in the Philippines, he made some anti-Semitic remarks. Bobby also had strong words for the U.S. government following the terrorist attacks of September 11, 2001. He was eventually granted political asylum in Iceland. Though a number of promoters attempted to draw Bobby back into competitive chess, he never played publicly again. He died in exile in 2008.

## Summary

Bobby Fischer had more books and articles written about him than any other player in the history of chess. His eccentric genius made him a tragic figure. His defenders point out that his accomplishments made him the greatest player in history. Because of his sharp and super-aggressive style of play, even his losses were interesting. Furthermore, his tournament demands were motivated not by money but by his desire to enhance the world's recognition of chess. As a consequence of his actions chess did become popular, and its prize money comparable to other sports. On the other hand, his critics point out that his antics were adolescent and detrimental to the dignity of the game. Mathematical studies of chess masters have put Bobby third—not first—in the list of all-time greats, behind Kasparov and Karpov. Despite mixed opinion about Bobby's place in the history of chess, the adventurous inventiveness of his games guaranteed that his legacy remained.

*Robert J. Paradowski*

## Additional Sources

Böhm, Hans, and Kees Jongkind. *Bobby Fischer: The Wandering King*. London: Batsford, 2005.

Edmonds, David, and John Eidinow. *Bobby Fischer Goes to War: How the Soviets Lost the Most Extraordinary Chess Match of All Time*. New York: Ecco, 2004.

Gufeld, Eduard Efimovich. *Bobby Fischer: From Chess Genius to Legend*. Davenport, Iowa: Thinkers Press, 2002.

Krauthammer, Charles. "Did Chess Make Him Crazy?" *Time* 165, no. 18 (May 2, 2005): 96.

Schiller, Eric, and Bobby Fischer. *Learn from Bobby Fischer's Greatest Games*. New York: Cardoza, 2004.

Soltis, Andy. *Bobby Fischer Rediscovered*. London: Batsford, 2003.

# *Gary Fisher*

**Born:** 1950
    Oakland, California
**Also known as:** Gary Christopher Fisher (full name)

## Early Life
Born in Oakland, California, in 1950, Gary Fisher spent the majority of his early life in Northern California with a great appreciation for the outdoors. At the age of twelve, Gary began competing in road and track bicycle races sponsored by the Amateur Bicycle League of America, the precursor to the United States Cycling Federation (USCF). In 1964, Gary discovered cyclocross, which is off-road bicycle racing over extremely rugged terrain, and immediately became enamored with the sport. He competed in five races and finished second in the intermediate age group in the Northern California District Road Championships. He excelled in all forms of cycling and enjoyed the competition, regularly racing in both road races and cyclocross. In 1968, he was suspended from the cyclocross because race organizers felt his hair was too long and violated racing standards. Refusing to cut his hair, Gary was ineligible for competition until 1972, at which point the archaic rule was repealed.

## The Road to Excellence
Once again able to compete, Gary returned to his first love, road racing. After finishing second in the Tour of Nevada City Bicycle Classic in 1973, Gary had achieved a category-one USCF status. His ranking was based on the difficulty of races and his placement within them.

In 1975, while deeply entrenched in racing, Gary began work on his famous Schwinn Excelsior X bicycle. A precursor to the modern mountain bike, this revolutionary 1930's-era-inspired bike included drum brakes, motorcycle brake levers and cables for better braking power, thumb shifters and derailleurs to help with climbing, and triple-front chain rings. All of these elements were collected from "junk bikes" that he and his friends picked up in bike shops.

By 1976, Gary had perfected his bike, and its popularity soared within his circle of friends and with cycling enthusiasts. Gary's roommate, Charlie Kelly, organized a downhill race called the "Repack"—its riders had to repack and grease their brakes constantly after using them continuously down the treacherous road on which the race occurred—in an area just north of San Francisco. Gary set the Repack record at 4 hours and 22 minutes. In the same year, Gary won the 125-mile Tour of Klamath Lake and placed twelfth in the National Road Championships. By this point, Gary had established a strong name within the racing circuit.

## The Emerging Champion
In 1980, Gary continued racing and compiling victories, winning the Reseda to the Sea, the Central Coast Clunker Classic, and the Whiskeytown Downhill off-road race. He placed second in the Northern California District Cyclocross Championships on a bike of his own creation. The following year, Gary won Reseda to the Sea again and sponsored a women's team in the Coors International Bicycle Classic stage race. In 1982, Gary won the Paradise Divide Criterium in Colorado and the first Rockhopper off-road race. In 1983, Gary helped create the National Off-Road Bicycle Association. He also organized a cycling team which had won 70 percent of all off-road races by 1984, including six consecutive wins in the Rockhopper race.

## Continuing the Story
In addition to racing and encouraging others to do the same, Gary continued to create and improve upon his early mountain bikes. Kelly first coined

### *Mountain Bike Race Victories*

| Year | Race |
|---|---|
| 1976 | Tour of Klamath Lake |
| 1980 | Central Coast Clunker Classic |
| | Whiskeytown Downhill |
| 1980-81 | Reseda to the Sea |
| 1982 | Paradise Divide Criterium |
| | Rockhopper |
| 1997 | XC Masters Category U.S. national championships |
| 1998 | Trans Alp eight-day stage race |

the term "mountain bike," and he and Gary cofounded Mountain-Bikes in 1979. The company was the first to specialize in mountain bikes, producing 160 its first year, each of which sold for $1,300. The company dissolved in 1983, freeing Gary to establish Fisher MountainBikes, which was purchased by Trek in 1993. Trek increased production, introducing ten new competitive models in the United States at varying costs to meet all budgets and skill levels.

By 1997, Gary turned his focus to the BMX circuit and founded a BMX racing team. He also created and produced ten BMX bike models, including an ultra-lightweight aluminum-frame model. Gary won the XC Masters Category U.S. national championships and earned a place on the U.S. Masters team. The following year, Gary won the Trans Alp eight-day stage race in Europe, solidifying his place in international cycling history.

## Summary

Gary Fisher is widely considered the founder of mountain biking. His devotion to cycling allowed him to excel competitively. Through individual training and support, and by founding and sponsoring cycling teams, he encouraged others to compete in the sport. His mountain bike creation introduced a new set of adventurers to cycling, and his commitment to improving his bike models ensured the sport would continue to grow.

Gary was inducted into the Mountain Bike Hall of Fame in 1988 and was named one of the top fifty people to leave their mark on mountain biking by

---

## Honors, Awards, and Milestones

| | |
|---|---|
| 1975 | Designed Schwinn Excelsior X bicycle |
| 1976 | Set Repack downhill-race record (4 hours 22 minutes) |
| 1979 | Cofounded MountainBikes—the first company to specialize in mountain bikes |
| 1983 | Cocreator of the National Off-Road Bicycle Association |
| | Founded Fisher MountainBikes |
| 1987, 2000 | *Outside* magazine "fifty people to leave their mark on mountain biking" |
| 1988 | Inducted into Mountain Bike Hall of Fame |
| 1994 | *Smithsonian* Award: The Founding Father of Mountain Bikes |
| | Korbel Night of Champions lifetime achievement award |
| 1999 | Inducted into Snow Bike Hall of Fame |

---

*Outside* magazine in 1987 and 2000. In 1994, *Smithsonian* magazine named him the "Founding Father of Mountain Bikes." That same year, Gary received the lifetime achievement award at the Korbel Night of Champions. In 1998, he was recognized by *Popular Mechanics* for the continuous innovations he offered mountain-bike technology and the sport, and he was inducted into the Snow Bike Hall of Fame in 1999.

*Sara Vidar*

## Additional Sources

Andrews, Guy, and Gary Fisher. *Mountain Bike Maintenance.* San Ramon, Calif.: Falcon Books, 2006.

Berto, Frank J. *The Birth of Dirt: Origins of Mountain Biking.* San Francisco: Van der Plas, 1999.

Brink, Tim. *The Complete Mountain Biking Manual.* New York: International Marine/Ragged Mountain Press, 2007.

Worland, Steve. *The Mountain Bike Book.* St. Paul, Minn.: Motorbook International, 2003.

Zinn, Lennard. *Zinn and the Art of Mountain Bike Maintenance.* Boulder, Colo.: VeloPress, 2005.

# *Emerson Fittipaldi*

**Born:** December 12, 1946
São Paulo, Brazil
**Also known as:** Emmo

### Early Life

Emerson Fittipaldi was born in São Paulo, Brazil, on December 12, 1946. His family admired the United States and loved racing. His father and his older brother were both named Wilson in honor of President Woodrow Wilson, and Emerson was named for the American poet Ralph Waldo Emerson. The fact that every family member, including Emerson's mother, raced automobiles, motorcycles, or go-karts illustrates the family's love for racing.

*Emerson Fittipaldi being interviewed after winning the British Grand Prix in 1972. (Popperfoto/Getty Images)*

Emerson's family was relatively well-to-do, and his father, a journalist, was able to finance a teen-age race career for Wilson, Jr., and Emerson on both 50-cubic-centimeter motorcycles and go-karts. Emerson began competitive racing at the age of seventeen, the youngest legal age for such activity in Brazil. By age nineteen, Emerson was driving open-wheel cars; he won the Formula Five Championship in 1966. The following year, he entered Grand Touring competition and finished second in the championship.

### The Road to Excellence

In 1969, Emerson felt he was ready for European Grand Prix racing, so he set off for England. In 1970, the death of another driver on his team gave Emerson a promotion to Formula One racing. In only his fourth race, Emerson won the United States Grand Prix. In 1972, driving a Lotus, he had five Grand Prix victories, winning the World Driver's Championship as the youngest driver ever to win that title. Two years later, he repeated as champion.

In 1975, Emerson made a mistake that almost ruined his racing career. With his brother, he formed his own team to design, build, and race cars. The price of oil was beginning to increase rapidly, and the economy of Brazil was suffering. Convincing Brazilian companies to invest in a racing team proved impossible. Even with Emerson investing more than $1 million of his own money, the team never had enough capital to test its car designs thoroughly or to purchase all the spare parts necessary. However, Emerson remained a great hero in his native Brazil and managed to finish second in the 1978 Brazilian Grand Prix, in what some have called his greatest race, one in which he confronted temperatures of 150 degrees Fahrenheit and dehydration inside his car. His racing team still needed money, however.

### The Emerging Champion

Emerson retired from racing in 1981. He owned an automobile dealership and a citrus farm in Brazil, and he concentrated on these businesses to recoup some of the money his racing team had lost. Dur-

## CART, Grand Prix, and Other Victories

|  |  |
|------|---------|
| 1966 | Formula Five Championship |
| 1969 | British Formula Three Championship |
| 1970 | United States Grand Prix |
| 1972 | Italian Grand Prix |
| | Race of Champions |
| | Austrian Grand Prix |
| 1972-73 | Spanish Grand Prix |
| 1972, 1974 | Belgian Grand Prix |
| | World Championship of Drivers |
| 1972, 1975 | British Grand Prix |
| 1973-74 | Brazilian Grand Prix |
| 1973, 1975 | Argentine Grand Prix |
| 1974 | Canadian Grand Prix |
| 1985 | Michigan 500 |
| 1986, 1988 | Road America 200 |
| 1986, 1992 | Elk Hart Lake |
| 1987 | Toronto 183 |
| 1987, 1989, 1992 | Cleveland Grand Prix |
| 1988, 1993 | Mid-Ohio 200 |
| 1989 | PPG Indy Car World Series Championship |
| 1989-90 | Nazareth Grand Prix |
| 1989, 1991 | Detroit Grand Prix |
| 1989, 1993 | Indianapolis 500 |
| | Portland 200 |
| 1992 | Australia |
| 1994 | Phoenix Slick-50 200 |
| | Marlboro Challenge |

ing this time, he drove go-karts for fun in local races. Brazilian go-karts are true racing machines, not toys. They have two engines and are capable of speeds up to 100 miles per hour. The financial success of his businesses and the fun he had racing go-karts convinced Emerson to return to professional racing. In 1984, he drove in the Miami Grand Prix and began to look for ways to enter the Championship Auto Racing Teams (CART) circuit.

In 1985, "Emmo," as American fans began to call him, was back in full force. He competed with Al Unser, Sr., Tom Sneva, and Al Unser, Jr. The race season was an exciting duel among all these drivers. Emerson won the Michigan 500 race, beating Unser, Sr., by a few car lengths. Just two days later, Emerson lost to Unser, Jr., at New York's Meadowlands Grand Prix by half a minute. These duels, particularly with the Unsers, continued for many years but, in the end, produced respect among the competitors rather than ill will.

## Continuing the Story

By 1989, Emerson had achieved major goals in several important areas of racing, but one goal still eluded him: He had never won the Indianapolis 500. When the Memorial-Day-weekend race arrived, Emerson and his car, "The Flying Beauty," were ready. From the green flag that signaled the start of the race, Emerson had the field covered. He led for 156 of the first 195 laps of the 200-lap race. In the process, he set a new speed record for a single lap, 221.370 MPH. As the race drew to a close, Emerson drove into the pit to take on just enough fuel to finish the race. Through a misunderstanding, his pit crew filled the tank. This extra weight slowed "The Flying Beauty" just enough for Emerson's rival, Unser, Jr., to catch up. On lap 196, Unser gained the lead. Both men were using all their skill and determination as they came into the last few laps. On lap 198, only a few miles from the finish, both Unser and Emerson caught up with slower cars from behind. As Emerson and Unser, Jr., tried to force their way through, their automobiles collided. Unser crashed into the wall and Emerson slid sideways. Luck and skill brought Emerson back on the track. As he passed the site of the wreck on his way to the finish, Unser was there giving Emerson a "thumbs up" salute. Later, Emerson said, "There's no doubt it was the most important single win of my career." Before the season was over, Emerson had won five CART races and was named CART champion driver of the year.

In 1990, Emerson was back at Indianapolis. Again he set a track record for a single lap, 225.58 MPH, and broke the track speed record for the entire race. However, as often happens in racing, record setting does not mean winning. Two other drivers set speed records also, and Emerson finished third. After a win at Detroit in 1991 and five first-place finishes in 1992, including the Marlboro Challenge, in 1993, Emerson won his second Indy

## Honors, Awards, and Records

|  |  |
|------|-------|
| 1972 | Won the World Championship of Drivers at 25 years 273 days of age—the youngest winner ever |
| 1989 | CART DeVilbiss Finish Line Award |
| 1990 | Set record for the fastest one-lap qualifying speed at the Indianapolis 500 (225.575 miles per hour) |
| | Set record for the fastest four-lap qualifying speed at the Indianapolis 500 (225.301 miles per hour) |
| 2000 | Chosen as Legend of the Indianapolis Motor Speedway |
| 2001 | Inducted into Motorsports Hall of Fame of America |

500. With his 1994 win at Phoenix, Emerson extended his streak of Indy car wins to ten consecutive seasons. Emerson suffered a devastating crash during the 1996 Michigan 500, in which he sustained severe neck injuries. Subsequent injuries to his back from a light-aircraft accident convinced Emerson that his long and distinguished career was at an end. Nearly ten years after his retirement, Emerson surprised the racing world when he competed in the Grand Prix Masters at the Kyalami racetrack in Gauteng, South Africa.

## Summary

Emerson Fittipaldi has had a lifelong love of racing. His career led him to try many kinds of vehicles, with mixed luck. Even when his career was not going well, Emerson retained an optimistic outlook and was an appealing personality. His determination, courage, and skill took him to the top of his field.

*Michael R. Bradley*

## Additional Sources

Higham, Peter, and Bruce Jones. *World Motor Racing Circuits: A Spectator's Guide.* London: Andre Deutsch, 1999.

Hinton, Ed. "Emerson Fittipaldi." *Sports Illustrated* 87, no. 18 (November 3, 1997): 74-76.

Ludvigsen, Karl E. *Emerson Fittipaldi: Heart of a Racer.* Newbury Park, Calif.: Haynes, 2002.

Nye, Doug. *Formula One Legends.* Leiccster, East Midlands, England: Magna Books, 1994.

# *John Force*

**Born:** May 4, 1949
Bell Gardens, California

### Early Life

The youngest of five children born to Harold and Betty Ruth Force, John Force was born into poverty and stricken with polio at a young age. With the help of leg braces and hot baths, John recovered enough to be quarterback on his high school football team in Bell Gardens, California, even though one of his legs was shorter than the other. Typical of the stubborn nature he later displayed in drag racing, John did not give up on his team, even though it had a 0-29 record in three years. John briefly attended Cerritos Junior College, where he played football.

Early on, John's passion was drag racing. As a child, he hung around the Lions Drag Strip in Los Angeles, California, to watch "Big Daddy" Don Garlits, Tom "The Mongoose" McEwen, and Don "The Snake" Prudomme, John's personal hero. However, John also admired his father, a truck driver who hauled goods throughout California. John married at nineteen and was a father at twenty. To support his family, he became a truck driver like his dad. John's first professional race car was an Oldsmobile that he bought for $150. John's first Funny Car was a Mustang Mach 1 built during the early 1970's.

### The Road to Excellence

Using money from his tax return and from selling an organ his mother-in-law won on the game show *Let's Make a Deal*, John purchased a broken Vega Funny Car from his cousin. Funny Cars, the type of dragsters John raced throughout his career, are handmade, high-horsepower cars that can reach speeds of more than 300 miles per hour (MPH) in approximately five seconds. Funny Cars launch from the starting line like a rocket. The cars run on nitromethane and are loud, emit a lot of smoke, have flames shoot from their tailpipes, and sometimes explode before they reach the end of the quarter-mile track. Stopping the car takes more time than running the race.

Success did not come easily to John. He started racing in 1975, and he joined the National Hot Rod Association (NHRA) in 1978. In 1987, in Montreal, Canada, nine years after joining the circuit, John won his first event. Three years after his initial victory, John won his first title. In 1985, John's fortunes began to change when he joined with crew chief Austin Coil. In fact, from 1990, the year of John's first championship, until 2004, John Force Racing won fourteen of fifteen championships, losing only in 2003. John won ten straight championships, dominating his sport. He was the first driver to win more than ten championships in his division. As of 2008, John had 126 career event victories in more than 500 career starts. Early in 2008,

*Funny-car driver John Force in 2008.* (Scott Sewell/CSM/Landov)

on his fifty-ninth birthday, John won his 1,000th individual heat.

## The Emerging Champion

In his long career, John had two severe accidents. In 1992, in Memphis, Tennessee, while traveling at more than 300 MPH, John hit the wall. After the accident, John, a huge Elvis Presley fan, was quoted as saying that he "saw Elvis at 1,000 feet." John became a fan favorite not only for his winning ways but also for his larger-than-life personality. He talked nonstop, telling stories and entertaining anyone who would listen. With four Mustangs in its stable of dragsters, John Force Racing consisted of John, his daughter Ashley, his son-in-law Robert Hight, and Mike Neff.

In 2007, John Force Racing had one of its worst years. The team lost Eric Medlen, who died in a Funny Car test run. Then in September, John was involved in the worst crash of his life. Racing at the Texas Motorplex in Ennis, Texas, near Dallas, John's car collided with driver Kenny Bernstein's car after both cars had crossed the finish line. John was airlifted to nearby Baylor University Medical Center in Dallas, where he was treated for a severely broken left ankle, a deep cut on his right knee, a broken and dislocated left wrist, and abrasions to his right hand. John recovered from his injuries in four months.

## Continuing the Story

John's mother was once quoted as saying that John was the dumbest of her five children, but he was also the richest. John, admittedly, went through most of his life believing Abraham Lincoln was the first president. John and his family became more famous because of the A&E reality show *Driving Force*, which chronicled the lives of the Force clan. John Force Racing was a family business: John's oldest daughter Adria, from his first marriage, ran

### Records and Milestones

First Funny Car racer to achieve 1,000 qualifying victories (2008)

Most wins in drag-racing history (126)

Set record for fastest quarter mile (4.665 seconds)

Set record for highest speed (333.58 mph)

### Honors and Awards

| | |
|---|---|
| 1990-2002, 2004, 2006 | National Hot Rod Association (NHRA) Champion |
| 1993-2002 | American Auto Racing Writers and Broadcasters Association all-American |
| 2000 | Second on NHRA's top fifty drivers list |
| 2005 | John Bolster Award |

his office; his other three daughters, from his second marriage—Ashley, Brittany, and Courtney—were all involved in some level of racing. John Force Racing has its own museum, located in Yorba Linda, California.

## Summary

A fifteen-time NHRA champion, John Force was often called "the Richard Petty of drag racing." Along with "Big Daddy" Don Garlits, he is one of the legends of his sport. The first NHRA driver to exceed 320 MPH, John won at twenty of the twenty-one venues on the NHRA circuit. The tour was where John felt most satisfied, racing with his family and friends.

*Randy L. Abbott*

## Additional Sources

Arneson, Erik. *John Force: The Straight Story of Drag Racing's Three-Hundred-MPH Superstar.* St. Paul, Minn.: Motorbooks, 2006.

Wilkinson, Alec. "Wheels on Fire." *Rolling Stone* 771 (October 16, 1997): 45-51.

# A. J. Foyt

**Born:** January 16, 1935
   Houston, Texas
**Also known as:** Anthony Joseph Foyt, Jr. (full
   name); Fancy Pants

### Early Life
Anthony Joseph "A. J." Foyt, Jr., was born on January 16, 1935, in Houston, Texas. A. J.'s father, Anthony Joseph, Sr., owned a garage and was a successful midget-car racer, so the young Foyt was around automobiles and racing from birth. A. J., Sr., built a racer for his son when the boy was five. A. J. learned to drive it at local tracks in between the races. He attended Lamar High School in Houston, but he dropped out in his junior year to begin a full-time racing career.

### The Road to Excellence
A. J.'s first victory came in a midget-car race at a Nebraska fair. By the time he was twenty-two, he had

*A. J. Foyt in 1970.* (RacingOne/Getty Images)

begun to compete on the United States Auto Club (USAC) circuit. A. J. competed in midgets and stock car races across the Midwest, on speedways and dirt tracks, honing his skills and earning a reputation as one of the country's most promising young drivers.

By 1958, A. J. had compiled enough racing credentials to take the Indianapolis Speedway's rookie driver test. On his first day at "Indy," A. J. sped around the track at 141.13 miles per hour and qualified for the Indianapolis 500, the premier event in American auto racing. At his first Indy 500, A. J. was in contention until the 148th lap of the 200-lap race, when his car hit an oil slick and spun out of control. The spin took A. J. out of the running for first, but he recovered to finish in sixteenth place, an impressive performance for a rookie driver.

### The Emerging Champion
A. J. won his first major race that year at the Sacramento Fairgrounds in California, and his performances were so good that he was offered a chance to compete on Europe's prestigious Grand Prix circuit. A. J. chose to keep racing in the United States, though, and, in 1959, he won ten USAC races. At Indianapolis, he improved on his first-year performance; he stayed in contention for most of the race and finished tenth. In 1960, A. J. won the USAC national driving championship for the best overall performance in that season's races. At the age of twenty-four, the stocky, 6-foot Texan was recognized as the country's top driver, but he still had not won the big prize. To cement his reputation, A. J. needed to win at Indianapolis.

In 1961, A. J. got his chance. He and the legendary Eddie Sachs hooked up in one of the most memorable Indy races ever. The two racers ran neck-and-neck for most of the race, and A. J. had opened up a ten-second lead with just fifteen laps to go. A. J., though, was running low on gas; his fueling apparatus was broken, and he needed to make a pit stop in order to finish the race. When he pulled over, Sachs zoomed past, and it seemed as though A. J. would have to be content with second place. Just five laps from the finish, though, Sachs's

## CART and Other Victories

| | |
|---|---|
| 1960-61, 1963-64, 1967 | DuQuoin 100 |
| 1960-61, 1963-64, 1967, 1975, 1979 | USAC Champion Driver |
| 1960-61, 1964-65, 1968, 1970 | Hoosier 100 |
| 1960, 1962, 1964, 1967-68 | Sacramento 100 |
| 1960, 1964 | Phoenix 100 |
| 1961, 1964, 1967, 1977 | Indianapolis 500 |
| 1961-64 | Langhorne 100 |
| 1962-64 | Trenton 100 |
| 1962, 1964 | Milwaukee 100 |
| 1963-65, 1973-74 | Trenton 150 |
| 1963, 1965, 1967, 1975 | Trenton 200 |
| 1964-65 | Firecracker 400 |
| 1964-65, 1967 | Springfield 100 |
| 1965 | Phoenix 200 |
| 1967 | Twenty-Four Hours of Le Mans |
| 1968 | Castle Rock 150 |
| | Hanford 250 |
| 1970 | Winston Western 500 |
| 1971 | Coca-Cola 500 |
| | National Dirt Car Champion |
| 1971, 1975 | Phoenix 150 |
| 1972 | Daytona 500 |
| | Valvoline Silver Crown Series Champion |
| 1973, 1975, 1979, 1981 | Pocono 500 |
| 1974-75 | Ontario 100 |
| 1975 | Michigan 200 |
| | Ontario 500 |
| 1975, 1979 | Milwaukee 150 |
| 1976 | Michigan 150 |
| | Texas 150 |
| 1977 | Mosport 300 |
| 1977, 1979 | Ontario 200 |
| 1978 | USAC Stock Car Champion Driver |
| | Daytona 500 100-mile Qualifying Race |
| | Silverstone 150 |
| 1978-79 | Texas 200 |
| 1983, 1985 | Twenty-Four Hours of Daytona |
| 1985 | Twelve Hours of Sebring |

came upon an accident on the track involving two other drivers. Rather than hit the stalled cars and risk injuring other drivers, A. J. made a courageous, split-second decision. Swerving off course, A. J. flipped and rolled his Ford stock car; the resulting injuries put him in a hospital. When he returned to racing later that year, he was still not strong, and he lost his USAC championship title for only the second time in five years. In 1966, he failed to win the championship again; Mario Andretti won both seasons, and A. J.'s dominance looked as though it might be a thing of the past.

In 1967, A. J. came roaring back, reclaiming the USAC title and winning his third Indy 500. A. J. had regained his spot as the United States' top racer, and he even extended his triumphs overseas. That season, A. J. and Dan Gurney became the first Americans to win the Twenty-Four Hours of Le Mans race in France, setting a new course record of more than 135 miles per hour.

**Continuing the Story**

A. J.'s success continued through the 1970's, and he proved to be a versatile driver, capable of winning in any type of car and on any sort of racecourse. He took the USAC title again in 1975 and 1979, winning repeatedly in each of the four major categories of competition: sprint, stock, midget, and championship car races. In 1977, he became the first four-time winner in Indianapolis 500 history when he edged past Gordon Johncock with fifteen laps to go. In 1983 and 1985, A. J. was on winning teams at the Twenty-Four Hours of Daytona, and, in 1985, he won the

car began to swerve. A rear tire had started to come apart, and it was impossible to tell if it would hold up long enough for Sachs to finish the race. Three laps from the finish, Sachs admitted defeat, pulling over for a tire change while A. J. drove on to his first Indianapolis 500 victory. A. J. had broken the Indy record by completing the course at an average speed of 139.13 miles per hour, and he stood firmly atop the racing world.

In 1964, A. J. won again at Indy, raising the track's speed record to 147.35 miles per hour. In January, 1965, though, A. J.'s career took a sudden detour. In a stock car race in Riverside, California, A. J. was chasing the leader when he

## Honors and Awards

| | |
|---|---|
| 1967, 1975-76 | Driver of the Year |
| 1968 | CART STP Most Improved Driver |
| 1975 | Jerry Titus Memorial Award |
| 1977 | First four-time winner of Indy 500 |
| 1978 | Inducted into Indianapolis Motor Speedway Hall of Fame |
| 1989 | Inducted into Motorsports Hall of Fame of America |
| 1999 | Associated Press Driver of the Century |

Twelve Hours of Sebring, giving him victories in all three of the world's major endurance races—Le Mans, Daytona, and Sebring.

A. J. was highly successful off the track as well. In the late 1960's, he began to design his own line of racing cars, called Coyotes, and soon began running his own racing teams. In addition to his considerable racing prize money, A. J. earned millions of dollars by endorsing automotive products, and by the mid-1970's he had acquired a fifteen-hundred-acre ranch near Houston with a huge mansion and more than one hundred thoroughbred racehorses. Despite his enormous success, A. J. continued to compete at small tracks around the country, drawing crowds wherever he raced. In explaining his willingness to enter small-time races, A. J. noted that in his early days as a racer he had been very poor. "I slept in my car and had trouble getting together enough money for food," he said. "Some of the promoters helped me out with cash, and I've never forgotten them. This is my way of paying them back." Back in those days, at the age of twenty, A. J. had married Lucy Zarr, and the couple had three children, including a son named A. J. III.

## Summary

A. J. Foyt became famous by accruing unprecedented victory totals at Indianapolis and in USAC competition. Not content with those impressive credentials, though, he competed in and won some of the toughest races in Europe and every type of domestic racing. He proved to be an all-around champion.

*Brook Wilson*

## Additional Sources

Arute, Jack, and Jenna Fryer. *Jack Arute's Tales from the Indy 500*. Champaign, Ill.: Sports, 2006.

Levine, Leo. "A. J. Foyt." *Road and Track* 56, no. 6 (February, 2005): 126-131.

Reed, Terry. *Indy: The Race and Ritual of the Indianapolis 500*. Washington, D.C.: Potomac Books, 2005.

# *Don Garlits*

**Born:** January 14, 1932
　　Tampa, Florida
**Also known as:** Donald Glenn Garlits (full name);
　　Big Daddy

## Early Life

Donald Glenn Garlits was born on January 14, 1932, in Tampa, Florida, to Helen and Edward Garlits. The son of an engineer turned farmer, Don, even as a boy, showed a knack for fixing and building things. Along with his brother Ed, he ran a bicycle repair shop from home to earn extra money. The Garlits brothers learned from their father that any task worth undertaking was worth doing well. Consequently, it was not uncommon to see the teenage Don working in his backyard until the early morning hours fixing car engines. After graduation from high school, Don took a job in the accounting department of a large store in Tampa; after only a few months, however, he realized that desk work was not for him. He quit the job to find something more exciting.

## The Road to Excellence

Knowing how Don enjoyed working with automobiles, his stepfather, Alex Weir, got Don a job in his brother's paint and body shop. Don took the job, stayed until the work ran out, and then spent the better part of two years moving from job to job, putting most of his earnings into his car. While working in a Tampa paint and body shop, Don met hot-rodder Grady Pickle. From that moment, Don was hooked on hot-rodding. For the next several years, Don and his friends spent all of their free time building fast cars and racing on the streets of Tampa.

In the summer of 1952, while boating with some friends, Don met and began dating Pat Bieger. Don was spending more time with Pat and less time with his racing friends. He felt uncomfortable about his hot-

rodder lifestyle and decided it was time to grow up. He sold his hot rod and bought a sedan. In February of 1953, Don and Pat were married. After he had been out of racing for the better part of a year, Don took Pat to watch the local competition at a nearby drag strip. By the end of the day, Don had entered his car and won his first racing trophy. He was hooked again.

## The Emerging Champion

During the next two years, Don toured along the East Coast learning how to compete and win. Life as a dragster during the early years was not glamorous. Don had no sponsors to help with the costs. Many hours were spent on the road, and if the car needed repairs, Don had to make them. On top of that, he earned money only when he won.

On November 11, 1957, in Brookville, Florida, Don established the first of his many world records. Driving the first of his thirty-two dragsters named Swamp Rat, he broke the 170-mile-per-hour barrier for the quarter mile. His West Coast competition questioned his times, however; he knew that the only way to silence his critics was to meet them head to head. The meeting took place at the neutral location of Houston, Texas. When the smoke

*Don Garlits in 1972.* (AP/Wide World Photos)

had cleared, the young upstart from Florida had beaten the Californians three straight times. In 1958, Don became the first dragster to break the 180-mile-per-hour mark.

Don differed from other racers in his intense desire to win and his ability to get more speed out of what he was driving. He became not only a great racer but also an innovative designer. He was never afraid to modify his car or try something new. He was the first to install an air spoiler on a dragster and the first to use port injection. After a near-fatal accident, he designed a rear-engine dragster for greater driver safety. During a California racing tour, artist Ed Roth gave Don the nickname "Big Daddy." Promoters and fans liked the name, and it stuck. In 1964, Don accomplished what many people compared to running the first sub-four-minute mile: He became the first man to break the 200-mile-per-hour barrier in a dragster.

### Continuing the Story

Don gained fame and fortune on the drag strip, but life was not always easy. Early in his career, he was nearly burned to death when his motor exploded in a race, engulfing him in flames. Modern protective gear was not yet in use; Don's leather jacket was all he had for protection. His face and hands were badly burned, and he spent weeks in the hospital recuperating. Had it not been for lifetime friend and fellow racer Art Malone, who convinced him to return to the sport he loved, Don would have retired.

Several years later, in Long Beach, California, another major accident occurred. While he accelerated off the starting line, his transmission exploded, sending parts through the floorboard, severing his toes and half of the arch on his right foot. Undaunted by the injury, Don healed and raced again.

## AHRA Championships

| | |
|---|---|
| 1958,1978-80,1984 | AHRA Summernationals |
| 1969,1971-73 | AHRA World Championships |
| 1970,1973,1978-80,1982,1984 | AHRA Springnationals |
| 1970,1973,1978,1981-83 | AHRA Winternationals |
| 1971-73,1979,1982,1984 | AHRA World Finals |
| 1971-74,1978-80,1982-84 | AHRA Top Fuel World Champion |
| 1971-74,1979,1983 | AHRA Nationals |
| 1974 | AHRA Grand Nationals |

## IHRA Championships

| | |
|---|---|
| 1972,1975 | IHRA Springnationals |
| 1972,1975,1979 | IHRA Winternationals |
| 1973,1976 | IHRA U.S. Nationals |
| 1975-78 | IHRA Top Fuel World Champion |
| | IHRA World Nationals |
| | IHRA Summernationals |
| 1976 | IHRA Winter Classic |
| | NHRA Championship |

## NHRA Championships

| | |
|---|---|
| 1963,1971,1973,1975,1986-87 | NHRA Winternationals |
| 1964,1967-68,1975,1984-86 | NHRA U.S. Nationals |
| 1968,1971,1979 | NHRA Springnationals |
| 1973-74 | NHRA Supernationals |
| 1975,1979,1984 | NHRA World Finals |
| 1975,1985 | NHRA Grandnationals |
| 1975,1985-86 | NHRA Top Fuel World Champion |
| 1979 | NHRA Fall Nationals |
| 1985 | NHRA Summernationals |

In 1992, after a career that lasted more than four decades, "Big Daddy" was forced to retire when the gravitational force from a test car he was driving caused retinal damage to both of his eyes. During his forty-three years of racing, Don won 112 national event titles, seventeen fuel world championships, and at least one national event for twenty consecutive years. His career-best speed was 287.11 miles per hour.

A devoted family man, Don always wanted to be a positive role model. He never accepted sponsorships from companies that did

## Honors and Awards

| | |
|---|---|
| 1969-70, 1972-73, 1975-77, 1985-86 | *Car Craft* magazine Top Fuel Driver of the Year |
| 1971-74 | AHRA Top Fuel Driver of the Year |
| 1972 | *Popular Hot Rod* magazine Driver of the Decade (1960-1970) |
| 1989 | Inducted into Motorsports Hall of Fame of America |
| 1997 | Inducted into International Motorsports Hall of Fame |
| 2004 | Inducted into Automotive Hall of Fame |

not convey positive family values. In 1984, Don opened the world's first drag-racing museum in Ocala, Florida. In 1987, Don's Swamp Rat 30 became the first drag-race vehicle to be put on display in the Smithsonian National Museum of American History. "Big Daddy" was inducted into the Motorsports Hall of Fame of America in 1989, the International Motorsports Hall of Fame in 1997 and the Automotive Hall of Fame in 2004.

## Summary

Few men in any sport have been as successful and as innovative as Don Garlits. His name became synonymous with drag racing, and his records became a legend. Often called the "father of drag racing,"

Don was number one on the National Hot Rod Association's list of top fifty drivers, 1951-2000.

*Randy J. Dietz*

## Additional Sources

Garlits, Don, and Bill Stephens. *Big Daddy Don Garlits: Tales from the Drag Strip*. Champaign, Ill.: Sports, 2004.

Koby, Howard V. *Top Fuel Dragsters of the 1970's: Photo Archive*. Hudson, Wis.: Iconografix, 2004.

Mueller, Mike. *The Garlits Collection: Cars That Made Drag Racing History*. North Branch, Minn.: CarTech, 2004.

Reisler, Jim. "Big Daddy Still Loves Speed." *Sports Illustrated* 86, no. 24 (June 16, 1997): 18.

# *Jeff Gordon*

**Born:** August 4, 1971
      Vallejo, California
**Also known as:** Jeffrey Michael Gordon (full
   name); Rainbow Warrior; Wonder Boy

## Early Life

Jeffrey Michael Gordon began racing at the age of five, when his stepfather, John Bickford, brought home two, quarter midget race cars for Jeff and his sister. Jeff loved the race car. He and his stepfather made a makeshift racetrack on a nearby fairgrounds and spent all their free time practicing laps.

Not content to simply practice, Jeff entered races, and he began winning right away. In 1977, he won the Western States Championships in his class, and two years later, he won his first Grand National Championship and Pacific Northwest Indoor Championship. By the age of nine, he was already beating drivers who were in their late teens.

In 1982, he won another national championship race, and then he moved on to racing go-karts. Undeterred by the change in vehicle, Jeff won all twenty-five events he entered in his first year and all twelve the next year. By 1984, at the age of thirteen, he was ready to move on to sprint cars, an unusual move for someone of that age. The move did not slow him down as he won twenty-two races that year.

## The Road to Excellence

By 1985, Jeff was ready to compete with adults instead of with other teens. However, California had age restrictions that would not allow Jeff to race against adults. His family, ready to put Jeff's budding racing career first, decided to move, in 1986, to Pittsboro, Indiana, a small town not far from Indianapolis, where the family could live economically, but Jeff could have access to racetracks and competitions.

Jeff joined the United States Auto Club (USAC) at the age of sixteen, becoming its youngest driver ever when he received his race driver's license on his sixteenth birthday. Before he was old enough to have a regular driver's license, he had already won three sprint car championships.

In 1989, Jeff moved on to midget-car racing, and at the age of eighteen, he was named the USAC midget-car rookie of the year. The following year, Jeff became the youngest driver ever to win the national USAC midget championship. He moved up to the Silver Crown Division, involving bigger cars, and became its youngest winner.

## The Emerging Champion

In 1990, with his stepfather's encouragement, Jeff made a deal to be filmed by the Entertainment and Sports Programming Network (ESPN) at the Buck Baker driving school in Rockingham, North Carolina. In exchange, Baker taught Jeff free of charge. While there, Jeff took his first lap in a stock car and was immediately hooked. At that moment, stock cars, racing on pavement instead of dirt tracks, became Jeff's racing vehicle of choice.

In 1991, Jeff teamed with car owner Bill Davis and began competing in the National Association for Stock Car Auto Racing (NASCAR) Busch Series

*Jeff Gordon spraying champagne to celebrate his victory at the Bank of America 500 in 2007.* (Rusty Jarrett/Getty Images)

Grand National Division, later called the Nationwide Series, and finished second three times and third once in his first year. Jeff was named, for the second straight year, to the all-American team by the American Racing Writers and Broadcasters Association and was also named rookie of the year.

In 1992, Jeff again drove for Bill Davis racing. Winston Cup car owner Rick Hendrick, of Hendrick Motorsports, noticed Jeff during a race in Atlanta. While watching Jeff's car, Hendrick saw that it was moving rather wildly, and he kept watching, waiting for it to crash. Instead Jeff won the race. Hendrick immediately decided he wanted Jeff on his team. In early May of 1992, Hendrick signed Jeff to a NASCAR Winston Cup Series (later the Sprint Cup) contract. Jeff was able to bring his Busch Series crew chief, Ray Evernham, with him. This partnership became the backbone of Jeff's early Cup career.

Jeff first raced the Number 24 DuPont Automotive Refinishes Chevrolet at Atlanta Motor Speedway, in the 1992 Hooters 500, starting twenty-first and finishing thirty-first, after crashing on lap 164.

Many considered this race to be one of the best in NASCAR history: It decided a championship between six drivers and featured Jeff driving in his first Cup race and Richard Petty driving in his final Cup race.

**Continuing the Story**

In 1993, at the age of twenty-one, Jeff won the Gatorade 125-mile qualifying race for the Daytona 500. That was not the only major event of that day, as Jeff met Brooke Sealy, who became his first wife.

That year, Jeff's first full season in the Winston Cup, showed that he belonged. He finished fourteenth overall and was named the Winston Cup rookie of the year. The following year, Jeff won his first race, the Coca-Cola 600 at Lowe's Motor Speedway. In 1995, he won his first championship in the Winston Cup, the youngest driver to do so in modern years. This championship win was followed by noted victories in the 1997 and 1999 Daytona 500s, a race he again won in 2005. In 1998, another championship, year, Jeff won a record-tying thirteen races and was also named driver of the year. As

## NASCAR Circuit Victories

| | | | | | |
|---|---|---|---|---|---|
| 1994 | Coca-Cola 600 | 1998 | Goodwrench 400 | 2001 | Brickyard 400 |
| | Brickyard 400 | | Food City 500 | (*cont.*) | Global at the Glen |
| 1995 | Goodwrench 500 | | Coca-Cola 600 | | Protection One 400 |
| | Purolator 500 | | Save Mart 350 | 2002 | Sharpie 500 |
| | Food City 500 | | Pennsylvania 500 | | Southern 500 |
| | Pepsi 400 | | Brickyard 400 | | Protection One 400 |
| | Slick 50 300 | | Bud at the Glen | 2003 | MBNA 500 |
| | Southern 500 | | Pepsi 400 | | Virginia 500 |
| | MBNA 500 | | CMT 300 | 2004 | Aaron's 499 |
| 1996 | Pontiac 400 | | Southern 500 | | Auto Club 500 |
| | TranSouth Financial 400 | | Pepsi 400 | | SaveMart 350 |
| | Food City 500 | | AC Delco 400 | | Daytona 500 |
| | Miller 500 | | NAPA 500 | | Brickyard 400 |
| | UAW-GM 500 | 1999 | Daytona 500 | 2005 | Daytona 500 |
| | DieHard 500 | | Atlanta 500 | | Advance Auto 500 |
| | Mountain Dew Southern 500 | | California 500 | | Aaron's 499 |
| | MBNA 500 | | Save Mart 350 | | Subway 500 |
| | Hanes 500 | | Frontier at the Glen | 2006 | SaveMart 350 |
| | Holly Farms 400 | | NAPA Autocare 500 | | USG Sheetrock 400 |
| 1997 | Daytona 500 | | UAW-GM Quality 500 | 2007 | Subway 500 |
| | Goodwrench 400 | | Save Mart 350 | | Aaron's 499 |
| | Food City 500 | | Chevrolet 400 | | Dodge 500 |
| | Goody's 500 | 2000 | DieHard 500 | | Pocono 500 |
| | Coca-Cola 600 | | SaveMart Kragen 350 | | UAW-Ford 500 |
| | Pocono 500 | | Chevrolet 400 | | Coca-Cola 600 |
| | California 500 | 2001 | UAW-Dodge 400 | | |
| | Bud at the Glen | | Autism Speaks 400 presented by Visa | | |
| | Southern 500 | | Kmart 400 | | |
| | CMT 300 | | | | |

## Awards, Honors, and Records

| | |
|---|---|
| 1993 | Rookie of the Year |
| 1994, 1997 | Busch Clash winner |
| 1995 | Won all three segments of the Winston Select all-star race |
| 1995, 1997-98, 2001 | Winston Cup Champion |
| 1996, 2001 | True Value Man of the Year for charity involvement |
| | Premier 1996 Indiana Professional Athlete |
| 1997-2000 | Won a record-breaking six consecutive road races |
| 1998 | Recorded the largest payday in racing history by winning $1.6 million at the Brickyard 400 |
| | Won four consecutive races from late July to late August, tying a modern-era record |
| | Tied modern-era record with thirteen wins in a season |
| | Driver of the Year |
| 2000 | Won his fiftieth career race at Talladega |
| 2001 | First driver to win $10 million in a single season |
| 2002 | Three hundreth career start, sixtieth career win |
| | Won the AARWBA Jerry Titus Memorial Trophy for a third time |

bosch. Ingrid gave birth to the couple's first child, Ella Sofia, on June 20, 2007.

Another big change for Jeff and his teammates at Hendrick Motorsports occurred when they welcomed NASCAR's most popular driver, Dale Earnhardt, Jr., to their team for the 2008 season. Often perceived to be rivals on the track, the two now share race strategies—along with two-time champion Jimmie Johnson.

### Summary

Jeff Gordon was a child prodigy in racing, beginning at a young age and consistently piling up wins in whatever kind of vehicle he drove. Strongly supported by his family, he was able to concentrate on racing throughout his childhood so that by the time he was a young man, he was already a champion. As Jeff's career flourished, he helped to make NASCAR racing a mainstream sport. He was able to move outside the sport by developing charities and even selling his own wine. Jeff became one of the most admired and successful drivers in NASCAR history.

*Eleanor B. Amico, updated by P. Huston Ladner*

of 2008, he had won four Cup titles, in 1995, 1997, 1998, and 2001. He finished second overall twice.

Jeff focused on more than just racing. In 1996, he was awarded the True Value man of the year for his charitable contributions. He supported several charities, including Kids and the Hood, the National Marrow Foundation, and Cure 2000, which all worked toward combating leukemia—a disease fought and conquered by Hendrick. Jeff also contributed to the Starlight Foundation and Make-A-Wish Foundation, which help to brighten the lives of seriously ill children.

In 1999, Jeff established the Jeff Gordon Foundation, which aimed to help children with chronic or life-threatening ailments. He also developed the Jeff Gordon Children's Hospital, part of the Carolinas Medical Center.

As Jeff's stature grew, details about his personal life became more widely known. In 2002, his divorce from Brooke made headlines—as did his engagement and subsequent marriage to Ingrid Vande-

### Additional Sources

Anderson, L. "Fired Up." *Sports Illustrated* 108, no.7 (February 18, 2008): 72-78.

Cain, Anthony B. *Jeff Gordon*. Chanhassen, Minn.: Child's World, 1999.

Gordon, Jeff, and Steve Eubanks. *Jeff Gordon: Racing Back to the Front—My Memoir.* New York: Atria Books, 2003.

Powell, Phelan. *Jeff Gordon*. Childs, Md.: Mitchell Lane, 2000.

Savage, Jeff. *Jeff Gordon: Racing's Superstar.* Minneapolis: Lerner, 2000.

Steenkamer, Paul. *Jeff Gordon: Star Race Car Driver.* Springfield, N.J.: Enslow, 1999.

# *Royce Gracie*

**Born:** December 12, 1966
        Rio de Janeiro, Brazil

## Early Life

Royce Gracie was born on December 12, 1966, in Rio de Janeiro, Brazil. Royce (pronounced "Hoyce") was one of nine children, including eight boys. Royce's father Helio and uncle Carlos Gracie are regarded by many as the creators of Brazilian or "Gracie" jiujitsu. As an amateur in Brazil, Royce began competing in jiujitsu tournaments at the age of eight and compiled a record of 51-3. Royce earned his blue belt in jiujitsu at the age of sixteen and his black belt before his eighteenth birthday. Along with his father and his uncle, Royce's older brothers Rorion, Relson, and Rickson were all instrumental in teaching Royce jiujitsu.

## The Road to Excellence

In 1985, while still a teenager, Royce moved to the United States on an invitation from his brother Rorion to babysit his brother's children. Having been taught jiujitsu since birth, Royce also helped

*Royce Gracie.* (Kevin Terrell/WireImage/Getty Images)

his brother teach the martial art from Rorion's garage.

On November 12, 1993, Rorion and business executive Art Davie created the first Ultimate Fighting Championship (UFC) tournament, which was an eight-man single-elimination event with no weight classes, no gloves, no time limits, and few rules other than the prohibition of biting and eye-gouging. For the Gracies, the UFC provided an opportunity to show how different styles of martial arts fared against each other.

Royce was chosen to participate in the tournament and to represent the art of Brazilian jiujitsu for the Gracie family. At the time, Royce was twenty-six years old and weighed 176 pounds. He and his family viewed the tournament as a means of showing the capabilities of Gracie jiujitsu to the entire world.

During the tournament, Royce defeated three opponents on the same night. After having already defeated two challengers, Royce advanced to the final bout of the tournament, in which he defeated French savate (a type of boxing) champion Gerard Gordeau by a rear choke submission, even though Gordeau outweighed Royce by 40 pounds. Royce's victory in this inaugural tournament illustrated the egalitarianism of mixed martial arts. Royce showed that traditional, strike-oriented martial artists underestimated the importance of grappling. His win over the championship kick-boxer Gordeau helped to support his argument that an experienced ground fighter could beat an experienced stand-up fighter.

## The Emerging Champion

After UFC 1, Royce won two additional UFC titles in UFC 2 and UFC 4 and became the first man in UFC history to successfully defeat four opponents in one night. At UFC 5, time limits were introduced, and Royce fought to a draw with Ken Shamrock in a thirty-five-minute bout. This was Royce's last UFC fight until 2006.

One of the most famous of Royce's fights actually ended in a loss. After leaving the UFC and joining the Japanese Pride Fighting Championships (PRIDE), Royce fought former amateur and professional wrestler Kazushi Sakuraba in PRIDE's Grand Prix tournament. In the match between Royce and Sakuraba, Royce could no longer continue and had his brother throw in the towel after 90 minutes of fighting. At the end of the longest bout in mixed-martial-arts history, Royce could no longer stand and had endured a broken femur.

In November, 2003, Royce and Shamrock were the first fighters to be inducted into the UFC Hall of Fame. On New Year's Eve in 2004, in a K-1 fight, Royce faced his largest opponent: sumo Grand Champion Akebono, who was 6 feet 8 inches and 486 pounds. Royce defeated Akebono in only 2 minutes 13 seconds with a shoulder lock. Royce considered this victory to be one of his most impressive in his career. He showed that leverage and the right technique were more valuable assets than size.

In 2006, Royce returned to the UFC to face Matt Hughes, the welterweight champion of the time. Hughes defeated Royce by technical knockout in the first round. In 2008, Royce had a much awaited rematch with Sakuraba and won by a unanimous judge's decision in the K-1/Elite XC "Dynamite" card. However, after the fight, the California State Athletic Commission revealed that Royce had tested positive for Nandrolone, an anabolic steroid. Because of the commission's rules at the time, though, the win was not overturned.

## Continuing the Story

Royce has established more than fifty Gracie Jiujitsu Network affiliate schools in the United States and in such countries as Israel, Canada, Japan, and the United Kingdom.

In addition to teaching jiujitsu, Royce also taught a vast array of reality-based, hand-to-hand combat techniques to private individuals and organizations such as the Central Intelligence Agency, the Federal Bureau of Investigation, the Drug Enforcement Administration, the Secret Service, Army Rangers, Army Special Forces, Navy SEALs, and many sheriff and police departments. Royce's main focus in his training within these organiza-

### Mixed Martial Arts Victories

| Date | Opponent | Competition |
|---|---|---|
| Nov. 12, 1993 | Gerard Gordeau | UFC 1 |
| | Ken Shamrock | UFC 1 |
| | Art Jimmerson | UFC 1 |
| Mar. 11, 1994 | Patrick Smith | UFC 2 |
| | Remco Pardoel | UFC 2 |
| | Jason Delucia | UFC 2 |
| | Minoki Ichihara | UFC 2 |
| Sept. 9, 1994 | Leopoldo | UFC 3 |
| Dec. 16, 1994 | Dan Severn | UFC 4 |
| | Keith Hackney | UFC 4 |
| | Ron van Clief | UFC 4 |
| Jan. 30, 2000 | Nobuhiko Takada | PRIDE Grand Prix 2000 |
| Dec. 31, 2004 | Akebono | K-1 Premium/Dynamite |
| June 2, 2007 | Kazushi Sakuraba | K-1/Dynamite |

tions was to help officers develop skills needed when they were engaged in physical confrontations that ended up on the ground without weapons. In addition to large organizations, Royce privately trained celebrities such as Chuck Norris, Guy Ritchie, and Nicholas Cage. Royce settled in Torrance, California, with his wife, Marianne, and three sons, Khonry, Khor, and Kheydon.

## Summary

In 1993, when Royce Gracie entered "the Octagon," the mixed-martial-arts ring, and won the first UFC tournament, martial arts in the United States changed forever. Royce introduced the power and effectiveness of his father Helio's style of Brazilian jiujitsu to a new generation of mixed martial artists across the world.

*Ryan K. Williams*

## Additional Sources

Gracie, Royce, and Charles Gracie. *Brazilian Jiujitsu: Street Self-Defense Techniques.* Montpelier, Vt.: Invisible Cities Press, 2002.

Krauss, Erich, and Bret Aita. *Brawl: A Behind-the-Scenes Look at Mixed Martial Arts Competition.* Toronto: ECW Press, 2002.

Peligro, Kid. *The Gracie Way: An Illustrated History of the World's Greatest Martial Arts Family.* Montpelier, Vt.: Invisible Cities Press, 2003.

Wall, Jeremy. *UFC's Ultimate Warriors: The Top Ten.* Toronto: ECW Press, 2005.

# *Dan Gurney*

**Born:** April 13, 1931
      Port Jefferson, New York
**Also known as:** Daniel Sexton Gurney (full
   name)

## Early Life

Daniel Sexton Gurney was born on April 13, 1931, in Port Jefferson, New York, a small suburban community on the north shore of Long Island. Dan's father was a professional opera singer who sang for a number of years at the Metropolitan Opera in New York. In 1948, shortly after Dan graduated from Manhasset High School, his parents relocated to Riverside, California, settling near the famous Riverside Raceway that was to become Dan's "home" racetrack for years to come. Soon after arriving, Dan enrolled in Riverside Junior College.

As a teenager, Dan found the wide-open desert near Riverside ideal for hot-rod racing, a passion he shared with his high school friends. After high school, Dan attended Menlo College near San Francisco, where he studied liberal arts. Later, he joined the Army and served part of his enlistment in Korea. Following his discharge from the service, he again took up the sport he learned on the desert flats near his home.

## The Road to Excellence

Driving his own Triumph TR2 sports car, Dan took part in his first real road race at Torrey Pines, California, in November, 1955, when he was twenty-four. Soon he graduated to larger, faster cars. At first he piloted a Porsche Speedster and later a Corvette, moving up quickly into the faster sports car categories on the Southern California racing circuit. Within two years, Dan raced a Ferrari to a second-place finish—after veteran driver/designer Carroll Shelby—in an event at Riverside Raceway. In the spring of 1958, he won his first important road race at Palm Springs. In June of that same year, Dan went to Europe to try his hand at international competition.

Teaming up with fellow Californian Bruce Kessler, he entered a three-liter Ferrari in the twenty-four-hour endurance race at Le Mans, France. In such events, each driver races approximately twelve hours in installments of two or more hours. Weather conditions were poor throughout the race; Kessler lost control of the car, and the team was unable to finish. Dan suffered a similar disappointment two weeks later in the twelve-hour event at Reims, France, when his teammate, Andrew Pilette, flipped their Ferrari coupé, resulting in another forfeit for the young American. Neverthe-

American race-car driver Dan Gurney, who competed in Formula One and NASCAR. (Courtesy of Amateur Athletic Foundation of Los Angeles)

## Sports Car, NASCAR, and Other Victories

| | |
|---|---|
| 1962 | Daytona Continental |
| 1962, 1964 | French Grand Prix |
| 1963-66, 1968 | Winston Western 500 |
| 1964 | Mexican Grand Prix |
| 1966 | Can-Am Challenge Cup Race (Bridgehampton Race Circuit) |
| 1967 | Le Mans Grand Prix d'Endurance Cochampion |
| | Race of Champions Champion Driver |
| | Belgian Grand Prix |
| 1968 | Manufacturer's World Championship |
| 1970 | Can-Am Challenge Cup Race (Mosport Park) |
| | Can-Am Challenge Cup Race (Mont-Treblant Circuit) |

less, it was apparent to racing insiders that Dan was a driver to watch. When he went to Europe in the spring of 1959, Dan arrived as a member of the Ferrari sports car team. In mid-season, however, he switched from sports cars to Formula One machines, and by the end of his first Grand Prix racing season, he had placed seventh in the World Championship of Drivers standings.

### The Emerging Champion

Dan continued to divide his racing time between the United States and the international circuits and to drive both Formula and sports cars. Dan's best year on the World Championship of Drivers circuit was 1961. Driving a Porsche Formula racer, he drove to second-place finishes in the French, Italian, and U.S. Grand Prix, and ultimately placed second overall—his career best—in the championship standings. The 1962 French Grand Prix at Rouen was to be his first—and Porsche's only—Formula One victory. He placed fifth in the overall standings in both 1962 and 1963.

Back in the United States, Dan was quickly becoming one of the most popular drivers of both stock cars and Indianapolis-style racers. His preeminence on the stock car circuit was demonstrated by his victories in 1963, 1964, 1965, 1966, and 1968 at the Winston Western 500. His involvement with Indianapolis in the early 1960's revealed Dan's deep and continuing interest in automobile design and construction. After seeing the effectiveness of rear-engine Formula One cars, Dan was convinced

that a rear-engine design might be effective against the front-engine Offenhauser racers that had dominated Indianapolis for years. He invited English designer Colin Chapman, of Lotus, to the 1963 Indy and met with executives from Ford. From those meetings, the idea for a Ford-powered, Lotus-designed Indianapolis racing car was born. Between 1965 and 1973, rear-engine cars powered by Ford won the Indianapolis 500 five times.

### Continuing the Story

Dan's interest in a winning car design did not stop there, however. In 1964, at the age of thirty-three, Dan teamed with Carroll Shelby to form All-American Racers, a manufacturing firm whose first product was the rear-engine, Gurney-built Eagle. This Indianapolis car was the first in a long line of competitive machines. At the 1968 Indianapolis race, Eagles finished first, second—with Dan driving—and fourth. Later, at the 1973 Indianapolis 500, twenty-one of the thirty-three cars in the starting lineup were Eagles, including the winner.

Dan continued to race competitively in Europe over the next few years. Teamed with Indy veteran A. J. Foyt, Dan won the 1967 Le Mans endurance race. A week later, in Spa, Belgium, Dan made racing history by becoming only the second American to drive an American-built car, his own V-12 Eagle, to victory in a European Grand Prix. Also, Dan's victory at Spa had been the fastest Grand Prix to that point. He finished the year in eighth position in the international World Drivers standings. That year, Dan became the first driver ever to capture championship victories in all four major racing categories: Formula One, sports cars, Indianapolis-type cars, and stock cars.

In 1968, he gave up Formula One racing to concentrate on stock cars and Indianapolis-style racing. In both that year and the next, he drove to second-place finishes at Indianapolis. In 1970, af-

## Honors, Awards, and Records

| | |
|---|---|
| 1967 | First driver to win championship races in every major racing category |
| 1988 | Inducted into Indianapolis Motor Speedway Hall of Fame |
| 1990 | Inducted into International Motor Sports Hall of Fame |
| 1991 | Inducted into Motorsports Hall of Fame of America |

ter a season that brought him a third-place finish at Indy and a number of victories on the sports car circuit, Dan announced his retirement from professional racing.

## Summary

Dan Gurney continued to design and develop a number of prototype racing machines, including the Toyota-powered Eagle HF89, a car designed for the international sports car circuit. Thoughtful, articulate, and farsighted, Dan was a true renaissance man of racing. His reputation will endure as an innovative designer and as possibly the finest all-around driver in racing history.

*Tony Abbott*

## Additional Sources

Considine, Tim. "The House That Dan Built." *Road and Track* 56, no. 1 (September, 2004): 128.

Ienatsch, N. "RideCraft: Dan Gurney's Two-Wheel Survival Tips." *Cycle World* 45, no. 8 (August, 2006): 72-74.

Kirby, Gordon. *Dan Gurney: All American Racer.* Phoenix, Ariz.: David Bull, 2006.

Ludvigsen, Karl E. *Dan Gurney: The Ultimate Racer.* Newbury Park, Calif.: Haynes North America, 2000.

Zimmerman, John. *Dan Gurney's Eagle Racing Cars: The Technical History of the Machines from All-American Racers.* Sparkford, Somerset, England: Haynes, 2007.

# Janet Guthrie

**Born:** March 7, 1938
      Iowa City, Iowa
**Also known as:** Janet the First

### Early Life

Janet Guthrie was born on March 7, 1938, in Iowa City, Iowa. Her father was then an operator at a local airport but later in his work career became an Eastern Airlines captain and moved his family to Miami, Florida. Janet took after her father in many ways. Like him, Janet was a hard worker and was always motivated by challenges. She also inherited her father's fascination with flying.

At the age of thirteen, Janet began flying lessons. In only three years, after reaching the legal age, she got her official pilot's license. By age nineteen, she had also obtained a commercial pilot's license.

### The Road to Excellence

Janet continued to fly while attending the University of Michigan. After graduating with a degree in

*Janet Guthrie, who, in 1977, became the first woman to race in the Indianapolis 500. (SCCA)*

physics, she began her first job as a technical editor. With her first year's salary, Janet bought herself a sports car, a Jaguar XK 120 coupe.

Janet knew little about cars or about driving, so she enrolled in a touring school. Gordon McKenzie, one of her instructors, was immediately impressed by her skillful handling of the car and suggested that she try auto racing.

The next year, Janet enrolled at a race car drivers' school in Marlboro, Maryland, officially sponsored by the Sports Car Club of America (SCCA). Janet also moved up to a Jaguar XK 140, a better-quality racing car. She learned to tear down and reassemble the engine of her XK 140.

Janet's first season as an auto racer was in 1964, when she entered thirteen races. Her best performance was in a six-hour endurance race at Watkins Glen in New Jersey. Against excellent competition, Janet came in fifth place overall and second place in her auto class.

However, racing was not Janet's only interest during this time. She also aspired to be one of the first women astronauts. Because she was both a pilot and a physicist, Janet seemed to have a good chance at making this dream come true. In 1965, at the age of twenty-seven, she was one of only four women to pass the National Aeronautics and Space Administration's preliminary tests for their scientist-astronaut program, but she was never selected for the program.

### The Emerging Champion

Over the next decade, Janet entered many SCCA-sponsored competitions across the United States, also racing as a member of an all-female team sponsored by Macmillan Ring Free Oil. She won races in many different kinds of cars, such as Mustangs and Chevrolets. Her most impressive wins were in the under-two-liter prototype class at Sebring, Florida, and in the B sedan class in the 1973 North Atlantic Road Racing Championship.

In 1976, at the age of thirty-eight, Janet made sports history by becoming the first woman to earn the right to compete in the qualifying rounds of the Indianapolis 500. She won qualifying rights for this

## Major Championships

| | |
|---|---|
| 1964 | Watkins Glen Six-Hour Race overall sixth-place finisher (sports cars) |
| 1964-65 | Watkins Glen Six-Hour Race, finishing second in her class (sports cars) |
| 1970 | Sebring Under Two-Litre Prototype Champion |
| 1973 | North Atlantic Road Racing B Sedan Champion |
| 1976 | World 600 fifteenth-place finisher |
| 1978 | Indianapolis 500 ninth-place finisher |

prestigious auto race by passing the "rookie test," which involved racing twenty laps at the Indianapolis Speedway under the careful scrutiny of four veteran United States Auto Club drivers. Janet passed with honors.

In 1977, Janet raced in the Indianapolis 500 in a green, turbocharged, Offenhauser-powered car sponsored by Bryant Heating and Cooling. She did not do as well in the race as she had hoped, but she established a reputation as a skillful driver among the majority of the racers and the 450,000 spectators. Her performance also impressed Rolla Vollstedt, an independent car designer and builder, who asked Janet to join his racing team.

### Continuing the Story

Not everyone appreciated Janet's love for auto racing. Janet was criticized by some as a publicity seeker, and others suggested that women simply did not have the strength to compete in the grueling sport of auto racing. Janet, standing at 5 feet 9 inches and weighing 135 pounds, answered these critics by saying, "I drive the car, I don't carry it."

Janet acknowledged that racing was difficult to break into, but she was not the only woman who succeeded in this male-dominated sport. She said many times that auto racing "depends more on reflexes and planning than it does on physical strength." The sport also demands concentration, emotional detachment, good judgment, commitment, and intense desire. These are all qualities that both men and women share.

Janet also understood the risks of auto racing. During her career, she saw many spectacular accidents but was fortunate never to have one herself. She always knew that she could be hurt while competing for the flag, but she insisted that auto racing was less dangerous than sports such as football.

Janet continued to race for several years after her Indianapolis debut. She was dubbed "Janet the First" by the media because she was the first woman to compete in many of the major auto races in the United States. She was highly sought after for public appearances and speaking engagements, but, because racing was her real love, Janet never let these engagements conflict with a race. In fact, each speaking contract contained a cancellation clause in case she got an opportunity to race.

Janet retired to New York City to work full time as a physicist. However, in her spare time she worked on car engines and continued to enjoy driving sports cars. In 2005, she published an autobiography. The following year, she was inducted into the International Motorsports Hall of Fame.

### Summary

Janet Guthrie won her place in sports history as the first American woman to compete successfully in the traditionally male sport of auto racing. She is best known for her 1977 and 1978 appearances in the Indianapolis 500, one of the most prestigious and competitive of all auto races. Janet always thrived on challenges. She was an auto racer, a pilot, and a parachutist and nearly became one of the first women astronauts.

*Kathleen Tritschler*

### Additional Sources

Guthrie, Janet. *Janet Guthrie: A Life at Full Throttle.* Wilmington, Del.: Sport Media, 2005.

Poole, David, and James McLaurin. *NASCAR Essential: Everything You Need to Know to Be a Real Fan!* Chicago: Triumph Books, 2007.

Reed, Terry. *Indy: The Race and Ritual of the Indianapolis 500.* Washington, D.C.: Potomac Books, 2005.

## Records

First woman to compete in the World 600 (1976)
First woman to compete in the Daytona 500 (1977)
First woman to qualify for and compete in the Indianapolis 500 (1977)
First woman to complete the Indianapolis 500, finishing ninth (1978)

## Honors and Awards

| | |
|---|---|
| 1976 | World 600 Rookie of the Year |
| 1980 | Inducted into Sudafed International Women's Sports Hall of Fame |
| 2006 | Inducted into International Motorsports Hall of Fame |

# Mika Häkkinen

**Born:** September 28, 1968
    Martinlaakso, Vantaa, near Helsinki,
      Finland
**Also known as:** Mika Pauli Häkkinen (full name);
    the Flying Finn; the Ice Man

### Early Life

Mika Häkkinen was born September 28, 1968, in Martinlaakso, a town near Helsinki, the capital of Finland. His parents, Harri and Aila, had one other child, a daughter, Nina. Like many race-car drivers, Mika began driving go-karts at a young age. He competed in his first kart race when he was only five years old. Harri Häkkinen recognized his son's talent and soon took a second job to help pay for the cost of renting go-karts.

In 1975, when Mika was seven, he won a go-kart race for the first time. Eventually, the Häkkinens purchased a kart for 1,000 Finnish marks (approximately $300) from a famous Finnish rally driver, Henry Toivonen. With his own kart, Mika began winning consistently. Racing in the FK 85cc Mini class, Mika won the Keimola Regional Karting Championship in both 1978 and 1979.

### The Road to Excellence

Over the next decade, Mika built a reputation as a talented driver, working his way up the automobile-racing hierarchy until he reached what many fans consider to be the top of open-wheel racing: Formula One. Open-wheel race cars, such as the cars raced at the Indianapolis 500, do not have fenders. Unlike the Indianapolis 500, which is run on an oval track, Formula One Grand Prix races are road races. The courses include both right and left turns as well as changes in grade. Formula One racing is more popular in Europe than in the United States, but Formula One races are held all over the world.

In 1991, Mika qualified as a Formula One driver and began driving for the Lotus-Judd team at the U.S. Grand Prix in Phoenix, Arizona. He did not have an auspicious beginning: His car's engine broke down, and he could not complete the race. His highest finish during his first Formula One season came at Imola, Italy; he placed fifth.

Mika's standing improved during his second season. He finished fourth in two races and climbed to eighth in championship points. His manager, Keke Rosberg, a former auto-racing champion and fellow Finn, negotiated a contract with the McLaren team for 1993. Despite the steady improvement in his performance as a Formula One driver during the preceding two years, Mika had to earn the right to be one of McLaren's two starting drivers. McLaren hired a more experienced starting driver, Michael Andretti from the Indy Car series, while using Mika as a test driver. Andretti's performance proved disappointing, however, and Mika took over as a starting driver for the final three races of 1993. The best finish of Mika's Formula One career up to that point, a third place, came in the final race of the year, the Japanese Grand Prix.

The next few years with McLaren proved difficult for Mika. In 1994, the team experienced reliability problems with its Peugeot engines. Mika failed to win any races, although he did finish second once and third five times. He ended the season in fourth place overall in championship points. In 1995, McLaren changed to a Mercedes-Benz engine and made changes in chassis design. The team continued to struggle to solve reliability and handling problems, and Mika slipped to seventh in championship points.

In November, 1995, during the final race of the season, Mika was in a serious accident. A rear tire blew out during the Grand Prix race in Adelaide, Australia, sending the McLaren car into the barricades. When rescuers reached the crash scene, Mika was unconscious and not breathing; he suffered severe head trauma and was comatose. Doctors feared he might not survive, let alone race again, but by February, 1996, Mika was back behind the wheel of a McLaren car.

As the 1996 season progressed, Mika's standing climbed in the championship ratings. He finished the year with 31 points and a fifth-place rating. However, Mika did not achieve his first Formula One victory until the end of the 1997 season, in a race at Jerez, Spain.

## The Emerging Champion

The McLaren team started the 1998 season well. The problems that had plagued McLaren and Mika during the previous seasons were gone; the car was fast and handled smoothly. Although Mika was known for signing autographs as "The Flying Finn," his composure and control while racing earned him the nickname "The Ice Man" among fellow drivers.

By the close of the racing season, Mika had qualified to start in the pole position nine times and had won eight races, including the Monaco Grand Prix in Monte Carlo. Nonetheless, the battle between Mika and rival driver Michael Schumacher for the world championship remained tight until the final race of the year. In that race, Schumacher got off to a poor start, from which he never recovered, making Mika's victory look easy. Finns greeted the news of Mika's Formula One championship with enthusiasm. The government issued a postage stamp in his honor, without the knowledge that Mika would repeat as the Formula One world champion the following year.

### Formula One and Other Finishes

| Year | Series | Place |
| --- | --- | --- |
| 1978-79 | Keimola Regional Karting Championship | |
| 1980 | Lapland Karting Championship | 4th |
| 1981 | Finnish Karting Championship | 1st |
| 1982 | Ronnie Peterson Memorial Championship | 1st |
| | Finnish Karting Championship (F-mini series) | 2d |
| 1983 | Finnish Karting Championship (FN series) | 1st |
| 1984 | Finnish Karting Championship (FA series) | 1st |
| 1985 | Finnish Karting Championship (FA series) | 1st |
| 1986 | Finnish Karting Championship (FA series) | 1st |
| 1987 | Finnish, Swedish, and Nordic Countries Formula Ford Championships | 1st |
| 1988 | GM Opel Lotus Euroseries | 1st |
| | British GM-Vauxhall Lotus | 2d |
| 1989 | British Formula Three | 7th |
| | Brands Hatch Cellnet Superprix | 1st |
| 1990 | British Formula Three | 1st |
| 1991 | World Formula One | 15th |
| 1992 | World Formula One | 8th |
| 1993 | World Formula One | 15th |
| 1994 | World Formula One | 4th |
| 1995 | World Formula One | 7th |
| 1996 | World Formula One | 5th |
| 1997 | World Formula One | 5th |
| 1998 | World Formula One | 1st |
| 1999 | World Formula One | 1st |
| 2000 | World Formula One | 2d |
| 2001 | World Formula One | 5th |
| 2005 | Deutsche Tourenwagen Masters (DTM, German Touring Car Masters) | 5th |
| 2006 | Deutsche Tourenwagen Masters (DTM, German Touring Car Masters) | 6th |
| 2007 | Deutsche Tourenwagen Masters (DTM, German Touring Car Masters) | 8th |

## Continuing the Story

Although Mika enjoyed two incredible years of racing success, in the 2000 season, he finished second behind Schumacher. Mika won the Spanish Grand Prix for the third year in a row, but rumors spread that he planned to retire at the end of the year. In interviews, he admitted that as he grew older the possibility of accidents weighed more heavily on his mind. Still, he insisted that he planned to continue participating in Formula One races for at least another two years.

In 2001, Mika had another disappointing season; he finished fifth in championship points. When the season ended, Mika decided to take a break from racing. As time passed, his sabbatical looked more and more like retirement from Formula One. However, in 2005, Mika returned to automobile racing as a driver for Mercedes-Benz in the Deutsche Tourenwagen Masters (DTM) series. Success eluded Mika; each year he drove, he finished lower in the championship points than the previous season. In November, 2007, after three seasons in DTM, Mika formally announced his retirement from professional motorsports.

## Summary

Mika Häkkinen enjoyed a long racing career. Although his most notable years in auto racing were from 1997 to 2000, his career began twenty-five years before he won his first world championship. Achieving success as a race-car driver took decades of hard work and determination. After his retirement as a driver, he remained active in the sport as a consultant and a commentator.

*Nancy Farm Männikkö*

## Additional Sources

Boccafogli, Robert, and Bryn Williams. *Formula One: 1999 World Championship Yearbook, Behind the Scenes World Championship Photographic Review.* New York: Voyageur Press, 1999.

Glick, Shav. "Nothing Retiring About Hakkinen at Indy." *Los Angeles Times,* October 1, 2001, p. D1.

Hilton, Christopher. *Mika Häkkinen: Doing What Comes Naturally.* Newbury Park, Calif.: Haynes, 1997.

Rendall, Ivan. *The Power Game: The History of Formula One and the World Championship.* New York: Cassell, 2000.

# Lewis Hamilton

**Born:** January 7, 1985
     Stevenage, Hertfordshire, England
**Also known as:** Lewis Carl Davidson Hamilton
     (full name)

### Early Life

Lewis Carl Davidson Hamilton was born into a mixed-race family: His mother's side was Caucasian, and his father's side was Caribbean of African descent. His father, Anthony, was an information technology manager. Lewis was named after legendary American sprinter, Carl Lewis. His parents split when he was only two years old. For a while, he lived with his mother, Carmen, and two half-sisters. However, Lewis rejoined his father after the latter remarried.

Lewis Hamilton, who was the Formula One champion in 2008. (Gero Breloer/dpa/Landov)

Lewis went to a local Catholic secondary school (the British equivalent of high school), where he excelled in sports, representing his school in soccer and cricket. However, from an early age, his real love was motor racing. When Lewis was six years old, his father gave him a radio-controlled car. A year later, he finished second in the British Radio-Controlled Cars Championship, competing against adult drivers.

Next, Lewis's father bought him a go-kart. Lewis began competing at the age of eight and started winning immediately. When he was only ten years old, he met Ron Dennis, the chief executive officer of racing team McLaren, and told him he wanted to race for the team one day. In fact, Lewis had such a successful go-kart season in 1996-1997, that McLaren-Mercedes Benz signed him three years later for its young driver support program. Thus, Lewis gained funding, which greatly relieved the burden of financial support from his father, who often had to work three jobs at a time. Lewis became the youngest driver in the program.

### The Road to Excellence

In 1998, Lewis progressed through the junior go-kart Yamaha division and entered the Junior Intercontinental A division the next year. These quick promotions were the result of Lewis's precocious talent. In 2000, he raced in Formula A and became the European champion with the maximum number of points in the drivers' order of merit. All of this occurred while he was still a secondary school student and too young to hold a British driver's license.

In 2001, Lewis raced in the Formula Super A. Driving champion Michael Schumacher raced against Lewis and saw his potential. In 2002, Lewis finally graduated from go-karts to cars. He entered the British Formula Renault series, where he finished third overall in the winter series, despite some early crashes. The next year, he won the class title with two rounds remaining. That season, he had ten victories and was in pole position eleven times. This enabled him to advance to the Formula Three Euro Series the following year. He finished fifth overall despite a disagreement with McLaren, which dropped him temporarily.

In 2005, at the age of twenty, Lewis dominated the Formula Three Euro Series, taking the title with fifteen wins and thirteen pole positions out of a possible twenty. He was also the Monaco Formula Three support race winner of the year.

### The Emerging Champion

Lewis was moving rapidly toward the top rank of Formula One driving. However, he had to pass through the GP2 Series first. McLaren-Mercedes had taken the GP2 title in 2005 with Nico Rosberg. Lewis was promoted to Rosberg's place and emulated his results in 2006, beating another talented young driver, Nelson Piquet, Jr., the son of a famous Brazilian Formula One driver. Lewis had particularly impressive races at the Nürburgring in Germany and on his home turf of Silverstone, where his ability to overtake the competition was exemplified at the extremely difficult Beckett's Corner.

In 2006, the McLaren-Mercedes team lost its two best drivers, Juan Pablo Montoya and Kimi Räikkönen. The team recruited Fernando Alonso from Renault. Then, at the end of September, Lewis was chosen to be McLaren's second driver. This was his biggest break.

The 2007 season was Lewis's first Formula One season. Designated to be a backup to Alonso, as race followed race, he soon passed him. Lewis's Formula One debut was at the Australian Grand Prix, where he qualified in fourth pole position and finished third, thus appearing on the winners' podium, becoming only the thirteenth rookie driver to accomplish this feat. At Bahrain, Lewis gained his first front-row start, finishing second behind Felipe Massa; he repeated this finish at the

---

## Major Competitions

| Year | Series | Place |
|------|--------|-------|
| 2000 | European Formula A Championship | 1st |
| 2002 | British Formula Renault | 3d |
| 2003 | British Formula Renault | 1st |
| 2004 | Formula Three Euro Series | 5th |
| 2005 | Formula Three Euro Series | 1st |
| 2006 | GP2 | 1st |
| 2007 | Formula One | 2d |
| 2008 | Formula One | 1st |

---

Spanish Grand Prix. He took the lead in the drivers' championship and held it until near the end of the season, the youngest driver ever to lead the championship. His first outright victory in Formula One was at the Canadian Grand Prix at Montreal. He earned his second win a week later in the United States, becoming only the second person to win more than one race in a rookie season. In the end, Lewis, with four wins and nine times on the podium, finished second in the drivers' championship to Räikkönen. The result was outstanding and made Lewis a national celebrity in Britain, even though he decided to live in Switzerland to avoid undue publicity and heavy tax laws.

### Continuing the Story

Lewis's success caused a great deal of tension with fellow driver Alonso, forcing one driver to depart. In the end, Alonso went, and Lewis stayed. Finnish driver, Heikki Kovalainen replaced Alonso. Again, Lewis scored a number of early victories, including a memorable one at Hockenheim in Germany. In that race he struggled from fifth to first with only eight laps to go, overtaking Massa and Piquet, Jr. More than halfway through the season he had already scored four first-place finishes and was leading the drivers' championship again, just ahead of Räikkönen in a somewhat faster Ferrari. In October, in Shanghai, China, Lewis won the Chinese Grand Prix. In total, he won five races in the 2008 season and became the youngest driver to win the Formula One championship when he outlasted Felipe Massa of Brazil by 1 point.

### Summary

Lewis Hamilton has been compared to the great golfer Tiger Woods. Both athletes showed precocious talent in their sport and gained invaluable

---

## Honors and Awards

| | |
|------|------|
| 2003 | *Autosport* British club driver of the year |
| 2005 | Monaco Formula Three Support Race Winner of the Year |
| 2007 | *Autosport* rookie of the year |
| | Hawthorn Memorial Trophy |
| 2008 | Laureus World Breakthrough of the Year |

support from their fathers. Furthermore, the issue of ethnicity played a role in each of their careers. Both golf and motor racing have traditionally been white sports, and for a black competitor to rise to the number-one position in exclusive environments was a tremendous achievement. Early in his career, Lewis became a rich man, gaining publicity and celebrity. With his tremendous desire and talent, Lewis possessed the skill to become a legend in his sport. He was the first black driver to win the Formula One championship.

*David Barratt*

## Additional Sources

Burgt, Andrew van der. *Lewis Hamilton: A Portrait of Britain's New F1 Hero*. London: J. M. Haynes, 2007.

Hamilton, Lewis. *Lewis Hamilton: My Story*. London: Harper Sport, 2007.

Hughes, Mark. *Lewis Hamilton: The Full Story*. London: Icon Books, 2008.

Jones, Bruce. *Lewis Hamilton: The People's Champion*. London: Carlton Books, 2007.

Worrall, Frank. *Lewis Hamilton: The Biography*. London: John Blake, 2007.

# Chip Hanauer

**Born:** July 1, 1954
   Seattle, Washington
**Also known as:** Lee Edward Hanauer (full name)

### Early Life

Lee Edward "Chip" Hanauer was born on July 1, 1954, in Seattle, Washington, to Stan Hanauer, a sales manager, and Lillian Hanauer. Chip, as Lee came to be called, was the younger of two sons. When he was nine, his mother fell to her death at home. Heartbroken by Lillian's death, Stan, Chip, and his older brother Scott took refuge in one another. A few months before Lillian's death, Chip had earned the $250 needed to purchase his first racing boat. With the support of his father and brother, ten-year-old Chip finished fifth nationally in the nine-to-twelve-year-old class of junior stock hydroplanes.

### The Road to Excellence

Chip realized at a young age that he loved hydroplane racing. His father knew about the dangers associated with the sport, but he also understood Chip's desire to compete. Stan was a supportive father; he even went so far as to build Chip's early boats. As Chip got older, he advanced through the outboard racing classes and eventually began racing inboard hydroplanes, which were powered by automobile engines. When Chip was eighteen, he was given a chance to test Ernie Lauber's new 145-cubic-inch-class hydroplane, the *Little Rambler.* Lauber was an industrial-arts teacher who also built hydroplanes. He was so impressed with Chip's racing skills that he asked him to be his driver. Lauber was not disappointed with his decision. Driving *Little Rambler,* Chip went on to win the American Powerboat Association (APBA) National High Point Championship in the 145 class.

Chip did not limit his racing to only one class. At some races, he would race in as many as four different classes. There were occasions when Chip would have to change

from boat to boat without even pausing or stepping on land. In his second year with Lauber, Chip won the 145 National High Point Championship again; he also won the 98 National High Point Championship while driving Gordy Cole's boat *Thunder Chicken.*

There was more to Chip, though, than merely hydroplane racing. After high school, he went to Washington State University, where he majored in education and was an excellent student. In 1976, he graduated cum laude with a bachelor of arts degree. After graduation, Chip became a teacher of emotionally disturbed children at a junior high school in Port Townsend, Washington. However, Chip did not give up racing. In 1976, he began rac-

*Chip Hanauer after winning the Madison Regatta in 1999.* (AP/ Wide World Photos)

## Major Championships

| Year | Competition | Place |
|------|-------------|-------|
| 1977 | APBA Gold Cup | 7th |
| 1978 | APBA Gold Cup | 4th |
| 1979 | APBA Gold Cup | 3d |
| 1981 | APBA Gold Cup | 3d |
| 1982 | APBA Gold Cup | 1st |
|      | APBA National Championship | 1st |
| 1983 | APBA Gold Cup | 1st |
|      | APBA National Championship | 1st |
| 1984 | APBA Gold Cup | 1st |
| 1985 | APBA Gold Cup | 1st |
|      | APBA National Championship | 1st |
| 1986 | APBA Gold Cup | 1st |
| 1987 | APBA Gold Cup | 1st |
| 1988 | APBA Gold Cup | 1st |
| 1989 | APBA Gold Cup | 6th |
|      | APBA National Championship | 1st |
| 1990 | APBA Gold Cup | 3d |
|      | APBA National Championship | 1st |
| 1992 | APBA Gold Cup | 1st |
|      | APBA National Championship | 1st |
| 1993 | APBA Gold Cup | 1st |
|      | APBA National Championship | 1st |
| 1995 | APBA Gold Cup | 1st |
| 1999 | APBA Gold Cup | 1st |

ing unlimited class hydroplanes for Tad Dean. His first unlimited boat, *Barney Armstrong's Machine*, was old. During his high school and college years, Chip had won seven inboard national championships, but the unlimited class constituted his biggest challenge to that point.

### The Emerging Champion

Chip was a dedicated teacher, but he could not ignore his love of hydroplane racing. He may have desired to teach youth who needed special care and understanding, but racing was in his blood. In 1978, Chip decided to become a full-time hydroplane racer. Chip was hired by Bob Steil, the owner of The Squire Shop chain of clothing stores, to be the driver for The Squire Shop team. In 1979, at Ogden, Utah, Chip won his first Unlimited race, driving the Allison-powered boat *The Squire Shop* in the Golden Spike Governor's Cup race. Chip won at Ogden again in 1980, and in 1981, he won the Columbia Cup in Pasco, Washington.

There were a number of great drivers at the time with whom

Chip had to compete, but the two who stood out were the legendary Bill Muncey and Dean Chenoweth. In 1981, Muncey was killed in a racing accident when his boat flipped over backward—an accident known in powerboat racing as a "blow-over." Muncey had been a champion powerboat racer for many years. In 1982, the Atlas Van Lines team asked Chip to take Muncey's place as its driver. Chip was greatly honored to be named to succeed Muncey. Racing for Atlas allowed him to drive for one of the best teams in the sport. The boat that he piloted was powered by a Rolls-Royce airplane engine. In 1982, Chip made the most of his opportunity by winning five races, including his first American Powerboat Association (APBA) Gold Cup Championship race, which he won in dramatic come-from-behind fashion. In 1983 and 1984, he won the Gold Cup in the boat *Atlas Van Lines* again. Chip had finally established himself as the premier powerboat racer.

### Continuing the Story

In 1985, Miller Brewing Company took over sponsorship of the team. Behind the wheel of *Miller American*, Chip continued his domination of the sport, winning the Gold Cup race three times in a row from 1985 to 1987. Unlimited hydroplanes—which weigh more than 5,000 pounds—can reach speeds of 200 miles per hour during a race; the slightest miscalculation or mechanical malfunction can result in the driver's death. Skill, instinct, and sometimes sheer luck help drivers to survive the dangerous sport of hydroplane racing. Chip proved that he could control his own fears during a race and still win. He was not reckless. He took calculated chances, but he would not endanger himself or others unnecessarily. Never considered arrogant, he was always polite and somewhat shy, preferring to remain apart from the racing crowd.

After the 1990 hydroplane season, Chip felt the need for a change. Always a fan of auto racing, Chip tried his hand at the sport. In 1991, he drove in the Firestone Firehawk series and did extremely well.

## Honors and Awards

| | |
|---|---|
| 1983, 1985, 1987, 1989-90, 1992-93 | APBA Hall of Champions |
| 1995 | Inducted into Motorsports Hall of Fame |
| 2005 | Inducted into International Motorsports Hall of Fame |

However, he could not get sponsorship for a car in 1992. Chip returned to hydroplane racing somewhat reluctantly. In 1992 and 1993, Chip won the Gold Cup race piloting *Miss Budweiser.* The 1993 win was Chip's ninth Gold Cup, breaking the record held by Bill Muncey. Chip had moved ahead of one of his idols, and in so doing had set a standard that secured his place as one of the truly great drivers of all time. In1994, Chip fractured four vertebrae while warming up for the Detroit Gold Cup, but he returned to racing only three weeks later. In 1995, he became the youngest inductee to the Motorsports Hall of Fame. Two more Gold Cup victories, in 1995 and 1999, solidified his reputation as one of the most dominant and enduring champions in hydroplane racing history. He was inducted into the International Motorsports Hall of Fame in 2005.

## Summary

Chip Hanauer combined talent, courage, and instinct to succeed in the dangerous sport of hydroplane racing. He dominated his competition as few others have done, earning recognition as one of the best racers in motorsports history.

*Jeffry Jensen*

## Additional Sources

Garrity, Jerry. "Dancing with the Devil." *Car and Driver* 44, no. 12 (1999).

Williams, David D. *Hydroplane Racing in Seattle.* San Francisco: Arcadia, 2006.

# Lee Haney

**Born:** November 11, 1959
Spartanburg, South Carolina
**Also known as:** Lee Marvin Haney (full name)

## Early Life

On November 11, 1959, Lee Marvin Haney was born in Spartanburg, South Carolina. His father was a truck driver, and his mother was a homemaker. When he was twelve, his parents gave him a set of plastic dumbbells and barbells for Christmas; Lee began lifting weights four days a week.

As a teenager, Lee continued lifting weights and played football in high school. At sixteen years old, he lost the Mr. South Carolina bodybuilding contest, but the mature bodybuilders encouraged Lee to continue. He received a football scholarship to Livingstone College in Salisbury, North Carolina, but a previous ankle injury from high school made playing football too painful. Lee decided to become a professional bodybuilder. He transferred to Spartanburg Methodist College in South Carolina.

## The Road to Excellence

In 1979, at the age of nineteen, the 212-pound, 5-foot 11-inch, Lee won the Amateur Athletic Union's Teen Mr. America contest. At 218 pounds, he placed fourth in the 1980 Mr. USA contest. In 1981, Lee graduated from Spartanburg Methodist College with a degree in youth counseling. That year, he also had surgery to remove a painful cyst on his left wrist.

In 1982, Lee became firmly established as a bodybuilder. He won the National Physique Committee (NPC) Junior Nationals Championship. Months later, he won the overall and heavyweight prizes at the NPC National Bodybuilding and Fitness Championships. He also won first prize in the heavyweight division at both the International Federation of Bodybuilders (now International Federation of Bodybuilding and Fitness) (IFBB) North American Championships and the IFBB World Amateur Championships (previously known as the Mr. Universe contest).

In 1983, Lee won his first professional titles. He won the IFBB Grand Prix Las Vegas and the IFBB Night of Champions. That year, Lee also competed in the Mr. Olympia contest, an event held annually by the IFBB. Winning this competition was considered the ultimate achievement in professional bodybuilding. Although in great shape at 233 pounds, Lee placed third. He realized he needed to refine his posing routine.

## The Emerging Champion

Lee worked intensely on his presentation and posing routine and on gaining weight and building more muscle. The training proved successful, and, in 1984, in New York, Lee won his first Mr. Olympia title. A huge crowd of 5,000 attended the finals. At 243 pounds, he was impressive, with beautifully sculpted muscles, and he easily defeated the other contestants. In 1985, in Brussels, Belgium, Lee repeated as Mr. Olympia. The next year, his winning onstage presentation in Columbus, Ohio, was considered possibly the best Mr. Olympia performance ever, and Lee received a perfect score.

In 1987, in Götenborg, Sweden, Lee easily defeated all challengers to win his fourth Mr. Olympia title in a row. That year, he also won first prize at the IFBB Grand Prix Germany. In 1988, the Mr. Olympia contest, held in Los Angeles, California, was attended by more than 6,000 people. Lee won easily again, for his

---

### Titles and Championships

| | |
|---|---|
| 1979 | Teen Mr. America |
| | Amateur Athletic Union (overall winner) |
| 1982 | National Physique Committee Junior Nationals (overall winner, heavyweight winner) |
| | National Physique Committee Nationals (overall winner, heavyweight winner) |
| | International Federation of Bodybuilding World Amateur heavyweight champion |
| 1983 | International Federation of Bodybuilding Grand Prix (Las Vegas) |
| | International Federation of Bodybuilding Night of Champions |
| 1984-91 | Mr. Olympia |
| 1987 | International Federation of Bodybuilding Grand Prix (Germany) |

fifth consecutive victory. With his well-defined large muscle mass, symmetry, and separation, he seemed unbeatable.

The 1989 Mr. Olympia in Rimini, Italy, was a difficult contest, with formidable challengers such as Lee Labrada and Vince Taylor. However, Lee won a sixth consecutive Mr. Olympia, equaling a record set by Arnold Schwarzenegger, who was Mr. Olympia from 1970 to 1975. In 1990, in Chicago, Illinois, Lee, Labrada, and Shawn Ray were strong contenders, but Lee won his seventh consecutive Mr. Olympia title and thus beat Schwarzenegger's record.

## Continuing the Story

Schwarzenegger had come out of retirement in 1980 to win a seventh Mr. Olympia contest, so Schwarzenegger and Lee each had seven wins. At the 1991 contest in Orlando, Florida, Lee was determined to win his eighth. Although Lee's main challenger, Dorian Yates, was comparable in height and weight, Lee won his eighth consecutive Mr. Olympia and set a new world record. After this victory, Lee decided to retire and did not compete in 1992.

From 1982 to 1991, Lee appeared on the covers of major bodybuilding magazines, including *Flex, Muscle Mag International, Iron Man,* and *Muscle Training Illustrated.* After retirement, he continued to write articles and advice columns for magazines. In 1989, Lee had published an exercise book, *Totalee Awesome.* In 1993, he published a second book, *Ultimate Bodybuilding,* which included comprehensive advice on weight training and nutrition. He also had an educational television show called *TotaLee Fit* on the Trinity Broadcasting Network.

In 1994, Lee fulfilled a dream by establishing Harvest House, a nonprofit, forty-acre nature retreat for children of all ages and nationalities. He was appointed a member of the President's Council on Physical Fitness and Sports in December, 1998. Lee Haney's World Class Fitness Center, the official wellness clinic for Atlanta, Georgia, provided supervised weight and aerobic training and nutritional counseling for eighteen years, until it closed in 2007. Lee designed training, nutrition, and injury-rehabilitation programs for professional athletes, such as boxer Evander Holyfield, baseball player Gary Sheffield, and basketball player Shawn Bradley. Lee also created his own brand of nutritional supplements and Awesomewear fitness apparel.

## Summary

An icon in the bodybuilding industry, Lee Haney set a world record by holding the title of Mr. Olympia for eight consecutive years. Known as the black bodybuilder who surpassed Arnold Schwarzenegger's seven-title record, Lee's elegant, chiseled physique made him one of the most memorable bodybuilders ever. He also became renowned as an author, philanthropist, fitness and nutrition teacher, and television-show host.

*Alice Myers*

## Additional Sources

Barber, Marchel'le Renise. "The Black Bodybuilder Who Beat Arnold Schwarzenegger's Record." *Ebony* 46, no. 5 (March, 1991).

Haney, Lee. *Totalee Awesome: A Complete Guide to Body-Building Success.* Wellingborough, Northamptonshire, England: Stephens, 1989.

Haney, Lee, and Jim Rosenthal. *Lee Haney's Ultimate Bodybuilding Book.* New York: St. Martin's Press, 1993.

O'Connell, Jeff. "Lee Haney: Winning the Mr. Olympia Eight Times in a Row Was But an Opening Act for This Southern Ambassador of the Fitness Lifestyle." *Muscle and Fitness* 66, no. 10 (October, 2005).

# *Bill Hartack*

**Born:** December 9, 1932
  Ebensburg, Pennsylvania
**Died:** November 26, 2007
  near Freer, Texas
**Also known as:** William John Hartack, Jr. (full
  name); Willie Hartack

### Early Life
William John Hartack, Jr., was born on December 9, 1932, in Ebensburg, Pennsylvania, and grew up on a farm in Belsano, Pennsylvania. His father, William Hartack, Sr., was a Slavic immigrant from Central Europe who worked in the Pennsylvania coal mines. Bill's mother, Nancy (Rager) Hartack, was killed in an automobile accident when he was eight years old. He grew up in a strict Catholic environment with no mother and a harsh, domineering father. In school, he loved team sports but was too small to play. He was a good student and graduated at the top of his high school class. After he finished school, he planned to work at Bethlehem Steel Company, but he met a jockey's agent who arranged for Bill to work as a stable hand at a horse racing track in West Virginia. The small, handsome young man—standing about 5 feet 3 inches and weighing 112 pounds—realized that horse racing was a sport for which he was well suited.

### The Road to Excellence
Norman Corbin hired Bill as a stable hand at the Charles Town Race Track in West Virginia. His employer noticed that Bill was strong and courageous and that he was good with horses. Corbin soon made him an exercise boy, and, after two years, he decided to train Bill as a jockey. Bill's racing debut was unspectacular. He finished near last in his first two races because he forgot to wear his goggles and the dirt blinded him. He shocked some observers with his unconventional riding style, sometimes even failing to grip his mount with his knees. Whatever his technical deficiencies, his ferocious determination and his ability to concentrate soon made him a top jockey. Few jockeys equaled Bill, with his quick reflexes and his ability to control and communicate with his mount.

Bill was determined to conduct his career and his life in his own way. He cared only about winning, not about what people thought of him. He had many suspensions for various racing infractions. His terrible temper created bad relations with agents, stable owners, and the press. After he won a race, he wanted to be by himself and not be bothered for at least an hour. If he lost, his anger was uncontrollable. His difficult personality caused him to have six different agents. His obsession with winning was both his greatest strength and his greatest weakness.

### The Emerging Champion
Although Bill Hartack had to ride against some of the greatest jockeys in history, including Eddie Arcaro and Willie Shoemaker, in the 1950's, he emerged as a great champion. Bill was effective at anticipating the strategy of the other jockeys. His

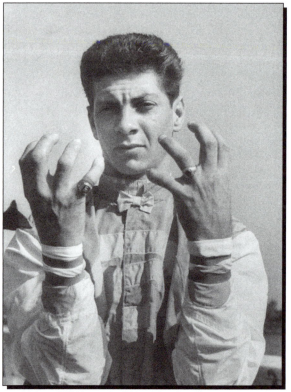

*Jockey Bill Hartack.* (Eliot Elisofon/Getty Images)

## Major Championship Victories

| Year | Race | Horse |
|------|------|-------|
| 1956 | Preakness Stakes | Fabius |
| 1957 | Kentucky Derby | Iron Liege |
| 1960 | Belmont Stakes | Celtic Ash |
|      | Kentucky Derby | Venetian Way |
| 1962 | Kentucky Derby | Decidedly |
| 1964 | Kentucky Derby | Northern Dancer |
|      | Preakness Stakes | Northern Dancer |
| 1969 | Kentucky Derby | Majestic Prince |
|      | Preakness Stakes | Majestic Prince |

incomparable reflexes allowed him to move rapidly to take advantage of openings on the track. He was physically tough and able to recover quickly from the many injuries jockeys suffer.

Bill rode 1,200 to 1,700 horses a year. In 1953, he had 328 wins, second to Willie Shoemaker. By age twenty, Bill had made enough money to buy his father a farm near Charles Town, allowing him to quit the coal mines. In 1954, Bill left Corbin and his contract was sold to Ada L. Rice, who brought Bill into the forefront of stake racing on her horse, Pet Bully. Bill worked for Mrs. Rice for about one year; in 1955, he became a freelance jockey. He teamed with agent John Charles (Chick) Lanz to form one of the most successful teams in horse racing. In 1955, Bill's busiest year, he had 417 wins. In 1956, he had 347 wins, moving ahead of Eddie Arcaro, and in 1957, he had 341 wins. He won national riding championships in 1955, 1956, 1957, and 1960. In 1957, Bill earned more than three million dollars, a record that stood until 1967. He won the Kentucky Derby five times: on Iron Liege (1957), Venetian Way (1960), Decidedly (1962), Northern Dancer (1964), and Majestic Prince (1969).

Despite his winning record, his difficult personality continued to be costly. In 1958, his high temper lost him his contract with Calumet Farms. In 1960, Bill won 307 times, but as the years passed he began to find it difficult to get mounts to ride because of his inability to keep good agents.

## Continuing the Story

Bill continued to win in the 1960's, but his record became more checkered. In 1969, he reached the peak of his career with his fifth Kentucky Derby victory, on Majestic Prince. The last time Bill rode in a Derby was 1974, when he came in eleventh on Warbucks. In the mid-1970's, as his career in the United States declined, he went to Hong Kong where he stayed for three seasons. Bill was then in his mid-forties, and he had a weight problem.

Despite the controversies that always surrounded him, Bill's skill and determination paid off financially. He won a purse total of $26,322,700. He became wealthy, able to afford a fine home in Florida, sports cars, and expensive boats. He also bought his father a farm and paid for his sister's college education. Bill was not as serious away from the racetrack—he liked to dance, swim, fish, and date women. After he retired in 1980, he worked as a racing official, acted as an ABC television commentator, and served as a technical adviser for racing movies. He died in November, 2007.

## Summary

Bill Hartack was considered arrogant, sullen, and highly emotional. He turned a good part of the horse racing world against him. He cared little about other people's opinions, nor did he care about the money; winning races was his only concern. His obsession paid off in terms of success. He won 25 percent of his races and was one of only two jockeys to win the Kentucky Derby five times.

*Martha E. Pemberton*

## Additional Sources

Brodowsky, Pamela K., and Tom Philbin. *Two Minutes to Glory: The Official History of the Kentucky Derby.* New York: Collins, 2007.

Drager, Marvin. *The Most Glorious Crown: The Story of America's Triple Crown Thoroughbreds from Sir Barton to Affirmed.* Chicago: Triumph Books, 2005.

Morgan, Bert, Eric Rachlis, and Blossom Lefcourt. *Horse Racing: The Golden Age of the Track.* Darby, Pa.: Diane, 2004.

*The Ten Best Kentucky Derbies.* Lexington, Ky.: Eclipse Press, 2005.

## Milestones

Annual money leader (1956-57)
21,309 mounts
4,250 victories

## Honors and Awards

1959   Inducted into Jockeys' Hall of Fame

# *Tony Hawk*

**Born:** May 12, 1968
     San Diego California
**Also known as:** Anthony Frank Hawk (full name)

## Early Life

Anthony "Tony" Frank Hawk was born in 1968, in San Diego, California, to Frank and Nancy Hawk. His parents were both more than forty years old when he was born and had three other children who were significantly older than Tony. At the time of Tony's birth, his two sisters, Lenore and Patricia, had already graduated from high school, and his brother, Steve, was a teenager. As a young child, Tony was extremely intelligent but not accom-

plished at any sport. He became frustrated by athletics, though he desired to compete.

After trying many different sports, Tony was given a blue fiberglass banana skateboard by his brother. Although he was not a great skateboarder when he first started, he was determined to learn to make his brother proud. Tony's father also wanted him to succeed and supported him by building several half-pipes in the family's backyard. Tony had his own ramps and half pipes to practice on every day. As Tony outgrew his backyard ramps, he spent time at the local skateparks. He said later that the local skateparks were wonderful places to work on his skills and think about life. Tony spent most of his time after school, weekends, and summers practicing his technique and developing new tricks on his skateboards.

## The Road to Excellence

At the age of twelve, Tony earned competitive sponsorship from Dogtown Skateboards. At the age of fourteen, he became a professional skateboarder. In his early years of competition, he invented some aerial skateboard tricks, including "airwalk"; "stale fish"; "gymnast plant"; "540," in which the rider spins 540 degrees while in the air; "frontside blunt"; "720," in which the rider spins 720 degrees while in the air; and many others. Later in his life, he accomplished the "900." The airwalk is a grab trick in which the skater holds the front end of the skateboard while in the air and walks a step or two. Tony won many competitions early in his career. From 1982 to 1986, he won first place in competitions from California to Vancouver, British Columbia. By the age of sixteen he was one of the best skateboarders in the world. He was doing so well in competition and earning so many endorsements that he was able to buy his own house at the age of seventeen.

## The Emerging Champion

In the late 1980's and early 1990's, competitive skateboarding became less popular than it had

*Tony Hawk, who revolutionized skateboarding in the 1980's and the 1990's. (Jamie McDonald/Getty Images)*

been previously. Therefore, in 1992, Tony started a skateboard company called Birdhouse, which sold skateboards and accessories. By 1995, Tony started competing again and won numerous gold and silver medals at the X Games from 1995 through 2003. In 1998, he started a children's skate-clothing company called Hawk Clothing. In 1999, he created the video game *Tony Hawk's Pro Skater,* which became a best seller. Also in 1999, he won best trick at the X Games. From 2000 to 2003, he won four gold medals in doubles and best-tricks categories at the X Games. During his career as a skateboarder, he competed in 103 competitions, winning 73 and placing second in 19.

## Continuing the Story

Tony retired from skateboarding competitions at the age of thirty-one after he performed the 900 at the 1999 X Games. The 900 consists of two and one-half, 900 degree, midair spins. Tony did not stop skating, he only stopped competing. In 2002, he started the "Boom Boom HuckJam" a tour that highlighted the best skateboarders, BMX riders, and motocross riders. Later, "Boom Boom Huck-Jam" became a ride at Six Flags amusements parks. Also in 2002, Tony created the Tony Hawk Foundation to assist low-income communities in the development of skateparks. In its first four years, the foundation gave away $1 million. Tony helped 336 communities build new skateparks. Furthermore, he made numerous appearances on television shows and in commercials and movies. In 2007, he released another video game.

## Summary

Tony Hawk is married with three sons and a daughter. His boys all showed interest in skateboarding.

### Milestones

Sponsored by Dogtown Skateboards at twelve

Turned professional at fourteen

Created many popular skateboard tricks (such as "airwalk," "gymnast plant," "540," "frontside blunt," and "720")

First person to perform the "900" (spinning 900 degrees in the air)

### X Games Statistics

| Year | Event | Place |
|------|-------|-------|
| 1995 | Street | Silver |
|      | Vert Singles | Gold |
| 1996 | Vert Singles | Silver |
| 1997 | Vert Singles | Gold |
|      | Vert Doubles | Gold |
| 1998 | Vert Singles | Bronze |
|      | Vert Doubles | Gold |
| 1999 | Vert Doubles | Gold |
|      | Vert, Best Trick | Gold |
|      | Vert Singles | Gold |
| 2000 | Vert Doubles | Gold |
| 2001 | Vert Doubles | Gold |
|      | Vert, Best Trick | Silver |
| 2002 | Vert Doubles | Gold |
|      | Vert, Best Trick | Bronze |
| 2003 | Vert, Best Trick | Gold |

Tony was fortunate enough to be at the forefront of an emerging sport. He put all his effort into learning the sport and developing new tricks for others to try. He proved himself through two decades of competition, and he inspired the generation of skateboarders who came after him. His love for skateboarding was exemplified through his public appearances, product endorsements, and commitment to the community. Although Tony stopped competing, his life continued to revolve around skateboarding.

*Pamela D. Doughty*

## Additional Sources

Blomquist, Christopher. *Skateboarding in the X Games.* New York: PowerKids, 2003.

Braun, Eric. *Tony Hawk.* Minneapolis: Lerner Sports, 2004.

Christopher, Matt, and Glenn Stout. *Tony Hawk.* Boston: Little Brown, 2001.

Davis, James. *Skateboarding Is Not a Crime: Fifty Years of Street Culture.* Buffalo, N.Y.: Firefly Books, 2004.

Hawk, Tony, and Sean Mortimer. *Hawk: Occupation, Skateboarder.* New York: ReganBooks, 2000.

Roberts, Michael. "The Birdman Versus the Flying Tomato." *Outside* 32, no. 2 (February, 2007): 54-59.

# *Damon Hill*

**Born:** September 17, 1960
    London, England
**Also known as:** Damon Graham Devereux Hill
    (full name)

## Early Life

Damon Graham Devereux Hill was born on September 17, 1960, in London and grew up in Shenley, England, just north of London. His father, Graham Hill, was not present at the birth but was away racing, as he would be throughout most of Damon's childhood. Young Damon was not impressed by racing: He believed that winning the Monaco Grand Prix was just his father's job. Graham Hill won Monaco five times and was Formula One world champion in 1962 and 1968, leaving an impressive legacy against which his son would often be measured. Damon's father survived his career as a race driver but was killed in the crash of his small airplane shortly after his retirement. Damon's first love was motorcycles, and he began racing them at the rather advanced age—for a professional driver—of twenty-one. In 1984, he was the champion of the track at Brands Hatch, winning forty races. His mother, Bette, urged him to switch to racing cars, however, because she considered them safer.

## The Road to Excellence

Damon's first experience racing cars, in 1983, was less than successful. He felt that racing cars was more difficult than racing motorcycles. Nevertheless, in 1984, he won his first race in a formula Ford. In 1985, he raced a full season to finish third in one series and fifth in another. That year he also tested a Formula Three car belonging to team owner

## Honors and Awards

| | |
|---|---|
| 1993-96 | Hawthorn Memorial Trophy |
| 1994, 1996 | BBC Sports Personality of the Year |
| 1997 | Order of the British Empire |
| | Blue Peter badge (British children's television show) |
| | *Sun* newspaper Sunshine Award |

Eddie Jordan, for whom he would later drive in Formula One. Attempting to be a full-time driver in Formula Three, Damon learned hard lessons about the racing business, including the dangers of his chosen profession. His prospective teammate, Bertrand Fabi, was killed in a violent testing accident, and the team then withdrew from competition. After some soul-searching following Fabi's death, Damon renewed his determination to become a successful racer.

Damon found another Formula Three team and finished ninth in the British championship in 1986, a respectable result for his first year. The following year he was fifth, and by 1988 he had worked his way up to a third-place finish. The next year he graduated to Formula 3000, beating a rival for the job because the team sponsor thought they could capitalize on Damon's famous name. In both 1989 and 1990, Damon struggled with inferior machines, but Eddie Jordan, who recognized Damon's skill, hired him for the 1991 Formula 3000 season. In another difficult year, Damon finished seventh in the championship.

## The Emerging Champion

Damon's big break came in 1991, when he was hired as test driver for the front-running Frank Williams Formula One team. In 1992, he continued the Williams testing and simultaneously drove for the financially troubled Brabham team, where he qualified in only two races. Williams's world champion driver, Nigel Mansell, chose to race Indy cars in 1993, leaving an opening, alongside three-time champion driver Alain Prost, for Damon. His experience and skill as a test driver prepared Damon for his debut season, and he often qualified well. He won three races, finishing the season in third place behind his teammate Prost and racing legend Ayrton Senna.

In 1994, Prost retired, and Damon's new teammate was Senna. The Williams cars were still the best in the field, and great things were expected. Then, in the Grand Prix of San Marino in May, Senna was killed in a high-speed crash. Under these stressful circumstances, Damon was thrust

## Formula One and Other Victories

| Year | Series | Place |
|------|--------|-------|
| 1984 | Formula Ford debut | 10th |
| 1985 | Formula Ford | (Six wins during season) |
| 1986 | British Formula Three | 9th |
| 1987 | British Formula Three | 5th |
| 1988 | British Formula Three | 3d |
|      | Formula 3000 debut | 3d |
| 1989 | Formula 3000 | — |
| 1990 | Formula 3000 | — |
| 1991 | Formula 3000 | 7th |
| 1992 | Formula One debut | — |
| 1993 | World Formula One | 3d |
| 1994 | World Formula One | 2d |
| 1995 | World Formula One | 2d |
| 1996 | World Formula One | 1st |
| 1997 | World Formula One | 12th |
| 1998 | World Formula One | 6th |
| 1999 | World Formula One | 11th |

into the position of team leader and faced the task of rebuilding the team's morale. He responded by winning the Spanish Grand Prix four weeks later. Helped by the disqualification of his chief rival Michael Schumacher in three races, Damon took the championship fight to the last race. Because of a controversial crash between the Damon and Schumacher in the Australian race, which some considered deliberate on Schumacher's part, Damon finished second in the championship behind his rival.

In 1995, Damon finished second again behind Schumacher, and the fans and press began to wonder if Damon could become champion. In 1996, however, Schumacher moved to Ferrari, whose car that year was not as competitive, and Damon's only serious competition came from his new teammate, Jacques Villeneuve, fresh from his championship-winning season in Indy cars. Damon started the year well, but a mid-season slump caused team owner Frank Williams to not renew Damon's contract for 1997. In spite of losing his job, Damon rallied and finished 1996 by winning the world championship.

### Continuing the Story

In 1997, Damon tried to bring success to the struggling, second-level team of Arrows. He surprised himself and race fans by leading the race at Hungary, finally finishing second. The rest of the season's results left him in twelfth place overall, however. The Jordan team hired Damon for the 1998 and 1999 seasons, and this position with a more competitive team provided Damon with more success. Although 1998 began poorly, three fourth-place finishes toward the end of the year and a win in the rain at Spain left him with a respectable sixth place in the championship. In 1999, he finished the year in eleventh place, while his teammate Heinz-Harald Frentzen was third after scoring two wins. Damon retired at the end of the 1999 season. After retiring, Damon stayed involved in the racing world. He cofounded the P1 International club and wrote articles for the magazine *F1 Racing*. In 2006, he became the president of the British Racing Drivers' Club.

### Summary

Many critics felt that Damon Hill lacked the natural racing talent of many of his fellow champions and that much of his success was a result of luck. One cannot reach the level of world champion wholly through good luck, though, and Damon's intelligence, emotional control, skill, and hard work left him with an excellent Formula One record of 22 wins in 115 races and earned him the world championship in 1996.

*Joseph W. Hinton*

### Additional Sources

Arron, Simon, and Mark Hughes. *The Complete Book of Formula One.* St. Paul, Minn.: Motorbooks International, 2003.

Bickerstaffe, Simon. "Under the Spotlight." *Environmental Engineering* 19, no. 3 (Autumn, 2006): 42.

Hill, Damon. *My Championship Year.* Boston: Little, Brown, 1997.

Hill, Damon, and Keith Sutton. *F1: Through the Eyes of Damon Hill—Inside the World of Formula One.* Boston: Little, Brown, 2000.

# *Lynn Hill*

**Born:** 1961
Detroit, Michigan

## Early Life

The fifth of seven children, Lynn Hill was born in Detroit, Michigan, to James Alan Hill and Suzanne Biddy Hill. The family relocated to Southern California, where Lynn grew up. As a child, Lynn was a natural athlete and excelled in both gymnastics and swimming. In 1975, when she was fourteen years old, her older sister and her sister's fiancé, Chuck Bludworth, introduced her to climbing when they invited her on a climbing trip to California's Big Rock and Joshua Tree National Park.

## The Road to Excellence

On that first trip, Lynn fell in love with the sport of climbing and began to participate in the sport regularly. Bludworth became her mentor, and by the time she was fifteen years old, Lynn was successfully climbing the smaller mountains of the Sierra Nevada range. By then, Lynn had a special talent for climbing. At 5 feet tall and barely 100 pounds, Lynn used her small frame to her advantage; it allowed her to climb and grasp rocks that larger individuals could not. When her parents divorced when she was a teenager, Lynn hid from the pain and the disruption to her life by spending more time climbing. During the early 1980's, she lived in the Yosemite Valley, located in California, with other mountain climbers and climbed every day. She particularly enjoyed "bouldering," which is a type of rock climbing performed without ropes and usually done on small cliffs or boulders. During this period, Lynn earned her bachelor of science degree in biology from the State University of New York at New Paltz.

## The Emerging Champion

In 1979, when Lynn was nineteen years old, she became the first woman to scale the

Ophir Broke in Telluride, Colorado. Throughout the 1980's, Lynn took her mountain climbing to a higher level by competing professionally on the World Cup climbing circuit. She supported herself financially by working as a rock-climbing guide and as a contestant on the television show *Survival of the Fittest.* The show, which had contestants compete physically against each other on an obstacle course, awarded a cash prize to the season's winner. Lynn, who was successful on the show, won the grand prize four consecutive years. Other television shows

*Lynn Hill.* (Tony Duffy/Getty Images)

on which she performed included *The Guinness Game, That's Incredible!*, and *Ripley's Believe It or Not.*

From 1986 through 1992, Lynn was one of the world's greatest rock climbers. She won more than thirty international climbing titles, including five at the prestigious Arco Rock Master competition, held yearly in Arco, Italy. By 1989, she had won more competitions than any other female competitor in the sport and was ranked number one internationally in women's sport climbing. On May 9 of that same year, she was injured while on a climb in Buoux, France; she fell 85 feet and broke her foot and dislocated her shoulder. In 1990, in Cimai, France, she became the first woman to successfully complete a grade 5.14 climb. In 1991, she was the first woman to climb the Mass Critique in Cimai, France. In 1992, she retired from competitive climbing.

### Continuing the Story

After retiring from the sport, Lynn continued to climb recreationally. In 1993, she became the first person ever to complete a "free" ascent—one in which the climber does not use any climbing equipment but instead, uses only hands, feet, and other body parts—on "the Nose" on El Capitan in Yosemite Valley. The climb took her four days to complete. In 1994, she completed the same climb in only twenty-three hours and by doing so set a new standard for climbing "the Nose" on El Capitan. In 1999, she completed a grade 5.13 climb of the Tête de Chou in Morocco. That same year, Lynn, as a member of an all-women expedition team, completed a grade 5.13 ascent of the 17,500 foot wall of the Tsaranoro Massif in Madagascar. In 2005, Lynn founded the Lynn Hill Climbing Camps in Eldorado Springs, Colorado, where she taught others how to climb. She continued to participate in climbing expeditions around the world.

## Climbing Milestones

| | |
|---|---|
| 1979 | Ophir Broke, Colorado (first ascent) |
| 1990 | Cimai, France (first woman to complete grade 5.14 climb) |
| 1991 | Mass Critique, Cimai (first female ascent) |
| 1992 | El Capitan, Yosemite Valley, California (first free ascent) |
| 1994 | Nose of El Capitan, Yosemite Valley (free ascent) |
| 1995 | Clodhopper Direct IV, Central Pyramid, Kyrgyzstan (first ascent) |
| | Perestroika Crack, Peak Slesova, Kyrgyzstan (first free ascent) |
| 1997 | Tête de Chou, Todra Gorge, Morocco (first ascent) |
| 1998 | Midnight Lightning, Yosemite Valley |
| | King Cobra, Yosemite Valley (first female ascent) |
| 1999 | Scarface, Smith Rocks, Terrebonne, Oregon (first female ascent) |
| | Tête de Chou, Morocco (grade 5.13 ascent) |
| | Tsaranoro Massif, Madagascar (grade 5.13 ascent) |
| 2004 | Viva la Liberdad, Vinales, Cuba, (first ascent) |
| | Sprayathon, Rifle, Colorado (first female ascent) |

### Summary

Lynn Hill achieved an enormous amount of success as a rock climber. She broke climbing records previously held by both men and women and set new records that had never been achieved by either sex. Her talent and determination as a rock climber brought the sport into the mainstream. Her accomplishments as a female climber also eradicated many of the sexist attitudes associated with the sport and made Lynn a role model for other female athletes. Even after she retired from professional competition, Lynn remained one of the best climbers in the sport.

*Bernadette Zbicki Heiney*

### Additional Sources

Hill, Lynn, and Greg Child. *Climbing Free: My Life in the Vertical World.* New York: Norton, 2002.

Horton, Ron. *Awesome Athletes.* San Diego, Calif.: Lucent Books, 2004.

Osius, Alison. "Free and Clear." *Shape* 14, no. 2 (October, 1994).

Prichard, Nancy. "The Climb of Her Life." *Women's Sports and Fitness* 19, no. 4 (May, 1997).

# Sir Edmund Hillary

**Born:** July 20, 1919
Auckland, New Zealand
**Died:** January 11, 2008
Auckland, New Zealand
**Also known as:** Edmund Percival Hillary (full name); Edmund Hillary

### Early Life

Edmund Percival Hillary was born on July 20, 1919, in Auckland, New Zealand, to Percival Augustus Hillary, a bee farmer, and Gertrude (Clark) Hillary, a schoolteacher. Edmund's education in Auckland and his work in his father's thriving apiarian business consumed most of his time while he was growing up, but a weekend trip in the winter of 1935 to Mount Ruapehu, a large New Zealand volcano, introduced Edmund to a mountain world of rock, ice, and snow that he found exhilarating. He endured two years at Auckland University College, chiefly to convince his parents that he was ill-suited to any profession requiring academic preparation. He preferred beekeeping, since it provided a life of outdoor physical labor. As he often said, he kept bees for a living and climbed mountains for fun.

### The Road to Excellence

When Edmund was twenty years old, he climbed to the top of a towering mountain in New Zealand's Southern Alps. This experience, he said, was the happiest day of his life, and it stimulated him to study mountaineering and to return periodically to the South Island's mountains to develop his climbing skills. World War II intervened, however, and, in 1943, he joined the Royal New Zealand Air Force. He served as a navigator on flying boats in the South Pacific, where he was seriously wounded. Fully recuperated after the war, he became a partner with his brother in an apiary and resumed mountain climbing.

In 1950, Edmund traveled to Europe and climbed in the Austrian and Swiss Alps; among other climbs, he made successful ascents of five peaks in the Bernese Oberland on five successive days. When he returned to New Zealand, he joined an organization planning to climb in the central Himalayas. At first, he and his companions hoped to climb Kanchenjunga, the world's third-tallest mountain. Failing to get permission for the climb, however, they settled on Mukut Parbat in the Garhwal Himalaya, the 23,760-foot summit of which Edmund and a partner reached, after arduous struggles, on July 11, 1951. This initial experience in the Himalayas taught Edmund many valuable lessons not only about high-altitude climbing but also about dealing with the Nepalese. When Edmund returned to his hotel in Ranikhet, he received a cablegram inviting him and one of his companions to join Eric Shipton, a famous Himalayan climber, on a reconnaissance of the world's tallest mountain, known as Sagarmatha in Nepal, Qomolangma in Tibet, and Everest everywhere else.

### The Emerging Champion

Before World War II, all attempts to climb Mount Everest had been made from the north, following a

*Sir Edmund Hillary.* (Library of Congress)

tortuous route from India through Tibet. After the Chinese communists invaded Tibet in 1950, the country was closed to foreigners. The purpose of the British reconnaissance expedition was to investigate the feasibility of a southern ascent of Everest. At the end of August, 1951, Edmund joined Shipton's group near the India-Nepal border. They then traveled to the Everest region and spent September and October exploring possible routes up Everest. Their explorations indicated that the Khumbu Icefall was the key to any southern attempt. This cascade of ice was created by the Khumbu Glacier's change of direction as it veered around the southern slopes of Everest. Though the ice fall presented severe dangers, Edmund concluded that it could be scaled safely.

When Shipton's group returned to Katmandu on November 17, 1951, they learned that the Nepalese had granted a Swiss team permission for an attempt on Everest in the spring of 1951. Although this news jeopardized the future plans of the Joint Himalayan Committee of the Royal Geographical Society and the Alpine Club, its members nevertheless decided to proceed with a British expedition to Everest in 1953. Part of the group's plan included a training expedition to the Himalayas in the summer of 1952. Edmund participated in this expedition, the purpose of which was to discover climbers who could function effectively in the Himalayan environment, to experiment with oxygen apparatuses, and to study physiological problems at high altitudes. In the course of the group's explorations and experimentations, Edmund climbed to within five thousand feet of the summit of Cho Oyu, the world's seventh-highest peak, and he made the first ascent of a formidable mountain pass, Nup La, from which he was able to observe Everest.

By the time the members of the Shipton expedition returned to India in June of 1952, they learned that the Swiss had failed to reach the summit of Everest but planned to try again in the autumn. Because of bad weather, this second attempt also failed, and the way was clear for the 1953 British expedition.

John Hunt, a British Army officer and mountain climber, assumed leadership of the expedition when Eric Shipton withdrew. With his army background, Colonel Hunt organized the expedition comprehensively with the care for detail of a commander planning a major military operation. By the time Hunt's party reached Nepal in March, 1953, all the members, including Edmund, were well trained and well supplied for a massive assault on the 29,028-foot mountain. Edmund helped to choose the site for the base camp on April 12, 1953. Colonel Hunt then sent him ahead to establish a route through the Khumbu Icefall. It took several weeks for Hunt's climbers, porters, and Sherpas to establish and supply a series of nine camps through the icefall and at various heights on the mountain. Climbers and porters on the upper slopes were aided by new lightweight oxygen equipment. The team established and supplied Camp IX at about a thousand feet from the summit, and Colonel Hunt chose two assault parties, the second of which was Edmund Hillary and his Sherpa partner, Tenzing Norgay. The first assault pair managed to reach Everest's South Summit at 28,700 feet and saw for the first time the final ridge leading to the top, but lack of time forced them to turn back.

Early in the morning of May 29, 1953, Edmund and Norgay set out from Camp IX, reached the South Summit at about 9:00 A.M., and finally reached the top at 11:30 A.M. Overjoyed at their success, the beekeeper and the Sherpa stayed on the peak for twenty minutes before descending. Their ascent of Everest made news around the world; several hours before she was to be crowned Queen of England, Elizabeth II learned that the British Everest Expedition had presented her with an extraordinary coronation gift. One of her first official acts as queen was to knight Sir John Hunt and Sir Edmund Hillary.

## Continuing the Story

Although the first ascent of Everest is the accomplishment for which Edmund is remembered, the

---

### Honors and Awards

| | |
|---|---|
| 1953 | Knight Commander of the Order of the British Empire |
| | Nepalese Order of the Strong Right Arms of the Gurkhas |
| | Royal Geographical Society Founder's Gold Medal |
| 1954 | American Geographical Society Cullum Geographical Medal |
| | National Geographic Society Hubbard Medal |
| 1958 | British Ministry of Defence Polar Medal |
| 1959 | Royal Society of Tasmania R. M. Johnston Memorial Medal |
| 1975 | James Wattie Award |
| 1995 | Honored with the Knight of the Order of the Garter (KG) |

exploit was not the last of his adventures. In the 1950's, he led a New Zealand expedition to the Himalayas and participated in a successful project to cross the Antarctic continent. In the 1960's, he led a series of expeditions to the Everest region, some to climb mountains and one to search for the legendary yeti—Edmund found no evidence for the creature's existence. These trips to the Himalayas heightened his concern for the people of the region, and he set up a foundation to provide them with hospitals, schools, roads, bridges, potable water, and an airfield.

During the 1970's, Edmund became aware of the tremendous damage done to the Himalayan environment by the thousands of foreign tourists and climbers who were visiting the Everest region. For example, the great demand for wood for construction and fuel was causing escalating deforestation and severe erosion of the steep slopes. Edmund supported Nepalese and United Nations advisers who were trying to develop a national park to safeguard the region's unique plant and animal life. He managed to get the New Zealand Ministry of Foreign Affairs involved; by 1975, Sagarmatha National Park was a reality, with a plan for reforestation and protection of the life of this beautiful but fragile mountain environment.

Even though helping others to an improved standard of living had become his primary concern, Edmund still found time for adventures. In 1977, he went on a jet-boat expedition up the Ganges River to establish its source in the Himalayas. As he traveled to Alaska, the Canadian Arctic, the Antarctic, Tibet, and Nepal, however, he became increasingly troubled about the environmental degradation he witnessed. Whenever he returned to the Himalayan valleys and ridges, which were pristine when he first saw them in the early 1950's, he found whole mountainsides scarred, eroded, and littered with garbage. He thus began participating in conferences on the environment and writing about his concern that human beings were abandoning their duty to the earth.

## Summary

Edmund Hillary, who with Tenzing Norgay first climbed Mount Everest, was an energetic, technically skilled, and courageous mountaineer and explorer. His many explorations all over the world convinced him that the places and people he came to love through his adventures must be vigorously protected.

*Robert J. Paradowski*

## Additional Sources

Barber, Terry. *Edmund Hillary and Tensing Norgay.* Edmonton, Alta.: Grass Roots Press, 2007.

De Porti, Andrea. *Explorers: The Most Exciting Voyages of Discovery, from the African Expeditions to the Lunar Landing.* Richmond Hill, Ont.: Firefly Books, 2005.

Fleming, Fergus, and Annabel Merullo. *The Explorer's Eye: First-Hand Accounts of Adventure and Exploration.* London: Phoenix, 2007.

Hillary, Edmund. *The View from the Summit.* London: Doubleday, 1999.

Holden, Andre. *Hillary and Everest: Fiftieth Anniversary Special.* Christchurch, Canterbury, New Zealand: The Press, 2003.

Johnston, Alexa. *Sir Edmund Hillary: An Extraordinary Life—The Authorized, Illustrated Biography.* Camberwell, Vic.: Penguin Group, 2005.

Keiser, Anne B., and Cynthia Russ Ramsey. *Sir Edmund Hillary and the People of Everest.* Kansas, Mo.: Andrews McMeel, 2003.

Unsworth, Walt. *Everest: The Mountaineering History.* 3d ed. Seattle, Wash.: The Mountaineers, 2000.

Venables, Stephen, and the Royal Geographical Society. *Everest: Summit of Achievement.* Crows Nest, N.S.W.: Allen & Unwin, 2003.

# *Bernard Hinault*

**Born:** November 14, 1954
Yffiniac, France
**Also known as:** The Badger; Le Blaireau

### Early Life
Bernard Hinault was born on November 14, 1954, in the Brittany town of Yffiniac in northern France. Bernard was raised in a simple but happy family. His father worked on the French railroads. Bernard was a keen bicyclist as a youngster. While attending the Collège de Saint-Brieuc, however, he decided to specialize in automotive engineering. Bernard seemed destined for a career as a mechanic.

In May, 1971, Bernard's destiny was dramatically altered following a victory in his first cycle race. No one witnessing this triumph could have foreseen the awesome career that was to follow. This victory inspired Bernard, and he embarked on a path from which he eventually emerged as the successor to the legendary French cyclist Jacques Anquetil.

### The Road to Excellence
In the early 1970's, Bernard competed regularly in amateur cycle races, especially in the Brittany area. In June, 1972, Bernard came into greater prominence, winning both the Junior Championship of Brittany and the French National Junior Championship. These promising displays caught the attention of Cyrille Guimard, a former professional cyclist whose career was hampered by various injuries. Guimard recognized talent and believed Bernard could go all the way to the top.

In 1974, Bernard turned professional and competed under Guimard's expert management. Guimard had a great influence on Bernard's career. He steered Bernard away from major races until Bernard had served his ap-prenticeship in the less prominent races of the professional circuit. Between 1974 and 1977, Bernard successfully competed in a variety of minor road racing competitions. In both 1975 and 1976, he was the pursuit champion of France. Then in 1977, Bernard completed his cycling education with victories in the Liège-Bastogne-Liège and Flèche-Wallonne classic road races.

Already, Bernard was dubbed the new Anquetil. Certainly no Frenchman since the "Maître" (the "master," Anquetil's nickname) had made such an impact upon cycling. Bernard even acquired his own nickname, "Le Blaireau" (the "badger"). This title was apt because, like a badger, Bernard was shy and retiring until confronted—at which point he would fight to the end. By the end of the 1977 season, Guimard was convinced that Bernard was the equal of any professional road racer. The ambitious young cyclist was ready for the bigger prizes in cycling, especially the Tour de France.

### The Emerging Champion
Bernard started the 1978 season confident that he could defeat the best road racers in the world. His

## *Major Championships*

| Year | Competition | Place |
|---|---|---|
| 1972 | Junior Championship of Brittany | 1st |
| | French National Junior Championship | 1st |
| 1975-76 | French Individual Pursuit Championship | 1st |
| 1977 | Liège-Bastogne-Liège Classic Road Race | 1st |
| | Flèche-Wallonne Classic Road Race | 1st |
| 1978 | French Road Racing Championship | 1st |
| 1978-79, 1981-82, 1985 | Tour de France | 1st |
| 1978, 1983 | Tour of Spain | 1st |
| 1979, 1984 | Tour of Lombardy | 1st |
| 1980 | World Road Championships, Professional Road Race | Gold |
| 1980, 1982, 1985 | Tour of Italy | 1st |
| 1982 | Tour of Luxembourg | 1st |
| 1986 | Tour de France | 2d |
| | Coors Classic | 1st |

confidence was vindicated by victories in the Tour of Spain and at the French Road Racing Championship. In his first season in elite competition, Bernard was setting the cycling world on fire. All that remained was the ultimate prize, the Tour de France.

Even though the 1978 Tour de France was Bernard's first, his career had been handled so astutely by Guimard that he was widely favored to win the race. The twenty-three-year-old Bernard shouldered the hopes of all of France. Not since Anquetil had a Frenchman won the Tour de France, and in the months leading up to the race public interest and expectation reached fever pitch. However, despite his relative inexperience, Bernard was confident. He was determined to win for France.

The 1978 Tour de France began in The Hague in the Netherlands, and wound its way through the Parisian suburbs and on to Bordeaux. In the early stages of the race Bernard kept a low profile, staying back in the group of riders. His position worried French onlookers. They need not have been concerned, however, for Bernard had the situation under control. Bernard made his decisive move in the eighth stage of the race, a fifty-nine-kilometer time trial. Although he failed to take the lead, Bernard demonstrated his capabilities. Following grueling climbs in the Pyrenees, Bernard had moved up to second place behind the Belgian Joseph Bruyere. After the Tour's stages in the Alps, the race came down to a head-to-head struggle between Bernard and the Dutchman Joop Zootemelk. Bernard knew he could defeat Zootemelk, and the long time trial stage that finished in Metz sealed his victory. At the end, Bernard arrived in Paris, the final stage, with a four-minute overall lead. Bernard lived up to all expectations and became the pride of France.

## Continuing the Story

The 1979 Tour de France featured Le Blaireau's triumphant return to Brittany. A stage of the race finished near Bernard's hometown, and much of Brittany came out to welcome its hero. Once again the Tour became a tussle between Bernard and Zootemelk. Although Bernard started slowly, he knew he could win the race and waited until the Alps before making his move. Zootemelk simply could not keep up and the steely Bernard won his

---

### Record

Won the Tour de France five times

### Honors and Awards

1986    Awarded the Légion d'Honneur

---

second Tour de France by a margin of more than thirteen minutes.

The year 1980 was one of triumphs and disasters for Bernard. Having won the world road racing championship, he entered the Tour de France seeking a third victory. However, Bernard was forced to retire from the race because of a knee injury. At the time of his withdrawal, he had been leading the race. The knee required surgery, but Bernard vowed to return the following year.

In the 1981 Tour de France, Bernard was again victorious; he followed up with a fourth win in 1982. Bernard was on the threshold of joining the "5" club—the members of which—Jacques Anquetil and Eddy Merckx—had won the Tour five times each. However, another Frenchman, Laurent Fignon, proved to be a thorn in Bernard's side by winning the Tour in 1983 and 1984. Bernard was back to his winning ways in 1985, however, winning a close race from American teammate Greg LeMond. Bernard had become a member of a very exclusive club.

Bernard's final year in competitive cycling was 1986. He finished second to LeMond in the Tour, after having won the King of the Mountains title. Bernard's last race victory came in the Coors Classic. He retired on his thirty-second birthday to tend to his newly acquired farm and to concentrate on his part-time posts of technical adviser to the Tour de France and consultant to a sports equipment company.

## Summary

Bernard Hinault rose from humble beginnings to become one of the greatest cyclists and one of the most popular French athletes of all time. Although he won numerous other races, Bernard was best known for his exploits in the Tour de France. In eight starts, Le Blaireau won five times, finishing second twice. This incredible record was a testament to Bernard's skill, courage, and determination, all of which elevated him to legendary status in the world of cycling.

*David L. Andrews*

## Additional Sources

Delanzy, Eric. *Inside the Tour de France: The Pictures, the Legends, and the Untold Stories of the World's Most Beloved Bicycle Race.* Emmaus, Pa.: Rodale, 2006.

Fife, Graeme. *Inside the Peloton: Riding, Winning, and Losing the Tour de France.* Edinburgh: Mainstream, 2002.

McGann, Bill, and Carol McGann. *The Story of the Tour De France.* Indianapolis, Ind.: Dog Ear, 2006.

Ollivier, Jean Paul. *The Giants of Cycling.* Boulder, Colo.: VeloPress, 2002.

Thompson, Christopher S. *The Tour de France: A Cultural History.* Berkeley: University of California Press, 2006.

# *Chris Hoy*

**Born:** March 23, 1976
    Edinburgh, Scotland
**Also known as:** Christopher Hoy (full name); the
    Real McHoy; the Hoycanator

### Early Life
On March 23, 1976, Christopher Hoy was born to David Hoy, a surveyor, and his wife Carol, a nurse. At the age of six, Chris became interested in bicycles when he watched Steven Spielberg's classic science fiction film, *E.T.: The Extra Terrestrial* (1982). Chris was fascinated with the BMX bicycle scenes in the movies. He was determined to be a bicyclist, so his mother bought him his first BMX for £5.

### The Road to Excellence
Chris became passionate about bicycling and broke the frames of his first two bicycles doing jumps from wooden planks onto bricks. At the age of seven, he became a competitive cyclist in BMX racing, which occurs on off-road racetracks. Chris's parents bought him a better bicycle, the Raleigh Super Burner BMX, which Chris rode in his races with the Danderhall Wolves, an Edinburgh club. For the next seven years, Chris was a BMX racer. When he was ten, he won his first major medal by finishing second in the BMX nationals. At the age of thirteen, he declared his ambition to become an Olympic champion.

From 1984 to 1986, Chris raced with the Scotia BMX team, affiliated with an Edinburgh bicycle shop. Chris's parents supported his cycling activities. His father served as coach, mechanic, and chauffeur. Chris and his father drove to races throughout Scotland and Britain on weekends. Each week, Chris's father dismantled and rebuilt the bike for the next race. From 1986 to 1991, Chris raced with the GT Factory BMX team, and his sponsors included Kwik-Fit and Slazenger. He competed internationally in the United States and Europe, and he became the Scottish champion, ranked first in Scotland for five years. He was ranked second in Britain, fifth in Europe, and ninth in the world.

### The Emerging Champion
Chris completed his secondary education at George Watson's College, an independent school in Edinburgh. Activities included rowing, rugby, and chess. In 1996, he began studies at the University of St. Andrews and then transferred to the University of Edinburgh. In 1999, he graduated with a degree in sports science.

Meanwhile, Chris continued racing. As the BMX craze was ending, mountain biking became

*Chris Hoy, who won three gold medals in cycling at the 2008 Olympic Games in Beijing, China.* (Martin Bernetti/Getty Images)

popular. In 1992, he joined the Dunedin Cycling Club, directed by Ray and Doreen Harris. He competed in road and track, mountain bike, and time trials. In 1994, Chris decided to focus on track cycling, which occurs in a velodrome, or sports arena with banked tracks. He joined the City of Edinburgh Racing Club, Britain's best track-racing club.

In 1996, Chris joined the Great Britain national squad; in 1997, he joined Great Britain's World Cup team. During the early years, British track cycling operated on a shoestring budget, but eventually lottery funding, long-range planning, and infrastructure development transformed British teams into world-class competitors.

Beginning in 1999, Chris won either an individual or team award each time he competed in a major event, such as the World Cup, the Track Cycling World Championships, the Commonwealth Games, and the European Track Cycling Championships. At the 2000 Olympic Games in Sydney, Australia, Chris won a silver medal in the team sprint. In 2004, at the Olympics in Athens, Greece, he won a gold medal in the men's 1-kilometer time trial and set Olympic, world, and British records.

## Continuing the Story

Chris was the Olympic Games kilometer record holder, but in 2005, the International Cycling Union (UCI) replaced the kilometer event with the keirin event in Olympic competition. The keirin is a cycling event with eight laps in which sprinters jockey for position, steadily accelerating before the final 625 meters. Chris trained intensively in the keirin and became the international Japanese keirin champion in 2007.

At the Track Cycling World Championships in Manchester, England, in March, 2008, Chris won two gold medals and a silver medal. Thus, he had

### Major Championships

| Year | Competition | Event | Place |
|---|---|---|---|
| 1999 | World Championships | Team sprint | 2d |
| 2000 | World Championships | Team sprint | 2d |
| | Olympic Games | Team sprint | Silver |
| 2001 | World Championships | Team sprint | 3d |
| 2002 | World Championships | Time trial | 1st |
| | World Championships | Team sprint | 1st |
| | Commonwealth Games | Time trial | 1st |
| | Commonwealth Games | Team sprint | 3d |
| 2003 | World Championships | Team sprint | 3d |
| 2004 | World Championships | Time trial | 1st |
| | World Championships | Team sprint | 3d |
| | Olympic Games | Time trial | Gold |
| 2005 | World Championships | Team sprint | 1st |
| | World Championships | Time trial | 3d |
| 2006 | World Championships | Time trial | 1st |
| | World Championships | Team sprint | 2d |
| | Commonwealth Games | Team sprint | 1st |
| | Commonwealth Games | Time trial | 3d |
| 2007 | World Championships | Time trial | 1st |
| | World Championships | Keirin | 1st |
| | World Championships | Team sprint | 2d |
| 2008 | World Championships | Sprint | 1st |
| | World Championships | Keirin | 1st |
| | World Championships | Team sprint | 2d |
| | Olympic Games | Sprint | Gold |
| | Olympic Games | Team sprint | Gold |
| | Olympic Games | Keirin | Gold |

won medals in ten successive Track Cycling World Championships. In April, 2008, BT, a communications provider, chose Chris to be an ambassador for the London Olympic Games in 2012. The ambassadors encourage people to become mentors, volunteers, and coaches for young athletes.

As the 2008 Beijing, China, Olympic Games began, Chris was the reigning world champion in the keirin and sprint. On the first day in the Laoshan Velodrome, Chris anchored the British sprint team. Surprisingly, the team defeated the French squad, which had been favored to win the gold medal. Chris also won gold medals in the men's keirin and the men's individual sprint. His triple-gold performance, passion for cycling, and inspirational story of hard work and perseverance firmly established his superstar status. In three Olympic Games, he had won a total of five medals.

The velodrome built in Glasgow for Scot-

### Honors and Awards

| | |
|---|---|
| 2002 | Scottish sports personality |
| 2003 | BBC Scottish sports personality of the year |
| 2003-05, 2007 | Scottish sports personality (Commonwealth Games Council) |
| 2005 | Honored as Member of the British Empire (MBE) |
| | Honorary doctorate from Edinburgh University |
| | Cyclingnews.com track cyclist of the year |
| 2007 | Glasgow Sportsperson of the Year |

land's 2014 Commonwealth Games was named in Chris's honor. Chris continued to be an ardent supporter of The Braveheart Cycling Fund, launched in 2003 to raise funds to support young Scottish cyclists.

## Summary

Chris Hoy became a world-famous cyclist and had numerous athletic achievements. He won the Track Cycling World Championships nine times. At the World Cup, he earned twenty-six gold medals, ten silver medals, and four bronze medals. Furthermore, he won the European Track Cycling Championships and the Commonwealth Games twice. With his three gold medals at the 2008 Bei-

jing Olympics, Chris became a British cycling hero, Scotland's greatest Olympian, and the most successful Olympic male cyclist of all time.

*Alice Myers*

## Additional Sources

Burnside, Anna. "Team Hoy Keeps Chris on His Bike." *The Times* (London), August 31, 2008, p. 5.

Longmore, Andrew. "Hoy Has High Hopes for New Golden Age; Olympics Countdown." *The Times* (London), August 3, 2008, p. 10.

Moore, Richard. *Heroes, Villains and Velodromes: Inside Track Cycling with Chris Hoy.* London: HarperSport, 2008.

# Miguel Indurain

**Born:** July 16, 1964
  Villava, Spain
**Also known as:** Miguel Angel Indurain Larraya
  (full name)

## Early Life

Miguel Angel Indurain Larraya was born in the small town of Villava, near Pamplona, Spain. He was the second of five children in his family, with an older sister, two younger sisters, and a younger brother. He grew up on the family farm. Persuaded by his cousins, Miguel entered his first bicycle race when he was eleven years old. He finished second in that race and first in his next. He thought he was still too young for the sport and turned his attention to soccer. Team sports, however, did not appeal to him, so he tried running and became the district champion in the 400-meter event. He returned to cycling when he was sixteen years old.

## The Road to Excellence

Soon after returning to cycling competition, Miguel competed in several low-level races a year. Few people knew of him until he won the Spanish national amateur road championship in 1983, his first major win as an amateur. At the age of nineteen, he became the leader of the Reynolds amateur team. The next year, he won two stages in the Tour de l'Avenir. Fellow cyclist Pedro Delgado commented that Miguel had everything necessary to become a great cyclist: strength, concentration, and dedication.

Miguel learned to be realistic in his goals from his first coach, Eusebio Unzue. He met Unzue in 1983 before winning the national amateur championship. With Unzue's help, he won fourteen races in 1984 and competed in the Los Angeles Olympics. His skill continued to develop under the coaching of José Echavarri. In 1985, Miguel turned professional. In that year, he led the Tour of Spain for four days, becoming the youngest cyclist ever to lead that race, and competed in his first Tour de France. In 1986, he won the Tour de l'Avenir. His victory in a mountain stage in the Alps proved his incredible strength.

In his early professional career, Miguel worked as a team rider, or domestique, supporting the team leader. He earned respect riding in the peloton, or main pack of riders, by respecting others and displaying proper cycling courtesy. At the same time, he already displayed some of the amazing strength that later would make him almost unbeatable in individual time-trial stages, in which cyclists

*Miguel Indurain, who won the Tour de France five times.* (Mike Powell/Getty Images)

## Major Championship Victories

| Year | Competition |
|---|---|
| 1983 | Spanish Amateur Road Championship |
| 1986 | Tour de l'Avenir |
| 1988, 1991-92 | Tour of Catalonia |
| 1989-90 | Paris-Nice |
| 1990 | San Sebastian Classic |
| 1991 | Tour of Vaulcluse |
| 1991-95 | Tour de France |
| 1992 | Spanish National Championship |
| 1992-93 | Tour of Italy |
| 1993 | Castilla-León Trophy |
| 1994 | Tour de L'Oise |
| 1995 | Tour of Rioja |
| | Tour of Galicia |
| | World Time Trial Championship |
| 1996 | Tour of Asturias |
| | Olympic Time Trial Championship |

ride alone against the clock. At 6 feet 2 inches and about 175 pounds, he was one of the larger competitive cyclists.

### The Emerging Champion

Miguel supported teammate Pedro Delgado for years, helping Delgado in his many victories. Echavarri and Unzue polished Miguel's skills, bringing him along slowly. In 1986, they took him to see Francesco Conconi, the medical scientist who had prepared Francesco Moser to set the world record for distance traveled in an hour. Conconi agreed that Miguel had the potential for greatness.

Miguel objected to the training regimen prescribed by Conconi, which involved losing weight while retaining muscle mass. Repeated tests showed that he had phenomenal physical capacity. His resting heart rate was only twenty-eight beats per minute, and his lungs had 30 percent greater capacity than those of the average athlete. He began to prove his potential, winning the 1989 and 1990 Paris-Nice races and the 1990 San Sebastian Classic. He competed in the Tour de France, cycling's premier event, each year, but he rode in support of Banesto team leader Delgado. In 1990, his assistance to Delgado probably cost him one of the top three positions. He ended up in tenth place. Miguel's chance came in the 1991 Tour de France,

when he was allowed to compete to be the team leader. Miguel came out on top for the Banesto team and won the race, beating Gianni Bugno by 3 minutes and 36 seconds.

### Continuing the Story

Following his first victory in the Tour de France, Miguel appeared to be unbeatable. By winning the three-week 1992 Tour of Italy by an impressive five minutes over Claudio Chiappucci, he became the favorite for that year's Tour de France. The win, and his performance in various stages, moved him to first place in the world rankings, replacing world champion Bugno. However, he remained worried by Delgado and others. He was reaching the peak in his personal as well as in his professional life, as he had become engaged to marry his girlfriend, Marisa López de Goicoechea.

The 1992 Tour de France was Miguel's seventh, and as the returning champion, he started the race wearing the traditional yellow jersey of the leader. The race began in San Sebastian with a short time trial, the prologue. Miguel, as returning champion, was the last rider to enter the course. He vowed to win the time trial, and he did, by two seconds. Later, he won the ninth stage of the race, another time trial, beating his nearest competitor by three minutes over the course of 65 kilometers. He also won the Tours-Blois individual time trial. These stage wins helped him to win his second Tour de France, defeating Claudio Chiappucci by 4 minutes and 35 seconds.

In 1993, Miguel returned to the Tour de France as the favorite. That year, he was joined on the Banesto team by his younger brother, Prudencio, who was competing in the event for the first time. Once again, Miguel won the prologue. He competed with the sprinters in the early stages, never falling far out of the lead. Miguel pulled ahead at the ninth stage, his seventh straight win of a time-trial stage. Prudencio finished the stage in last

### Record

1994   World hour record, 53.040 km

### Honors and Awards

1992   *VeloNews* International Cyclist of the Year

place, 17 minutes behind. Miguel stayed even with Switzerland's Tony Rominger on the toughest climbs of the mountain stages that followed. Rominger proved to be Miguel's main competition; he was in second place when the race concluded in Paris, 4 minutes and 59 seconds behind Miguel, who had taken his third straight victory.

Miguel admitted that he was nearing the end of his peak years, but he still had the potential to win another Tour de France or two. In 1994, he won his fourth straight Tour de France, becoming only the third man in history to do so. Even in a mountain time trial designed to beat him, his time was near the winner's.

In addition to his fourth Tour de France victory, Miguel won the Tour de l'Oise and set a world hour record of 53.040 kilometers in 1994. He showed no sign of letting up in 1995 when he won his fifth consecutive Tour de France as well as the Tour of Rioja and the Tour of Galicia. He also claimed the World Time Trial Championship.

In 1996, Miguel's incredible string of Tour de France victories came to an end. However, he remained impressive in other races, finishing first in the Tour of Asturias and winning a gold medal in the time trials during the 1996 Olympic Games in Atlanta. Having accomplished so much and want-ing to leave while he was still at the peak of his abilities, Miguel retired in 1997.

## Summary

Miguel Indurain was the first cyclist to win five consecutive Tour de France races, placing him among the pantheon of cycling's greatest riders, such as Jacques Anquetil, Eddie Merckx, and Bernard Hinault, all five-time Tour de France winners. Miguel's incredible physical capacity inspired awe and respect among his competitors, and his humility and generosity as a team rider earned him the regard of teammates as well as fans throughout Spain and Europe.

*A. J. Sobczak*

## Additional Sources

Delanzy, Eric. *Inside the Tour de France: The Pictures, the Legends, and the Untold Stories of the World's Most Beloved Bicycle Race.* Emmaus, Pa.: Rodale, 2006.

Muñoz, Pablo. *Miguel Indurain: A Life on Wheels.* Translated by Adrian Bell. Norwich, Norfolk, England: Mousehold Press, 1998.

Thompson, Christopher S. *The Tour de France: A Cultural History.* Berkeley: University of California Press, 2006.

# *Anatoly Karpov*

**Born:** May 23, 1951
      Zlatoust, Soviet Union (now in Russia)
**Also known as:** Anatoly Yevgenyevich Karpov (full name)

### Early Life

Anatoly Yevgenyevich Karpov grew up in Zlatoust, a metal fabricating center in the southern Ural Mountains, where his father was an engineer. When Anatoly was four years old, his father taught him to play chess. Anatoly loved the game; he played children and adults at every opportunity and enjoyed reading chess books at bedtime. By the age of eleven, Soviet chess authorities realized

Anatoly Karpov considering his next maneuver at the Hastings International Chess Tournament in 1972. (Popperfoto/Getty Images)

Anatoly was a chess prodigy and encouraged his development.

### The Road to Excellence

Former world champion Mikhail Botvinnik tutored Anatoly during school vacations in 1963 and 1964. When he was fifteen, Anatoly's chess victories earned him the title of Soviet master, and he began receiving monthly stipends from the Soviet sports federation; thereafter, he earned his living from chess. In 1967, he won the European Junior Championships at Groningen, Netherlands. He entered Moscow State University in 1968, winning the university championship the following year. Soviet chess authorities then sent Anatoly to the 1969 World Junior Chess Championships tournament in Stockholm, Sweden, where his victories brought him recognition as an international master. In 1970, Anatoly's success in a Caracas, Venezuela, tournament earned him the title of international grand master.

### The Emerging Champion

In 1974, the world chess organization, Fédération Internationale des Échecs (FIDE), arranged a competition to choose an official challenger for world champion Bobby Fischer. Anatoly won by decisively defeating Lev Polugaevsky in the quarterfinals and Boris Spassky, the 1969-1972 world champion, in the semifinals and narrowly edging Victor Korchnoi in the final round. When FIDE rejected his demands concerning the structure of the championship match, Fischer refused to defend his title. In 1975, FIDE's president ruled that Fischer thereby forfeited the title and declared Anatoly world champion by default.

Many commentators doubted that Anatoly could have defeated Fischer. To prove his right to the championship, Anatoly undertook an extremely active tournament career. Few previous champions had played as often or as well. In the next ten years, Anatoly entered thirty-three tournaments, placing first 28 times and losing only 18 of the 405 games he played.

## Major Chess Championships

| | |
|---|---|
| 1967 | European Junior Champion |
| 1969 | World Junior Champion |
| 1975-85 | World Champion |
| 1976, 1983 | USSR Champion |
| 1977 | West German Champion |
| 1993, 1999 | FIDE World Champion |

In 1978, Anatoly successfully defended his title against Korchnoi. Both players felt intense political pressure to win. Korchnoi had recently defected from the Soviet Union and claimed he had long been the target of discrimination, while Anatoly was an active member of the Russian Communist Party. The match was plagued by many unusual events. Korchnoi complained that the Soviets had planted a hypnotist in the audience who used mental force to distract him; in response, he had two members of an Asian religious sect sit in lotus position near the Soviet delegation. Nevertheless, Anatoly won 6-5 with 21 draws. His 1981 title defense, once more against Korchnoi, was less bizarre, and Anatoly won 6-2 with 10 draws.

**Continuing the Story**

In September, 1984, Anatoly faced a new challenger, Garry Kasparov, born in Azerbaijan, then part of the Soviet Union. Anatoly won four of the first nine games, seeming well on his way to victory, but an unprecedented 17 consecutive draws followed before he won a fifth game. Although the match lasted five months and extended to a record forty-eight games, Anatoly could not achieve the one win he needed to retain his title. Kasparov fought back, winning three games, including the last two played. Kasparov was furious when the president of FIDE canceled the entire match, claiming that both players were exhausted.

When the match was replayed with a twenty-four-game limit in 1985, Kasparov won 5-3, becoming the new champion. Had Anatoly been able to win the last game of the match, he would have retained his title, since a tied match went to the defending champion. Anatoly's contract entitled him to a rematch in 1986, but Kasparov again prevailed, 5-4. Anatoly was unwilling to surrender. He entered the 1987 FIDE competition and, by winning one match, was given the right to challenge Kas-

parov. Kasparov barely achieved a 4-4 tie by winning the twenty-fourth and final game and retained the title. In 1990, Anatoly once more won the challenge series. Facing Kasparov for a fifth time, he lost 4-3.

In 1993, Anatoly again attempted to regain his championship, but Nigel Short of England eliminated him in the semifinal round. Kasparov and Short, discovering they could assemble a larger prize-purse on their own, declined to play under the jurisdiction of FIDE and organized the Professional Chess Association to sponsor their match. FIDE ruled that Kasparov thereby forfeited his title and arranged a match between Jan Timman of the Netherlands and Anatoly—the two had placed second and third in the candidate series. Both Anatoly and Kasparov easily won their matches, and the world of chess had two champions.

In 1996, Anatoly successfully defended his FIDE title 6-3 against Gata Kamsky, a Russian who had immigrated to the United States. In 1998, Anatoly defeated Viswanathan Anand of India 5-3. However, attempts to arrange another Anatoly-Kasparov match to unify the world chess championship failed.

FIDE's new system of selecting a world champion further confused the situation by producing a third claimant to the title in 1999. FIDE decided to hold an annual tournament in which the one hundred best players in the world competed in short elimination matches; the eventual winner became world champion for the year. Anatoly and Kasparov were offered special placement in the semifinals.

Kasparov declined to participate, claiming that a brief match was not an acceptable replacement for the long, demanding encounters that had previously decided the championship. Anatoly also refused, asserting that his 1998 contract guaranteed he would remain champion until the year 2000. He sued unsuccessfully in the Swiss courts to invalidate the 1999 Las Vegas tournament won by Alexander Khalifman of Russia.

In the new millennium, Anatoly began to sink in

## Honors and Awards

| | |
|---|---|
| 1965 | Soviet chess master |
| 1969 | International chess master |
| 1970 | International chess grand master |

the world ratings of chess players. In 2001, he had an opportunity to play against Kasparov and Vladimir Kramnik, Kasparov's successor as world champion outside FIDE jurisdiction. Anatoly decided against participating in view of the likelihood of his finishing third after the other two "K's." His continued play on the world stage tended to specialize in rapid chess, which included faster time limits than in ordinary tournaments. The fatigue that bothers older players in long tournament games was less of a factor for games that lasted 10 minutes.

Anatoly also continued to write and to teach. In addition to books on chess openings and endgames, he also was one of the authors of a book on the application of chess strategy to the business world. He gave his name to a chess school in the United States and was personally involved in the creation of an academic chess department at the Russian State University; the first class graduated in 2008. While Kasparov spent the years after giving up his title on political matters, Anatoly restricted his attention to the world of chess.

## Summary

Along with Bobby Fischer and Garry Kasparov, Anatoly Karpov was one of the dominant chess grand masters of the late twentieth century. Although he was sometimes criticized as unimaginative, his style of play had no noticeable weaknesses.

When once asked about his methodology, he denied having one. Anatoly preferred to play conservatively, slowly, and inexorably, accumulating minute positional advantages that destroyed his opponents. In a total of 144 games in five matches against Kasparov, the net result was plus two for Kasparov. Anatoly considered the 1994 tournament at Linares, Spain, his masterpiece. Against a field including six of the strongest players in the world—including Kasparov—Anatoly won nine of thirteen games and lost none.

*Milton Berman, updated by Thomas Drucker*

## Additional Sources

Damsky, Yakov. *The Batsford Book of Chess Records.* London: Batsford, 2005.

Karpov, Anatoly. *Anatoly Karpov's Best Games.* Translated by Sarah J. Young. New York: Henry Holt, 1996.

_____. *Karpov on Karpov: Memoirs of a Chess World Champion.* Translated by Todd Bludeau. New York: Atheneum, 1991.

Karpov, Anatoly, Jean-François Phélizon, and Bachar Kouatly. *Chess and the Art of Negotiation: Ancient Rules for Modern Combat.* Westport, Conn.: Praeger, 2006.

Pandolfini, Bruce, ed. *The Best of Chess Life and Review: Volume Two, 1960-1988.* New York: Simon & Schuster, 1988.

# *Garry Kasparov*

**Born:** April 13, 1963
    Baku, Soviet Union (now in Azerbaijan)
**Also known as:** Garry Kimovich Kasparov (full name); Garry Kimovich Weinstein (birth name)

### Early Life

Garry Kasparov, was born Garry Kimovich Weinstein, on April 13, 1963, in Baku, the capital of the former Soviet republic Azerbaijan, to Kim Moiseyevich Weinstein, a teacher, and Clara Shagenova Kasparov, an Armenian engineer. After the five-year-old Garry tried to solve a chess problem that his parents were pondering in the local paper, his father taught him the game. Soon the son was beating his teacher. Only two years later, Garry's father died of cancer; the boy and his mother went to live with her parents, whose family name he adopted when he was twelve on the advice of a former world chess champion, who felt that Soviet anti-Semitism would hurt Garry's career.

### The Road to Excellence

By his third year in school, Garry was participating in chess tournaments. In 1973, he won his first prize, for his performance in the Azerbaijan youth team championship. Impressed, the national team trainer, Alexander Sergeyevitch Nikitin, urged Garry to enter the prestigious Botvinnik School. In August, 1973, Garry passed difficult exams to study under former world champion Mikhail Moiseyevich Botvinnik. In the past, Botvinnik had taught Anatoly Karpov, who became world champion in 1975.

    Garry confirmed his reputation as a childhood prodigy in January, 1976, by winning the Soviet Junior Championships at Tbilisi, Soviet Union (now in Georgia), against much older opponents. In July, he played abroad for the first time, in the World Junior Championships in Wattignes, France. At thirteen, Garry was the youngest player ever to represent the Soviet Union internationally, and, although he lost, he was on his way to earning an international reputation. In the next few years, fellow chess players started comparing him with two teenage predecessors who had gone on to become world champions: Boris Spassky and Bobby Fischer, the American who had taken the world title from Spassky in 1972.

    In spring, 1979, in Banja Luka, Bosnia (now in Bosnia and Herzegovina), Garry's first adult international tournament put him in a competition with fourteen grand masters. To his delight, he played well enough to earn not only his international master's norm but also his first grand-master title, two major strides in one tournament. The start of the following decade brought him gold medals from Olympic competitions and an international rating of 2,625, only 65 below Karpov's. A Kasparov-Karpov confrontation became almost inevitable.

### The Emerging Champion

On September 10, 1984, in Moscow, the twenty-one-year-old Garry confronted Karpov for a world

*Chess champion Garry Kasparov.* (Ted Thai/Getty Images)

championship match that turned into an endurance contest. Losing four of the first nine games, Garry seemed defeated. However, the next seventeen games were a draw. The competition created unprecedented problems in financing, logistics, and public relations as it dragged out to forty-eight games over the next five months. The forty-seventh game gave Garry his second victory.

In February, the Philippine president of the Fédération Internationale des Échecs (FIDE), Florencio Campomanes, canceled the match because of concern over the players' exhaustion. Garry objected in vain. In 1985, when the two opponents resumed play in a London-Leningrad (now St. Petersburg) return match, Garry won a twenty-four-game match by a narrow margin to become the thirteenth world champion—the youngest ever at the age of twenty-two. Both men donated their earnings from this match to a relief fund for victims of the Chernobyl atomic power-station disaster.

In 1986 and 1990, Garry beat Karpov again, while their 1987 match resulted in a draw. In 1991, for his fifth match with Karpov, Garry did not have the full one hundred days he usually devoted to championship training because of political instability in Azerbaijan. Nevertheless, he again won in the New York-Lyon matches against Karpov.

In 1993, Garry left FIDE to create the Professional Chess Association (PCA) with British chess player Nigel Short. He promptly defeated Short, his new challenger, in the first PCA-sponsored match. Meanwhile, Karpov played against, and defeated, a Dutch grand master, Jan Timman, under the supervision of FIDE. Predictably, after winning these separate matches, Karpov and Garry both claimed the title of world champion. In 1995, Garry followed up his win with another PCA match

| Major Chess Championships | |
|---|---|
| 1980, 1982, 1986, 1988 | Chess Olympiads (with USSR team) |
| 1981, 1990, 1992-94, 1997, 1999-2002, 2005 | Linares Tournament |
| 1992, 1994, 1996 | Chess Olympiads (with Russian national team) |
| 1995 | Super Classic series |
| | 2d Intel Grand Prix |
| 1998-99 | World Cup series |
| 2001 | Corus Wijk aan Zee |

in which he overcame Viswanathan Anand, an Indian competitor.

## Continuing the Story

While rising to the peak of chess sportsmanship, Garry had also completed his high school studies with honors and then graduated from Baku's Institute of Foreign Languages in 1986. In the following year, he wrote an autobiography dedicated to his father and focused on exploring his competition with Karpov. Later, Garry used his clout as an international celebrity to become a respected authority on postcommunist reform, speaking at world conferences and contributing articles on Russia to the *Wall Street Journal*. Besides creating the Kasparov Foundation for charitable causes, Garry founded the Kasparov International Chess Academy to promote his game's importance worldwide.

In 1996, Garry amazed the chess world by playing against Deep Blue, a computer built by International Business Machines (IBM) according to standard time regulations. Processing millions of chess moves in seconds, Deep Blue won the first game only to lose the match 4-2. In 1997, an updated Deep Blue with even faster processing capacities defeated Garry, winning three and a half out of six games. The machine's victory did not threaten Garry's status as perhaps the greatest chess genius in the game's history, but his contact with IBM did advance his cause of promoting the acceptance of computers in the former Soviet Union. In 2000, Garry's winning matches included the Bosnia 2000 Tournament for the "triple crown" and an Internet on-line competition with the world's strongest female player, Judit Polgar of Hungary.

In the second half of 2000, at a match in London, Garry lost his title, which he had held for fifteen years, to Vladimir Kramnik, who won 8.5 to 6.5. Nevertheless, during the early years of the twenty-first century, Garry won a number of major

| Honors and Awards | |
|---|---|
| 1980 | Grand master |
| 1985 | World Champion |
| 1985-93 | FIDE World Champion |
| 1985-2000 | Classical World Chess Champion |
| 2004 | Russian Chess Champion |

tournaments and maintained his rating as the top player in the world. However, because of financial and political problems, he was unable to play in a match that would have allowed him to regain his title as World Chess Champion. In January 2005, frustrated by FIDE's inability to organize a viable match, he decided to stop trying to regain his title, and, a few months later, he announced that he was retiring from high-level competitions, though he continued to enter and triumph in blitz events.

Garry increasingly devoted his time to business and politics. He wrote and lectured about the requirement for corporate leaders and chess grand masters to exhibit similar kinds of preparation, discipline, and strategy. Politically, Garry became the most prominent opponent of Russian president Vladimir Putin's policies. Despite Garry's Armenian-Jewish background, he tried to become a candidate in Russia's 2008 presidential race, but he was outmaneuvered by Putin, whose hand-picked successor, Dmitry Medvedev, easily won.

## Summary

Garry Kasparov was called "the greatest player in the history of chess," an appellation with which he agreed. From the time he became the youngest ever World Chess Champion in 1985, to his retirement in 2005, he was almost always the top player in the world. His rating of 2,851 was the all-time highest, and he also held the record for consecutive tournament victories. After his retirement, he concentrated his efforts on writing, business ventures, and political activism.

*Margaret Bozenna Goscilo,*
*updated by Robert J. Paradowski*

## Additional Sources

Kasparov, Garry. *Garry Kasparov on My Great Predecessors.* 5 vols. Guilford, Conn.: Globe Pequot Press, 2006.

_____. *How Life Imitates Chess: Making the Right Moves, from the Board to the Boardroom.* New York: Bloomsbury, 2007.

Kasparov, Garry, and Dmitry Plisetsky. *Garry Kasparov on Modern Chess, Part One: Chess Revolution in the Seventies.* Lyndon, Wash.: Everyman Chess, 2007.

Kasparov, Garry, and Donald Trelford. *Unlimited Challenge: The Autobiography of Garry Kasparov.* New York: Grove Weidenfeld, 1987.

Khodarkovski, Michael. *A New Era: How Garry Kasparov Changed the World of Chess.* New York: Ballantine Books, 1997.

Remnick, David. "The Tsar's Opponent." *The New Yorker* (October 1, 2007): 65-77.

Waitzkin, Fred. *Mortal Games: The Turbulent Genius of Garry Kasparov.* New York: Putnam, 1993.

Yudovich, Mikhail. *Garri Kasparov: His Career in Chess.* Translated by Oleg Zilbert. Moscow: Raduga, 1988.

# *Evel Knievel*

**Born:** October 17, 1938
   Butte, Montana
**Died:** November 30, 2007
   Clearwater, Florida
**Also known as:** Robert Craig Knievel, Jr. (full name)

### Early Life

Born on October 17, 1938, Robert Craig "Evel" Knievel, Jr., was raised by his grandparents in Butte, Montana. He was interested in sports and daredevil racing from an early age, and he excelled in ski jumping and ice hockey in high school. In 1957, he won the Northern Rocky Mountain Ski Association Class A Men's Ski Jumping Championship. As a young man, Evel played professional and semiprofessional hockey, worked as a miner and as a field guide for hunters, and served briefly in the U.S. Army. He also raced and sold motorcycles, was a political advocate for hunters, and worked as an insurance salesman.

### The Road to Excellence

His public career as a daredevil began in 1965, when he formed Evel Knievel's Motorcycle Daredevils group, using a nickname from his youth. His act included motorcycle jumping over dangerous animals such as rattlesnakes and mountain lions, riding through fire, and other death-defying actions. He soon went solo and started extending the length of his jumps. To make his jumps more interesting for the public, and to help them visualize the lengths of these jumps, he lined up parked cars, approached them with a ramp, and landed on another ramp on the other side.

Evel began by charging $500 for a jump over two cars and gradually increased the number of cars and his performance fees as his fame continued to spread. In 1968, on New Year's Day, he jumped across the fountains in front of Caesars Palace in Las Vegas, a distance of 151 feet, but crashed on the other side, sustained severe injuries, and was in a coma for a month.

### The Emerging Champion

As Evel became more popular, his flamboyant public image attracted a great deal of attention from the media. He wore colorful costumes like those of comic-book heroes and was admired by children. This was a period of turmoil in American society, and for many parents, his patriotic and antidrug statements outweighed concerns about

*Evel Knievel, who performed numerous dangerous motorcycle stunts.* (Michael Ochs Archives/Getty Images)

whether children would try to imitate his dangerous activities.

During the 1970's, the Ideal Toy Company began making a series of action figures and other toys based on Evel and his stunts. These toys and accessories—including lunch boxes and Thermos bottles—were extremely popular and generated a great deal of income for Evel. Also during this time, he became friends with other celebrities, such as singer Elvis Presley and boxer Muhammad Ali. Because of his dangerous vocation, he became a prominent advocate of motorcycle safety, especially crash helmets.

In 1971 Warner Bros. released a biographical film, *Evel Knievel,* with George Hamilton portraying Evel and Evel himself serving as Hamilton's stuntman. In 1977 Warner Bros. released a second film, *Viva Knievel,* an action film in which Evel appeared as himself along with Gene Kelly, Lauren Hutton, and others. Evel appeared also on television, both as a dramatic subject and as a guest star.

Many athletes, especially in high-contact sports such as football, have endured repeated sports injuries, but Evel holds the record. Although he personally claimed to have broken only thirty to thirty-five bones, some biographers have claimed that the figure is actually in the hundreds. He was made the American Orthopedic Association's Man of the Century and was listed in the 1984 *Guinness Book of World Records* for his many fractures.

### Continuing the Story
On September 8, 1974, Evel attempted to use the Sky-Cycle X-2, a special steam-powered vehicle invented by engineer Robert Truax, to jump over the Snake River Canyon at Twin Falls, Idaho. The highly publicized event took place before approximately fifteen thousand fans and a much larger television audience. Although a premature parachute opening prevented him from reaching the other side, Evel was unhurt and earned $6 million for the stunt.

On May 31, 1975, Evel broke his pelvis upon landing after jumping over thirteen double-decker buses at Wembley Stadium in London, England. After recovering from this crash, he tried an even more ambitious challenge, and on October 25, 1975, jumped fourteen buses at King's Island in Ohio. This performance captured a record 52 percent share of the television viewing audience for

## Major Stunt-jumping Events

|  |  |
|------|-------|
| 1968 | Crashed in an attempt to clear the fountains at Caesar's Palace in Las Vegas |
| 1970 | Cleared thirteen cars in Seattle |
| 1971 | Cleared thirteen cars in front of a then-record crowd at Houston Astrodome |
| | Set world record at Ontario, California, by jumping nineteen cars |
| | Crashed in an attempt to clear thirteen trucks in Yakima, Washington |
| 1973 | Taking off from the highest ski-style jump ramp ever used, flew over fifty cars stacked in the center of the Los Angeles Coliseum |
| 1974 | Soared 135 feet over thirteen 8-foot-wide trucks at Canadian National Exposition |
| | Jumped a specially constructed rocket-powered "Sky-Cycle" over the Snake River Canyon in Idaho |
| 1975 | Cleared thirteen double-decker buses, then crashed upon landing, breaking his pelvis, at Wembley Stadium in London |
| | Jumped over fourteen buses at King's Island in Ohio |

the ABC network. In 1976, he and a bystander were seriously injured at the Chicago Amphitheater when he attempted to do a motorcycle jump over a tank full of live sharks. This was his last major stunt-jumping event. While recovering from the Chicago accident, he began studying painting with artist Jack Ferriter.

After his retirement from stunt jumping, he traveled the country playing golf, signing autographs at public appearances, and painting Western scenes. He became involved in philanthropy, especially the Make-A-Wish Foundation. Years after his retirement, Evel found out that he had contracted the hepatitis C virus, probably as a result of contamination during one of his many blood transfusions and operations, and underwent a related liver transplant in 1999.

One of his sons, Robbie, continued in his father's footsteps as a professional daredevil motorcyclist. In 1989, Robbie Knievel used a lighter bike to duplicate his father's jump over the Caesars Palace fountains in Las Vegas, but without falling.

Evel continued to be discovered by younger audiences through video releases of his films. In November 1999, Rockstar Games released an interactive Evel Knievel video game, so that virtual daredevils could experience his stunts in the safety of their living rooms. In addition, one of Evel's mo- torcycles is exhibited at the Smithsonian's National Museum of American History in Washington, D.C. At the time of his death in November, 2007, Evel was still in the news. A rock opera based on his life premiered in September.

## Summary

Through determination and years of systematic risk-taking and experience, Evel Knievel built a reputation for daredevil motorcycle jumping that few others would dare to emulate. He is remem- bered as pop culture icon, an athlete, and a show- man. He captured the imagination of many Ameri- cans during the late-1960's and early 1970's, and he remains a hero to many.

*Alice Myers*

## Additional Sources

Barker, Stuart. *Life of Evel: Evel Knievel.* London: CollinsWillow, 2005.

Collins, Ace. *Evel Knievel: An American Hero.* New York: St. Martin's Press, 2001.

Knievel, Evel. *Evel Ways: A Daring Approach to Life.* Minneapolis: GraF/X, 2000.

Mandich, Steve. *Evel Incarnate: The Life and the Leg- end of Evel Knievel.* London: Sidgwick & Jackson, 2000.

# Vladimir Kramnik

**Born:** June 25, 1975
  Tuapse, Russia, Soviet Union (now in
    Russia)
**Also known as:** Vladimir Borisovich Kramnik (full
  name)

## Early Life

Vladimir Borisovich Kramnik was born on June 25, 1975, in Tuapse, Russia, Soviet Union (now in Russia), in the Krasnodar region on the northeast corner of the Black Sea. His father, Boris Kramnik, was a respected sculptor. His mother, Irina, was a music teacher. Russian players have dominated championship chess since World War II, with only a few exceptions. Vladimir learned to play chess at the age of five. He studied at the famous chess school established by the Soviet Union's first world chess champion, Mikhail Botvinnik. Excellence in competitive chess requires many years of intense preparation and study. A young chess player must compete in tournaments with other outstanding players. Vladi-

*Vladimir Kramnik playing against Deep Fritz, a German chess computer, in 2006.* (Juergen Schwarz/Bongarts/Getty Images)

mir practiced diligently, and his enormous talent for chess was quickly recognized.

## The Road to Excellence

The International Chess Olympiad is held every four years. More than one hundred countries send their best players to compete in this team event. When former world champion Anatoly Karpov could not play for the Russian team in the 1992 Manila Olympiad, the reigning champion, Gary Kasparov, recommended sixteen-year-old Vladimir to take his place. Kasparov had been impressed with the confident and mature play Vladimir had already exhibited. Vladimir's selection was controversial because of his age. However, Vladimir silenced his critics with an outstanding performance. He won a gold medal by winning eight games while losing none and drawing one against strong competition. The chess world was on notice: A budding star had arrived.

The following year, Vladimir joined the world's best players in the highly competitive Linares tournament in Spain. His fifth-place finish established him among the leading players in the world. He was named a grand master, a title awarded to the world's strongest chess players. Vladimir's chess style was strong and aggressive, featuring powerful attacks against his opponent's king. In addition, he was known for profound preparation of his opening maneuvers.

Over the next few years, Vladimir continued to excel in the most competitive grand-master tournaments. He came in first in numerous tournaments: in Chalkidiki, Greece, in 1992; in Belgrade, Yugoslavia (now in Serbia), in 1995; in Monaco, in 1996; in Tilburg, the Netherlands, in 1997; in Wijk aan Zee, the Netherlands, in 1998; and numerous times at Dortmund, Germany. Internationally competitive chess players are ranked by the Fédération Internationale des Échecs (FIDE), the world chess organization, according to tournament and match results. Despite his aggressive style, Vladimir was difficult to beat. In 1999 and the first half of 2000, he set a world record by playing more than eighty consecutive games without a loss. By the end of the 1990's, Vladimir's rating was approaching 2800, one of the highest in chess history.

## The Emerging Champion

By 2000, Vladimir had earned the right to play for the world chess championship in a match against Kasparov, who had been world champion since 1985, when, at the age of twenty-two, he defeated Karpov. Kasparov, widely acknowledged as the strongest player in chess history, was the heavy favorite to beat Vladimir. Kasparov had already defended his title against Karpov in several rematches and against the grand masters Nigel Short and Viswanathan Anand. The sixteen-game championship match began on October 8, 2000, in the Riverside Studios in London, England. The match was sponsored by the BrainGames Network, which was offering the winner a $2 million prize and the solid silver Howard Staunton trophy crafted by Asprey and Garrard, jewelers to Queen Elizabeth II.

The match was broadcast on the Internet; the moves of each game were followed by chess enthusiasts throughout the world. Kasparov had the white pieces for game one and Vladimir the black. Vladimir stunned the chess world on move three by playing the "Berlin Defense" to Kasparov's aggressive "Ruy Lopez" opening. The Berlin Defense, considered to give white too strong an advantage, had rarely been played for a century. However, it proved a solid defensive opening system, and the queen pieces were exchanged—captured and taken off the board—on move eight. Kasparov could not break through Vladimir's stodgy defense. Game one ended in a draw.

In game two, Vladimir shocked the chess world by defeating Kasparov in a well-played endgame,

## Major Chess Victories

| | |
|---|---|
| 1990 | Russian Championship |
| 1992 | Chalkidiki (Greece) Tournament |
| 1994 | PCA Intel Grand Prix |
| 1995, 1997, 2007 | Dortmund Festival |
| 1996, 1998-99, 2007 | Monaco Tournament |
| 2004 | Linares (Spain) Tournament |

when the game pieces have been greatly reduced. In game three, Kasparov aimed for revenge with an improved opening move but again could not break through Vladimir's Berlin Defense. The pattern repeated throughout the match. Vladimir's defense was impenetrable.

With the white pieces, Vladimir won the tenth game brilliantly, in only twenty-five moves, and took a two-game advantage. On November 2, 2000, Vladimir won the match with a final score of 8.5 points to Kasparov's 6.5 points and was crowned the seventeenth world champion in chess history. Although stunned, Kasparov was gracious in defeat.

## Continuing the Story

Vladimir's victory over Kasparov in 2000 was notable for many reasons. At the time, Kasparov seemed nearly unbeatable. In defeating him, Vladimir did not lose a single game, a feat last accomplished by Jose Raoul Capablanca in his 1921 World Championship match against Emanuel Lasker. In addition, Vladimir achieved his victory with his startling use of the antiquated Berlin Defense, which stymied Kasparov's power of attack. Vladimir successfully defended his world title against Peter Leko, in 2004, and against Veselin Topalov, in 2006. He also won several grand-master tournaments. He played matches against the world's most advanced chess computers, which had reached strengths comparable to the best human chess players. Vladimir was admired for his gentlemanly behavior and sportsmanship as world champion. His accomplishments earned him the prestigious Russian title "Master of Sport."

On December 30, 2006, Vladimir married Marie-Laure Germon. He was also diagnosed with a form of arthritis, which made sitting for long periods uncomfortable and hampered his chess play. In September, 2007, he lost the world chess champi-

## Honors and Awards

| | |
|---|---|
| 1991 | Under-18 World Championship |
| 2000-07 | World Chess Champion |
| 2000, 2006 | Chess Oscar |
| 2006 | Highest score, Chess Olympiad |
| 2006–07 | FIDE World Chess Champion |

onship to the brilliant grand master Anand. In October, 2008, in Bonn, Germany, Anand defeated Vladimir in a world championship rematch by a final score of 6.5 points to 4.5 points.

## Summary

Vladimir Kramnik reigned as world chess champion from 2000 to 2007. Excelling at chess requires not only intense mental and theoretical preparation but also physical training in order to sustain concentration and stamina during grueling matches. Vladimir's rise to the world championship at the age of twenty-four was a remarkable achievement. Vladimir joined a historic group of world chess champions including such illustrious players as Mikhail Tal, Boris Spassky, and Bobby Fischer.

*Howard Bromberg*

## Additional Sources

Bareev, Eugeny, and Ilya Levitov. *From London to Elista: The Inside Story of the World Championship Matches That Vladimir Kramnik Won Against Garry Kasparov, Peter Leko, and Veselin Topalov.* Alkmaar, Netherlands: New In Chess, 2008.

Cox, John. *The Berlin Wall: The Variation That Brought Down Kasparov.* Gothenburg, Sweden: Quality Chess, 2007.

Keene, Raymond, and Ron Morris. *The BrainGames World Chess Championship.* London: Everyman Chess, 2000.

Kramnik, Vladimir, and Iahov Damsky. *Kramnik: My Life and Games.* London: Everyman Chess, 2000.

Topalov, Veselin, and Zhivko Ginchev. *Topalov-Kramnik 2006 World Chess Championship: On the Edge in Elista.* Milford, Conn.: Russell Enterprises, 2007.

# *Julie Krone*

**Born:** July 24, 1963
     Benton Harbor, Michigan
**Also known as:** Julieanne Louise Krone (full
   name)

## Early Life

Julieanne Louise Krone was born on July 24, 1963, in Benton Harbor, Michigan. She grew up on a farm in the nearby town of Eau Claire. Her father was an art and photography teacher, and her mother, who was a former state equestrian champion, bred and showed Arabian horses and taught riding.

Julie always wanted to be around horses. She was first put on a horse when she was only two; at the age of three, she was making half-mile trips on her horse. By the time Julie was five, her mother was entering her in horse shows for contestants under twenty-one years of age. Julie won again and again. At the age of fourteen, she was riding in horse shows every summer and winning in every available category.

## The Road to Excellence

In 1979, at only fifteen years of age, Julie rode in her first professional races at fairground tracks in Michigan. In December of that year, she dropped out of high school and moved to Tampa, Florida, to live with her grandparents and to seek an opportunity to race at the Tampa Bay Downs racetrack. Julie's self-confidence and determination won her the help of trainer Jerry Pace, who arranged for her to compete. On Julie's eleventh mount, she won her first race, and she won eight more times in her first forty-eight races.

Julie then met Julie Stellings, another person who was to help her realize her dreams. Stellings was a former jockey who introduced Julie to many horse owners and arranged for her brother-in-law to become Julie's trainer. Stellings also persuaded Chick Lang, an agent from Baltimore, to take Julie as a client. In Baltimore, Julie raced at Pimlico and two other Maryland tracks, Laurel and Bowie.

During one race at Laurel, Julie experienced the first of many injuries she would suffer as a jockey. She was thrown from her horse and broke her back. She spent two months in bed and thought that she would never race again. When she did return to the track, she went eighty races without winning. In the fall and winter of 1981, however, she recaptured her form, riding more than one hundred winners.

## The Emerging Champion

In 1982, Julie moved to Atlantic City, New Jersey, where she won more races than any other jockey, becoming the first woman to win a racing title at a major track. She performed the same feat the following year. She was making a mark in a sport that had always been dominated by men. To overcome the prejudice against women jockeys, Julie needed not only natural talent but also a strong will and a fighting spirit. On one occasion, the 4-foot 10-inch, 100-pound Julie was involved in a fight with a male jockey who had slashed her across the face with a whip during a race. Both jockeys were fined as a result of the incident, but Julie had shown that she was not going to be pushed around.

Although Julie was feisty in dealing with the horse racing fraternity, aggression was not the hallmark of her riding style. According to many trainers, Julie had a knack for getting a horse to relax and the ability to communicate with it. Legendary jockey Bill Shoemaker has said that Julie had a sixth sense that enabled her to communicate with the horse. Julie's friend and fellow jockey Richard Migliore pointed out that Julie's success stemmed not from her aggressive attitude but from her patience.

## Continuing the Story

In the mid-1980's, Julie left Atlantic City and began racing at three New Jersey tracks: the Meadowlands, Monmouth Park, and Garden State Park. Her success continued. In 1986, she earned $2.3

### *Major Championship Victory*

| Year | Race | Horse |
|------|------|-------|
| 1993 | Belmont Stakes | Colonial Affair |

million, the highest earnings for a woman jockey that year. During the following year, Julie recorded 130 wins at Monmouth Park and 124 wins at Meadowlands, totals that were the most of any jockey at those tracks. In December, 1987, she began racing at the Aqueduct track in New York City, where she became the first woman to ride four winners in one day. In 1988, her ability to coax the best out of her horses was confirmed yet again when she rode Gaily Daily, a 75-1 long shot, to victory in the Flower Bowl Handicap at Belmont Park, the most dramatic upset in racing that year. Also in 1988, Julie became the leading female jockey in history by riding her 1,205th winner. By 1992, she had ridden more than two thousand winners.

Julie was injured many times in her riding career. In April, 1988, she fell from her horse and was so bruised that she could hardly move for three days. She recovered within a month, but only a few days after returning to competition, she took another fall and suffered a concussion. In a 1990 collision at the Meadowlands, Julie broke her left forearm and needed eight and a half months to recover. In August, 1993, she sustained multiple fractures of her right ankle after falling from her horse on the final day of the Saratoga racing season. This setback came only a few months after her career reached another pinnacle. In June, 1993, at Belmont Park, she became the first woman to win a triple crown race—the triple crown races are the Kentucky Derby, the Preakness Stakes, and the Belmont Stakes. Julie rode Colonial Affair, a 13-to-1 outsider, to victory in the Belmont.

Along with her success as a jockey, Julie suffered several serious injuries. Two months after her historic win at Belmont, she crushed her ankle and was kicked in the heart in an accident at Sarasota. In 1995, she went down again at Gulfstream Park and injured both her hands. Four years later she decided to retire from racing. In her farewell race, in 1999, she finished with three winners and two second-place finishes, capping a ground-breaking career that spanned nineteen years. In 2000, she became the first woman inducted into the Jockeys' Hall of Fame.

---

## Records and Milestones

Leading female jockey in history, with 3,545 career wins

First female jockey to win a Triple Crown race

Champion jockey titles at Atlantic City, Monmouth Park, The Meadowlands, and Gulfstream tracks

First woman inducted into Jockeys' Hall of Fame, 2000

---

In 2002, Julie came out of retirement. The following year she became the first female jockey to win a Breeders' Cup event; however, later in the year, she suffered another injury, and unofficially retired in 2004. She gave birth to her first child in 2005.

## Summary

Julie Krone combined her natural riding talent with unlimited dedication and ambition. Overcoming the prejudice against women that existed in the horse racing world, she forced her way to the top by winning nearly four thousand races. By the mid-1990's, she was not only the leading woman jockey in the country but was also considered by many to be the biggest attraction in racing. More than her $81 million in career winnings, or her numerous career riding titles, Julie's impact on the male-dominated world of horse racing was profound. Her inspiration to women athletes in all sports is incalculable.

*Bryan Aubrey*

## Additional Sources

Hoffer, Richard. "Lady's Day." *Sports Illustrated* 99, no. 17 (November 3, 2003): 98.

Krone, Julie, and Nancy Ann Richardson. *Riding for My Life*. Boston: Little, Brown, 1995.

LaFontaine, Pat. *Companions in Courage: Triumphant Tales of Heroic Athletes*. New York: Warner Books, 2001.

O'Neil, Dana Pennett, and Pat Williams. *How to Be Like Women Athletes of Influence: Thirty-one Women at the Top of Their Game and How You Can Get There Too*. Deerfield Beach, Fla.: Health Communications, 2007.

# *Marion Ladewig*

**Born:** October 30, 1914
        Grand Rapids, Michigan
**Also known as:** Marion Van Oosten (birth name)

## Early Life

Marion Van Oosten was born on October 30, 1914, in Grand Rapids, Michigan, where her father was a police officer. In her early teens, she was a champion sprinter, winning the 100-yard dash four years in a row at the West Side Businessmen's Picnic. She played first base on her brother's baseball team before becoming a shortstop and pitcher for a softball team. The sponsor of the softball team was Bill Morrissey, owner of the Fanatorium bowling alley in Grand Rapids, who became a key person in Marion's bowling career.

*Marion Ladewig, who was the female American bowler of the year nine times. (Courtesy of Amateur Athletic Foundation of Los Angeles)*

## The Road to Excellence

One evening, after watching Marion pitch, Morrissey suggested that she might also be a good bowler. Marion accepted his invitation to try, and, after scoring a respectable 81 in her first game, was hired by Morrissey as a cashier in his bowling lanes. In addition to her three-dollar-per-night salary, she received an hour of free bowling every afternoon. Morrissey instructed her in bowling and instilled in her the habit of daily practice, which would carry her through her entire career.

Bowling lanes were not automated in the 1940's. Instead of having machines to set up the pins, pinsetters had to wait in an area behind the pins and set them up by hand. One March evening in 1945, a pinsetter did not show up for work, so Marion set pins all evening. Although she had been bowling for nine years, from behind the pins, she could see the ball coming in and noticed that a bowler who was putting spin on the ball was more successful than a bowler who was simply rolling the ball hard. She began to put spin on her ball, and her scores began to improve.

Even before she changed her bowling style, Marion had begun to have competitive success in Grand Rapids, then in the state of Michigan, and finally at the Midwest regional level. Her first notable victory was the singles title at the 1940-1941 Western Michigan Gold Pin Classic. Throughout the 1940's, her average steadily rose up into the 190's. Her national dominance began in 1949, when she won the first Bowling Proprietors Association of American (BPAA) women's all-star title.

## The Emerging Champion

In the 1950's, Marion became the dominant force in women's bowling. Over a career that lasted until 1965, she won the all-star title eight times, the women's title of the World's Invitational Championship five times, the National Doubles title twice, and the Women's International Bowling Congress (WIBC) all-events title twice. Furthermore, she was selected nine

## Major Championship Victories

| | |
|---|---|
| 1949-53, 1957, 1959, 1963 | BPAA Women's All-Stars |
| 1950, 1955 | WIBC All-Events |
| 1955 | WIBC Doubles (with Wyllis Ryskamp) |
| 1957, 1960, 1962-64 | World's Invitational |
| 1958-59 | National Doubles (with LaVerne Carter) |

times as woman bowler of the year by the Bowling Writers Association of America (BWAA). In 1950, she captured the WIBC team title with the Fanatorium Majors. The Fanatorium team, with Marion as captain, also won the national team match game title in 1957 and 1958.

Marion's career average was 204, but she was capable of much higher, as she demonstrated in the 1951 all-star tournament during a string of games considered one of the greatest in bowling history. She entered the third day of the tournament in second place. In her first two games on Saturday, December 15, she rolled a 255 and a 279. This set a two-game all-star record of 534. She then followed this up on the same day with scores of 247, 227, 247, 224, 255, and 247. Her eight-game average was 247.6. The highest possible score is 300. With this performance, she won her third straight women's all-star title and outscored all 160 men in the men's tournament as well.

There was no professional league for women during much of Marion's career. In December, 1959, she was one of twenty-three charter members of the Professional Women's Bowling Association (PWBA). Nine months later, one hundred women participated in the first PWBA tournament in Miami. The winner of that tournament was Marion.

### Continuing the Story

Two words were often used to describe Marion: "consistency" and "class." Her consistency led to her success as a bowler, and her "class" made her a wonderful ambassador for bowling. In 1950, she entered into a contract with Brunswick and became a part of their advisory staff. In this role, she gave bowling clinics and exhibitions and taught courses in the United States and throughout much of the rest of the world.

According to other bowlers, Mari-

on's accuracy set her apart. She did not throw the most powerful ball, but she was always in the pocket. She was also described as a great competitor who took advantage of every opportunity. After her retirement from competitive bowling in 1965, Marion became part-owner of a bowling establishment near her home in Grand Rapids. In addition to the daily operations of the lanes, she continued helping others with the game she loved by teaching bowling. At the age of sixty-five, she was still bowling between 170 and 174 in three leagues.

The honors and awards did not end when she retired. In 1973, she was voted the greatest woman bowler of all time. In 1984, she was inducted into the International Women's Sports Hall of Fame.

### Summary

Marion Ladewig only began learning her sport at the age of twenty-two and did not begin serious competition until she was thirty-five. She showed that one could continue participating and enjoying a sport well into the retirement years. She was a tough competitor whose secret to success was practice. She did not, however, sacrifice style and class for success.

*Jan Rintala*

### Additional Sources

Miller, Ernestine G. *Making Her Mark: Firsts and Milestones in Women's Sports.* Chicago: Contemporary Books, 2002.

Sherrow, Victoria, ed. *Encyclopedia of Women and Sports.* Santa Barbara, Calif.: ABC-Clio, 1996.

Woolum, Janet. *Outstanding Women Athletes: Who They Are and How They Influenced Sports in America.* Phoenix, Ariz.: Oryx Press, 1998.

## WIBC Records

Highest doubles score, 1,264 (1955, with Wyllis Ryskamp)

## Honors and Awards

| | |
|---|---|
| 1950-54, 1957-59, 1963 | BWAA Woman Bowler of the Year |
| 1953 | Michigan Woman Athlete of the Year |
| 1962-64 | *Bowlers Journal* First Team All-American |
| 1964 | Inducted into WIBC Hall of Fame |
| 1973 | Greatest Woman Bowler of All Time |
| 1982 | John O. Martino Award |
| 1984 | Inducted into International Women's Sports Hall of Fame |
| 1991 | National Bowling Hall of Fame Salute to Champions Award |

# Niki Lauda

**Born:** February 22, 1949
 Vienna, Austria
**Also known as:** Andreas Nikolaus Lauda (full
 name)

## Early Life

Andreas Nikolaus "Niki" Lauda was born on February 22, 1949, into a wealthy industrial family in Vienna, the capital city of Austria. With all the entertainment of a large city at hand, as well as the sports available on the nearby lakes and Alps, it would have been easy for Niki to grow up a lazy, rich playboy. Instead, he grew up willing to work hard driving and testing race cars.

## The Road to Excellence

At the age of eighteen, after finishing the Austrian equivalent of high school, Niki turned down his father's offer to send him to college and insisted instead that he wanted to drive race cars. His father was not happy with this idea and refused to provide the money for a race car. Niki went instead to his grandmother, who gave him the money for a Mini Cooper, used in hill-climbing events.

## Grand Prix Victories

| | |
|---|---|
| 1974 | Spanish Grand Prix |
| 1974, 1977, 1985 | Netherlands Grand Prix |
| 1975 | Swedish Grand Prix |
| | United States Grand Prix |
| 1975-76 | Belgian Grand Prix |
| | Monaco Grand Prix |
| 1975, 1977, 1984 | World Champion of Drivers |
| 1975, 1978, 1984 | Italian Grand Prix |
| 1975, 1984 | French Grand Prix |
| 1975, 1985 | Dutch Grand Prix |
| 1976 | Brazilian Grand Prix |
| 1976-77, 1984 | South African Grand Prix |
| 1976, 1982-84 | British Grand Prix |
| 1977 | German Grand Prix |
| 1984 | Austrian Grand Prix |
| 1985 | Dutch Grand Prix |

Niki was good at competitive driving and soon worked his way up the ranks of Formula Three, and then Formula Two, cars. When he thought he was ready, Niki convinced the March Racing Team to hire him as a Formula One driver and persuaded an Austrian bank to sponsor him. His grandfather wanted Niki to enter the family business and convinced the bank to withdraw its sponsorship. Niki, with the determination typical of his character, then borrowed $100,000 to begin Formula One racing. Within two years, he had repaid the money with interest.

In 1974, Niki signed a contract with the Ferrari Company to test drive and race its cars. It is an unusual combination for a driver to be good at both test and race driving. The skills needed are similar, but the understanding of the car is different. As a race driver, Niki was able to drive fast; as a test driver, he was able to tell how to make the car perform better.

## The Emerging Champion

By 1975, Niki was already at the top of his chosen field. Although he had finished fourth in Formula One Grand Prix points in 1974, his association with Ferrari gave him the cars and the focus he wanted. Often, he worked ten hours a day perfecting the cars for Ferrari and preparing to race. Formula One Grand Prix racing takes much work. The season typically lasts ten months and includes sixteen races on six continents. In 1974, Niki had been leading the race for the championship when he entered the British Grand Prix, losing that race and the championship. In 1975, however, he was ready to win.

Many types of automobile races are not run in the rain, but Formula One races usually continue under almost any circumstances. The British Grand Prix of 1975 was run in a flood. Eleven cars crashed, and the lead changed hands nine times. Finally, the weather became so severe that the officials stopped the race with Niki in eighth place. Critics immediately began to suggest that Niki did not have the courage or the skill to be a champion, but he proved them wrong. He held on to his lead in points and at the end of the season was crowned as the World Champion of Drivers.

In 1976, Niki was eager to repeat his win. Instead, he proved he was a champion in another way. After winning several races and taking the lead in points, Niki and the other drivers came to Nürburgring for the German Grand Prix. The Nürburgring race course is the longest of the Grand Prix courses. With 172 corners, it is considered the most difficult, and with a number of drivers killed there, the most dangerous.

On the second lap of the race, a wheel came off Niki's car and two other vehicles slammed into the wreckage, which burst into flames. For more than sixty seconds, Niki struggled to free himself from the inferno, inhaling the flames and fumes deep into his lungs. At last released and carried to the hospital, even the best doctors gave him no chance to live. A priest was called in, and Niki was given the last rites of the Roman Catholic Church, but he refused to die. Even though he knew death would mean an end to the pain, he refused to give in. Almost miraculously, he got up within a week of the accident and began walking. In only a few days, he had returned to his country home near Salzburg, Austria, and begun a rigorous program of physical training. Only ten weeks later, he was back on the racetrack.

Soon Niki had the point lead again, but just barely. The championship would be decided by the final race of the season, the Japanese Grand Prix. When race day came on the Fuji, Japan, course, the rain had been pouring down for eight hours. After a two-hour delay, the officials ordered the race to begin despite the terrible weather. Niki took the track but two laps later pulled into the pit and left the race. This guaranteed that Jim Hunt would be the new champion.

## Continuing the Story

By leaving the race and giving away the championship, Niki invited, and received, vast amounts of criticism. Many people concluded that he had lost his courage and said so in unflattering terms. Niki kept working with Ferrari.

When the 1977 season began, Niki was back on the track. He won the South African Grand Prix, the third race of the season, and he continued from there. Three races before the end of the season, at the United States Grand Prix at Watkins Glen, New York, Niki pulled so far ahead in points no one could catch him. For the second time, he was world champion and his courage was beyond question.

Niki went back to his home near Salzburg to enjoy his championship in the beautiful Austrian Alps with his wife, Marlene.

## Summary

Niki Lauda never had the dash and flamboyance of many Formula One drivers. He was a technical genius but preferred a quiet life. He rarely drank, never smoked, and had no use for idle rich people. Although he struck many people as cold, he simply preferred privacy. He kept only one trophy in his house, the first he received. Above all, he was a driver of great courage.

*Michael R. Bradley*

## Additional Sources

Henry, Alan. *Four Seasons at Ferrari: The Lauda Years.* Derby, Derbyshire, England: Breedon, 2002.

Ménard, Pierre, and Jacques Vassal. *Niki Lauda: The Rebel.* St. Sulpice, Switzerland: Chronosports, 2004.

Rusz, Joe. "Pole Position." *Road and Track*, April, 2004, 116.

# *Bruce Lee*

**Born:** November 27, 1940
     San Francisco, California
**Died:** July 20, 1973
     Hong Kong
**Also known as:** Lee Jun Fan (birth name); Li
   Xiaolong

## Early Life

Bruce Lee was born Lee Jun Fan in San Francisco's Chinatown in 1940—the Year of the Dragon. His father, Lee Hoi Chuen, was a well-known Hong Kong opera singer who happened to be on tour in the United States at the time Bruce was born. A hospital staff member attending the boy's birth suggested calling him Bruce.

Back home in Kowloon, Hong Kong, the infant was almost immediately thrust into the career path that would make him a child film star. Bruce was barely three months old when he appeared briefly in a Chinese film shot in San Francisco. At the age of eight, he played his second role— under the new nickname of Lee Siu Lung (Lee Little Dragon), the name by which he became known best in Hong Kong and on the Mandarin film circuit of Southeast Asia. By his eighteenth birthday, Bruce had acted in twenty films, including a starring role in *The Orphan*, made about 1958.

As a youngster, Bruce showed little aptitude for school, preferring to spend his days as a member of one of the many street gangs roaming through the crowded, noisy colony. With a weapon, a toilet chain, wrapped around his waist, he soon became one of the toughest of his bunch. He and his cohorts got into frequent, bloody scrapes with English schoolboys.

## The Road to Excellence

About this time, Bruce decided to take up martial arts, to learn how to defend himself, he told his mother, who agreed to pay for the lessons. After observing several styles, he chose the Chinese art of *wing chun*, a comparatively simple style of kung-fu only a few hundred years old. His teacher was the international grandmaster Yip Man, probably the twentieth century's most revered *wing chun* practitioner. Even in adolescence, Bruce's newfound love of this style was all-consuming, and he threw himself into his daily lessons with a fiery passion. Like a wild, unbroken colt, he released his energy unpredictably, anywhere and everywhere: Walking along the streets, he would startle people by suddenly launching a flurry of punches and kicks at them.

Not long after joining Yip Man's school, Bruce was eager to test his prowess by taking on all challengers. Such rivalries were not uncommon among

*Bruce Lee.* (Michael Ochs Archives/Getty Images)

the pupils of competing kung-fu *kwoons* (training halls). Informal contests of skill and courage, carried out in secret, helped decide which boys—and therefore which styles—were "the best" on the island. These matches, combined with constant practice, enabled Bruce to perfect his increasingly formidable combat skills. In 1958, he competed in the Hong Kong interscholastic boxing championships. In the finals, Bruce, applying *wing chun*, handily defeated his opponent, a British boy who, using classic boxing techniques, had been champion three years running.

### The Emerging Champion

In early 1959, Bruce, at the urging of his parents, sailed for the United States in search of better opportunities. Landing eventually in Seattle, Washington, he worked in a restaurant and set about earning his high school diploma. He then enrolled at the University of Washington as a philosophy major.

Bruce soon opened his own kung-fu studio, the Jun Fan Gung Fu Institute, in Seattle. He also began to formulate the combat principles that eventually became the basis for his own style, which he called *jeet kune do* (the way of the intercepting fist). In all of his years of study, he had come to see that the classical forms of kung-fu were artifice unsuited for actual and unpredictable street combat. With their misplaced emphasis on stances, set responses, and mechanically rehearsed techniques, such forms were, he believed, too complicated to be of any use in a real situation. "I always say that actual combat is never fixed, has no boundaries or limits, and is constantly changing from moment to moment," he declared. The practitioner who blindly adheres to the classical methods is "merely 'performing' his stylized blocks and listening to his own screams. . . . After all, how many ways are there to come in on an opponent without deviating from the natural and direct path?"

Rejecting tradition, the streamlined techniques of *jeet kune do* were, by contrast, short, fast, and to the point, with no wasted motion. The practitioner did not so much "oppose" an opponent as "react" to him or her with direct, rapid-fire punching and kicking. The object, he told an interviewer, is a "maximum of anguish with a minimum of movement."

Bruce and Linda Lee Emery were married in

| Martial Arts Films | |
|---|---|
| 1971 | *Fists of Fury* |
| 1972 | *Chinese Connection* |
| | *Return of the Dragon* |
| 1973 | *Enter the Dragon* |
| 1978 | *Game of Death* |

1964; they had two children, Brandon and Shannon. Later that same year, Bruce and his wife moved to Oakland, California, where he started a second studio and, after more experimentation and refinement, began teaching his new fighting method. A third studio was opened in 1966, in Los Angeles, where Bruce and Linda had relocated so that he could begin work on a new television series.

Bruce's life and career had taken a fateful turn in 1964, when he demonstrated his method at the first International Karate Championships held in Long Beach, California. His dazzling performance persuaded many of the experts in attendance of the merits of *jeet kune do*. The exhibition also brought him to the attention of Hollywood television producer William Dozier, who subsequently cast Bruce in the short-lived series *The Green Hornet* (1966-1967). With that exposure, Bruce became a household name in many parts of the world, including the United States and Southeast Asia. Television work on other series followed, including a recurring role on *Longstreet* (1971-1972).

Bruce continued to give lessons and to demonstrate his art at clubs, exhibitions, and tournaments across the country. Celebrity clients such as actors Steve McQueen and James Coburn, screenwriter Sterling Siliphant, and professional basketball star Kareem Abdul-Jabbar, as well as renowned karate champions Chuck Norris, Joe Lewis, and Mike Stone, paid as much as $250 an hour for private classes. A script written by Siliphant, *Marlowe* (1969), led to Bruce's first role in a full-length U.S. feature film. That year Bruce, Siliphant, and Coburn collaborated on an idea Bruce had for a martial arts film to be titled "The Silent Flute," which was later shot as *Circle of Iron* (1979) and starred actor David Carradine in the part written for Bruce.

In 1970, Bruce injured his lower back during a training exercise. Forced into immobility for the first time in his adult life, and full of restless energy, he began writing out and diagramming the basics of his innovative style of self-defense, eventually filling up eight 2-inch-thick notebooks. These were later condensed into a single volume and published after his death as *Tao of Jeet Kune Do* (1975).

## Continuing the Story

In the early 1970's, as the martial arts became more popular in the United States, Bruce conceived the idea for a new television series based on the wanderings of an exiled Shaolin priest and kung-fu master in the lawless American West of the 1870's. The result was the popular *Kung Fu* (1972-1975)—with Carradine in the role that Bruce had hoped to play.

With Bruce's Hollywood acting career temporarily stalled, Bruce accepted the offer of Hong Kong film producer Raymond Chow to shoot a series of films overseas. In 1971, the Lee family left for Hong Kong, where Bruce made several films, each of which earned millions of dollars at box offices throughout Southeast Asia. Next he shot a few spectacular fight scenes (displaying, among other things, his mastery of the lethal nunchaku) for *Game of Death*, another Hong Kong venture, but died well before its completion in 1978. Meanwhile he made what was easily his best film and one of the best martial arts films of all time. *Enter the Dragon* (1973), a Warner Bros.-produced effort in which Bruce plays a secret agent who infiltrates a mysterious island fortress involved in drug smuggling and prostitution, solidified his status as an international superstar.

Nearing the end of postproduction on that film, Bruce was physically and emotionally exhausted. In May, 1973, he collapsed while dubbing sound at Golden Harvest studios. He recovered, only to lapse into a coma about five weeks later while at the apartment of Taiwan actor Betty Ting-pei. Hours later he was dead, at the age of thirty-two, of a cerebral edema, a swelling of the brain.

## Summary

Bruce Lee emerged from humble roots to become one of his sport's most captivating and explosive practitioners. Through years of intensive experimentation, refinement, and application, he invented his own controversial but effective method of combat, one that stressed the ability to respond realistically to the situation at hand. Finally, he parlayed his phenomenal success at martial arts into an internationally successful, if brief, motion-picture career that included the definitive martial arts film of the time. In 1993, he received a star on the Hollywood Walk of Fame, shortly before the Los Angeles premiere of the film biography *Dragon: The Bruce Lee Story*.

*Philip Wong*

## Additional Sources

Bishop, James. *Bruce Lee: Dynamic Becoming*. Carrollton, Tex.: Promethean Press, 2004.

Hunter, Jack. *Intercepting Fist: The Films of Bruce Lee and the Golden Age of Kung-Fu Cinema*. London: Glitter Books, 2005.

Lee, Bruce, and John R. Little. *Bruce Lee: Artist of Life*. Boston: C. E. Tuttle, 2001.

Little, John R. *Bruce Lee: A Warrior's Journey*. Chicago: Contemporary Books, 2001.

Miller, Davis. *The Tao of Bruce Lee: A Martial Arts Memoir*. New York: Harmony Books, 2000.

Statan, Andrew J. *Bruce Lee: Memories of a Master*. New York: Health 'n Life, 2007.

Thomas, Bruce. *Bruce Lee: Fighting Words*. Berkeley, Calif.: Frog, 2003.

# Jeanette Lee

**Born:** July 9, 1971
    Brooklyn, New York
**Also known as:** The Black Widow

## Early Life

Jeanette Lee was born in Brooklyn, New York, of Korean heritage. At the age of thirteen, she was diagnosed with scoliosis, a disorder marked by a curvature of the spine. She underwent surgery to join the vertebrae along the curve of her spine, and steel rods were inserted to allow her vertebrae to fuse together.

A good student, Jeanette was accepted to and attended the Bronx High School of Science but later dropped out. After high school, Jeanette attended various colleges, hoping to earn a bachelor's degree in early childhood development and elementary education. However, at the age of eighteen, Jeanette was working as a waitress and uncertain about her future plans. She had seen *The Color of Money,* a film about pool hustlers, starring Paul Newman and Tom Cruise. Jeanette became fascinated by billiards. Walking around the neighborhood one spring day in 1989, Jeanette strolled into Chelsea Billiards, a local pool room. From her very first day in the local pool hall, Jeanette was hooked on the game.

## The Road to Excellence

Jeanette dedicated herself to the sport. For the next five years, she had virtually no life outside of playing pool. Skipping breakfast, makeup, and a shower, Jeanette hurried the three blocks between her home and Chelsea Billiards, playing fifteen or sixteen straight hours every day. One day, Jeanette played thirty-seven hours consecutively until her back collapsed, and she had to be carried home. She was briefly hospitalized. However, after her release, she was still obsessed, imagining games in her head and visualizing billiard balls careening off the walls of her bedroom. Jeanette knew that, with practice, she could be a great pool player. Beyond skill, a billiards player relies on geometry and physics. Jeanette's all-consuming passion and studious approach to the game paid off, and she made her professional debut at the age of twenty-one.

Jeanette became known as "The Black Widow," a name she earned because of her appearance. Jeanette had long black hair and dark brown eyes and always dressed in black. In tournament play, she exuded a serious, calculating attitude. She used her persona as a psychological advantage over her opponents. Her first victory came at the Baltimore Billiards Classic, the World Professional Billiard Association (WPBA) opening tournament. By the end of her second season on the tour, Jeanette was named player of the year by *Billiards Digest.*

## The Emerging Champion

During the 1990's, Jeanette became the most recognized, successful, and popular player in her sport. The WPBA thrived, in large measure because of television coverage. In 1993, the association had its first television exposure, four hours, at its tournament of champions. Within five years, women's billiards was televised for more than fifty hours. The women's game became more successful than the men's game, both in popularity and in

---

### WPBA and Other Championships

|  |  |
|------|-------------|
| 1994 | U.S. Open 9-Ball |
| | Baltimore Billiards Classic |
| | Kasson Classic |
| | San Francisco Classic |
| | WPBA Nationals |
| 1995 | Olhausen Classic |
| | Brunswick Classic |
| 1997 | Huebler Classic |
| | Olhausen Classic |
| 1998 | Penn Ray Classic |
| | Cuetec Cues Hawaii Classic |
| 1999 | Ultimate Shootout |
| | ESPN Ladies' Tournament of Champions |
| 2004 | Atlanta Women's Open |
| | ESPN Ultimate Challenge |
| | World Trick Shot Championships |
| | BCA Open |
| 2005 | China Invitational |
| 2007 | World Team Cup |
| | Empress Cup |
| | International Skins Billiard Championship |

earnings. Pool is a game in which women can compete equally with men, since size and strength are not important.

Jeanette's competitive nature paid off: In 1994, she won the WPBA Nationals and the U.S. Open 9-Ball tournament. As of 2008, Jeanette had claimed more than thirty WPBA-sponsored national and international tournaments and titles in her fourteen-year professional career. At one time ranked the number-one player in the world, she was named the WPBA sportsperson of the year in 1998. In 2001, representing the United States at the World Games, Jeanette won the gold medal; she won two silver medals at separate World Games. A versatile player, Jeanette won in every type of game. In 2004, she won the World Trick Shot Challenge Championship, and in 2005, she won the China Invitational. Furthermore, Jeanette won the World Team Cup, Empress Cup, and the International Skins Billiard Championship with her doubles partner and husband, George Breedlove.

### Continuing the Story

A national spokesperson for the Scoliosis Association, Jeanette settled in Indianapolis, Indiana, with her husband and children. She served as a trustee of the Women's Sports Foundation and was fea-

tured on ESPN's list of "Sexiest Female Athletes" in the world and *Esquire* magazine's "Ten Women We Love." She also made commercials and appeared on television, guesting on such programs as *Today, The Late Show with David Letterman*, and *Live with Regis and Kelly*. Jeanette oversaw the building of Black Widow Billiards at Carolina Crossroads in Roanoke Rapids, North Carolina, which opened in 2008 and was equipped for televised tournaments and corporate and charity events.

### Summary

The most successful and recognizable billiards player of her generation, Jeanette Lee's great determination and dedication to her craft provided an example of what women athletes can achieve. By August, 2005, she had undergone nine surgeries on her back, neck, and shoulders, all related to scoliosis. The chronic pain associated with her condition served as an obstacle to overcome.

Within a few months of joining the professional tour, Jeanette was ranked among the top ten players. Competing and winning at straight pool, 9-ball, trick shots, and speed pool, Jeanette became a legend in her sport.

*Randy L. Abbott*

### Additional Sources

Lee, Jeanette, and Adam Scott Gershenson. *The Black Widow's Guide to Killer Pool: Become the Player to Beat.* New York: Three Rivers Press, 2000.
Reilly, Rick. "Doing the Hustle." *Sports Illustrated* 103, no. 1 (July 4, 2005): 82.

# Greg LeMond

**Born:** June 26, 1961
Lakewood, California
**Also known as:** Gregory James LeMond (full
name)

### Early Life

Gregory James LeMond was born in Lakewood, near Los Angeles, California, on June 26, 1961. At the age of seven, he moved to Lake Tahoe, California, and a few years later to Nevada, where his father began a real estate business.

One of three children of Bertha and Robert LeMond, Greg grew up in an athletic family. Greg's sister was a superior gymnast and his father was a serious senior amateur cyclist. Greg loved freestyle skiing. He practiced hard to improve his skills. After learning that cycling was the best off-season training for skiing, he turned to it with a vengeance. A lack of snow in the 1975-1976 season kept Greg on wheels rather than on skis. He discovered that he really liked cycling and began to race.

### The Road to Excellence

Greg's success in competitive cycling was instantaneous. He won the California Junior Championship in 1976, his first year of competition, and went on to win the National Junior Championship in 1977.

The support of Greg's family was crucial to his success. The whole family attended his races. His mother provided him with special meals, his sister cheered him on, and his father often raced alongside him. At the age of fifteen, Greg mapped out his cycling career goals. Before many years had passed he had achieved every one of them, except for the Olympic victory that became impossible when the United States boycotted the 1980 Olympic Games.

Greg dropped out of high school so he could dedicate himself more fully to cycling. Only later did he earn his degree through correspondence courses. In 1979,

he realized his dream of winning the World Junior Championship in Argentina.

Successful cycling takes coaching, but there were few American coaches who were capable of helping Greg shape his impressive talents. Fortunately for Greg, he came under the wing of Eddie Borysewicz, a Polish coach who was crucial in providing him with a systematic training program. Soon Greg was ready for bigger things.

*Greg LeMond competing in 1994.* (Mike Powell/Getty Images)

## The Emerging Champion

Greg set his sights on turning pro, but it was a difficult road. A young American like Greg had a tough time making it in a sport that had always been dominated by Europeans.

In 1980, while still an amateur, Greg won the Circuit de la Sarthe race, the first time in history that an American had ever won a major stage race. He soon signed his first professional contract with Renault, a French cycling team, after its coach, Cyrille Guimard, had seen Greg race.

Greg was a natural cyclist. He had a huge lung capacity that helped him perform magnificently in the mountains of the European circuit and a physical frame that provided both strength and speed. However, he still had to mature—to learn more racing tactics and how to compete on the world-class circuit, where psychology and group strategy are as important as raw skill.

Greg's first major international victory was the Coors Classic in 1981. Two years later, he won the World Road Championships Professional Road Race, the first American ever to do so. His string of outstanding performances the same year earned him the Super Prestige Pernod Trophy. In 1985, Greg finished second in the most important and grueling cycling event in the world, the Tour de France. With Greg's assistance, teammate Bernard Hinault won the event.

Competitive cycling is a sport that demands a rare combination of individual excellence and teamwork. Greg, however, felt that he had not been given the chance for individual victory in the Tour

| | Major Championships | |
|---|---|---|
| Year | Competition | Place |
| 1976 | California Junior Championships, Road Race | 1st |
| 1977 | U.S. Nationals, Junior Road Race | 1st |
| 1979 | World Road Championships, Junior Road Race | Gold |
| | World Cycling Championships, Junior Individual Pursuit | Silver |
| | World Road Championships, Junior Team Time Trials | Bronze |
| 1980 | Circuit de la Sarthe | 1st |
| 1981, 1985 | Coors Classic | 1st |
| 1982 | Tour de l'Avenir | 1st |
| 1983, 1989 | World Road Championships, Professional Road Race | Gold |
| 1985 | World Road Championships, Professional Road Race | Silver |
| | Tour de France | 2d |
| 1986, 1989-90 | Tour de France | 1st |
| 1990 | Championship of Zurich | 2d |
| 1992 | Tour du Pont | 1st |

de France. He vowed to win it the following year. In 1986, after a twenty-four-day, 2,500-mile race marred by savage competition with his own teammate, Hinault, Greg became the first American ever to win the Tour de France. Finally the American public began to find the sport interesting.

The bright picture changed in 1987. Greg's cycling career appeared to be finished. He broke his wrist in an early season race, and then on April 20 he was nearly killed in a hunting accident. While on a turkey shoot in California, he was accidentally struck by sixty shotgun pellets that pierced his vital organs. Only rapid evacuation by a helicopter saved his life.

## Continuing the Story

Greg's recovery was complicated by an emergency appendectomy and other injuries. In 1988, while competing on the tour, he suffered the indignity of having to be pushed along by his teammates. However, Greg showed heart in one of the most spectacular comeback finishes in sporting history. In 1989, Greg won the Tour de France. Entering the last stage, he was fifty seconds behind his main rival, Laurent Fignon, and no one thought Greg could possibly win. However, he roared into Paris at the unheard-of average speed of thirty-four miles per hour and won by only eight seconds, the narrowest winning margin in the race's history. Greg went on to victory once again in the 1989 World Road Championships. In 1990, he won the Tour de France for the third time.

## Records and Milestones

First American cyclist to capture victories in the Tour de France and the World Road Championships Professional Road Race

First cyclist to win three medals in any world championship competition

## Honors and Awards

| | |
|---|---|
| 1983 | Super Prestige Pernod Trophy |
| 1984 | Tour de France White Jersey (best rookie cyclist) |
| 1989 | *Sports Illustrated* Sportsman of the Year |
| 1991 | Jesse Owens International Trophy |

Though he made an astonishing recovery from the injuries sustained in 1987, Greg was never the same afterward. Following his third victory in the Tour de France, he struggled to maintain his form, winning only one race in 1992, the Tour du Pont. In 1994, Greg decided to retire after he was diagnosed with a rare muscular disease called mitochondrial myopathy.

## Summary

Greg LeMond's stature as an all-time cycling great will never be in doubt. Because of Greg, American cyclists for the first time had to be taken seriously on the international scene. His career shows how important family support, individual dedication, and focused planning are to the realization of athletic goals. Moreover, Greg's heroic surmounting of adversity is a magnificent inspiration for others who yearn for success in the face of long odds.

*Ronald C. Sawyer*

## Additional Sources

Abt, Samuel. *Up the Road: Cycling's Modern Era from LeMond to Armstrong.* Boulder, Colo.: VeloPress, 2005.

LeMond, Greg. *Time Trials: My Life.* London: Yellow Jersey, 2004.

Startt, James. *Tour de France, Tour de Force: A Visual History of the World's Greatest Bicycle Race.* San Francisco: Chronicle Books, 2003.

Whittle, Jeremy. *Le Tour: The History of the Tour de France.* London: Collins, 2007.

# *Johnny Longden*

**Born:** February 14, 1907
      Wakefield, England
**Died:** February 14, 2003
      Banning, California
**Also known as:** John Eric Longden (full name);
  the Pumper; the Fox

## Early Life
John Eric Longden was born in Wakefield, England, on February 14, 1907, and his family later

*Jockey Johnny Longden, who earned horse racing's triple crown with victories in the Kentucky Derby, the Belmont Stakes, and the Preakness Stakes in 1943.* (Courtesy of Amateur Athletic Foundation of Los Angeles)

immigrated to Canada. Great athletes generally arise in two ways: Some first take up their sport as an avocation; others seize the chance their ability offers to extricate themselves from poverty. Johnny belonged to the latter group. He had little formal education and in his teens worked in a coal mine.

Johnny turned what many would perceive as a handicap into an asset, enabling him to raise his prospects of success. He was short, standing 4 feet 11 inches, and weighed only 110 pounds. Although short people often are at a disadvantage, in one occupation they have an edge: Horse racing requires riders of Johnny's dimensions. Horses that have to race with a jockey weighing 150 pounds have severe disadvantages. Johnny saw that a future far superior to that of a coal miner awaited him if he could become a jockey.

## The Road to Excellence
Johnny acquired his earliest experience as a trick rider in Canadian fairs. His riding ability and his talent for handling horses convinced him to try his hand as a professional jockey. In 1927, he began his career and immediately started an intensive program of hard work. He arrived at the track each day by 8:00 A.M. and mingled with the trainers, exercise boys, and walkers. He did not confine himself to learning to ride but endeavored to master every sort of work at the track. To that end, he was willing to perform unpleasant tasks, such as "mucking out" a stable and bandaging a horse's legs. By doing so, he acquired a comprehensive knowledge of racing. Joe Hernandez, Johnny's California agent from 1931 to 1966, noted that Johnny excelled not only as a jockey but also in every aspect of the sport.

Meanwhile, Johnny developed a style of racing that enabled him to realize his riding potential to the fullest. He had an unusual ability to break his horse fast at the start of a race. Taking advantage of the

## Major Championship Victories as a Jockey

| Year | Race | Horse |
|------|------|-------|
| 1943 | Belmont Stakes | Count Fleet |
| | Kentucky Derby | Count Fleet |
| | Preakness Stakes | Count Fleet |

## Major Championship Victories as a Trainer

| Year | Race | Horse |
|------|------|-------|
| 1969 | Kentucky Derby | Majestic Prince |
| | Preakness Stakes | Majestic Prince |

quick start, he tried to keep his horse ahead for the entire race. Because of his style, he was nicknamed "The Pumper" by fans; he was also called "The Fox." Not all horses like to charge immediately to the front, and if Johnny's mount preferred to keep back of the pack initially, he was perfectly capable of riding in this fashion. A breakneck dash from the starting gate to the finish was, however, his trademark.

### The Emerging Champion

Throughout his long career, Johnny was based in California. His first appearance in the state was in the 1931-1932 season, in which he rode at the Tanforan track near San Francisco. His success was immediate: He rode fifty-four winners in fifty-one days.

Southern California became the hub of Johnny's activities during the mid-1930's. He rode at the first meeting of the Santa Anita Race Track in 1936; his first victory there was aboard War Letter on December 26, 1936. Through nearly his entire career, Johnny ranked among the best California jockeys.

Two obstacles confronted Johnny in his efforts to reach the top. Because of the speed and power of racehorses, the chance of injury to a jockey is considerable. Johnny suffered breaks in both arms, both legs (one five times), his collarbone, both feet, two vertebrae, and several ribs. However, even after reaching an age above that of most jockeys, Johnny never let injuries halt his career. Injuries were a part of the price he had to pay to remain a leading rider.

Another difficulty stemmed from Johnny's decision to center his career in California. Most major American racing events during the 1930's, 1940's,

and 1950's took place in the eastern states. A major victory at Santa Anita counted for much less in prestige and financial rewards than a win in an eastern stakes race. Among Johnny's contemporaries was Eddie Arcaro, generally considered the greatest of all jockeys in major stakes races; Johnny was also eclipsed by a younger rival, Willie Shoemaker, in this type of race.

Johnny refused to be discouraged. He did not concentrate on key races but instead aimed to build a consistent run of winners. Because of his extraordinary longevity as a rider—his forty years in the saddle was surpassed only by Shoemaker's forty-one years—he outranked nearly all other riders in purses and number of wins.

### Continuing the Story

Johnny's peak as a jockey was in the early 1940's. In 1943, he rode one of the twentieth century's greatest horses, Count Fleet, to victory in the triple crown. The triple crown consists of the Kentucky Derby, the Preakness Stakes, and the Belmont Stakes, the most important races for three-year-olds. Johnny's wins in 1943 were his only victories in these events as a jockey. He was also the leading money-winner in 1943, a feat he repeated in 1945.

Afterward, Johnny returned to his usual steady, rather than spectacular, path. In 1950, he once again found himself in the limelight. His adept riding of Noor enabled his mount to upset Citation, the 1948 triple crown winner, in four successive races.

Johnny closed his career in triumph. His last mount was in the March 13, 1966, San Juan Capistrano Handicap, the eighth race of the day. His horse, George Royal, had not won all year, and Johnny, aged fifty-nine, was well past his prime. George Royal was a come-from-behind horse, unamenable to Johnny's front-running style. Johnny

### Records and Milestones

Only person to ride and train Kentucky Derby winners
Annual money leader (1943, 1945)
Triple Crown winner aboard Count Fleet (1943)
6,032 career victories

### Honors and Awards

1958    Inducted into Jockeys' Hall of Fame

responded to the challenge. He won the race, nosing out Bobby Unser, a much younger jockey.

In 1966, Johnny retired with 6,032 wins, at the time the world's record. The total purses won by his horses were more than $24 million. After his riding career, he worked for many years as a trainer. He died in 2003.

## Summary

After a hard youth working as a coal miner in Canada, Johnny Longden decided to become a jockey. Careful study of all aspects of racing enabled him to attain his goal. He was a leading rider for forty years, centering his activities in California. Although he did not specialize in major stakes races, he won the triple crown aboard Count Fleet in 1943. He closed his career with a victory in his final race.

*Bill Delaney*

## Additional Sources

Beckwith, Brainerd Kellogg. *The Longden Legend.* South Brunswick, N.J.: A. S. Barnes, 1976.

Drager, Marvin. *The Most Glorious Crown: The Story of America's Triple Crown Thoroughbreds from Sir Barton to Affirmed.* Chicago: Triumph Books, 2005.

Jacques, L. L., and Sue Morton. *Joey: Calgary's Horse and Racing's Hall of Famers.* Calgary, Alta.: Puckshot Press, 2006.

# *Jeannie Longo*

**Born:** October 31, 1958
     Annecy, France
**Also known as:** The Cannibal

## Early Life

Jeannie Longo was born on October 31, 1958, in Annecy, a French city located 20 miles south of Geneva, Switzerland. Jeannie was the youngest of three girls born to athletic parents. Her father was a competitive runner and rugby player; her mother taught sports in school. The family moved to Grenoble, and Jeannie began following her parents down the ski slopes at a young age. She also developed a talent for the piano, which she studied seriously for ten years.

At the age of seventeen, Jeannie enrolled in college and began devoting more time to studying and to skiing. She began cycling during the warmer seasons as a way to stay in shape for skiing. The sports complemented each other, and she became French university champion in skiing. She met her future husband, Patrice Ciprelli, during her competitive skiing career, and he helped coach her in both sports.

## The Road to Excellence

Jeannie began to concentrate on cycling, and she won the French National Road Racing Championship in 1979. The next year, she successfully defended that title, picking up the France National Pursuit Championship as well. Both titles were hers for the rest of the 1980's. She became known for riding at the front of the pack, even though the riders in front work hardest, cutting the wind for the riders behind them.

The 1981 World Championships in Prague, Czechoslovakia (now Czech Republic), marked Jeannie's emergence to world prominence. Jeannie missed the gold medal by inches. She had promised Ciprelli that she would marry him when she was world cham-

pion; she added jokingly that people said she lost the race to avoid fulfilling her promise. Jeannie also took third place in the individual pursuit competition in 1981. She continued to compete in both skiing and cycling events, earning two more bronze medals in the individual pursuit at the World Championships in 1982 and 1983.

Jeannie's breakthrough came in 1984, when she won the Tour of Texas, a series of events that drew riders from all over the world. She took a silver medal in the individual pursuit at the 1984 World Championships and then repeated her win at the Tour of Texas the following year. Also in 1985, she earned her first World Championships Road Race, along with another second-place finish in the individual pursuit. Soon after, she married Ciprelli. She continued to compete using her maiden name, under which she had become famous.

## The Emerging Champion

Jeannie had been a champion almost since her entry into the sport of cycling, but after her first world championship, she dominated the sport. In 1986, she won the World Championships Road Race and

### *Major Championship Victories*

| Year | Competition | Place |
|---|---|---|
| 1979-89, 1992, 1995, 2006 | French National Road Racing Championship | 1st |
| 1980-89, 1992, 1994 | French National 3-kilometer Pursuit | 1st |
| 1984-85 | Tour of Texas | 1st |
| 1985-87, 1989, 1995 | World Championships Road Race | 1st |
| 1986, 1988-89 | World Championships 3-kilometer Pursuit | 1st |
| 1987 | Coors Classic | 1st |
| | Tour of Colombia | 1st |
| | Tour of Norway | 1st |
| 1987-89 | Tour de France Féminin | 1st |
| 1988-89 | World Championships 30-kilometer Points Race | 1st |
| 1991 | Ore-Ida Women's Challenge | 1st |
| 1992 | Olympic Games Road Race | Silver |
| | Olympic Games Pursuit | 5th |
| 1995, 1999, 2001-03, 2006 | French National Time Trial Championship | 1st |
| 1995-97 | World Championships Time Trial | 1st |
| 1996 | Olympic Games Road Race | Gold |
| | Olympic Games Time Trial | Silver |
| 2000 | Olympic Games Time Trial | Bronze |

the 3-kilometer Pursuit, earning two gold medals in the space of a week and beating Rebecca Twigg of the United States at the latter's home track in Boulder, Colorado.

Jeannie extended her stay in Colorado to take advantage of the thin air at the high altitude. She set a world record for distance traveled in 1 hour by a female cyclist. Few accomplishments had eluded her, but she still lacked an Olympic medal and a victory in the Tour de France Féminin (later known as Grande Boucle), a multiday race run in conjunction with the men's Tour de France. In 1985 and 1986, she finished second to Italy's Maria Canins in the Tour de France Féminin, an event that Jeannie had pushed to get established. The race was first run in 1984.

Training for the 1987 event began in January, with Jeannie riding up mountain roads in the Alps while her husband followed her in a car. She began the year's racing by winning the week-long Tour of Colombia, the week-long Tour of Norway, and the two-week Coors Classic. When the Tour de France Féminin began in July, she was ready for mountain riding. She dueled with Canins for days and then won a decisive stage of the race in the Alps. That stage win effectively clinched the race for her; Canins finished second.

Jeannie had her eye on further world records, and she returned to Colorado. She set a new world hour record as well as four other records to bring her total to eleven. The records were erased, however, when she tested positive for the drug ephedrine. She had never tested positive before, and she claimed that traces of the drug came from herbal therapy she had undergone in France. Nevertheless, her records were stripped from her, and she faced a one-month suspension from cycling. No major events were held during her suspension, and she returned ready to prove herself.

Jeannie continued to win major championships. She won the Tour de France Féminin in 1988 and 1989. She also won the World Championships 3-kilometer Pursuit in 1988 and 1989, Road Race in 1989, and the 30-kilometer Points Race in 1988 and 1989. After her amazing 1989 season, she retired from the sport, as did Canins.

## Continuing the Story

Jeannie's retirement lasted only one year. Many people believed that she missed cycling and the

---

### Record

| | |
|---|---|
| 2000 | Broke world one-hour women's record (44.767 kilometers) |

---

spotlight, particularly after compatriot Catherine Marsal won the 1990 World Championships Road Race. Jeannie began her comeback with the 1991 Ore-Ida Women's Challenge road race in Idaho. To maintain a low profile, she entered under the name Jane Ciprelli, using her husband's last name. She won the race.

An Olympic medal was the one major cycling prize that Jeannie had not yet won. A minor accident that broke her bicycle's derailleur had dropped her to sixth place in the 1984 road race, and in 1988, she had tired while chasing the leader, dropping back to finish in twenty-first place. Another chance came in 1992. She finally won her medal, finishing second in the road race to Kathryn Watt. She also placed fifth in the 3,000-meter individual pursuit. She continued to take on challenges, even experimenting with racing mountain bikes in off-road races. She placed second in the 1993 World Championship Mountain Bike road race. Always a fierce competitor, she was fined for her disregard of the winner's national anthem at the awards ceremony.

In 1994 and 1995, Jeannie put together a string of impressive victories: The French National 3-kilometer Pursuit, the World Championships Road Race, and the French National Road Racing Championship. After losing the gold medal in the 1988 Olympics because of a broken derailleur, Jeannie took the 1996 Olympic Games in Atlanta, Georgia, by storm, winning the gold medal in the road race competition and the silver in the time trials. She added another win at the 1997 World Championships Time Trial to her considerable list of victories, bringing her total of World Championships titles to thirteen. At the age of forty-one, Jeannie competed in her fourth Olympic Games in Sydney, Australia, taking the bronze medal in the time-trial event.

Though Jeannie took issue with the Chinese government, especially concerning its occupation of Tibet, in 2008, she competed in a record-tying seventh consecutive Olympics, finishing in fourth place in the women's time trial. At the age of forty-nine, she was still competitive on the world stage.

Pushing herself against much younger cyclists, she came close to capturing a medal in the 23.5-kilometer race, even while hampered by a sciatic nerve in the back of her leg. Jeannie, who had not missed an Olympics since 1984 when women's cycling debuted, refused to stay in the Olympic Village accommodations and criticized the International Olympic Committee for awarding the Games to Beijing, claiming the decision was made for "marketing reasons." Having gained four Olympic medals over the years, Jeannie decided to participate in the 2008 Olympics, believing that boycotting the Games would prove nothing. However, she refused to do any sightseeing while in China and only competed in her events and then went home after narrowly missing a bronze medal in the road time trial.

Feisty and opinionated, Jeannie was dubbed "The Cannibal" by fans because of her insatiable hunger for success. At 5 feet 4 inches and 105 pounds, Jeannie's strength and stamina seemed out of proportion to her appearance. Her enormous competitive drive alienated competitors and fans over the years. Though some see cycling as a team sport, Jeannie was never one to sacrifice her success if it meant giving less than her best. Jeannie and her husband, who was also her coach, settled near Grenoble, France, where Jeannie raised chickens and organic vegetables and sold her own line of vitamins.

## Summary

Jeannie Longo is arguably the greatest women's cyclist ever to compete. She won more than 900 races in all. Her persistent charges to the front and consistent strength made her a formidable competitor. She won fifty-five national titles, set thirty-eight world records, earned a combined thirteen world road and track titles, and was victorious in three women's Tour de France competitions.

*A. J. Sobczak, updated by Randy L. Abbott*

## Additional Sources

Abt, Samuel. "Longo Renounces Retirement Plans." *The New York Times*, October 9, 1997, p. C6.

Levinson, David, and Karen Christensen, eds. *Encyclopedia of World Sport: From Ancient to Present.* Santa Barbara, Calif.: ABC-Clio, 1996.

Lipoński, Wojciech. *World Sports Encyclopedia.* St. Paul, Minn.: Motorbooks International, 2003.

Thompson, Christopher S. *The Tour de France: A Cultural History.* Berkeley: University of California Press, 2006.

Wallechinsky, David, and Jaime Loucky. *The Complete Book of the Olympics: 2008 Edition.* London: Aurum Press, 2008.

# Ellen MacArthur

**Born:** July 8, 1976
   Whatstandwell, Derbyshire, England
**Also known as:** Dame Ellen Patricia MacArthur
   (full name)

## Early Life

Ellen Patricia MacArthur was born July 8, 1976, to parents who were both teachers. Although Derbyshire is far from any coast, Ellen dreamed of the sea. She was inspired by Arthur Ransome's stories from the 1930's about the summer adventures, including sailing, of schoolchildren in the lush Lake District. When Ellen was four years old, her aunt took her on boating trips off England's east coast. Before she was ten years old, Ellen was navigating along the canals of Whatstandwell in her own dinghy, an extravagance she earned by saving her lunch money. She was set to matriculate at a local university when she came down with mononucleosis. During her convalescence, she decided to pursue sailing. In 1994, she moved to Hull to establish her reputation, which was difficult, given her diminutive frame, in a sport widely regarded as requiring extraordinary strength. However, she never thought of giving up; in 1995, she sailed a 21-foot yacht around Great Britain single-handedly and was recognized as the young sailor of the year.

## The Road to Excellence

Unable to find sponsorship in England, Ellen moved to France. Although she lived in a shed at a boatyard for several years, she was determined to find patronage. At twenty-two years old, Ellen sailed solo across the Atlantic. Kingfisher, a retail home-improvement chain, sponsored her. Her breakthrough success came with her first-place finish in the 1998 Route du Rhum, a race in monohulls every four years from Brittany, France, to Guadeloupe. Commentators marveled at Ellen's tenacity and her ability to maintain the difficult maneuvers of competitive solo sailing in the open Atlantic Ocean, given her physical build and her gender—solo sailing had seldom been a woman's sport. For her achievement, Ellen was named, ironically, the 1999 yachtsman of the year. For the re-

mainder of 1999 and most of 2000, Ellen continued to race. In June, 2000, Ellen set a new world record for an Atlantic crossing in a monohull: just under fifteen days.

## The Emerging Champion

Ellen's performance in the 2000-2001 Vendée Globe catapulted her into international prominence. The grueling race, run every four years, is an around-the-world competition for single-handed yachts. Unlike other circumnavigational races, the Vendée Globe is nonstop, and the sailors can receive no outside assistance. With its inception in the late 1980's, the race, traversing some of the most treacherous stretches of navigation, became the premiere event in open-ocean racing, demanding extraordinary endurance, stamina, and mental sharpness over a period of nearly four months. Few took Ellen's entry seriously, but during the race, she challenged for the lead consistently. Although Ellen did not win, she finished second—a little

*Ellen MacArthur.* (Charles Platiau/Reuters/Landov)

## Sailing Records

| Year | Event/Location | Time | Record |
|---|---|---|---|
| 2000 | England to Rhode Island | 14 days, 23 hours, 11 minutes | East to west in a single-handed monohull |
| 2000-01 | Vendée Globe | 94 days, 4 hours, 25 minutes, 40 seconds | Continuous circumnavigation by a woman in a monohull |
| 2004 | New York to England | 7 days, 3 hours, 50 minutes | Fastest transatlantic crossing by a woman |
| 2005 | Around the world | 71 days, 14 hours, 18 minutes, 33 seconds | Single-handed, continuous circumnavigation |

more than a day off the pace—in ninety-four days, four hours, twenty-five minutes, and forty seconds, the fastest time a woman had ever achieved. She was the youngest woman to complete a solo circumnavigation. Her celebrity was magnified when reports stated she had lost valuable time at a critical moment when she assisted a competitor whose boat had been damaged.

Although Ellen continued to race—she acquired another victory and another record in the 2002 Route de Rhum—she set her sights on the world record for solo, nonstop circumnavigation, a notoriously difficult undertaking. She had to contend with a range of weather events, tricky currents, unforeseeable technical problems, and the heavy toll of fatigue and isolation. Ellen agreed to maintain a live Web site in which she broadcast most of the journey for a mesmerized international audience. When she crossed the finish line on February 7, 2005—after seventy-one days, fourteen hours, eighteen minutes, and thirty-three seconds—she had eclipsed the previous mark by more than a full day. Critics quickly pointed out that improvements in technology had greatly aided Ellen, and reporters often found Ellen joyless and tiresomely self-promoting. Nevertheless, Ellen received international recognition. She was made a Dame by Queen Elizabeth II, the youngest so recognized, and *Time* magazine named her among the year's one hundred heroes and icons.

## Continuing the Story

At twenty-eight years old and at the pinnacle of a sport that had been dominated by men for centuries, Ellen continued to pursue racing opportunities. In 2008, she announced the formation of the BT Team Ellen, a racing conglomerate set to compete in Continental contests. Given the rapid developments in sailing technology and that open-ocean crossing depends on the unpredictable turns of weather and currents, Ellen's circumnavigation

record did not hold for long. France's legendary sailor Francis Joyon broke the record in January, 2008, shattering Ellen's record by more than two weeks with a run of fifty-seven days, thirteen hours, thirty-four minutes, and six seconds. However, Ellen's place in the history of sailing was secured. She wrote inspirational and riveting books about both her sailing career and her world-record run, both of which became best sellers. She became a motivational speaker, challenging women to defy limits and resist stereotypes. Using her considerable celebrity, she established the Ellen MacArthur Trust, a charity that gives children recovering from cancer the chance to experience life on a boat for four days.

## Summary

A lone figure crossing the ocean: few images in sports are more romantic or inspirational. Courage, strength, mental acuity, and stamina all became part of Ellen MacArthur's legend. Although she never joined environmental movements seeking to protect the world's waterways, Ellen created, in her copious writings and on her Web site, a stirring sense of the power and beauty of the ocean. Given her single-minded dedication to her career, savvy entrepreneurial instincts, confidence at a young age, and celebrity status, Ellen redefined a sport that had long been the preserve of wealthy middle-aged men and muscle-bound sailors.

*Joseph Dewey*

## Additional Sources

Compton, Nic. *Sailing Solo: The Legendary Sailors and the Great Races.* Camden, Maine: International Marine/McGraw-Hill, 2003.

Dewar, Oliver. *Extreme Sail.* London: Pavilion, 2006.

MacArthur, Ellen. *Race Against Time.* New York: Penguin, 2006.

_____. *Taking on the World: A Sailor's Extraordinary Solo Race Around the Globe.* Camden, Maine: International Marine/McGraw-Hill, 2005.

# Chris McCarron

**Born:** March 27, 1955
    Dorchester, Massachusetts
**Also known as:** Christopher John McCarron (full name)

### Early Life

Christopher John McCarron was born on March 27, 1955, in Dorchester, Massachusetts, a Boston suburb. Chris was one of nine children of Herbert and Helen McCarron. His father worked as secretary for the Massachusetts Knights of Columbus. Chris grew up in Dorchester, and, in 1972, he graduated from Christopher Columbus High School, where he played varsity ice hockey. He dreamed of playing professional hockey for the Boston

*Chris McCarron smiling after winning the Santa Anita Handicap in 2001. (AP/Wide World Photos)*

Bruins and idolized the team's star defenseman Bobby Orr.

Chris's 5-foot, 2-inch, 95-pound frame, along with the success of his older brother, jockey Gregg McCarron, shifted Chris's sights toward thoroughbred racing. He did not see a racetrack until he was fifteen years old but soon began watching Gregg ride horses. In 1972, Gregg landed Chris a job with leading trainer Odie Clelland.

### The Road to Excellence

In 1973, Odie patiently taught Chris thoroughbred racing at his St. Matthews, South Carolina, farm. Chris was terrified the first time he ever mounted a horse, staying on it for only 4 seconds. He eventually learned the qualities of a genuine horseman, however, while he earned $90 a week for grooming and walking horses. On January 24, 1974, Chris entered his first race as an apprentice jockey. His filly finished last at Bowie Race Track in Maryland. Chris rode in unusual fashion, tucking his right leg higher up in the irons than his left leg.

### The Emerging Champion

In 1974, Chris tirelessly accepted 2,199 mounts and earned about $250,000. His first victory came on February 4, aboard his eleventh mount. Within several weeks, eighteen-year-old Chris had made an impact on the Maryland racing circuit. On March 21, Chris triumphed on four of six mounts. He consistently rode at least three daily winners and even recorded six victories one day at Pimlico Race Track in Baltimore, Maryland. In the fall season, Chris raced six days a week in Maryland and competed Saturday nights and Sunday afternoons at Penn National Race Track in Grantville, Pennsylvania.

On December 17, 1974, Chris broke Canadian Sandy Hawley's record for the most victories by a jockey in one year. He set the record, 516 victories, aboard Ohmylove at Laurel Race Track in Maryland. Chris's record lasted until jockey Kent Desormeaux rode 597 winners in 1989. Chris ended 1974 with 546 winners, earning his first Eclipse Award as the nation's top apprentice jockey. The competition facing Chris, however, did not rival that of California or New York racetracks.

## Continuing the Story

In 1975, Chris repeated as the nation's winningest jockey with 468 triumphs. Two years later, he moved to California and faced stiffer competition at Hollywood Park in Inglewood. Racing style adjustments brought him immediate success upon arriving. In 1980, Chris led the nation for the first time in money earned by a jockey, with $7,663,300, and also won his second Eclipse Award. Also in 1980, his busy fall schedule of eight daily races at Aqueduct Race Track in Ozone Park, New York, and nightly races at the Meadowlands in New Jersey, helped him become only the fourth rider to lead the nation's jockeys in both wins and earnings. Chris also paced all jockeys in money earned in 1981, with $8,397,604, and 1984, with $12,045,813. Seagram's, using a computerized analysis of performances, rated Chris as the best jockey in 1982, 1983, and 1984. In 1983, Chris became the youngest jockey to reach $50 million in purses and also the youngest to ride 3,000 career winners. He rode John Henry during the last four years of the great gelding's career and guided Precisionist to the Breeders' Cup Sprint title in 1985.

Chris did not win a triple crown race until 1986. At the 1983 Preakness Stakes, his mount, Desert Wine, finished second. Another mount, Eternal Prince, placed third in 1985. In 1986, he guided Bold Arrangement to second place in the Kentucky Derby, Broad Brush to third in the Preakness, and Danzig Connection to first on a sloppy track in the Belmont Stakes.

Chris was injured by a terrible accident in October, 1986, at the Santa Anita Race Track in Arcadia,

## Major Championship Victories

| Year | Race | Horse |
|------|------|-------|
| 1974 | Kentucky Derby | Go for Gin |
| 1985 | Breeders' Cup Sprint | Precisionist |
| 1986 | Belmont Stakes | Danzig Connection |
| 1987 | Kentucky Derby | Alysheba |
|      | Preakness Stakes | Alysheba |
| 1988 | Breeders' Cup Classic | Alysheba |
| 1989 | Breeders' Cup Classic | Sunday Silence |
| 1992 | Preakness Stakes | Pine Bluff |
|      | Breeders' Cup Distaff | Paseana |
|      | Breeders' Cup Juvenile | Gilded Time |
| 1994 | Kentucky Derby | Go for Gin |
| 1995 | Breeders' Cup Turf | Northern Spur |
| 1996 | Breeders' Cup Classic | Alphabet Soup |
| 1997 | Belmont Stakes | Touch Gold |
| 2000 | Breeders' Cup Classic | Tiznow |
| 2001 | Breeders' Cup Classic | Tiznow |

California. Three thoroughbreds suddenly fell about six lengths in front of Chris, causing him to be thrown from his horse. Jockey Laffit Pincay, Jr., fell on Chris, breaking Chris's leg in four places. During surgery, a twelve-inch stainless steel rod was attached to the thigh bone of his left leg. Chris courageously resumed racing two months later.

Alysheba was the best horse Chris ever rode. In 1987, Chris won his first Kentucky Derby when Alysheba defeated Bet Twice by three-quarters of a length. Alysheba was clipped by Bet Twice and nearly fell, but won the race in a brilliant final stretch duel. Chris earned his third triple crown victory when Alysheba edged out Bet Twice by one-half length in the Preakness. After finishing a disappointing fourth in the Belmont Stakes, Alysheba won the $1 million Super Derby at Louisiana Downs in September, 1987. Chris then steered Alysheba to victory in the 1988 Breeders' Cup Classic at Churchill Downs. Alysheba earned Eclipse Awards in 1987, as best three-year-old colt, and in 1988, as horse of the year.

In November 1989, Chris replaced suspended jockey Pat Valenzuela aboard Sunday Silence in the Breeders' Cup Classic at Gulfstream Park in Florida. Sunday Silence, who was the 1989 horse of the year, edged archrival Easy Goer by a neck. In June, 1990, Chris took a spill at Hollywood Park that resulted in a broken right arm and two fractured legs, requiring surgery; but in less than three months, he was riding and winning again.

## Milestones

Annual money leader (1980-81, 1984, 1991)
7,141 victories—through 1999, the tenth-highest all-time record

## Honors and Awards

| | |
|------|------|
| 1974 | Eclipse Award, Outstanding Apprentice Jockey |
| 1980 | Eclipse Award, Outstanding Jockey |
|      | George Woolf Memorial Jockey Award |
| 1989 | Inducted into Jockeys' Hall of Fame |
| 1991 | Mike Venezia Memorial Award |
| 1993 | Big Sport of Turfdom Award |

Chris won his second Preakness Stakes in 1992, aboard Pine Bluff, and won his second Kentucky Derby in 1994, aboard Go for Gin. In 1997, he foiled Silver Charm's bid for the triple crown by riding Touch Gold to victory at the Belmont Stakes. At the age of forty-five, Chris won the 2000 and 2001 Breeders' Cup Classics aboard Tiznow, bringing his Breeders' Cup win total to nine.

On June 23, 2002, at the age of forty-seven, Chris officially retired from racing. During his twenty-eight-year career, he won a total of 7,141 races. In 2003, he worked as a race designer for the motion picture *Seabiscuit* and also starred in the film, playing the jockey of legendary horse War Admiral. From 2003 to 2004, Chris served as the general manager of Santa Anita Park and worked for Magna Entertainment Corporation, an owner and operator of horse racetracks, from 2004 to 2005. In October of 2006, Chris opened the North American Racing Academy, a training school for jockeys. In addition, he worked extensively with charity organizations dedicated to helping disabled jockeys.

## Summary

Chris McCarron was one of the finest jockeys in racing history. At the time of his retirement, he ranked in the top ten in career victories. He also won purses totaling $264 million. The Jockeys' Hall of Fame inducted him in August, 1989. Chris won won a bevy of the most important races in the thoroughbred industry, and, in retirement, gave back to the industry.

*David L. Porter, updated by Michael Stellefson*

## Additional Sources

Nack, William. "Silence Roars Once More," *Sports Illustrated* 71 (November 13, 1989): 28.

Pierce, Charles P. "Psycho." *Gentlemen's Quarterly* 63, no. 5 (1993).

Reed, William F. "Rolling in Clover." *Sports Illustrated* 76 (May 25, 1992): 66.

Shulman, Lenny. *Ride of Their Lives: The Triumphs and Turmoil of Today's Top Jockeys.* Lexington, Ky.: Eclipse Press, 2002.

Williams, Gene. "Chris' Craft." *Louisville Magazine* 47, no. 5 (1996).

# *Floretta Doty McCutcheon*

**Born:** July 22, 1888
Ottumwa, Iowa
**Died:** February 2, 1967
Pasadena, California
**Also known as:** Mrs. Mac; Floretta Doty (birth name)

## Early Life

Floretta Doty McCutcheon was born in Ottumwa, Iowa, on July 22, 1888. In 1901, her family moved to Denver, Colorado. In 1921, they moved again to Pueblo, Colorado, where Floretta lived for many years. In Pueblo, she met and later married Robert McCutcheon, a clerk for Colorado Fuel and Iron Corporation. They soon had their only child, Barbara.

For many years, Floretta was a housewife who enjoyed quilting and an occasional round of golf. Unlike so many sports champions, she did not enter her sport until late in life. She began to bowl in Pueblo as a hobby, and on November 23, 1923, at the age of thirty-five, Floretta rolled a 69 in her first game.

## The Road to Excellence

Floretta continued to bowl in Pueblo, participating in two leagues, but then stopped bowling until 1926, when she joined league play again. Her career as a bowler was enhanced when an accomplished and well-known bowler, Jimmy Smith, gave an exhibition in Pueblo. Soon thereafter, Floretta adopted a style similar to Smith's, and a year later, she defeated the hall of famer in a three-game exhibition, 704 to 687. With this victory, "Mrs. Mac," as she became known, began a tour of exhibition matches, traveling through New York, Ohio, Missouri, Minnesota, Michigan, California, Oregon, and Colorado. In 1930, at the age of forty-two, Mrs. Mac began the Mrs. McCutcheon School of Bowling with her partner, C. J. Cain, who had been Jimmy Smith's manager. She continued to travel to major cities throughout the United States, giving exhibition matches and conducting teaching clinics for women. Mrs. Mac was far superior to other women bowlers, as bowling had not been widely popular with women in the United States. Her competitors were men, many of whom she defeated.

## The Emerging Champion

Mrs. Mac weighed 185 pounds when she began bowling. A year after her tour began, she had lost 42 pounds. In 1935, she traveled eighteen thousand miles, giving exhibitions, running bowling "schools," and competing in tournaments.

Mrs. Mac continued her tours and exhibitions and compiled an impressive list of records. She bowled ten 300-pin games, eleven 800-pin three-game series, and more than one hundred series above 700 pins. In Morris, Minnesota, on January 20, 1931, she rolled her highest three-game total of 832 pins. Once, she hit 248 in twelve-game blocks. She averaged 201 for 8,076 games over a ten-year period. No woman had ever scored better than her 248 twelve consecutive games.

Mrs. Mac also placed first among the women in the 1932 Olympic Games, and, during the 1938-1939 season, she averaged 206 pins in New York, a record that stood until the 1963-1964 season. None of Mrs. Mac's records is included in Women's International Bowling Congress (WIBC) records because she scored in instructional exhibitions or unsanctioned match play.

In spite of the many records she set, Mrs. Mac's greatest contribution to bowling was her school. She traveled extensively throughout the United States and is credited with instructing as many as 300,000 women in bowling. She maintained that women would eventually bowl as well as men because bowling required rhythm, control, timing, and coordination rather than strength and speed. Although bowling had been popular with women, its popularity increased dramatically among women

---

## Honors and Awards

| | |
|---|---|
| 1956 | Inducted into WIBC Hall of Fame |
| 1973 | Inducted into Colorado Sports Hall of Fame |
| 1988 | Inducted into Iowa Sports Hall of Fame |

thirty-five and older because of Mrs. Mac's tours, exhibitions, and instruction. Her contributions made bowling the most popular amateur sport in the United States during the Depression.

## Continuing the Story

Mrs. Mac continued to travel, compete, and instruct during the decade of the 1930's. She was a spot bowler who used the four-step delivery and was highly regarded because of her consistent accuracy. She made further contributions to the game by writing bowling booklets, organizing leagues, and creating an instructional series for female bowlers.

In 1939, she became an instructor at the Capital Health Center in New York City. In 1944, she moved to Chicago, Illinois, where she continued her instruction at the Bowlium. In 1954, she announced her retirement and moved to San Gabriel, California, to help care for her two grandchildren. She left the game after dominating bowling for fifteen years and molding champions for fifteen more years. Although she held all of the bowling records for women, she never won a tournament. However, for her many contributions as teacher and athlete, she was inducted into the WIBC Hall of Fame in 1956 as a Star of Yesteryear and was later named as an honorary member of WIBC. She died in 1967.

## Summary

Floretta "Mrs. Mac" Doty McCutcheon was known as both a teacher and an athlete. She began her career late in life, at the age of thirty-five. After defeating Jimmy Smith, a well-known champion, she established herself as the dominant woman bowler of the 1930's. For many years, she toured the United States, giving exhibitions and conducting clinics for women. She also wrote booklets advocating the four-step delivery and spot bowling. During this time, she bowled more than eight thousand matches, averaging more than 200 per game. In the 1938-1939 season, she set a WIBC league average of 206, a record that stood for twenty-five years. She helped open the door for women in athletics.

*Susan J. Bandy*

## Additional Sources

Layden, Joseph. *Women in Sports: The Complete Book on the World's Greatest Female Athletes.* Los Angeles: General, 1997.

McIntosh, Ron. *Bowler's Handbook: A Guide to (Almost) Everything in Bowling.* Elfers, Fla.: McIntosh, 2006.

Miller, Ernestine G. *Making Her Mark: Firsts and Milestones in Women's Sports.* Chicago: Contemporary Books, 2002.

Woolum, Janet. *Outstanding Women Athletes: Who They Are and How They Influenced Sports in America.* Phoenix, Ariz.: Oryx Press, 1998.

# *Larry Mahan*

**Born:** November 21, 1943
Salem, Oregon

## Early Life

Larry Mahan was born on a farm near Salem, Oregon, on November 21, 1943. Larry's love for riding horses was evident early in his life. By the time he was ten years old, he was spending most of his time at the Oregon State Fairgrounds, breaking every colt he could find. At the age of twelve, he entered his first junior rodeo, roping and riding calves, where he won six dollars and a belt buckle. By the time he graduated from high school, he was ready to trade his job sacking groceries for a chance to make it big in rodeo.

## The Road to Excellence

Even though Larry was a good rider, he had his fair share of injuries. After graduating from high school, he entered a rodeo in Stockton, California, where he rode a bull named Rattler. A few seconds out of the chute, Larry flew off and learned why they called the bull Rattler. Once he was off the bull, it came after him and stepped on his jaw, breaking it in five places. This injury kept Larry from riding for several months while he was recuperating. During this time, he married Darlene, and they moved to Arizona, where they attended Arizona State University. Like most newlyweds, they had little money, so Larry went to what he knew best—the rodeo—to earn money for tuition.

Larry Mahan, who was the World All-Around Champion in rodeo six times from 1966 to 1973. (ProRodeo Hall of Fame and Museum of the American Cowboy)

## The Emerging Champion

Larry broke into the professional rodeo circuit in 1965. As a new face in rodeo, he attracted attention quickly when, during his rookie year, he took first place in the Professional Rodeo Cowboys Association (PRCA) bull riding category and seventh in the All-Around Cowboy Championship. Larry soon became widely recognized because of his frequent exposure at rodeos. To participate in as many rodeos as he could, he flew his own plane to rodeos across the country, often competing in two a day.

Larry's success involved some serious injuries. For example, he was kicked by a bull in the back of his neck, breaking three vertebrae. When he was X-rayed at the hospital, the doctor did not see the broken bones and told Larry it was all right to ride. A month and about twelve bull rides later, the doctor discovered that he had missed the broken vertebrae. Larry's neck had healed on its own; he simply complained of a stiff neck.

## Milestones, Honors, and Awards

| | |
|---|---|
| 1965, 1967 | PRCA Bull Riding Champion |
| 1966 | Inducted into Rodeo Hall of Fame, the National Cowboy Hall of Fame |
| 1966-70, 1973 | PRCA World Champion All-Around Cowboy |
| 1967 | NFR Saddle Bronc Riding Average Winner |
| 1979 | Inducted into Pro Rodeo Hall of Fame |
| 1985 | Inducted into Oregon Sports Hall of Fame |

Larry competed in professional rodeo for about thirteen years. The late 1960's were his glory years. He held the record for the most consecutive PRCA World Champion All-Around Cowboy titles from 1966 to 1970. He emerged at the top again in 1973, taking a record six All-Around Cowboy Championships. He consistently won first to fourth place in bull riding, bareback riding, and saddle bronc riding.

### Continuing the Story

Larry differed from other rodeo athletes in that he was also a successful businessman and public relations manager. He was called "Goldfinger" because, unlike other cowboys who spent what money they earned, Larry invested in different businesses. He had a talent for making money out of almost anything. Jim Shoulders, another well-known cowboy, once suggested that Larry had been important in promoting rodeo by using the media and promoting himself in business.

After his rodeo career, Larry became involved in a wide range of activities. For a while, he broke into television to assist with rodeo commentary, and he even formed his own group as a singer, touring the country and playing during rodeos. His business ventures kept him busy as well; he established the "Larry Mahan Collection" of boots and western clothing. He was also involved in the longhorn cat- tle business, and in the early 1980's, he bought a cattle ranch in Colorado. He became interested in horse cutting (training horses to "cut" or separate cattle from a herd) and bought another ranch in Bandera, Texas.

Larry had learned an important lesson when he was competing on the rodeo circuit: To get to the top, he had had to put aside many other things in his life. His dedication to rodeo cost him a marriage, and his two children grew up without seeing much of their father. He remarried after retiring from rodeo, and his goals centered more on spending time with his wife, Robin.

### Summary

Larry Mahan was different from other cowboys. While in the arena, he became one of the most successful rodeo athletes, with six All-Around Cowboy titles plus numerous other individual event titles. Outside the arena, he was able to promote himself and rodeo while investing his money in business. By the end of his rodeo career, he had learned that fame, money, and success were not everything. The more important things in his life became his family and ranching.

*Rodney D. Keller*

### Additional Sources

Ehringer, Gavin, and Gary Vorhes. *Rodeo Legends: Twenty Extraordinary Athletes of America's Sport.* Colorado Springs, Colo.: Western Horseman Magazine, 2003.

St. John, Bob. *On Down the Road: The World of the Rodeo Cowboy.* Austin, Tex.: Eakin Press, 1983.

Wade, Bob. *Ridin' and Wreckin'.* Salt Lake City, Utah: Gibbs Smith, 1996.

# *Valentin Mankin*

**Born:** August 19, 1938
Kiev, Soviet Union (now in Ukraine)

## Early Life

Valentin Mankin was born on August 19, 1938, in Kiev, a port city on the Dnieper River and the capital of the Ukraine. Not all of the citizens of Kiev are of Ukrainian heritage; such is the case of Valentin, who is of Russian descent. Kiev, which recovered well from immense damage sustained during World War II, is considered one of the most beautiful in Europe. Along with its parks and gardens, it is well known for its wealth of medieval art and architecture. Valentin, an only child, was raised in this atmosphere. He attended school in Kiev and planned to become a building engineer.

Legend has it that, as a young man, Valentin was concerned that certain activities, such as running, would cause blood to be concentrated in his feet, thereby limiting the flow to his brain. The resultant lack of oxygen to his brain, he reasoned, could lead to diminished intelligence. He therefore looked to activities that might stimulate a stronger blood flow to his head.

One sport that Valentin felt might accomplish this was water polo, and as a young teenager he looked forward to the challenge of playing on the water polo team. However, he was not selected for the team, because his hands were considered too small to handle the ball effectively. Little did Valentin realize what a blessing those small hands would be in shaping the course of his brilliant future.

## The Road to Excellence

As Valentin walked dejectedly along the banks of the Dnieper pondering his failure to make the water polo team, he saw young rowers practicing on the river. Spotting a man whom he thought was the rowing coach, the ambitious youngster asked what it would take to be a rower. The man responded that he did not know, because he was the sailing coach, whereupon the undaunted Valentin asked what he needed to do to be on the sailing team. The coach, no doubt taken with the enthusiasm and hopefulness of the boy, directed him to the sailing team.

While Valentin enjoyed the mere act of sailing, he set himself apart from other young sailors because he was mature enough to learn everything he could about the principles underlying the practice of sailing. His complete dedication to the sport was rewarded when he won his first race within a year of his talk with the coach along the banks of the Dnieper. Three years later, at the age of nineteen, he qualified for the Soviet national team. He won his first national championship when he was twenty-one.

Valentin was racing Finn-class boats. These boats are 14 feet 9 inches long and weigh 314 pounds. Having only one sail and a center board—a structure that hangs down into the water from the bottom center of the boat for stability in currents—the Finn is a small craft that requires only one person to sail it in competitive events.

## The Emerging Champion

In 1964, at the age of twenty-six, Valentin was selected as an alternate to the Tokyo Olympics. Four years later, in 1968, he represented the Soviet Union at the Mexico Olympics, thus beginning one of the most brilliant records in Olympic sailing history. In Mexico, he won the gold medal in the Finn class.

During the ensuing four years, Valentin switched to a Tempest-class boat. The Tempest, at 977 pounds and almost 22 feet in length—with a jib, the small forward sail on sloop-styled boats; a mainsail; and a spinnaker, a large balloon-like sail used in racing—requires a racing crew of two people. In the 1972 Munich Olympics, Valentin won his second gold medal with his crewman, Vitalii Drydyra.

---

### Major Championships

| | | |
|---|---|---|
| 1968 | Olympic gold medalist (winning score of 11.7; Finn class) | |
| 1972 | Olympic gold medalist (winning score of 28.1; Tempest class) | |
| 1973 | World Championship (Finn class) | |
| 1976 | Olympic silver medalist (score of 30.40; Tempest class) | |
| 1980 | Olympic gold medalist (winning score of 24.7; Star class) | |

In the 1976 Olympics at Montreal, Valentin and his new crewman, Vladislav Akimenko, were beaten in the Tempest competition by a team from Sweden and finished with a silver medal. In preparation for the 1980 Olympics in Moscow, Valentin moved up to a Star-class boat. The Star is about 9 inches longer and five hundred pounds heavier than the Tempest and has a jib and mainsail. Valentin took the gold medal in the Star class at Moscow, and in so doing, he became the first Olympic sailor in history to win a gold medal in his home waters.

Valentin, who retired from competitive sailing in 1980, has other championships to his credit, including the 1973 World Championship in the Finn class.

## Continuing the Story

By the time he retired from the Soviet national team, Valentin was regarded by his peers as a sailor of legendary strength and intelligence. He had elevated competitive sailing to a sport requiring elegant precision and technical and strategical superiority, as well as courage, stamina, and physical strength. He continued his valuable contributions to Soviet sailing by establishing an Olympic training camp on the Black Sea. In 1988, he was named head coach of the Soviet national team and moved to Moscow. In 1990, he moved to Alassio, Italy, a coastal village near the port city of Genoa, home of the Italian Sailing Federation. Here the delightful Valentin was warmly welcomed, as much for his wit and gracious enthusiasm as for his immense, well-earned sailing wisdom.

## Summary

As a fifteen-year-old Russian boy, rejected from a Kiev water polo team he had earnestly hoped to join, Valentin Mankin showed the maturity and cheerful fortitude that destined him for one of the finest sailing records in Olympic history. His complete devotion to sailing for more than thirty-five years earned him the genuine respect of his peers, as well as a permanent place among the world's finest competitive sailors.

*Rebecca J. Sankner*

## Additional Sources

Cardwell, Jerry D. *Sailing Big on a Small Sailboat.* 3d ed. Dobbs Ferry, N.Y.: Sheridan House, 2007.

Greenberg, Stan. *Whitaker's Olympic Almanack: An Encyclopaedia of the Olympic Games.* Chicago: Fitzroy Dearborn, 2000.

Kukushkin, V. *Valentin Mankin.* Moscow: Progress, 1979.

Siegman, Joseph. *Jewish Sports Legends: The International Jewish Hall of Fame.* Washington, D.C.: Potomac Books, 2005.

# Nigel Mansell

**Born:** August 8, 1953
Upton-upon-Severn, Worcestershire,
England
**Also known as:** Nigel Ernest James Mansell (full
name)

## Early Life
Nigel Ernest James Mansell was born on August 8, 1953, in Upton-upon-Severn, Worcestershire, England, a village ninety miles northwest of London. Nigel became involved with motor-cart racing through his father, Eric, an engineer with some small-time racing experience. When Nigel was thirteen, he sailed through a fence at a track while going one hundred miles per hour in a cart. Upon arriving at the hospital, Nigel's condition was so severe that a priest administered last rites. Nigel gave an indication of his toughness when he regained consciousness and told the priest to leave.

## The Road to Excellence
Nigel was no stranger to adversity. In a Formula Ford race in 1979, he broke his neck in two places when his car left a racecourse going backward at 120 miles per hour. Unfortunately for Nigel, he had just resigned from an engineering job at an aerospace company to pursue racing full time. He found himself with no job and no money, and for a period of time he had no movement in his arms and legs. Nigel, though, was not one to quit.

Nigel was told that he had to remain flat on his back or risk permanent paralysis. Ignoring his doctor's advice, Nigel discharged himself from the hospital and was back racing in less than two months. Wearing a neck brace, he won the Formula Ford driving championship by winning thirty-two of forty-two starts, despite driving at times in great pain.

Nigel's family was not wealthy enough to sponsor his jump to the next level of competition, so he wrote four hundred letters pleading for financial backing from potential sponsors. In 1978, unable to secure a sponsor, he sold his house and many of his belongings to buy a race car. After four races, Nigel was out of money.

Nigel, a fully qualified engineer, took a job as a window washer in the middle of winter so he could keep racing. Finally, in 1979, he signed on with an established racing team. The move provided him with cash and some valuable exposure.

## The Emerging Champion
In 1980, Nigel made the jump to Formula One, the top level of racing. He quickly established himself as one of the finest drivers in British racing history. He was admired by many for his determination and tenacity, as demonstrated in a race in Dallas, Texas, in 1984. In that race, he pushed his car across the finish line to wind up in sixth place, then collapsed from heat exhaustion.

Nigel was at or near the top of Formula One racing during the 1980's and early 1990's. During

*Nigel Mansell.* (PA Photos/Landov)

191

1985 and 1986, he won a total of thirteen races and narrowly missed the world driving championship. In 1987, Nigel won six races and broke a thirty-four-year-old record by qualifying on the front row for fifteen consecutive races. A late-season crash relegated him to another second-place finish in the world driving championship.

In 1992, Nigel set several records (which were later broken), including most wins (nine), most pole position starts (fourteen), and most consecutive wins at the start of a season (five). This tremendous string of success helped Nigel to clinch the Formula One championship in August, the earliest the crown had been won since 1971.

In 1993, Nigel did something that no other reigning Formula One champion had ever done: He switched to Indy car racing. In his first Indy car race, in Australia, Nigel won both the pole position and the race, both at record average speeds. His first full year of Indy car racing was an unbelievable success. Nigel won the championship by posting five wins in fifteen starts. He also won seven pole positions, captured nine top-five finishes, and eleven top-ten finishes, and led an incredible 603 out of a possible 2,112 laps.

## Continuing the Story

Nigel's accomplishments in the 1993 Indy car series are even more impressive when considering that, prior to the 1993 Indianapolis 500, Nigel had never raced on an oval track. Furthermore, Nigel had to overcome serious back injuries incurred in a crash during his attempt to qualify for a race in Phoenix, Arizona. Doctors had to clean out his lower back with hypodermic needles and vacuum tubes, then surgically repair damaged muscle. One hundred sutures were left deep inside his lower back to reduce swelling. During the week of practice and qualifying before a race in Long Beach, California, a doctor drained one hundred cubic centimeters of blood from his back almost every

### Grand Prix and Other Victories

| | |
|---|---|
| 1985 | European Grand Prix |
| 1985, 1992 | South African Grand Prix |
| 1986 | Belgian Grand Prix |
| | Canadian Grand Prix |
| 1986-87, 1991-92 | French Grand Prix |
| | British Grand Prix |
| 1986, 1990, 1992 | Portuguese Grand Prix |
| 1987 | Austrian Grand Prix |
| 1987, 1991-92 | Spanish Grand Prix |
| 1987, 1992 | San Marino Grand Prix |
| | Mexican Grand Prix |
| 1989 | Hungarian Grand Prix |
| 1989, 1992 | Brazilian Grand Prix |
| 1991 | Italian Grand Prix |
| 1991-92 | German Grand Prix |
| 1993 | Australian Grand Prix |
| | Miller 200 |
| | Marlboro 500 |
| | New England 200 |
| | Bosch Grand Prix |

morning to reduce the swelling. Nigel left the United States after the 1993 season. In 1994, he returned to Formula One and joined the British Touring Car Championship in 1998. In 2005, he briefly returned to racing, competing in the Grand Prix Masters series.

## Summary

Nigel Mansell will be remembered as one of history's greatest racing drivers. He was made an officer of the Order of the British Empire for his services to British motorsports. On the Isle of Man, his name is on the currency and his face appears on postage stamps. He was inducted into the International Motorsports Hall of Fame in 2005.

*William R. Swanson*

## Additional Sources

Arron, Simon, and Mark Hughes. *The Complete Book of Formula One.* St. Paul, Minn.: Motorbooks International, 2003.

Doodson, Mike. *Nigel Mansell: A Photographic Portrait.* Newbury Park, Calif.: Haynes, 2007.

Hilton, Christopher. *Inside the Mind of the Grand Prix Driver: The Psychology of the Fastest Men on Earth—Sex, Danger, and Everything Else.* Newbury Park, Calif.: Haynes, 2003.

Jones, Bruce. *ITV Sport Complete Encyclopedia of Formula One.* London: Carlton, 2007.

### Honors and Awards

| | |
|---|---|
| 1990 | Made an officer of the Order of the British Empire |
| 1992 | World Championship of Drivers |
| 1993 | CART/PPG Indy Car Championship |
| | CART Rookie of the Year |
| | Royal Automobile Club Gold Medal |
| 2005 | Inducted into International Motorsports Hall of Fame |

# *Roland Martin*

**Born:** March 14, 1940
Maryland

## Early Life

Roland Martin was born on March 14, 1940, and grew up wanting to become a wildlife photographer. His parents died in a car crash in Europe, and he joined the Army, becoming an officer. After he left the Army, he went to the University of Maryland and became a schoolteacher after graduation. However, his greatest pleasure was fishing in the great outdoors. In 1963, at twenty-three years old, he became a guide in the Santee Cooper Country, a recreation area in South Carolina that comprises Lakes Marion and Moultrie. During those years, he developed maps of the lakes and coined the term "pattern fishing." A fish pattern in a specific body of water denotes the conditions that attract fish to a particular area. Therefore, by knowing the depth, cover temperature, clarity, and currents to which a species of fish is attracted, a specific fish could be found in any area with similar conditions. Developing pattern fishing helped Roland understand the significance of knowing his prey. Because he understood where fish congregate, he had an advantage in competing in Bass Anglers Sportsman Society (BASS) tournaments.

## The Road to Excellence

Roland became part of BASS in 1969 and joined Ray Scott on his "seminar" tour in 1970. He quit his job as a guide in the Santee Cooper to work for Scott. Roland was reluctant to join Scott when he saw that he and his partner brought in 178 pounds of fish in a competition. However, Scott persuaded Roland to join his tour; Roland was soon winning BASS tournaments. In 1970, he placed in seven BASS tournaments, winning one competition and finishing second in three other. His first BASS tournament victory came on Lake Seminole, which straddles Florida, Georgia, and Alabama. In 1971, Roland qualified for the first Bass Master's Championship. In 1971 and 1972, he won the BASS angler of the year award.

## The Emerging Champion

From 1971 to 1973, Roland never finished lower than sixteenth place and won three tournaments during that period. From 1971 through 1985, he was BASS angler of the year ten times. In 1976, he did not qualify for the Bass Master's Championship, although he competed in five tournaments that year. The season was the worst of his fishing career. However, in 1977, Roland was back and competed in the Bass Master's Championship, although he did not win. In the first years of the 1980's, Roland won three consecutive BASS tournament titles, the first time anyone had accomplished such a feat. During the same era, he purchased Clewiston Marina on Lake Okeechobee, located in central Florida. During the late 1980's, he had his own television show called *Fishing with Roland Martin*. He continued to compete in BASS tournaments until 1992.

## Continuing the Story

In 1992, Roland retired from professional tournaments only to return the following year. Competing in fishing tournaments was something he enjoyed too much to give up. When he was forty years old, he told reporters that he planned to retire at the age of fifty because he would be too old to compete with younger men. However, Roland continued to compete at the age of sixty-eight. His score card includes 19 BASS titles, 92 top-ten BASS finishes, 132 top-twenty finishes, and 25 Bass Master's Championship titles. As of 2008, Roland's television shows could be viewed five times a week on Versus, a cable and satellite channel. Roland developed his own line of fishing equipment including the famous "rocket rod," which propels the line into the water rather than using the traditional

## Statistics

BASS titles, 19
Top-ten BASS tournament finishes, 92
Top-twenty BASS tournament finishes, 132
Bass Master's Championship titles, 25

casting technique. Roland and his wife Judy had two children: Scott, also a fisherman, and Laura Ann. Roland and his son were the first fisherman from the United States to visit Cuba after Fidel Castro gained control. They did an episode of *Fishing with Roland Martin* in Cuban waters.

## Summary

Roland Martin set the record for the most BASS angler of the year titles, ten, and the record for the number of BASS titles, nineteen. His career earnings exceeded $1.5 million. In 2005, he was voted second to Rick Clunn as the greatest angler of all time. Roland was not the top vote-getter because of his lack of Classic Championships. He was the first angler to enter all three angler halls of fame: International Game Fishing Association Fishing Hall of Fame, Freshwater Fishing Hall of Fame, and Professional Bass Fishing Hall of Fame. Through his television show and his personal appearances, he encouraged people from all over the world to enjoy fishing and conserve the environment to allow the continuation of fishing for future generations.

*Pamela D. Doughty*

## Additional Sources

*Hooked! America's Passion for Bass Fishing.* New York: Simon and Schuster, 2001.

Martin, Roland. *Roland Martin's One Hundred and One Bass-Catching Secrets.* 2d ed. New York: Skyhorse, 2008.

# *Rick Mears*

**Born:** December 3, 1951
    Wichita, Kansas
**Also known as:** Rick Ravon Mears (full name)

### Early Life
Rick Ravon Mears was born on December 3, 1951, in Wichita, Kansas, to Bill Ravon Mears and Mae Louise (Simpson) Mears. As a boy, Rick was quiet and shy, so shy that in school he would take an "F" rather than speak in front of a group. However, Rick was very competitive.

Rick entered the world of racing in 1968, when he started racing motorcycles in the California desert. He was successful, winning more than sixty trophies before he switched to racing sprint buggies in the Mojave Desert. Rick soon graduated to off-road races and even competed in the famous Pikes Peak Hill Climb. In 1973, Rick captured

*Rick Mears celebrating his second Indy win in 1984.* (AP/Wide World Photos)

seven off-road victories and started racing sportsman stock cars at local California speedways.

### The Road to Excellence
In 1976, Rick jumped into the world of big-time racing, making his Indy car debut with an eighth-place finish in the California 500. He finished ninth in each of the final two events of the 1976 season and was named rookie of the year by the United States Auto Club.

In 1977, Rick attempted to qualify for the Indianapolis 500 for the first time, sacrificing his job and home in California. He did not qualify for the race; however, he picked up four top-ten finishes in the eight Indy car races in which he competed that year.

Rick's fortunes as a professional racer took off through a chance occurrence. While participating in a motorcycle expedition in the Colorado Rockies, he met Roger Penske, a highly successful race-car owner who offered him an opportunity to drive for his team during the 1978 racing season. Rick jumped at the chance.

### The Emerging Champion
The 1978 racing season was the beginning of one of the most successful owner-driver teams in automobile racing history. Rick's driving talent and the near-military ambitiousness of the Penske program proved to be a formidable combination for the next fourteen years.

Rick qualified on the outside of the front row, in third position, for the 1978 Indianapolis 500. He was the first rookie to break 200 miles per hour in qualifying and was named the Indianapolis 500 rookie of the year. Rick won his first Indy car race in Milwaukee, Wisconsin, that year, then went on to capture two more wins and three second-place finishes.

In 1979, Rick captured the pole position for the Indianapolis 500 and recorded the first of his four Indianapolis 500 victories. Rick won two other races that year and finished in the top ten in all fourteen races in which he competed.

## Continuing the Story

During the remainder of his racing career, which ended with his retirement after the 1992 season, Rick was a model of consistency. Perhaps no other driver in racing devoted as much time to understanding his car's handling. During testing sessions, Rick closely examined the computer data between runs, working with engineers to perfect a car's handling. On the road, Rick sat in his hotel room with a computer, playing with the numbers, trying to make connections between the computer readouts and what he felt on the track. He constantly strove for perfection.

Rick also had to overcome some serious accidents during his career. While competing in the 1981 Indianapolis 500, Rick narrowly escaped a potentially fatal burning. In 1985, the condition of his feet limited his racing to oval tracks, as road racing requires more footwork for braking and shifting.

Competition, not a love of speed, was the motivating factor for Rick's success. He was not a gambler on the track but took calculated risks when the situation called for it. With Indy cars typically traveling more than the length of a football field each second, a driver must understand when a risk can be taken. Rick's judgment rarely was wrong. Rick's

### Milestone

Only driver to win six Indy 500 poles

### Honors and Awards

| | |
|---|---|
| 1976 | USAC Rookie of the Year |
| 1978 | Indianapolis 500 Rookie of the Year |
| 1979 | Jerry Titus Memorial Award |
| 1979, 1981-82 | CART National Champion |
| 1989 | Associated Press Driver of the Decade |
| 1997 | Inducted into International Motorsports Hall of Fame |
| 1998 | Inducted into Motorsports Hall of Fame of America |

success won the respect of his fellow drivers as well as the media. Indy car driver Danny Sullivan stated, "Rick is the best guy I've ever seen on an oval . . . he's the yardstick for all of us." In 1989, Rick was named the driver of the decade by the Associated Press. In 1992, he was the youngest of ten drivers named "Champions for Life" at the driver of the year awards ceremony. He was inducted into the International Motorsports Hall of Fame in 1997 and the Motorsports Hall of Fame of America in 1998.

## Summary

Rick Mears always maintained that he was not motivated by records. He was true to his words when he announced his retirement in 1992. By retiring at the relatively young age of forty-one, he passed up the chance to establish some new racing records, including the chance to become the first driver to win the Indianapolis 500 five times.

*William R. Swanson*

## CART and Other Victories

| | |
|---|---|
| 1978 | Brands Hatch |
| 1978-79, 1981-82 | Atlanta |
| 1978,1988-91 | Milwaukee |
| 1979 | Trenton |
| 1979, 1984, 1988, 1991 | Indianapolis 500 |
| 1980-81 | Mexico City |
| 1981 | Watkins Glen |
| 1981-82 | Riverside |
| 1981, 1983 | Michigan |
| 1982, 1985 | Pocono 500 |
| 1982, 1989-90 | Phoenix |
| 1989 | Laguna Seca |

## Additional Sources

Arute, Jack, and Jenna Fryer. *Jack Arute's Tales from the Indy Five Hundred*. Champaign, Ill.: Sports, 2006.

McKenna, A. T. *Indy Racing*. Edina, Minn.: Adbo & Daughters, 1998.

Shaffer, Rick. *CART: The First Twenty Years: 1979-1998*. Richmond, Surrey, England: Hazleton, 1999.

Sowers, Richard. *Stock Car Racing Lives*. Phoenix, Ariz.: David Bull, 2000.

# Eddy Merckx

**Born:** June 17, 1945
     Meensel-Kiezegem, Belgium
**Also known as:** Edouard Louis Joseph Merckx
    (full name); the Cannibal

### Early Life

Edouard Louis Joseph Merckx (pronounced "merks") was born in the small Belgian village of Meensel-Kiezegem, approximately twenty-five miles from the French border, on June 17, 1945. His father worked as a grocer. Eddy decided at a young age that cycling was his great love. He found it hard to concentrate on his schooling and preferred to be out working on his cycling. Eddy finally convinced his mother that he should try his hand at professional cycling. At the age of sixteen, Eddy dropped out of school to devote himself full time to cycling.

### The Road to Excellence

Eddy did not waste any time in his pursuit. In between races, he learned quickly the value of hard work. Conditioning was important to him. Throughout his career as a cyclist, he always kept in great shape. Conditioning, combined with desire, made Eddy a powerful rider. Eddy also developed an amazing amount of stamina. In 1962, he won his first title, the Junior Championship of Belgium. Two years later he won the amateur World Road Championship. At this point, Eddy knew that he was ready to turn professional.

In 1965, he began competing as a professional cyclist. In that first year Eddy proved that he was on the verge of greatness. He won a number of races, including ones at Vilvoorde, Torhout, Visé, and Saint Jansteen. Eddy also finished second in the Belgian Pro National Championship. For his next challenge, he decided to compete in classic cycling events. In 1966, Eddy won the 180-mile Milan-San Remo race that has been dubbed the King of the Classics.

Eddy won the Milan-San Remo race again the next year. He was beginning to look like the great rider that his coach of 1962, Felicien Vervaecke, had predicted. In 1967, Eddy won his first professional World Road Championship at Heerlen, Netherlands. He had not won the Tour de France yet, but he was about to break through to the top of the cycling elite. Eddy amazed a number of critics

*Eddy Merckx racing at the 1972 Tour de France.* (AFP/Getty Images)

## Major Championships

| Year | Competition | Place |
|---|---|---|
| 1962 | Belgian Junior Championships | 1st |
| 1964 | World Road Championships, Amateur Road Race | Gold |
| 1965 | Belgian Pro National Championship | 2d |
| 1966-67, 1969, 1971-72, 1975-76 | Milan-San Remo | 1st |
| 1967, 1971, 1974 | World Road Championships, Professional Road Race | Gold |
| 1968, 1970, 1972-74 | Tour of Italy | 1st |
| 1969-71 | Paris-Nice | 1st |
| 1969-72, 1974 | Tour de France | 1st |
| 1973 | Tour of Spain | 1st |

with his win in the 1968 Tour of Italy. The race is 2,400 miles long and lasts twenty-three days. Eddy proved that he had the physical stamina for such a grueling race.

### The Emerging Champion

In 1969, Eddy became the world's premiere cyclist by winning three classic events and his first Tour de France. He was the first cyclist to be so successful in the classic races and win the 2,600-mile Tour de France in the same year. The Tour de France is considered the leading road race in the world. It is an event of just longer than twenty days that takes the rider through the European countryside and ends in Paris. Eddy not only won the race but also finished first in six stages of the race. Because of his success during the year, Eddy won the top cycling award: The Super Prestige Pernod Trophy. He had compiled a total of 412 points, which was almost 130 points higher than the previous record.

Because of his stamina, Eddy was at his best in the long-distance road races. In 1970, he won the Tour de France again and his second Tour of Italy.

## Records

One of five cyclists to win the Tour de France at least five times

One of only two cyclists to capture competitive cycling's unofficial version of the Triple Crown, winning the Tour de France, the Tour of Italy, and the World Road Championships Professional Road Race in 1974

Set world record for the most first place finishes in Milan-San Remo race, 7

Most career Tour de France Yellow Jerseys, 96

Most career Tour de France stage wins, 34

## Honors and Awards

1969-75  Super Prestige Pernod Trophy

Eddy was in top form and, seemingly, no other cyclist was in his class. From 1969 to 1975, he won the Super Prestige Pernod Trophy. In 1971, Eddy amassed a point total of 570 to win the trophy. Even though he was the premiere cyclist, winning the Tour de France did not come easily. In the 1971 race, Eddy was several minutes behind Luis Ocaña in total time, but the Spaniard crashed while descending the Pyrenees Mountains, causing Eddy and another cyclist to crash into Ocaña. Ocaña was unable to resume the race because of his injuries, but Eddy recovered from his fall and pedaled to his third victory at the Tour de France. He won his fourth Tour de France in a row in 1972.

### Continuing the Story

Eddy decided to go to Mexico City to attempt to set a world's record for one-hour cycling. At Mexico City's Velodrome, he was able to cover thirty miles and 1,231 yards on the wood track in the one-hour time limit. In this particular event Eddy's only opponent was the clock—a new type of challenge for him.

During his career, Eddy won most of the classic events in which he raced. The classics were the important short races of the season. He was at his best, however, in the multistage long races that are known as tours. The tours were the most demanding, since they covered more than 2,000 miles.

In 1973, Eddy won his fourth Tour of Italy. He also won the Tour of Spain that year, which put him in line to become the first cyclist ever to win the three most prestigious tours in the same year. The season took too much out of Eddy, however, and he decided not to compete in the Tour de France. This broke his string of Tour de France victories at four. Eddy knew that he could not extend himself anymore for the season. In 1974, though, he came back to win both the Tour de France and the Tour of Italy. Eddy also won his third professional World Road Championship race that year. He had proven to be one of cycling's greatest road race champions. There are few athletes whose careers can compare with Eddy's. What he did as a cyclist is considered phenomenal. In 1978, Eddy retired from racing and became a respected bicycle designer and businessman.

## Summary

Eddy Merckx won the Tour de France five times, the Tour of Italy five times, the professional World Road Championships race three times, and the Milan-San Remo Classic seven times. He won countless other races. Eddy always believed in the importance of conditioning. Eddy left a cycling legacy to which all subsequent cyclists could aspire.

*Jeffry Jensen*

## Additional Sources

Delanzy, Eric. *Inside the Tour de France: The Pictures, the Legends, and the Untold Stories of the World's Most Beloved Bicycle Race.* Emmaus, Pa.: Rodale, 2006.

Fife, Graeme. *Inside the Peloton: Riding, Winning, and Losing the Tour de France.* Edinburgh: Mainstream, 2002.

Vanwalleghem, Rik. *Eddy Merckx: The Greatest Cyclist of the Twentieth Century.* Translated by Steve Hawkins. Boulder, Colo.: Velo Press, 2000.

Wadley, J. B. *Eddy Merckx and the 1970 Tour de France.* Silsden, West Yorkshire, England: Kennedy Brothers, 1970.

# *Reinhold Messner*

**Born:** September 17, 1944
        Bressanone, Italy

## Early Life

Reinhold Messner was born the second of nine children of Josef Messner and Maria Messner. When Reinhold was only five years old, his father introduced him to mountaineering through a family climb up the 3,025-meter (almost 10,000-foot) Sass Rigais in the Dolomites, a mountain range in Italy. Based on that experience, Reinhold became increasingly passionate about climbing, and, by age thirteen, he and his eleven-year-old brother Günther were committed climbing partners. A few years later, he and Günther returned to the Sass Rigais and climbed to the summit of the difficult north face—a route their father had failed to climb. Reinhold had a sometimes stormy relationship with his father, who did not consider climbing to be a realistic career for his son. Reinhold eventually earned a degree in architecture.

## The Road to Excellence

Reinhold's experience grew as he and Günther climbed extensively in the nearby Dolomites and then, beginning in 1965, by repeating classic rock and ice climbs in the Alps. From 1965 to 1970, Reinhold made a number of solo ascents in addition to the numerous climbs he made with his brother and others. Reinhold was perfecting the art of the light and fast, alpine-style, ascent. He learned to go without food and trained by running; he was known for his speedy ascents. By the age of twenty-five, Reinhold was an exceptionally skilled rock climber and alpinist, having made more than fifty first ascents and twenty difficult solo climbs.

## 8,000-Meter Peaks Climbed

| Year | Peak | Elevation | Notes |
|------|------|-----------|-------|
| 1970 | Nanga Parbat | 8,125 meters (26,657 feet) | |
| 1972 | Manaslu | 8,156 meters (26,759 feet) | |
| 1975 | Gasherbrum I (Hidden Peak) | 8,068 meters (27,470 feet) | |
| 1977 | Dhaulagiri | 8,167 meters (26,795 feet) | |
| 1978 | Mount Everest | 8,848 meters (29,029 feet) | First ascent without auxiliary oxygen |
| | Nanga Parbat | 8,125 meters (26,657 feet) | First solo ascent of an 8,000-meter peak |
| 1979 | K2 | 8,611 meters (28,251 feet) | |
| 1980 | Mount Everest | 8,848 meters (29,029 feet) | First solo ascent |
| 1981 | Shisha Pangma | 8,012 meters (26,286 feet) | |
| 1982 | Kanchenjunga | 8,598 meters (28,209 feet) | |
| | Gasherbrum II | 8,035 meters (26,362 feet) | |
| | Broad Peak | 8,048 meters (26,404 feet) | |
| 1983 | Cho Oyu | 8,201 meters (26,906 feet) | |
| 1984 | Gasherbrum I | 8,068 meters (26,470 feet) | Climbed both peaks before returning to base camp |
| | Gasherbrum II | 8,035 meters (26,362 feet) | |
| 1985 | Annapurna | 8,091 meters (26,545 feet) | |
| | Dhaulagiri | 8,167 meters (26,795 feet) | |
| 1986 | Makalu | 8,485 meters (27,838 feet) | |
| | Lhotse | 8,516 meters (27,940 feet) | |

In 1970, Reinhold and Günther were invited on a fateful expedition to climb their first 8,000-meter (more than 26,000-foot) peak in the Himalayas: Nanga Parbat. After several weeks of labor, the two Messners and a third teammate were first in line at Camp Five, poised for a summit attempt. Given the weather conditions, Reinhold was to make a solo bid for the summit. However, as he climbed upward early the next morning, he noticed someone following him. Günther caught up, and together the two made the first ascent of the difficult Rupal Face of Nanga Parbat.

## The Emerging Champion
After an hour atop Nanga Parbat, the Messners started down. Darkness overtook them, and they endured a high, cold bivouac. Eventually, to avoid the difficulties of the Rupal Face, they traversed the mountain and headed down the other side into a different valley. Günther was lost on the descent. Reinhold barely survived the ordeal himself, and most of his toes and some of his fingertips were later amputated because of severe frostbite. Once recovered from his amputations, Reinhold climbed three 8,000-meter peaks: Manaslu in 1972, Gasherbrum I (Hidden Peak) in 1975, and Dhaulagiri in 1977. Additionally, Reinhold and his climbing partner, Austrian Peter Habeler, made a record, ten-hour ascent of the infamous north face of the Eiger, a mountain in the Swiss Alps, in 1974.

In 1978, Reinhold turned his attention to the highest of the 8,000-meter peaks: Mt. Everest, standing at 8,848 meters (29,029 feet). Most physiologists felt that the air was too thin at the peak of Mt. Everest to allow for an ascent without using supplemental oxygen. However, Reinhold, thought making the ascent without oxygen was possible and teamed with his longtime partner Habeler to make an attempt by "fair means," without oxygen. After careful planning and much effort, Reinhold and Habeler became the first to make an oxygenless ascent of Mt. Everest.

Next, Reinhold conceived of a bold project: a solo climb of Nanga Parbat. His team consisted of only two others, who stayed at base camp, a medical student and a liaison officer. His climbing equipment consisted primarily of crampons and an ice axe. Despite these self-imposed limitations, Reinhold successfully

made a solo, oxygenless climb of Nanga Parbat in 1978. In 1979, Reinhold and a partner climbed the Abruzzi Spur on K2, the world's second-highest mountain.

## Continuing the Story
In 1980, Reinhold embarked on perhaps the ultimate mountaineering challenge: ascending Mt. Everest's north face solo and without oxygen. As before, his base-camp team was small, consisting of only three others. After a superhuman effort, Reinhold succeeded in making the summit, a feat at the extreme limits of human capability.

During the next few years, Reinhold climbed the remainder of the fourteen 8,000-meter peaks: Shisha Pangma in 1981; Kanchenjunga, Gasherbrum II, and Broad Peak in 1982; Cho Oyu in 1983; Annapurna and Dhaulagiri in 1985; and Makalu and Lhotse in 1986. With the ascent of Lhotse, Reinhold became the first person to climb all fourteen of the 8,000-meter peaks. Furthermore, in 1984, Reinhold and a companion completed the first traverse of two 8,000-meter peaks, Gasherbrum I and Gasherbrum II, without returning to base camp.

Seeking other adventures, Reinhold turned to the horizontal world. In 1990, he and a teammate made the first ski traverse of Antarctica. In 2002, at the age of 60, he hiked across the Gobi Desert. From 1999 to 2004, Reinhold held political office as a member of the European parliament. In the latter part of the 2000's, he focused his energies on the development of a series of museums dealing with mountains and mountain culture. Contrary to his father's objections, Reinhold made a career out of mountaineering, supporting himself over the years by lecturing, writing books, and engaging in various other mountain-related business activities.

## Summary
Reinhold Messner is widely regarded as the world's greatest mountaineer. In 1978, he and Peter Habeler were the first men to climb Mt. Everest with-

---

### *Other Endurance Accomplishments*

1989   Traversed the South Pole
2004   Traversed the Gobi Desert, China (2,000 miles)

out supplementary oxygen. Taking this a step further, in 1980, Reinhold became the first man to
solo Mt. Everest, again, doing it without oxygen.
He was the first to climb all fourteen of the 8,000-
meter peaks and went on to make significant arctic
and desert crossings by foot. He lives in his castle
home called Schloss Juval, near Merano, Italy, and
oversees a series of museums dealing with mountains.

*Russell N. Carney*

## Additional Sources

Alexander, Caroline. "Murdering the Impossible."
*National Geographic*, November, 2006, 42-67.

Messner, Reinhold. *Free Spirit: A Climber's Life*. Translated by Jill Neate. Seattle, Wash.: The Mountaineers, 1991.

_____. *The Naked Mountain*. Translated by Tim
Carruthers. Ramsbury, Marlborough, Wiltshire,
England: Crowood Press, 2003.

Wetzler, Brad. "Reinhold Don't Care What You
Think." *Outside*, October, 2002.

# *Dave Mirra*

**Born:** April 4, 1974
     Syracuse, New York
**Also known as:** David Michael Mirra (full name)

### Early Life

David Michael Mirra was born on April 4, 1974, in Syracuse, New York. His parents separated when he was young, and Dave grew up with his father and brother in the small, nearby town of Chittenango. Ironically, Dave, the most decorated freestyle bicycle motocross (BMX) rider of all time grew up in a small town where the winters were harsh. By comparison, most of Dave's BMX competitors grew up in California and were able to ride year-round, thus avoiding a battle with the elements.

At the age of four, Dave was already beginning to ride bicycles. He often chased his older brother, Tim, or got into races with other children in the neighborhood. With these other children, Dave and his brother started jumping curbs and building ramps. These jumps encouraged Dave to start riding in a different way.

### The Road to Excellence

As exciting as jumping curbs and ramps was, Dave was looking to push himself further. Over the next couple of years, a number of circumstances inspired him to do so. First, during the mid-1980's, freestyle BMX riding became popular. With the emergence of this sport, bike manufacturers began sending their riders on tours. In 1984, Team Haro visited upstate New York. Seeing the factory riders in person was the dramatic moment that caused Dave to commit to riding. He began by focusing on "flatland" riding, which is comparable to dancing with the bicycle on flat, paved surfaces.

### The Emerging Champion

At the age of thirteen, Dave visited "The Plywood Hoods," a group of riders who were considered the

*Dave Mirra performing at the T-Mobile Ramps and Amps Invitational in 2003.* (Mark Mainz/Getty Images)

## X Games Statistics

| Year | Event | Place | Year | Event | Place |
|---|---|---|---|---|---|
| 1996 | Street | Bronze | 2001 | Vert | Gold |
|  | Vert | Gold | 2002 | Vert | Gold |
| 1997 | Street | Gold | 2003 | Street | Bronze |
|  | Vert | Gold |  | Vert | Silver |
| 1998 | Vert Doubles | Gold | 2004 | Bike Park | Gold |
|  | Street | Gold |  | Bike Street | Gold |
|  | Vert | Gold | 2005 | Vert, Best Trick | Silver |
| 1999 | Vert | Gold |  | Bike Park | Gold |
| 2000 | Vert | Silver | 2007 | Bike Park | Bronze |
|  | Street | Gold |  |  |  |

underground kings at that time. Based in York, Pennsylvania, this collection of riders had developed a following through a brash riding style and a continual effort to develop new tricks. This group provided one of the few havens for freestyle riders on the East Coast.

Though young, Dave was featured in the Plywood Hoods' video *Dorkin' in York*. This appearance helped catapult him to prominence in the sport. Haro signed Dave to be one its riders. However, as good as Dave was getting, by late 1988, the sport was in trouble. Dave was dropped from Haro in a cost-cutting measure. That he had finished eleventh, out of twelve, in his first contest might have been a factor in his dismissal.

However, Dave was not without a sponsor long, as Dyno, a subdivision of GT Bicycles, signed him. He did not have immediate success with Dyno. He still had not won a contest, but he started to focus aggressively on becoming a "vert," or ramp rider. On the ramps, he began to distinguish himself, becoming more successful than he had been before. With Dave's growing popularity and ability, Dyno kept him busy. He was soon touring the country and competing in a number of contests.

## Continuing the Story

In December of 1993, Dave's life changed in a profound way. While crossing a street in Chittenango, Dave was hit by a drunk driver. He suffered a fractured skull and a torn shoulder. There was a serious concern that he might die. After recovering, he faced six months of rehabilitation.

Quite possibly, BMX riding gave Dave a goal to help overcome his accident. However, once healed, he still had not achieved anything he wanted. His sponsor, who at that time had changed to GT Bicy-

cles, suggested that he move to California. Two weeks after doing so, he moved back to New York. He still was not happy. His brother, who had moved to Greenville, North Carolina, to go to school, encouraged Dave to move closer to him. Relocating to Greenville restarted his career. He began riding with the desire that he had before the accident, and he returned to Haro.

The X Games was the event that made Dave a public figure. The first X Games took place in 1995, and though Dave finished with a silver medal, the competition was a career-defining moment. It was a springboard to his future success and popularity. Afterward, he won nearly every possible freestyle award, in flatland, vert, and street riding. He won numerous gold medals at the X Games; was the NORA Cup ramp rider of the year in 2001, 2002, and 2003; and won an ESPN ESPY award.

## Summary
Dave Mirra was one of the best freestyle bike riders ever. His ability to overcome his earlier injuries was just one way in which he showed championship form. In addition to his riding, he started his own bike company, released a video game, was named one of *People* magazine's fifty hottest bachelors, and made an appearance on *The Late Show with David Letterman*. In 2006, Dave married his longtime girlfriend, Lauren Blackwell. They settled in Greenville with their two daughters, Madison and Mackenzie. When not riding, Dave helped out with children's charities, including the Dream Factory, an organization that grants wishes to critically ill children.

*P. Huston Ladner*

## Additional Sources
Mahaney, Ian. *Dave Mirra: Bicycle Stunt Riding Champion*. New York: PowerKids Press, 2005.
Rosenberg, Aaron. *Dave Mirra: BMX Superstar*. New York: Rosen, 2004.

## Honors and Awards

| | |
|---|---|
| 2001-03 | NORA Cup ramp rider of the year |
| 2005 | ESPN ESPY: action sports athlete of the year |
| | Teen Choice Awards: extreme male athlete of the year |
| | *BMX Plus* freestyler of the year |
| 2008 | *BMX Plus* third-place freestyler of the year |

# *Willie Mosconi*

**Born:** June 27, 1913
     Philadelphia, Pennsylvania
**Died:** September 16, 1993
     Haddon Heights, New Jersey
**Also known as:** William Joseph Mosconi (full name); Mr. Pocket Billiards

### Early Life

William Joseph Mosconi was born in Philadelphia on June 27, 1913. He learned to play billiards in his father's pool hall. However, his father, Joseph William Mosconi, wanted him to join the Dancing Mosconis on the vaudeville entertainment circuit. To discourage him from playing billiards, Willie's father locked up the cues. Undaunted, Willie improvised by using a broomstick to shoot potatoes into the pockets.

By the age of six, the pocket-billiards prodigy was playing exhibition matches in New York City and Philadelphia for money. Willie never took lessons to learn how to play billiards. Instead, he mastered billiards by watching other people play the game. The hustlers who came to Philadelphia sought Willie out just so they could brag they had beaten the child star, but, by Willie's account, the hustlers often left town broke. When Willie was six, he scored a victory in which he sank forty consecutive balls. However, he became bored with billiards and retired at the age of seven.

### The Road to Excellence

Willie believed most of the great billiards players—including himself—were born with the talent. They were also showmen who knew how to please spectators. From the time he was a teenager, billiards provided him with his livelihood. He never thought of the game as a pastime. He only played for the money, which he used to feed his family.

In 1933, at the age of twenty, Willie won a sectional tournament, finished third in the national championships, and earned a place, but no title, in the world championships. Despite the fact he finished fifth, Brunswick Corporation, a manufacturer of billiards equipment, hired him to demonstrate its products. While traveling the country giving exhibitions on behalf of Brunswick, he perfected his famous trick shots.

After several unsuccessful attempts at the world championships title, Willie sought employment outside the world of professional billiards. In 1941, when no job offer materialized, he returned to Philadelphia and competitive billiards.

### The Emerging Champion

Willie won his first world championship in a marathon tournament of 224 games that lasted from

*Willie Mosconi.* (Time Life Pictures/Getty Images)

November 26, 1940, to May 2, 1941. Between 1942 and 1953, Willie held the world title ten out of twelve possible times.

On many occasions, Willie said the best advice about billiards that anyone ever gave him was to hate the person he was playing. What Willie hated most was not the player, but rather the possibility of his own defeat. The killer instinct, the desire to beat an opponent by a score of 125-0, was critical to his success. Pocket billiards, he said, is a game of concentration played shot by shot. It is all about the control of the cue stick, the cue ball, the balls, the rails, and the pocket. A champion knows where all the balls will go from the first shot.

Willie rarely ever practiced more than an hour or two at a time. Billiards, he said, could only be mastered in competition against better players. The best lesson every player must learn is not to miss, because then he or she does not have to worry about anything else. Willie once beat thirteen-time world champion Ralph Greenleaf in a 1948 match that lasted only seventeen minutes because he did not want to miss a play at the Strand Theater in Times Square in New York City.

## Continuing the Story

By 1950, Willie was a national celebrity. His rapid-fire play and trademark sports jacket and slacks only enhanced his image. His stardom won him a new role in the world of billiards. He was a technical adviser on the set of *The Hustler* (1961), which starred his friend Jackie Gleason as a character named Minnesota Fats. Willie again served as a technical adviser for the sequel, *The Color of Money* (1986). Looking back on his career as a professional billiards player, Willie often said there was nothing he could not do with a billiard ball. He told journalists he retired after winning his fifteenth world championship because he got bored beating the same players year in and year out.

On December 27, 1956, Willie suffered a stroke at the billiards room he owned in Philadelphia. Sixteen months later, he was back playing billiards, however. His family said his recovery was so rapid because he was a relentless competitor who could not tolerate the idea of losing. After retiring from competition at the age of forty-three, Willie frequently played in exhibitions. In 1978, he played

---

### Records and Milestones

| | |
|---|---|
| 1942-53 | Ten World Championships in twelve years |
| 1950 | Best grand average: 18.34 balls per inning (Chicago, World Tournament) |
| 1954 | High run: 526 balls (Springfield, Ill., exhibition game) |
| 1956 | Best game: run of 150 in one inning (Kinston, N.C., game vs. Jimmy Moore) |

---

and defeated Minnesota Fats, Rudolph Wanderone, Jr., in a series of lucrative televised matches. Willie died of a heart attack on September 16, 1993, in his home in Haddon Heights, New Jersey.

## Summary

Willie Mosconi ranks as one of the greatest pocket billiards players in the history of the sport. He won 77 percent of his tournament competitions, compared with a 71 percent record for billiards champion Ralph Greenleaf. Between 1941 and 1957, Willie won the world championship in straight pool fifteen times. In 1954, he ran 526 consecutive balls without a miss in a straight-pool exhibition calling the ball and pocket before every shot. His other heralded records included his best game ever, in which he sank 150 balls in a row in 1 inning (a perfect game) in 1956.

Willie was a tough competitor in tournament-length contests of 125 or 150 points and a veritable conqueror in longer challenge matches. He won twelve of his thirteen challenge matches by a combined score of 42,625 to 28,108, finishing, on average, more than 1,000 points ahead of his opponents. For him, billiards was an honorable and reputable profession, not a game for hustlers and suckers. Both in legend and fact, he ranks as a true gentleman of the sport.

*Fred Buchstein*

## Additional Sources

Dyer, R. A. *The Hustler and the Champ: Willie Mosconi, Minnesota Fats, and the Rivalry That Defined Pool.* Guilford, Conn.: Lyons Press, 2007.

Mosconi, Willie. *Willie Mosconi's Winning Pocket Billiards: For Beginners and Advanced Players with a Section on Trick Shots.* New York: Crown, 1995.

Mosconi, Willie, and Stanley Cohen. *Willie's Game: An Autobiography.* New York: Macmillan, 1993.

Stein, Victor. *The Billiard Encyclopedia: An Illustrated History of the Sport.* Minneapolis: Blue Book, 1996.

# *Shirley Muldowney*

**Born:** June 19, 1940
     Schenectady, New York
**Also known as:** Shirley Roque Muldowney (full
  name); Shirley Roque (birth name)

### Early Life

Shirley Roque Muldowney was born on June 19, 1940, in Schenectady, New York. Her mother, Mae Roque, was a laundress, and her father, Belgium Benedict "Tex" Roque, was a professional prize-fighter. Shirley's father taught her how to defend herself against bullies at her tough neighborhood school.

In 1956, Shirley met Jack Muldowney, the best hot-rodder in town. At sixteen, she began to drive Jack's Mercury and then quit school to marry him. To keep a promise to her father, she got her di-

*Shirley Muldowney.* (Courtesy of National Hot Rod Association)

ploma eight years later. Jack built Shirley's first fast car and got her interested in drag racing.

### The Road to Excellence

One year after Shirley married, she had a son. Shirley kept driving, and her husband worked on her cars. Shirley's reputation as a hot-rodder and her fascination with speed grew.

During the 1960's, Shirley raced stock cars, developing her driving technique and reaction time. She also fought authorities from the National Hot Rod Association (NHRA) because they did not want to give women professional status. Shirley and other women persisted until they got the right to apply for NHRA approval.

In 1971, Shirley won her first major race and finished the season ranked in the top five. Touring constantly was difficult, however. Whereas Shirley wanted to race full time, her husband wished for a quieter life at home. They divorced in 1972.

Then, Conrad "Connie" Kalitta, a top drag racer, became Shirley's crew chief and agent. He promoted Shirley as "Cha Cha" Muldowney and booked her in drag strips all over the country. Shirley's driving impressed the crowds. Even after suffering two serious track fires in 1972 and 1973, Shirley went on. She decided to enter Top Fuel drag racing.

### The Emerging Champion

Shirley was proud to have three drag racing greats sign her application for a Top Fuel license in 1974: Kalitta, Don Garlits, and Tommy Ivo. Kalitta remained her crew chief, and Rahn Tobler became her mechanic. Shirley's main interest was speed. Top Fuel cars could cover one-quarter mile in 6 seconds or less.

Shirley's dragster, which looked like a 25-foot hot-pink arrow on wheels, shot her into stardom. She was the first woman to qualify for a national Top Fuel event and win the final round. In 1976, she became the first woman to win an NHRA title. Also, she was the first woman to run the quarter mile in less than 6 seconds, win a Winston Championship, and earn a place on the auto-racing all-

American team. In 1977, after twenty-one years of driving, she won the NHRA World Championship in Top Fuel.

Even so, some racers doubted her skill, claiming that her low weight gave her an advantage. Others, however, recognized her strengths: her ability to focus, her quickness, and her studious approach to driving. Most important, she remained cool under stress.

Shirley had to fight for her future, however. In 1977, when her partnership with Kalitta ended, the racing world did not think she could keep winning. Worse, she could not get a sponsor. She had always had to fight for acceptance in the male-dominated world of racing, and this situation was no different.

Shirley had to enter many more races to support herself and her young pit crew. At the 1980 opening race, Shirley and her team won their first big

## NHRA Top Fuel Victories

| | |
|---|---|
| 1976-77, 1980 | Spring Nationals |
| 1977 | Summer Nationals |
| | Grand Nationals |
| 1977, 1980, 1982 | Top Fuel World Championship |
| | Winston World Finals |
| 1980 | Fall Nationals |
| 1980, 1982-83 | Winter Nationals |
| 1981 | Southern Nationals |
| 1981-82 | Gatornationals |
| 1982 | North Star Nationals |
| | U.S. Nationals |

victory without Kalitta and set a 255-mile-per-hour record. That year, Shirley clocked 5.705 seconds at the Gatornationals and won eleven national events. She had more runs over 250 miles per hour and under 6 seconds than any other driver. Her 1980 world title silenced her critics. She became the first person ever to win the NHRA Top Fuel World Championship more than once. In 1982, she won it again and beat Kalitta to win the U.S. Nationals at Indianapolis, Indiana. She had become the best in the sport. Also in 1982, Shirley raced against Top Fuel driver Lucille Lee in the NHRA's first all-women final round. Shirley took the win.

**Continuing the Story**

Shirley's life was chronicled in the 1983 film *Heart Like a Wheel*. The forty-four-year-old racer was at the height of success when her career took a violent turn. In June, 1984, outside Montreal, Canada, a front-tire blowout threw her pink dragster into a destructive 600-foot-rollover near the end of a drag strip. Her legs, pelvis, and right hand were shattered. Her left knee was bent backward, and her right thumb and left foot were almost severed. It took eighteen months of operations, therapy, misery, and determination before she could walk again.

With her left ankle permanently fused and one leg shorter than the other, a triumphant Shirley returned to racing in January, 1986, at the Firebird International Raceway in Phoenix, Arizona. She had returned to racing, she said, because driving dragsters was what she did best.

In 1989, Shirley broke the four-second drag-racing barrier at Maple Grove Raceway in

## Records

First woman to be licensed to drive as a Top Fuel drag racer by the NHRA (1973)

First woman driver to win an NHRA title event (1976)

Only woman driver to win the U.S. Nationals (1982)

First driver to win three NHRA Top Fuel World Championships

Twice set record for the fastest speed in drag racing history, the second time at 319.22 miles per hour (1998)

## Honors and Awards

| | |
|---|---|
| 1975-77, 1980, 1982 | American Auto Racing Writers and Broadcasters Association Auto Racing All-American Team |
| 1976-77 | *Drag News* Top Fuel Driver of the Year |
| 1977 | U.S. House of Representatives Outstanding Achievement Award |
| 1979 | Charter Member, NHRA 250-Mile-an-Hour Club |
| 1981-82 | *Car Craft* magazine All-Star Team, Top Fuel Driver |
| 1982 | Jerry Titus Memorial Award |
| 1985 | *Car Craft* magazine Ollie Award |
| 1986 | American Auto Racing Writers and Broadcasters Association Comeback Driver of the Year |
| 1989 | Charter Member, Cragar Four-Second Club |
| 1990 | Inducted into Motorsports Hall of Fame of America |
| 1997 | U.S. Sports Academy's Top 25 Pro Female Athletes, 1972-97 |
| 2001 | Fifth on NHRA top fifty drivers list |
| 2003 | Inducted into Michigan Sports Hall of Fame |
| 2004 | Inducted into International Motorsports Hall of Fame |

Reading, Pennsylvania. Shirley also became the first female member of the Cragar Four-Second Club. In 1990, Shirley left the NHRA to compete in match racing in the United States and overseas. During the early 1990's, she set twelve track records for speed throughout the United States. She returned to NHRA competition in 1995, and in 1996, she won three consecutive national events and finished second in Top Fuel points.

In 1998, at the northern nationals, Shirley continued her record-breaking career, logging the fastest run in the history of NHRA competition. In 2000, she improved her best career speed to 319.22 miles per hour, a track record at the nationals in Cordova, Illinois.

In January, 2003, Shirley announced her farewell tour. She competed in six races during the season. In September, 2003, at Route 66 Raceway in Joliet, Illinois, Shirley clocked a run of 4.579 seconds at 327.66 miles per hour, a career-best time. She ran her final race on November 9, 2003, at the Raceway at Pomona.

Shirley won many honors during her illustrious career. In 1990, she was inducted into the Motorsports Hall of Fame of America. In 2001, she was number five on the NHRA's fifty greatest drivers list. In 2004, she was inducted into the International Motorsports Hall of Fame. She was also listed as one of the top thirty outstanding women by the New York Senate.

## Summary

Shirley Muldowney's comeback from a near-fatal crash in 1984 demonstrated her superb skill, stamina, and mental toughness. Her passion for racing inspired fans and fellow drivers alike, and her belief that she could go faster than anyone else made her not only a champion driver but also a true racer. Shirley's stellar career in a male-dominated sport served as inspiration for female athletes everywhere.

*JoAnn Balingit, updated by Caitlin Moriarity*

## Additional Sources

McGovern, Kieran. *The Shirley Muldowney Story.* Hemel Hempstead, Hertfordshire, England: Phoenix, 1996.

Muldowney, Shirley, and Bill Stephens. *Shirley Muldowney's Tales from the Track.* Champaign, Ill.: Sports, 2005.

Post, Robert C. *High Performance: The Culture and Technology of Drag Racing, 1950-2000.* Baltimore: Johns Hopkins University Press, 2001.

Woolum, Janet. *Outstanding Women Athletes: Who They Are and How They Influenced Sports in America.* Phoenix, Ariz.: Oryx Press, 1998.

# Bill Muncey

**Born:** November 12, 1928
    Royal Oak, Michigan
**Died:** October 18, 1981
    Acapulco, Mexico
**Also known as:** William Edward Muncey (full
    name); Mr. Unlimited

## Early Life

William Edward "Bill" Muncey was born in Royal Oak, Michigan. His father was a Chevrolet dealer in Detroit. After high school, Bill attended the General Motors Institute of Technology and did his postgraduate work in marketing at Rollins College in Winter Park, Florida. Introduced to music by his mother, Bill became an accomplished jazz saxophonist and could also play the piano and clarinet. He played with the Guy Lombardo Orchestra, the U.S. Navy concert band, and the Seattle Orchestra. Bill's background in marketing led him to Atlas Van Lines, where he was vice president of marketing for several years. Later, Bill drove the Atlas Van Lines hydroplane.

## The Road to Excellence

Bill became a member of the American Power Boat Association (APBA) as a young adult. Over Bill's long career, power boats were transformed into hydroplanes, a combination of boat and airplane. The boats were propelled by World War II jet engines, usually Rolls-Royce and Allison models. The jet engines enabled the boats to reach speeds in excess of 200 miles per hour. The boats rode the water on the tips of their sponsons, projections from the boat located in the rear hull, with half of the propeller out of the water.

Hydroplanes have always been loud, and the sport is often referred to as "thunderboating." Speedboat racing is almost as old as automobile racing, dating to the early 1900's. All across the United States, hydroplane racers have met in large cities—such as Detroit, Michigan; Seattle, Washington; Miami, Florida; and Washington, D.C.—or in smaller towns on the Ohio River—such as Madison and Evansville, Indiana, and Owensboro, Kentucky. The races have taken place on rivers, lagoons, and lakes. Tens of thousands to hundreds of thousands of fans have lined the shores to watch these three-ton boats with 3,000 horsepower jet engines race, during which boats shoot off plumes of water called "roostertails" that climb 75 feet in the air and measure 100 yards long.

In 1946, Bill's father asked musician Guy Lombardo, who was a speedboat racer and owner, to sell his son a boat in order to keep him busy and away from bad influences. "I sold him a boat that had never won a race," said Lombardo. Within one year, Bill was driving hydroplanes, and within five years, he was racing them.

Bill was trained on limited boats, those that used automotive engines. In 1948, on the Detroit River, Bill drove an unlimited boat, those powered by jet engines, for the first time, in a race for the Harmsworth Trophy, one of the most important awards in motorboat racing. Bill, nineteen years old, borrowed an engine from legendary boat racer and wealthy industrialist Gar Wood. Bill's boat, the *Miss Great Lakes*, sank to the bottom of the Detroit River. Bill did not get another ride in an unlimited hydroplane for four years.

## The Emerging Champion

Over nearly thirty years, Bill's racing career had its ups and downs. The late 1950's was an era of dominance for Bill. Driving the *Miss Thriftway* for Willard Rhodes, Bill won the APBA Gold Cup in 1956 and 1957 and again in 1961 and 1962. In 1972, Bill was unstoppable. Out of seven races held that year, he won six and finished second in the other one.

Two regions of the United States, centered in Detroit and Seattle, created the East-West rivalry in unlimited hydroplanes. Bill was born and raised in the Detroit area but his loyalty was to Rhodes and Seattle. He made his home in the West as well, living in La Mesa, California. Not only did Bill drive his boat fast, but he also drove it intelligently. To win championships in unlimited hydroplanes, a driver must know when to go all out and when to back off.

Early in his career, Bill learned that victory did not always go to the swiftest boat and driver. Hydro-

## Honors and Awards

| | |
|---|---|
| 1956-57, 1961-62, 1972, 1977-79 | APBA Gold Cup |
| 1960-62, 1972, 1976, 1978-79 | U.S. National Champion |
| 1989 | Inducted into Motorsports Hall of Fame of America |
| 2004 | Inducted into International Motorsports Hall of Fame |

planes are sensitive machines: The engine burns out if the boat goes too fast; conversely, the boat stalls if the boat goes too slowly. Bill was an intelligent driver and an innovator. In addition to the jumpsuit, helmet, and parachute, the life jacket was a piece of essential equipment used by the driver. Bill designed his own life jacket, one which saved his life on more than one occasion.

### Continuing the Story

By 1977, Bill had been racing in unlimited hydroplanes for twenty-seven years and had forty-one career victories—his closest competitor had won twenty. Furthermore, Bill had won five APBA Gold Cups, tying the all-time record set by Wood. Bill eventually won eight.

Like any high-speed-racing vehicles, unlimited hydroplanes are dangerous. Responding to the safety issues surrounding his sport, Bill once said, "Dangerous? This is defined as one of the cruel sports. We figure anything less than death is a minor accident." The boats weigh more than three tons and measure more than 30 feet long. They travel in excess of 200 miles per hour and are powered by 3,000 horsepower. Skimming the water in the straightaway, going tightly into a turn, the hydroplane can disintegrate around the driver: the engine can explode and catch fire, and the boat can flip over or lose its steering. Bill had a number of encounters with out-of-control boats. In a 1958 Seattle race, Bill's boat lost its rudder, and Bill was unable to steer his boat out of the path of a Coast Guard cutter. Traveling 100 miles per hour, Bill hit the ship broadside, puncturing its hull. Both boats sank in a matter of minutes. On another occasion, Bill fell off his boat's trailer and broke his foot, and his crew had to carry him and place him in the cockpit of the boat. Bill ran the entire race with a broken foot.

In his twenty-ninth season, on an October day in 1981, Bill was in the final heat of the $175,000 world championship race in Acapulco, Mexico. Bill's Atlas Van Lines boat moved ahead of a pack of rival boats, only to flip in the air at full speed and land upside down. Bill's spine severed as a result of the impact with the water, and he died.

### Summary

Bill Muncey dominated the sport of hydroplane racing in the same way that Michael Jordan dominated professional basketball or Tiger Woods dominated professional golf. Over a nearly thirty-year career in one of the most dangerous sports in the world, Bill won more hydroplane races and more Gold Cup trophies than any other driver.

*Randy L. Abbott*

### Additional Sources

Fishman, Joanne A. "The Muncey Era Comes to a Sad End." *The New York Times*, October 25, 1981, p. A3.

Garey, Stephen A. *Bill Muncey, Boat Racing Legend.* Author, 1982.

Hogg, Tony. *Thunderboating with Bill Muncey.* Newport Beach, Calif.: Author, 1978.

Keese, Parton. "Muncey Rallies in Final Heat to Retain World Hydro Crown." *The New York Times*, June 30, 1969, p. 51.

# Ty Murray

**Born:** October 11, 1969
Phoenix, Arizona
**Also known as:** Ty Monroe Murray (full name);
King of Cowboys

## Early Life

Ty Monroe Murray was born in Phoenix, Arizona, the youngest of three children and only son of Butch and Joy Murray. Ty's father trained horses and broke colts for a living, and his mother won bull-riding trophies in her youth. Ty and his sisters learned to rope and ride as naturally as they learned to walk and talk. Ty's first shoes were cowboy boots, and by the time he was three, he was riding calves unaided.

Ty's early passion for riding and his desire for excellence marked him as special from early childhood. In third grade, Ty was given a writing assignment in response to the question: "If you could accomplish anything in the world, what would it be?" Ty's answer was specific and lofty: He wrote that he wanted to top the record of Larry Mahan, who won the Professional Rodeo Cowboy Association's (PRCA's) All-Around Cowboy title six times. At that time, during the mid-1970's, no one thought that Mahan's record could ever be broken.

## The Road to Excellence

Ty never wanted to be anything but a cowboy; virtually every activity in which he engaged, and every decision he made, was bent toward that goal. To improve his balance, he walked along the tops of fences. He taught himself to ride a unicycle and, when that became easy, rode it while carrying weights in each hand. He saved money he earned doing chores and bought a bucking machine, which he rode until his thighs bled. At night, according to his mother, he slept in the "spurring position" used in bronc riding: toes out, heels in.

Ty began riding small bulls when he was

nine years old. The second bull he ever rode threw and stepped on him, breaking his jaw. When Ty was thirteen, rodeo legend Mahan saw him ride at the Little Britches national finals in Colorado. The boy, Mahan remarked, was riding better at thirteen than Mahan had as a world champion. At this early stage, the style that distinguished Ty was evident: clean, smooth, precise, and, in Mahan's words, "almost Zcn-like."

*Ty Murray, who won a record seven World All-Around Championships.* (ProRodeo Hall of Fame and Museum of the American Cowboy)

## Major Championships and Honors

| | |
|---|---|
| 1988 | PRCA Resistol Overall and Bareback Rookie of the Year |
| 1989 | Inducted into Rodeo Hall of Fame |
| 1989-94, 1998 | PRCA World All-Around Cowboy Champion |
| 1993, 1998 | PRCA World Bull-Riding Champion |
| 1999 | PBR Finals Champion |
| 2000-02 | Reserve PBR Bud Light Cup World Champion |
| 2000 | Inducted into Pro Rodeo Hall of Fame |

In high school, Ty continued to compete in rodeo and to hone his skills. He joined his school's gymnastics team expressly because he thought it would improve his coordination and balance. Although only in his late teens, he was already pushing the envelope of athleticism in his sport and honing what many consider the most disciplined physical machine in rodeo. In 1987, he won the National High School All-Around Cowboy title, competing in saddle bronc, bareback, and bull riding.

After completing high school, Ty moved to Texas and enrolled at Odessa College, a small, two-year school with a premier rodeo program and conveniently located on the PRCA circuit. In 1989, he claimed the National Intercollegiate Rodeo Association's all-around title and also competed in his first PRCA national finals, where he won his first professional PRCA All-Around Cowboy title, making him, at twenty, the youngest all-around winner in PRCA history.

### The Emerging Champion

Ty returned to the PRCA finals for the next five years (1990-1994), and each year, he walked away with the All-Around Cowboy championship title. This consistency was remarkable enough in itself but even more so when considering that Ty competed in the most grueling "roughstock" events—bareback, saddle bronc, and bull riding. The physical toll and sky-high injury rates these events exact tend to weed out all but the toughest competitors. Ty's ability to withstand pain and excel in these events was testimony to his discipline and toughness. Timed events—calf roping, team roping, and steer wrestling—while requiring terrific skill and speed, are less physically arduous. Ty's choice of events amounted to a particularly grueling triathlon.

When Ty began riding professionally, he partnered, or shared driving and traveling expenses, with veteran cowboy and longtime family friend Cody Lambert. Lambert had known Ty since his babyhood and mentored him in his riding. Lambert was known as one of the sharpest minds and most solid business heads in the sport. He was eight years older than Ty.

Lambert's intimate inside knowledge of stock contractors and events allowed him to know which rodeos were worth entering, based not only on the prize money but also on the quality of the stock. A good rider has a better chance to make money if the stock is tough. With Lambert's help, Ty not only won and continued winning but also prospered financially. Ty's talent and grit probably predestined a rise to the top of his profession. There is no question, however, that Lambert's presence in Ty's life—as friend and adviser—sped his ascent.

### Continuing the Story

Despite his extraordinary athleticism, Ty was not exempt from injuries. He was sidelined repeatedly for damage to his knees and shoulders, for which he had to undergo reconstructive surgery. What distinguished him was his ability to rebound after each setback, with skills and riding confidence seemingly unfazed by enforced layoffs. After having to take time off because of a shoulder injury, in 1998, Ty came back to win the PRCA All-Around Cowboy title for a record-breaking seventh time, topping the previous record of six held by Mahan. A short time later, Ty received an engraved trophy buckle at the ProRodeo Hall of Fame from Mahan recognizing his achievements.

In 1999, Ty shifted his attentions from the PRCA and focused more on bull riding and on the highly lucrative Professional Bull Riders (PBR) World Championship. This move allowed him not only to focus his energies but also to spend less time on the road. He won the PBR finals in 1999 and finished as reserve champion from 2000 to 2002. In 2000, Ty was inducted into the ProRodeo Hall of Fame. Two years later, he retired from rodeo.

After his retirement, Ty remained active on the rodeo scene. He served frequently as an announcer for televised PBR bull-riding events. In July of 2004, he became the president of PBR and helped guide the organization to become more recognized and

**213**

grow in popularity. Its events were broadcast on mainstream television both in the United States and abroad. He also hosted a reality show on Country Music Television, entitled *Ty Murray's Celebrity Bull Riding Challenge.*

## Summary

Ty Murray became known as the "King of Cowboys" and the Michael Jordan of professional rodeo. He was a rarity: a child prodigy who fulfilled the promise of his youth. From early childhood he was consumed by a love of rodeo and a driving ambition to break records and set new ones. He progressed steadily from youth rodeos to high school and college events, on to the professional circuit, gathering virtually every honor the sport has to bestow. By virtue of his innate talent, rigorous self-discipline, and steady determination, he became one of the greatest athletes rodeo has ever seen.

*Christel Reges, updated by Lamia Nuseibeh Scherzinger*

## Additional Sources

Coplon, Jeff. *Gold Buckle: The Magnificent Obsession of Rodeo Bull Riders.* San Francisco: HarperCollinsWest, 1995.

Hollandsworth, Skip. "Sweetheart of the Rodeo." *Texas Monthly,* May, 1999, 118.

Murray, Ty, and Steve Eubanks. *King of the Cowboys.* New York: Atria Books, 2003.

Murray, Ty, and Kendra Santos. *Roughstock: The Mud, the Blood, and the Beer.* Austin, Tex.: Equimedia Corporation, 2003.

# *Paula Newby-Fraser*

**Born:** June 2, 1962
      Salisbury, Southern Rhodesia (now
        Harare, Zimbabwe)
**Also known as:** Iron Queen; Queen of Kona

## Early Life

Paula Newby-Fraser was the second of two children born to South African nationals in Salisbury, Southern Rhodesia (now Harare, Zimbabwe). When Paula was four, her parents, Brian and Betty Newby-Fraser, moved the family to Durban, South Africa, because of political upheaval after Southern Rhodesia declared its independence. There, Paula's father established the second-largest industrial-painting business in the country. Paula credits her mother—a sociologist, educator, and progressive liberal—as a role model for her ability to extend herself beyond boundaries.

Although her parents were not athletic, Paula took ballet and swimming lessons, played field hockey, and practiced Spanish dance. In middle school she began swimming competitively, and by high school she had achieved national ranking. From the ages of eight to sixteen, Paula swam ninety minutes before school and two hours after school each day.

At the age of sixteen, Paula stopped swimming because she could advance no further as an amateur. South Africa, because of its apartheid policy, was banned from the Olympics. Paula did not believe she could support herself as a professional swimmer. She attended the University of Natal for the next six years, completely abandoning sports.

## The Road to Excellence

While working full time, Paula began jogging to lose the excess weight she had gained in college. She soon added weightlifting and aerobics classes to her routine. Late in 1984, she heard about triathlons, so she and her boyfriend purchased bicycles and began riding daily. Only eight weeks later, she entered her first triathlon. She not only won the women's division but also set a new course record. Three months later, she won a national-level Ironman Triathlon—a 2.4-mile swim, a 112-mile

bike race, and a marathon run—which earned her a free trip to the Hawaii Ironman Triathlon Championships.

Paula's training for the Hawaii Ironman was casual compared to that of professional triathletes. She ran 25 to 30 miles a week, swam 2 or 3 miles a week, and occasionally rode her bike. Amazingly, she finished third—a fact that is often mentioned as evidence of her natural ability and her strong training base. After leaving Hawaii she spent some time in the triathlete community of San Diego, Cal-

Paula Newby-Fraser crossing the finish line to win the women's division of the 1992 Ironman Triathlon. (AFP/Getty Images)

## Major Championships

| Year | Race |
| --- | --- |
| 1986, 1988-89, 1991-94, 1996 | Hawaii Ironman Triathlon (world championship) |
| 1988, 1990-92, 2002 | Ironman Japan |
| 1989 | World Duathlon |
| 1989-92 | Nice International Triathlon |
| 1991 | Powerman Duathlon |
| 1991-92 | Escape from Alcatraz |
| 1992, 1994-95 | Ironman Europe |
| 1994-95, 1997 | Ironman Lanzarote |
| 1996 | Ironman Canada |
| 1996-97 | Ironman Australia |
| 2000 | Ironman South Africa |
| 2002 | Superfrog XXIX Triathlon |
| | Ironman Japan |
| 2004 | Ironman Korea |

ifornia. Enchanted by the lifestyle, she moved, at the age of twenty-three, to California, settling in Encinitas.

### The Emerging Champion

After her impressive finish in her first Hawaii Ironman Triathlon Championships, Paula continued to improve her frequency of competition and her race results. She finished second in the 1986 Hawaii Ironman, but the winner was later disqualified, leaving Paula in first place in the women's division with $17,000 in prize money. She asked Paul Huddle, a professional triathlete and trainer, to help her increase her running and biking mileage.

Paula's 1988 Hawaii Ironman win has been called the greatest performance in endurance sports history. Her time in the women's division broke the women's course record by thirty-four minutes and was beaten by only ten men.

### Continuing the Story

Paula's 1988 Hawaii win was the start of an impressive string of accomplishments. Her 1992 Hawaii Ironman win—besides representing the first time a woman had completed the Ironman in less than nine hours—was the first perfect race in triathlon history. She performed the fastest swim, fastest bike, and fastest run in the women's division of the race. Her winning time in the 1994 Ironman Europe competition, 8 hours 50 minutes 24 seconds (8:50:24), set a women's world record for the event. She began to be called the "Iron Queen" and "Queen of Kona," winning an unequaled eighth

Hawaii Ironman Triathlon Championship in 1996. One honor in which she took great pleasure was the 1990 professional sportswoman of the year award, given by the Women's Sports Foundation. This international award, she felt, garnered broader recognition for her sport.

After winning her eighth world championship, Paula continued racing and training, although not as frequently or as intensely. Between 1986 and 2004, she won twenty-four Ironman competitions—more than twice as many as triathletes Mark Allen, Erin Baker, Natascha Badmann, and Dave Scott—including the inaugural Ironman South Africa in 2000.

In 2002, at the age of thirty-nine, Paula won the Ironman Japan competition, making her the oldest person ever to win an Ironman. Then, in August, 2004, she won Ironman Korea, which had to be limited to biking and running to avoid the rough waters caused by bad weather. She was forty-two years and two months old. Paula said, "Why does forty happen to be a defining age for women? It's not. It doesn't faze me to stand on the line next to a twenty-five-year-old."

Paula overcame many obstacles. If her bike got a flat tire during a race, she could change the tire within two minutes. One time during a race in Thailand, a whole herd of huge water buffalo blocked her path. Paula saw that the other runners were gaining on her. She had to keep going and contemplated charging into the herd. Instead, she yelled, "Get out of the way!" The water buffalo

## Records and Milestones

| | |
| --- | --- |
| 1992 | Hawaii Ironman course women's record time: 8:55:28 |
| 1994 | Ironman women's world record time: 8:50:24 |

## Honors and Awards

| | |
| --- | --- |
| 1990 | Women's Sports Foundation Professional Sportswoman of the Year |
| 1990, 1996 | *Triathlete Magazine* Triathlete of the Year |
| 1996 | Inducted into Ironman Hall of Fame |
| | *Inside Triathlon* Triathlete of the Year |
| | U.S. Sports Academy, CNN, and *USA Today* Top 5 Professional Women Athletes of the Last 25 Years |

slowly ambled off the road, and Paula continued, eventually winning the race. The *Los Angeles Times* and *ABC's Wide World of Sports* acclaimed Paula as the greatest all-around female athlete in the world. In 1996, the United States Sports Academy named her as one of the top five professional women athletes of the previous twenty-five years. Paula was inducted into the Breitbard Hall of Fame of the San Diego Hall of Champions in 2000.

Besides competitions, Paula's activities included writing her training guide, *Peak Fitness for Women* (1995); cofounding the MultiSport School of Champions, which offered training camps for triathletes; providing race-day analysis over the Internet for the 1999 Hawaii Ironman; and acting as host of both the CEO Ironman Challenge events at Ironman Coeur d'Alene and Ironman USA Lake Placid. In 2006, she was named president of North America Sports, which organizes eight Ironman-sanctioned events in the United States and Canada and raises money for charity and nonprofit groups.

On October 5, 2005, Paula, married Paul Huddle in San Diego. Paul worked with Paula at the MultiSports School of Champions as a triathlon coach. Paula became a U.S. citizen in 1996. In 2007, she won the Partner Speed Golf World Championship.

## Summary

Paula Newby-Fraser's impressive list of accomplishments qualifies her as the greatest triathlete in the sport's history. She contributed more to the sport than setting records and winning world championships, however. She was an articulate and dedicated spokesperson for her sport, particularly for female competitors. She was also an innovator as the first to use 24-inch-diameter bike tires and as the first female to incorporate weightlifting into her training. Her training routine focused on speed and rest at a time when other triathletes practiced "megamileage." Other professional triathletes commended her consistency in training and her mental toughness in a sport that is psychologically as well as physically demanding. She did not allow age to be a barrier. Paula felt fortunate to be able to make a living at a sport she loved.

*Glenn Ellen Starr Stilling,*
*updated by Chrissa Shamberger*

## Additional Sources

Burgess, Todd. "Having Iron Will to Finish Ironman." *Rocky Mountain News,* July 3, 2007.

Cook, Jeff. *The Triathletes: A Season in the Lives of Four Women in the Toughest Sport of All.* New York: St. Martin's Press, 1992.

Johnson, Anne Janotte. "Paula Newby-Fraser." In *Great Women in Sports.* Detroit: Visible Ink Press, 1996.

McAlpine, Ken. "Ironwoman." *Sports Illustrated* 87, no. 14 (October 6, 1997): 127.

McDowell, Dimity. "The Veterans. Into Their Fifth (and Sixth) Decades, Some Champions Just Keep Getting Stronger." *Sports Illustrated Women* 4, no. 8 (December, 2002/ January, 2003).

"Paula Newby-Fraser." *Outside* 29, no. 1 (January, 2004): 44.

Ridge, Julie. "Enduring Greatness." *Women's Sports and Fitness* 11, no. 5 (June, 1989): 24-26, 28-29.

# *Barney Oldfield*

**Born:** January 29, 1878
Near Wauseon, Ohio
**Died:** October 4, 1946
Beverly Hills, California
**Also known as:** Berna Eli Oldfield (full name);
Daredevil Promoter; Speed King of the World

## Early Life

Berna Eli Oldfield was born on January 29, 1878, near Wauseon, Ohio. When he was eleven, his parents, Henry Clay and Sarah (Yarnell) Oldfield, moved to Toledo, Ohio, where Berna soon revealed his daredevil nature by catching rides on city fire wagons. When he was fourteen, he bought a bicycle, which he raced through the streets of Toledo.

In 1893, Berna quit school to become a bicycle racer. He learned fast, studying ways to reduce wind resistance, build his physical stamina, and pace himself. The turning point in his life came in 1894, when he rode in the Ohio State Championship races in Canton, Ohio. After he finished second in three events, the Stearns bicycle factory hired him to ride for its racing team. He acquired the nickname "Barney," which he soon made synonymous with daredevil speed racing.

## The Road to Excellence

Barney Oldfield was born as the United States was entering the Industrial Revolution, an era of technological advancement, when telephones, electric lights, and, soon, automobiles were changing American life. In 1902, when Barney started racing automobiles, the United States was still in the horse-and-buggy era, and few people sensed the automobile's importance. Most rural Americans had never heard of the automobile, and there were only 178 miles of paved roads in the entire country.

Although Barney was not well educated, he helped change American life. He was an important

*Barney Oldfield in a Ford 999.* (Courtesy of Amateur Athletic Foundation of Los Angeles)

matchmaker in the fast-developing American love affair with the automobile. His success in reaching the public imagination stemmed from his mix of flamboyant daredevil feats with an unmatched gift for self-promotion.

Early automobile manufacturers realized that car racing would provide dramatic advertising for their new product. In 1901, Tom Cooper, a bicycle racing friend, urged Barney to come to Detroit, Michigan, where Tom was helping Henry Ford build two high-speed racing cars. At Grosse Point, Michigan, in October, 1902, Barney drove the Ford 999 car to his first victory, breaking a speed record held by Alexander Winton, considered the greatest racer of that time. In June, 1903, Barney used the 999 racer to become the first American to cover a mile in less than one minute. These feats made Barney famous, boosted Ford's career, and helped popularize the automobile in the United States. Barney was a natural showman who barnstormed the nation; people flocked to see the famous mile-a-minute man race the newest machines.

**The Emerging Champion**

In August, 1903, Barney left Tom Cooper to work for Alexander Winton. His salary was $2,500 a year plus maintenance, expenses, and prize money. He soon drove the Winton Bullet Number Two to a three-mile record and went on to set record after record, driving with his trademark cigar clenched between his teeth. There were bad times. In September, 1903, for example, he blew a tire and veered into the crowd, killing one spectator and injuring himself.

Barney entered racing when it was an unorganized sport dominated by flamboyant showmen running match races against one another. Barney rebelled against attempts to bring organization to racing, and he was in constant trouble with the new American Automobile Association (AAA), which often suspended him from official events.

Suspensions did not hurt his popularity. In mid-1904, Barney went to work for the Peerless Company and drove the "Green Dragon." Money poured in, which he spent on lavish parties. He toured the United States and Canada and won international acclaim. By the end of the year, he held all dirt-track records from one to fifty miles. In

---

### Honors and Awards

1946   Honored at the Detroit Golden Jubilee as an automobile industry pioneer
1952   Inducted into Indianapolis Motor Speedway Hall of Fame
1953   Inducted into Automobile Racing Hall of Fame
1989   Inducted into Motorsports Hall of Fame of America
1990   Inducted into International Motor Sports Hall of Fame

---

1905, he stayed in the headlines by winning races and continuing to have narrow escapes from death. On March 16, 1906, he set a new record at Daytona Beach with a speed of 131.7 miles per hour. He was called the "Speed King of the World."

Barney's name was synonymous with racing and with speed. He raced farm tractors and pitted cars against locomotives and airplanes. He drove the most famous cars of his day: Fiat, Mercer, Maxwell, Stutz, the Ford 999, a French Delage, and a Christie. Few people could beat Barney on dirt tracks, and he was also a master of long-distance road racing.

AAA suspensions kept him out of some of the early Indianapolis 500 races, but in 1914, he took fifth place driving a Stutz; he took fifth again in 1916. In November, 1914, he won the Cactus Derby, a race of 671 miles from Los Angeles, California, to Phoenix, Arizona, that won him the title of "Master Driver of the World."

**Continuing the Story**

The Indianapolis races symbolized a new day, with dedicated professionals eclipsing the undisciplined daredevils. In 1918, Barney retired to pursue other interests.

At the end of his auto racing career, he formed an alliance with the Firestone Tire and Rubber Company that led to its continuing involvement in racing. The company named a tire after Barney, called the "Oldfield." Barney made money on this venture, selling out in 1924.

Barney became a millionaire and lived lavishly. He was married four times. His friends included many famous millionaires and film stars. Although the stock market crash in 1929 wiped out his fortune, he remained famous to the end of his life. He earned money as a consulting engineer and spokesperson for automobile products, and as a celebrity at fairs and other public events. He appeared in a film about his life and wrote his autobiography.

In May, 1946, at the Detroit Golden Jubilee celebrating a half century of motoring, Barney was honored as one of the great pioneers in automobile history—a fitting end to his story. He died on October 4, 1946, of a cerebral hemorrhage.

## Summary

Few sports figures have had as much impact on the American imagination as Barney Oldfield. Part sportsman and part huckster, he helped establish the automobile as the technological innovation that most changed American life in the twentieth century.

During Barney Oldfield's long racing career, he drove in thirty-six championship events and set numerous speed records. He helped create the first successful racing drivers' union and eventually became a pioneer in establishing automobile safety regulations. He was named to the Automobile Racing Hall of Fame in 1953 and the Indianapolis Motor Speedway Hall of Fame in 1952.

*Martha E. Pemberton*

## Additional Sources

Kernan, Michael. "Wow! A Mile a Minute! Automobile Racing Driver Barney Oldfield Set Many Speed Records." *Smithsonian* 29, no. 2 (May, 1998): 28-29.

Nolan, William F. *Barney Oldfield: The Life and Times of America's Legendary Speed King.* Reprint. Carpinteria, Calif.: Brown Fox Books, 2002.

Oldfield, Barney. *Barney Oldfield's Book for the Motorist.* Boston: Small, Maynard, 1919.

"Track Record." *Popular Mechanics* 182, no. 9 (September, 2005): 20.

# *Connie Paraskevin-Young*

**Born:** July 4, 1961
     Detroit, Michigan
**Also known as:** Connie Paraskevin (birth name);
    Connie Young
**Other major sport:** Speed skating

## Early Life

On July 4, 1961, while the United States celebrated its Independence Day with sparklers and fireworks, the Paraskevin family celebrated the birth of its sixth and last child, Connie. The name Paraskevin is Russian in origin; Connie's grandfather had immigrated to the United States from the Soviet Union.

Connie came from an athletic family. Her father played Canadian football in high school, and her mother was a golfer and skier. One sister played tennis while another was a speed skater. Her two brothers played hockey. While growing up in Detroit, Michigan, Connie played a variety of sports: tennis, golf, skiing, speed skating, and cycling. Her first introduction to pedal power came at the age of two atop a red tricycle.

## The Road to Excellence

Connie began track cycling for her hometown Wolverine Club at the age of ten. Track cycling is held in a velodrome, a stadium with a banked track. She won her first national cycling championship as an eleven-year-old in the omnium, also known as the overall track category. To win the omnium one must compete in a series of events, each at distances ranging from one-quarter mile to two miles.

From 1973 through 1978, Connie dominated the junior age groups, capturing national omnium titles each year. In addition to her two-wheeled accomplishments, Connie achieved success on the ice. As a member of the U.S. national speed skating team, she won a bronze medal in the sprints at the World Championships in 1978.

## The Emerging Champion

Connie discovered that she could gain Olympic recognition through speed skating. She made two Olympic teams (1984 and 1988) and was on the national speed skating team for eight consecutive years (from 1977 through 1984). She stopped competing as a cyclist for two years prior to the 1980 Winter Olympic Games to concentrate entirely on speed skating. In 1981, she returned to cycling and made the national team that same year.

Match sprint cycling, held in a velodrome, enjoys its greatest visibility every four years at the Olympic Games. The event pits two cyclists against each other and is an audience favorite. It is comparable to the 100-meter dash in track and field competitions. It combines speed, strategy, quickness, strength, and daring. Each sprint is 1,000 meters in length, but only the last 200 meters are timed. Match sprint cyclists ride a fixed-gear (one-speed) bicycle without brakes. These bikes cannot coast and go only as fast as the rider can pedal.

Connie's many years of competing in both cycling and speed skating caused her to develop shin problems in 1981. She sought help from her new coach Roger Young, and this proved to be a successful partnership. Connie won her first match sprint World Track Championship the following year.

*Connie Paraskevin-Young.* (AP/Wide World Photos)

221

## Major Championships

| Year | Competition | Place |
|---|---|---|
| 1973-78 | U.S. Nationals, sprint speed skating junior championship | 1st |
| 1978 | World Championships, sprint speed skating | 3d |
| 1981 | U.S. National Criterium Championships, match sprint cycling | 1st |
| 1982-83, 1985, 1987-89, 1992, 1994 | U.S. Nationals, match sprint cycling | 1st |
| 1982-84, 1990 | World Track Championships, match sprint cycling | 1st |
| 1985 | World Track Championships, match sprint cycling | 2d |
| | 7-Eleven Cup Series Finals, match sprint cycling | 1st |
| 1986-87 | World Track Championships, match sprint cycling | 3d |
| 1987 | Pan-American Games, match sprint cycling | 1st |
| 1988 | Olympic Trials, match sprint cycling | Gold |
| | Olympic Games, match sprint cycling | Bronze |
| 1990 | Goodwill Games, match sprint cycling | 1st |
| 1991 | Pan-American Games, match sprint cycling | 3d |
| 1995 | Pan-American Games, match sprint cycling | 1st |

During the 1987 World Track Championships, Connie was suffering mysterious head and neck aches but still managed to take the bronze medal. U.S. trainers packed her head and spine in ice before she raced. "The pain was so severe, there were literally times when I couldn't see," she said. Though she sustained injuries throughout her athletic career, she never used them to explain subpar performances.

### Continuing the Story

"On the track," said Connie, after the 1990 Goodwill Games,

> I see my opponent as a faceless person. They are the competition, and I want to beat them no matter who they are. But once the race is over, they get their face back and we're friends again. A lot of athletes make their opponent the enemy. Not me.

Connie's sense of good sportsmanship and her desire to help fellow cyclists, even her toughest competitors, were demonstrated when she helped a Soviet rider come to the United States to train. Erika Salumae, one of Connie's closest rivals, lived, trained, and competed with her for months.

Connie competed in two more Olympic Games, in 1992 and 1996, though without winning medals. During her distinguished cycling career, she won many U.S. national championship titles and world championships, and she was ranked among the top three cyclists in the world for ten years. After the 1996 Olympic Games, Connie retired from competition. She and husband, coach Roger Young, remained active in cycling as sports marketing consultants and trainers. Connie also works as a motivational speaker.

### Summary

Sheila Young-Ochowicz, a longtime friend, competitor, and sister-in-law, had this to say about Connie Paraskevin-Young: "Her talent has always existed. She's dedicated herself to be the best sprinter possible, and has overcome obstacles that include prejudice towards women in cycling. Her attitude is way beyond that of surviving."

*Greg Woo*

### Additional Sources

Levinson, David, and Karen Christensen, eds. *Encyclopedia of World Sport: From Ancient Times to the Present*. Santa Barbara, Calif.: ABC-Clio, 1996.

Miller, Ernestine G. *Making Her Mark: Firsts and Milestones in Women's Sports*. Chicago: Contemporary Books, 2002.

Wallechinsky, David, and Jaime Loucky. *The Complete Book of the Olympics: 2008 Edition*. London: Aurum Press, 2008.

## Honors and Awards

| | |
|---|---|
| 1988 | U.S. Cycling Federation Cyclist of the Year |
| 1990 | *VeloNews* Female Cyclist of the Year |

# *Danica Patrick*

**Born:** March 25, 1982
Beloit, Wisconsin
**Also known as:** Danica Sue Patrick (full name)

## Early Life
Danica Sue Patrick was born on March 25, 1982, in Beloit, Wisconsin. Shortly thereafter her family moved to Roscoe, Illinois, where Danica grew up in a small-town atmosphere. Her parents, T. J. and Bev, both had strong competitive sports backgrounds and met at a snowmobile race where Bev was acting as a friend's mechanic. In addition to racing snowmobiles, T. J. raced midget cars and motocross bikes.

## The Road to Excellence
Danica was ten years old when she and her younger sister Brooke first visited a local go-kart track. Go-karts, open-frame vehicles powered by small gasoline engines, are often starting places for race-car

*Danica Patrick, who was the first woman to win an Indy race in 2008.* (Brian Lawdermilk/MCT/Landov)

drivers' careers, but Danica's introduction to them was inauspicious. Inexperienced in handling the machine, she had difficulty simply keeping up with the parade lap, let alone actually racing. However, the experience did not discourage her and, if anything, made her determined to learn. By the end of the summer, she was in second place in a field of twenty drivers.

In 1994, she won the World Karting Association's Grand National Championship and followed her success with additional titles the following two years. By 1997, she was seriously contemplating a professional racing career. Her next logical step was to go to England, where she had better training opportunities in open-wheel racing than in the United States. She gained the sponsorship of the Mecoms, a Texas racing family, and lived with a host family in England. Suddenly on her own with minimal supervision, she began to lose her focus and spend too much time socializing. As a result, the Mecoms threatened to withdraw her funding; only by agreeing to severe restrictions was Danica able to continue for a second year of training at Jaguar Racing.

## The Emerging Champion
When Danica returned from England, she was approached by Bobby Rahal of Rahal Letterman Racing, who offered her a place on his development team. For the next several years she drove in the Toyota Atlantic series, compiling an impressive record of top-five finishes. In 2005, she was moved up to the Indy Racing League (IRL), and on May 29, 2005, she started fourth in the Indianapolis 500. Although she was not the first woman to drive in that famous race, she quickly made her mark as the first woman to lead the race, if only briefly. However, her success was marred by several rookie mistakes, and, in the end, she had to work hard to finish fourth.

## Continuing the Story
After her spectacular debut, which resulted in the rookie of the year award, Danica had mixed results in the 2006 racing season. In the 2007 season, she

switched to a new team, Andretti-Green, and gained new corporate sponsors. Although she finished four races in the top five, she still could not win a race. As a result, considerable controversy surrounded her. Some people felt that her status as a woman worked to her benefit and that a male driver with similar racing results would have lost sponsorship. Her partisans point out her high rankings in the IRL points system, which rose steadily over the first three years of her IRL career, as evidence of genuine, developing talent. Michael Andretti, of Andretti-Green, regarded her as a rookie even past her first season, on the grounds that Rahal-Letterman gave her relatively little opportunity to become acquainted with the tactics of driving. Danica refused to allow the controversy around her career to disturb her. Finally, on April 20, 2008, Danica earned her first victory, the Indy Japan 300. She was the first woman to win an IndyCar race.

When not racing, Danica lives quietly with her husband, Paul Hospenthal, whom she met when he helped with her injury rehabilitation and training. Although Danica was raised in a household that paid little attention to formal religion, when she married Hospenthal, she converted to Catholicism, his faith.

## Summary

Although Danica Patrick was not the first woman to drive in the Indianapolis 500—that distinction belongs to Janet Guthrie, who qualified in 1977—her outstanding performance in the 2005 race made her newsworthy as a rookie driver and not as a woman driver only. However, Danica's image and physical attractiveness have allowed her to parlay her athletic success into endorsement opportunities. She has posed for the *Sports Illustrated* swimsuit edition but has concentrated on ensuring that her appearance enhances, rather than detracts from, her professional reputation.

*Leigh Husband Kimmel*

| Milestones | | |
|---|---|---|
| 1994 | World Karting Association Manufacturers Cup points champion | |
| | World Karting Association Grand National Championship (Yamaha class) | |
| 1994, 1995 | World Karting Association Great Lakes Sprint Series victory | |
| 1997 | World Karting Association Grand National Championship (HPV and Yamaha classes) | |
| 2001 | Gorsline Scholarship Award | |
| | Long Beach Grand Prix pro/celebrity race winner | |
| 2004 | First pole position (Portland) | |
| 2005 | *USA Today* Female Athlete of the Year | |
| | Indianapolis 500 Rookie of the Year | |
| 2005-07 | IndyCar most popular driver | |
| 2008 | First IndyCar victory (Indy Japan 300) | |

## Additional Sources

Ingram, Jonathan, and Paul Webb. *Danica Patrick: America's Hottest Racer.* St. Paul, Minn.: Motorbooks International, 2005.

Patrick, Danica, with Laura Morton. *Danica: Crossing the Line.* New York: Fireside, 2006.

# *David Pearson*

**Born:** December 22, 1934
    Whitney, South Carolina
**Also known as:** David Gene Pearson (full name);
    Silver Fox

## Early Life
David Gene Pearson was born on December 22, 1934, in Whitney, South Carolina. His parents were cotton-mill workers. David grew up in the town of Spartanburg, South Carolina. The Pearson family was poor, and it was expected that David would also work in a cotton mill as soon as he was old enough. His life changed, though, after he went to his first car race. David was only ten, but he knew even at that young age that he wanted to be a race-car driver. At every opportunity, David tinkered with old cars, but he kept his dream of racing to himself so as not to worry his mother. By the time David was a teenager, he was mechanically adept enough to build his own engine. He dropped out of high school and, in 1952, he raced for the first time, driving a 1940 Ford at Woodruff Speedway in Woodruff, South Carolina.

## The Road to Excellence
David was certain after his first race that he did not want to do anything with his life except race. Soon, he was considered a celebrity on the dirt track circuit. Throughout the 1950's, David continued to improve as a driver, hoping that one day he could join the Grand National circuit of the National Association for Stock Car Auto Racing (NASCAR).

In 1959, David won thirty of the forty-two dirt track races he entered. At the time, he was working in a gas station to supplement his meager race winnings. The owner of the station, along with some of David's friends, located a 1959 Chevrolet that had been used on the Grand National circuit. David did not have enough money to buy the car himself, so friends started a fan club to help raise the funds needed to purchase the car. As a result, David was able to start racing his 1959 Chevrolet on the Grand National circuit in 1960.

David's first year on the circuit was frustrating because the Chevy was unable to perform well enough for David to win any races. He competed in twenty-two races that year and finished in the top ten in only seven. This was not up to the David's dirt-track performance standards, but it was good enough for him to capture rookie of the year.

## The Emerging Champion
David had thoughts of going back to the minor circuit, where he could win. He knew that he was a good driver, but he needed someone to put his car in racing condition. Ray Fox, a car builder and master mechanic, came along to fill the gap and make David's car competitive. David could concentrate on racing to win because he knew that his car had been properly overhauled. In 1961, David came away with wins in the World 600, the Firecracker

David Pearson, who was NASCAR's top driver in 1966, 1968, and 1969. (Courtesy of Amateur Athletic Foundation of Los Angeles)

250, and the Dixie 400. No second-year driver on the Grand National circuit had ever before won three races in one year.

The next two years were disappointing for David because he did not win any of the fifty-three races in which he competed. In 1964, David's luck changed after he switched to a Dodge car owned by Cotton Owens. David won eight times during the year, although he was frustrated by not winning any

## NASCAR Circuit Victories

| | |
|---|---|
| 1961 | Firecracker 250 |
| | Dixie 400 |
| 1961, 1974, 1976 | World 600 |
| 1964, 1966, 1968-69 | Richmond 500 |
| 1965-66 | Capital City 400 |
| 1966, 1968-69 | NASCAR Grand National Championship |
| 1967-68, 1971 | Southeastern 500 |
| 1968 | Nashville 420 |
| | Staley 400 |
| 1968-69 | Volunteer 500 |
| 1968, 1970, 1972 | CRC Chemicals Rebel 400 |
| 1969 | Wilkes 400 |
| | Champion Spark Plug 600 |
| 1969, 1971, 1975 | Daytona 500 100-Mile Qualifying Race |
| 1969, 1973, 1978 | Carolina 500 |
| 1972-73 | Delaware 500 |
| 1972-73, 1975-76 | Gabriel 400 |
| 1972-74 | Winston 500 |
| 1972, 1974, 1976, 1978 | Champion Spark Plug 400 |
| 1972-74, 1978 | Firecracker 400 |
| 1973 | Atlanta Journal 500 |
| | Virginia 500 |
| 1973-74 | American 500 |
| 1973-74, 1976 | CRC Chemicals Rebel 500 |
| 1973, 1975, 1978 | Mason-Dixon 500 |
| 1973, 1976 | Coca-Cola 500 |
| 1974 | National 500 |
| 1975 | Purolator 500 |
| 1976 | Daytona 500 |
| | World 600 |
| | Southern 500 |
| | Western 500 |
| | Riverside 400 |
| 1976-77 | Heinz Southern 500 |
| | Winston Western 500 |

of the major races. The 1966 season turned out to be one of David's best. He won fifteen Grand National races that year and, along with the points he had earned in the superspeedway races, came away with the year's NASCAR Grand National championship. This was the first of three driving championships that David would win.

Before the 1967 season ended, David decided to switch to Ford. By the time he started racing the following year, he had a whole new team behind him that included Dick Hutcherson as his crew chief and Ralph Moody as his overall supervisor. With the help of his new team, David was in top form for the year. He managed to win sixteen times and finish in the top five another thirty-six times, capturing his second NASCAR Championship.

What David wanted next was to match Lee Petty's achievement of back-to-back championships. In 1969, he did not disappoint himself or his fans. David captured eleven victories and was in the top five in forty-two additional races. He won his third NASCAR Championship and equaled the record of Lee Petty, who had won the championship in 1954, 1958, and 1959.

## Continuing the Story

Starting in 1970, David began to cut back on the number of races in which he competed during the year so that he could concentrate on the major races. During the early 1970's, he averaged only eighteen races per year. In 1971, David began having trouble with his team after Ford Motor Company pulled its support from racing. He knew it was time to become affiliated with a new team. Glen and Leonard Wood of Stuart, Virginia, sought out David and made a deal with him to drive for the Woods-Purolator Mercury team in 1972. In 1973, David won eleven of the eighteen races he entered and was voted by the National Motorsports Press Association as the American driver of the year. In 1976, David became the first man to receive this award a second time. In that year, David also became the first driver to win the Western 500 and the Daytona 500 in the same year, and only the second driver to win the NASCAR triple crown: The Daytona 500, the World 600, and the Southern 500.

From 1960 through 1985, David won a total of 105 Grand National titles. At the time of his retirement, he held the record for the best career winning percentage on the NASCAR circuit, winning one out of every five and a half races in which he started. He and his wife, Helen, were married in 1952, and they had three sons. Their oldest son, Larry, has continued the family racing tradition.

## Honors and Awards

| | |
|---|---|
| 1960 | NASCAR Grand National Rookie of the Year |
| 1963-64, 1971-72, 1975-76 | Union 76-Darlington Record Club Award |
| 1973, 1976 | National Motorsports Press Association American Driver of the Year |
| 1979-80 | Most Popular Winston Cup Driver |
| 1980 | Winston West Grand National Most Popular Driver |
| | Grand American Stock Car Most Popular Driver |
| 1991 | Inducted into National Motorsports Press Association Stock Car Racing Hall of Fame |

## Summary

David Pearson was one of the most popular and successful NASCAR drivers of all time. His determination and driving skills pulled him out of childhood poverty and took him to the top of his chosen profession. Throughout the ups and downs of his racing career, David remained a respected individual and competitor; he will be remembered as one of the greats of racing.

*Jeffry Jensen*

## Additional Sources

Golenbock, Peter. *NASCAR Confidential: Stories of the Men and Women Who Made Stock Car Racing Great.* St. Paul, Minn.: Motorbooks International, 2004.

Hembree, Michael. *NASCAR: The Definitive History of America's Sport.* New York: HarperEntertainment, 2000.

Huff, Richard M. *Stock Car Racing: Running with NASCAR's Best.* Chicago: Bonus Books, 2000.

Hunter, Jim, and David Pearson. *Twenty-one Forever: The Story of Stock Car Racer David Pearson.* Huntsville, Ala.: Strode, 1980.

Poole, David, and James McLaurin. *NASCAR Essential: Everything You Need to Know to Be a Real Fan!* Chicago: Triumph Books, 2007.

Sowers, Richard. *Stock Car Racing Lives.* Phoenix, Ariz.: David Bull, 2000.

# Kyle Petty

**Born:** June 2, 1960
Randleman, North Carolina
**Also known as:** Kyle Eugene Petty (full name)

## Early Life
Kyle Eugene Petty was born on June 2, 1960, to Richard "the King" Petty, a race-car driver, and Lynda Petty. Kyle's grandfather, Lee Petty, was one of the earliest stars of North American Stock Car Auto Racing (NASCAR). As the son and grandson of drivers, Kyle was strongly influenced by the racing world as he was growing up. He frequently traveled with his father and grandfather to the track and watched them race; as he grew older, he often helped build their cars. However, his father and grandfather neither pushed him into racing nor sought to discourage him from following in their footsteps. As a result, Kyle explored a wide variety of interests, including the possibility of a country music career. However, even the lure of Nashville's Grand Ole Opry could not compete with the call of the racetrack.

## The Road to Excellence
In 1979, Kyle entered and won his first race at the Daytona Automobile Racing Club of America competition. Although he was an aggressive and talented driver, he did not possess the same level of skill as his father, who won his seventh and last Daytona 500 the following day. As a result, Kyle spent the first years of his Winston Cup career with several different racing teams, including the Wood Brothers and Felix Sabates.

Kyle's corporate sponsors also changed over the years as he struggled to build his career. An aspect of his family's deep religious convictions included

### Notable Victories

| Year | Location |
|------|----------|
| 1979 | Daytona (Automobile Racing Club of America) |
| 1986 | Richmond |
| 1987 | Charlotte |
| 1990-91 | North Carolina |
| 1993 | Pocono |
| 1995 | Dover |

never accepting corporate sponsorship from companies that made or sold alcoholic beverages. Although this decision made finding wealthy corporate sponsors difficult, Kyle was always able to gain sufficient financial backing to continue racing professionally. For instance, during the early 1990's, his principal sponsor was Mello Yello, a soft drink manufacturer. He bore the company's logo on his firesuit, on the hood of his race car, and across the sides of his transport trailer.

## The Emerging Champion
In 1991, Kyle survived an injury at Talladega Speedway that nearly destroyed his career. His leg was so badly broken that nine inches of bone protruded out of the flesh. Even after the surgeons pinned his broken femur back together, infection occurred and, for a time, raged throughout his body. Once he overcame both the injury and the subsequent infections, he began rehabilitating himself to be ready to race the next year.

Kyle's brush with death left a permanent mark on his personality. Before the injury, some experts questioned his determination, given his wide-ranging interests. However, after the 1991 accident, he was clearly focused upon becoming the best driver he could be. He never allowed his competitive side to erase his fundamental humanity. When Ernie Irvan, the driver blamed for Kyle's near-fatal wreck, was injured in the following season, Kyle visited Irvan in the hospital. That act allowed Irvan to realize how important simple courtesies were in the NASCAR circuit.

## Continuing the Story
On May 12, 2000, Kyle's eldest son Adam died in a racetrack wreck, ending the possibility of the first fourth-generation professional athlete in the United States. Although Kyle was devastated by the loss of his son, three weeks later, he got behind the wheel of one of his son's cars and raced. Since that day, Kyle has driven the #45 car without his name written on the driver's side door as a memorial to his son. Kyle's #44 car was driven subsequently by Bobby Labonte.

The Pettys found other ways to memorialize Adam as well, including the Victory Junction Gang camp, one in the network of Hole in the Wall Gang camps sponsored by actor Paul Newman for seriously and chronically ill children. Kyle also joined a cross-country motorcycle race for charity in which Adam had participated previously. Kyle's second son, Austin, also became involved in auto racing, reviving the possibility that a Petty could become the first fourth-generation athlete in the United States. Kyle assumed managerial control of Petty Enterprises, the company that supports his racing efforts, which is based out of the same rural North Carolina community where his extended family lives.

## Summary

Although Kyle Petty is the third generation of champions and the son of the man who won 200 NASCAR races, he regards that legacy as an obligation rather than a source of entitlement. In an era in which star athletes often fall short of heroic status, Kyle's humility and old-fashioned Southern courtesy distinguish him.

*Leigh Husband Kimmel*

| Honors and Awards | |
|---|---|
| 1998, 2000 | NASCAR USG Person of the Year |
| 1999-2000 | *NASCAR Illustrated* Person of the Year |
| 2000, 2004 | Myers Brothers Award |

## Additional Sources

Fleischman, Bill, and Al Pearce. *The Unauthorized NASCAR Fan Guide 2002.* Detroit: Visible Ink, 2002.

Gaillard, Frye, with Kyle Petty. *Kyle at Two Hundred MPH: A Sizzling Season in the Petty NASCAR Dynasty.* New York: St. Martin's Press, 1993.

Petty, Patti, and Kyle Petty. *The Petty Family Album: In Tribute to Adam Petty.* New York: Universe, 2002.

# *Lee Petty*

**Born:** March 14, 1914
      Near Randleman, North Carolina
**Died:** April 5, 2000
      Greensboro, North Carolina
**Also known as:** Lee Arnold Petty (full name)

## Early Life

Lee Arnold Petty was born on March 14, 1914, near Randleman, North Carolina. His was a farm family who had lived around the area for generations The Toomes, his mother's family, were farmers who grew tobacco and grain. Lee's father, Judson Petty, was descended from Quakers who had settled the area before the American Revolution. Judson was a "jack-of-all-trades" who grew tobacco, cut and hauled logs, ran a trucking line, and worked on cars.

Lee grew up doing what rural boys did at that time—working, hunting, swimming, and fishing. Lee liked competition and raced, even on a bicycle, whenever he had the chance. Although the family moved around, they always lived in the area of Randleman and Level Cross, North Carolina, where family and friends were nearby. Lee married just as the Great Depression was beginning, in 1929, but the new couple got by. They soon had two sons, Richard and Maurice. Richard became one of the most famous stock-car race drivers in the history of the sport, and Maurice, who had polio as a child, became an outstanding crew chief and mechanic.

## The Road to Excellence

Lee was always tinkering with his automobiles to make them go faster. His business as a truck driver helped him to develop excellent driving skills. Soon he was putting the two skills together to race other drivers from the area down deserted stretches of local highways. These informal contests always took place at night so that oncoming headlights would warn contestants when to give way to approaching traffic. Lee was soon the acknowledged champion of this dangerous and illegal activity.

At about the same time, racing cars on dirt tracks was becoming popular all over the South. Lee and his family began to attend these races, and in 1947, Lee and his brother, Julie, began to enter the events. In his first race, Lee finished first; in his second race, second; and in his third race, third. This disgusted Lee, who made as his motto: "There is no second place. You either win or lose. That's the only two parts there are to racing." The racing bug had bitten him too hard to be ignored, however. In 1948, a trip to see the race at Daytona Beach, Florida, brought Lee back into racing, with his sons as his pit crew. By 1950, Lee was racing every weekend and sometimes during the week as well.

There was not much money in these victories. When the entire family went to a race, they stayed in a tourist home and packed enough food from home to eat on the trip. However, Lee

*Lee Petty.* (AP/Wide World Photos)

## NASCAR Circuit Victories

| | |
|---|---|
| 1954 | Daytona 4.1-Mile Beach/Road Race |
| 1954, 1958-59 | NASCAR Grand National Championship |
| 1958 | NASCAR Late-Model Short Track |
| 1959 | Daytona 500 |
| | Virginia 500 |
| | Wilkes 400 |
| 1959-60 | Staley 400 |
| 1960 | Richmond 500 |

was building his skill and was establishing a reputation as a good driver.

### The Emerging Champion

In 1953, racing began to pay off for Lee. He was driving Dodge cars, always with the number 42, and always painted the soon-to-be famous "Petty blue."

The race cars of this period were supposed to be true stock cars, automobiles taken off the dealer's lot just as the factory delivered them. Experience was showing that these cars could not stand up to the stress of racing, so changes began to be allowed by the National Association for Stock Car Auto Racing (NASCAR). Lee and his assistants were good at these modifications, and their mechanical skill boosted Lee's driving ability. As a result, in 1954, Lee rose to the top of his sport as NASCAR champion for the year, beating his nearest competitor by more than three hundred points.

Also in 1954, Lee inherited the farm of his father-in-law and moved the family to the old house where he had met his wife. A barn was converted into an auto shop so that, for the first time, Lee could work on several cars at the same time. Success was mixed with tragedy, however. In 1957, at the Darlington 500 race, Lee was involved in a serious accident in which his friend Bobby Goldsmith was killed.

### Continuing the Story

Twice more, in 1958 and in 1959, Lee won the NASCAR Championship. He was a fair, clean, but hard competitor. His son Richard began his racing career during this period. Though Lee was willing to help his son prepare for a race, once on the track, it was every Petty for himself. For example, at

the Atlanta race in 1959, Richard crossed the finish line, apparently winning his first race. In a few minutes, an official approached him to say that he had been disqualified after another driver had filed a protest that had been upheld. That driver was Lee.

In 1961, Lee's active racing career came to an end at the Daytona 500 race. While battling for the lead toward the end of the race, Lee was struck broadside by another car and both vehicles went over the fence. Lee suffered internal bleeding, a punctured lung, and a leg so badly broken he wore a brace until the end of his life. He spent four months in the hospital and was firmly told, "no more racing." Lee retired, having won fifty-four of the fastest races ever run in NASCAR competition.

Not driving did not mean leaving the sport he loved, however. Lee became one of the best racing engineers in the business, modifying and setting up the chassis for races. He also established the Petty Enterprises racing team. He died in 2000.

### Summary

Lee Petty came up in car racing when it was not as popular or respectable as it is now. Even when he was NASCAR champion, most newspapers did not cover the sport extensively. As a result, Lee never became a household name like his son Richard, but he prepared the way for all the famous and wealthy drivers who followed him.

*Michael R. Bradley*

### Additional Sources

Bechtel, Mark. "The Patriarch: Lee Petty, 1914-2000." *Sports Illustrated* 92, no. 116 (April 17, 2000): 26.

Golenbock, Peter. *NASCAR Confidential: Stories of the Men and Women Who Made Stock Car Racing Great.* St. Paul, Minn.: Motorbooks International, 2004.

Petty, Richard, and William Neely. *King Richard I: The Autobiography of America's Greatest Auto Racer.* New York: Macmillan, 1986.

## Honors and Awards

| | |
|---|---|
| 1990 | Inducted into International Motor Sports Hall of Fame |
| 1996 | Inducted into Motorsports Hall of Fame of America |

# *Richard Petty*

**Born:** July 2, 1937
      Level Cross, North Carolina
**Also known as:** Richard Lee Petty (full name);
   King Richard; King of the Road

## Early Life

Richard Lee Petty was born on July 2, 1937, in Level Cross, North Carolina. Richard was born into the world of stock car racing. His father, Lee Petty, was three times National Association for Stock Car Auto Racing (NASCAR) Champion, in 1954, 1958, and 1959. When Richard was born, a race car was always parked in the yard of the family home. Weekends were spent traveling to various towns for races.

As a teenager, Richard helped on the family farm and helped his father build and repair race car engines. He also found time to play on the high school football, basketball, and baseball teams. Through these sports, Richard met his wife, Lynda, who was a cheerleader. At the age of twenty-one, Richard drove in his first official race at Columbia, South Carolina, finishing sixth.

## The Road to Excellence

The Petty family—Lee, Richard's younger brother Maurice, and cousin Dale Inman—formed a close-knit team to build and race stock cars, modified versions of automobiles available to the general public at new car dealerships. While Lee had the experience and Maurice and Dale were excellent mechanics, Richard had the courage and skill to drive the cars. The major car manufacturers sponsored various stock car drivers with parts and money because the racing modifications often produced technological improvements for cars intended for highway use. For many years, Richard drove Chrysler cars.

As a driver, Richard developed the racing technique of "drafting," in which a driver stays directly behind and extremely close to the car in front. Although dangerous because of the high speeds in-

volved, this "nose to tail" technique allows the cars to go faster and use less gasoline. The number-two spot is favored by drivers until near the end of the race, at which time the second car tries to pass. Richard became good at both passing and, if he was in the lead, holding off the car attempting to pass him. This technique was new when Richard began racing, but today, "drafts" of up to thirty and more cars can be seen in major races.

Richard also developed the physique to drive long distances at high speeds under hot conditions. Before developing ulcers, Richard weighed 190 pounds and stood 6 feet 2 inches tall. On an asphalt track, the air temperature may be above 90 degrees Fahrenheit, and the temperature in a race car, nearly 140 degrees.

## The Emerging Champion

In 1964, Richard won his first NASCAR Championship. In his first fifteen years of racing, he won 150 races, more than twice the wins of any other driver

*Richard Petty in 1970.* (RacingOne/Getty Images)

then in competition. The highest point of his career came in 1967, when Richard won 27 of the 48 races he entered that year.

There were some periods, such as 1976, when nothing seemed to go right for the Petty race team, but then a new mechanical idea would surface or, as Richard said, "My luck would get good," after which the famous number 43, painted "Petty blue," would be a regular sight in the winner's circle again at race tracks all over the nation. Richard attributed his success to teamwork. Mechanics have to build tough engines to hold up for 500 miles at speeds close to 200 miles per hour. Furthermore, the pit crew must work fast to change the tires, fill the gas tank, and make necessary repairs when a car leaves the track during the race. The Petty team was recognized as the best in racing, and Richard gave them full credit.

This teamwork was displayed at the Daytona 500 race in 1981. Changes in NASCAR rules meant that everyone was driving a smaller car that year. Richard's car, a Buick Regal, was not quite as fast as the Pontiac driven by Bobby Allison. For 173 laps, Richard trailed. On laps 173 and 174, all the leading cars pulled into the pits for tires and gas, spending an average 19 seconds off the track. Richard's crew had him out of the pit and back on the track in 6.8 seconds. Richard used this advantage, along with his driving skill, to win the prestigious race for the seventh time.

In 1988, at Daytona, skill and luck almost ran out. On lap 106, Richard was involved in an accident in which his car stood on its nose, rolled more than six times, and was hit broadside by another racer. Some luck remained, because Richard walked away from the wreck.

### Continuing the Story
In the 1970's, Richard was nicknamed "King Richard" or, sometimes, "King of the Road." By 1988, he

| NASCAR Circuit Victories | |
|---|---|
| 1960, 1962-63, 1967, 1969, 1971-72, 1975, 1979 | Virginia 500 |
| 1961, 1967, 1971-73, 1975 | Richmond 500 |
| 1962-63, 1970-75 | Staley 400 |
| 1962, 1967-68, 1972, 1975 | Wilkes 400 |
| 1964-67, 1969, 1971 | Nashville 420 |
| 1964, 1966, 1971, 1973-74, 1979, 1981 | Daytona 500 |
| 1964, 1967 | NASCAR Grand National Championship |
| 1964, 1974, 1980 | Music City 420 |
| 1966 | Atlanta Journal 400 |
| 1966-67 | CRC Chemicals Rebel 400 |
| 1967 | Heinz Southern 500 |
| 1967-68, 1970-74 | Capital City 400 |
| 1967-70, 1972-73 | Old Dominion 500 |
| 1967, 1970-71, 1974, 1976-77 | Carolina 500 |
| 1967, 1975 | Volunteer 500 |
| 1968, 1971, 1976, 1979 | American 500 |
| 1969-70 | Mason-Dixon 300 |
| 1969, 1972 | Winston Western 500 |
| 1970-71, 1974 | Atlanta Journal 500 |
| 1970, 1975, 1977 | Riverside 400 |
| 1971 | Texas 500 |
| 1971, 1974-75 | Delaware 500 |
| 1971-72, 1974-75, 1979 | NASCAR Winston Cup Championship |
| 1974 | Talladega 500 |
| | Gabriel 400 |
| 1974, 1976 | Purolator 500 |
| 1975 | Southeastern 500 |
| | National 500 |
| 1975, 1977 | Coca-Cola 500 |
| | World 600 |
| | Firecracker 400 |
| 1975, 1979, 1981 | Champion Spark Plug 400 |
| 1979 | CRC Chemicals 500 |
| 1980-81 | Northwestern Bank 400 |
| 1983 | Winston 500 |

had started in 500 consecutive NASCAR races and was grossing more than two million dollars a year for his company, Petty Enterprises. He had won every important race on the NASCAR circuit several times. Success had not come without a high price. Richard had 40 percent of his stomach removed because of ulcers, lost 75 percent of his hearing, broke his neck twice, shattered his hip, and cracked his ribs several times.

The secrets of winning races are skill and teamwork, but the secret of Richard's popularity among race fans was his personality. Richard always had time to talk with fans and to sign autographs. Nine times in his career, racing fans voted him most popular NASCAR driver. In the years following his retirement from racing, Richard received numerous honors. In 1992, he was awarded the Medal of Freedom, the highest U.S. civilian award. In 1997, he was inducted into the International Motor Sports Hall of Fame. Even after his retirement, he remained one of NASCAR's most popular and recognizable racers.

## Summary

The ability to win races is a necessary component of a champion, but living as a winning person is more important. Richard Petty always made time for his family and his fans. He stayed away from drugs and alcohol and remained positive off the track. These characteristics made him King of the Road.

*Michael R. Bradley*

## Additional Sources

Blake, Ben, and Dick Conway. *Richard Petty: Images of the King.* St. Paul, Minn.: Motorbooks International, 2005.

Chandler, Charles. *Quotable Petty: Words of Wisdom, Success, and Courage by and About Richard Petty, the King of Stock-Car Racing.* Nashville, Tenn.: Towle House, 2002.

Petty, Richard. *King of the Road.* New York: Macmillan, 1977.

Petty, Richard, and William Neeley. *King Richard I: The Autobiography of America's Greatest Auto Racer.* New York: Macmillan, 1986.

Vehorn, Frank. *A Farewell to the King: A Personal Look Back at the Career of Richard Petty, America's Winningest and Most Popular Driver.* Asheboro, N.C.: Down Home Press, 1992.

## Records

Won seven NASCAR series championships

Most victories on the NASCAR circuit, 200

Most pole positions won on the NASCAR circuit, 127

Most victories at the Daytona 500, 7

## Honors and Awards

| | |
|---|---|
| 1959 | NASCAR Rookie of the Year |
| 1959-62, 1964, 1966-67, 1972-75 | Union 76-Darlington Record Club Award |
| 1962, 1964, 1968, 1970, 1974-78 | NASCAR Most Popular Driver |
| 1989 | Inducted into Motorsports Hall of Fame of America |
| 1992 | Medal of Freedom |
| 1997 | Inducted into International Motor Sports Hall of Fame |
| | Inducted into North Carolina Auto Racing Hall of Fame |
| 1998 | Inducted into National Motorsports Press Association Hall of Fame |

# *Lester Piggott*

**Born:** November 5, 1935
      Wantage, Berkshire, England
**Also known as:** Lester Keith Piggott (full name)

## Early Life

On November 5, 1935, Lester Keith Piggott was born into a family already well known in horse racing. His parents, Keith Piggott and Iris (Rickaby) Piggott, both came from families whose involvement in horse racing stretched back four generations.

Lester's childhood was filled with the sport and business of horse racing. His father had rented a stable in the town of Letcombe Regis and had begun to train horses. Lester was a natural athlete and, by the age of ten, was participating in local amateur horse racing events. He read everything he could about racing, from old memoirs of nineteenth-century racing to the daily newspapers. It thus came as no surprise to his family when Lester began to assist at morning exercise for the racehorses in his father's stable. In the spring of 1948, Lester officially began a racing career by becoming legally apprenticed to his father.

*Lester Piggott.* (PA Photos/Landov)

## The Road to Excellence

By this time, the Piggott family had moved to the town of Lambourn, where Lester spent most of his time working in his father's stable. Keith Piggott was the most influential teacher of Lester's life, correcting his errors and praising his hard work. Lester's first professional race was an apprentice event at Salisbury, Wiltshire, England, on April 7, 1948. Although he did not win, Lester continued to participate in many racing events throughout the summer.

On August 18 of 1948, Lester won his first race on The Chase, a horse owned by Betty Lavington. Seeing Lester's potential, Lavington chose Lester to race many of her horses, including Lester's first three winners: The Chase, Forest Glade, and Secret Code.

By the 1950 racing season, more and more trainers were requesting Lester as jockey, and his wins became more frequent. That year, he finished with more wins than many established jockeys and was named Britain's leading apprentice. In 1951 and 1952, Lester won such prestigious events as the Blue Riband Derby Trial Stakes, the Great Metropolitan, and the Eclipse Stakes. At the end of 1952, Lester was taken off the apprentices' list and given full jockey status.

Lester, though, was becoming too heavy for flat racing. His family had assumed that he would turn to jump racing when his weight exceeded the normal allowances for flat racing. Determined to continue in flat racing, however, Lester developed the discipline he would need to keep his body weight low.

## The Emerging Champion

Many changes occurred in Lester's life in 1954. In June, he won the English Derby, one of the most prestigious British races. Moreover, as a result of an incident during

235

## Major Championship Victories

| Year | Race | Horse |
|------|------|-------|
| 1954 | Epsom Derby | Never Say Die |
| 1957 | Two Thousand Guineas | Crepello |
|      | Epsom Derby | Crepello |
|      | Epsom Oaks | Carrozza |
| 1959 | Epsom Oaks | Petite Étoile |
| 1960 | Epsom Derby | St. Paddy |
|      | St. Leger | St. Paddy |
| 1961 | St. Leger | Aurelius |
| 1966 | Epsom Oaks | Valoris |
| 1967 | St. Leger | Ribocco |
| 1968 | Two Thousand Guineas | Sir Ivor |
|      | Epsom Derby | Sir Ivor |
|      | St. Leger | Ribero |
| 1970 | Two Thousand Guineas | Nijinsky II |
|      | One Thousand Guineas | Humble Duty |
|      | Epsom Derby | Nijinsky II |
|      | St. Leger | Nijinsky II |
| 1971 | St. Leger | Athens Wood |
| 1972 | Epsom Derby | Roberto |
|      | St. Leger | Boucher |
| 1975 | Epsom Oaks | Juliette Marny |
| 1976 | Epsom Derby | Empery |
| 1977 | Epsom Derby | The Minstrel |
| 1981 | One Thousand Guineas | Fairy Footsteps |
|      | Epsom Oaks | Blue Wind |
| 1983 | Epsom Derby | Teenoso |
| 1984 | Epsom Oaks | Circus Plume |
|      | St. Leger | Commanche Run |
| 1985 | Two Thousand Guineas | Shadeed |
| 1992 | Two Thousand Guineas | Rodrigo de Triano |

the King Edward VII Stakes, he was required by the Stewards of the Jockey Club to leave his father's service and go to work for another trainer. This gave him the opportunity to begin what became a great partnership with the trainer Noel Murless.

Murless's stable contained some of the great horses of racing history, such as Crepello, Carrozza, and Petite Étoile. On these horses, Lester won many prestigious races, including the Two Thousand Guineas, the Derby, and the Oaks. In addition, Lester developed the unique skill of understanding the different temperaments of horses, which allowed him to coax the best out of the horses he rode. In 1959, Lester won the Oaks, the Sussex Stakes, the Yorkshire Oaks, and the Champion Stakes with Petite Étoile because he knew the horse's abilities. She was at her best in a race when coming up with late acceleration; Lester knew that

he had to hold her back until they were near the end of the course. With St. Paddy, the horse on which he won the Dante Stakes and the Derby in 1960, Lester realized that the high-strung horse became frightened if ridden with too loose a rein. A tight rein encouraged him to run. Lester had the most wins of any British jockey that season, and he was named Britain's champion jockey.

Throughout the 1960's, Lester continued to collect victories with horses from Murless's stable. By 1967, however, Lester was feeling confined by his contract. He decided to freelance as a jockey. This was generally considered a mistake by the racing community, as no British jockey had ever really been successful at freelancing. However, of Lester's 191 wins in 1966, 156 of them were for trainers other than Murless. Lester was confident that his abilities as a jockey were great enough to attract offers from trainers. In 1967, he silenced his critics when he won the Irish Sweeps Derby and the St. Leger and finished the year with 117 wins, maintaining his position as champion jockey.

### Continuing the Story

Beginning in 1958, when Lester had won the Ascot Gold Cup on the horse Gladness, the Irish trainer Vincent O'Brien asked Lester to ride his horses. This arrangement grew into a great partnership after Lester became a freelancer. Lester rode many of O'Brien's great horses, including Sir Ivor, Nijinsky II, and Roberto. In the 1970's, Lester frequently won many of the "English Classics," the most prestigious British races, including four Derby wins and three victories at the St. Leger.

During the 1980's, Lester won six more races in the English Classics, bringing his total of Classic wins to twenty-nine. By then, his total surpassed Frank Buckle's record of twenty-seven, a record that had stood for 157 years. At the end of the 1985 racing season, Lester retired and began training racehorses at his stables at Newmarket.

In 1987, Lester was prosecuted for failure to pay income tax, and he was convicted and given a two-

## Honors and Awards

| | |
|---|---|
| 1960, 1964-71, 1981-82 | Champion Jockey of Great Britain |
| 1975 | Order of the British Empire (revoked in 1985 because of tax evasion) |

year sentence. When he was released from prison in 1989, he found, surprisingly, that his popularity had actually increased. Bored with training, he returned to the saddle in October, 1990. He not only added another English Classic win to his record but also continued to win top-name races at the age of fifty-nine.

Lester appeared in the Emirates Airlines Legends Race in Melbourne, Australia, in 2000. At sixty-five years of age, he rode to a third-place finish amid cheers from the many fans who still adored the former champion.

## Summary

Lester Piggott exhibited a determination to succeed that took him to the top of horse racing. He possessed an athletic ability and an understanding of his profession that enabled him to become one of the greatest jockeys in racing history.

*Margaret Debicki*

## Additional Sources

Karter, John. *Lester: Return of a Legend.* Rev. ed. London: Headline, 1993.

Piggott, Lester. *Lester: The Autobiography of Lester Piggott.* London: Corgi, 1996.

_____. *Lester's Fifty to Follow for the Flat.* Alderley Edge, Cheshire, England: Winning Line, 1997.

Piggott, Lester, and Sean Magee. *Lester's Derbys.* London: Methuen, 2004.

Tanner, Michael. *Lester Piggott: Return to the Saddle.* London: Ebury, 1996.

# Laffit Pincay, Jr.

**Born:** December 29, 1946
    Panama City, Panama
**Also known as:** Laffit Alejandro Pincay, Jr. (full
  name)

## Early Life

Laffit Alejandro Pincay, Jr., was born to Laffit and Rosario Pincay on December 29, 1946, in Panama City, Panama. Panama City is the capital of Panama, so Laffit was exposed to big-city life early on, and he immediately was drawn toward the racetrack.

Life was difficult for Laffit and his three brothers and sisters. When his parents divorced, his father, a horse trainer, moved to Venezuela. As a child, Laffit hardly ever saw him. At fifteen, Laffit got a job at the track cleaning out stalls, but he did not get paid. Even though he had to work hard, he loved it because he was around horses. He worked for a whole year and then got promoted to a job with a bit of pay and the duty of exercising horses. Then, a year later, he moved up again and was able to ride the horses out of the gate in practice. At the track, he met his mentor, Bolivar Moreno, who started a small school for promising young boys and increased Laffit's self-confidence. That pushed him to begin riding, and his real racing career began.

## The Road to Excellence

Laffit began to race at the track, and, in less than two years, he rode four hundred winners and was Panama's leading rider. Fred Hooper, who helped numerous jockeys get their start, brought Laffit to the United States. In 1965, Hooper brought Laffit to race at Arlington Park in Chicago; Laffit could barely speak English but enjoyed immediate success against some tough competitors. The first year, he won eight races and, even though he came to Chicago late in the season, he finished the year the third-ranked rider overall. He then moved to Hawthorne Park, where he became top rider, and then on to the best racetrack in New York, where he finished third for the season.

Laffit rode well whether he was behind or ahead, which was an unusual trait. He did not get excited, and he was a logical rider. He was quick to learn English, becoming fluent in less than a year. Laffit credited his success to three things early on: hard work, desire, and a man named Vince DeGregory.

DeGregory was an agent who had earlier helped Ángel Cordero, Jr. Once De-

*Laffit Pincay, Jr., astride Millennium Wind after their 2001 win.* (AP/
Wide World Photos)

## Major Championship Victories

| Year | Race | Horse |
|------|------|-------|
| 1982 | Belmont Stakes | Conquistador Cielo |
| 1983 | Belmont Stakes | Caveat |
| 1984 | Belmont Stakes | Swale |
|  | Kentucky Derby | Swale |
| 1985 | Breeders' Cup Juvenile | Tasso |
| 1986 | Breeders' Cup Juvenile | Capote |
|  | Breeders' Cup Classic | Skywalker |
| 1988 | Breeders' Cup Juvenile | Is It True |
| 1989 | Breeders' Cup Distaff | Bayakoa |
| 1990 | Breeders' Cup Distaff | Bayakoa |
| 1993 | Breeders' Cup Juvenile Fillies | Phone Chatter |

Gregory saw Laffit, he became his agent. DeGregory strove hard to get the best mounts he could for Laffit. Eventually, after several years at the top of his field, Laffit began to get depressed. He was not satisfied with anything, and, even though he was still winning at least four races a day, he was not happy.

## The Emerging Champion

Not all the pressure was self-imposed. Laffit's agent wanted riding championships and pressured Laffit to snap out of his depression. The major problem facing Laffit was that he always had to struggle with his weight. Jockeys must be weighed before each race and, if they are too heavy, they are not allowed to race.

Because horse racing was his profession, and because he loved racing so much, Laffit was willing to starve to do it. He would have a few nuts for breakfast, a cup of broth for lunch, and a piece of skinless chicken for dinner, if he had anything. He would also spend at least an hour a day in the sweatbox.

In early 1974, he fainted in the jockeys' room and was rushed to the hospital. After a series of tests, it was discovered that he was so dehydrated that he had almost died. Laffit realized that he needed to find a safer way to keep his weight down and, with a doctor's help, he did. He ate a bit more each day, stopped using sweatboxes, drank plenty of water, and did aerobic exercise.

## Continuing the Story

Laffit did what came naturally to him, but he worked to keep on top of his profession. A really good horse will win at times with anyone riding, but to win consistently and to win the big races, the jockey must have ability and confidence and must instill it in the horse. Laffit considered getting up at 4:00 A.M. to work horses as much a part of his job as riding a stakes winner at 4:00 P.M.

In 1985, Laffit had to overcome the emotionally devastating suicide of his wife. He was such a professional that he came back two weeks later to win again. His aim was to be strong physically and mentally in both his professional and personal life. He gave a 100 percent effort whether it was a weekday race or the Kentucky Derby.

Laffit won the Eclipse Award for outstanding jockey six times in his career—the last time coming in 1999. In the same year, he surpassed Willie Shoemaker's record of 8,834 career victories by riding Irish Nip to an easy win in the sixth race at Hollywood Park in California. In 2000, he extended his career wins total to 8,848 and broke the $200 million mark in career purses—a figure that made him the second all-time leader in winnings. In 2003, he retired with 9,530, a career-win total that was eventually surpassed by Russell Baze in 2006. Laffit won the Kentucky Derby in 1984, the Breeders' Cup Classic in 1986, and the Belmont Stakes in 1982, 1983, and 1984.

## Summary

Laffit Pincay, Jr., was one of the best jockeys ever to ride in the United States. He will forever be a part of horse racing. In 2004, Hollywood Park created the Laffit Pincay, Jr., Award given annually to the

## Milestones

Annual money leader (1970-74, 1979, 1985)

9,530 victories—highest all-time record at time of retirement in 2003 (record later broken)

## Honors and Awards

| | |
|---|---|
| 1970 | George Woolf Memorial Jockey Award |
| 1971, 1973-74, 1979, 1985, 1999 | Eclipse Award, Outstanding Jockey |
| 1975 | Inducted into Jockeys' Hall of Fame |
| 1985, 2000 | Big Sport of Turfdom Award |
| 1996 | Mike Venezia Memorial Award |

jockey who most personifies "integrity, extraordinary dedication, determination, and distinction." Laffit became a commentator for Horse Racing Television (HRTV) and the Entertainment and Sports Programming Network (ESPN).

*Brooke K. Zibel*

## Additional Sources

Blood-Horse Publications. *Horse Racing's Top One Hundred Moments.* Lexington, Ky.: Author, 2006.

Hoffer, Richard. "It Takes a Hungry Man." *Sports Illustrated* 95, no. 9 (September 3, 2001): 66.

Kindred, Dave. "Feeling Like a Kid Again." *Sporting News* 225, no. 20 (May 14, 2001): 62.

Reeves, Richard Stone, and Edward L. Bowen. *Belmont Park: A Century of Champions.* Lexington, Ky.: Eclipse Press, 2005.

Shulman, Lenny. *Ride of Their Lives: The Triumphs and Turmoil of Today's Top Jockeys.* Lexington, Ky.: Eclipse Press, 2002.

# *Martin Potter*

**Born:** October 28, 1965
     Blythe, Northumberland, England
**Also known as:** Eggy Potter; Potz

## Early Life

Martin Potter was born in Blythe, Northumberland, England, on October 28, 1965. When he was two, his family moved to Orange Free State, South Africa, but Martin did not see the ocean until he was ten years old. He started surfing at South Beach, Durban, South Africa on a foam board with an old surfboard fin stuck into it. When that board snapped two years later, his father bought him a new 6-foot 8-inch surfboard, and Martin discovered his gift for surfing.

## The Road to Excellence

At twelve, Martin surfed in his first contest, held at South Beach. Martin was allowed to surf in the novice section and won. His performance also won him the support of Ernie Tomson, a surfboard sponsor and enthusiast. Tomson was the father of Shaun Tomson, the South African hero who had won the Association of Surfing Professionals (ASP) 1977 World Tour Championship. Ernie Tomson encouraged Martin to compete in other contests, for example, at the Bay of Plenty, eight miles from South Beach. By age fourteen, Martin was the national junior champion.

When he was not skipping class to surf, Martin took carpentry classes at George Campbell Technical School. Surfing, however, had become his priority. Soon he made the South African touring team and went on a tour of the United States. At fifteen, still relatively unknown, Martin entered two South African international professional contests and beat former champ Shaun Tomson in both. He placed second in these events and stunned the surf world with his spectacular debut. Thus, Martin's professional surfing career began in 1980, around the same time his parents' divorce was finalized.

Immediately after the divorce, Martin went on tour, worried that his surfing would suffer if he did not. He traveled the surfing tour circuit through Brazil, Japan, the United States, Hawaii, and Australia, finishing eighth in the world after the 1981 season. His explosive surfing—the unique powerful attacks and aerial maneuvers—caught everyone's eye. At sixteen, he had earned a world reputation as surfing's brilliant new wunderkind.

## The Emerging Champion

Martin's powerful surfing, called radical at the time, earned him both spectacular successes and spectacular failures in competition. His was a style not suited to competition demands for consistency and safety. Furthermore, in contests, the surfer must be attuned to his rivals' performances and disciplined enough to respond to them even while seeking his own inspiration. Martin's temperament, however, was suited to a free-form approach: free-surfing, or surfing for the fun of it. He did not give in to demands for dedication or discipline.

As a result, his acrobatic style impressed but did not convince the surfing establishment, who claimed he was too inconsistent and made too many mistakes in events. Judging panels never treated his falls kindly. Thus, the teenager who had been pegged as world-champion material ever since his professional debut delivered uneven yearly performances through the early and mid-1980's, as he grew into adulthood. His reputation, however, seemed to maintain itself. Year after year, he was ranked with the top sixteen seeds at the beginning of each tour, by virtue of his natural talent alone and with, he admits, "no effort whatsoever" on his part.

In 1983, he rose to fifth place, and in 1984, he won three major

| ASP Tour and Other Victories | |
|---|---|
| Year | Competition |
| 1979 | National Junior Championship |
| 1983 | Stubbies Classic |
| 1984 | Fosters Surfmasters |
|  | Hang Ten California |
| 1984, 1989 | Marui Japan Open |
| 1987 | Hot Tuna UK Surfmasters |
| 1988 | MBF Headstart |
| 1989 | O'Neill/Pepsi Cold Water Classic |
|  | Rip Curl Swan Classic |
|  | Coca-Cola Classic |
|  | Quicksilver Lacanau Pro |
|  | Arena Surfmasters |
|  | ASP World Tour Championship |
| 1990 | Life's a Beach Classic |
|  | Rip Curl Pro Landes |

events and helped his family move to Newquay, England. There his mother and two brothers lived in a house he bought, and Martin tried to sort out his career. The result was an extended "safari" to Indonesia in midseason with three Brazilian friends, and a farewell to the 1985 competition tour.

Martin returned from Indonesia weary but changed. He began to look for a place where he could apply his talents to winning. He was no longer satisfied with his reputation as the best free-surfer in the world, but one who could scarcely win a contest. He decided to settle in Whale Beach, Australia, on Sydney's north side. Sydney's waves were known as the training ground for world champions.

In Sydney, Martin lived with his new manager, Peter Colbert, who had guided Tom Carroll to two world championships. He found stability, a circle of close friends, and a way to control his powerful surfing. He decided to sell the house in Newquay and applied for Australian residency. His mother, however, refused to live in Australia and took legal action against him. Despite the tense separation from his family, he managed to come in fifth in 1986 and captured impressive wins in 1987 and 1988. His performance flourished as he faced the rigors of the contest trail.

Martin's spontaneity while riding and his willingness to take risks finally paid off during the 1989 season. He started off with a phenomenal win in the season's opening event, the O'Neill/Pepsi Cold Water Classic off Santa Cruz, California. Out of the first five world-tour events that year, Martin won four. No surfer had ever opened a year so successfully. In the middle of the season, he spent two months in fitness training and four hours a day surfing. Back by August, he easily took two more big wins. His decision to join an antiapartheid boycott of South Africa's once-prestigious Gunston 500 competition was a painful one, not only because he was fond of friends and the waves there, but also because he risked falling behind in the ratings by staying home. Soon afterward, however, the 1989 ASP World Tour Championship was his, by the widest margin of points in professional surfing history. Martin also became the first surfer to win more than $100,000 in one season, doubling his total career earnings.

---

### Record

First professional surfer to win more than $100,000 in a season

---

### Continuing the Story

Winning the world title was important to Martin. Many times he had been written off as too erratic for serious competition. However, throughout the eight seasons of professional surfing, during which he grew up and fulfilled his promise, Martin never let others' skepticism spoil his intense love of stylish and innovative surfing. His need to surf for his own satisfaction, on his own terms, survived. Even after winning the title, he still believed that if he were a leader in anything, it was in free-surfing, not competition surfing.

Perhaps Martin's greatest legacy was his influence on how surfing competitions are judged. In 1989, his daring maneuvers forced the ASP to expand judging criteria continually. His world title came at a time when surfers were questioning whether contest results were really the best measure of talent. There was no questioning either the purity or the credentials of Martin after his fabulous title year, when he showed his accomplishments in all facets of the sport, on big and small waves alike.

Martin remained in the top ten on the ASP Tour until 1995, when he decided to retire. He became a surfing instructor and put out a training video with fellow surfing champ Barton Lynch. In 2000, he joined Gotcha as a marketing manager in France. In November, he returned to competition at the Biarritz Surf Trophé competition, where he missed the final round by a narrow margin.

### Summary

Martin Potter's fans considered him a renegade in the surf world, which has only recently achieved a fairly wholesome reputation. He would probably not mind if his nonconformity inspired future surfers in their approach to the sport. Accepting his world championship trophy, he said, "I'll be very happy if the way I surf means that from now on the guys will be able to be themselves."

*JoAnn Balingit*

### Additional Sources

Martin, Andrew. *Walking on Water.* London: John Murray, 1991.

Reilley, Mike. "New-Look Potter Looking for a Victory in O. P. Pro Surfing." *Los Angeles Times* (Orange County edition) July 29, 1990, p. 18.

Young, Nat. *The History of Surfing.* Salt Lake City, Utah: Gibbs Smith, 2006.

# *Alain Prost*

**Born:** February 24, 1955
      Lorette, near Saint-Chamond, France
**Also known as:** Alain Marie Pascal Prost (full
   name); the Professor

## Early Life

Alain Marie Pascal Prost was born on February 24, 1955, in the Loire region of France's heartland, in an area of farms and small villages. He grew up dreaming of having an illustrious career like those of his two idols, Charles de Gaulle and Jackie Stewart.

Alain was a fierce competitor even when he was in school. He started playing soccer, as all the other boys did. In high school, however, he discovered the thrills of competing as a sprinter. Before long, though, he reached the conclusion that his future in track and field after high school was not promising. His thoughts turned to a new passion: kart racing, which he had discovered on a family vacation. At the age of fifteen, he envisioned himself racing not on foot but in a high-speed vehicle.

After school, he worked in his father's furniture shop. Although the work was boring, he knew that this was the only way he could make his dream come true. When he was sixteen, Alain bought his first go-kart with $100 that he had managed to save. He remained in school only two more years before quitting and signing on as a professional go-kart driver. After becoming European Junior Karting Champion in 1975, Alain felt that he was ready to enter the world of professional auto racing.

## The Road to Excellence

Realizing that he had much to learn about professional auto racing, Alain spent the next year at a racing school outside Marseilles. As soon as he graduated in 1976, he swept the French Formula Renault Championship, winning twelve of thirteen races and setting eleven track records. Alain then proved to the racing world that his early victories were not a fluke by becoming the European Formula Three driving champion just three years later. This brought him to the attention of several of the "big league" teams of Formula One racing.

Filled with self-confidence, Alain joined the prestigious McLaren team. However, when he made his Formula One debut in 1980 in Argentina, he was introduced not only to the glamour but also to the harsh realities of professional auto racing. Upon his arrival, mechanics called him "The Little Frog" and scrawled "Tadpole" on the side of his car. Instead of feeling demoralized by this rude treatment, Alain became more determined than ever to prove himself. He ended the race by placing among the top six drivers, thus becoming one of the few racers to score points in a debut race.

What began as a promising year for Alain ended in disappointment. He suffered a broken wrist in a race in South Africa and had to sit out several races.

*Alain Prost celebrating his victory at the 1987 Brazilian Grand Prix.* (Simon Bruty/Getty Images)

At the end of the racing season, he suffered a concussion from a collision at Watkins Glen, New York. Frustrated with himself and with the team's cars, he resigned from McLaren and even considered retiring.

Luck plays an important role in the lives of many champions, and this was also true for Alain. In 1981, he joined the Renault team just as it was winning one Grand Prix after another. His first Formula One victory came that season, in his home race, the French Grand Prix. Even though Alain won a number of races in 1982, he lost six contests in 1983 because of a faulty electrical part. Moreover, he became involved in increasingly unpleasant disagreements with the team management. After losing the 1983 championship he was made a scapegoat and fired by Renault. He avoided sinking into depression, as he had two years before, because he was supported and advised by Stewart, Jack Nicklaus, and Arnold Palmer. His morale was also given a sizable boost when his wife Anne-Marie gave birth to their son, Nicolas.

In 1984, McLaren gave Alain a second chance, and he set about reestablishing himself as a future world champion. Although he narrowly lost the championship that year, he gained the knowledge and experience that enabled him to clinch the world championship in 1985. He learned that aggression on the track wastes gasoline, rubber, and nerves. He also became the greatest French hero since Jean-Claude Killy, despite the fact that he was driving a German-built car and living in Switzerland.

## The Emerging Champion

For the next three years, Alain concentrated on breaking Stewart's 1973 record of twenty-seven Grand Prix wins. This goal motivated him to win the world championship again in 1986. In 1987, Alain finally tied and then broke Stewart's record when he won his twenty-eighth race at the Portuguese Grand Prix. He ultimately went on to win fifty-one races, his final race victory coming in the Australian Grand Prix in 1993. His record of most wins stood until 2001.

In France, Alain's achievement was treated like a moon landing, even though it went almost unnoticed in the United States, where Formula One racing is relatively unknown. One Parisian newspaper went so far as to claim that Alain had earned himself a seat at the right hand of God. Even Formula One drivers, who are normally stingy with their compliments, began calling Alain a superman. The entire time that Alain was winning world championships and breaking records, he never forgot that he was a member of the McLaren team. Any personal glory that he achieved was always, he felt, secondary to the glory that he brought to his team.

## Grand Prix and Other Victories

| Year(s) | Event |
|---|---|
| 1975 | European Junior Karting Championship |
| 1976 | French Formula Renault Championship |
| 1979 | European Formula Three Driving Champion |
| 1981, 1983, 1988, 1990, 1993 | French Grand Prix |
| 1981, 1984 | Netherlands Grand Prix |
| 1981, 1985 | Italian Grand Prix |
| 1982, 1984-85, 1987-88, 1990 | Brazilian Grand Prix |
| 1982, 1993 | South African Grand Prix |
| 1983, 1985-86 | Austrian Grand Prix |
| 1983, 1985, 1990 | British Grand Prix |
| 1983, 1987 | Belgian Grand Prix |
| 1984 | European Grand Prix |
| 1984-86, 1988 | Monaco Grand Prix |
| 1984-86, 1993 | San Marino Grand Prix |
| 1984, 1987-88 | Portuguese Grand Prix |
| 1984, 1993 | German Grand Prix |
| 1985-86, 1989-90, 1993 | World Championship of Drivers |
| 1986, 1988, 1993 | Australian Grand Prix |
| 1988, 1990 | Mexican Grand Prix |
| 1988, 1990, 1993 | Spanish Grand Prix |
| 1990, 1993 | English Grand Prix |
| 1993 | Canadian Grand Prix |

## Continuing the Story

At the same time that Alain was reaching his pinnacle as a driver, he received intense pressure from a fierce competitor who was, ironically, his teammate at McLaren. Ayrton Senna, who barely beat Alain for the world championship in 1988, was an entirely different breed of driver. Alain was a conservative driver who preferred to out-think his opponents not out-dare them. Senna, on the other hand, was an aggressive driver who won by taking risks that Alain would never have considered. In 1989, Alain's cerebral approach to racing paid off and he beat Senna on points to claim his third world championship. The rivalry that divided these two men partially accounted for Alain's de-

---

### Honors and Awards

1985   Légion d'Honneur
1988   Champion of Champions Trophy
1993   Order of the British Empire (OBE)
1994   Autosport Gregor Grant Award
1995   Autosport International Racing Driver Award
1999   World Sports Awards of the Century

---

cision to leave McLaren and drive for Ferrari in 1990.

Though Alain did not win many races in his first year with Ferrari, he finished in the top five in eight of his fifteen starts in 1991. He did not race in 1992 but returned in 1993 as a member of the Williams-Renault Team and won seven Grand Prix competitions in addition to his fifth world championship.

Rather than become Senna's teammate the following season, Alain retired from Formula One at the end of 1993. He remained active in the racing world, both as a television commentator and as an advisor for his former teams. He even had a period as a team owner, forming the Alain Grand Prix team in 1997. Although the Alain team had many difficulties, failed to achieve any real success, and folded after the 2001 racing season, this did nothing to dent Alain's reputation as one of the finest racing drivers ever. He remained highly respected in retirement.

By the end of the 1980's, Alain had attained folk-hero status in Europe. He had also become the richest driver on the circuit, with an annual income of $5 million. In addition to the money and titles that he received over the years, Alain was given the Légion d'Honneur, France's highest civilian award, in 1985. Despite all these accolades, Alain felt that his greatest honor was a private audience with the pope. His enduring nickname, "The Professor," underlines his sublime discipline, intelligence, and skill behind the wheel. His driving style was an inspiration for many subsequent racing drivers.

### Summary

Alain Prost established himself as the greatest driver on the Formula One circuit during the late 1980's. His superb combination of car control, race tactics, and strategy helped him to break Jackie Stewart's Grand Prix record of twenty-seven wins in 1987. Despite the adulation and praise that were heaped upon him, Alain was a calm, cool, thoughtful, and cautious driver. Unlike some of his more flamboyant competitors, Alain survived by always taking into account the possibility of death.

*Alan Brown, updated by Thomas McGrath*

### Additional Sources

Chimits, Xavier, and François Granet. *Williams-Renault Formula One Motor Racing Book.* New York: Dorling Kindersley, 1994.

Henry, Alan. *Alain Prost.* London: Kimberley's, 1986.

Menard, Pierre, and Jacques Vassal. *Formula One Legends: Alain Prost—The Science of Racing.* St. Sulpice, France: Chronosports, 2004.

Rendall, Ivan. *The Power Game: The History of Formula One and the World Championship.* New York: Sterling, 2000.

Small, Steve, ed. *The Grand Prix Drivers: Racing Heroes from Fangio to Prost.* Osceola, Wis.: Motorbooks International, 1987.

# *Don Prudhomme*

**Born:** April 6, 1941
      San Fernando, California
**Also known as:** Snake

## Early Life

Don Prudhomme was born on April 6, 1941, in San Fernando, not far from where drag racing in the United States was born. From his earliest days, Don was a part of the world of cars. His father owned an automobile repair shop. While Don was going to school, he worked in the shop at night and on weekends. At the age of seventeen, Don left high school to work with his father full time.

Don was soon caught up in the world of informal drag racing. In 1958, after buying a 1950 Oldsmobile, he joined local hot-rod enthusiasts in a racing club called the Road Kings. Like many other unofficial car clubs in Southern California at the time, the Road Kings raced on back roads and abandoned airport runways. Don and his fellow hot-rodders marked off quarter-mile strips and raced against one another or the clock to test whose car was fastest.

## The Road to Excellence

In 1960, Don's first break came when, at the age of nineteen, he was asked by fellow Road King member Tommy Ivo, who had recently turned professional, to accompany him on a drag-racing tour through the East. Don agreed and, even though he ended up doing mostly odd jobs like pushing Ivo's car up to the starting line and assisting the mechanics before and after each race, he knew that the experience would be invaluable in his own future career.

When the tour was over, and with his sights set on becoming a professional, Don went back to working in his father's shop, learning about cars from racing mechanics, and frequenting the local drag racing meets sponsored by the National Hot Rod Association (NHRA).

The NHRA was founded in 1951 to govern the growing sport of drag racing. Among its first actions was to sanction drag strips in and around the Los Angeles area where Don grew up. The NHRA moved quickly to regulate all aspects of the sport: It established guidelines for races, defined categories of racing cars, and administered the competitive events that made up the racing season.

Finally, when he was twenty-three years old, Don got his chance to race in NHRA-sanctioned events. In a series of challenges that pitted him against his old street-racing buddy Tommy Ivo, Don was beaten consistently in what, for many, would have signaled the finish of a short professional career.

## The Emerging Champion

Despite those early defeats, however, Don entered as many meets as he could, worked relentlessly on his car, and developed into a first-rate mechanic and driver. His determination to succeed earned him some victories, a nickname—"The Snake"— and a solid reputation as a driver capable of competing with the most formidable competition.

While still a rookie, Don came to the attention of Roland Leong, a drag-racing enthusiast and car promoter. Leong's Chrysler-powered dragster,

### NHRA Victories

|  |  |
|---|---|
| 1965 | Winternationals, Top Fuel |
| 1965, 1969-70 | U.S. Nationals, Top Fuel |
| 1967 | Springnationals, Top Fuel |
| 1973-74, 1977, 1989 | U.S. Nationals, Funny Car |
| 1974-76, 1980, 1987 | Gatornationals, Funny Car |
| 1975-76 | Fallnationals, Funny Car |
| | Winston World Finals, Funny Car |
| 1975-76, 1978 | Springnationals, Funny Car |
| 1975-76, 1978-79, 1981-82, 1988 | Grandnationals, Funny Car |
| 1975-78 | Winternationals, Funny Car |
| 1976-77, 1980-82, 1988 | Summernationals, Funny Car |
| 1989 | California Nationals, Funny Car |
| | Chief Nationals, Funny Car |
| 1991-92 | Springnationals, Top Fuel |
| 1991, 1994 | Chief Auto Parts Nationals, Top Fuel |
| 1992 | Autolite Nationals, Top Fuel |
| | Fram Southern Nationals, Top Fuel |
| 1994 | Champion Auto Nationals, Top Fuel |
| | Slick 50 Nationals, Top Fuel |

## Records

First Funny Car driver to finish a race in under 6 seconds, 5.98 (1975)
First Funny Car driver to reach a top speed of 250 miles per hour (1982)

## Honors and Awards

1991   Inducted into Motorsports Hall of Fame of America
1997   Inducted into *Hot Rod* magazine Hall of Fame
2000   Inducted into Drag Racing Hall of Fame

dubbed "The Hawaiian," gave Don just the vehicle he needed to compete against the major competitors on the NHRA circuit.

In 1965, Don burned his way to the winner's circle of drag racing's Top Fuel category, driving The Hawaiian to victory at both the NHRA Winternational races in Pomona, California, in February, and the U.S. Nationals in Indianapolis, Indiana, in September. With those wins, he secured a place in the record books as the first driver to capture two consecutive NHRA national events.

Two years later, in Tennessee, at the wheel of another Top Fuel racer, Don captured the Spring Nationals in the first official run of under 7 seconds with a record top speed at that strip of 222.76 miles per hour. He went on to take the Top Fuel victories at the Indianapolis Nationals in both 1969 and 1970, becoming only the second driver in history, after Don Garlits, to earn three Top Fuel national wins.

In 1973, Don switched from dragsters to funny cars, which are cars with a dragster chassis on which a lightweight plastic body resembling a modified street sedan is fitted. Don won the U.S. Nationals that year and in 1974, bringing his career victories in that prestigious NHRA event to five. Don's wins in six out of eight championship funny-car events in the 1975 season began a remarkable four-year streak of championship victories that established Don as one of the all-time greats of the sport.

### Continuing the Story

Through the 1980's, Don continued to race funny cars, earning twelve championship victories and high finishes in the standings. In 1990, he again turned his attention to Top Fuel, fielding his own 300-inch-wheelbase rear-engine dragster. From 1991 to 1994, Don won nine NHRA competitions. In 1994, he retired from competition with forty-nine career NHRA wins. He had recorded the third quickest time in drag racing history at 4.73 seconds. Don won thirty-five championship events, which, at the time of his retirement, was the highest win total for a funny car driver in NHRA history. Those victories, along with his early five in Top Fuel, earned him second place on the all-time win list at the time of his retirement.

The victories Don Prudhomme achieved, and his endurance as a competitive racer, are testament to a single-mindedness and a will to succeed that few sports figures attain. His success did not come easily, however. In drag racing, maintaining a competitive presence means promoting oneself constantly. Throughout his career, Don spent long hours booking match races, organizing his appearances, and lining up sponsors. Don was a dedicated master driver. In a sport whose competitive events last for only five seconds, winning is what counts. Don was inducted into *Hot Rod* magazine's hall of fame in 1997 and the Drag Racing Hall of Fame in 2000. After his retirement, he headed his own racing team, which won Top Fuel championships in 2002 and 2003.

### Summary

When Don Prudhomme was a child, drag racing was in its infancy. When he began racing professionally in the mid-1960's, hot rods averaged 200 miles per hour on the quarter-mile strip. In the 1970's and 1980's, speeds increased, times dropped, and Don was the record setter. Into the early 1990's, with speeds advancing to 300 miles per hour on that same short quarter-mile, Don remained a champion and a competitor.

*Tony Abbott*

### Additional Sources

Genat, Robert. *Top Fuel Dragsters*. St. Paul, Minn.: Motorbooks International, 2002.

Higdon, Hal. *Six Seconds to Glory: Don Prudhomme's Greatest Drag Race*. New York: Putnam, 1975.

Muldowney, Shirley, and Bill Stephens. *Shirley Muldowney's Tales from the Track*. Champaign, Ill.: Sports, 2005.

# Bobby Rahal

**Born:** January 10, 1953
   Medina, Ohio
**Also known as:** Robert Woodward Rahal (full name)

### Early Life

Robert Woodward Rahal was born on January 10, 1953, in Medina, Ohio, a small city near the shores of Lake Erie. As a boy, Bobby learned that success was extremely important to his Lebanese American family. His father, Michael Rahal, had become wealthy as an international food merchant. Also, Bobby's father raced sports cars in both Canada and the United States. Growing up around racing gave Bobby a head start learning the inner workings of both automobiles and the racing business.

In 1970, when Bobby was only seventeen years

*Bobby Rahal.* (AP/Wide World Photos)

old, he told his father he would like to drive. His father took Bobby to a racetrack in Canada and, in order to enter him in the race, convinced race officials that he was eighteen. The race was held at Harewood Acres, and Bobby drove his father's Elva-Porsche. Bobby's enthusiasm for racing got the better of him, though, when he drove his car off the track and into a wet field. Not easily discouraged, Bobby returned to Canada a year later and won his first race behind the wheel of the family Porsche 906. His career as a race driver was off to an early start.

### The Road to Excellence

By 1973, Bobby was old enough to join the Sports Car Club of America (SCCA). His first SCCA race was in May, 1973. He drove his father's Lotus. He was soon racing in the Chicago region at SCCA-sponsored events. First driving a Lotus 47, then a Lola T-290, Bobby became the Chicago region's rookie of the year. Bobby had also begun attending Denison University, where he earned a bachelor's degree in history. His ambition was to enter a profession such as law or medicine, because he felt racing was too uncertain a career.

By 1974, Bobby had learned to drive well enough to become the SCCA's Division B Sports Racing Champion. He had planned to attend law school but, with his newfound success in racing, he decided to postpone his plans and become a professional racer.

On the road toward becoming a champion, Bobby continued competing in the SCAA American amateur series and the Formula Atlantic series. A watershed year in his career was 1978, when he turned in a brilliant performance in the Formula Atlantic opener held at the United States Grand Prix in Long Beach, California.

Although Bobby had qualified for the pole, or lead starting position, in this race, his car was struck by another racer on the warm-up lap, forcing Bobby to start the race in last place. He drove like a champion, climbing back to third place before a mechanical problem forced him out of the race. His performance impressed Walter Wolf, a

## CART and Sports Car Victories

| | |
|---|---|
| 1974 | SCCA Division B Sports Racing |
| 1975 | Formula Atlantic |
| | SCCA President's Cup |
| 1976 | North American Formula Atlantic |
| 1979 | Can-Am Challenge Cup Race (Laguna Seca) |
| 1982 | Cleveland 500 kilometers |
| | Michigan 150 |
| 1983 | Riverside 500k |
| 1984-87 | Laguna Seca 186 |
| 1984, 1992 | Phoenix 150 |
| 1985 | Michigan 200 |
| 1985-86 | Mid-Ohio 200 |
| 1986 | Indianapolis 500 |
| | Toronto 186 |
| | Montreal 187 |
| | Michigan 250 |
| 1986-87, 1992 | PPG Indy Car World Series Championship |
| 1987 | Portland 200 |
| | Meadowlands 168 |
| 1988 | Pocono 500 |
| 1989 | Meadowlands 180 |
| 1991 | Marlboro Grand Prix |
| 1992 | Detroit |
| | New England |
| | Nazareth |

Canadian Formula One team owner, Wolf offered Bobby a chance to drive the Wolf Team Formula Three racer.

Bobby's first Formula Three race driving for the Wolf Team was at Monaco, where he qualified for the pole. Although he did not win the race, he placed third in his next two races. This start was impressive enough for Wolf to offer Bobby a ride in the team's spare Formula One car. His first Formula One race was at Watkins Glen, New York, in 1978, where he finished twelfth.

At this stage in his career, Bobby was seen as more than a promising rookie by other team owners, but finding a team that would give him a chance to drive a Formula One car regularly was difficult. Bobby knew that to be offered a chance to drive for a Formula One team, he would have to prove himself on the European circuit. In the 1979 season, he drove a Formula Two car for Chevron in eleven races, doing well enough to earn him three stars in the *Autosports* yearly driver ratings.

Bobby's main goal, however, was to drive Indy cars. Rather than sign with a team that lacked the fi-

nancial resources to compete consistently, Bobby decided to continue driving in the Canadian-American (Can-Am) circuit during 1979 and 1980. With no offers on the horizon for Formula One, this period was one of the lowest in his career.

## The Emerging Champion

In 1980, Bobby met his wife, Debi, at a race in Canada, and they were married a few months later. Bobby's professional disappointment continued, however. At one point, he even quit racing and took a job in a Chicago advertising agency. Five months later, he was back in pursuit of his dream, although 1981 did not bring him any nearer the driver's seat of either a Formula One or an Indy car. Then fortune and an old friend intervened.

In 1982, Jim Trueman, a longtime friend and racing associate of Bobby's father, decided to race Indy cars and offered Bobby a chance to drive. Trueman, founder and president of Red Roof Inns and of the Truesports racing team, was well known in racing circles for his support of struggling and deserving drivers. His backing for Bobby was repaid in championship style.

As soon as Bobby climbed behind the wheel of his Truesports Indy car, he began to do what he knew all along he could. By winning at Cleveland that year, Bobby became the first rookie in twelve years to win an Indy car race. As a result, he was voted the Championship Auto Racing Team's (CART) rookie of the year.

Trueman's relationship with Bobby was one of mutual trust and affection. In the next several years, Bobby climbed toward the peak of auto racing honors with Trueman's backing. In 1983, he placed in the top ten in nine out of twelve events. In 1984, he took back-to-back wins at Phoenix and Monterey, and in 1985, he placed in the top five six times and set a record-breaking lap speed of 215.202 miles per hour in qualifying for the Michigan 500.

All this set the stage for Bobby's year of greatest

## Honors and Awards

| | |
|---|---|
| 1973 | SCCA Chicago Region Rookie of the Year |
| 1982 | CART Rookie of the Year |
| 1983 | CART Goodwill Ambassador Award |
| 2004 | Inducted into Motorsports Hall of Fame of America |

achievement as a driver. In 1986, he became the first driver since 1981 to win three straight races (Mid-Ohio, Montreal, Michigan 250) and was victorious in the first Toronto event. He became the first Indy driver to earn one million dollars in a single season. His greatest win came on Memorial Day at Indianapolis, when he shot past Kevin Cogan for the lead with just two laps to go. On his final lap, Bobby drove 209.152 miles per hour, the then-fastest race lap recorded at Indianapolis.

Winning the Indianapolis 500 is every professional driver's dream, but when it finally came true for Bobby, the victory was bittersweet. Trueman had been fighting a losing battle with colon cancer for two years, and just before the race, Bobby told him, "This one's for you, Jim." Trueman was in Victory Lane to celebrate one last win with his driver. Less than two weeks later, Trueman died, leaving a saddened Bobby to race the rest of the season with the memory of his lost friend and sponsor to inspire him.

### Continuing the Story

The years following his championship season of 1986 continued to bring victories and success to Bobby both on and off the racetrack. He and his wife Debi finally realized another dream in the adoption of a baby daughter, Michaela. The couple also had two sons, Jarrad and Graham Robert.

Bobby's growing family and his desire to do something for his community became increasingly important to him. Bobby became the founder and chair of Central Ohio's Children's Charities and sponsored the Annual Bobby Rahal Columbus Charities Pro-Am Golf Tournament.

Bobby's ambitions in business were realized when he opened a Honda dealership in 1988 and a Lexus dealership in 1990. On the racetrack, he continued to be a formidable competitor, winning races in 1987, 1988, and 1989. In 1990, he took home purses totaling more than $1 million. After thirty-one winless starts, Bobby broke his streak with a victory at Meadowlands in 1991 and followed in 1992 with his third PPG Indy Car World Series Championship and four Grand Prix victories. Bobby retired from competition following the 1994 season. In 2004, he was inducted into the Motorsports Hall of Fame of America.

### Summary

For Bobby Rahal, racing was never solely an end in itself. It brought him financial success and the knowledge that he could be the best at what he wanted to do. These achievements were, in typical Bobby style, the result not just of luck, but also of careful planning, dedication, and hard work. The desire for success and the qualities instilled in him by his family enabled him to become a winner on and off the racetrack.

*Francis Poole*

### Additional Sources

Kirby, Gordon. *Bobby Rahal: The Graceful Champion.* Phoenix, Ariz.: David Bull, 1999.

_____."CART: Bobby's Back at Work." *Road and Track* 53, no. 4 (December, 2001): 128.

Lamm, John. "Like Father, Like Son . . . Again." *Road and Track* 57, no. 10 (June, 2006): 16.

Sakkis, Tony. *Indy Racing Legends.* Osceola, Wis.: Motorbooks International, 1996.

# Steve Reeves

**Born:** January 21, 1926
   Glasgow, Montana
**Died:** May 1, 2000
   Escondido, California
**Also known as:** Steven Reeves (full name)

## Early Life

On January 21, 1926, Steven Reeves was born in Glasgow, Montana, a tiny town a few miles from the Canadian border, where the northern plains stretch for miles in every direction. Steve's father, Lester, was a farmer who worked the stubborn Montana soil. He was killed in a farming accident before his son was two years old, leaving Steve's mother, Golden, with a young son and an uncertain future.

Steve Reeves, who was the National Amateur Bodybuilders Association "Mr. Universe" in 1950 and went on to star in numerous Hollywood films. (Tony Lanza)

## The Road to Excellence

When Steve was ten years old, he and his mother moved to Oakland, California. In an attempt to bolster the family finances, Steve found employment as a newspaper delivery boy. Even while he was on the job, Steve found time to exercise his young muscles. He pedaled his bicycle furiously up the steep Oakland hills attempting to build his calf muscles. He practiced his coordination by throwing his papers precisely on the top step of every porch.

Steve enjoyed wrist wrestling and could beat every opponent who challenged him except for one smaller rival who had a strength far in excess of his stature. Steve was mystified until he visited his adversary's home one day and found him working out with weights in his backyard. This was Steve's first encounter with barbells, and it made a great impression on him.

Steve began to work out with his friend, but his serious weightlifting had to wait until he entered Castlemont High School, where he began working out with weights on a regular basis. Steve found that his young muscles responded quickly to the exercise, but he needed more direction than his school coaches could give him.

By a stroke of luck, Oakland was also the home of Ed Yarick, who ran one of the best bodybuilding gymnasiums in the world. Yarick took Steve under his wing and began training him. After two years of intensive instruction under Ed's care, Steve began to put on more muscle than ever before.

World War II put a temporary halt to Steve's career. As soon as he graduated from high school, he joined the U.S. Army and was sent to fight in the Philippines. Nothing could stop Steve's meteoric rise, however, and when he returned from fighting in 1946, he came back to Yarick's gym and redoubled his efforts. His hard work began to pay off when he won the Mr. Pacific Coast title in both 1946 and 1947.

## The Emerging Champion

Steve's greatest triumph in bodybuilding occurred in 1947, when he won the top prize in the world of

251

## Major Championships

| Year | Competition | Place |
|------|-------------|-------|
| 1946-47 | Mr. Pacific Coast | 1st |
| 1947 | Mr. America | 1st |
| 1948 | Mr. Universe | 2d |
|  | Mr. USA | 2d |
| 1948, 1950 | Mr. World | 1st |
| 1949 | Mr. USA | 3d |
| 1950 | Mr. Universe | 1st |

bodybuilding at that time. In that year, he was crowned Mr. America. Suddenly, the handsome young athlete became a celebrity. Photographs showing his broad shoulders, massive arms, and slender waist seemed to be everywhere.

Steve did not escape the notice of filmmakers. One of the first to contact him was Cecil B. De Mille, the director of many screen epics. He needed someone to play the biblical hero Samson in his next extravaganza, and Steve seemed just the one for the job.

When De Mille asked him to shed 20 pounds of hard-earned muscle, however, Steve rebelled, and the role was given to someone else. Despite this setback, Steve continued to pursue bodybuilding and to hope for a career in films. In 1948, he placed second in both the Mr. Universe and Mr. USA contests and gained top honors in the Mr. World competition. Two years later, he traveled to London, England, and was judged Mr. Universe for 1950.

## Continuing the Story

After Steve won these competitions, he was pursued again by filmmakers, this time with greater success. In 1954, he played a small but important part in *Athena*, but it was not until 1957 that Steve finally graduated to lead roles. In that year, he was asked to play the muscular lead in an Italian production called *Hercules*, and from then on, his career as a film muscleman went full speed ahead.

Most of the films Steve starred in were "sword-and-sandal" pieces set in the time of ancient Greece and Rome and full of action and special effects. The films were instant hits with the fans, and Steve devoted most of his energy to satisfying the public's demand for more of these popular films. In all, Steve starred in sixteen motion pictures between 1954 and 1968.

Unknown to his many fans, however, was that the muscular movie star had suffered from a terrible injury. During the 1959 filming of *The Last Days of Pompeii* (1960), Steve's chariot slammed into a tree, dislocating his shoulder. Despite the agonizing pain, Steve was able to snap the shoulder back into its socket. He continued filming, but at a terrible price. From then on, each stunt he performed in every succeeding movie injured the shoulder a little more until finally he was forced to retire forever from his strenuous film career.

Steve returned to the West Coast after his cinematic career was cut short. In 1963, he had married a Polish countess, Aline Czarzawicz, and the two retired to a ranch in Southern California, where they began to breed Morgan horses.

Because he could no longer work out with heavy weights, Steve devised other methods of exercise. He became interested in "power walking," his term for strenuous walking while swinging light weights in either hand.

## Summary
As a bodybuilder and later as a popular film star, Steve Reeves demonstrated that a muscular build and a healthy lifestyle can translate into a successful career. His masculine good looks, combined with his powerful physique, provided a model for the young bodybuilders of an entire generation.

*David Chapman*

## Additional Sources

Dowling, Dave, and George Helmer. *Steve Reeves: His Legacy in Films*. Malibu, Calif.: Classic Image, 2003.

LeClaire, Chris. *Steve Reeves: Worlds to Conquer, An Authorized Biography*. Chatham, Mass.: Monomoy Books, 1999.

Moore, Milton T., Jr. *Steve Reeves: A Tribute*. Dallas, Tex.: Author, 1982.

_____. *Steve Reeves: One of a Kind*. Dallas, Tex.: Author, 1983.

Reeves, Steve, John Little, and George Helmer. *Dynamic Muscle Building*. Malibu, Calif.: Classic Image, 2003.

Reeves, Steve, John Little, and Bob Wolff. *Building the Classic Physique the Natural Way*. 2d ed. Malibu, Calif.: Steve Reeves International, 1995.

Reeves, Steve, and James A. Peterson. *Power Walking*. Indianapolis, Ind.: Bobbs-Merrill, 1982.

# Willy T. Ribbs

**Born:** January 3, 1955
   San Jose, California
**Also known as:** William Theodore Ribbs, Jr. (full name)

## Early Life

William Theodore Ribbs, Jr., the first African American to compete in the Indianapolis 500 auto race, was born on January 3, 1955, in San Jose, California. At that time, although a number of black drivers did compete locally in both drag and stock car races, no African Americans had succeeded in reaching American automobile racing's highest levels. Role models, however, were not completely lacking: Willy's family friends included successful race-car driver Dan Gurney.

Willy, believing that he had a better chance of breaking into the upper echelons of auto racing in Europe than in the United States, paid his own way to England at the age of twenty-one. There he acquired the experience necessary to succeed.

## The Road to Excellence

Willy began his racing career in Great Britain in 1977, driving rented formula Ford racing cars, open-wheel race cars configured similarly to Formula One vehicles but with smaller engines and less power. He enjoyed an exceptionally good sea-

son for an inexperienced driver, with six first-place finishes out of eleven starts. Willy was named series champion. In 1978, he returned to the United States, hoping to secure a position on a racing team, but met with little success.

After Willy drove in the Long Beach Formula Atlantic, a promoter invited him to North Carolina to race at the Charlotte Motor Speedway. However, he was unable to obtain a competitive car, and things looked bleak. Willy's racing career seemed to have ended.

## The Emerging Champion

By 1982, however, Willy was back on the fast track in Formula Atlantic racing, with both a sponsor—Red Roof Inns—and a competitive car. He won the pole position at Long Beach in qualifying laps against Michael Andretti and Al Unser, Jr. The following year, Willy progressed to the Trans-Am circuit, where he won five of twelve races. The Sports Car Club of America (SCCA) named Willy rookie of the year for 1983. A meeting with Edsel Ford led to Ford Motor Company sponsorship. During the next two years, Willy won more Trans-Am races than any other driver on the circuit, with a total of seventeen victories.

At the same time, Willy continued to try to advance to racing Indy cars. In 1985, boxing promoter Don King put together a deal for Willy to compete at the Indianapolis 500. However, preparations had begun too late; the car handled poorly and lacked power. Winning Indy cars are the result of many years of teamwork among designers, sponsors, and drivers—a successful race car cannot be acquired in a few short weeks. Willy and King canceled without attempting to qualify.

In 1987, Willy began driving for his friend Dan Gurney's racing team. After a successful season, Willy was named International Motor Sports Association (IMSA) driver of the year, an honor he repeated the following year. By 1989, Willy felt confident enough to form his

---

### Racing Career Highlights

| | |
|---|---|
| 1977 | Formula Ford series champion |
| 1982 | Won pole position in qualifying laps at Long Beach Grand Prix |
| 1983 | Sports Car Club of America rookie of the year |
| 1984 | Won more races than any driver on the Trans-Am circuit |
| 1987, 1988 | International Motor Sports Association driver of the year |
| 1991 | Became first African American to start at the Indianapolis 500 |
| 1993 | Qualified for the Indianapolis 500 |
| 1999 | Made Indy Racing League debut |
| 2000 | Finished second at the Long Beach Grand Prix |
| 2001 | Joined NASCAR Craftsman Truck Series; became first African American to be a full-time participant in a major NASCAR subdivision |

own racing team to field an Indy car. Entertainer Bill Cosby provided financial support. In 1990, with his career still climbing, Willy drove in the PPG Cup series for the first time at Long Beach. The PPG Cup series helped him prepare for qualifying at the Indianapolis 500.

## Continuing the Story

In 1991, Willy enjoyed a better PPG Cup season than in 1990. More important, McDonald's restaurants had come on board, giving him a major corporate sponsor for his attempt at the Indianapolis 500. Willy became the first African American driver to race in the event. In 1991, he finished in the points in five Indy car races, with his best finish a sixth place at Denver. He continued to drive for Gurney in IMSA events.

Willy continued driving Indy cars through 1995, but to many observers it appeared his career had peaked in the early 1990's. In 1993, he started thirteen races but managed only five points-paying finishes and no wins. In 1994, he started fifteen races but finished in the points only four times. His best showing in 1994 was a sixth-place finish at Michigan. By 1995, Willy was having difficulty finding sponsors, and his racing career entered a prolonged hiatus. Unwilling to retire from the sport he loved, Willy attempted a comeback in 1999. He entered an Indy car race in Las Vegas but crashed. In 2001, he joined the National Association for Stock Car Auto Racing's (NASCAR's) Craftsman Truck Series. He finished the season sixteenth in points.

## Summary

Willy T. Ribbs made racing history when he became the first African American to race in the Indianapolis 500. Although he enjoyed considerable success in automobile racing, he never became as well known as figures in other, more popular sports. Indy car racing is an expensive endeavor, and sponsors can be fickle. If Willy had been a pop culture icon, he might have enjoyed a lengthier racing career. As it was, when he began slipping in the points standings, both corporate and individual sponsors became impossible to find.

*Nancy Farm Männikkö*

## Additional Sources

Franchitti, Dario. "Driver Willy T. Ribbs Tries Comeback." *The Washington Post*, September 26, 1999, p. M12.

Garrett, Jerry. "Tell 'Em Willy T. Is Back." *Car and Driver*, February, 2000, 123-129.

Jess, Tyehimba. *African American Pride: Celebrating Our Achievements, Contributions, and Enduring Legacy.* New York: Citadel Press, 2003.

Sakkis, Tony. *Indy Racing Legends.* Osceola, Wis.: Motorbooks International, 1996.

Sessler, Peter C., and Nilda Sessler. *Indy Cars.* New York: Rourke Press, 1999.

# *Valentino Rossi*

**Born:** February 16, 1979
Urbino, Italy
**Also known as:** Rossifumi; Valentinik; the Doctor

## Early Life

Valentino Rossi was born in Urbino, Italy, on February 16, 1979. His father, Graziano Rossi, a motorcycle racer, introduced Valentino to the sport, which became a lifelong passion. By the time Valentino reached his fifth birthday, he was racing go-karts. Though Valentino, with the support of his father, wanted to race motorcycles, his mother insisted racing go-karts was safer. His mother prevailed until Valentino won the regional go-kart championship at the age of eleven. At that time, racing go-karts became too expensive for his family. Valentino officially entered the world of motorcycle racing with "mini moto," miniature motorcycles. After winning many regional mini-moto races between 1991 and 1993, Valentino, based partially on his father's advice, decided to enter the Italian Sport Production Championship.

## The Road to Excellence

Valentino's first year of motorcycle racing was difficult. He used 125cc motorcycles, the largest he had raced up to that time. After a first year in which he gained valuable knowledge and finished in the top three in the final race of the season, Valentino was given the opportunity to ride for the Italian motorcycle team Aprilia and spent the next several years refining his riding skills. In 1996, Valentino won his first Grand Prix World Championship race but finished ninth overall for the season.

By 1997, Valentino dominated the 125cc racing world. He won eleven of the fifteen races that season and captured the Grand Prix World Championship title. Valentino outgrew his competition and moved to 250cc motorcycle racing in 1998. Adjusting to a larger motorcycle was difficult. However, he soon dominated, winning the Grand Prix Championship in 1999. During this era, Valentino earned the nickname "Valentinik," a combination of his name and "Paperinik," a superhero duck from an Italian comic book.

## The Emerging Champion

Not long after his win at the 250cc level, Valentino was offered the opportunity to ride for Honda at the 500cc level, the top tier of motorcycle racing. Valentino soon became a world renowned champion and household name. However, a full season transpired before Valentino became successful. In 2000, Valentino rode hard and often, ending the season in second place. In 2001, Valentino captured the title by winning eleven races in the World Championship Grand Prix. This was the final season of the World Championship Grand Prix; the competition shifted to MotoGP. The difference between the World Championship Grand Prix and the MotoGP was the motorcycles used in the races. Before MotoGP, racing motorcycles were composed of improved versions of street bikes. However, motorcycles used in MotoGP were designed specifically for racing and could never be ridden legally on city streets. This change allowed for heightened competition but was an adjustment for all riders in the 500cc class.

*Valentino Rossi in 2008.* (Bazuki Muhammad/Reuters/Landov)

In 2001, Valentino competed in an eight-hour endurance race called the "Suzuka 8 Hours," in which racers rode on a three-and-one-half mile figure-eight track with an overpass. This track, in Japan, is one of the world's most dangerous, and claimed the life of rider Daijiro Kato in 2003. In the 2001 race, Valentino and his teammate, Colin Edwards, finished first.

Still riding for Honda, Valentino won back-to-back MotoGP titles, bringing his consecutive world championship wins to three by 2003. The last race of 2003, in Australia, was Valentino's best. Entering the race, Valentino needed a victory to clinch the world championship title; the pressure to win was extreme. Valentino overtook a racer while a yellow flag was present. The yellow flag is used in motorcycle racing when an accident occurs and instructs the riders to slow their speed and not to pass. For passing one of his fellow riders during this time, Valentino was penalized 10 seconds. Valentino could have lost the race and the season's championship if he had finished the race less than 10 seconds ahead of the nearest competition. Valentino exhibited the skills of a true champion and finished the race 15 seconds ahead of the second-place rider, securing the 2003 MotoGP title.

## Continuing the Story

After winning three consecutive titles with Honda, critics said Valentino was only as good as the bike he rode. With his contract coming to a close with Honda, Valentino switched to Yamaha. Even though Yamaha's motorcycle was inferior to Honda's, Valentino was confident he could win on any motorcycle he rode. Tensions were high in the first race of the 2004 season, as Valentino prepared to ride his first MotoGP race aboard a Yamaha. To the astonishment of the crowd, Valentino finished first in this South African race, ahead of his former teammates at Honda, thus removing any doubt about Valentino's championship abilities. Valentino captured both the 2004 and the 2005 championships.

---

### Career Statistics

Wins, 91
Poles, 50
Podium standings, 140

---

### World Championships

| | | | |
|---|---|---|---|
| 1997 | 125cc division | 2001 | 500cc division |
| 1999 | 250cc division | 2002-05 | MotoGP |

---

The move from Honda to Yamaha showed how much Valentino had grown. During the early stages of his career, his comfort level on an unfamiliar motorcycle took him most, if not all, of a season to establish. However, at the apex of his career, Valentino was able to ride any motorcycle competitively.

Valentino entered the final race of 2006, in Valencia, Spain, needing a win to secure another championship season. However, in the middle of the race, he crashed his bike and was forced to leave the track. Though he was not seriously injured, he ended the 2006 season in second place. He finished the 2007 season in third place.

## Summary

Valentino Rossi was one of the most successful motorcycle racers of all time. He won a total of seven World Championship Grand Prix titles, six as MotoGP. Valentino achieved victory through determination and hard work. In his career, he struggled with each change—whether motorcycle class, team, or sponsor—but at the end of each season, he emerged at or near the top of the final rankings. His dedication showed most clearly in the number 46 he wore. Normally, world-champion racers wear the number 1, signifying their ranking. However, he wore number 46 as a tribute to his father who used the number when he won his first championship in 1978.

*Pamela D. Doughty*

## Additional Sources

Falsaperla, Filippo. *Valentino Rossi: Legend.* London: Yellow Jersey, 2006.

Gifford, Clive. *Racing: The Ultimate Motorsports Encyclopedia.* New York: Kingfisher/Houghton Mifflin, 2006.

Oxley, Mat. *The Valentino Rossi Book.* Newbury Park, Calif.: Haynes, 2005.

_____. *Valentino Rossi: MotoGenius.* Newbury Park, Calif.: Haynes, 2006.

Rossi, Valentino. *What if I Had Never Tried It: The Autobiography.* St. Paul, Minn.: MotorBooks, 2006.

# *Johnny Rutherford*

**Born:** March 12, 1938
    Coffeyville, Kansas
**Also known as:** John Sherman Rutherford III
    (full name); Lone Star J. R.

### Early Life
John Sherman Rutherford III, was born on March 12, 1938, in Coffeyville, Kansas. He would not have been a race-car driver if his mother had had her way. She wanted him to take advantage of the booming business environment as he was growing up in the Dallas, Texas, area, but Johnny enjoyed racing even then. As a child, he wanted to compete and to go fast, even if on a bicycle.

Johnny started racing in 1959, driving modified stock cars in the Dallas area. He raced at Indianapolis for the first time in 1963, but the transmission on his car failed, and he finished in twenty-ninth place, three places farther back than he had begun the race. In 1964, Johnny crashed his car and had no back-up car in which to continue the race. Although he won the U.S. Auto Club Sprint Car Championship in 1965, his car broke down at Indianapolis. In 1966, there was another crash; in 1969, his fuel tank ruptured; in 1970, his engine failed; in 1971, he was ordered off the track because of an oil leak; and in 1972, he broke a connecting rod. Johnny's early career could have given him the nickname "Hard Luck Johnny."

### The Road to Excellence
By 1964, Johnny was a challenger for the big wins in Indy-style auto racing. He had worked his way up through the ranks of rookies and beginners to earn the opportunity to race the fastest cars against the best drivers. Something always went wrong, however. In some years, money from sponsors was not available; at other times, bones were broken in acci-

*Race-car driver Johnny Rutherford, who, from 1973 to 1980, won the Indianapolis 500 three times.* (Courtesy of Amateur Athletic Foundation of Los Angeles)

## CART and Other Victories

| | |
|---|---|
| 1963 | Daytona 500 Twin 125 Qualifying Race |
| 1965 | USAC Sprint Club Championship |
| | Atlanta 250 |
| 1973 | Pocono 500 |
| | Michigan 125 |
| 1973-74 | Ontario 100 |
| 1973, 1977 | Milwaukee 150 |
| 1974, 1976, 1980 | Indianapolis 500 |
| 1975, 1977-78, 1981 | Phoenix 150 |
| 1976 | Trenton 200 |
| | Texas 200 |
| 1978, 1980 | Michigan 200 |
| 1979 | Atlanta 125 |
| 1980 | California 200 |
| | Mid-Ohio 156 |
| | Milwaukee 200 |
| | PPG Indy Car World Series Championship |
| 1985 | Montreal 187 |
| 1986 | Michigan 500 |

dents that took Johnny out of competition for weeks at a time. In other years, Johnny had sponsors to pay the bills and good health for driving, but his cars broke down. All in all, Johnny faced a considerable amount of frustration. This frustration did not necessarily extend to his personal life, however. In 1968, Johnny and his wife, Betty, became the parents of a son, John, and in 1971, a daughter, Angela Ann, was born.

In 1970, Johnny looked like a sure winner at the Indianapolis 500 race, losing the pole position to Al Unser by only two and one-half feet over a distance of ten miles. When the actual race began, however, Johnny's car let him down, and he was never in contention. In 1973, Johnny took the pole position, this time by beating Bobby Unser by 52 feet over the 10-mile trial course. Johnny set a track record of more than 198 miles per hour. Despite this accomplishment, victory escaped him again.

The good news came in 1974. Although Johnny started in the twenty-fifth position, he carefully and patiently worked his way past one car after another. This time, his car and his luck were both good. Although seven cars dropped out of the race within a few minutes and fourteen of the thirty-three starters would never

complete the race, Johnny pushed on. He held the lead for 122 laps of the 200-lap race and finished ahead of Bobby Unser by 23 seconds. Victory had come to Johnny at Indy at last.

### The Emerging Champion

Johnny did not always experience good luck, but he was an experienced and established driver who never needed to doubt his own ability.

In 1975, the Indianapolis 500 was once more run in the rain, and once more Johnny was competing with the best. All day, he dueled with Bobby Unser for the lead. Late in the race, Johnny pulled into the pit for fuel, and, just after he had reentered the track and regained the lead, the rain poured down. Cars were sliding around the track when the officials stopped the competition with Johnny in second place.

In 1976, Johnny was fully ready. Again the rain poured down, but this time it worked to his advantage. The major competitor Johnny had to face was A. J. Foyt. The race was different because new rules had limited engine size, making the cars run slower. That led to more passing on the corners instead of passing only on the straightaways. Time and again Johnny and Foyt passed each other, but shortly before 1:00 P.M. the rain fell in torrents and the race was stopped with Johnny 12 seconds in the lead. Those 12 seconds were worth more than $256,000 in first-prize money. The race was the shortest Indianapolis 500 in history.

### Continuing the Story

Although Johnny and his family were all concerned about accidents, Johnny was at the peak of his career. The smaller engines and slower speeds had made timing and driver judgment more important than ever, and Johnny was good at both of those. In 1980, skill and determination led Johnny to victory at Indianapolis again. This third victory made him the first driver to win the race twice when starting from the pole position. The way Johnny won showed his sense of timing.

## Honors and Awards

| | |
|---|---|
| 1974, 1980 | Jerry Titus Memorial Award |
| 1987 | Inducted into Indianapolis Motor Speedway Hall of Fame |
| | Inducted into Automobile Racing Hall of Fame |

After refueling on lap 169, Johnny carefully figured he had just enough gas to finish the race without going into the pit again. His judgment as a driver also helped him to properly handle cars equipped with ground effects, which channeled air under them to make the machines hug the track.

## Summary

Unlike many drivers, Johnny Rutherford did not own his cars. He drove under contract with designers and owners and was paid a retainer as well as a percentage of his winnings. Even when he could not seem to win, Johnny always had a cheerful personality, and that won and him thousands of loyal fans and hundreds of personal friends. He was one of the most popular drivers ever to race Indy-style cars.

*Michael R. Bradley*

## Additional Sources

Higdon, Hal. *Johnny Rutherford: Indy Champ.* New York: Putnam, 1980.

Reed, Terry. *Indy: The Race and Ritual of the Indianapolis 500.* Washington, D.C.: Potomac Books, 2005.

Rutherford, Johnny. *Lone Star J. R.: The Autobiography of Racing Legend Johnny Rutherford.* Chicago: Triumph Books, 2000.

Syken, Bill. "Johnny Rutherford, Racer." *Sports Illustrated* 102, no. 9 (February 28, 2005): 10.

# Wanda Rutkiewicz

**Born:** February 4, 1943
       Plungė, Lithuania
**Died:** May 12 or 13, 1992
       Kangchenjunga, Himalaya, Nepal
**Also known as:** Wanda Blaszkiewicz (birth name)

## Early Life
Wanda Rutkiewicz was one of four children born to Zbigniew Blaszkiewicz and Maria Blaszkiewicz. She spent her early years in Wroclaw, Poland. A natural athlete, she participated in a variety of sports and eventually earned a degree in electrical engineering from Wroclaw's polytechnic institute. Wanda began serious rock climbing at the age of eighteen. In climbing, Wanda found her passion, and she climbed throughout Poland, Czechoslovakia, and East Germany. Beginning in 1964, at the age of twenty-one, Wanda made the first of several trips to the Alps, sharpening her alpine skills.

## The Road to Excellence
In 1970, Wanda married her first husband, fellow climber and mathematician Wojtek Rutkiewicz. During the early 1970's, Wanda made several significant climbs, including Lenin Peak, at 7,134 meters (23,406 feet), in the Russian Pamirs (now in Tajikistan); Noshaq, 7,492 meters (24,580 feet), in the Hindu Kush Range; and the second ascent of the difficult North Pillar in the Alps. Notably, the first ascent had been made by elite mountaineers Peter Habeler and Reinhold Messner in 1968. Messner went on to become the first man to climb all fourteen of the 8,000-meter mountains—a goal to which Wanda aspired.

In 1975, Wanda led the "Polish Women's Karakoram Expedition" to the world's highest unclimbed mountain: Gasherbrum III, at 7,952 meters (26,089 feet), located in Pakistan's Karakoram Range. The climbers reached the summit, and this became the highest "first ascent" made by women.

In 1978, Wanda joined an expedition to Mt. Everest, 8,848 meters (29,028 feet), as a climber and a documentary filmmaker. She reached the summit on October 16, becoming the first Western woman, and third woman overall, to stand atop the world's highest mountain. Wanda, a strikingly attractive woman, had became a hero and a celebrity in Poland. She began to plan a women's expedition to K2, 8,611 meters (28,251 feet), the world's second highest mountain. However, during a winter climb in 1981, Wanda sustained a compound fracture of the femur—a serious injury. Surgery was performed, but the bone was not set properly. She eventually turned to Dr. Helmut Scharfetter for further treatment, and he became her second husband.

## The Emerging Champion
Despite the injury to her leg, Wanda was determined to accompany the 1982 women's expedition to K2, which she had planned; she made the eleven-day hike to base camp on crutches. The expedition did not go well. Wanda was unable to climb, one of her close friends collapsed and died on the moun-

*Wanda Rutkiewicz was the first European woman to Climb Mt. Everest.* (AP/Wide World Photos)

tain, and the team eventually quit because of the weather.

By 1984, Wanda was able to walk without pain. In 1985, she climbed the south face of Aconcagua, 6,960 meters (22,835 feet), in South America, and Nanga Parbat, 8,126 meters (26,660 feet), in the Himalayas. In 1986, Wanda joined a small, French team that was planning to attempt K2 in "alpine" style—light and fast, without fixed high camps or ropes. Accordingly, the four climbers were stretched to their limits but eventually reached the top. Wanda arrived first, on June 23, becoming the first woman to ascend the summit of K2. Wanda and one teammate returned to safety, but the other two perished during their descent. This was a particularly deadly summer on K2, as chronicled in Jim Curran's classic account, *K2: Triumph and Tragedy.*

In 1987, Wanda climbed Shisha Pangma, 8,013 meters (26,289 feet). In 1988, she married her third husband, German cardiologist Kurt Lyncke. Sadly, in 1990, he died from a fall on Mt. Broad, 8,047 meters (26,400 feet). In 1989, Wanda climbed Gasherbrum II, 8,035 (26,362 feet), as part of the British women's expedition, and in 1990, she climbed Gasherbrum I, 8,080 meters (26,509 feet).

### Continuing the Story

At this point, Wanda announced her goal to become the first woman to climb the fourteen 8,000-meter mountains. She had climbed six, and she proposed to climb the remaining eight in a little more than a year. She called this project her "caravan of dreams." Her strategy was to rely on other expeditions to have established camps and ropes in advance. Thus, she could arrive to begin her climb, still acclimatized from the last summit. Wanda's time line was unrealistic. By the end of 1991, she had added only two more peaks to her list, Cho Oyu, 8,153 meters (26,749 feet), and Annapurna, 8,078 meters (26,503 feet). On Annapurna, she was injured by a falling rock but made the summit.

In 1992, she set out to climb her ninth 8,000-meter peak, Kangchenjunga, 8,585 meters (28,166 feet). She joined the team of a young Mexican

### 8000-Meter Mountain Peaks Climbed

| | | | |
|---|---|---|---|
| 1978 | Mount Everest | 1989 | Gasherbrum II |
| 1985 | Nanga Parbat | 1990 | Gasherbrum I |
| 1986 | K2 | 1991 | Cho Oyu |
| 1987 | Shisha Pangma | | Annapurna I |

couple, Carlos and Elsa Carsolio. Eventually, only Carlos and Wanda were poised to reach the summit. Wanda was moving slowly, so Carlos went ahead of her to the summit. Coming down, he found her dug into the slope, prepared to spend a freezing cold night in the elements without bivouac gear, such as a sleeping bag and a stove. He suggested that she go down with him, but she refused, hoping to make an attempt on the summit the next morning. Carlos descended alone, the weather closed in, and Wanda died either May 12 or 13, high on Kangchenjunga. She was forty-nine years old.

### Summary

At a time when mountaineering was predominantly a male activity, Wanda Rutkiewicz rose from the grim world of post-war Poland to become, perhaps, the greatest woman mountaineer of all time. She was the third woman, and the first Western woman, to climb the world's highest mountain, Mt. Everest. She was the first woman to climb the infamous K2, the world's second highest mountain, which is considered technically more difficult than Mt. Everest. At the time of her death in 1992, she had climbed eight of the fourteen 8,000 meter peaks—more than any other woman of her era. In addition to her climbing, she was a mountain photographer, filmmaker, and writer. She received the Star of Distinction award from Pakistan and the Albert Medal of the Royal Society of Arts from England.

*Russell N. Carney*

### Additional Sources

Curran, Jim. *K2: Triumph and Tragedy.* Boston: Houghton Mifflin, 1987.

Jordan, Jennifer. *Savage Summit: The True Stories of the First Five Women Who Climbed K2, the World's Most Feared Mountain.* New York: HarperCollins, 2005.

Reinisch, Gertrude. *Wanda Rutkiewicz: A Caravan of Dreams.* Mukilteo, Wash.: Carreg, 2000.

### Milestones

First Western woman to reach the summit of Mount Everest (1978)

First woman to climb K2 (1986)

# Lyn St. James

**Born:** March 13, 1947
   Willoughby, Ohio
**Also known as:** Evelyn Gene Cornwall (birth
   name); Evelyn Caruso (married name)

## Early Life

Lyn St. James was born Evelyn Gene Cornwall, the only child of Albert and Maxine Cornwall, in Willoughby, Ohio. Her father's family was in the sheetmetal business, and Lyn visited her father's shop often, showing an early interest in machines. Lyn's mother suffered from multiple sclerosis, and she encouraged Lyn to appreciate the independence that driving a car could bring, teaching Lyn to drive on long car trips through Ohio and the Midwest. Shy and studious, Lyn attended St. Andrew's School for

*Lyn St. James.* (Steve Swope/Getty Images)

Girls, where she excelled in sports. She was also an excellent student of the piano, having taken lessons for thirteen years. She received a teacher's certificate from the St. Louis Institute of Music.

## The Road to Excellence

Though her mother took Lyn to see the Indianapolis 500 in 1966, Lyn's first real experience with racing came at the age of seventeen when she attended a drag-racing event in Indiana. A young male friend of Lyn was racing in the event, and Lyn kidded him about his lack of success. He challenged her to do better. Strapped into the cockpit with a helmet on, Lyn found herself in a race car for the first time. She made the most of her experience, winning her first race. Trophy in hand, Lyn went home. Her mother made Lyn promise never to race again, a pledge she kept for ten years.

Four years after her marriage to John Carusso, a fellow racing enthusiast, Lyn got the urge to race again. Her husband was racing in regional, amateur Sports Car Club of America (SCCA) events in Florida, where the couple owned an electronics business. Lyn was a member of her husband's pit crew, and she watched as Carusso drove a Ford Pinto and a Chevy Corvette on racetracks every weekend.

Unable to keep her promise to her mother, Lyn earned her competition license through SCCA driving schools. In her first sanctioned race, Lyn spun her car, a Ford Pinto, into a corner, and it jumped the fence and landed in a pond near the track. Lyn was unharmed, but she stood by helplessly as her car slowly sank into the muck.

## The Emerging Champion

Despite her discouraging start, Lyn persisted. She switched to a Chevrolet Vega, and in 1976 and 1977, she was the SCCA Florida Regional Champion in the showroom stock class. In 1978, she was runner-up in the Southeast SCCA competition. She drove her husband's Corvette in the famous twelve-hour race at Sebring, Florida.

## Milestones

1987, 1991   Entered the 24 Hours of Daytona race
1989, 1991   Entered the 24 Hours of Le Mans race
   1992-97   Six consecutive Indianapolis 500 starts

## Records

Recorded fastest time on closed-course by a women, 225.72 mph (1995)
First woman to win an International Motor Sport Association solo GT race

Lyn, known as Evelyn Carusso at the time, was becoming well-known in the racing world, but her husband suggested she find a new name, one that sounded more like a race-car driver. One night while watching the television show *Macmillan and Wife*, starring Susan St. James, Lyn settled on her new racing name. The thirty-two-year-old Evelyn Carusso became Lyn St. James.

Lyn and her husband divorced in 1979, and she continued to race on weekends while owning and operating an auto-supply store during the week. Lyn's free time was spent raising money to race. In the 1980's, Lyn's career began to take off. She was named *Autoweek* magazine's rookie of the year in International Motor Sports Association (IMSA) Grand Touring (GT) racing. Lyn found a sponsor in Ford Motor Company and won several events, including the 1985 Watkins Glen, New York, IMSA GT race.

At thirty-eight years old, Lyn thought back to the 1966 Indianapolis 500 she attended with her mother, and she decided to compete in open-wheel racing. Lyn's friend and mentor in Indy car racing was Dick Simon, a veteran race-car driver and owner. Simon gave Lyn her first experience in an Indy car, allowing her to run practice laps at the Texas World Speedway.

## Continuing the Story

In 1992, Lyn qualified for and drove in her first Indianapolis 500, finishing eleventh, and she was named rookie of the year. In 1993, Lyn married Roger Lessman, an Idaho real-estate developer and land-speed-record competitor. Lyn continued racing at Indianapolis, making the field a total of seven times, including six consecutive

years. She once qualified as high as sixth in the thirty-three-car field, at a faster speed than racing legends Nigel Mansell, Mario Andretti, Arie Luyendyk, and Bobby Rahal. In addition to her successes at Indianapolis, Lyn drove on winning teams in the 1987 24 Hours of Le Mans and the 1990 24 Hours of Daytona.

Lyn's last Indianapolis 500 was bittersweet. In 2000, her car was built from scratch. During a practice run, a wheel separated from a tire on the next-to-last qualifying day, and the car was destroyed. With only one day to prepare, Simon's team supplied a backup car, and Lyn drove it fast enough to qualify for her seventh and last Indy race. At the age of fifty-three, Lyn was the oldest driver in the field, but she was not the only woman. Sarah Fisher, nineteen years old, was a rookie in 2000. Lyn, who had followed Fisher's development closely, was proud of the young driver. In a strange circumstance, the two drivers were involved in a crash during the race, signaling the end of Lyn's career at the Indianapolis 500.

## Summary

Lyn St. James came to Indy car racing late in life, but she left an important legacy for women drivers. She was the second woman to race in the Indianapolis 500 and the first woman to be named rookie of the year, in 1992, at Indianapolis. She was also the first woman to drive a race car in excess of 200 miles per hour, and after she retired, her influence on the sport continued in her role as teacher to both young men and women drivers.

*Randy L. Abbott*

## Additional Sources

Olney, Ross R. *Lyn St. James: Driven to Be First.* Minneapolis: Lerner, 1997.
St. James, Lyn. *Ride of Your Life: A Race Car Driver's Journey.* New York: Hyperion, 2002.
Stewart, Mark. *Lyn St. James.* New York: Children's Press, 1996.

## Honors and Awards

1992   Indianapolis 500 Rookie of the Year
1996   *Working Women* one of 350 women who changed the world between 1976-1996
2000   *Sports Illustrated for Women* top 100 Women Athletes of the Twentieth Century
2001   National Association for Girls and Women in Sports: Guiding Women in Sports award

# Carmen Salvino

**Born:** November 23, 1933
  Chicago, Illinois
**Also known as:** Carmen Mario Salvino (full name)

## Early Life

Carmen Mario Salvino, the second of four children, was born on November 23, 1933, in Chicago, Illinois. His parents, poor and hardworking, moved their family to Dania, Florida, north of Miami, when Carmen was five. One day, walking alongside a ditch, he spotted something shiny. Because he liked the shape and the white finish of the cracked wooden object, he took it home for a toy. He had never before seen a bowling pin.

In Dania, the family worked on a vegetable farm that belonged to Carmen's grandfather, an Italian immigrant. They lived in a simple wooden apartment building without electricity or indoor plumbing. The second year there, vegetable prices dropped so low that the farm could not support everyone, and so the family moved back to Chicago.

Carmen's father, Michael Salvino, who had only a third-grade education, could not find steady work in Chicago, so he decided to start his own farm and bought land near Davie, Florida, a few miles inland from Dania. When ten-year-old Carmen was not in school, he worked hard on this farm, where the soft, mucky earth made planting and harvesting difficult. In 1944, after a disastrous tomato crop, Mr. Salvino moved his family back to Chicago for good.

## The Road to Excellence

In Chicago, Carmen and his brothers worked hard to help support the family. The bitter winter weather was one reason for young Carmen's interest in the job setting pins for two dollars a day at the Amalgamated, an indoor bowling center. The twelve-year-old pinboy naturally began to bowl too. His first ball ever was a strike, and his first full-game score, 75, made him want to try again.

Carmen's only instruction was from Joe Ronosky, a tailor who bowled in the top local league. Ronosky gave Carmen his first ball. At fourteen,

Carmen was averaging more than 160—bowling's perfect score, a 300 game, represents 12 strikes in a row—and getting better. In his first experience with league play, Carmen, the only boy on a team of working-class men, was bowling more than 180 by season's end.

In 1950, Carmen was recruited to be in charge of pinsetters at Schueneman & Flynn's, a bigger

---

## PBA Tour Victories

| | |
|---|---|
| 1961 | Empire State Open, Albany, New York |
| 1962 | Pontiac Open, Pontiac, Michigan |
| | National Championship at Philadelphia |
| 1963 | Jacksonville Open, Jacksonville, Florida |
| 1964 | Rockford Open, Rockford, Illinois |
| 1965 | Paramus Open, Paramus, New Jersey |
| | Birmingham Open, Birmingham, Alabama |
| 1967 | St. Paul Open, St. Paul, Minnesota |
| | Mobile Open, Mobile, Alabama |
| 1968 | Caracas Invitational, Caracas, Venezuela |
| 1973 | Lincoln-Mercury Open, New Orleans |
| 1974 | New Jersey Open, Edison, New Jersey |
| 1975 | Showboat Invitational, Las Vegas |
| | Pittsburgh Open, Pittsburgh, Pennsylvania |
| 1976 | Quad Cities Open, Davenport, Iowa |
| 1977 | Houston Open, Houston |
| 1979 | Miller High Life Classic, Anaheim, California |
| 1984 | National Seniors Championship, Canton, Ohio |
| 1988 | Senior/Touring Pro Doubles Championship, Buffalo, New York (with Randy Pedersen) |

## Other Major Victories

| | |
|---|---|
| 1952 | Dom DeVito Classic Singles |
| | BPAA National Doubles (with Joe Wilman) |
| 1954 | ABC National Championship Team member |
| 1954, 1957 | Chicago Individual Match Game |
| 1954, 1960 | Chicago Classic League Championship Team member |
| 1955 | Petersen Masters Round Robin |
| 1956 | Illinois State All-Events |
| 1972 | ABC National Doubles (with Barry Asher) |

and more prestigious bowling center. There Carmen spent every spare minute perfecting his strike ball. With the help of Jim Flynn, co-owner of the bowling alley, Carmen entered another league and bowled so well that his reputation spread beyond the neighborhood. An article in *The Chicago Daily News* dubbed him the "boy wonder" of bowling in Chicago. He was seventeen and an instant celebrity.

### The Emerging Champion

Carmen was still in high school when he turned professional. Rudy Hazucha, a team captain in the Classic League, invited Carmen to join his team during the 1950 Illinois state tournament held at Schueneman & Flynn's. Carmen had barely accepted when he was asked to join the lineup to fill in for a team member. As it happened, the American Bowling Congress tournament, one of bowling's biggest annual championships, equivalent to baseball's World Series, was scheduled for that week.

Carmen got permission to miss school and took a train to St. Paul, Minnesota, for the tournament, where he won $1,000, the fourth-place prize. The money was split five ways for the team members, and Carmen came home feeling like a hero. He became confident enough to disagree with Hazucha on the best throwing style and stuck to his own way, throwing his ball in a huge hook, or curve, from the left of the lane.

In 1952, Carmen won his first major tournament, the Dom DeVito Classic. Just eighteen, he was the youngest player ever to win such an important tournament. By 1955, Carmen had won five major titles. That year, he married Virginia Morelli. Their daughter Corinne was born in 1956.

During the late 1950's, Carmen participated in the new, popular television bowling shows and saw the sport blossom with the growth of professional tournament circuits, like the Professional Bowlers Association (PBA). Through the late 1960's, he competed on the road, even playing in Japan and Venezuela.

### Continuing the Story

In 1968, Carmen turned thirty-five. He began to feel the physical and psychological challenges middle-aged athletes recognize. Although bowling

---

### PBA Record

Highest 16-game score, 4,015 (1980)

### Honors and Awards

| | |
|---|---|
| 1963, 1967, 1973-74 | *Bowling* magazine Second Team All-American |
| 1975 | *Bowlers Journal* First Team All-American |
| | Inducted into PBA Hall of Fame |
| 1976 | *Bowling* magazine First Team All-American |
| 1979 | Inducted into ABC Hall of Fame |
| 1980 | Inducted into Chicago Sports Hall of Fame |
| 1985 | Inducted into Italian-American Sports Hall of Fame |
| 1985-86 | President of PBA |

---

does not require the same quick reactions or the strength that some other sports demand, Carmen found the constant touring and competition more stressful as he grew older.

Furthermore, bowling was changing. The lanes were no longer coated with shellac, but with lacquer and, by the mid-1960's, with polyurethane plastic. The change in the basic lane surface made Carmen's characteristic "big hook" release unsuccessful—the high spin of the ball made it slide uncontrollably on the slick polyurethane, which had less friction than shellac.

After a few dismal years, Carmen agreed to be tutored by Hank Lahr, an old friend from Chicago. Lahr offered Carmen support and friendship and taught him technique, including a mathematical formula for calculating the motion and energy of the ball, which replaced the instinctual approach the bowler had always relied on. With Lahr's help, Carmen reshaped his game and made a comeback, which climaxed with his victory at the 1973 Lincoln-Mercury Open in New Orleans. Carmen's famous "equation" was primarily his new ability to think about bowling scientifically rather than in terms of luck or instinct.

Between 1973 and 1979, Carmen won seven PBA tour events and conducted experiments constructing bowling balls that resulted in successful collaborations to create more durable and better performing balls.

### Summary

Carmen Salvino's devotion to the sport and his ability to recognize and adapt to changing conditions granted him a long and satisfying career. In 1984, just turned fifty, he competed in his first seniors event and won. In 1985, he became president of the PBA for one year. Into the twenty-first century, he continued to bowl and write about bowling.

*JoAnn Balingit*

## Additional Sources

Bowman, Dale. "Salvino Keeps on Rolling." *Chicago Sun Times*, December 10, 2006, p. A71.

_____. "Salvino Knows, and Talks, a Good Game." *Chicago Sun Times*, September 26, 1999, p. 30.

Herbst, Dan. *Bowling Three Hundred: Top Pros Share Their Secrets to Rolling the Perfect Game.* Chicago: Contemporary Books, 1993.

Salvino, Carmen, and Frederick C. Klein. *Fast Lanes: Carmen Salvino and Professional Bowling Grew Up Together—Here Is Their Story.* Chicago: Bonus Books, 1988.

# *Magnus Samuelsson*

**Born:** December 21, 1969
    Linköping, Östergötlands län, Sweden
**Also known as:** King of the Stones; Giant Swede

## Early Life

Magnus Samuelsson was born in Sweden, on December 21, 1969, to a family of farmers. He learned the value of hard work and how to endure long hours of heavy lifting by performing the duties common to farms in the Swedish countryside. This farming life, in which Magnus engaged his entire life, instilled in both him and his brother the skills necessary to become champions. In 1985, Magnus and his brother, Torbjörn, watched a World's Strongest Man competition on television, and Magnus was determined to become as strong as Jón Páll Sigmarsson, the holder of the World's Strongest Man title that year. At this time, Magnus began lifting weights for fun, never knowing that thirteen years later he would hold that most coveted title.

## The Road to Excellence

As time passed, Magnus trained more and more, though he only trained after he completed his farming duties. He did not win a major tournament until 1995, when he was victorious in Sweden's Strongest Man competition. He continued to hold this title year after year. Also in 1995, he en-

### Competitive Record

| Year | Competition | Place |
|---|---|---|
| 1995 | World's Strongest Man | 10th |
| 1995-97, 1999-2001, 2003-05 | Sweden's Strongest Man | 1st |
| 1996, 2000 | World Muscle Power | 2d |
| 1997, 2000, 2004 | World's Strongest Man | 3d |
| 1998 | World's Strongest Man | 1st |
| | World's Strongest Team Contest | 3d |
| | World Strongman Challenge | 1st |
| 1999 | World's Strongest Man | 5th |
| | World's Strongest Team Contest | 2d |
| 2000 | Europe Strongman Classic | 2d |
| 2001 | Europe's Strongest Man | 3d |
| | Strongman Super Series | 1st |
| 2003, 2007 | World's Strongest Man | 4th |

tered the World's Strongest Man event and placed tenth among elite competitors. Though he was not victorious, he continued to train, hoping to capture the title.

During these first years on the competition circuit, Magnus settled into a training regimen that included consuming 8,500 calories a day. His caloric intake was four times the amount an average man needs for sustenance, but, at 6 feet 6 inches and more than 340 pounds, Magnus was not average. With this strict regimen in place, he won the Sweden's Strongest Man competition in 1996 and 1997. In 1997, Magnus stepped upon the podium, finishing third in the World's Strongest Man competition.

## The Emerging Champion

In 1998, in Morocco, Magnus won the World's Strongest Man competition. The contest included six events testing the different muscle groups of the competitors. A man who is simply strong cannot win this event. The World's Strongest Man competition tests endurance, speed, agility, and sheer, brute strength.

The two events featured in the competition for which Magnus was best known were the "Farmer's Walk" and the "McGlashen Stones." In the Farmer's Walk, competitors had to carry an item weighing between 275 and 375 pounds for a set distance. This event tested speed and agility, as the athlete with the fastest time won. The McGlashen Stones, (later known as the "Atlas Stones"), was one of the more difficult events in strongman competitions and the one for which Magnus earned his nicknamed, "King of the Stones." In this event, athletes shouldered giant, round stones weighing 220 to 350 pounds. The strongmen heaved these stones atop a platform a certain distance from their original starting point. With each stone heaved, the weight of the stone and the height of the platform were increased. This event tested speed, agility, and strength.

The events in which Magnus competed became more varied and interesting over the years. A few of the more exciting events were the "Keg Toss," in which athletes threw 50-pound kegs over a 13-foot wall; the "Car Carry," in which the competitors stood inside a car, with it resting on their shoulders, and carried it a certain distance; and the "Truck Pull," a timed event in which competitors were harnessed to an eighteen-wheeler and pulled the truck a certain distance. Again, the events were meant to be simple but varied enough to test many skills and muscle groups at the highest level. This superior level was where Magnus competed.

## Continuing the Story

With his 1998 win in Morocco, Magnus became recognized internationally. He continued to win Sweden's Strongest Man, finishing first nine times. He was on the podium, finishing in the top three, of World's Strongest Man four times and won numerous other strongman titles throughout Europe and the world. In 2004, he became one of only five men to close the fourth level of the "Captains of Crush" handgrip, which requires a man to exert 365 pounds of pressure with only his hand.

Magnus was known as having two of the world's strongest arms and has been Europe's best arm wrestler. During one arm-wrestling match, Magnus broke an opponent's arm in two places. Though he was known for his strength, Magnus was also one of the most honest and sportsmanlike athletes in the

world, refusing drugs and congratulating fellow competitors on their victories. In 2003 and 2004, Magnus's wife, a two-time strongest woman winner, gave birth to a son and daughter, respectively. As of 2008, Magnus continued to compete, and, after suffering a back injury in 2006, placed fourth in the 2007 World's Strongest Man competition.

## Summary

Despite his athletic career, Magnus Samuelsson continued to live the life of a farmer. He attributed his success to the skills he learned on the farm and stayed true to those methods. He reached the World's Strongest Man competition finals ten times, which set a world record. He became a testament to the fact that strength alone does not make a champion. Through changes in the strongman competition and injuries—such as slipped discs, separated biceps, and countless pulled tendons—Magnus showed that dedication and endurance are the qualities of a true champion.

*Pamela D. Doughty*

## Additional Sources

Bonner, Mike. *The Composite Guide to Strongman Competition.* Philadelphia: Chelsea House, 2000.

Cotal, Sharon. "Mighty Magnus Works Out." *Daily News,* January 13, 2001, p. SC1.

McCallum, Jack. "Titans of Testosterone." *Sports Illustrated* 91, no. 15 (October 18, 1999).

# Eugen Sandow

**Born:** April 2, 1867
      Königsberg, East Prussia (now Kaliningrad, Russia)
**Died:** October 14, 1925
      London, England
**Also known as:** Friedrich Wilhelm Müller (birth name)

### Early Life

On the cold shores of the Baltic Ocean, Eugen Sandow was born Friedrich Wilhelm Müller on April 2, 1867, in the city of Königsberg. Although the city later changed its name to Kaliningrad and became part of the Soviet Union, in the nineteenth century it was a distant outpost of the German Empire.

Eugen was the son of a modest greengrocer. Later in life, when he had become a professional athlete, he decided to switch his identity in order to cut off all contact with his humble past. Not much is known about Eugen's early days in Germany, but it is clear that the boy had a flair for athletics. He joined a gymnastics society and liked performing acrobatic tricks. Around 1885, Eugen left the city of his birth, became a tumbler, and joined a traveling circus that toured the cities of Europe.

### The Road to Excellence

By the time he was twenty, Eugen had been traveling through Europe for several years, but he had never achieved success. When he arrived in Brussels, Belgium, he was down on his luck. However, he was seen by a well-known coach and weightlifter named Professor Louis Attila, who took Eugen under his wing and helped him become a professional strongman.

In those days, an athlete with a good physique could make a living by performing feats of strength in a type of theater called a "music hall" in Europe and "vaudeville" in the United States. These theaters staged variety shows where many different entertainers performed, from singers and actors to jugglers and trained dogs.

Eugen discovered that he had a real talent in this line of work. Under the direction of Attila, Eu-

gen began to have some success as a professional strongman. People were eager to see the handsome young man lift heavy weights, bend iron bars, and balance heavy weights on his shoulders.

*Eugen Sandow, who was the founder of modern bodybuilding.* (Library of Congress)

**269**

## The Emerging Champion

Eugen and Attila knew, however, that the young athlete's greatest attraction was his wonderful physique. Thanks to his acrobatic stunts and Attila's coaching, Eugen had built his body to near perfection. His arms, shoulders, and especially his stomach muscles were hard and sinewy. He reminded audiences of the statues of Greek gods they had seen in museums, but Eugen's body was of flesh, blood, and muscle, not lifeless stone. For the first time ever, people were willing to pay to see a bodybuilder pose in front of them.

In 1889, Eugen got his first big break, in London, England. There he defeated two famous strongmen in a contest of strength and became the hero of the hour. This victory led to more and more theatrical engagements in England. In one of these performances in 1893, Eugen was scouted by an American agent who convinced Eugen to come to New York. In the United States, Eugen was discovered by the greatest of all his managers: Florenz Ziegfeld.

Ziegfeld later became famous for glorifying beautiful women in spectacular shows, but the young manager's first client was the German strongman. Ziegfeld whisked his new discovery off to Chicago, where a great World's Fair had just opened. Eugen became an instant sensation when he displayed his muscles at the Trocadero Theatre near the fairgrounds. It seemed as if everyone who visited the fair came to see Eugen perform his strength show also.

After the Chicago fair closed in 1894, Eugen and Ziegfeld embarked on several tours of the United States that took them all over the country. In every city they visited, Eugen tried to convince his audiences to take up exercise and a healthy lifestyle. He tried to show that anyone could have as muscular a body as he had. Not surprisingly, lifting weights, in an attempt to become as "strong as a Sandow," became popular.

## Continuing the Story

In 1896, Eugen broke with Ziegfeld and returned to Europe. He continued to perform, but there were other interests in his life now. Two years previously he had married Blanche Brooks, an English girl, and the two of them settled down in London.

Eugen had not retired, however, for his energy constantly ran full speed ahead. The strongman was particularly busy in the early years of the twentieth century. He began a string of gyms, started a mail-order exercise business, invented and marketed new exercise equipment, and sold food supplements. A few years earlier, he had begun one of the world's first physical culture publications, called *Sandow's Magazine of Physical Culture*. All of these enterprises became instant successes.

In 1901, Eugen gained further fame by holding the world's first bodybuilding contest. "The Great Competition," as it was called, was supposed to determine the best physique in the country. On the night of the event, more than fifteen thousand fans crowded into the auditorium to see the spectacle. The judges included Sir Arthur Conan Doyle, creator of the fictional detective Sherlock Holmes, and Eugen. The German muscleman was quickly making both himself and bodybuilding popular with the public.

If Eugen had one besetting fault, it was that he wanted to do too much too quickly. He seemed obsessed with transforming all of humanity into healthier, shapelier beings. In the early 1900's, Eugen embarked on several tours of the world in order to do just that. He visited Australia, India, South Africa, and the United States in succession, all the while trying to promote bodybuilding. He believed that he had no time to lose.

Back in England, the former muscleman concentrated on what he called "curative physical culture." Thanks to people like Eugen, doctors at the start of the twentieth century were just beginning to understand the part that regular, systematic exercise plays in human health. Eugen had no doubts about the helpful effects of working out. In fact, he believed that many diseases could be successfully treated by his particular system of calisthenics and weightlifting.

However, the strongman did not spend all of his time exercising or coaching. He was also fond of cars—especially fast ones. Eugen was never happier than when he was careening down the road at the then-outrageous speed of forty miles per hour. Ironically, it was his love affair with motoring that caused his death. According to the story his family later told, the fifty-eight-year-old strongman took a corner too quickly and overturned his car. When he attempted to right the car by himself, he burst a blood vessel in his brain and died several weeks later.

## Summary

Eugen Sandow lived life in high gear. He was convinced that his goals were good and that people needed to hear his message. Without that drive, Eugen might never have become the great popularizer of bodybuilding. He became a symbol of health and strength for the entire world.

*David Chapman*

## Additional Sources

Chapman, David L. *Sandow the Magnificent: Eugen Sandow and the Beginnings of Bodybuilding*. Rev. ed. Urbana: University of Illinois Press, 2006.

Daley, Caroline. "The Strongman of Eugenics, Eugen Sandow." *Australian Historical Studies* 33, no. 120 (October, 2002): 233-248.

Post, Robert C. "Sandow the Magnificent: Eugen Sandow and the Beginnings of Bodybuilding." *Journal of American History* 82, no. 1 (June, 1995): 283.

Sandow, Eugen. *Body-Building: Or, Man in the Making—How to Become Healthy and Strong*. London: Gale & Polden, 1904.

_____. *Sandow on Physical Training: A Study in the Perfect Type of the Human Form*. New York: J. S. Tait & Sons, 1894.

# Michael Schumacher

**Born:** January 3, 1969
      Hürth-Hermülheim, West Germany (now
         in Germany)

## Early Life
Michael Schumacher was born to a middle-class family in Hürth-Hermülheim, West Germany (now in Germany), on January 3, 1969. His father, Rolf, unintentionally started Michael on his career path when he added a motor to his son's pedal car. After Michael crashed into a light pole, his father decided he should drive on a track, so Michael became a member of the local go-kart club at the age of four.

At first, Michael go-karted just for fun, but as his love of racing and his skills developed, the hobby became a more serious one. By 1984, he became the German junior champion at the age of fifteen. He was champion again the next year and finished second in the World Junior Karting Championships at Le Mans, France. In 1987, he dominated the German Karting Championships and also won the European Karting Championships.

## The Road to Excellence
In 1988, Michael jumped to racing Formula König cars, considered the first level in single-seaters. He won nine of the ten races he entered in his first year. At the same time, he finished second in a series for the faster Formula Ford cars. His dazzling performance brought him to the attention of Willi Weber, who immediately signed Michael to drive his Formula Three car. Weber became his manager, guiding his career for the next ten years. Michael began to think that his hobby could become a profession.

In 1990, his second year in For-

mula Three, Michael won the championship, and Weber moved him into the next phase of his career, placing him on the Mercedes Group C sports-car team. This became the final course in Michael's professional racing education.

In the summer of 1991, the Jordan Formula One team needed a substitute driver for the Belgian Grand Prix. Weber arranged for Michael to fill the seat, and Michael surprised observers by qualifying seventh on one of Formula One's most challenging tracks. In the race he withdrew with mechanical problems on the first lap, but he was already recognized as a future star.

*Michael Schumacher hoisting the winner's trophy after finishing first in the Japanese Grand Prix in 2004.* (Eriko Sugita/Reuters/Landov)

## The Emerging Champion

Almost immediately, Michael was embroiled in a Formula One controversy, as the Jordan team and the Benetton team, for whom he had also driven, argued over his contract. Characteristically, Michael ignored the legal arguments and the interpersonal politics and concentrated on his driving; Benetton eventually won his contract.

Just one year after his debut, Michael got his first win at the Belgian Grand Prix and placed third in the championship for 1992. In 1993, he finished fourth, behind Alain Prost, Ayrton Senna, and Damon Hill. A verbal feud that had developed the previous year between Michael and three-time world champion Senna continued, demonstrating Michael's confidence and his growing skill in the psychological games often played among rival drivers.

In 1994, Michael and Formula One had tumultuous years. At the Grand Prix of San Marino, rookie Roland Ratzenberger was killed in a crash during a qualifying race. The next day, Senna crashed and was killed in the early laps of the race. Michael went on to win the race, not knowing until after the finish that Senna had died. After several days of serious thinking, Michael decided that racing was important enough to him to continue, and he won his next race, at Monaco. He also assumed leadership of the Formula One Racing Drivers Association and campaigned for greater safety measures.

Michael's difficult season continued as he was disqualified from four races for technical reasons. A war of words raged in the press between Michael and Hill, a new rival. The championship came down to the last race, in Australia. Though Michael collided with Hill in what many thought was a deliberate crash, he won the race and became world champion by one point. In 1995, he equaled Nigel Mansell's record of nine wins in one season and took the championship again, becoming the youngest-ever two-time champion.

## Continuing the Story

At the age of twenty-six, Michael had reached the top of his sport and challenged himself by moving to another team. He accepted an offer of $25 million a year from the famous Ferrari team and became one of the highest-paid athletes in the world. Ferrari had not won a championship since 1979

### Major Racing Finishes

| Year | Series | Place |
|------|--------|-------|
| 1984-85 | German Junior Karting | 1st |
| 1986 | European Karting | 3d |
| 1987 | German Karting | 1st |
| | European Karting | 1st |
| 1988 | German Formula König | 1st |
| 1989 | German Formula Three | 3d |
| 1990 | World Endurance | — |
| 1991 | German Formula Three | 1st |
| | World Endurance | — |
| | Formula One debut | — |
| 1992 | World Formula One | 3d |
| 1993 | World Formula One | 4th |
| 1994-95, 2000-04 | World Formula One | 1st |
| 1996 | World Formula One | 3d |
| 1997 | World Formula One | — |
| 1998 | World Formula One | 2d |
| 1999 | World Formula One | 5th |
| 2005 | World Formula One | 3d |
| 2006 | World Formula One | 2d |

and hoped Michael's skill and leadership would return the team to the forefront. In 1996, Michael battled Hill and newcomer Jacques Villeneuve to give Ferrari a third-place finish. The following year Michael was contending for the championship, with five wins, when he crashed into leader Villeneuve in the final race. Michael's aggressive style had failed him. The Formula One governing board ruled the crash deliberate and stripped Michael of his points for the year, taking away his second place in the world championship.

In 1998, Michael rebounded and finished second again, behind the superior McLaren car of Mika Häkkinen. At the 1999 British Grand Prix, a brake failure in Michael's car sent him into the tire barrier then to the hospital with a broken leg. He was out for seven races but returned to finish second at the race in Malaysia.

In 2000, Michael won five of eight races, then allowed Häkkinen to pass him in the standings. However, Häkkinen, was among the first to congratulate Michael when, at Suzuka, Japan, he won his third world championship. The Ferrari team had won for the first time in twenty-one years. With three world titles, Michael joined five other drivers on Formula One's all-time career list.

The 2000 championship was just the beginning of Schumacher's dominance; he and the Ferrari team continued to lead the sport. The 2001 season began with a forceful display of Ferrari power, as Michael won the first race of the season at Melbourne, Australia. Michael won eight more races and took his fourth world championship title. With these wins, he equaled the fifty-one Grand Prix victory record set by Prost.

In 2002, Michael continued to surpass the competition on the Formula One circuit. He improved upon his previous season's win total by taking first place on the podium in eleven races, setting a new record for most victories in a season. He earned the world championship for the fifth time, equaling the record set by Juan Manuel Fangio. In 2003, the championship was decided at the final race of the season in Japan. Michael's victory made him the only six-time world champion in the sport's history.

In 2004, Michael dominated again, storming his way to his seventh driver's championship and thirteen victories, only failing to finish in the points twice in the season. He appeared unbeatable. However, because of Federation Internationale de l'Automobile rule changes and Michelin's tire improvements, Michael's competition was able to chase him down the following season. In 2006, Michael came close to winning another championship, but an engine failure at the Suzuka track ended his hopes, as Ferenando Alonso and the Renault team triumphed.

## Summary

Michael Schumacher earned his racing reputation with hard work, determination, and natural skill. At a young age, he amazed the Formula One world with his talent and maturity. His self-confidence bordering on arrogance and aggressive style landed him in trouble more than once, but no one could deny his skill as a racer. He earned his seven world championship titles as well as his reputation as the best driver of his generation. His record was incomparable: 7 world championships, 91 victories, 154 podium finishes, 68 pole positions, and 76 fastest laps in sixteen seasons.

*Joseph W. Hinton, updated by Amanda J. Bahr-Evola*

## Additional Sources

Allen, James. *Michael Schumacher: Driven to Extremes.* London: Bantam, 2000.

Allsop, Derek. *Michael Schumacher: Formula for Success.* Osceola, Wis.: Motorbooks International, 1996.

Collings, Timothy. *Schumacher: The Life and Times of the New Formula One Champion.* Osceola, Wis.: Motorbooks International, 1996.

Domenjoz, Luc, and David Waldron. *Michael Schumacher: Rise of a Genius.* Bath, Somerset, England: Parragon, 2002.

Sparling, Ken. *Michael Schumacher.* Willowdale, Ont.: Firefly Books, 1999.

# *Arnold Schwarzenegger*

**Born:** July 30, 1947
  Thal, near Graz, Austria
**Also known as:** Arnold Alois Schwarzenegger
 (full name); the Austrian Oak; the Governator

## Early Life

Arnold Alois Schwarzenegger was born in the village of Thal, Austria, near the city of Graz, on July 30, 1947, to Aurelia and Gustav Schwarzenegger. While he was still a boy, Arnold shifted his interest from soccer to bodybuilding because it emphasized the individual. He worked out and displayed his already muscular body at the small lake in Thal. He used the primitive weightlifting equipment at the Graz Athletic Union, where Kurt Marnul, Mr. Austria, suggested that Arnold take anabolic steroids, then legally available and commonly used by bodybuilders. More important than the steroids, however, were Arnold's genetic tendency toward muscularity and his extreme determination. Having seen a magazine cover with bodybuilder Reg Park posing as Hercules, Arnold decided that he wanted to become Mr. Universe, a movie star, and a rich man.

## The Road to Excellence

Before he could achieve his goals, however, he had to serve in the Austrian army, which he entered on October 1, 1965. Late in that month he went absent without leave and traveled to Stuttgart, in Germany, to enter the junior division of the Mr. Europe competition. He won, and while there, he also met two men who became his close friends: Albert Busek and Franco Columbu. Busek invited Arnold

*Arnold Schwarzenegger, who was Mr. Olympia seven times.* (Hulton Archive/Getty Images)

## Major Championships

| Year | Competition | Place |
|------|-------------|-------|
| 1966 | Mr. Europe | 1st |
| | International Powerlifting Championship | 1st |
| | NABBA Amateur Mr. Universe | 2d |
| 1967 | NABBA Amateur Mr. Universe | 1st |
| 1968 | IFBB Mr. Universe | 2d |
| 1968-70 | NABBA Professional Mr. Universe | 1st |
| 1969 | IFBB Mr. Universe | 1st |
| | Mr. Olympia | 2d |
| 1970 | Mr. World | 1st |
| 1970-75, 1980 | Mr. Olympia | 1st |

to move to Munich, Germany, after he finished his military obligation and work out in facilities owned by Busek's boss. When Arnold returned to his army post, he spent a week in its prison. However, he had become a hero by daring to break a rule and winning a title. Thus, he served as part of a tank crew in the mornings and worked out in the afternoons. In January, 1966, he appeared on the cover of a bodybuilding magazine that Busek edited.

Arriving in Munich as a civilian on August 1, 1966, Arnold worked as a trainer in a gymnasium but preferred to be the one exercising. His appearance of immense strength was not illusory, as demonstrated by his win in the heavyweight class of the 1966 International Powerlifting Championships and his German Powerlifting Championship two years later. His focus, though, was still on bodybuilding, and he won the 1966 Mr. Europe and the amateur and professional Mr. Universe contests of the National Amateur Bodybuilders' Association in 1967 and 1968, respectively.

### The Emerging Champion

After his victory in London in 1968, Arnold traveled to the United States for the first time, intending to win the Mr. Universe title of the International Federation of Bodybuilders (IFBB). In Miami, however, he lost the contest to the lighter, shorter Frank Zane. Losing self-confidence and able to speak only German fluently, Arnold accepted an invitation from Joe Weider, a publisher of bodybuilding magazines, to travel to Los Angeles to train. In California, Arnold worked at Gold's Gym with his usual fanaticism not only to increase the size of his muscles but also to lose the flab that had counted against him in Miami. Soon, at Arnold's request, Weider

brought Columbu to the United States, and the two European bodybuilders shared an apartment. Weider intended to promote his magazines by making Arnold even more famous, and Arnold was happy to cooperate.

Arnold continued to win bodybuilding titles, including the Mr. Olympia contest, the most prestigious in the IFBB. After finishing second in 1969, Arnold went on to win the title six years in a row, from 1970 to 1975. As the documentary *Pumping Iron* (1977) shows, Arnold announced his retirement from competitive bodybuilding after his 1975 triumph. He did, however, make a surprising reappearance in the Mr. Olympia contest in 1980, achieving a controversial victory over Zane.

### Continuing the Story

Arnold's movie career had started with his title role in the low-budget *Hercules in New York* (1970). Before the release of *Pumping Iron*, he had also appeared in *The Long Goodbye* (1973) and *Stay Hungry* (1976). For the latter, he won a Golden Globe Award for the best motion picture debut by a man. Even though his talent as an actor was debatable, Arnold's compelling presence in front of cameras, like his presence on bodybuilding stages, led to other movie roles. He achieved Hollywood stardom in *Conan the Barbarian* (1982) and superstardom in *The Terminator* (1984). Thanks to his energetic promotion of his enterprises, his smart investments, and the huge payments for his screen performances, he became rich.

On September 16, 1983, Arnold became a U.S. citizen. With him at the ceremony was his close companion Maria Shriver, a television journalist and the niece of the late, former president John F. Kennedy. In 1986, Arnold and Maria married and eventually had four children. Despite his marital alliance with a prominent Democratic family, Arnold was a Republican and an admirer of President Ronald Reagan. Soon after taking office in 1989, President George H. W. Bush named Arnold the chair-

## Honors and Awards

| | |
|------|------|
| 1966 | Named Best Built Man of Europe |
| 1989 | Appointed chairman of President's Council on Physical Fitness |
| 2003 | Elected governor of California |
| 2006 | Reelected governor |

man of the President's Council on Physical Fitness and Sports. Arnold served with enthusiasm, as he also served Special Olympics, founded by his mother-in-law.

Eventually, when age seemed to be ending his career in action movies, Arnold turned even more toward public life. In a recall election in 2003, he overcame allegations of sexual misbehavior to win a plurality and become the thirty-eighth governor of California. Taking positions to the left of many Republicans and sometimes at odds with the Roman Catholic Church, to which he belonged, Arnold achieved another goal by winning a majority in his reelection campaign in 2006.

## Summary

As in bodybuilding, powerlifting, and movie-making, Arnold Schwarzenegger succeeded in politics. Although some observers saw him as mainly an outgoing entertainer whose most notable ability was to project a charming image, others saw him as a great American immigrant success story. For the latter group, he was the poor but gifted immigrant who, by hard and intelligent work, not only popularized bodybuilding but also rose to the top in all of his endeavors.

*David Chapman, updated by Victor Lindsey*

## Additional Sources

Andrews, Nigel. *True Myths: The Life and Times of Arnold Schwarzenegger from Pumping Iron to Governor of California.* New York: Bloomsbury, 2003.

Blitz, Michael, and Louise Krasniewicz. *Why Arnold Matters: The Rise of a Cultural Icon.* New York: Basic Books, 2004.

Leamer, Laurence. *Fantastic: The Life of Arnold Schwarzenegger.* New York: St. Martin's Press, 2005.

Mathews, Joe. *The People's Machine: Arnold Schwarzenegger and the Rise of Blockbuster Democracy.* New York: PublicAffairs, 2006.

# *Dave Scott*

**Born:** January 4, 1954
      Woodland, California
**Also known as:** David Forshee Scott

## Early Life

David Forshee Scott was born on January 4, 1954, in Woodland, California, to Verne H. Scott, a civil engineering professor, and Dorothy J. (Forshee) Scott. As one of three children, Dave learned to appreciate family activities, which included sports such as swimming. Growing up in Northern California, he also spent many hours in the vast wilderness of the region.

Dave went to Davis High School, where he excelled at water polo, swimming, and basketball. He was named an all-American in water polo, becoming the first all-American at Davis High School in any sport. After high school, Dave attended the University of California at Davis (UC Davis), where his father taught civil engineering. Dave majored in physical education and exercise physiology.

## The Road to Excellence

Dave continued to participate in water polo and swimming at UC Davis. During his college career, he earned all-American honors in swimming and made the all-conference team twice in water polo. Dave also played in two National Collegiate Athletic Association (NCAA) water-polo championships.

After graduation in 1976, he became the head coach for the Davis Aquatic Masters program. He had started with the program in 1974, when it had merely eleven members. Dave remained the head coach of the program until 1981; by that year, the membership had swelled to 425, making it the largest aquatic masters program in the United States. Sometimes, Dave coached and counseled as many as four hundred people a day. In ad-

Dave Scott, who won the Hawaii Ironman Triathlon six times from 1980 to 1987. (Courtesy of Dave Scott)

dition to the exercise Dave got at work, he liked to go on long runs during his free hours.

Dave was an enthusiastic spokesman for the virtues of physical fitness. He participated in clinics and spoke at club meetings and seminars. Dave had found an outlet for inspiring others to take physical fitness seriously, but he also needed some competitive outlets to challenge himself. He began entering long-distance swimming events, including the 2.4-mile Hawaiian Open Water Swim at Waikiki. Dave won the Waikiki event in 1978 and 1979. At the 1978 awards ceremony, he was asked to compete in the newly created Ironman Triathlon event. The Ironman consisted of a 2.4-mile swim, a 112-mile bike ride, and a 26.2-mile run, each completed in succession on a single day. The first Ironman was held in 1978. Dave was intrigued by the thought of competing, and in 1979, he trained for the Ironman.

## The Emerging Champion

Dave felt confident of his ability to handle the swimming portion of the Ironman, but he was less sure of his cycling and running skills. With the help of friends, Dave pushed himself until he felt confident that he could complete all three sections of the triathlon. In addition to physical training, he experimented with a special diet, high in complex carbohydrates but low in fat. Since the triathlon was such a new event, there had not been any studies done that could tell Dave how to train. The 6-foot 160-pound athlete took it upon himself to test the limits of what one person could do physically. Dave had to adapt both his mind and body in order to complete a superhuman task.

In 1980, Dave competed in his first Ironman. He surprised everyone but himself by not only winning the event but also setting a new record time of 9 hours, 24

## Major Championships

| | |
|---|---|
| 1980, 1982-84, 1986-87 | Hawaii Ironman Triathlon |
| 1982 | Hanover Hamptons Triathlon |
| | Southhampton Triathlon |
| | USTS Portland Triathlon |
| | USTS San Diego Triathlon |
| | USTS Seattle Triathlon |
| 1983, 1986 | Gulf Coast Triathlon |
| 1985, 1989 | Japan Ironman Triathlon |
| | USTS Miami Triathlon |
| 1988 | USTS Houston Triathlon |
| 1989 | USTS Phoenix Triathlon |

minutes, and 33 seconds. He shattered the old record by almost 2 hours. His workouts, which had lasted up to nine hours a day, had paid off. However, beyond the intense training, it had been Dave's passion to excel that had made him a champion.

Injuries forced Dave to miss the 1981 Ironman, but he was in prime shape for 1982. Whereas the 1980 Ironman competition was not billed as a world championship, the 1982 competition was, and the competition was renamed the Ironman Triathlon World Championship. The event had also been moved from the early part of the year to October and was held at Kono, Hawaii. The changes did not seem to affect Dave, who won easily, setting a new record with a time of 9 hours, 8 minutes, and 23 seconds.

### Continuing the Story

Dave was called the ultimate triathlete. In addition to 1980 and 1982, Dave went on to capture the Ironman title in 1983, 1984, 1986, and 1987. In 1984, he became the first to finish the Ironman in less than 9 hours. The first Ironman in 1978 attracted merely fifteen competitors, but by the 1990's, the Ironman was drawing nearly 1,500 triathletes. Competition had become so fierce that triathletes had to qualify for the world championship at Kono by doing well at other events.

Dave's principal rival during the late 1980's was Mark Allen. In 1986 and 1987, Dave prevailed at the Ironman, but in 1989, Allen won the first of his many Ironman championships. The 1989 race is considered one of the most dramatic duels in triathlon history. Dave finished with a remarkable time of just over 8 hours and 10 minutes, but Allen's time was 58 seconds faster. In 1989, Dave began to suffer from various injuries, including a painful knee condition, and in the summer of 1991, he retired from competition. Dave came out of retirement to compete in the Hawaii Ironman Triathlon two more times, in 1994 and 1996, finishing in second place overall and fifth overall, respectively.

Dave devoted himself to coaching, lecturing, conducting clinics, and writing, and he was able to spend more time with his wife and children. He also appeared as a commentator and analyst for triathlon competitions on several networks in the United States and Canada. For his extraordinary accomplishments, Dave was the first inductee of the Ironman Hall of Fame in 1993.

### Summary

Dave Scott combined intense training habits, a strict diet, and an iron will to become the first great triathlete. He helped to bring triathlons to the attention of the public, transforming the competitions from the hobby of a few fitness fanatics into a worldwide sport.

*Jeffry Jensen*

### Additional Sources

Finch, Michael. *Triathlon Training*. Champaign, Ill.: Human Kinetics, 2004.

Keegan, Paul. "Swim. Bike. Run. Repeat?" *Outside* 23, no. 11 (November, 1998): 171-173.

Noakes, Timothy. *Lore of Running*. Champaign, Ill.: Human Kinetics, 2003.

Scott, Dave, and Liz Barrett. *Dave Scott's Triathlon Training*. New York: Simon & Schuster, 1986.

## Honors and Awards

| | |
|---|---|
| 1982 | *City Sports* magazine Athlete of the Year |
| 1987 | *Triathlete* magazine Outstanding Performance Award |
| 1987-88 | *Triathlon Today* All-American |
| 1993 | Ironman Hall of Fame |
| 1999 | *Triathlete* magazine Hall of Fame |

# *Wendell Scott*

**Born:** August 28, 1921
Danville, Virginia
**Died:** December 23, 1990
Danville, Virginia

### Early Life

Wendell Scott was the founding father of African American stock-car racing. He was born on August 28, 1921, in Danville, Virginia, and studied at Danville High School, leaving after eleventh grade. He did not perform especially well in athletics or academics but played baseball enthusiastically. Baseball remained a lifelong interest.

During World War II, Wendell served in the U.S. Army from 1942 to 1945 and was stationed in Cheyenne, Wyoming, and Europe. An able mechanic, Wendell ended his war service in charge of a convoy of trucks. Many successful National Association for Stock Car Auto Racing (NASCAR) drivers bloomed under the same sort of apprenticeship. Wendell joined Grand National racing in 1961, at Spartanburg, South Carolina.

### The Road to Excellence

Wendell's initial success came in 1959, when he won the Sportsman Racing Championship at Southside Speedway in Richmond, Virginia. The same year, he captured the Virginia Championship for stock car drivers. During his early years, Wendell struggled for the financial backing necessary to turn out a competitive racing machine. In one race, he endured the frustration of a broken seat and gas pedal.

During the 1961 racing season, Wendell ranked thirty-second in national point standings. The next year, he demonstrated his true racing form. At the wheel of a 1961 Chevrolet, he started forty-one races and finished among the top ten on seventeen occasions. In 1963, Wendell started forty-seven races with fifteen top-ten finishes. Wendell still drove his faithful 1961 Chevrolet, logging 6,163.4 miles in competitive racing. He recorded his only 1963 NASCAR victory in a Jacksonville, Florida, race. His next-best performance that year was a fifth-place finish at Spartanburg, South Carolina.

### The Emerging Champion

In 1964, Wendell began the season in a 1962 Chevrolet. Halfway through the season, Wendell opted for a 1963 Ford and immediately enjoyed greater success. With the Ford, he generated greater acceleration. In 1966, he finished sixth in the Grand National standings, earning $16,780 in forty-five starts, finishing three times among the top five, and ranking seventeen times in the top ten. For many years, he occupied the spotlight as the only African American driver on the circuit.

Like many auto racers, Wendell possessed superstitions. He never wore green or allowed green coloring on his automobile or allowed peanuts to

*Wendell Scott, who earned his only NASCAR victory in 1964 at Speedway Park in Jacksonville, Florida.* (Courtesy of Betty Carlan/International Motorsports Hall of Fame)

be consumed in his pits or garage area. He did experience some prejudice as a black racer but never let it affect him.

Wendell launched his racing career just as NASCAR began to achieve momentum as a sport. The Daytona International Speedway opened in 1959, while speedways opened at Atlanta, Georgia, and Charlotte, North Carolina, in 1960. The 1961 Firecracker 400 race at Daytona Beach, Florida, was televised, signifying national coverage for the sport.

### Continuing the Story

Wendell's best NASCAR season came in 1969, when he finished eleven times in the top ten and collected $27,542 in prize money. In May, 1973, Wendell was involved in a nineteen-vehicle wreck during the Talladega race. Wendell's 1971 Mercury was demolished, and he suffered the first serious injuries of his racing career. He ended up with three fractured ribs, two fractures in the pelvic girdle, a fractured right knee, two fractures of the left knee, a fractured leg, and an arm laceration that necessitated sixty stitches.

Wendell died on December 23, 1990, at the age of sixty-nine, having suffered from spinal cancer, bilateral pneumonia, high blood pressure, and kidney ailments. He frequently described himself as an aging pugilist: "I guess I'm like a washed-up prize fighter. He knows it's the last round, and he knows he's beat, but he keeps trying to land that knockout punch." At his Danville, Virginia, funeral, many NASCAR drivers paid respects to the pioneer racer who started more than five hundred Grand National races and finished among the top five twenty times.

### Summary

In 1977 the film *Greased Lightning* reprised Wendell Scott's life, career, successes, and setbacks. Wen-

---

### Racing Record

| 1959 | Sportsman Racing Championship—Richmond, Virginia Virginia Championship |
|------|----------------------------|
| 1962 | Raced forty-one times, seventeen top-ten finishes |
| 1963 | Raced forty-seven times, fifteen top-ten finishes NASCAR win in Jacksonville, Florida |
| 1966 | Raced forty-five times, seventeen top-ten finishes |
| 1969 | Eleven top-ten NASCAR finishes |

dell's life was an example of how hard it was for any NASCAR racer, white or black, to succeed. It is of sociocultural significance that Wendell's successful years, in the late 1960's, occurred during the era of the Civil Rights movement, Martin Luther King, Jr.'s prominence and death, and racial tensions that threatened to pull the United States into major social disorder. Wendell battled to survive as a lone black driver in a culture of racial discrimination and segregation. As there were no African American drivers on the NASCAR circuit even at the start of the twenty-first century, Wendell's accomplishments seem all the more admirable.

*Scott A. G. M. Crawford*

### Additional Sources

Alleyne, Sonia, and T. R. Witcher. "The New Face of NASCAR." *Black Enterprise* 34, no. 9 (April, 2004): 108-118.

Black American Racers Association. *Black Racers Yearbook 1974: Official Annual of the Black American Racers Association.* Trenton, N.J.: The Association, 1974.

McLaurin, James. *NASCAR's Most Wanted: The Top Ten Book of Outrageous Drivers, Wild Wrecks, and Other Oddities.* Washington, D.C.: Brassey's, 2001.

Strosnider, J. Steve. *Tales from the Track: Stories from the Early Days of Racing.* Victoria, B.C.: Trafford, 2002.

# *Ayrton Senna*

**Born:** March 21, 1960
São Paulo, Brazil
**Died:** May 1, 1994
Bologna, Italy
**Also known as:** Ayrton Senna da Silva (full name)

## Early Life

Ayrton Senna da Silva was born on March 21, 1960, in São Paulo, Brazil. He was the oldest son of Milton da Silva, a well-to-do São Paulo businessman. Ayrton grew up in a loving family environment. At the age of four, his father built him his first go-kart. When Ayrton started school, his father let it be known that if Ayrton did not have good monthly school reports, then he would not be allowed to use the go-kart for a month.

In July, 1973, Ayrton made his debut in his first go-kart race. He started in the 100-cubic-centimeter category. After racing in that category for several years, Ayrton decided to contend for the Kart World Championship. In 1977, the championship was held at Le Mans, France, and Ayrton finished a respectable sixth. He finished second in 1979 and 1980 and fourth in 1981. During his years of go-kart racing, Ayrton won the South American Championship twice, in 1977 and 1978, and the Brazilian Championship four times, in 1978, 1979, 1980, and 1981.

## The Road to Excellence

After eight years of go-kart racing, Ayrton decided to try auto racing. Ayrton was a shy young man, but he was brimming with determination. In March, 1981, he competed in his first British Formula Ford 1600 car race, driving a Van Diemen RF80-Ford. His previous go-kart experience held him in good stead, and Ayrton had his first win in only his third race. By the end of the Formula Ford season, he had won twelve of his twenty races.

For all of his talent on the track, however, Ayrton was having difficulty understanding how the racing business functioned. He needed to find financing to advance to more competitive circuits. Moreover, his marriage to his childhood sweetheart Liliane was damaged by his racing frustrations. By the time

the 1982 racing season began, Ayrton had overcome his doubts about continuing to race and had found the necessary funding, but his marriage was dissolved after only six months.

In 1982, Ayrton began racing in Formula Ford 2000 races, driving a Van Diemen RF82-Ford for Rushen Green Racing. He competed in both the British and European races, entering twenty-seven and winning twenty-one. Ayrton graduated to British Formula Three races for the next season, driving for West Surrey Racing in a Ralt RT3-Toyota. Ayrton won the first nine races of the season and a total of twelve rounds of the British Formula Three Championship on his way to dethroning titleholder Martin Brundle. Racing experts were amazed by Ayrton's racing talent, as well as by his complete refusal to accept anything less than victory.

## The Emerging Champion

With his Formula Three exploits, Ayrton had impressed various Formula One sponsors. After much thought, Ayrton decided to team up with Toleman Group Motorsport. He drove in his first Formula One competition on March 25, 1984, at the Brazilian Grand Prix in Rio de Janeiro, driving a Toleman TG183B-Hart. Although Ayrton did not win a Grand Prix race during the 1984 season, he im-

---

### *Grand Prix Victories*

| | |
|---:|---|
| 1985 | Portuguese Grand Prix |
| 1985, 1988-91 | Belgian Grand Prix |
| 1986-88 | Detroit Grand Prix |
| 1986, 1989 | Spanish Grand Prix |
| 1987, 1989-93 | Monaco Grand Prix |
| 1988-89, 1991 | San Marino Grand Prix |
| 1988-90 | German Grand Prix |
| 1988, 1990 | Canadian Grand Prix |
| 1988, 1991-92 | Hungarian Grand Prix |
| 1988, 1993 | British Grand Prix |
| | Japanese Grand Prix |
| 1989 | Mexican Grand Prix |
| 1990-91 | U.S. Grand Prix |
| 1990, 1992 | Italian Grand Prix |
| 1991, 1993 | Australian Grand Prix |
| | Brazilian Grand Prix |

## Honors and Awards

1988, 1990-91   World Championship of Drivers
1994   Brazilian Grand Cross of Merit

pressed larger and wealthier racing teams. Ayrton could not resist the chance to join John Player Team Lotus for the 1985 season, since Lotus could afford more sophisticated equipment. Driving a Lotus 97T-Renault, Ayrton won his first Grand Prix race in Portugal on April 21, 1985.

Ayrton's first year with Team Lotus was relatively successful; he won two races and finished fourth in Formula One world championship points. Ayrton, though, was disappointed with the results. He made it clear that for next season he was to be Team Lotus's number-one driver. Ayrton finished fourth again in world championship points in 1986 and third in 1987, however, and he came to the conclusion that he was never going to contend for the world championship unless he changed teams. In 1988, Ayrton joined the Honda Marlboro McLaren team. Alain Prost, a former world champion, also drove for McLaren, but Ayrton nevertheless captured his first Formula One championship by winning eight of the sixteen Grand Prix in which he was entered.

### Continuing the Story

Ayrton and Prost were once again teammates for the 1989 season. Both were intense competitors, and relations between the two were not always civil. Ayrton was always an aggressive driver, and his racing tactics were sometimes questioned by those with whom he competed. In 1989, Prost won the championship, and Ayrton finished second. Prost was well liked by the media, whereas Ayrton had no interest in talking to the press. A deeply religious man, he remained close to his family and guarded his privacy. All of his energy was funneled into his racing. Ayrton found little or no time for the added commitments of a world champion driver.

In 1990, Prost left the McLaren team and joined Ferrari. The two drivers again contended for the championship, but this time Ayrton won the title, and Prost had to settle for second place. Ayrton won his third world championship in 1991, while

Prost finished a distant fifth. Nigel Mansell captured the title in 1992, and Prost came back to win it in 1993, with Ayrton finishing second.

After the 1993 season, Prost announced his retirement; Mansell had left the Formula One circuit to race Indy cars. Ayrton was thus the odds-on favorite for the 1994 title. Early in the 1994 season, however, Ayrton was leading the field at the San Marino Grand Prix when his car left the course at full speed and crashed into a concrete wall. He was rushed to a nearby hospital, but his injuries were severe, and he was pronounced dead hours after the accident. The Brazilian government declared three days of national mourning in his honor, and hundreds of thousands of fans attended his funeral services in São Paulo. Even his most bitter rivals mourned him publicly, conceding that he had been one of the top drivers in Formula One history. At the time of his death, his career total of forty-one Formula One victories left him second only to Prost.

### Summary

Ayrton Senna combined remarkable racing technique with a fiery spirit to reach the top of Formula One competition. His untimely death was a major loss to auto racing.

*Jeffry Jensen*

### Additional Sources

Cahier, Paul-Henri. *Senna by Cahier.* Richmond, Surrey, England: Hazleton, 2004.

Henry, Alan. *Ayrton Senna: One Year On.* Osceola, Wis.: Motorbooks International, 1995.

Hilton, Christopher. *Ayrton Senna: As Time Goes By.* Newbury Park, Calif.: Haynes, 1999.

_____. *Ayrton Senna: The Whole Story.* Newbury Park, Calif.: Haynes North America, 2004.

_____. *Memories of Ayrton.* Newbury Park, Calif.: Haynes North America, 2003.

Ménard, Pierre, and Jacques Vassal. *Ayrton Senna: Above and Beyond.* St. Sulpice, Switzerland: Chronosports, 2003.

Rubython, Tom. *The Life of Senna.* London: BusinessF1, 2004.

Senna, Ayrton. *Ayrton Senna's Principles of Race Driving.* Osceola, Wis.: Motorbooks International, 1993.

# Willie Shoemaker

**Born:** August 19, 1931
  near Fabens, Texas
**Died:** October 12, 2003
  San Marino, California
**Also known as:** William Lee Shoemaker (full name); the Shoe; Bill Shoemaker

## Early Life

William Lee "Willie" Shoemaker was born on August 19, 1931, in a farmhouse near Fabens, Texas, a west Texas farm town. The child of Babe, a cotton-mill worker, and Ruby Shoemaker, Willie was born prematurely and weighed only 2½ pounds. The doctor told the Shoemakers that Willie would not live through the night and that he would make arrangements for the funeral. Willie's grandmother put the baby in a shoebox and placed him in the oven, leaving the door of the oven ajar so that he could breathe. Miraculously, he lived.

Willie's parents were divorced when he was four years old, and his mother took him to Winters, in central Texas, to live with her parents, who were sharecroppers. On his grandparents' farm, Willie rode his first horse at the age of six.

At the age of ten, Willie moved to the San Gabriel Valley in California to live with his father and stepmother. At El Monte High School, Willie failed to make the football and basketball teams but wrestled in the 95-105-pound division, finishing undefeated. He dropped out of school in the eleventh grade at the age of sixteen.

## The Road to Excellence

After leaving school, Willie took a job cleaning stalls at the Suzy Q Ranch in La Puente, California, where he earned $75 a month plus room and board. Willie soon advanced to a new position at the ranch: exercising horses and breaking yearlings. Trainer George Reeves soon realized that Willie had potential as a jockey and arranged for him to ride in his first race on March 19, 1949, aboard Waxahachie at Golden Gate Fields in Albany, California. At the age of seventeen, the 4-foot, 100-pound jockey finished fifth in his first race.

Willie's first victory came shortly thereafter, on April 20, 1949, when he rode Shafter V. That was only the first of the 219 races that Willie won in 1949. In 1950, he tied with Joe Culmone for the national riding championship with 388 wins. Willie's mounts earned $844,040, while his great predecessor and friend, Eddie Arcaro, earned $1,410,160. Willie won more money than any other jockey in 1951, 1953, and 1954, losing to Arcaro in 1952.

## The Emerging Champion

In 1955, Willie won his first Kentucky Derby, riding Swaps to a 1½-length victory and defeating Arcaro. A year later, Willie became the first jockey to win more than $2 million in purse money.

Although Willie became a champion soon after his career began and experienced much success as

Willie Shoemaker, who won the Kentucky Derby four times, along the way earning recognition as perhaps the greatest jockey of all time. (Courtesy of Amateur Athletic Foundation of Los Angeles)

a young jockey, his career was not without adversity. He suffered a humiliating defeat in the Kentucky Derby in 1957, riding Gallant Man. He was locked in a struggle with Iron Liege, ridden by Bill Hartack, when he mistook the sixteenth pole for the finish line and briefly stood up in the saddle; as a result, Gallant Man was passed and defeated by Iron Liege.

Willie rebounded quickly from that embarrassing defeat and won his first Belmont Stakes the next month aboard Gallant Man. The next year, Willie won his second Kentucky Derby aboard Tomy Lee and his second Belmont Stakes aboard Sword Dancer. From 1958 to 1964, he led the nation in money won and in victories.

In 1962, Willie won the Belmont Stakes riding Jaipur, and in 1963, he won the Preakness Stakes on Candy Spots. In 1965, he won the Kentucky Derby, and in 1967, he won both the Preakness and the Belmont and rode Damascus to the horse of the year title. That year, Willie's mounts earned more than $3 million.

Beginning in 1968, Willie could not compete for thirteen months because he broke a leg when a horse fell on him at the Santa Anita track. His convalescence was difficult, and he had become somewhat bored with racing. His bad luck continued into the next year. He entered competition again in February of 1969, but on April 30, a horse flipped over backward on him, crushed his pelvis, tore his bladder, and damaged nerves in his legs. Willie was out for another three months, and there was doubt that he would ever ride again. In 1970, however, at the age of thirty-nine, he surpassed Johnny Longden as the jockey with the most victories in the history of horse racing, 6,033 wins.

---

### Major Championship Victories

| Year | Race | Horse |
| --- | --- | --- |
| 1955 | Kentucky Derby | Swaps |
| 1957 | Belmont Stakes | Gallant Man |
| 1958 | Belmont Stakes | Sword Dancer |
|  | Kentucky Derby | Tomy Lee |
| 1962 | Belmont Stakes | Jaipur |
| 1963 | Preakness Stakes | Candy Spots |
| 1965 | Kentucky Derby | Lucky Debonair |
| 1967 | Belmont Stakes | Damascus |
|  | Preakness Stakes | Damascus |
| 1975 | Belmont Stakes | Avatar |
| 1986 | Kentucky Derby | Ferdinand |
| 1987 | Breeders' Cup Classic | Ferdinand |

---

Willie seemed to be rejuvenated, and he continued his career far beyond the age when most jockeys retire. On March 3, 1985, he became the first jockey to earn $100 million in purse money, riding Lord at War in the Santa Anita Handicap. He earned his 8,446th career win and his 917th stakes victory. In 1986, at the age of fifty-four, Willie won the Kentucky Derby, riding Ferdinand, for his fourth Derby win. With this victory, he became the oldest rider by a dozen years to win the Kentucky Derby. The next day, he won the John Henry Handicap at the Santa Anita Race Track, riding Palace Music, and later rode Ferdinand to a second-place finish in the Preakness and a third-place finish in the Belmont Stakes. In December, he brought Ferdinand from last place to win the Malibu Stakes.

In February of 1987, Willie had arthroscopic surgery to repair torn cartilage in his left knee. He recovered quickly to record a victory in the San Luis Obispo Handicap two weeks after his surgery. In 1987, he finished sixth in the Kentucky Derby and did not compete in any other triple-crown races during that year.

### Continuing the Story

In June of 1987, at Hollywood Park in Inglewood, California, Willie, once again atop Ferdinand, defeated the 1987 Kentucky Derby winner, Alysheba, to win his first Breeders' Cup Classic. At the end of 1987, Willie had ridden in five different decades, had won 8,706 races, and had earned $110 million in prize money. He had won 983 stakes victories and 245 races

---

### Records and Milestones

8,833 victories—the highest total of all time until broken by Laffit Pincay in 1999
Annual money leader (1951, 1953-54, 1958-64)

### Honors and Awards

| | |
| --- | --- |
| 1958 | Inducted into Jockeys' Hall of Fame |
| 1971 | National Turf Writers' Association Joe Palmer Award |
| 1976 | Eclipse Award, Special Award |
| 1981 | Eclipse Award, Outstanding Jockey |
|  | Eclipse Award, Award of Merit |
| 1990 | Mike Venezia Memorial Award |

worth more than $100,000. He had won four Kentucky Derbys, five Belmonts and Woodward Stakes, ten Santa Anita Handicaps, and eight Hollywood Gold Cups.

Willie retired from racing in 1990. His had 8,833 career wins, 1,009 stake victories, 257 stake races with values of $100,000 or more, and more than $123 million in purses. After retiring, Willie continued his career in horse racing as a horse trainer.

In April of 1991, Willie was involved in an automobile accident that left him paralyzed from the neck down. He would never ride again but worked as a trainer until 1997. He died in 2003. His career is commemorated at Santa Anita with a life-size statue.

## Summary

Willie Shoemaker was one of the greatest riders who ever raced, yet for many years he was always known as the jockey who misjudged the finish line in the 1957 Kentucky Derby. His victory at the 1986 Kentucky Derby at the age of fifty-four, however, erased that humiliating defeat.

Willie was highly praised by his peers, who said that he did everything well, having good strength and skill. He was most noted, however, for his "touch" with the horses. Willie was once known as the "Silent Shoe," but now most jockeys think that he talked exceptionally well to the horses.

*Susan J. Bandy*

## Additional Sources

Blood-Horse Publications. *Horse Racing's Top One Hundred Moments.* Lexington, Ky.: Author, 2006.

Ennor, George, and Bill Mooney. *The World Encyclopedia of Horse Racing: An Illustrated Guide.* London: Carlton, 2001.

Shoemaker, Willie. *Shoe: Willie Shoemaker's Illustrated Book of Racing.* Chicago: Rand McNally, 1976.

Stevens, Gary, Mervyn Kaufman, and Bill Shoemaker. *The Perfect Ride.* Secaucus, N.J.: Citadel Press, 2002.

# *Jim Shoulders*

**Born:** May 13, 1928
     Tulsa, Oklahoma
**Died:** June 20, 2007
     Henryetta, Oklahoma
**Also known as:** James Arthur Shoulders (full
  name)

### Early Life

James Arthur Shoulders was born on May 13, 1928, in Tulsa, Oklahoma. Ironically, the boy who was to become one of the all-time great rodeo stars was not raised on a ranch. His father, Jim Shoulders, was an auto mechanic who worked in the city. Jim did spend much of his early childhood on his grandfather's farm, however.

Jim first became interested in rodeo when his older brother, Marvin, began entering amateur contests. When he was thirteen, Jim was given his first chance to ride a bull at a rodeo near Collinsville, Oklahoma. Jim begged his brother to let him sit on the bull. The instant the bull made its first lunge in the chute, Jim clambered to safety. Marvin shoved him back on and said, "All right, kid, you want to rodeo. It's now or never." Jim accepted his brother's challenge and spurred his bull out before cheering onlookers. That day was the beginning of a long career.

### The Road to Excellence

Not content to live with the thrilling memory of just one rodeo performance, Jim decided to enter the rodeo at Oilton, Oklahoma, in the summer of 1942. Even though he was only fourteen years old, he competed well enough to win $18 in prize money. This small victory convinced him that he had the talent to become a professional rodeo cowboy.

After graduating from Tulsa East Center High School, Jim became a professional rodeo cowboy. He was convinced that performing in the rodeo was the only way that a "green country boy" like him could make a lot of money. Shortly after marrying his high school sweetheart, Sharon, in 1947, he scored his first national triumph at Madison Square Garden, winning two championships and $5,000. Two years later, he earned his first World Champion All-Around Cowboy title and $21,495 in winnings.

Because there were no rodeo schools for training rodeo cowboys when Jim started out, he learned how to ride bulls and broncs by experience and observation. He had not competed long before discovering that balance is much more important than strength for a rodeo performer. Like a baseball pitcher, Jim learned to keep a book "in his head," first figuring out the bronc's style and then conditioning his reactions. He also realized that, in order to stay in top shape, he had to resist the temptation to smoke and drink like the other cowboys.

*Jim Shoulders, who suffered numerous injuries in a record-setting rodeo and bull-riding career.* (ProRodeo Hall of Fame and Museum of the American Cowboy)

## The Emerging Champion

Jim was at the height of his career from 1949 through 1959. For eleven years, Jim was the best all-around cowboy on the professional circuit. During this time, he was the biggest money winner, not because he entered more rodeos than anyone else but because he always won something. Even when he did not win the big prizes, he at least walked away with second place. By the end of this period, Jim had collected sixteen world championships. Seven times, he was best in the world in bull riding, five times the all-around king, and four times bareback bronc winner.

The only year in the period of his heyday in which he was not one of the top bull riders was 1953. Jim had to sit out much of the season after a bull fell on him in Midland, Texas, and broke his collarbone. The next year, though, Jim bounced back and regained his title as champion bull rider.

Jim's success can be attributed to the fact that he was probably the toughest man in the history of rodeo competition. After breaking his collarbone in 1953, Jim participated in eight more rodeos, even though doctors had inserted a steel pin to stabilize his collarbone. In 1957, a twisting bronc snapped Jim's right collarbone again, but Jim managed to finish the ride and win the event. By 1960, his knees were in such bad shape that he had to bind them with elastic bandages before he could ride. That same year, he had to undergo plastic surgery after a spinning bull gored him in the face. Although many people would have quit after suffering only one of these injuries, Jim characteristically downplayed the severity of the pain following each mishap and then put forth his best effort. Before Jim retired, he had paid a dear price for his achievements, breaking his collarbone three times, both arms twice, both knees twice, and an ankle once.

## Continuing the Story

Although Jim officially retired from Professional Rodeo Cowboys Association (PRCA) competition in the mid-1960's, he never really quit rodeo. As director of the Mesquite Shoulders corporation, Jim produced the Mesquite Championship rodeo, which he started in 1958. This rodeo, which he operated with his family, ran every weekend from April to September. He also bred rodeo stock on his 500-acre ranch near Henryetta, Oklahoma, and became one of the top professional stock contrac-

### Record

Captured a total of sixteen individual world championship titles on the professional circuit—the most in professional rodeo

### Milestones

| | |
|---|---|
| 1949 | World Champion All-Around Cowboy |
| | Inducted into Rodeo Hall of Fame, the National Cowboy Hall of Fame |
| 1950 | Bareback Riding Champion |
| 1951 | Bull Riding Champion |
| 1954-59 | PRCA Bull Riding Champion |
| 1955 | Inducted into Rodeo Hall of Fame |
| 1956-58 | PRCA Bareback Riding Champion |
| 1956-59 | PRCA World Champion All-Around Cowboy |
| 1959 | National Finals Rodeo (NFR) Bull Riding Average Winner |
| 1974 | Inducted into Madison Square Garden Hall of Fame |
| 1975 | Inducted into Oklahoma Sports Hall of Fame |
| 1979 | Inducted into Pro Rodeo Hall of Fame |

tors. Jim perhaps derived the most pleasure from his Rodeo Riding School, which was the first of its kind. He was particularly proud of the champions that he trained, including world champion George Paell and two-time World Champion All-Around Cowboy Phil Lyne.

Jim's dominance of rodeo brought him recognition. In 1974, he became the first rodeo cowboy to enter the Madison Square Garden Hall of Fame, and in 1975, he was inducted into the Oklahoma Sports Hall of Fame. In fact, Jim's name was so identifiable to sports fans that he was featured as a Miller Lite celebrity in commercials with stars like the late Billy Martin, former New York Yankees' manager. He also endorsed such products as Wrangler jeans.

## Summary

Jim Shoulders was truly one of the legends of rodeo. He won an incredible sixteen world championships. He will be remembered as the first five-time All-Around Cowboy world champion in history. Jim's reign as champion cowboy is memorable, not only because of its duration, but also because of the tremendous endurance and determination that made it possible.

*Alan Brown*

## Additional Sources

Allen, Michael. *Rodeo Cowboys in the North American Imagination.* Reno: University of Nevada Press, 1998.

Coplon, Jeff. *Gold Buckle: The Grand Obsession of Rodeo Bull Riders.* New York: HarperCollins, 1995.

Ehringer, Gavin, and Gary Vorhes. *Rodeo Legends: Twenty Extraordinary Athletes of America's Sport.* Colorado Springs, Colo.: Western Horseman Magazine, 2003.

Fredriksson, Kristine. *American Rodeo from Buffalo Bill to Big Business.* College Station: University of Texas A&M Press, 1985.

"Jim Shoulders 1928-2007." *Sports Illustrated* 107, no. 1 (July 2, 2007): 21.

Steagall, Red, and Loretta Fulton. *Cowboy Corner Conversations.* Abilene, Tex.: State House Press, 2004.

Wooden, Wayne S., and Gavin Ehringer. *Rodeo in America: Wranglers, Roughstock, and Paydirt.* Lawrence: University Press of Kansas, 1996.

# Kelly Slater

**Born:** February 11, 1972
      Cocoa Beach, Florida
**Also known as:** Robert Kelly Slater (full name)

## Early Life

Robert Kelly Slater was born on February 11, 1972, in the small coastal town of Cocoa Beach, Florida. Though his father did not have the talent to be a top-notch surfer, he encouraged Kelly and his brothers to get out in the water. Kelly began his career at the age of five. At first, he started on boogie boards. He quickly moved onto the larger surfboards, and his career took off.

Kelly began by surfing the small waves of Cocoa Beach, an area not known for its surfing. Soon, by carpooling, he headed thirty minutes south to the Sebastian Inlet, where the waves were bigger than those at Cocoa Beach. In 1980, he entered, and won, his first contest. Two years later, he won the U.S. junior championships. He repeated as champion for the next five years.

Captivated by surfing, Kelly had traveled to the big waves of Hawaii's North Shore by the time he was twelve. Though his career was progressing, Kelly earned straight A's in high school. He turned professional two months prior to leaving high school.

## The Road to Excellence

In some ways, Kelly was a natural. He felt comfortable on small or big waves. However, he also brought a new attitude to surfing competition. At the time, most surfers approached competitions with a laid-back style. Kelly eschewed this approach. He liked to surf in a more aggressive manner. This new style led Kelly and a group of other surfers, notably Derek Ho and Shane Beschen, to be called the "New School." Kelly was the leader of this group. He often studied other surfers, analyzing what it took to beat them and trying to find weaknesses in their abilities. He took the best attributes from these surfers' styles and beat them at their own game. No one had approached competitive surfing like this before.

## The Emerging Champion

With his aggressive attitude and his intense work ethic, Kelly rose quickly in the ranks of professional surfing. In the first year he turned professional, he won one contest. Life on the Association of Surfing Professionals (ASP) Tour was an adjustment for Kelly. For him, winning a single contest was a big deal, which was a major contrast to the ease he had in winning contests at the junior level.

In his second year on the ASP Tour, Kelly seemed to regress. He did not win any contests and some speculated that he was not the prodigy that many believed him to be. The following year, he proved his doubters wrong by becoming the youngest ASP champion ever. Along the way, he won two more contests. In professional surfing, the champion does not have to win contests as much as he has to consistently finish near the top of the field.

The following year, Kelly surfed well, but Ho won the championship. That year, Kelly won one more contest. The following year, he emerged as the

*Kelly Slater in 2007.* (AP/Wide World Photos)

leading surfer on the tour. In 1994, he won six contests, including that prestigious Pipeline Masters and the ASP championship.

For the next five years, Kelly compiled impressive statistics, winning nineteen contests and four more world titles. In 1998, he won his sixth world title without winning a contest. Rather than winning contests and dominating in his previous fashion, he surfed contests in a way that consistently placed him second or third. After his sixth title, Kelly, at the age of twenty-six, abruptly retired from surfing.

### Continuing the Story

The pressure of touring around the world, as enjoyable as it might be envisioned, had gotten to Kelly. He took time to travel and to pursue other opportunities. Furthermore, he rekindled his relationship with his father. After his mother and father divorced when Kelly was eleven, Kelly and his father had become estranged. During Kelly's retirement, the two were able to mend their relationship.

Though Kelly was retired, he did not stop competing; he won nine more contests. In 2002, he announced that he was returning to the tour. He started the season strongly, but he missed contests to spend time with his father, who was dying of throat cancer. That year, Kelly finished ninth.

In 2003, Kelly returned energized. He surfed well, winning four contests, but could not top Andy Irons, an emerging talent. In a season that went to the final heat in the final contest, Kelly lost. The defeat affected him throughout 2004, and he was a nonfactor that season.

In 2005, in Tahiti, Kelly had an epiphany. After struggling through the miserable 2004 season, he realized that he was not having any fun surfing.

---

### Major Surfing Tournament Victories

|  |  |  |  |
|---|---|---|---|
| 1990 | Body Glove Surfbout Trestles | 1999 | Mountain Dew Pipe Masters |
| 1992 | Rip Curl Pro | 2000 | Gotcha Tahiti Pro |
| | Marui Masters | 2002 | The Quiksilver in Memory of Eddie Aikau |
| 1993 | Marui Pro | 2003 | Billabong Pro (Tahiti) |
| 1994 | Rip Curl Pro | | Billabong Pro (South Africa) |
| | Gotcha Lacanau Pro | | Billabong Pro (Spain) |
| | Chiemsee Pipe Masters | | Nova Schin Festival |
| | The Bud Surf Tour | 2004 | Snickers Australian Open |
| 1995 | Quiksilver Pro | 2005 | Billabong Pro |
| | Chiemsee Pipe Masters | | Globe Pro |
| 1996 | Coke Surf Classic | | Billabong Pro |
| | Rip Curl Pro Saint Leu | | Boost Mobile Pro |
| | CSI pres. Billabong Pro | 2006 | Quiksilver Pro |
| | U.S. Open | | Rip Curl Pro |
| | Rip Curl Pro | 2007 | Boost Mobile Pro |
| | Quiksilver Surfmasters | 2008 | Quiksilver Pro |
| | Chiemsee Pipe Masters | | Rip Curl Pro |
| 1997 | Coke Surf Classic | | Globe Pro |
| | Billabong Pro | | Billabong Pro |
| | Tokushima Pro | | Boost Mobile Pro |
| | Marui Pro | | |
| | Kaiser Summer Surf | | |
| | Typhoon Lagoon Surf Challenge | | |

---

Thus, he changed his attitude to enjoy what he was doing. By altering his outlook, he scored consecutive perfect scores, and three total, during one contest. After becoming the first to earn perfect scores on consecutive rides, he added two more championships.

### Summary

In the world of surfing, Kelly Slater stands alone. He was an eight-time world champion and won more contests than anyone in the history of surfing. He secured his place as one of the greatest surfers ever and continued to compete as of 2008. Beginning his career on the small waves of Cocoa Beach, Florida, Kelly became the greatest surfer of his time.

*P. Huston Ladner*

### Additional Sources

Grossman, Hillard. "Brevard's Own Kelly Slater: Surfing Superman, Regular Guy." *Florida Today*, May 26, 2002.

Slater, Kelly, and Jason Borte. *Pipe Dreams: A Surfer's Journey*. New York: ReganBooks, 2003.

Syken, B. "Second Wave." *Sports Illustrated* 103, no. 22 (December, 2005).

Tejada, J. "The Big Kahuna." *Sports Illustrated for Kids* 18, no. 4 (April, 2006).

---

### Milestones

Won eight Association of Surfing Professionals championships (1992, 1994-1998, 2005-2006; most ever)

Most Association of Surfing Professionals tour victories, 39

# *Jackie Stewart*

**Born:** June 11, 1939
      Milton, Dumbartonshire, Scotland
**Also known as:** Sir John Young Stewart (full
    name); the Flying Scot

### Early Life

John Young "Jackie" Stewart was born on June 11, 1939, in Milton, Dumbartonshire, Scotland. His parents were able to afford to send their youngest son to a good school. Living in the Scottish countryside, Jackie spent much time shooting and fishing, but it was motorsports that caught his imagination.

The Stewarts were a family dominated by motoring. Jackie's father had been a motorcycle racer before he set up a successful car dealership and garage. Even more of an inspiration to Jackie was his elder brother, Jimmy, who raced in the early 1950's.

### The Road to Excellence

Jackie yearned to drive race cars. However, as a result of Jimmy's numerous crashes, Jackie's parents were set against his emulating his brother. In 1961, unknown to his parents, Jackie started racing for a local sponsor named Barry Filer. Jackie's driving remained hidden from his parents until 1962, when he decided to get married. His marriage to Helen MacGregor was covered by the local press, which revealed his secret career. By this time Jackie could not be stopped.

Jackie's racing career took off quickly. Some fine performances in local races encouraged David Murray to invite Jackie to join the Ecurie Ecosse racing team. Jackie jumped at the chance. Joining this team gave Jackie exposure to the whole of the racing industry. In 1963, he won fourteen out of twenty-three starts, and in 1964, twenty-eight out of fifty-three starts.

After the impressive beginning of his career, Jackie moved up the motor racing ladder when he signed, with Ken Tyrrell, to race in Formula Three. In March, 1964, the first time he ever drove a single-seater, Jackie made his debut in Formula Three racing at Snetterton in England.

In his first outing, Jackie greatly impressed Tyr-

rell, who, two days later, offered him a ride in Formula One. As young as he was, Jackie was extremely shrewd and knew his own limitations. He turned down Tyrrell's offer, preferring to work his way slowly through Formula Three, then Formula Two. This meant that by the time he got to Formula One, he would be a more experienced, knowledgeable, and, he hoped, successful driver.

Jackie soon dominated Formula Three and Formula Two racing, and by the end of 1964, he was testing Formula One cars for the Lotus team. He had completed his driving apprenticeship and was ready for the big time.

### The Emerging Champion

Jackie's first Formula One season was 1965. He signed for the BRM team as second driver to the legendary Graham Hill. Jackie's learning process began all over again. As always, he did not take long

*Jackie Stewart after a racing victory at the German Grand Prix in 1973.* (AP/Wide World Photos)

## Grand Prix and Other Victories

| | |
|---|---|
| 1965, 1969 | Italian Grand Prix |
| 1966 | Tasman Cup Series Championship |
| 1966, 1971, 1973 | Monaco Grand Prix |
| 1968-69, 1973 | Netherlands Grand Prix |
| | Dutch Grand Prix |
| 1968, 1971, 1973 | German Grand Prix |
| 1968, 1972 | United States Grand Prix |
| 1969-70 | Race of Champions |
| 1969-71 | Spanish Grand Prix |
| 1969, 1971 | British Grand Prix |
| 1969, 1971-72 | French Grand Prix |
| 1969, 1971, 1973 | World Championship of Drivers |
| 1969, 1973 | South African Grand Prix |
| 1971 | Can-Am Challenge Cup Race (Mid-Ohio) |
| | Can-Am Challenge Cup Race (Mont-Treblant Circuit) |
| 1971-72 | Canadian Grand Prix |
| 1972 | Argentine Grand Prix |
| 1973 | Belgian Grand Prix |

to adjust to the higher level of competition. In his first Grand Prix, in South Africa, he finished sixth. Following three second-place finishes, Jackie astounded the racing world by winning the Italian Grand Prix at Monza. In his first season, Jackie could already compete with the best in the sport.

Winning the 1966 Monaco Grand Prix was a significant landmark in Jackie's career. Victory on the demanding Monte Carlo circuit confirmed his technical excellence as a driver. Everything was going according to plan for Jackie until the Belgian Grand Prix.

On a treacherously wet circuit, Jackie left the track at 150 miles per hour and plowed into a tree. He was trapped in the car with leaking fuel burning his skin. Jackie remained there for more than half an hour until he was finally freed from the wreckage. He had always been concerned with the safety aspect of racing. This incident made him determined that, however fast he raced, safety was of the utmost importance.

Jackie began the 1967 season as BRM's premier driver, Hill having moved to Lotus. However, the season proved to be disappointing; because of a succession of mechanical failures, Jackie failed to win a single Grand Prix.

When, in 1968, Tyrrell offered him a job, Jackie accepted. Not only was he glad to join a team with a reliable car, he also relished the opportunity of working again with the man who had given him his big break in racing.

## Continuing the Story

With Tyrrell, Jackie was transformed from a promising driver into a legitimate challenger for the world title. The 1968 season brought victories at the Dutch, German, and U.S. Grand Prix, and a respectable second-place finish in the driver's championship behind Hill.

Jackie's year was 1969. He won six Grand Prix and skated to the World Championship of Drivers. Ironically, it was his victory at Monza, where he had won his first Grand Prix, that won him his first world crown.

In 1970, the Tyrrell team had severe car trouble. With only a win in Spain, Jackie had no chance of regaining his title. He remained loyal to Tyrrell, and by the start of the 1971 season, he had a competitive car again. That was all he needed, and he won his second World Championship.

A stomach ulcer hampered the defense of his title in 1972, and the time he missed in midseason cost him dearly in his struggle to catch the young Emerson Fittipaldi. In 1973, however, in a new Tyrrell, Jackie was fit for the whole season and won his third World Championship. In the course of the season, he exceeded twenty-five Grand Prix wins, tying the number of victories set by Jim Clark, a fellow Scot. At the German Grand Prix at Nurburgring, Jackie set a new record mark with twenty-seven.

Jackie retired after the 1973 season. He had shown the world that he was one of the greatest drivers ever, and he had nothing else to prove in motor racing. Retirement did not mean inactivity for the likable Scotsman. He immersed himself in his business interests and still found plenty of time to indulge in his numerous hobbies, especially shooting, fishing, and golf. He also became a commentator for motor racing. In 2001, he was knighted.

## Honors and Awards

| | |
|---|---|
| 1966 | Indianapolis 500 Rookie of the Year |
| 1971 | Order of the British Empire |
| 1973 | *Sports Illustrated* Sportsman of the Year |
| | British Broadcasting Corporation Sports Personality of the Year |
| 1990 | Inducted into International Motorsports Hall of Fame |

## Summary

Although Jackie Stewart was almost destined to become a racing driver, he was not necessarily destined to become a great one. Jackie possessed a single-minded attitude toward his driving career. He was clinically efficient on the track, combining great technique with a fervent concern for safety. These qualities made him one of the best drivers ever.

*David L. Andrews*

## Additional Sources

Collings, Timothy, and Stuart Sykes. *Jackie Stewart: A Restless Life—The Biography.* London: Virgin, 2004.

Henry, Alan. *Grand Prix Champions: From Jackie Stewart to Michael Schumacher.* Osccola, Wis.: Motorbooks International, 1995.

Ludvigsen, Karl E. *Jackie Stewart: Triple-Crowned King of Speed.* Newbury Park, Calif.: Haynes North America, 1998.

Stewart, Jackie. *Jackie Stewart on the Road.* London: Collins, 1983.

_____. *Winning Is Not Enough: The Autobiography.* London: Headline, 2007.

Stewart, Jackie, and Eric Dymock. *Jackie Stewart: World Champion.* Chicago: Henry Regnery, 1970.

Stewart, Jackie, and Alan Henry. *Jackie Stewart's Principles of Performance Driving.* Richmond, Surrey, England: Hazleton, 1992.

Stewart, Jackie, and Peter Manso. *Faster! A Racer's Diary.* New York: Farrar, Straus and Giroux, 1972.

# Tony Stewart

**Born:** May 20, 1971
Columbus, Indiana
**Also known as:** Anthony Wayne Stewart (full name)

## Early Life

Anthony Wayne Stewart was born on May 20, 1971, in Columbus, Indiana. At the age of eight, he began racing go-karts in his backyard. In 1983, before he was even a teenager, Tony won the International Karting Federation national championship. Four years later, in 1987, he was victorious in the World Karting Association national championship.

## The Road to Excellence

In 1989, Tony graduated to three-quarter midget cars and then quickly extended his driving apprenticeship by taking the wheel of United States Automobile Club (USAC) midgets, silver-crown racers, and sprint cars. In 1995, he made automobile his-

tory by becoming the first driver to win the USAC triple crown, meaning he was the champion of the top three divisions in the same year.

In 1996, Tony felt he had the experience and competitive focus to join the Indy Racing League (IRL). He took the award for rookie of the year in the IRL's inaugural season. The following year he added to his 1996 successes by securing one victory, four pole positions, and the IRL championship. At this stage in his career, Tony had to decide whether he wanted to stay with the IRL; try lucrative Formula One Grand Prix racing, which required signing up with a European auto maker; or switch to National Association for Stock Car Auto Racing (NASCAR).

## The Emerging Champion

A key catalyst in Tony's decision to move to NASCAR was Joe Gibbs, who had been the head coach of the Washington Redskins football organization and led his team to three Super Bowl championships. In his post-football life, Gibbs enthusiastically embraced motorsports and built Joe Gibbs Racing.

In 1991, Joe Gibbs Racing started as a one-car operation with Dale Jarrett behind the wheel. In 1995, Bobby Labonte took over for Jarrett, but a few years later, Tony helped solidify the organization. In 1997, Gibbs began sponsoring a Busch Series (later Nationwide Series) car for Tony. This series is similar to the minor leagues in baseball. For two years, Tony continued to drive in both the IRL and the NASCAR feeder series. Very few drivers are able to successfully compete in different racing categories. In 1999, Tony finally committed to full-time Winston Cup racing as a member of the Home Depot Team under the tutelage of Gibbs.

In 1999, Tony won three Win-

*Tony Stewart poking his head out of his car at the Daytona International Speedway in 2008.* (Michael Bush/UPI/Landov)

ston Cup races. In that year, he took part in the Indianapolis 500 and the Coca-Cola 600. He finished ninth and fourth, respectively, and displayed uncommon resilience and stamina. He racked up NASCAR victories at Richmond, Virgina; Phoenix, Arizona; and Homestead, Florida. He was also named rookie of the year by NASCAR. In addition, his teammate, Labonte, won the Winston Cup Championship.

## Continuing the Story

In his rookie year with NASCAR, Tony was successful in the Winston Cup series. He competed in thirty-four races; had three wins, thirteen top-five positions, twenty-one top-ten finishes, and two pole

positions; and won $3 million in prize money. In 2000, Tony doubled his number of Winston Cup victories, achieving six, the most wins of any driver. His six wins broke the record for most wins by a sophomore driver, beating Dale Earnhart's 1980 record of four.

In the 2001 season, Tony really showed his talents as he won another three races, and, more important, finished second in the overall points standings. Building off the momentum of the previous year, Tony raced to another three wins in 2002. The wins helped give him the status that he really desired—that of overall champion. This championship helped to solidify him as one of best drivers in the United States, in any series.

After the 2002 season, Tony continued to stay on par with the high standards that he set for himself. He won another Winston Cup Championship in 2005. Two seasons later, he had amassed a total of thirty-two wins. During the 2007 season, Joe Gibbs Racing announced it was switching from Chevrolets to Toyotas for 2008. While some criticized the decision, Tony felt it was a good one, but in 2008, he announced he was leaving Joe Gibbs Racing.

Aside from Tony's NASCAR driving, he continued to race on dirt tracks when he had the chance. He became the owner of the most famous dirt track in United States, Eldora Speedway, in Rossburg, Ohio. He also founded Tony Stewart Racing, which fielded cars in USAC and the World of Outlaws series.

In addition to these exploits, Tony established the Tony Stewart Foundation to help children, drivers, and animals. One of the prime beneficiaries of his efforts was the Victory Junction Gang Camp, in North Carolina, which helped children ages seven to fifteen with life-threatening illnesses.

## Summary

Tony Stewart became known as one of the most talented drivers in NASCAR or any other series. His career statistics were comparable to any other driver's. His friends nicknamed Tony "Smoke," because before arriving at NASCAR, he "smoked" the field. While Tony became more outspoken, and at times drew the ire of NASCAR, fans loved his candid attitude and his passion for racing. He commonly down-

### Nascar and Other Victories

|  |  |
|------|---------|
| 1983 | International Karting Federation National Championship |
| 1987 | World Karting Association National Championship |
| 1995 | USAC Triple Crown |
| 1999 | Exide NASCAR Select Batteries 400 |
| | Dura Lube 500K |
| | Pennzoil 400 |
| 2000 | MBNA Platinum 400 |
| | Kmart 400 |
| | Jiffy Lube 300 |
| | MBNA Gold 400 |
| | NAPA 500 |
| | Pennzoil 400 |
| 2001 | Pontiac Excitement 400 |
| | Dodge/Save Mart 350 |
| | Sharpie 500 |
| 2002 | MBNA America 500 |
| | Chevy American Revolution 400 |
| | Sirius Satellite Radio at The Glen |
| 2002, 2005 | Winston Cup Championship |
| 2003 | Pocono 500 |
| | UAW-GM Quality 500 |
| 2004 | Tropicana 400 presented by Meijer |
| | Sirius at The Glen |
| 2005 | Dodge/Save Mart 350 |
| | Pepsi 400 |
| | New England 300 |
| | Allstate 400 at The Brickyard |
| | Sirius at The Glen |
| | Nextel Cup Championship |
| 2006 | DirecTV 500 |
| | Pepsi 400 |
| | Banquet 400 |
| | Bass Pro Shops 500 |
| | Dickies 500 |
| 2007 | USG Sheetrock 400 |
| | Allstate 400 at The Brickyard |
| | Centurion Boats at The Glen |
| 2008 | AMP Energy 500 |

played his charitable efforts, seemingly in contrast to the brash style that he sometimes displayed.

*Scott A. G. M. Crawford,*
*updated by P. Huston Ladner*

## Additional Sources

Craggs, T. "Quick in His Seat." *The New York Times*, March 2, 2008.

Mello, Tara Baukus. *Tony Stewart*. Philadelphia: Chelsea House, 2000.

Patrick, D. "Just My Type: Tony Stewart Goes Long." *Sports Illustrated* 108, no 7 (February 18, 2008): 29.

Pillsbury, Richard. "Stock Car Racing." In *The Theater of Sport*. Baltimore: Johns Hopkins University Press, 1995.

## Honors, Awards, and Milestones

|  | |
|---|---|
| 1995 | U.S. Auto Club Triple Crown winner; first driver to ever win the National Midget, Sprint, and Silver Crown championships in one year |
| 1996 | Indy Racing League Rookie of the Year |
| | Indianapolis 500 Rookie of the Year |
| | Indy 500 pole sitter |
| 1997 | Indy Racing League Champion |
| 1999 | NASCAR Rookie of the Year |
| 2002 | Winston Cup Champion |
| | NASCAR Driver of the Year |
| 2005 | NEXTEL Cup Champion |
| 2006 | Inducted into National Midget Auto Racing Hall of Fame |
| | Set fast lap record at Indianapolis for the IRL |

# Abbye Stockton

**Born:** August 11, 1917
Santa Monica, California
**Died:** June 26, 2006
Santa Monica, California
**Also known as:** Abbye Eville (birth name); Pudgy; America's Barbelle; the First Lady of Iron; the Queen of Muscle Beach

## Early Life

Abbye Stockton was born Abbye Eville on August 11, 1917, in Santa Monica, California. She was nicknamed "Pudgy" by her father because of her chubby appearance. Working as a telephone operator after graduation from high school, Abbye started going to Muscle Beach, south of the Santa Monica Pier, to shed some excess weight. On these exercise dates, Abbye and her boyfriend Les Stockton worked primarily on gymnastics. Large crowds flocked to Muscle Beach, the birthplace of the physical fitness boom of the twentieth century, to see weightlifting, hand balancing, human-pyramid building, gymnastics, acrobatics, and bodybuilding competitions and demonstrations. Abbye, Stockton, and their friend Bruce Conner performed an acrobatic act called *Three Aces* at football halftime shows and other venues.

Abbye and Stockton married in 1941. At about 115 pounds and 5 feet 2 inches, Abbye gradually became known as the most muscular blond beauty on Muscle Beach, with a "38-20-36" figure. She was a shocking spectacle because, at the time, women's participation in weightlifting and bodybuilding was unusual. Her custom-made, two-piece bathing suit was another novel point of attraction.

## The Road to Excellence

The public on Muscle Beach started paying attention to Abbye and Les when they performed a high-press routine. With a 100-pound barbell over her head, Abbye balanced herself on top of her husband's outstretched hands. Abbye became famous when she supported 180-pound Les over her head in a hand-to-hand stand. The media, fascinated by her strength, physical beauty, and charisma, quickly capitalized on her. She appeared in photo essays in pictorial magazines such as *Life, Pic,* and *Laff.* In a 1939 *Pic* issue, Conner threw Abbye through the air while Les waited to catch her. She appeared on the covers of more than forty magazines around the world. She was also featured in two newsreels—*Whatta Build* and *Muscle Town USA.* Finally, she received product endorsement contracts from the Ritamine Vitamin Company and the Universal Camera Company. She appeared on local and nationwide exhibition shows and, sometimes, with Mr. America winners Steve Reeves and George Eiferman.

## The Emerging Champion

From 1944 to 1954, Abbye wrote for *Strength and Health,* the most influential fitness magazine at that time. In her women's column, called "Barbelles," she used photographs of her and other women to argue for the benefits of weight training. Weights, she wrote, not only could enhance women's figures but also make women better athletes. She also exposed the myths that women working with weights lost femininity and were unable to become pregnant.

Also in *Strength and Health,* Abbye publicized the first sanctioned weightlifting contests, which she helped organize. Virtually nonexistent during the 1940's, these contests were sanctioned by the Amateur Athletic Union. The first contest was held at the Southwest Arena in Los Angeles on February 26, 1947. Here, Abbye pressed 100 pounds,

---

### Honors, Awards, and Milestones

| | |
|---|---|
| 1940's | Helped organize the first sanctioned weightlifting for women |
| 1947 | At the first AAU women's weightlifting competition, she pressed 100 pounds, snatched 105 pounds, and clean-and-jerked 135 pounds |
| 1948 | Miss Physical Culture Venus |
| 1998 | Steve Reeves International Society Pioneer Award |
| 2000 | Inducted into International Federation of Bodybuilding and Fitness Hall of Fame |
| 2002 | Spirit of Muscle Beach Award |

snatched 105 pounds, and clean-and-jerked 135 pounds. She won a $1,000 prize and was named 1948 Miss Physical Culture Venus by Bernarr Macfadden, *Physical Culture* magazine publisher.

## Continuing the Story

In 1948, the Stocktons opened the Salon of Figure Development, a women's gym, on Sunset Boulevard in Los Angeles. The Stockton Studios were opened in Beverly Hills two years later. From 1955 to 1960, Abbye retired from business and stayed home to raise her only child, who was born in 1953. After that, she spent the following twenty years instructing bodybuilding.

The Stocktons served as consultants for television documentaries and books on Muscle Beach. One of the books, published in 1999, was *Remembering Muscle Beach: Where Hard Bodies Began* by Harold Zinkin and Bonnie Hearn. Abbye received the Steve Reeves International Society Pioneer Award in 1998 and was elected to the International Federation of Bodybuilding and Fitness Hall of Fame in 2000. She received the Spirit of Muscle Beach award two years later. On June 26, 2006, Abbye died in Santa Monica of complications from Alzheimer's disease. Her husband had died in 2004.

## Summary

Abbye Stockton was part of the physical fitness culture that made Muscle Beach famous during the 1930's and 1940's. A pioneer in bodybuilding and the gym business, she inspired women to take up weight training during the 1940's and also fueled the fitness craze in the 1980's. As a role model for women bodybuilders, she proved that weightlifting did not make women less feminine and that weight training could enhance athletic ability.

*Anh Tran*

## Additional Sources

"A 'Lady of Iron' and a Model for Fitness." *Los Angeles Times*, January 7, 2008.

Black, Jane. "Abbye 'Pudgy' Stockton." *Milo* 12, no. 1 (June, 2004).

McCracken, Elizabeth. "The Belle of the Barbelle." *The New York Times*, December 31, 2006.

Thomas, Al. "Out of the Past . . . Fond Remembrance: Abbye 'Pudgy' Stockton." *Body and Power* 2 (March, 1981).

# *Junko Tabei*

**Born:** September 22, 1939
      Miharu Machi, Japan
**Also known as:** Junko Ishibashi (birth name)

### Early Life
Junko Ishibashi was born September 22, 1939, in Miharu Machi, a market town in northern Japan. The fifth of seven children, Junko's first taste of mountain climbing came at the age of ten. On a school field trip, Junko's teacher guided her and some of her classmates to the top of a 6,000-foot mountain. This experience led to a fascination with mountains and mountaineering that became her passion in the years to come.

### The Road to Excellence
After graduating from Tokyo's Showa Women's University in 1962, Junko took a job as a middle-school teacher. She also joined a men's climbing

*Junko Tabei, who was the first woman to climb Mt. Everest.* (Keystone/Getty Images)

club. Barely 5 feet tall and weighing 93 pounds, this bespectacled woman found that she was nonetheless the equal of many of the male climbers. Subsequently, she climbed several of Japan's best-known peaks, including its highest mountain, the 12,388-foot Mount Fuji. As her confidence and mountaineering skills grew, her goal became to climb what she termed the "white mountains" throughout the world.

In 1965, she met Masanobu Tabei, a fellow mountaineer. Despite her mother's objection—Tabei was not a college graduate—Junko and Tabei were married three years later. In the years to come, they raised two children: a daughter, Noriko, and a son, Shinya.

In 1969, Junko established a women's mountaineering club; in 1970, her club decided to climb 24,787-foot Annapurna III in the Himalayas. The expedition included 8 climbers, 14 sherpas, 114 porters, a doctor, and a reporter. The climbers arrived in Kathmandu in March of that year.

The traditional approach to climbing in the Himalayas is to lay siege to the mountain. That is, over a period of time, climbers—and especially sherpas—set up and stock a series of camps at higher and higher levels. This gradual movement up the mountain allows time for the human body to acclimatize to increasing elevation. Camp one was established at 14,370 feet. This was followed by other camps, culminating with Camp five at 22,300 feet. Junko, Hiroko Hirakawa, and two sherpas were selected by Eiko Miyazuki, the expedition leader, to make the final assault on the summit from Camp five. After a determined effort, the four reached the top on May 19, 1970.

### The Emerging Champion
Following their success on Annapurna III, Miyazuki and Junko decided to attempt Mount Everest, in the Himalayas, with an all-woman team. In 1971, they received a permit to climb Everest in 1975. Thus began a long period of extensive planning and fund-raising. The expedition was sponsored by the mountaineering club, and funds were secured from sources including *Yomiuri Shimbun*, the Tokyo

## Tabei's Conquest of the Seven Summits

| Year | Mountain | Elevation in feet | Location |
|------|----------|-------------------|----------|
| 1975 | Everest | 29,035 | Nepal |
| 1980 | Kilimanjaro | 19,340 | Tanzania |
| 1987 | Aconcagua | 22,834 | Argentina |
| 1988 | McKinley | 20,320 | United States |
| 1989 | Elbrus | 18,510 | Russia |
| 1991 | Vinson Massif | 16,066 | Antarctica |
| 1992 | Carstensz Pyramid | 16,023 | Indonesia |

newspaper, as well as Nikon Television. Also, in 1973, Junko resigned from her teaching job and used her retirement benefits to help pay for the expedition.

At 29,035 feet, Mount Everest is the highest point on Earth and has long been a target for world-class mountaineers. Despite determined British efforts in the 1920's to climb the mountain, the first confirmed ascent was not made until 1953, by Edmund Hillary, a beekeeper from New Zealand, and by Tenzing Norgay, a Nepalese sherpa. In the intervening years, a number of men had climbed the mountain—but no woman had done so.

The all-woman Japanese Everest expedition involved fourteen women, five hundred porters, twenty-three sherpas, and a doctor. On March 16, 1975, base camp was established at the foot of the Khumbu glacier. It took nearly two weeks to rig a route of aluminum ladders and fixed lines through the treacherous Khumbu ice fall. By April 3, they had established Camp one at the top of the ice fall. Over the following weeks, they established a series of camps higher up the mountain. On May 4, disaster struck. An avalanche rolled over seven climbers and six sherpas asleep in their tents. Two of the sherpas were seriously injured, as was Junko. It took several days for her to recover.

As a result of the lost time and equipment, only one summit attempt by two climbers could be supported. On May 13, Junko and sherpa Ang Tshering established Camp six at 27,887 feet. On May 15, the two left for the summit, only to be turned back by bad weather. On May 16, they tried again, leaving camp at 5:00 A.M. Junko's 31-pound load included cameras, drinks, flags, and oxygen cylinders. While the mountain has been climbed without us-

ing bottled oxygen, most climbers sleep wearing an oxygen mask at high camp and breathe a steady flow of the gas on summit day. At 8:30 A.M. Junko and Tshering reached the South Summit. With Tshering breaking a trail through deep snow, the pair finally reached the summit of Mount Everest at 12:30 P.M. At thirty-five years of age, and with a two-year-old daughter at home, Junko became the first woman to stand on the highest point on the earth.

### Continuing the Story

Junko continued to climb. In 1992, she became the first woman to complete the "Seven Summits." The Seven Summits represent the highest points on each of the earth's seven continents. Over the years, Junko climbed more than seventy major peaks all over the world and received numerous awards. Deeply concerned about the natural environment, Junko was directly involved in "cleanup" climbs in both Japan and the Himalayas and became director of the Japanese chapter of the Himalayan Adventure Trust, an organization whose goal is to preserve the mountain environment.

### Summary

As a successful Japanese woman in the male-dominated sport of mountaineering, Junko Tabei was an inspirational role model for women—and all mountaineers—in Japan and around the world. She followed a dream that took her to the tops of the "white mountains" and to the top of her sport.

*Russell N. Carney*

### Additional Sources

Birkett, Bill, and Bill Peascod. *Women Climbing: Two Hundred Years of Achievement.* London: A & C Black, 1990.

Horn, Robert. "No Mountain Too High for Her." *Sports Illustrated* 84, no. 17 (April 29, 1996).

Jordan, Jennifer. *Savage Summit: The True Stories of the Five Women Who Climbed K2, the World's Most Feared Mountain.* New York: William Morrow, 2005.

McLoone, Margo, and Kathryn Besio. *Women Explorers of the Mountains: Nina Mazuchelli, Fanny Bullock Workman, Mary Vaux Walcott, Gertrude Benham, Junko Tabei.* Mankato, Minn.: Capstone Press, 2000.

# Kōki Taihō

**Born:** May 29, 1940
      Karafuto Island, Japan (now Sakhalin
      Island, Russia)
**Also known as:** Naya Kōki (birth name)

## Early Life
On May 29, 1940, Naya Kōki was born to a Ukrainian father and a Japanese mother on the southern half of Karafuto Island, Japan (now Sakhalin Island, Russia). At the end of World War II, in August, 1945, the Soviet Union attacked Japan and conquered Karafuto. Like others fearing the Soviets, the family fled to Japan's northern island of Hokkaidō.

As a teenager living with his mother in Hokkaidō, Kōki trained as a logger. In 1956, at sixteen years old, he was discovered by a sumo scout impressed by his strength and moved to Tokyo. At the time, sumo was considered the quintessential Japanese sport. Even though Kōki was not a Japanese citizen, as this, at the time, required that one's father be Japanese, he felt thoroughly Japanese. To further Kōki's identification with Japan, Hokkaidō was attributed as his place of birth.

## The Road to Excellence
In Tokyo, Kōki joined the *Nishonoseki* stable and trained to become a *rikishi*, or sumo wrestler. He took the name of Taihō, meaning "great phoenix." Weighing only 155 pounds, Kōki trained hard and feasted on the *rikishi* diet of *chankonabe*, a Japanese stew, to gain strength and weight. Eventually, Kōki's fighting weight was 340 pounds.

Kōki made his official debut as a sumo wrestler in September, 1956. His *hatsu dohyō-iri*, or first entry into the sumo ring, was in November. Kōki rose swiftly through the lower divisions of sumo competition and entered the second division, *Jūryō*, in May, 1959, after fourteen competitive tournaments called *basho*. After eighteen more *basho*, in January, 1960, Taihō was promoted to the *Makuuchi* division, the matches of which are broadcast all over Japan.

In his first *Makuuchi* tournament, the *Hatsu basho* of Tokyo in January, 1960, Kōki won twelve of the fifteen regulation bouts. He was given the *kanto-sho* award for extraordinary fighting spirit. Losing in the *Haru* (spring) *basho* in March, Kōki came back to win, eleven to four, in the *Natsu* (summer) *basho* in May. By defeating the forty-sixth *Yokozuna* (grand champion) Asashio, Kōki won the *Kinboshi*, or gold, award, reserved for such a rare feat, in addition to his second *kanto-sho* award. He also rose into the elite group of *sanyaku*, or sumo-wrestler titleholders.

## The Emerging Champion
Kōki won the first of his thirty-two career *Makuuchi* championships in the Kyūshū *basho* of November, 1960, with a score of thirteen victories and two losses. After finishing the next three *basho* with more victories than losses, Kōki won the Nagoya *basho* in July, 1961. This victory helped Kōki to receive the title of *Yokozuna*, the top rank in all sumo, with his twelve to three victory in the *Aki* (fall) *basho* in September.

At twenty-one, Kōki became the forty-eighth *Yokozuna*, the youngest to earn this status at the time. Since 1630, *Yokozuna* have been elected from the top wrestlers. The counting of *Yokozuna* dates to 1789, and since 1950, *Yokozuna* have been chosen by the Japan Sumo Association. A *Yokozuna* is not only expected to excel at sumo but also have *hinkaku*, or dignity and grace. When his fighting prowess recedes, a *Yokozuna* is expected to retire. Very rarely are more than one *Yokozuna* active at the same time. During Kōki's career, there were at most four *Yokozuna* fighting at the same time and as few as two.

Kōki's career reached its zenith during the early

---

### Milestones

| | |
|---|---|
| 1959 | Promoted to *Jūryō* division |
| 1960 | Promoted to *Makuuchi* division |
| | Won the *kanto-sho* award, for "fighting spirit" |
| | Joined *sanyaku* (sumo title holders) |
| 1961 | Promoted to *Yokozuna*, sumo's top rank |
| | Youngest sumo wrestler to gain *Yokozuna* status |
| 1961-71 | Served as the forty-eighth *Yokozuna* |

1960's. As the first post-World War II *Yokozuna* to do so, from July, 1962, to May, 1963, Kōki won six consecutive *basho*. His record stood until 2005. He competed in the *basho* as East *Yokozuna*, considered more dignified than a West *Yokozuna*. In May, 1963, for the first time in his career, Kōki won the *Natsu basho* with a perfect score of fifteen victories. He repeated this extraordinary sumo feat seven times.

## Continuing the Story

At the peak of his career in the 1960's, Kōki enthralled Japan by winning an unprecedented series of championships. He won four of the six *basho* of 1964, the first two with perfect scores of fifteen.

The rigors of sumo took their toll on Kōki. He sat out the first match of 1966 because of injury. However, in March, he won his second series of six consecutive championships as East *Yokozuna*, the last two with perfect scores. Until 1971, missed bouts in a tournament were counted against the wrestler. Thus, in late 1967, Kōki's record deteriorated. He did not win the Nagoya or Kyūshū *basho* because of twelve and two absences, respectively. In the middle of 1968, Kōki sat out three *basho* because of severe injury.

Kōki made a stunning comeback in September, 1968, winning the *basho* as West *Yokozuna*. He also won the next two *basho* as East *Yokozuna*, both with perfect scores, and compiled an astonishing record of forty-five victories. After three more championships, the last of which was the first *basho* of 1971,

Kōki retired gracefully during the *Natsu basho* in May, 1971.

After his retirement, Kōki trained his own stable of sumo wrestlers but had little success. In 1975, at the age of thirty-five, he suffered a stroke. In 2000, as is the custom for any *Yokozuna* who survives to his sixtieth birthday, Kōki ceremoniously entered the sumo ring in a splendid *kanreki dohyō-iri* ritual, cheered by thousands of fans. In 2003, he turned over his sumo stable to his son-in-law Takatoriki, a former *rikishi*.

## Summary

Kōki Taihō was one of the greatest modern sumo wrestlers. His career record of 32 championships and 872 single-bout victories versus only 181 losses and 136 absences, and his participation in 69 top *Makuuchi* division tournaments from 1960 to 1971 are most impressive. His 1968 comeback after a severe injury inspired many, as did his grace and dignity in and out of the sumo ring.

*R. C. Lutz*

## Additional Sources

Cuyler, Patricia. *Sumo: From Rite to Sport*. New York: Weatherhill, 1979.

"The Giant Bird." *Time*, February 8, 1963.

Hall, Mina. *The Big Book of Sumo*. Berkeley, Calif.: Stone Bridge, 1997.

Newton, Clyde, and Gerald Toff. *Dynamic Sumo*. New York: Kodansha, 2000.

# Major Taylor

**Born:** November 26, 1878
    Indianapolis, Indiana
**Died:** June 21, 1932
    Chicago, Illinois
**Also known as:** Marshall Walter Taylor (full
    name); Dusky Wheelman

## Early Life

Marshall Walter Taylor was born on a dirt farm just outside Indianapolis, Indiana, on November 26, 1878. His African American parents, Gilbert and Saphronia Taylor, were children of Kentucky slaves.

Marshall was among the youngest of the Taylors' eight children. To make ends meet, his father supplemented the meager farming income by becoming a coachman for a wealthy white family; the family practically adopted young Marshall. Marshall lived with this family for the next four to five years, experiencing the privileges of the white upper class, including expensive clothes and toys and private tutoring.

From his parents, Marshall learned the value of hard work. From the family that unofficially adopted him, he learned self-confidence and the possibility of expanding his own horizons.

Marshall took to athletics naturally. He earned the respect of his playmates by holding his own in tennis, baseball, football, roller skating, and running. He could also ride a bicycle like the wind.

## The Road to Excellence

Marshall's white benefactors moved to Chicago when the youngster was about thirteen, and Marshall went home to his family's farm. In his spare time, he taught himself all kinds of bicycle stunts and tricks. Eventually, the owner of a local bicycle shop was so impressed with Marshall that he offered him the job of shop boy. Part of his duties, as a publicity stunt, was to dress up in a full soldier's uniform and entertain passersby with his nifty stunt riding. From then on Marshall's nickname became "Major."

Major began racing bicycles at the age of fifteen. He won his first race, a 10-mile event against amateur male cyclists. He also entered and usually won various boys' races in Indiana and Illinois. Because of his African American heritage, however, he could not belong to any of the exclusively white bicycling clubs.

Racial prejudice increased in Indianapolis in the late 1890's. Louis "Birdie" Munger, a white former racer and an Indianapolis bicycle manufacturer who saw potential greatness in Major, took the young cyclist under his wing. Munger invited Major to accompany him when he relocated his bicycle factory in the East, in Worcester, Massachusetts, a city more tolerant of African Americans.

Before Major had turned eighteen, he had gained a wonderful reputation as a graceful yet powerful sprint rider. In his professional debut at Madison Square Garden in New York, he created a sensation by defeating the reigning American sprint champion, Eddie Bald. The "Dusky Wheelman," as Major was sometimes called, was already on his way to cycling immortality.

*Major Taylor.* (Bob Thomas/Popperfoto/Getty Images)

## The Emerging Champion

At the end of his second year as a professional, Major established his international reputation when he beat the star Welsh cyclist Jimmy Michael. In the process, he broke the world record twice. Major's tenacious riding style set him apart from his competitors. His popularity with Northern racing fans and promoters soared with each successive victory.

However popular Major was with the racing supporters, he was openly disliked by his fellow professional circuit riders, mostly because he was black—and talented. Fearing that Major's successes threatened their assumed physical superiority, they conspired to prevent him from winning the national championship by riding against him in combinations. As a group, they could pocket him in, elbow and bump him, and otherwise frustrate any normal racing strategy Major might have used. Major decided to use his famous "gunpowder start," figuring that if they could not catch him from the start they could not prevent him from winning. It worked.

Major's natural gifts, combined with his poise, intelligence, and self-control, helped him to overcome the harassment. In 1899, at the age of twenty-one, he won the World Championship Mile; later in the year, and again in 1900, he won the coveted American sprint championship. No American rider before him had attained such a convincing level of excellence.

## Continuing the Story

In the early years of the twentieth century, cycling was big in the United States but even bigger in Europe. Major was lured to France to race against the world sprint champion Edmond Jacquelin and also to compete against other national champions throughout Europe.

Major was warmly received by the Europeans. In a short four months he achieved heroic stature, as the press celebrated his splendidly muscled body, his high character, his modesty and courtesy—and his winning ways. He rode in nearly every European capital and soundly beat all the European champions; he also met Jacquelin, losing the first match but winning the second.

Major continued racing for the rest of the decade. Eventually, physical fatigue and the stress of continued racial harassment in the United States, on and off the racing track, forced his retirement in 1910.

With his wife, Daisy, and his daughter, Rita Sydney Taylor, Major, then quite wealthy, continued to live in Worcester for the next twenty years. Former athletes then, however, could not capitalize much on their fame; it was doubly hard for African American athletes, as social discrimination severely limited their opportunities.

Major drifted into poverty as one business venture after another failed. Following his gradual financial collapse, his marriage also failed. He moved to Chicago in 1930, practically penniless. Without bitterness or self-pity, he died two years later in the Cook County Hospital charity ward at the age of fifty-three.

## Summary

In his day, the golden age of bicycle racing, Major Taylor was known as the fastest bicycle rider in the world. He was also the only professional African American in an otherwise white sport. The racial harassment he faced on and off the track demanded heroic personal qualities. In spite of these hardships, he became the first African American world champion rider and the second African American world champion in any sport. Major, the gentleman athlete, stands as an example of what it means to pursue and achieve athletic excellence against all odds.

*William Harper*

## Additional Sources

Balf, Todd. *Major: A Black Athlete, a White Era, and the Fight to Be the World's Fastest Human Being.* New York: Crown Publishers, 2008.

Nye, Peter. *Hearts of Lions: The History of American Bicycle Racing.* New York: W. W. Norton, 1988.

Ritchie, Andrew. *Major Taylor: The Extraordinary Career of a Champion Bicycle Racer.* Reprint. Baltimore: Johns Hopkins University Press, 1996.

Taylor, Major. *The Fastest Bicycle Rider in the World: The Autobiography of Major Taylor.* Reprint. Brattleboro, Vt.: S. Greene Press, 1972.

---

### *Honors, Awards, and Milestones*

| | |
|---|---|
| 1898-1900 | U.S. Professional Sprint Champion |
| 1899 | World Professional Sprint Champion |
| | 1-Mile World Champion |
| 1989 | Inducted into U.S. Bicycling Hall of Fame |

# *Casey Tibbs*

**Born:** March 5, 1929
      Mission Ridge, near Fort Pierre, South
      Dakota
**Died:** January 28, 1990
      Ramona, California
**Also known as:** Casey Duane Tibbs (full name)

## Early Life
Casey Duane Tibbs was born March 5, 1929, in Mission Ridge, near Fort Pierre, South Dakota, to John and Florence Tibbs. Casey was the youngest of ten children; he had five brothers and four sisters. Casey's father raised horses, and Casey took to the saddle almost immediately. He was breaking horses for six to ten dollars a head by the time he was thirteen. Casey soon decided to compete in rodeo full time. He entered an amateur contest and won four first prizes. This good beginning was soon followed by a broken ankle. Also, Casey's father saw no reason for any of his children to leave the ranch. He was opposed to life on the rodeo circuit. Still, Casey persevered and persuaded his mother to sign a letter of consent so he could enter professional competitions.

## The Road to Excellence
When he was fifteen, Casey won his first rodeo prize money riding a bucking horse at McLaughlin, South Dakota. He won only eighty-seven dollars, but Casey was hooked on the rodeo.

Rodeo competitions differ from most sports in that the contestants' entry fees become the prize money to be won or lost. Casey found it necessary to work part-time as a ranch hand to supplement his income. He was in fifth place in the saddle bronc competition by the time he was seventeen. He was in third place the next year, and number one by age nineteen.

In rodeo competition, there are two kinds of bronc riders, bareback and saddle. A bareback rider must stay on the horse for 8 seconds, whereas a saddle bronc rider must ride for 10 seconds. Needless to say, although the prize money is extremely generous in terms of the length of actual competition, the horse seldom cooperates with the rider. The rider is judged not only on his form but also on the ferocity of the horse's reaction. The judges award half the points for one criterion and half for the other.

Rodeo is a highly contested sport; even a modest competition may draw a hundred riders in the saddle and bareback categories. Moreover, big rodeos occur throughout the year, and riders have little time between contests.

*Actor and cowboy Casey Tibbs, who was a two-time World All-Around Champion in rodeo.* (ProRodeo Hall of Fame and Museum of the American Cowboy)

A rider must enter as many competitions as possible, because championships are assessed on the basis of prize money won in a year. Finally, while contestants may compete in a single event, most try to capture the all-around title awarded by the Professional Rodeo Cowboys Association (PRCA). In order to qualify for the all-around title, a rider must compete in at least three events.

### The Emerging Champion

Casey chose to concentrate on saddle bronc, bareback bronc, and bull riding. All three events are dangerous and injuries are common, but Casey was extremely successful as a rodeo performer. He won seven professional circuit saddle bronc and bareback riding championships and was the World Champion All-Around Cowboy on two occasions.

Admittedly, Casey paid for his triumphs with numerous broken bones and assorted fractures, but he obviously loved his work. The monetary rewards were substantial—he earned a then-record $42,065 in 1955—but the excitement and the ever-present danger were intoxicating as well.

Casey lived his life on the rodeo circuit at a rapid pace. Moreover, he stood out from the crowd with his flashy purple outfits and his Cadillac convertibles in the same color. For all his antics, Casey was an exceptional performer.

Casey developed an exemplary feeling for what could and could not be done with a horse. Indeed, he was often able to persuade even "bad" mounts to give him a winning ride. Riders are assigned mounts on the basis of a lottery system in which the luck of the draw dramatically affects chances for success.

Casey was not physically heavy in his active years, so he developed a riding style that involved "floating" a horse rather than "anchoring" himself to the saddle in the fashion of heavier, brawnier riders. This trademark rocking-chair style was often imitated, but none succeeded in matching the skill with which Casey forked a bronc coming out of the chute. In 1951, he won the professional titles in saddle bronc riding, bareback riding, and the all-around cowboy division. This took an unprecedented display of skill and stamina.

## Milestones

| | |
|---|---|
| 1949 | Professional Saddle Bronc Riding Champion |
| 1951 | PRCA Bareback Riding Champion |
| | Inducted into Rodeo Hall of Fame, the National Cowboy Hall of Fame |
| 1951-54, 1959 | PRCA Saddle Bronc Riding Champion |
| 1951, 1955 | PRCA World Champion All-Around Cowboy |
| 1955 | Inducted into Rodeo Hall of Fame |
| 1979 | Inducted into Pro Rodeo Hall of Fame |

## Records

Won six professional circuit saddle bronc riding championships—the most in professional rodeo

At age twenty, the youngest professional rodeo cowboy ever to win a world championship title in any event (record shared with Ty Murray)

### Continuing the Story

The time a bronc rider spends at work is short—Casey once remarked, "I'm on and off a bronc before I can take a deep breath"—but the working conditions are physically demanding. After thirty-nine breaks and fractures, Casey decided it was time to pursue a less-demanding regimen. As a star on the rodeo circuit, he earned a great deal of money, but his expenses were equally high.

The entry fees, hospital bills, transportation from contest to contest, and living expenses while competing make up a considerable investment for a rodeo performer. Casey's exotic outfits, his propensity for flashy automobiles, and his inclination to gamble with his life and his prize money left him rich in awards but short on cash. Furthermore, his reputation as a practical joker cost him a career as a film star.

Still, the toughness that sustained him on the circuit remained and the former Professional Rodeo Cowboys Association All-Around Cowboy survived. He undertook a career as a stuntman, raised horses on ranches in California and South Dakota, organized rodeos around the world, served as a representative for numerous corporations, and produced an award-winning film *Born to Buck* (1967). In 1990, he died of cancer at the age of sixty.

### Summary

Casey Tibbs was founder of the Professional Rodeo Cowboys Association and a charter member of the

ProRodeo Hall of Fame. He is credited with bringing professional rodeo to national attention. For more than a decade, he was America's best-loved cowboy.

*J. K. Sweeney*

## Additional Sources

Allen, Michael. *Rodeo Cowboys in the North American Imagination.* Reno: University of Nevada Press, 1998.

Ehringer, Gavin, and Gary Vorhes. *Rodeo Legends: Twenty Extraordinary Athletes of America's Sport.* Colorado Springs, Colo.: Western Horseman Magazine, 2003.

Melvin, Donna Maher. *Casey Tibbs: Nine-Time World Champion Pro-Rodeo Cowboy.* [South Dakota]: Author, 2008.

Wooden, Wayne S., and Gavin Ehringer. *Rodeo in America: Wranglers, Roughstock, and Paydirt.* Lawrence: University Press of Kansas, 1996.

# *Ted Turner*

**Born:** November 19, 1938
     Cincinnati, Ohio
**Also known as:** Robert Edward Turner III (full
  name)

## Early Life

Robert Edward Turner III, better known as Ted
Turner, was born on November 19, 1938, in Cincinnati, Ohio. The future yachtsman and businessman was the son of Ed Turner, a cotton farmer
turned salesman, and his wife Florence, whose

*Ted Turner shortly before skippering his boat in the 1977 America's
Cup race.* (George Silk/Time & Life Pictures/Getty Images)

grandfather had the first chain grocery store in Cincinnati. Ted's childhood was turbulent, marked by a
move to Georgia and frequent separations from his
family starting at the age of six.

Perhaps as a misguided effort to prepare Ted for
the competitive world of big business, his father
was unduly harsh in one moment, yet exceedingly
generous in another. The volatility of the father-
son relationship began to show early in Ted's personality. Always a bit mischievous, he earned the
nickname "Terrible Ted" at the McCallie School in
Chattanooga, Tennessee, one of sev-
eral boarding schools he attended in
his youth. Still, Ted was an outstanding
student, particularly interested in history and the classics. He proved early to
be an outstanding orator, becoming the
Tennessee state high school debating
champion when he was seventeen.

## The Road to Excellence

As a college student at Brown University in Providence, Rhode Island, Ted
wanted to major in the classics, but at
his father's insistence, he switched to
accounting. At Brown, Ted also had the
opportunity to hone the sailing skills he
had developed as a child. He loved sailing and won his first nine regattas as a
member of the school's sailing team.

Ted's abilities were not lost on the
members of the Noroton Yacht Club in
nearby Connecticut, who offered him a
chance to race lightning boats for them
during the summer. It seemed like the
perfect summer for Ted, but his father,
who had become the owner of an expanding outdoor advertising company,
wanted him at home. Ted expressed his
disappointment through rowdy behavior that eventually got him suspended
from Brown. The suspension led to a
stint in the Coast Guard, at the behest
of his father.

When Ted was twenty-five, his father

## Major Championship Victories

| | |
|---|---|
| 1963 | U.S. Y-Flyer Championship |
| 1965 | North American Flying Dutchman Champion |
| 1966 | Southern Ocean Racing Conference Champion |
| 1971 | World Championship (5.5-meter) |
| 1977 | America's Cup (as skipper) |
| 1979 | Fastnet Rock Championship (as skipper) |

committed suicide, and Ted took over the family business. At the time, the business was in serious trouble, but through a series of brilliant strategies, Ted turned it into not one but several thriving enterprises that included a cable television station, the Atlanta Braves baseball team, the Atlanta Hawks basketball team, and even the World Championship Wrestling organization. Ted's management style was so enthusiastic, creative, and high-profile that he gained a somewhat outrageous reputation among his peers.

### The Emerging Champion

The adjectives "courageous" and "tenacious"—both used by Ted as names for his yachts—more aptly explain his unusual success in sailing. In the years when Ted was developing his business skills, he was working equally hard to develop his sailing skills. He worked tirelessly to know all that he could about sailing and about the boats in which he raced, and he accepted nothing less than perfection from these boats and their crews.

Among Ted's many sailing victories were three U.S. 5.5-meter championships. These boats are about eighteen feet long, with a jib—which is a small sail forward of the mast—and a mainsail. In 1972, Ted finished first in the Australian Sydney-Hobart regatta, and won the Chicago to Mackinac race in 1973. Ted was best known, however, for his 1977 America's Cup victory over Australia in his 12-meter yacht *Courageous.*

The America's Cup race began in 1851, when the New York Yacht Club sent the schooner *America* to compete against a British schooner for the Hundred Guinea Cup. The *America* won the race, and the trophy was renamed the America's Cup. The race is the most venerable of all international yacht racing events. One must first defeat one's compatriots in trial races to earn the right to represent one's country in competition for the coveted cup.

Ted lost the trials in his 1974 attempt to defend the cup. However, even though he had expended immense time, effort, and money only to lose, Ted took the defeat as the true competitor he was, and he vowed to return for the next trials. His competitive spirit drove him to prepare excellently for the 1977 trials, which he won handily, as he did the America's Cup race against Australia later that year. For his fine performance in the 1977 race and his many previous victories, he won his third yachtsman of the year award.

### Continuing the Story

Ted continued to sail with exceptional intelligence and fearless enthusiasm. He also enjoyed a fair amount of good fortune, as in 1979, when he won the Fastnet Rock race off the coast of Ireland. In that race, a severe storm took the lives of fifteen of his fellow sailors. That year Ted also earned an unprecedented fourth yachtsman of the year award. After winning the Fastnet, Ted realized that competitive racing required an almost full-time schedule, which interfered with his business, and he decided to quit sailboat racing.

Ted's thriving business enterprises included Turner Broadcasting Systems (TBS), the first "superstation," and CNN, the twenty-four-hour cable-television news network. Ted's oratorical skills did not diminish, and he was a highly regarded speaker, particularly at business conventions. He used his influence and wealth to establish the Goodwill Games, an international athletic event based on the spirit of friendly competition. Ted's efforts in this area were aimed at improving relations between the United States and the Soviet Union through sports events.

In 2003, Ted resigned as vice chairman of AOL Time Warner and focused his time on his other businesses, including Ted's Montana Grill, a chain of bison-meat restaurants. He also started the Captain Planet Foundation, which funded and supported hands-on environmental projects for kids.

Widely known throughout the business and sports worlds as a mercurial and formidable competitor, Ted became the owner of a plantation near

### Honors and Awards

| | |
|---|---|
| 1970, 1973, 1977, 1979 | U.S. Yachtsman of the Year |

Atlanta, Georgia, the home base of his many enterprises. In 2005, he was inducted into the Advertising Hall of Fame by the American Advertising Federation. Divorced three times, once from actress Jane Fonda, he is the father of two daughters and three sons.

## Summary

Ted Turner was one of the most versatile competitors in the yachting world. He excelled in many different racing categories including the prestigious 12-meter class, in which he and his crew defended the America's Cup for the United States in 1977. This same versatility and excellence characterized his business career. He became one of the most influential names in cable television.

A brilliant, sensitive youngster, given to mischievous activities, Ted channeled his childhood insecurities into highly constructive accomplishments. Capable of accurately perceiving the smallest details or the broadest general concepts, Ted thrived on adversity. That he successfully mingled his diverse interests and abilities into a rich and purposeful life was a fitting testament to his ability to put dreams fearlessly into action.

*Rebecca J. Sankner, updated by Maryanne Barsotti*

## Additional Sources

Auletta, Ken. *Media Man: Ted Turner's Improbable Empire.* New York: Rigatoni, 2004.

Byman, Jeremy. *Ted Turner: Cable Television Tycoon.* Greensboro, N.C.: Morgan Reynolds, 1998.

Conner, Dennis, and Michael Levitt. *The America's Cup: The History of Sailing's Greatest Competition in the Twentieth Century.* New York: St. Martin's Press, 1998.

Goldberg, Robert, and Gerald Jay Goldberg. *Citizen Turner.* Orlando, Fla.: Harcourt Brace, 1995.

Hickok, Ralph. *A Who's Who of Sports Champions.* Boston: Houghton Mifflin, 1995.

Turner, Ted, and Gary Jobson. *The Racing Edge.* New York: Simon & Schuster, 1979.

Vaughn, Roger. *Ted Turner, Mariner, and the America's Cup.* Boston: Little, Brown, 1975.

# Jan Ullrich

**Born:** December 2, 1973
      Rostock, East Germany (now in Germany)
**Also known as:** Der Kaiser Ulle

### Early Life
Jan Ulrich grew up in Rostock, East Germany (now in Germany), and won his first bicycle race at the age of nine. He soon was matriculated into the sports training system of the German Democratic Republic and attended the SC Dynamo Sports School of East Berlin at the age of thirteen. After the fall of the Berlin Wall in 1989, Jan moved to Hamburg with his trainer, Peter Becker. Jan gained recognition in the cycling world when he entered the 1993 Union Cycliste Internationale World Amateur Road Race World Championship in Oslo, Norway, and became the world champion.

### The Road to Excellence
At the age of twenty-two, Jan signed on with Team Telekom, a professional cycling team competing in international road bicycle races. Becker acted as Jan's agent, and Belgian Walter Godefroot became Jan's manager.

During his first two years with Team Telekom, Jan trained hard and had a number of small accomplishments. He won the German national time trial in 1995. That year, he also finished first in the Tour de Suisse. In addition, Jan entered and placed in the top three of the German Hofbrau Cup. Also in 1995, Jan competed in, but did not finish, the Tour of Spain (known popularly as the Vuelta).

Jan passed up a place in the 1996 German Olympic cycling team to be a part of the Tour de France. Representing Team Telekom, Jan rode as lieutenant to teammate Bjarne Riis, who was the Tour de France champion that year. However, Jan finished second, only one minute and forty-one seconds behind Riis. During the event, Jan won the final individual time trial and thus entered into a new realm professionally. Five-time Tour de France champion Miguel Ángel Indurain, who in that year was deposed by Riis, famously predicted that Jan would win a Tour de France some year.

### The Emerging Champion
Jan catapulted to international attention with his dramatic win in the 1997 Tour de France. He started the race strongly and soon became a favorite with the media. The French press declared him *le patron* (the boss). As the 1997 event progressed, Jan solidified his lead. Jan wore both the yellow jersey, as overall leader, and the white jersey, as the

*Jan Ullrich racing in the 1997 Tour de France, which he won.* (Pascal Rondeau/Getty Images)

## Major Racing Competitions

| | |
|---|---|
| 1993 | Amateur World Road Race cycling champion |
| 1995 | Germany National Time Trial Champion |
| 1996 | Tour de France 2d place |
| 1997 | Tour de France winner |
| | Germany National Road Race Champion |
| 1997, 2003 | German Sportsman of the Year |
| 1998 | Tour de France 2d place |
| 1999 | World Time Trial Cycling Champion |
| | Winner Vuelta a España (Tour of Spain) |
| 2000 | Gold medal, Olympic games |
| | Silver medal, Olympic games |
| | Tour de France 2d place |
| | Coppa Agostoni |
| 2001 | World Time Trial Cycling Champion |
| | National Road Race Champion |
| | Tour de France 2d place |
| | Giro dell'Emilia |
| | Versatel Classic |
| 2003 | Tour de France 2d place |
| 2004, 2006 | Tour de Suisse winner |

leader of riders under the age of twenty-five. Not since Laurent Fignon in 1983 had a rider possessed both jerseys at the same time.

Though Jan had served as lieutenant to team-mate Riis in the previous year's Tour de France, he soon proved that he could better Riis's riding. Jan shot ahead in the second-mountain and tenth-overall stage of the competition. He was pitted against two of the Tour de France's strongest climbers, Marco Pantani and Richard Virenque. Jan finished more than a minute ahead of these two race favorites, for which he earned his first yellow jersey. The race finished dramatically, with Jan pulling ahead of Virenque to win the 1997 Tour de France.

At the age of twenty-three, Jan became the fourth youngest winner of the Tour since 1947. He also earned the respect and increased attention of the German press. He was credited with encouraging a surge in the popularity of cycling in Germany.

### Continuing the Story

Jan was the defending champion in the 1998 Tour de France. After a strong beginning, winning the yellow jersey in the ninth stage, Jan fell behind his great rival, the American cycling champion Lance Armstrong. Jan chased Armstrong for most of the remainder of his career.

In the 2000 Summer Olympics, held in Sydney,

Australia, Jan prevailed, beating Armstrong. He won a gold medal for overall performance and a silver medal in the individual time-trial event. Armstrong won a bronze medal that year. The next few years brought some victories and some defeats to Jan, with Armstrong close behind—or ahead of—him.

In 2002, Jan was implicated in drug and alcohol incidents. In May of that year, he had his driver's license revoked after a drunk-driving incident in which he plowed into a row of bicycles. In June of that year, he tested positive for amphetamines and lost his contract with Team Telekom; he was banned from racing for six months and missed the Tour de France. Jan became known for his partying lifestyle and was a frequenter of clubs and bars. He also gained weight in the off-season.

However, Jan did not end his career in cycling until 2007. He was implicated in the large doping scandal, Operación Puerto, which was an effort by Spanish authorities to curtail drug use in the sports world. Jan was one of several cyclists linked with Spanish physicians Dr. Eufemiano Fuentes and Dr. Jose Merino Batres. After weeks of media coverage, a complicated web unraveled: Several athletes, including Jan, had received blood transfusions with a full doping program that involved the performance-enhancing drugs Erythropoietin, anabolic steroids, human growth hormones, and insulin-like growth factor 1. At the age of thirty-three, Jan retired from cycling. He was retained as a consultant for the Austrian-based Volksbank cycling team.

### Summary

In the early 1990's, Jan Ulrich emerged as one of the world's youngest and strongest cyclists. His rise to the top of the premier international race, the Tour de France, helped to inspire an enthusiasm for the sport among the general populace. However, his career was tarnished by accusations of performance-enhancing-drug use.

*Alison Stankrauff*

### Additional Sources

Burke, Edmund R. *Serious Cycling*. 2d ed. Champaign, Ill.: Human Kinetics, 2002.

Rendell, Matt, and Nicolas Cheetham. *The Official Tour de France: 1903-2004*. London: Weidenfeld & Nicolson, 2004.

# Al Unser

**Born:** May 29, 1939
Albuquerque, New Mexico
**Also known as:** Alfred Unser (full name)

### Early Life

Alfred Unser was born on May 29, 1939, in Albuquerque, New Mexico, into a racing family. His father, Jerry, Sr., and his older brothers, Jerry, Louis, and Bobby, were all racers. His father ran a garage and allowed the boys to tinker with an old pickup truck, which they finally got to run. Informal races and driving around the desert gave Al his earliest contact with driving. The neighborhood was a rough one, with clashes between Hispanics and Anglos and between newcomers and old-time residents. Working in the family business and on the family racing team gave Al a constructive outlet for his energy.

The Unser family was involved in the annual Pikes Peak road race, and this event gave Al his racing groundwork. Al also gained experience with stock cars and sprint cars. During these years, Al was somewhat in the shadow of his older brother Bobby, who was rapidly establishing a racing reputation for himself.

### The Road to Excellence

In 1967, Al had his first success in an Indianapolis 500 race by finishing second. Bobby won the race the next year, so Al was still struggling for recognition.

In 1970, during the qualifying events for the Indianapolis 500, it appeared a close race was shaping up. At least four drivers were close in speed, and Al won the pole position by only two and one-half feet over a 10-mile race. In the actual race, both Unser brothers were at the front of the pack by lap 3. Their driving skill was enhanced by their pit crews, Al's crew consistently getting his car back on the track in about 20 seconds on each of his stops. This combined effort helped Al build a 32-second lead by the end of the race.

Al Unser, who won consecutive Indianapolis 500s in 1970 and 1971. He also won the race in 1978 and 1987. (Courtesy of Amateur Athletic Foundation of Los Angeles)

## The Emerging Champion

The next year, 1971, Indianapolis was marked by problems from the start. The pace car crashed into a photographers' stand as it was leaving the track. Early in the race, three drivers wrecked, leading to 17 laps under the caution flag. Other cars dropped out with mechanical problems and, after 118 laps, Al was in the lead to stay. Late in the race, a final fiery crash took out more cars and strewed the track with burning gas and wreckage. Still, Al steered clear and ended the race with a new track speed record, an average of 157.735 miles per hour. Al joined a select group of only three other back-to-back Indy winners.

In the 1972 season, Al's career slowed down. He won some races, but not on a consistent basis. He was frequently plagued with breakdowns and penalties. He was involved in a controversy with fans and other drivers about the tactics he used to win the 1973 Texas 200 race. In 1975 and 1976, Al had to work out problems with a new type of car, a Cosworth Ford eight-cylinder turbocharged engine, a powerful engine that won races when it did not break down. In addition to his racing problems, Al's mother died in 1975.

## Continuing the Story

1976 and 1977 were better racing years, but Al still was not winning the big races or taking the United States Auto Club (USAC) Championship. In 1978, however, all the pieces came together. After spending several years developing the new engine, Al ran away with the Indy 500. This win was aided by car designer Jim Hall, whose ground-effects design

caused the car to hug the ground more closely to take the corners at a higher speed. Al became only the third person to win at Indianapolis three times. Less than a month later, Al won the Pocono 500 race in the same car.

Al and several other drivers were dissatisfied with the way USAC regulated racing, so, at the end of 1978, twenty racing teams formed their own association to sponsor races, the Championship Auto Racing Teams (CART). It touched off a controversy between the two sponsoring groups that eventually had to be settled in court.

In 1979, Al again changed racing teams, this time joining Bobby Hillin's Chaparral Racing Team because the car designer attended races to see the car perform and to identify problems. Although this change was successful, Al soon faced a new competitor, his son Al, Jr.

Although father and son were in competition, they worked together, as in the 1983 Indianapolis 500, when Al, Jr., blocked driver Tom Sneva for 10 laps in an unsuccessful attempt to protect his father's lead.

---

### CART and Other Victories

|  |  |
|---|---|
| 1964-65, 1983 | Pikes Peak Hill Climb |
| 1968 | Nazareth 100 |
| 1969 | Phoenix 200 |
| 1969-70 | Duquoin 100 |
| 1969-70, 1976 | Milwaukee 200 |
| 1970 | Indianapolis Raceway Park 150 |
| | Springfield 100 |
| | Trenton 300 |
| | USAC National Champion |
| 1970-71, 1976, 1979, 1985 | Phoenix 150 |
| 1970-71, 1978, 1987 | Indianapolis 500 |
| 1970-73 | Hoosier 100 |
| 1970, 1972, 1975 | Tony Bettenhausen 100 |
| 1971 | Milwaukee 150 |
| 1973 | Texas 200 |
| | Valvoline/USAC Silver Crown Series Champion |
| 1974 | Michigan 250 |
| 1976, 1978 | Pocono 500 |
| 1977-78 | California 500 |
| 1980 | Can-Am Challenge Cup Race (Laguna Seca) |
| 1983 | Cleveland Grand Prix |
| | Cleveland 500 kilometers |
| 1983, 1985 | PPG Indy Car World Series Championship |

---

### Honors, Awards, and Records

|  |  |
|---|---|
| 1967 | USAC Rookie of the Year |
| 1970 | Jerry Titus Memorial Award |
| 1970, 1978 | Martini & Rossi Driver of the Year |
| 1986 | Inducted into Indianapolis Motor Speedway Hall of Fame |
| 1987 | One of only three drivers to capture the Indianapolis 500 four times |
| | At forty-seven years and eleven months of age, the oldest driver in history to capture the Indianapolis 500 |
| 1991 | Inducted into Motorsports Hall of Fame of America |
| 1998 | Inducted into International Motorsports Hall of Fame |

In 1985, Al, Sr., and Al, Jr., came into the last race of the season virtually tied for the championship. Al, Sr., had started the year with a contract for only three races. He consistently finished in the top five and came to the final race on the verge of the championship. Al, Jr., needed to beat Al, Sr., by two places to win the championship. Almost at the end, Al, Sr., charged past another driver, and, although finishing the race behind his son, won the championship by one point.

Perhaps the zenith of Al's career came in 1987, when he went to Indianapolis without a car to drive. The injury of another driver during the qualifying events gave him his chance. His skill and experience gave him the victory for the fourth time and made him the oldest person ever to win the Indy 500. With age beginning to take its toll, Al finished his racing career with a third-place finish in 1992 and a twelfth-place finish in his final race of 1993.

## Summary

Al Unser was both relaxed and competitive, with a rural manner of speaking and a wry sense of humor. Noted for clean living, sticking to his work, and finishing almost every race he entered, he enjoyed his children's company and his relationship with his racing "family."

*Michael R. Bradley*

## Additional Sources

Martin, J. A., and Thomas F. Saal. *American Auto Racing: The Milestones and Personalities of a Century of Speed.* Jefferson, N.C.: McFarland, 2004.

Reed, Terry. *Indy: The Race and Ritual of the Indianapolis 500.* Washington, D.C.: Potomac Books, 2005.

Sakkis, Tony. *Indy Racing Legends.* Osceola, Wis.: Motorbooks International, 1996.

Taylor, Rich. *Indy: Seventy-five Years of Racing's Greatest Spectacle.* New York: St. Martin's Press, 1991.

# Bobby Unser

**Born:** February 20, 1934
      Colorado Springs, Colorado
**Also known as:** Robert William Unser (full name)

### Early Life

Robert William Unser was born on February 20, 1934, in Colorado Springs, Colorado. He moved to Albuquerque, New Mexico, at the age of three when his parents, Jerry, Sr., and Mary, opened an automobile repair garage there. Bobby had older twin brothers, Jerry and Louis, and a younger brother, Al.

Bobby grew up during the later years of the Great Depression, so the Unser family did not have much money. Also, the boys were newcomers to town and had to fend for themselves against the more established youth.

The boys' father allowed them to rebuild an old pickup truck when Bobby was nine, so he learned about mechanics at an early age. The entire family became involved in racing. Bobby's father drove racers; one uncle did also. Jerry, Jr., was a United States Auto Club (USAC) stock car champion in 1957 and was killed in an auto race at Indianapolis in 1959. Louis won the Pikes Peak Hill Climb twice before he became confined to a wheelchair by multiple sclerosis. Younger brother Al was also a racer, as was his son Al, Jr.

At the age of fifteen, Bobby began racing in Albuquerque and soon established a reputation. In 1953, Bobby entered the Air Force but managed to combine his duties with auto racing. In 1957, he was discharged because of the death of his father. At that point, Bobby began to concentrate fully on his racing in the Pikes Peak Hill Climb.

### The Road to Excellence

In 1963, Bobby drove for the first time in the Memorial Day race at Indianapolis, Indiana. This race was not a long one for Bobby because he crashed his car on the third lap. In 1966, Bobby was back, finishing eighth, and in 1968, he hit the big time.

Turbine cars were supposed to win the Indy 500 in 1968, but with his mother Mary and second wife Norma watching from the same spot where his brother had been killed in 1959, Bobby stayed on the tail of these cars as, one after the other, they broke down. Coming into lap 191 of the 200 laps in the race, Bobby was still trailing when the last turbine sputtered to a stop, and he sprinted ahead. Because of his immense popularity on the race circuit, the fans cheered wildly. In winning the race, Bobby had set a new track record of 152.8 miles per hour.

With money from his prize and with an established reputation, Bobby began to attract sponsors who made available money, automobile parts, and backing. Bobby began an association with Roger Penske that lasted many years. Each season after

*Bobby Unser, who won the Indianapolis 500 in 1968, 1975, and 1981.* (Courtesy of Amateur Athletic Foundation of Los Angeles)

1968, Bobby did a little better, winning more of the big races. By 1972, he held speed records at seventeen of the eighteen race tracks on the United States Auto Club (USAC) circuit.

### The Emerging Champion

Bobby did not confine himself to Indy-style cars. In 1974, he set a new speed record in the Pikes Peak Hill Climb in a stock car. This 12½ mile race climbed to the top of Pikes Peak, 14,100 feet in height, over a road with more than five hundred turns. This race was almost an Unser family possession, because various family members won it twenty-eight times.

On Memorial Day in 1975, Bobby was back in Indianapolis. This time, there was no concern about turbo cars, but other drivers, such as archrival A. J. Foyt, were out to give Bobby a run for the money. Again, someone else led for most of the race, but as the race neared its end, several drivers pulled into the pit to get gas. Bobby had planned better and had gotten gas earlier and began to take the lead. Suddenly, the skies opened up in a heavy downpour. With Bobby ahead, the starter waved the checkered flag after only 174 laps. This win in the rain was Bobby's second at Indy.

Wins and championships continued to come to Bobby, and he kept on pushing hard. As he put it, he did what came naturally and was the easiest thing for him—going fast.

### Continuing the Story

In 1981, a third Indy win came to Bobby but only after a monthlong period of controversy. During the race, Bobby dueled with Mario Andretti and, as the race reached the three-quarters point at lap 148, both men pulled into the pits under a yellow flag to take fuel. Under a yellow flag, no driver is supposed to improve his position. As Bobby left the pit, he reentered the track in a way not clearly covered by the rules. At the end of the race, Bobby was ahead, but Andretti filed a protest. The next day, the USAC board upheld the protest and declared An-

dretti the winner. Bobby then protested because the rules called for a one-lap penalty to be assessed immediately. In October, 1981, the USAC agreed and officially awarded the race to Bobby. He became the oldest driver ever to win the Indianapolis 500—a record later broken by younger brother Al.

The controversy and its worry and tension caused Bobby to lose some of his enthusiasm for racing, and he decided to retire. He had earned almost three million dollars, three victories at Indianapolis, and two national championships. Retirement did not mean completely giving up racing because two of his sons, Robbie and Bobby, Jr., continued to

---

### NASCAR and Stock Car Victories

| | |
|---|---|
| 1950 | New Mexico Modified Stock Car Championship |
| 1956, 1958-62, 1966, 1968-69, 1974, 1976 | Pikes Peak Hill Climb |
| 1965 | Stardust 150 |
| 1968, 1972, 1976 | Phoenix 150 |
| 1968, 1974 | USAC National Driving Champion |
| 1968, 1975, 1981 | Indianapolis 500 |
| 1969-70 | Langhorne 150 |
| 1971 | Marlboro 300 |
| | Milwaukee 200 |
| | Trenton 200 |
| | Tony Bettenhausen 200 |
| 1972-73 | Milwaukee 150 |
| 1974 | Michigan 200 |
| 1974, 1976, 1979-80 | California 500 |
| 1979 | Michigan 126 |
| | Michigan 150 |
| 1980 | Pocono 500 |

---

### Honors, Awards, and Records

| | |
|---|---|
| 1974 | Martini & Rossi Driver of the Year |
| 1976 | Made the fastest pit stop ever, using only four seconds to refuel on lap ten of the Indianapolis 500 |
| 1990 | Inducted into Indianapolis Motor Speedway Hall of Fame |
| | Inducted into International Motorsports Hall of Fame |
| 1994 | Inducted into Motorsports Hall of Fame of America |
| 1997 | Inducted into National Sprint Car Hall of Fame |

drive racers, and Bobby still occasionally drove stock cars and four-wheel-drive dirt-road races.

## Summary

Bobby Unser paid a price for success. For years, he risked his life in every race. He spent more time away from his family than with it, and he suffered the physical injuries that are a part of race-car driving. Bobby had a strong personal motivation, however: "There is no such thing as a slow day in the life of Bobby Unser and I will go fast until the day I die."

*Michael R. Bradley*

## Additional Sources

Martin, J. A., and Thomas F. Saal. *American Auto Racing: The Milestones and Personalities of a Century of Speed.* Jefferson, N.C.: McFarland, 2004.

Sakkis, Tony. *Indy Racing Legends.* Osceola, Wis.: Motorbooks International, 1996.

Scalzo, Joe. *The Bobby Unser Story.* Garden City, N.Y.: Doubleday, 1979.

Unser, Bobby, and Paul Pease. *Winners Are Driven: A Champion's Guide to Success in Business and Life.* Hoboken, N.J.: J. Wiley & Sons, 2003.

# *Jacques Villeneuve*

**Born:** April 9, 1971
     St-Jean-sur-Richlieu, Quebec, Canada
**Also known as:** Jacques Joseph Charles Villeneuve
  (full name)

## Early Life

Jacques Joseph Charles Villeneuve was born on April 9, 1971, in St-Jean-sur-Richlieu, Quebec, Canada. His father Gilles Villeneuve was obsessed with racing both snowmobiles and cars. Jacques grew up in a world of speed, following his father to races around Canada and, later, Europe. When Gilles was hired to drive for Ferrari in Formula One races, he began to build a reputation as a daredevil. His over-the-edge style of driving thrilled racing fans and impressed his fellow competitors.

In 1983, Gilles Villeneuve was killed in a crash while qualifying for the Belgian Grand Prix. Jacques was eleven years old. Though he had won few races and never won a championship, Gilles had become one of the most famous drivers in racing history. His reputation both helped and hindered Jacques throughout his own driving career.

Through Gilles's racing success, the family was financially secure, and at the age of twelve, Jacques was sent from his home in France to a private boarding school in Switzerland. He excelled in his classes when he applied himself, but overall, he was less interested in school than in skiing. On snow he was fast, daring, and competitive; most likely, he could have become a ski champion had his interest not changed to cars. He made friends with his ski instructor Craig Pollock, who later became Jacques's manager and played an important role in his life and career.

## The Road to Excellence

In the summers, Jacques and his family returned to Canada. There his uncle Jacques, also a successful racing driver, encouraged young Jacques's interest in motor racing, first in go-karts, then with sessions at racing schools. His instructors praised his natural speed and declared that he had the family talent.

Back in Europe in 1988, Jacques entered three races in the Italian Touring Car Championship, a move made easier by the fame of his father in Italy. He finished tenth in his first race, a respectable result for a seventeen-year-old beginner with little driving experience. The next year he quit school before graduating to compete in the Italian Formula Three series. Here too he found sponsorship and patient instruction because of his name. He was a quick learner and dedicated himself to racing, finishing tenth in the championship in 1990 and sixth the following year.

Jacques was uncomfortable in Italy, as he was constantly compared to his famous father, so he moved to Japan to race in the Formula Three series. Living on his own far from home at the age of twenty helped Jacques mature and grow into the life of a professional racer. His driving continued to improve as well, and he finished second in the Formula Three Championship.

In 1992, Jacques made a "guest appearance" at a Formula Atlantic race in Montreal, Canada, racing

### Formula One and Other Victories

| Year | Series | Place |
|------|--------|-------|
| 1988 | Italian Touring Car Championship | 10th |
| 1989 | Italian Formula Three | — |
| 1990 | Italian Formula Three | 10th |
| 1991 | Italian Formula Three | 6th |
| 1992 | Japanese Formula Three | 2d |
|      | Formula Atlantic | 3d |
| 1993 | Formula Atlantic | 3d |
| 1994 | PPG IndyCar | 6th |
|      | Indianapolis 500 | 2d |
| 1995 | PPG IndyCar | 1st |
|      | Indianapolis 500 | 1st |
| 1996 | World Formula One | 2d |
| 1997 | World Formula One | 1st |
| 1998 | World Formula One | 5th |
| 1999 | World Formula One | — |
| 2000 | World Formula One | — |
| 2001 | Formula One | 7th |
| 2002 | Formula One | 12th |
| 2003 | Formula One | 16th |
| 2004 | Formula One | 21st |
| 2005 | Formula One | 14th |
| 2006 | Formula One | 15th |
| 2007 | NASCAR Nextel Cup | 42d |
|      | NASCAR Craftsman Truck Series | 59th |
| 2008 | Le Mans Series | 9th |

against his uncle Jacques. The younger Jacques finished third amid much media attention. This experience persuaded him to return to Canada for the 1993 season, driving in the Formula Atlantic series for the Players-Forsythe team.

## The Emerging Champion

The Formula Atlantic series took Jacques all over the United States and Canada and introduced him to oval tracks as well as to road and street courses. He had five first-place finishes in fifteen races and placed third in the overall championship. These results persuaded team owner Jerry Forsythe to enter him in the PPG Indy Car World Series for 1994.

Jacques was immediately comfortable in these faster and more powerful machines and started the year with impressive qualifying times. However, two accidents early in the season revived comparisons with the reckless style of his father. Jacques's race engineer, Tony Cicale, defended him, saying that he drove carefully and intelligently, never exceeding the limits of the car or his driving skill. Good results followed, including a second-place finish at the Indianapolis 500. He finished the year in sixth place overall and won rookie of the year honors for 1994.

In 1995, Jacques conquered the world of Indy cars, with an impressive come-from-behind win at Indianapolis. Four first-place finishes, along with consistent results in the rest of the seventeen races, brought Jacques the Indy car championship.

Jacques's impressive success in Indy cars brought him a job offer from the top-ranked Williams Formula One team. Adapting quickly to the differences in Formula One cars, Jacques nearly won his first race in Australia. Winning four races during the 1996 season, he finished a close second to his teammate Damon Hill for the championship. In 1997, Jacques drove again for Williams; this time, seven wins were enough to bring him the world championship at the age of twenty-six.

## Continuing the Story

In 1998, the Williams team had a difficult season, and Jacques finished fifth in the championship behind the cars of the McLaren and Ferrari teams. In 1999, Jacques took on the difficult job of helping to bring a new team to success, driving for British American Racing. This team, formed by his old friend and manager Pollock, had a dismal first year,

finishing few races and earning no points. Jacques finished twenty-second in the series, and his teammate Ricardo Zonta was last at twenty-fourth. The 2000 season started with better results, but Jacques admitted in magazine interviews that he might be interested in driving for another team in 2001 if his fortunes with British American Racing did not improve.

Instead, Zonta left the team and was replaced by Frenchman Olivier Panis. In 2001, Jacques finished on the podium twice, in Spain and Germany. Remaining in Formula One with British American Racing in 2002, Jacques's fortunes fell. Pollock was fired as team manager, and Jacques scored only four points the entire year. In 2003, Panis was replaced by Englishman Jenson Button. After tremendous early successes, Jacques's career seemed to be slowing down. His performance, even when compared to his younger, less experienced teammates, seemed noticeably worse. Without a ride in Formula One for most of 2004, Jacques was forced to step back and evaluate his participation in the series. Driving in the final three races that year for Renault, Jacques failed to finish any of the races on the lead lap.

After several disappointing years, Jacques began driving for the Swiss team Sauber, later bought by BMW. With his new team, Jacques rekindled his ability and consistently scored points in 2005-2006. However, Jacques never returned to the championship level in Formula One again. He left the series in 2006. Seeking new challenges, Jacques turned to the 24 Hours of Le Mans. Racing for Peugeot, he desired to win the third leg of the triple crown of motorsports, hoping to join Graham Hill as the only winners of Le Mans, Indianapolis, and the Formula One Championship.

With his successes in Formula One and Indy Car behind him, Jacques followed Juan Pablo Montoya, another former Indy winner and Grand Prix champion, into the NASCAR series. Along with Montoya, Dario Franchitti, and Sam Hornish, Jr., Jacques brought an open-wheel style to the stock-car tracks. He drove in the Nextel Cup series and the Craftsman Truck series. In 2007, only one month after his first truck-series race, Jacques made his NASCAR debut with Bill Davis Racing at Talladega Superspeedway in Alabama. Because of a lack of sponsorship and failure to qualify for the 2008 Daytona 500, Jacques's involvement with NASCAR, in both the truck and stock-car series, was brief. Seemingly drifting from one type of racing to another, Jacques spent the remainder of the 2008 series in SPEEDCAR, a series composed of road races and stock-car-type tracks. Outside racing, Jacques opened a trendy café in Montreal called Newtown, roughly an English translation of his last name. Jacques, an aspiring songwriter, released his first music album, *Private Paradise*, in 2007.

## Summary

In only eight years Jacques Villeneuve went from a beginning racer to the world champion. Along the way, he proved that he was an intelligent and calculating driver: a man who knew his limits and those of his car. He used that knowledge, along with courage and determination, to emerge from the shadow of his famous father to become a champion in his own right.

*Joseph W. Hinton, updated by Randy L. Abbott*

## Additional Sources

Collings, Timothy. *The New Villeneuve: The Life of Jacques Villeneuve*. Osceola, Wis.: Motorbooks International, 1997.

Hilton, Christopher. *Jacques Villeneuve: In His Own Right*. Osceola, Wis.: Motorbooks International, 1996.

James, Brant. "Villeneuve Hot on Montoya's New Trail." *St. Petersburg Times*, September 1, 2007, p. 8C.

Jenkins, Chris. "Villeneuve's Career Slowing, Future Uncertain: No Retirement for Ex-Indy, F1 Champ." *USA Today*, October 1, 2003, p. 10C.

Sparling, Ken. *Jacques Villeneuve: Born to Race*. Willowdale, Ont.: Firefly Books, 1999.

Voeglin, Rick. "The Son Also Races." *Sport*, September, 1998, 38.

# Dave Villwock

**Born:** February 10, 1954
 Bremerton, Washington
**Also known as:** David Villwock (full name)

## Early Life

The son of Gerald and Doris Villwock, David Villwock was born on February 10, 1954, in Bremerton, Washington. When Dave was five years old, he moved with his family to a farm in nearby Port Orchard, Washington. During Dave's childhood, his family participated in weekend boat races throughout the Pacific Northwest. In his uncle's shop, Dave helped his father and uncle, Al, build boats for racing, including stock outboards and hydroplanes. Dave's uncle encouraged him to race for recreational benefits as well as to develop his competitive nature.

*Dave Villwock standing on the bow of the* Miss Budweiser *after winning the General Motors Cup in 2000.* (AP/Wide World Photos)

## The Road to Excellence

In his early races, Dave learned to drive various boat types. Recognizing his potential, retired racers, including Steve Jones, served as mentors, teaching Dave driving and other techniques based on their experiences. Jones's philosophy of refusing to lose strengthened Dave's resolve to win despite any personal or financial obstacles or rough waters, wet engines, or poor starts.

Sometimes lacking sufficient equipment and money, Dave relied on his willpower for motivation and attributed his early victories to this positive attitude. He began his professional racing career driving 20-inch boats known as crackerboxes. Using these powerboats, he won several American Power Boat Association (APBA) national championships. Dave next piloted E racing runabouts and began setting world records. He accomplished similar feats in the superstock runabout, ski-racing runabout, and pro competition runabout classes and won national championships in all three categories in 1984. That year, he was inducted into the APBA Hall of Champions.

## The Emerging Champion

With Jerry Yoder, Dave built a hydroplane with which he competed in the 6-liter class. Known as the *Sunset Chevrolet Special*, this hydroplane enabled Dave to win every heat and race he entered with it in 1988, earning him another national championship and enabling him to set world records. Fran Muncey, representative of the Circus Circus Unlimited Hydroplane team, saw Dave race the 6-liter hydroplane in San Diego, California. She contacted him, and he began working as Circus Circus team manager in November, 1988.

## Major Championships

| | |
|---|---|
| 1974-75 | APBA National Championship |
| | High Point Championship |
| | Western Division Championship in crackerbox class |
| 1984 | APBA National Superstock Runabout Championship |
| | APBA Ski Runabout National Championship |
| | Pro Competition Runabout National Championship |
| 1987 | National High Point Championship in the 6-liter hydroplane class |
| | Ten Grand Prix Championship in the 7-liter class |
| 1988 | Western Division Championship for the 6-liter hydroplane class |
| | Western Division championship in the Superstock Runabout Class |
| 1990 | National Championship in the Unlimited Hydroplane Class as team manager of Circus Circus team with driver Chip Hanauer |
| 1996 | UHRA National Driver Championship |
| | APBA Gold Cup |
| 1997 | APBA Gold Cup |
| 1998 | UHRA National Driver Championship |
| | APBA Gold Cup |
| 1999 | UHRA National Driver Championship |
| 2000 | APBA Gold Cup |
| 2002 | APBA Gold Cup |
| 2005 | Bill Muncey Cup |
| 2006 | APBA Gold Cup |
| 2007 | APBA Gold Cup |

Unlimited hydroplanes were considered the world's fastest race boats.

In his new position, Dave worked with driver Chip Hanauer, who set a world speed record with the Circus Circus hydroplane, traveling 158.87 miles per hour on a 2.5-mile qualifying lap in 1989. This unlimited hydroplane was the first to surpass 150 miles per hour on a 2-mile lap. The following year, Dave's team earned a national championship.

Ron Jones, Jr., invited Dave to test-drive a powerboat with unique design features. Dave suggested ways to increase the boat's speed; he also designed and created a propeller. Piloting this craft, known as the *Coors Dry,* he won his first unlimited hydroplane race, in 1992, at San Diego. The next year, he agreed to drive for a reorganized Circus Circus team. His technical expertise benefited the team because of his innovations in hull structure.

In 1994, he won consecutive races in Seattle and San Diego. He continued to place first

or second in qualifying heats and races throughout 1996. Also that year, he drove the *PICO American Dream* to victory at the Unlimited Hydroplane Racing Association (UHRA) national driver championships and won the APBA Gold Cup championship, which has been compared to the Indianapolis 500 car race.

### Continuing the Story

Dave next agreed to drive the *Miss Budweiser* when Bernie Little, the boat's owner, asked him to replace Hanauer in 1996. After winning the first four races of the 1997 season and securing another APBA Gold Cup, Dave crashed the *Miss Budweiser* on the Columbia River near Pasco, Washington, and was hospitalized. His right arm was broken, and his hand was almost severed. Physicians amputated two infected fingers and told Dave that his professional hydroplane-racing career was over. He refused to accept that prognosis and underwent approximately twenty surgeries and eight months of physical therapy.

During his recovery, Dave and his team prepared for his return to racing. They reinforced the *Miss Budweiser* with a sturdier hull and redesigned the steering wheel. Dave returned to UHRA racing by winning the Pontiac Grand Am Thunder race on the Ohio River near Evansville, Indiana. The victory was his third consecutive in that race. He attained an average speed of 137.01 mph, proving that he was physically able to race hydroplanes. He finished ten races in one season and won eight of them, an unrivaled achievement in the sport. He won his third consecutive Gold Cup at a Detroit River race in Michigan,

## Records and Milestones

| | |
|---|---|
| 1979-82 | Set four world speed records in E Racing Runabout class |
| 1984 | Set fifth world speed record |
| 1986 | Set world speed record in the Superstock Runabout Class |
| 1988 | Set seventh and eighth world speed records |
| | Set record for winning eight seasonal races |
| 1999 | Set ninth world speed record |
| | Repeated record of eight seasonal victories |
| 2000 | Ten consecutive victories, Unlimited Class |
| 2004 | Set Unlimited hydroplane speed record |

earned his second UHRA national driver championship, and was inducted again into the APBA Hall of Champions in recognition of his accomplishments.

In 1999, Dave repeated his record of securing eight seasonal victories. He won his third UHRA national driver championship and set a world record when he attained a speed of 173.38 miles per hour in a race on Mission Bay, San Diego. Each time Dave won, he had to start the next race a lane farther from the course's center, adding extra mileage to his course.

In 2000, Dave won the first UHRA race at Lake Havasu, Nevada, giving boat owner Little a record 125 career wins. Dave's domination of the sport led to the UHRA practice of penalizing winning drivers with fuel decreases. The association's new policy meant that drivers started with 4.3 gallons of fuel per minute to power the engine, but lost one-tenth of a gallon per victory, effective at their next race.

*Miss Budweiser* was not the fastest boat on the circuit in 2001, but the team opened the season with a victory in Evansville, won sixty percent of its heats, and secured the championship on the last day of the season in San Diego. In the 2002 season, the team captured three victories in six races, enough to win a fourteenth APBA Gold Cup, the fifth for Dave. The *Miss Budweiser* team lost its captain when Little died prior to the 2003 campaign. Despite its success in winning the 2003 championship, *Miss Budweiser*'s twenty-third title since 1969, the team struggled and announced that the 2004 campaign was its last. The team finished in style, winning the 2004 championship. *Miss Budweiser* won its final race in 2004, winning all its heats to take the Bill Muncey Cup.

Dave found himself briefly unemployed until he signed on with Erick Ellstrom's *Miss E-LAM Plus* team in 2005. Though the team had won seven races with various drivers over the years, it had never won the championship. With Dave in the driver's seat, the team won its first championship. Favored to win the 2006 championship, Dave crashed during qualifications at St. Francis Bay, Quebec, Canada. At the Tri-Cities race, the same

year, Dave's boat went airborne and did one and one-half revolutions before hitting the water hard. The team was able to repair the boat and win the competition, marking only the second time in history a boat had flipped and came back to win the race in the same day. In 2007, Dave won the Evansville "Thunder on the Ohio" season opener for his tenth win in twelve years at Evansville. At Detroit, Dave won his sixth APBA Gold Cup and the first for team E-LAM.

## Summary

Dave Villwock won or placed in a record-setting percentage of races on the unlimited-hydroplane circuit. He ranked third all-time in victories behind only the late Bill Muncey and the retired Chip Hanauer. As driver or team manager of unlimited hydroplanes, Dave collected fifty-five victories in addition to his earlier racing titles earned while driving other types of boats. One of the few drivers to have been a crew chief first, his technical knowledge contributed to the advancement of hydroplane technology.

*Elizabeth D. Schafer, updated by Randy L. Abbott*

## Additional Sources

Armijo, Mark. "Can Anything Stop Villwock? Hydro Officials Plan New Rules." *The Arizona Republic*, May 19, 2000, p. C5.

Boeck, Scott. "'Miss Bud' Driver Undeterred: Villwock back from Horrific Crash in '97." *USA Today*, May 22, 1998, p. F15.

Riley, Jim. "Villwock: Elam Has Saved Its Best for Seattle." *The Seattle Times*, August 1, 2007, p. D3.

Savage, Jeff. *Hydroplane Boats*. Mankato, Minn.: Capstone Press, 2004.

# Lisa Wagner

**Born:** May 19, 1961
Hillsboro, Illinois
**Also known as:** Rocket

## Early Life

Lisa Wagner was born on May 19, 1961, in Hillsboro, Illinois. Bolstered by her parents' involvement in a local junior bowling league, Lisa began to bowl regularly by the age of six. After her parents finished their own games, Lisa threw practice balls. With tips and practical advice from her parents, the young bowler soon began to compete in local tournaments.

Lisa Wagner, whose bowling career coincided with the onset of television coverage of the sport, making hers one of the most recognizable faces in women's bowling. (International Bowling Museum)

When Lisa was fifteen, professional bowler Tommy Evans began coaching Lisa. The lessons that Lisa learned from her parents and from Evans remained with her throughout her career. After competing in and winning amateur tournaments, Lisa began a career as a professional bowler in 1980.

## The Road to Excellence

Although Lisa had been bowling from the time she was six years old, had the support of her family, and had been coached by a professional bowler, she still struggled for her first break in professional bowling. Even so, Lisa amassed enough money and experience in amateur tournaments to consider a career as a professional bowler. Because women bowlers' earnings were lower than men bowlers' earnings, when Lisa turned professional, she had to use the prize money she won in amateur tournaments to fund trips to her first several professional tournaments.

Early in her professional career, at a tournament in Las Vegas, Nevada, Lisa and her doubles partner Carolyn Dorin were so surprised to qualify for the tournament that they were unprepared when they did—they had not purchased team uniforms and had to make a spur-of-the-moment shopping trip to find matching clothes for the tournament. Despite their surprise qualification and hastily chosen outfits, the pair managed to win the tournament in the last frame of the final game.

## The Emerging Champion

Lisa proved herself early in her career by winning the Ladies Professional Bowlers Tour rookie of the year title in 1980. In her first ten years of professional competition, Lisa netted twenty titles and earned more than $360,000. In 1988, she reached an impressive milestone as the first woman bowler to reach $100,000 in earnings in one year.

By the end of the 1980's, Lisa won twenty titles and was named bowler of the decade by *Bowling Magazine*. She had become firmly established as a top bowler by the beginning of the 1990's. However, because of a hectic slate of personal appear-

| Honors and Awards | | |
|---|---|---|
| | 1980 | Ladies Pro Bowlers Tour Rookie of the Year |
| 1983, 1988, 1993 | | Ladies Pro Bowlers Tour Bowler of the Year |
| | 1989 | Bowler of the Decade |
| | 1999 | Inducted into Women's International Bowling Congress Hall of Fame |
| | | Inducted into Ladies Pro Bowlers Tour Hall of Fame |

ances, the fatigue of tournaments, and her work as a member of Brunswick's advisory staff, Lisa began to compete in fewer tournaments. Furthermore, she was still recovering from an ankle injury she had received in an automobile accident in 1988. While Lisa had fully recuperated from a sprained left ankle, she discovered that she was developing arthritis in the injured ankle. The champion bowler did not let the injury affect her game. Instead, her list of titles and achievements grew.

## Continuing the Story

Lisa's success continued into the next decade, and, in 1996, Lisa was inducted into the Ladies Pro Bowlers Tour Hall of Fame and had won the tour's bowler of the year award three times, in 1983, 1988, and 1993. The following year, she landed an endorsement contract with bowling-product manufacturer AMF. Along with fellow professional bowlers Wendy Macpherson, Marianne Dirupo, Dana Miller-Mackie, and Kim Adler, Lisa signed a $750,000, three-year sponsorship contract with AMF to represent the company and their products. Lisa also had endorsements with Mongoose Gloves.

Early in 1999, Lisa became the leading title-holder by winning her thirty-first title. She further secured her hold on the record by winning her thirty-second title in August of 1999. In 2000, Lisa led all other women's professional bowlers in the number of titles won. Having earned more than $900,000 in her career, Lisa entered the twenty-first century as one of the top money earners in women's bowling. She retired in 2002. Further adding to her achievements, she was inducted into the Women's International Bowling Congress Hall of Fame in October of 1999. After two decades on the professional bowling tour, Lisa added a new dimension to her career by becoming a broadcaster for her sport.

## Summary

Lisa Wagner, who began bowling early in life, had both the determination and stamina necessary to become a champion woman bowler. Although she had to struggle, she showed that hard work and determination are effective tools to reach goals. Having won many of bowling's highest honors, Lisa demonstrated exactly what it takes to become a champion.

*Kimberley H. Kidd*

## Additional Source

Miller, Ernestine G. *Making Her Mark: Firsts and Milestones in Women's Sports*. Chicago: Contemporary Books, 2002.

# *Rusty Wallace*

**Born:** August 14, 1956
   Fenton, near St. Louis, Missouri
**Also known as:** Russell William Wallace, Jr. (full
   name)

### Early Life

Russell William "Rusty" Wallace, Jr., was born on August 14, 1956, in Fenton, near St. Louis, Missouri, into a family of stock-car racers. Russ Wallace, Rusty's father, raced as a hobby into the late 1970's and won three St. Louis track championships. Rusty's mother, Judy Buckles Wallace, also raced occasionally and had a winning record. All three of the Wallace boys—Rusty, Mike, and Kenny—participated in the Craftsman Truck, Nationwide, and Sprint Cup division of the National Association for Stock Car Auto Racing (NASCAR).

### The Road to Excellence

On August 12, 1972, Rusty and his mother went to court to obtain an order to allow Rusty to begin racing cars. He was sixteen years old and therefore legally entitled to drive, but the local track required that competing drivers under eighteen years of age have a court order and parental permission. Although Rusty had already been competing in go-kart racing and in motocross events, he was eager to race cars. Six days later, Rusty debuted at Lake Hill Speedway in St. Louis by winning his heat. However, in his excitement, he forgot to fill the tank for the actual race and ran out of gas.

   In their ongoing struggle to provide funds for their racing, Rusty and his brothers delivered newspapers and worked at the family's vacuum-cleaner shop. Later, they joined with Charlie Chase and Don Miller, who was a local representative for Penske Racing products, and other friends to found the Poor Boy Chassis Company, which produced and sold race-car chassis. The company's staff,

deemed the "Evil Gang" by famed racer Bobby Allison, was made up of volunteers whose compensation was going to races and working on race cars.

### The Emerging Champion

Rusty was racing full time by his twenty-first birthday. In 1979, he chose to compete on the United States Auto Club circuit because of its larger markets and the publicity generated by its renowned star A. J. Foyt. That season, Rusty was named the rookie of the year.

   For Rusty, the year 1980 was memorable and significant for two reasons. First, he married his girlfriend, Patti Hall, on January 16. Second, at the urging of Don Miller, Rusty drove Roger Penske's car in the 1980 Winston Cup spring race at Atlanta, Georgia. Though Rusty finished second, the next year, Penske opted to concentrate on his Indy car program rather than run in NASCAR. Rusty returned to competing on other circuits and won the 1983 American Speed Association championship with three first-place and fourteen top-ten finishes.

   In 1984, Cliff Stewart, a longtime Winston Cup car owner, hired Rusty to drive his car. The rookie received a salary of $40,000 and 40 percent of

*Rusty Wallace preparing to race at the Sharpie 500 in 2005.* (Nell Redmond/UPI/Landov)

his winnings—his first salary since his days in the vacuum-cleaner shop. Though the year was not completely successful, Rusty still finished a respectable fourteenth in the Winston Cup Championship points standings and earned rookie of the year honors. However, the next year, the relationship between Stewart and Rusty deteriorated as the team struggled.

As a result, Rusty moved to Raymond Beadle's Blue Max racing operation for the 1986 season. In the fifth race of the season, at Bristol, Tennessee, Rusty finally earned his first Winston Cup victory. The win solidified his racing reputation and caused his popularity with fans and sponsors to surge. He followed this with a win at Martinsville, Virginia, sixteen top-ten finishes, and more than $500,000 in prize money to end the year in sixth position in the points standings.

Rusty won twice in 1987 and led the points race briefly during the 1988 season. However, in a practice run at Bristol Motor Speedway, the right front tire on his car blew, causing the car to flip five times. Rusty, unconscious and not breathing, was resuscitated. Though the crash cost him the championship, he was left with only severe bruises and a major headache.

In 1989, Rusty achieved the pinnacle of stock-car racing success: the Winston Cup Championship. He said, "In 1989, we made the decision to win," and the team did so despite its precarious financial situation, which led to bounced payroll checks, difficulty in obtaining needed supplies, and constant duns from creditors. Rusty filed a lawsuit against Beadle to obtain back pay and release from his contract. The suit was eventually settled, with Rusty agreeing to race for Blue Max the next year. Despite the continuing turmoil, Rusty was able to win five times during the season to clinch the championship.

**Continuing the Story**
In 1990, with Blue Max, Rusty struggled, His two wins were offset by six incomplete races and continuing financial problems, even though the Miller Brewing Company sponsored the team. Rusty, his old friend Miller, and Penske formed a new partnership, Penske Racing South, for the 1991 season. Momentum for success began to build over the next few years despite spectacular and frightening crashes at Daytona and Talledega in 1993. Crashes

### Major Races and Championships

|  |  |
|---|---|
| 1972 | First amateur stock-car race and win |
| 1980 | First Winston Cup race |
| 1983 | American Speed Association Championship |
| 1986 | First Winston Cup wins |
| 1989 | Winston Cup Championship |
| 2000 | Fiftieth Winston Cup win |
| 2004 | 55th NEXTEL Cup win |

notwithstanding, Rusty won ten races in 1993, eight in 1994, two in 1995, five in 1996, one in 1997, one in 1998, and one in 1999, leading to his fiftieth Winston Cup win in 2000 at Bristol, the site of his first Winston Cup victory.

In 2003, Rusty collected his fifty-fifth win at the short-track Martinsville Speedway in Virginia. The victory, his last, established Rusty as the eighth winningest driver in NASCAR history. He retired at the conclusion of the 2005 season, in which he finished eighth overall.

After his retirement, Rusty kept busy. He began broadcasting and developing his own race team. In 2006, he was part of the team that broadcasted the Indy Racing League events on ESPN and ABC. Later in the year, Rusty covered NASCAR. While his transition to commentator was not always smooth, he continued to improve.

Rusty's race team also demonstrated progress. In 2005, the first year of competition, Rusty Wallace, Inc. was abysmal. After that year, his Nationwide Series team got better. In 2006, Rusty put his

### Honors and Awards

|  |  |
|---|---|
| 1973 | Central Auto Racing Association Rookie of the Year |
| 1979 | U.S. Auto Club Rookie of the Year Award |
| 1984 | Winston Cup Rookie of the Year |
| 1988, 1993 | NMPA Driver of the Year |
| 1998 | Inducted into Missouri Sports Hall of Fame |
| 2005 | Received the National Motorsports Press Association (NMPA) Myers Brothers Award |
| | Received American Auto Racing Writer and Broadcasters Association (AARWBA) Rick Mears "Good Guy" Award |
| | Selected *NASCAR Illustrated* Person of the Year |

son Steven in one of the cars. Though he struggled at times, Steven began to show promise in 2008, when he was ranked in the top fifteen. Rusty entered another aspect of motorsports, helping to develop the Iowa Speedway near Des Moines. Indy Racing League and the Nationwide Series events have been held there.

## Summary

With fifty-five wins, Rusty Wallace is considered among the best ever in NASCAR. He demonstrated amazing car control and tenacity on the racetrack. In addition, he earned more than $21 million in prize money in his Winston Cup racing career. After retiring from the sport, Rusty did not stray far from the track. As a commentator and race-track

designer, Rusty displayed the same characteristics that made him a championship driver.

*Susan Coleman, updated by P. Huston Ladner*

## Additional Sources

Mello, Tara Baukus. *Rusty Wallace.* Philadelphia: Chelsea House, 2000.

Ryan, Nate. "Life Is Busier than Ever for Wallace Since Cup 'Retirement.'" *USA Today,* May 10, 2006.

_____. "Wallace Trains Son Stephen, Eighteen." *USA Today,* Feb 17, 2006.

White, Ben. *Rusty Wallace: Stats and Standings.* Phoenix, Ariz.: Futech Interactive Products, 1999.

Zeller, Bob, and Rusty Wallace. *Rusty Wallace: The Decision to Win.* Phoenix, Ariz.: David Bull, 1999.

# *Bobby Walthour*

**Born:** January 1, 1878
　　　　Walthourville, Georgia
**Died:** September 2, 1949
　　　　Boston, Massachusetts
**Also known as:** Robert Walthour (full name);
　Dixie Flyer

## Early Life

Robert "Bobby" Walthour was born on the first day of January, 1878, in Walthourville, Georgia. His birthplace was named after his grandfather William L. Walthour, a famous general in the Civil War. Bobby's family heritage was of the Southern aristocracy, but following the Civil War his grandfather's vast landholdings were confiscated for tax reasons. Consequently, the family's wealth did not transfer into Bobby's hands.

Bobby was one of nine children. His childhood was not much different from that of youngsters in other rural families of the time: plenty of religion, homegrown food, daily chores, and a good deal of neighborhood play. What did somewhat separate Bobby from his playmates was his attraction to the newest sporting sensation of the nineteenth century: the bicycle. Even though it was cumbersome and hard to ride, Bobby mastered riding solo on this newfangled contraption by the time he was three years old. From the beginning, he was destined to ride.

## The Road to Excellence

Before he was fifteen, Bobby was drawn to the world of bicycle racing. He set out for Atlanta, Georgia, the southern center of cycling competition. He landed a job as a bicycle messenger to support himself while he began his self-coached competitive training.

At the first opportunity he entered a local race. He competed in the boys' event and the five men's events and won them all. For the next two years Bobby raced throughout the South, winning the Georgia and the southern sprint titles in the same year. His fame began to spread.

While racing in Birmingham, Alabama, Bobby met a young girl named Daisy Blanche Bailey. As the story goes, Bobby and Daisy, both underage, were determined to get married. One night they eloped, pedaling their way on a two-seat bicycle into a rural community, where they convinced the village parson to perform the ceremony. The press picked up the romantic story, as did poets. In turn, these poets inspired some songwriters, and the world was given the famous song, "On a Bicycle Built for Two."

By the turn of the century, Bobby had begun to scrape out a meager living as a professional bicycle racer. To become really successful in the sport, Bobby had to prove himself in the North, in places like Newark, New Jersey, and New York City, where racers from all over the world competed against each other.

## The Emerging Champion

In the North, Bobby was successful enough at the short sprints, but what caught his attention were

*Bobby Walthour.* (Library of Congress)

two other forms of racing: the six-day indoor endurance races and motor-paced racing, the newest of the racing events.

In Boston, he won a ten-hour individual event that helped him qualify for the six-day race at New York's Madison Square Garden. In these races, the riders competed in teams of two. One of the two riders had to be on the track every minute of the twenty-four-hour-day, six-day week. With his teammate Archie McEachern, Bobby won his first six-day race.

What especially attracted Bobby was motor-paced racing, in which the cyclist rode a few inches behind a huge, powerful motorcycle. The motors, as they were called, gave the riders windshields and a constant pace. Rider and motor, almost touching, whizzed around small, banked, oval tracks at speeds from thirty to fifty miles per hour.

Bobby's physical and mental toughness combined to make him the top U.S. motor-paced racer by the time he was twenty-four years old. He was invited to Europe to compete for the world championship title. In 1904, he won sixteen of seventeen starts, including the world championship, a 62.5-mile event in London. He repeated as world champion in 1905. Bobby, "the Dixie Flyer," was becoming the premier motor-paced racer of his day.

## Continuing the Story

Motor-paced racing was extremely dangerous. If the motor broke a chain or blew a tire, the bicycle racer crashed directly into the back of the motor. If the cyclist went down on the track because of a collision or a flat tire on his own bike, he could be run over by the other motors or cyclists.

During his some twenty years of racing, Bobby had broken almost every bone in his body at one time or another. He broke his collarbone twenty-nine times. He was twice pronounced dead by doctors after track smashups. A number of his racing friends were killed during these races. Bobby's broken bones, stitches, and scars never proved fatal.

### Honors, Awards, and Milestones

| | |
|---|---|
| 1901, 1903 | New York Six-Day Indoor Cycling Cochampion |
| 1902-03 | Professional Motor-Paced Cycling U.S. Champion |
| 1904-05 | Professional Motor-Paced Cycling World Champion |
| 1932 | Named one of Georgia's three greatest athletes |
| 1989 | Inducted into U.S. Bicycling Hall of Fame |

Bobby was a captain in the Army during World War I, serving as the secretary to the Young Men's Christian Association (YMCA) division in France. He raced for a few years after the war, mainly in Europe, eventually giving up competition after a nasty track accident in the late 1920's. The Germans had confiscated his racing winnings and personal savings during the war. When he finally returned to the United States in the 1930's, he took up work with a New York sporting goods company, and, later, he worked in Boston for an automobile magazine publisher. In 1949, Bobby contracted cancer and died of pneumonia later that year at the age of seventy-one.

## Summary

For the first two decades of the twentieth century, Bobby Walthour was the world's most famous motor-paced cyclist. At a celebration given in his honor in Atlanta in 1932, Bobby was ranked with baseball star Ty Cobb and golfer Bobby Jones as one of the three greatest athletes to come out of Georgia. His world championships and his inspirational, record- and bone-breaking rides, made him one of the greatest and hardiest racing cyclists the sport has ever had. It is generally agreed that Bobby was to cycling what Babe Ruth was to baseball.

*William Harper*

## Additional Sources

Hickok, Ralph. *A Who's Who of Sports Champions.* Boston: Houghton Mifflin, 1995.

Nye, Peter. *Hearts of Lions: The History of American Bicycle Racing.* New York: W. W. Norton, 1988.

# Dick Weber

**Born:** December 23, 1929
Indianapolis, Indiana
**Died:** February 13, 2005
Florissant, Missouri
**Also known as:** Richard Anthony Weber

## Early Life

Richard Anthony "Dick" Weber was born on December 23, 1929, in Indianapolis, Indiana. He was the son of Carl John Weber, a gas station attendant and bowling alley manager, and Marjorie Wheeler Weber, a schoolteacher. Bowling was a popular sport during the Depression, and Dick often went to the bowling alley with his father, who bowled in a weekly league. When Dick was ten, his family joined a family league so that Dick could bowl with them.

Dick attended Indianapolis Technical High School, where he played basketball and baseball. He also spent a considerable amount of time at the local bowling alley. He took a job as a pinsetter, and when he was not setting pins, he was bowling. He graduated from high school in 1948, earning letters in both basketball and baseball.

After graduation, Dick married Juanita "Neet" Dirk and took a job in a post office sorting mail. To supplement his salary from the post office, he began to work at night as a professional bowling shop operator.

## The Road to Excellence

Dick gained experience bowling in local leagues in Indianapolis for several years while he continued to work in the post office during the day and the bowling alley at night. He was small, weighing about 125 pounds, but he soon grew to 5 feet 9 inches and 140 pounds. His increased size enabled him to establish an average of 200 pins per game.

Dick's appearance in professional bowling came rather suddenly, even though he had worked to improve his game for many years. In 1954, he was competing in Chicago in an all-star tournament. On the lane next to him was the famous professional team known as the "Budweiser Five." The captain of the team, Don Carter, was impressed with Dick's bowling and invited him to join the team. Dick immediately accepted the offer.

To compete with the famous team, Dick had to travel from Indianapolis to St. Louis, and he had no money for the trip. A longtime friend and local bowling lane owner Carl Hindel came to his rescue. He lent him a loud, pin-striped

*Dick Weber in 1961.* (Olen Collection/Diamond Images/Getty Images)

## PBA Tour Victories

| | |
|---|---|
| 1959 | Paramus; Dayton |
| 1960 | Albany |
| 1961 | Dallas; Shreveport; Houston; Redondo Beach; San Jose |
| 1962 | Chicago; Puerto Rico |
| 1963 | New Brunswick; Las Vegas |
| 1964 | Dallas |
| 1965 | Wichita; Houston |
| 1966 | Denver; Fresno |
| 1969 | New Orleans; Altoona |
| 1970 | Hawaii |
| 1971 | Denver; Toledo; Hawaii |
| 1973 | Toledo |
| 1976 | Garden City |
| 1977 | Kansas City |
| 1983 | Senior Championship at Canton |
| 1986 | Senior Invitational at Las Vegas |
| 1989 | Senior/Touring Pro Doubles at Buffalo |

## Other Major Victories

| | |
|---|---|
| 1962-63, 1965-66 | U.S. Open |

suit with wide lapels and gave him money to make the trip. With his wife and small baby, named Richard, Dick drove to St. Louis to join Carter, Ray Bluth, Whitey Harris, Pat Patterson, and Tom Hennessey for his first professional competition.

### The Emerging Champion

Dick replaced Don McLaren and had a wonderful first year with the "Buds." He teamed with Bluth to win the first of four national doubles titles and helped his team capture the Bowling Proprietors Association of America (BPAA) national title in 1955.

Dick's brilliant first year began a career that extended more than thirty years. The Budweiser team won the BPAA national title in 1956, 1958, 1959, 1961, and 1965 and the BPAA all-star championship in 1962, 1963, 1965, and 1966. With Bluth, he won the national doubles title in 1960, 1961, and 1964.

In 1961 and 1962, Dick accomplished an amazing feat—he had a string of seven Professional Bowlers Association (PBA) victories out of nine competitions that included the nation's best bowlers. He was the American Bowling Congress (ABC) tournament-average leader and was chosen bowler of the year by the Bowling Writers Association of America (BWAA) in 1961. In the same year, he was also the year's top money-winner, earning nearly

$100,000. By the age of thirty-one, he had won eighteen major tournaments and had earned a major reputation.

Dick had his best year in 1965. He averaged 211 pins per game for 960 games and was the ABC tournament-average leader for the second consecutive year. During the Houston Open, he became the first professional bowler to roll three perfect games in one tournament. For his accomplishments in the first half of the 1960's, Dick was named the bowler of the year by the BWAA three times, in 1961, 1963, and 1965.

### Continuing the Story

In 1970, Dick became the youngest man ever to be elected into the ABC Hall of Fame. In 1975, he became one of the eight charter members of the PBA Hall of Fame.

Beginning in the 1970's, Dick competed in only half of the major tournaments on the tour. In 1976, however, his earnings passed the $500,000 mark, and he ranked first in all-time winnings. In 1977, he won his 26th professional tournament to place second on the all-time PBA list.

In addition to touring as a professional, Dick became part owner of a St. Louis bowling establishment and served as an adviser for American Machine and Foundry (AMF). His interest in bowling also led him to give exhibitions and clinics and appear on a television series dealing with bowling techniques. He also wrote articles and books on bowling. He became the president of the PBA in 1969-1970 and was elected to the Indiana and St. Louis Halls of Fame.

Dick was a popular star, and his career extended

## PBA Records

Most consecutive top-five finishes, 7 (1961)
Most consecutive top-twenty-four finishes, 23 (1963)
Most 300 scores in a tournament, 3 (1965)

## Honors and Awards

| | |
|---|---|
| 1960-67, 1969, 1971 | *Bowler's Journal* All-American Team |
| 1961, 1963, 1965 | BWAA Bowler of the Year |
| 1965 | PBA Player of the Year |
| 1969-70 | President of PBA |
| 1970 | Inducted into ABC Hall of Fame |
| 1975 | Inducted into PBA Hall of Fame |

over an unusually long period of time. His long career was the result of his ability to adapt to the changing conditions of the game. When he first began his career, lacquer was used on the lanes, and the big hook was the most successful delivery. Years later, lacquer was replaced with harder finishes, which required a different style of delivery. Dick adopted a straighter, softer pitch, which allowed him to continue to be a champion. Dick continued to win tournaments well into the 1980's. He won the Showboat Invitational tournament for three consecutive years from 1986 to 1988. In 1987, he was named professional bowling host at the Showboat Center in Atlantic City, New Jersey.

Dick and his wife, Juanita, had four children. Dick's son Pete also became a successful, hall-of-fame bowler. After his retirement, Dick continued an active lifestyle by playing golf. He died in 2005.

## Summary

In 1955, Dick Weber's first year as a professional bowler, Dick helped the Budweisers to the first of six national team titles and four all-star championships. With Bluth, he won the first of four national doubles titles in the same year. He was named bowler of the year three times by the Bowling Writers Association of America. *Bowler's Journal* chose him ten times to the all-American first team and five times to the second team. He was selected to the ABC Hall of Fame in 1970, and, in 1975, became a charter member of the PBA Hall of Fame. He was voted the second-greatest bowler of all time by sportswriters in a 1970 poll. He established a 202-pin lifetime average, rolled eighteen sanctioned 300-pin games, and rolled high-pin series scores of 815, 814, 804, and 800 during his long and distinguished career.

*Susan J. Bandy*

## Additional Sources

Bechtel, Mark, and Stephen Cannella. "Striking Presence." *Sports Illustrated* 102, no. 8 (February 21, 2005): 19.

Porter, David L., ed. *Biographical Dictionary of American Sports: Basketball and Other Indoor Sports.* Westport, Conn.: Greenwood Press, 1989.

Weber, Dick. *Bowling.* New York: Cornerstone Library, 1971.

_____. *The Champion's Guide to Bowling.* Rev. ed. New York: Simon and Schuster, 1981.

Weber, Dick, and Roland Alexander. *Weber on Bowling.* Englewood Cliffs, N.J.: Prentice-Hall, 1981.

# *Pete Weber*

**Born:** August 21, 1962
   St. Ann, Missouri
**Also known as:** Peter David Weber (full name);
   PDW

## Early Life

Peter David Weber was born in St. Ann, Missouri, on August 21, 1962, to bowling icon Richard "Dick" Weber and Juanita Weber. The youngest of four children who were all seemingly natural bowlers, Pete began bowling at the age of two and developed the same passion and vigor for the sport held by his father throughout his legendary career. At the age of four, Pete received a 6-pound custom-made ball. At the age of eight, he was able to bowl a 200 game; he bowled a 300 by age twelve. In his early teens, he began a rigorous daily practice schedule and triumphed over adult players in local bowling tournaments.

## The Road to Excellence

As a teenager, Pete was not committed to his education and rebelled in ways. He skipped class, got into fights, ran with the wrong crowd, smoked marijuana, and participated in underaged drinking. This behavior eventually led to his decision to drop out of school in the tenth grade to work at a local bowling alley. Seeing his potential, Pete's father successfully petitioned the Professional Bowlers Association (PBA) to allow high school graduates under eighteen to join the PBA Tour. In 1980, Pete received the PBA rookie of the year award and became the youngest player in PBA history, at the age of twenty-five, to reach the ten-title plateau. Pete adopted a strong hook style, patterned after bowling great Mark Roth, rather than his father's traditional style. Also, some deemed his persona to be unprofessional and inappropriate. He battled drug and alcohol addiction for years and became known for his antics on and off the lanes. His outbursts and gestures were unpredictable and unacceptable to the previous leaders of the PBA Tour. Many felt that he received special privileges because of his family legacy.

## The Emerging Champion

A fan of the Word Wrestling Federation (now World Wrestling Entertainment) pro wrestler Robert Van Dam (RVD), Pete gave himself the nickname PDW and often celebrated victory by taunting his opponents verbally and sometimes making a "V" sign in the direction of his crotch. Though some of his more seasoned and conservative colleagues in the PBA detested this type of display, the new leadership recognized its potential marketability. Pete's fan base continued to grow. Under the new PBA leadership team, tours, prize funds, media coverage, and, inevitably, respect for the sport increased. During the change in management in 2000, Pete was finishing up a six-month suspension that resulted from an altercation during a professional-amateur event in Michigan. He disagreed with the suspension, but the ruling was upheld because of prior infractions of a similar nature. Later, Pete admitted that his third wife Tracy helped him change his behavior to deal with the pressures of life on the road.

## Continuing the Story

At 5 feet 7 inches and 140 pounds, Pete earned his place in history as an outstanding bowler with more than $3 million in career earnings, thirty-four career PBA titles, and admission to both the PBA Hall of Fame (1998) and the United States Bowling Congress Hall of Fame (2002). When he won the Etonic Championship in 2006, he became the second bowler to exceed $3 million in earnings. Pete, who wore sunglasses while bowling, triumphed over his doubters. He won the PBA's triple crown: the U.S. Open, Tournament of Champions, and PBA National Championship. After a serious

---

## *Honors and Awards*

|  |  |
|------|-------|
| 1980 | PBA rookie of the year |
| 1989 | George Young High Average Award |
| 1998 | Inducted into Professional Bowlers Association Hall of Fame |
| 2002 | Inducted into United States Bowling Congress Hall of Fame |
| 2006 | Most career bowling titles, 42 |

## Major Titles

|  |  |
|------|-------|
| 1987 | Tournament of Champions |
| 1988 | Bowling Proprietors Association of America (BPAA) U.S. Open |
| 1989 | Professional Bowlers Association (PBA) National Championship |
|      | BPAA U.S. Open |
| 1992 | Touring Players Championship |
| 1998 | PBA National Championship |
| 2004 | BPAA U.S. Open |
| 2007 | BPAA U.S. Open |

comeback, Pete lost his father on February 13, 2005. The entire bowling community mourned Dick Weber's death. At the 2005 Bowlersparadise.com Classic in Hammond, Indiana, which was televised by ESPN, Pete gave an emotional tribute to his father on camera after his title win as he silently stared into the camera and pointed to the "DW" patch on his sleeve. Later, Pete suffered two major defeats to rival Walter Ray Williams, as the two competed in the 2006 PBA World Cup Championship and the Dydo Japan Cup title matches.

## Summary

Pete Weber endured many life struggles and overcame hardships to which many athletes succumb. In 2004, he was featured in the documentary *A League of Ordinary Gentlemen.* He settled in St. Ann, Missouri, with his wife and three children. In the summer of 2008, Pete and his father Dick Weber were named among the fifty greatest players in PBA history.

*Vikki M. Armstrong*

## Additional Sources

Friedman, Steve. *The Agony of Victory: When Winning Isn't Enough.* New York: Arcade, 2007.

"The Questions with Pete Weber." *Sports Illustrated* 105, no. 19 (November 13, 2006): 43.

# Simon Whitfield

**Born:** May 16, 1975
     Kingston, Ontario, Canada
**Also known as:** Simon St. Quentin Whitfield (full
name)

## Early Life

Simon St. Quentin Whitfield was born in Kingston,
Ontario, Canada, on May 16, 1975. He gained dual
citizenship, Canadian and Australian, because his
father was from the latter country. As a boy, Simon
was an avid soccer player. However, by the age of
eleven, he became interested in becoming a multisport athlete as the result of a five-dollar wager with
a boyhood friend on a four-mile swimming race
across a lake north of Kingston. In 1987, when Simon was only twelve, he competed in his first triathlon. At the time, he did not have any special

Simon Whitfield competing in the Olympic triathlon in
2008. (Adam Pretty/Getty Images)

equipment and later recalled that he raced in a
pair of boxer shorts imprinted with little cows. Furthermore, instead of a fancy racing bicycle, he used
his mountain bike. Even without specialized equipment, Simon was an instant fan of the event. At that
moment, in his own words, he became a "triathlon
groupie." By the time he had reached his fifteenth
birthday, he was a serious competitor in his chosen
sport.

## The Road to Excellence

In the fall of 1992, Simon left Canada to attend
Knox Grammar School in Sydney, Australia. His
father, Geoff, raised in Sydney, had also been
schooled at Knox. Geoff had accepted a scholarship to Canada's University of Alberta, eventually
settling in Kingston. Simon headed in the opposite
direction, returning to his father's birthplace. He
finished high school at Knox while continuing to
train in the triathlon. After graduation, he returned to Canada. In 1995, he became a member
of Canada's junior national triathlon team and was
the Canadian junior triathlon champion that same
year. In 1996, he became a full-fledged member of
Canada's national team.

By 1997, Simon had established credentials as
an international competitor with whom to be reck-
oned. He placed ninth that year at the Triathlon
World Championships in Perth, Australia. He not
only raced in Australia but also returned there to
train during the difficult Canadian winters. Australia always held a fond place in his heart, especially
after the 2000 Olympics.

## The Emerging Champion

After his showing at the 1997 Triathlon World
Championships, Simon steadily continued moving
up the ranks at national and international competitions. Still a member of the Canadian national
team, he competed around the world. In 1998, he
raced in locales as diverse as Hungary and Mexico,
eventually becoming the Canadian triathlon championship.

By this time, he also began thinking of competing at the 2000 Olympics, the first time the men's

triathlon event was included in the Games. He started putting all his efforts not only into the sport but also into earning the right to race in his adopted country.

The year preceding the Olympics, 1999, was a successful one for Simon. He made strong showings in the Triathlon World Championships in Montreal and the International Triathlon Union World Cup. He was becoming known for performing spectacularly under pressure. He added to his previous performances by winning a bronze medal at the Pan-American Games, a win he said was one of the highlights of his career. In 1999, he was again Canadian triathlon champion and earned the Triathlon Canada athlete of the year award.

Prior to the Olympics in September, 2000, Simon had a number of other races to occupy his attention. Although the preparation and training culminated in the Olympics, races earlier in the year had established his reputation and standing when he arrived in Sydney.

Simon placed second in the Rio World Cup and second in the Corner Brook World Cup in Canada. He was also named rookie of the year at the 2000 Aussie Grand Prix. Although he placed only fourth in the 2000 Toronto World Cup, he was part of an increasingly competitive field of world-class athletes, a good test for the upcoming Olympics. By the time he arrived in Sydney for the Olympic Games, he was the top North American triathlete and ranked twenty-first in the world.

## Continuing the Story

After the first leg of the Olympic triathlon, a 1,500-meter (the metric mile) swim, Simon emerged from the 61-degree waters in Sydney Harbor in twenty-eighth place. The swim was followed by the 40-kilometer (25-mile) bike ride. During this leg of the race tragedy almost struck when a pileup spilled riders across the course. The bikers in front of Simon had

## Major Championships

| Year | Competition | Place |
|------|-------------|-------|
| 1996 | Canadian Duathlon Championships | 1st |
| 1997 | Triathlon World Championships | 9th |
|  | Stage 4 French IronTour | 1st |
| 1998 | Canadian Triathlon Championships | 1st |
|  | Canadian Duathlon Championships | 1st |
|  | Ontario Provincial Championships | 1st |
|  | sea2summit Adventure Race | 1st |
| 1999 | Pan-American Games | 3d |
|  | Triathlon World Championships | 7th |
|  | International Points Race Zundert, Holland (Olympic qualifying race) | 1st |
|  | Canadian Triathlon Championships (Olympic qualifying race) | 1st |
|  | Nike/Tag Heuer Eliminator | 1st |
|  | Stage 5 French IronTour | 1st |
|  | World Cup, Noosa, Australia | 9th |
| 2000 | World Cup, Rio | 2d |
|  | World Cup, Corner Brook, Canada | 2d |
|  | World Cup, Toronto | 4th |
|  | Olympic Games: Triathlon | Gold |
| 2001 | World Championships | 6th |
|  | World Cup, Toronto | 1st |
|  | World Cup, St. Petersburg, Florida | 1st |
| 2002 | World Championships | 1st |
|  | World Cup Corner Brook, Canada | 1st |
|  | World Cup Edmonton | 1st |
| 2003 | World Cup Makuhari, Japan | 12th |
|  | World Cup, New York | 1st |
|  | World Cup, Corner Brook, Canada | 4th |
|  | World Cup Edmonton | 1st |
|  | World Cup, Tongyeong, South Korea | 9th |
| 2004 | Olympic Games | 11th |
|  | World Cup, Mazatlan | 1st |
| 2005 | World Championships, Gamagori, Japan | 6th |
|  | World Cup Edmonton | 9th |
| 2006 | World Cup, Cancun | 6th |
|  | World Cup, Corner Brook, Canada | 2d |
|  | Pan-American Cup, Brampton, Canada | 1st |
|  | World Cup Mazatlan | 9th |
| 2007 | World Cup, Cancun | 1st |
|  | World Cup, Beijing | 5th |
|  | Triathlon World Championships | 4th |
|  | World Cup Kitzbuhel, Austria | 1st |
|  | World Cup, Des Moines | 6th |
|  | World Cup, Vancouver | 1st |
|  | World Cup, Lisbon | 10th |
|  | World Cup, Ishigaki, Japan | 8th |
| 2008 | Olympic Games | Silver |

lost their concentration, nearly leading to disastrous results for Simon. He jumped off his bike, yelled at the other riders, and then remounted. By the end of this leg he was still more than 1 minute behind the leaders, with the 10-kilometer (6.2-mile) run remaining.

At that point, the race was a contest between Olivier Marceau of France and Stephan Vuckovic of Germany. Vuckovic pulled ahead of Marceau and seemed assured of the win. Simon, however, was an incredible runner, and he moving steadily up on the pack one runner at a time. He surged ahead, nearly catching Vuckovic. The German was not ready to concede the race, however, and increased his speed. With only a few hundred feet to go, Simon sprinted ahead of Vuckovic, who no longer had the reserves to retake the lead. Simon won the race in 1 hour, 48 minutes, and 24.02 seconds, beating Vuckovic by 13.56 seconds. Simon's family—including his 92-year-old grandmother—cheered for him at the finish. In addition to winning the gold in the triathlon's debut, Simon received another honor when he received a call from Canadian Prime Minister Jean Chrétien congratulating him. Simon won the first gold medal for the Canadians in the 2000 Olympics.

After his Olympic victory, Simon followed up with another gold medal in the 2002 Commonwealth Games in Manchester, England. With more and better triathletes competing, he did not fare as well at the 2004 Olympics in Athens, Greece, finishing in eleventh place, because of the weakest portion of his game, swimming.

Simon trained hard and was ready for the 2008 Games in Beijing, China. He was one of three Canadians that qualified for the Olympic men's triathlon event. The others were Paul Tichelaar of Edmonton, Alberta, and Colin Jenkins of Hamilton, Ontario. This time, strategy played a key role. With Jenkins playing the part of a *domestique*, a pacesetter, Simon was able to draft in his teammate's wake in the bicycling portion of the race and thus conserved energy for the swimming and running parts of the triathlon. The tactic paid off, as Simon took the silver medal, just 5 seconds behind the winner, Jan Frodeno of Germany. In gratitude for Jenkins's outstanding teamwork, Simon gave the twenty-five-year-old half of the $15,000 bonus money that the Canadian Olympic Committee gives to Canadian athletes who win medals.

Married to wife Jennie, and with a young daughter, Pippa Katherine, Simon settled with his family on Salt Spring Island, near Victoria, in British Columbia, Canada. He continued to train, in hopes of competing in the triathlon at a fourth consecutive Olympics in London, England, in 2012.

## Summary

A natural athlete, Simon Whitfield gravitated toward the triathlon because he loved the variety of the event. Both in his native Canada and in his adopted Australia, homeland of his father, Simon trained diligently, slowly inching up in the ranks with solid performances in international meets. The winner of the Olympic gold medal in triathlon at its debut at the 2000 Sydney Games, Simon finished out of the medals at the 2004 Olympics in Athens before returning to the victor's stand with a silver medal at the 2008 Beijing Olympics. He aspired to qualify for the triathlon again at the next Olympic venue, London, in 2012.

*Deborah Service, updated by Jack Ewing*

## Additional Sources

Allen, Karen. "Teamwork Earns Olympic Triathlon Slot." *USA Today,* July 26, 1999, p. C8.

Crockford, Ross. *Victoria: The Unknown City.* Vancouver, B.C.: Arsenal Pulp Press, 2006.

Fish, Mike. "Men's Triathlon: Whitfield Gets First Gold for Canada." *The Atlanta Journal-Constitution,* September 17, 2000, p. F6.

Kearns, Brad. *Breakthrough Triathlon Training.* New York: McGraw-Hill, 2005.

Wallechinsky, David, and Jaime Loucky. *The Complete Book of the Olympics: 2008 Edition.* London: Aurum Press, 2008.

Weir, Tom. "Canadian Winner Feels Right at Home." *USA Today,* September 18, 2000, p. E7.

# Walter Ray Williams, Jr.

**Born:** October 6, 1959
Eureka, California
**Other major sport:** Horseshoes

### Early Life
Walter Ray Williams, Jr., was born on October 6, 1959, in Eureka, California. His interest in bowling began when he was eleven years old, when a fellow competitor at a horseshoe-pitching tournament took him and his younger brother bowling. He enjoyed bowling and connected with the game immediately. As a result of this early bowling experience, the Williams brothers joined a bowling league later that year. Walter was only able to bowl sporadically because his family did not have the financial means to allow him to practice as much as he would have liked.

Walter was unable to bowl seriously until his senior year in high school, when he took bowling as a physical education credit. Skipping the usual junior bowling league route, Walter began to compete in adult men's bowling leagues when he was seventeen. In addition to a busy schedule competing in both bowling and horseshoe pitching, Walter found time to earn a bachelor of science degree in physics from California State Polytechnic University at Pomona.

### The Road to Excellence
Walter maintained a busy schedule, entering both bowling tournaments and horseshoe-pitching tournaments, putting him in the unusual position of competing in and winning titles in two different sports. The young bowler joined the Professional Bowlers Association (PBA) in 1980 and steadily increased his earnings on the tour.

In 1993, Walter was still known as much for his horseshoe-pitching championships as for his bowling. He continued to compete in bowling tournaments, and, in 1993, his perseverance paid off. By the end of the year, Walter had bowled four 300 games, 1,300 games in one year, and sixty-one-successive 200 games.

All three achievements set PBA records. In addition, he won seven titles and had total earnings of more than $290,000, winning the George Young high average award for the first time. Then, in 1994, Walter won two titles, stayed at the top of the points battle, and finished in second place for the season with winnings topping $195,000.

### The Emerging Champion
Walter continued his impressive streak into 1995, when he won one title and took home more than $153,000 in earnings. He was also inducted into

*Walter Ray Williams, Jr., bowling in the final round of the 2003 Professional Bowlers Association World Championship.* (AP/Wide World Photos)

the PBA Hall of Fame that year. The best years statistically for Walter were from 1996 through 1998, during which time he won thirteen titles and emerged as points leader and high-average-award winner. In addition, he claimed the PBA's bowler of the year award for those three years.

By 1998, he had won the PBA bowler of the year award five times, in 1986, 1993, 1996, 1997, and 1998; the George Young high average award again in 1996 and 1997; and the Harry Smith point leader award in 1993, 1994, 1996, and 1997. A high point in his career came when he was named the PBA player of the decade for the 1990's. Walter was elected president of the PBA for the 1995-1997 term. He ended the 1997 season as the PBA's top-ranked player.

**Continuing the Story**

By early 1998, Walter had become the first bowler to garner career earnings of more than $2 million. He was named one of the twenty greatest players of the twentieth century by *Bowling* magazine, and, with total winnings more than $2.4 million, Walter held the record as the PBA's top money winner.

However, in 1999, knee problems hampered Walter's play, and he began to fall in the rankings. Though he had suffered no injury to his knee, he began wearing a knee brace to help correct the effects of his knee problems. Characteristically, Walter made no excuses for his faltering game and persevered through the next few years. Though he continued to bowl and to win during the 1999-2000 season, he did not perform up to his previous standards, falling from first to seventh in the rankings.

Although 1999 was not Walter's best year, the five-time bowler of the year did become one of only three players to win thirty titles. Walter, who won only one title in 1999, seemed to have lost his momentum. However, by the end of 2000, he was once again racking up impressive victories in PBA tournaments. In addition to his bowling titles, he had won a total of six World Horseshoe Pitching Championships by the end of 2000.

Even though Walter was a successful and top-ranked bowler, he set difficult goals for himself. One such goal was to score more first-place than

**Honors and Awards**

| | |
|---|---|
| 1986, 1993, 1996-98, 2003 | Professional Bowlers Association Player of the Year |
| 1993-94, 1996-97, 2003 | Harry Smith Point Leader Award |
| 1993, 1996-97, 2003, 2005 | George Young High Average Award |
| 1995 | Inducted into Professional Bowlers Association Hall of Fame |
| 1995-96, 2001-02 | President, Professional Bowlers Association |
| 1998-99, 2001, 2003, 2005-06 | ESPY Award winner |
| 1999 | Victor Award |
| 2005 | Inducted into United States Bowling Congress Hall of Fame |

second-place finishes, a goal that he achieved and maintained at the end of the 2000 season. Another goal was to win both the World Horseshoe Pitching Championship and the PBA player of the year award in the same year. Walter continued to dominate his sport throughout the first years of the twenty-first century. In 2006, he won his forty-second title, passing fellow champion Earl Anthony for the PBA record. He added two more titles to his resume, for a total of forty-four. By the end of the 2007-2008 season, Walter had also claimed the second-highest season average score with 228.43, narrowly missing Norm Duke's record 228.47 season average from the previous year.

In 2006, Walter added a movie credit to his resume. He appeared in a sports documentary entitled *A League of Ordinary Gentlemen*, which focused on the history of competitive bowling in the United States. The film contained clips from all eras of modern bowling and addressed both the popularity of the sport and its difficult years, including the sport's low point during the middle 1990's. Walter's role in this documentary illustrated his status as a top bowler.

In the 2007-2008 season, Walter added even more winnings to his record-breaking career earnings. In addition to his forty-four titles, he had winnings of more than $4 million. At the end of that season, he was ranked number one and had bowled seventy-five 300 games in his career.

Walter made history again when he joined the U.S. team that competed in the 2008 World Tenpin Bowling Association's Championships held in Bangkok, Thailand. Until 2008, professional bowlers were not allowed to participate in the championships, but a change in rules allowed them to compete. During the championships, he earned three gold medals—in masters, singles, and team competitions—and one bronze medal—in trios.

## Summary

Throughout his career, Walter Ray Williams, Jr., showed that hard work and dedication to a sport could produce championships. Though he did not follow the typical route to his victories, he achieved his goals in both bowling and horseshoe pitching. By winning championships in both sports, Walter served as an inspiration to aspiring bowlers and horseshoe pitchers alike.

*Kimberley H. Kidd,*
*updated by Kimberley M. Holloway*

## Additional Sources

Campos, Johnny. "Aiming for Deadeye: Walter Ray Williams, Jr., Fresh off a Record-Breaking Campaign, Has His Sights Set on an All-Time Best Seventh Player of the Year Award—But Getting There Won't Be Easy." *Bowling Digest* 21, no. 4 (October, 2003): 38-42.

Clark, Tom. "'Deadeye' Dominates Bowling, Horseshoes." *USA Today*, February 3, 2003.

_____. "Williams Aims to Tie Legend's Mark." *USA Today*, December 10, 2004.

Deitsch, Richard, Kostya Kennedy, and Mark Bechtel. "Q and A: Walter Ray Williams, Jr." *Sports Illustrated* 99, no. 20 (November 24, 2003): 28.

Fischer, David, and William Taffe. *Sports of the Times: A Day-by-Day Selection of the Most Important, Thrilling, and Inspired Events of the Past 150 Years.* New York: St. Martin's Press, 2003.

"Who's Hot, Who's Not." *Sports Illustrated* 104, no. 14 (April 3, 2006): 21.

# Cale Yarborough

**Born:** March 27, 1939
       Timmonsville, South Carolina
**Also known as:** William Caleb Yarborough (full name)

### Early Life

William Caleb Yarborough was born on March 27, 1939, in Timmonsville, South Carolina. He grew up on his parent's tobacco farm in Sardis, South Carolina, a small rural community. Cale had a happy home life and loved to play and explore on the family farm. Even as a young boy, Cale liked to be at the wheel of a car or truck. He often sat on the lap of one of his father's farmworkers as they drove errands in the pickup. By the age of eight, he was driving around the farm on his own.

Cale's first taste of driving competition came in 1950, when he entered a local soapbox race. Cale spent hours preparing his racer and looked forward to competing against other children. In the end, Cale did not win the race. Losing was a terrible feeling, and from that moment, Cale decided that he wanted to be a winner. This competitive edge ultimately enable Cale to become one of the greatest stock-car racers of all time.

### The Road to Excellence

From an early age, Cale loved anything having to do with cars and driving, but he was also an outstanding all-around athlete while attending Timmonsville High School. Cale won the South Carolina Golden Gloves welterweight boxing title and he was also an all-state running back. Clearly, Cale had many athletic talents and it was by no means certain that he would end up in auto racing.

At one stage, it appeared that Cale was headed for a career in professional football. After attending Clemson University on a football scholarship for a short while, Cale played semiprofessional football for the Sumter, South Carolina, Generals. He was even offered a tryout with the Washington Redskins. Cale declined the offer and decided that he was going to make a career in his first love—auto racing.

By the age of seventeen, Cale was an accomplished stock-car driver, having won the South Carolina Stock Car Sportsman Championship. This level of racing allowed Cale to make enough money to support himself and his new bride, but he had a burning ambition to get to the top of the sport.

Cale Yarborough acknowledging his fans after winning the Daytona 500 in early 1968. (AP/Wide World Photos)

To make it big in stock-car racing, Cale had to be successful on the highly competitive Grand National Circuit of the National Association for Stock Car Auto Racing (NASCAR). For a long time, NASCAR success eluded Cale; he went seven years on the circuit without a win. Finally, in 1965, Cale secured his first victory, and in that season, he finished in the top ten in thirty-four races. He also amassed $25,140 in prize money. After years of patient learning, Cale had arrived on the NASCAR circuit.

### The Emerging Champion

Between 1965 and 1970, Cale won fourteen NASCAR Championship races. His big year came in 1968, when he won six NASCAR races and $136,786 in prize money. Probably his most satisfying victory of the 1968 season came in the Southern 500, held in Darlington, South Carolina, near his home. In a grueling race, Cale eventually outlasted David Pearson to record an emotional victory on the track he had frequented as a child.

Having come to dominate the NASCAR circuit, Cale became restless and looked for a new challenge. In the early 1970's, Cale tried his hand at single-seater racing on the United States Auto Club (USAC) circuit. Although not a total failure, Cale found it difficult to adjust to this form of competition. After two frustrating seasons, he returned to stock-car racing.

In 1973, Cale returned to the NASCAR circuit with great enthusiasm, and in the following two years, he won a total of seventeen NASCAR races. His aggressive driving and fierce will to win, which hampered his performances in single-seater racing, once again made him a dominating force in stock-car competition.

Cale was reaching his peak as an auto racer and was about to embark upon the most successful phase of his career. Between 1976 and 1978, Cale dominated the stock-car scene like no one else before him. In these three seasons, Cale won twenty-eight NASCAR races and won the Winston Cup—the NASCAR circuit driving title—three times. These triumphs earned him nearly $1.5 million in prize money.

### Continuing the Story

Following his three-year domination of the stock-car world, Cale gradually concentrated less and less on racing. Between 1979 and his retirement in 1986, he competed in an average of only sixteen races a year.

## *NASCAR and Other Victories*

|  |  |
|---|---|
| 1957 | South Carolina Stock Car Sportsman Championship |
| 1967-68, 1976, 1981 | Pepsi 400 |
| 1967-69, 1974, 1981, 1983 | Coca-Cola 500 |
| 1968, 1973-74, 1978, 1982 | Southern 500 |
| 1968, 1974, 1977 | Virginia 500 |
| 1968, 1977, 1983-84 | Daytona 500 |
| 1969 | Miller Genuine Draft 500 |
| 1970, 1974, 1977, 1982, 1984-85 | Daytona 500 Twin 125 Qualifying Race |
| 1970, 1975, 1978, 1980 | Nationwide 500 |
| 1970, 1977 | Miller Genuine Draft 400 |
| 1973-74, 1976-77 | Valleydale Meats 500 |
| 1973, 1976, 1978-79 | Music City 420 |
| 1973, 1979 | National 500 |
| 1974 | Riverside 400 |
| 1974-75 | Nashville 420 |
| 1974, 1976-78, 1980 | Busch 500 |
| 1974, 1976, 1978 | Wilkes 400 |
| 1974, 1977 | Mason-Dixon 500 |
| 1975, 1980, 1982 | Carolina 500 |
| 1976 | Delaware 500 |
| | Capital City 400 |
| 1976-77 | Staley 400 |
| 1976, 1978 | Old Dominion 500 |
| | NASCAR Winston Cup Champion |
| 1977, 1979 | Richmond 400 |
| 1978, 1982-83 | Gabriel 400 |
| 1978, 1984 | Winston 500 |
| 1979 | Mountain Dew 500 |
| 1980 | Texas 400 |
| | Atlanta Journal 500 |
| 1980, 1983 | Champion Spark Plug 400 |
| 1984 | International Race of Champions |
| | Van Scoy Diamond Mines 500 |
| 1985 | Miller High Life 500 |
| | Talladega 500 |
| 1986 | Budweiser International Race of Champions, third-round winner |

## Honors, Awards, and Records

| | |
|---|---|
| 1967 | NASCAR Winston Cup Most Popular Driver |
| 1968 | Ford Motor Company Man of the Year |
| 1968-69, 1978-79 | Union 76-Darlington Record Club |
| 1977 | Olsonite Driver of the Year |
| 1978 | Only driver to win three consecutive NASCAR Winston Cup Championships |
| 1982 | Only driver to win the Southern 500 five times |
| 1991 | Inducted into American Auto Racing Writers and Broadcasters Association Hall of Fame |

Despite his relative inactivity, Cale was still successful, winning twenty-four more races, to bring his career total to eighty-eight NASCAR victories. In 1982, Cale's victory at the Southern 500 gave him an unprecedented fifth triumph in that race. Perhaps fittingly, Cale dominated the race held in his own "backyard."

Throughout his racing career, Cale displayed a single-minded confidence in his own ability and a fierce competitive spirit. These attributes enabled him to amass $5,003,616 in prize money by the time of his retirement in 1986. Cale invested his earnings wisely and managed his numerous thriving business interests with the same drive and determination that characterized his racing career. In 1993, he was inducted into the International Motorsports Hall of Fame. His racing team continued to compete into the 2000's.

## Summary

Cale Yarborough always believed in his ability to make it to the top as a stock-car driver. He kept this self-confidence even through the long, unsuccessful learning phase of his career. As a result of his patience and perseverance, Cale ultimately realized his dream, becoming one of the best stock-car racers the sport has ever seen.

*David L. Andrews*

## Additional Sources

Burt, William. *NASCAR's Best: Stock Car Racing's Top Drivers Past and Present.* Osceola, Wis.: Motorbooks International, 2004.

Hawkins, Jim. *Tales from the Daytona 500.* Champaign, Ill.: Sports, 2002.

Hinton, Ed. *Daytona: From the Birth of Speed to the Death of the Man in Black.* New York: Warner Books, 2001.

Huff, Richard M. *Stock Car Racing: Running with NASCAR's Best.* Chicago: Bonus Books, 2000.

McCullough, Bob. *My Greatest Day in NASCAR.* New York: St. Martin's Press, 2000.

Sowers, Richard. *Stock Car Racing Lives.* Phoenix, Ariz.: David Bull, 2000.

Spencer, Reid. "Title Track." *Sporting News* 227, no. 35 (September 1, 2003): 58-59.

Yarborough, Cale, and William Neeley. *Cale: The Hazardous Life and Times of America's Greatest Stock Car Driver.* New York: Times Books, 1986.

# Resources

# Bibliography

## Contents

## Angling

Frazier, Ian. *The Fish's Eye: Essays About Angling and the Outdoors.* New York: Farrar, Straus and Giroux, 2002.

Henshall, James A. *Book of the Black Bass: Comprising Its Complete Scientific and Life History Together with a Practical Treatise on Angling and Fly Fishing and a Full Description of Tools, Tackle and Implements.* 1881. Reprint. Kessinger Publishing, 2007.

McClane, A. J., ed. *McClane's New Standard Fishing Encyclopedia and International Angling Guide.* New York: Gramercy Books, 1998.

McDonald, John. *The Origins of Angling.* New York: Lyons & Burford, 1997.

Martin, Darrel. *The Fly Fisher's Craft: The Art and History.* Guilford, Conn.: Lyons Press, 2006.

Martin, Roland. *Roland Martin's One Hundred and One Bass-Catching Secrets.* 2d ed. New York: Skyhorse, 2008.

Reiger, George. *Profiles in Saltwater Angling: A Tribute to Great Fish and Great Fishermen.* 2d ed. Camden, Maine: Silver Quill Press, 1999.

VanDam, Kevin. *Secrets of a Champion: Bass Superstar Reveals His Winning Tips.* Jones, Mich.: KVD Publications, 2002.

VanDam, Kevin, with Louie Stout. *Kevin VanDam's Bass Strategies: A Handbook for All Anglers.* Jones, Mich.: KVD Publications, 1995.

## Auto Racing

Arron, Simon, and Mark Hughes. *The Complete Book of Formula One.* St. Paul, Minn.: Motorbooks, 2003.

Boccafogli, Robert, and Bryn Williams. *Formula One: 1999 World Championship Yearbook, Behind the Scenes World Championship Photographic Review.* New York: Voyageur Press, 1999.

Burt, William. *NASCAR's Best: Stock Car Racing's Top Drivers Past and Present.* Osceola, Wis.: Motorbooks, 2004.

Chimits, Xavier, and François Granet. *Williams-Renault Formula One Motor Racing Book.* New York: Dorling Kindersley, 1994.

Daly, Derek, and Mario Andretti. *Race to Win: How to Become a Complete Champion Driver.* St. Paul, Minn.: Motorbooks, 2008.

Garner, Joe. *Speed, Guts, and Glory: One Hundred Unforgettable Moments in NASCAR History.* New York: Warner Books, 2006.

Genat, Robert. *Top Fuel Dragsters.* St. Paul, Minn.: Motorbooks, 2002.

Gifford, Clive. *Racing: The Ultimate Motorsports Encyclopedia.* New York: Kingfisher/Houghton Mifflin, 2006.

Gillispie, Tom. *Racing Families: A Tribute to Racing's Fastest Dynasties.* Dallas, Tex.: Beckett, 2000.

Golenbock, Peter. *NASCAR Confidential: Stories of the Men and Women Who Made Stock Car Racing Great.* St. Paul, Minn.: Motorbooks, 2004.

Hawkins, Jim. *Tales from the Daytona 500.* Champaign, Ill.: Sports, 2002.

Hembree, Michael. *NASCAR: The Definitive History of America's Sport.* New York: HarperEntertainment, 2000.

Henry, Alan. *Grand Prix Champions: From Jackie Stewart to Michael Schumacher.* Osceola, Wis.: Motorbooks, 1995.

Higham, Peter, and Bruce Jones. *World Motor Racing Circuits: A Spectator's Guide.* London: Andre Deutsch, 1999.

Hill, Damon, and Keith Sutton. *F1: Through the Eyes of Damon Hill—Inside the World of Formula One.* Boston: Little, Brown, 2000.

Hilton, Christopher. *Inside the Mind of the Grand Prix Driver: The Psychology of the Fastest Men on Earth—Sex, Danger, and Everything Else.* Newbury Park, Calif.: Haynes, 2003.

Hinton, Ed. *Daytona: From the Birth of Speed to the Death of the Man in Black.* New York: Warner Books, 2001.

Huff, Richard M. *Stock Car Racing: Running with NASCAR's Best.* Chicago: Bonus Books, 2000.

Jones, Bruce. *ITV Sport Complete Encyclopedia of Formula One.* London: Carlton, 2007.

Koby, Howard V. *Top Fuel Dragsters of the 1970's: Photo Archive.* Hudson, Wis.: Iconografix, 2004.

Latford, Bob. *Built for Speed: The Ultimate Guide to Stock Car Racetracks, a Behind-the-Wheel View of the Winston Cup Circuit.* Philadelphia, Pa.: Courage Books, 1999.

McGee, David M., and Kenny Bernstein. *Bristol Dragway.* Charleston, S.C.: Arcadia, 2007.

McGee, Ryan. *Ultimate NASCAR: One Hundred Defining Moments in Stock Car Racing History.* New York: ESPN Books, 2007.

McKenna, A. T. *Indy Racing.* Edina, Minn.: Adbo & Daughters, 1998.

McLaurin, James. *NASCAR's Most Wanted: The Top Ten Book of Outrageous Drivers, Wild Wrecks, and Other Oddities.* Washington, D.C.: Brassey's, 2001.

Martin, J. A., and Thomas F. Saal. *American Auto Racing: The Milestones and Personalities of a Century of Speed.* Jefferson, N.C.: McFarland, 2004.

Menard, Pierre, and Jacques Vassal. *Formula One Legends: Alain Prost—The Science of Racing.* St. Sulpice, France: Chronosports, 2004.

Miller, Timothy, and Steve Milton. *NASCAR Now!* 3d ed. Richmond Hill, Ont.: Firefly Books, 2008.

Mueller, Mike. *The Garlits Collection: Cars That Made Drag Racing History.* North Branch, Minn.: Car-Tech, 2004.

Nye, Doug. *Formula One Legends.* Leicester, East Midlands, England: Magna Books, 1994.

Poole, David, and James McLaurin. *NASCAR Essential: Everything You Need to Know to Be a Real Fan!* Chicago: Triumph Books, 2007.

Post, Robert C. *High Performance: The Culture and Technology of Drag Racing, 1950-2000.* Baltimore: Johns Hopkins University Press, 2001.

Reed, Terry. *Indy: The Race and Ritual of the Indianapolis 500.* Washington, D.C.: Potomac Books, 2005.

Rendall, Ivan. *The Power Game: The History of Formula One and the World Championship.* New York: Sterling, 2000.

Sakkis, Tony. *Drag Racing Legends.* Minneapolis: Motorbooks, 1996.

_____. *Indy Racing Legends.* Osceola, Wis.: Motorbooks, 1996.

Senna, Ayrton. *Ayrton Senna's Principles of Race Driving.* Osceola, Wis.: Motorbooks, 1993.

Sessler, Peter C., and Nilda Sessler. *Indy Cars.* New York: Rourke Press, 1999.

Shaffer, Rick. *CART: The First Twenty Years: 1979-1998.* Richmond, Surrey, England: Hazleton, 1999.

Small, Steve, ed. *The Grand Prix Drivers: Racing Heroes from Fangio to Prost.* Osceola, Wis.: Motorbooks, 1987.

Sowers, Richard. *The Complete Statistical History of Stock Car Racing: Records, Streaks, Oddities, and Trivia.* Phoenix: David Bull, 2000.

_____. *Stock Car Racing Lives.* Phoenix, Ariz.: David Bull, 2000.

Stewart, Mark. *Auto Racing: A History of Fast Cars and Fearless Drivers.* New York: Franklin Watts, 1998.

Strosnider, J. Steve. *Tales from the Track: Stories from the Early Days of Racing.* Victoria, B.C.: Trafford, 2002.

Taylor, Rich. *Indy: Seventy-five Years of Racing's Greatest Spectacle.* New York: St. Martin's Press, 1991.

White, Ben, and Nigel Kinrade. *The Drivers of NASCAR.* Rev. ed. St. Paul, Minn.: Crestline, 2006.

Zimmerman, John. *Dan Gurney's Eagle Racing Cars: The Technical History of the Machines from All-American Racers.* Sparkford, Somerset, England: Haynes, 2007.

## Billiards

Alciatore, David G. *The Illustrated Principles of Pool and Billiards.* New York: Sterling Publishing, 2004.

Billiard Congress of America. *Billiards: The Official Rules and Records Book.* New York: Lyons & Burford, 1992.

Byrne, Robert. *Byrne's Wonderful World of Pool and Billiards: A Cornucopia of Instruction, Strategy, Anecdote, and Colorful Characters.* San Diego: Harcourt Brace, 1996.

Koehler, Jack H. *The Science of Pocket Billiards.* Laguna Hills, Calif.: Sportology Publications, 1989.

Laurance, Ewa Mataya, and Thomas C. Shaw. *Complete Idiot's Guide to Pool and Billiards.* 2d ed. Indianapolis: Alpha Books, 2004.

Lee, Jeanette, and Adam Scott Gershenson. *The Black Widow's Guide to Killer Pool: Become the Player to Beat.* New York: Three Rivers Press, 2000.

Mizerak, Steve, with Joel Cohen. *Billiards for Advanced Players.* Merrillville, Ind.: ICS Books, 1996.

Mosconi, Willie. *Willie Mosconi's Winning Pocket Billiards: For Beginners and Advanced Players with a Section on Trick Shots.* New York: Crown, 1995.

Shamos, Michael Ian. *The New Illustrated Encyclopedia of Billiards.* New York: Lyons Press, 1999.

Stein, Victor. *The Billiard Encyclopedia: An Illustrated History of the Sport.* Minneapolis: Blue Book, 1996.

## Bodybuilding and Strongman

Bonner, Mike. *The Composite Guide to Strongman Competition.* Philadelphia: Chelsea House, 2000.

Chapman, David L. *Sandow the Magnificent: Eugen Sandow and the Beginnings of Bodybuilding.* Rev. ed. Urbana: University of Illinois Press, 2006.

Haney, Lee. *Totalee Awesome: A Complete Guide to Body-Building Success.* Wellingborough, Northamptonshire, England: Stephens, 1989.

Haney, Lee, and Jim Rosenthal. *Lee Haney's Ultimate Bodybuilding Book.* New York: St. Martin's Press, 1993.

Hughes, Mary. *The Composite Guide to Bodybuilding.* Philadelphia, Pa.: Chelsea House, 2000.

Reeves, Steve, John Little, and George Helmer. *Dynamic Muscle Building.* Malibu, Calif.: Classic Image, 2003.

Reeves, Steve, John Little, and Bob Wolff. *Building the Classic Physique the Natural Way.* 2d ed. Malibu, Calif.: Steve Reeves International, 1995.

Reeves, Steve, and James A. Peterson. *Power Walking.* Indianapolis, Ind.: Bobbs-Merrill, 1982.

Schwarzenegger, Arnold, with Bill Dobbins. *The New Encyclopedia of Modern Bodybuilding.* New York: Simon and Schuster, 1998.

Thompson, Daley, and Peter Walker. *Going for Gold: Daley Thompson's Book of Total Fitness and Body Care for Young People.* London: Unwin Paperbacks, 1987.

Torres, John Albert. *Legends of Health and Fitness: Fitness Stars of Bodybuilding.* Hockessin, Del.: Mitchell Lane, 2000.

Webster, David Pirie. *Sons of Samson.* Nevada City, Calif.: IronMind Enterprises, 1998.

## Bowling

Anthony, Earl, and Dawson Taylor. *Winning Bowling.* Chicago: Contemporary Books, 1994.

Carter, Don. *Bowling the Pro Way.* New York: Viking Press, 1975.

Herbst, Dan. *Bowling Three Hundred: Top Pros Share Their Secrets to Rolling the Perfect Game.* Chicago: Contemporary Books, 1993.

Jowdy, John. *Bowling Execution.* Champaign, Ill.: Human Kinetics, 2002.

McIntosh, Ron. *Bowler's Handbook: A Guide to (Almost) Everything in Bowling.* Elfers, Fla.: McIntosh, 2006.

Weber, Dick. *Bowling.* New York: Cornerstone Library, 1971.

_____. *The Champion's Guide to Bowling.* Rev. ed. New York: Simon and Schuster, 1981.

Weber, Dick, and Roland Alexander. *Weber on Bowling.* Englewood Cliffs, N.J.: Prentice-Hall, 1981.

## Chess

Damsky, Yakov. *The Batsford Book of Chess Records.* London: Batsford, 2005.

Karpov, Anatoly, Jean-François Phélizon, and Bachar Kouatly. *Chess and the Art of Negotiation: Ancient Rules for Modern Combat.* Westport, Conn.: Praeger, 2006.

Kasparov, Garry. *Garry Kasparov on My Great Predecessors.* 5 vols. Guilford, Conn.: Globe Pequot Press, 2006.

Kasparov, Garry, and Dmitry Plisetsky. *Garry Kasparov on Modern Chess, Part One: Chess Revolution in the Seventies.* Lyndon, Wash.: Everyman Chess, 2007.

Keene, Raymond, and Ron Morris. *The BrainGames World Chess Championship.* London: Everyman Chess, 2000.

Khodarkovski, Michael. *A New Era: How Garry Kasparov Changed the World of Chess.* New York: Ballantine Books, 1997.

Pandolfini, Bruce, ed. *The Best of Chess Life and Review: 1960-1988.* New York: Simon & Schuster, 1988.

Schiller, Eric, and Bobby Fischer. *Learn from Bobby Fischer's Greatest Games.* New York: Cardoza, 2004.

## Cycling

Abt, Samuel. *Up the Road: Cycling's Modern Era from LeMond to Armstrong.* Boulder, Colo.: VeloPress, 2005.

Burke, Edmund R. *Serious Cycling.* 2d ed. Champaign, Ill.: Human Kinetics, 2002.

Delanzy, Eric. *Inside the Tour de France: The Pictures, the Legends, and the Untold Stories of the World's Most Beloved Bicycle Race.* Emmaus, Pa.: Rodale, 2006.

Fife, Graeme. *Inside the Peloton: Riding, Winning, and Losing the Tour de France.* Edinburgh: Mainstream, 2002.

_____. *Tour de France: The History, the Legend, the Riders.* Updated. Edinburgh: Mainstream, 1999.

McGann, Bill, and Carol McGann. *The Story of the Tour De France.* Indianapolis, Ind.: Dog Ear, 2006.

Moore, Richard. *Heroes, Villains and Velodromes: Inside Track Cycling with Chris Hoy.* London: HarperSport, 2008.

Nye, Peter. *Hearts of Lions: The History of American Bicycle Racing.* New York: W. W. Norton, 1988.

Ollivier, Jean Paul. *The Giants of Cycling.* Boulder, Colo.: VeloPress, 2002.

Perry, David B. *Bike Cult: The Ultimate Guide to Human-Powered Vehicles.* New York: Four Walls Eight Windows, 1995.

Phinney, Davis, and Connie Carpenter. *Training for Cycling: The Ultimate Guide to Improved Performance.* New York: Putnam, 1992.

Rendell, Matt, and Nicolas Cheetham. *The Official Tour de France: 1903-2004.* London: Weidenfeld & Nicolson, 2004.

Startt, James. *Tour de France, Tour de Force: A Visual History of the World's Greatest Bicycle Race.* San Francisco: Chronicle Books, 2003.

Thompson, Christopher S. *The Tour de France: A Cultural History.* Berkeley: University of California Press, 2006.

Whittle, Jeremy. *Le Tour: The History of the Tour de France.* London: Collins, 2007.

Woodland, Les. *The Unknown Tour de France: The Many Faces of the World's Biggest Bicycle Race.* San Francisco: Van der Plas, 2000.

## Horse Racing

Blood-Horse Publications. *Horse Racing's Top One Hundred Moments.* Lexington, Ky.: Author, 2006.

Bowen, Edward. *At the Wire: Horse Racing's Greatest Moments.* Forestville, Calif.: Eclipse Press, 2001.

Brodowsky, Pamela K., and Tom Philbin. *Two Minutes to Glory: The Official History of the Kentucky Derby.* New York: Collins, 2007.

Chew, Peter. *The Kentucky Derby: The First One Hundred Years.* Boston: Houghton Mifflin, 1974.

Drager, Marvin. *The Most Glorious Crown: The Story of America's Triple Crown Thoroughbreds from Sir Barton to Affirmed.* Chicago: Triumph Books, 2005.

Ennor, George, and Bill Mooney. *The World Encyclopedia of Horse Racing: An Illustrated Guide.* London: Carlton, 2001.

Gruender, Scott A. *Jockey: The Rider's Life in American Thoroughbred Racing.* Jefferson, N.C.: McFarland, 2006.

Hotaling, Edward. *The Great Black Jockeys: The Lives and Times of the Men Who Dominated America's First National Sport.* Rocklin, Calif.: Forum, 1999.

Jacques, L. L., and Sue Morton. *Joey: Calgary's Horse and Racing's Hall of Famers.* Calgary, Alta.: Puckshot Press, 2006.

Mooney, Nan. *My Racing Heart: The Passionate World of Thoroughbreds and the Track.* New York: Harper Paperbacks, 2003.

Morgan, Bert, Eric Rachlis, and Blossom Lefcourt. *Horse Racing: The Golden Age of the Track.* Darby, Pa.: Diane, 2004.

Privman, Jay. *Breeders' Cup: Thoroughbred Racing's Championship Day.* Liguori, Mo.: Triumph Books, 2001.

Reeves, Richard Stone, and Edward L. Bowen. *Belmont Park: A Century of Champions.* Lexington, Ky.: Eclipse Press, 2005.

Shoemaker, Willie. *Shoe: Willie Shoemaker's Illus-*

*trated Book of Racing.* Chicago: Rand McNally, 1976.

Shulman, Lenny. *Ride of Their Lives: The Triumphs and Turmoil of Today's Top Jockeys.* Lexington, Ky.: Eclipse Press, 2002.

Simon, Mary, and Mark Simon. *Racing Through the Century: The Story of Thoroughbred Racing in America.* Irvine, Calif.: BowTie Press, 2002.

Stevens, Gary, Mervyn Kaufman, and Bill Shoemaker. *The Perfect Ride.* Secaucus, N.J.: Citadel Press, 2002.

Sugar, Bert Randolph, and Cornell Richardson. *Horse Sense: An Inside Look at the Sport of Kings.* Hoboken, N.J.: John Wiley & Sons, 2003.

*The Ten Best Kentucky Derbies.* Lexington, Ky.: Eclipse Press, 2005.

Von Borries, Philip. *Racelines: Observations on Horse Racing's Glorious History.* Lincolnwood, Ill.: Masters Press, 1999.

## Martial Arts

Gaines, Ann Graham. *The Composite Guide to Martial Arts.* Philadelphia, Pa.: Chelsea House, 2000.

Gracie, Royce, and Charles Gracie. *Brazilian Jiu-jitsu: Street Self-Defense Techniques.* Montpelier, Vt.: Invisible Cities Press, 2002.

Hunter, Jack. *Intercepting Fist: The Films of Bruce Lee and the Golden Age of Kung-Fu Cinema.* London: Glitter Books, 2005.

Krauss, Erich, and Bret Aita. *Brawl: A Behind-the-Scenes Look at Mixed Martial Arts Competition.* Toronto: ECW Press, 2002.

Metil, Luana, and Jace Townsend. *The Story of Karate: From Buddhism to Bruce Lee.* Minneapolis: Lerner Publishing, 1995.

Peligro, Kid. *The Gracie Way: An Illustrated History of the World's Greatest Martial Arts Family.* Montpelier, Vt.: Invisible Cities Press, 2003.

Smith, Robert W. *Martial Musings: A Portrayal of the Martial Arts in the Twentieth Century.* Erie, Pa.: Via Media, 1999.

## Motocross and Extreme Sports

Booth, Douglas, and Holly Thorpe, eds. *Berkshire Encyclopedia of Extreme Sports.* Great Barrington, Mass.: Berkshire Publishing Group, 2007.

Casper, Steve. *Motocross.* St. Paul, Minn.: Motorbooks, 2006.

Dixon, Franklin W. *Motocross Madness.* New York: Aladdin Paperbacks, 2005.

Gorr, Eric. *Motocross and Off-Road: Performance Handbook.* 3d ed. St. Paul, Minn.: Motorbooks, 2004.

Milan, Garth. *Freestyle Motocross: Jump Tricks from the Pros.* Osceola, Wis.: Motorbooks, 2000.

Powell, Ben L. *Extreme Sports Skateboarding.* Hauppauge, N.Y.: Barron's Educational Series, 1999.

Reynolds, Tom, and Dale Kiefer. *The Buzz on Xtreme Sports.* New York: Lebhar-Friedman Books, 2001.

Roberts, Ben. *Extreme Sports In-line Skating.* Hauppauge, N.Y.: Barron's Educational Series, 1999.

Rohrer, Russ. *Ten Days in the Dirt: The Spectacle of Off-Road Motorcycling.* Osceola, Wis.: Motorbooks, 2004.

Ryan, Ray. *Motocross Racers: Thirty Years of Legendary Dirt Bikes.* St. Paul, Minn.: Motorbooks, 2003.

Scott, Michael. *Motocourse 2007-2008: The World's Leading MotoGP and Superbike Annual.* Silverstone, England: Crash Media Group, 2008.

Thompson, Mark. *Motocross and Off-Road Training Handbook: Tune Your Body for Race-Winning Performance.* St. Paul, Minn.: Motorbooks, 2006.

Todhunter, Andrew. *Dangerous Games: Ice Climbing, Storm Kayaking, and Other Adventures from the Extreme Edge of Sports.* New York: Doubleday, 2000.

## Mountain Biking

Andrews, Guy, and Gary Fisher. *Mountain Bike Maintenance.* San Ramon, Calif.: Falcon Books, 2006.

Behr, Steve. *Extreme Sports: Mountain Biking.* Hauppauge, N.Y.: Barron's Educational Series, 1998.

Berto, Frank J. *The Birth of Dirt: Origins of Mountain Biking.* San Francisco: Van der Plas, 1999.

Brink, Tim. *The Complete Mountain Biking Manual.* New York: International Marine/Ragged Mountain Press, 2007.

Worland, Steve. *The Mountain Bike Book.* St. Paul, Minn.: Motorbooks, 2003.

Zinn, Lennard. *Zinn and the Art of Mountain Bike Maintenance.* Boulder, Colo.: VeloPress, 2005.

## Mountaineering

Birkett, Bill, and Bill Peascod. *Women Climbing: Two Hundred Years of Achievement.* London: A & C Black, 1990.

Holden, Andre. *Hillary and Everest: Fiftieth Anniversary Special.* Christchurch, Canterbury, New Zealand: The Press, 2003.

Jordan, Jennifer. *Savage Summit: The True Stories of the First Five Women Who Climbed K2, the World's Most Feared Mountain.* New York: HarperCollins, 2005.

McLoone, Margo, and Kathryn Besio. *Women Explorers of the Mountains: Nina Mazuchelli, Fanny Bullock Workman, Mary Vaux Walcott, Gertrude Benham, Junko Tabei.* Mankato, Minn.: Capstone Books, 2000.

Messner, Reinhold. *Free Spirit: A Climber's Life.* Translated by Jill Neate. Seattle, Wash.: Mountaineers Books, 1991.

_____. *The Naked Mountain.* Translated by Tim Carruthers. Seattle, Wash.: Mountaineers Books, 2003.

Unsworth, Walt. *Everest: The Mountaineering History.* 3d ed. Seattle, Wash.: Mountaineers Books, 2000.

Venables, Stephen, and the Royal Geographical Society. *Everest: Summit of Achievement.* Crows Nest, N.S.W.: Allen & Unwin, 2003.

## Powerboat Racing

Desmond, Kevin. *A Century of Outboard Racing.* Osceola, Wis.: MBI, 2001.

Farley, Fred, and Ron Harsin. *A Century of Gold Cup Racing.* Harrisburg, Pa.: Bristol Fashion Publications, 2004.

Greene, David. *David Greene's Statistical History of Major League Boat Racing.* Seattle, Wash.: Author, 1993.

Hunn, Peter. *The Golden Age of the Racing Outboard.* Marblehead, Mass.: Devereux Books, 2000.

Kunz, Phillip, and William G. Holder. *Prop Riders: Sixty Years of Racing Hydroplanes.* Marblehead, Mass.: Devereux Books, 2003.

Savage, Jeff. *Hydroplane Boats.* Mankato, Minn.: Capstone Press, 2004.

Williams, David D. *Hydroplane Racing in Seattle.* San Francisco: Arcadia, 2006.

## Rodeo

Allen, Michael. *Rodeo Cowboys in the North American Imagination.* Reno: University of Nevada Press, 1998.

Bernstein, Joel. *Wild Ride: The History and Lore of Rodeo.* Layton, Utah: Gibbs Smith, 2007.

Campion, Lynn. *Rodeo: Behind the Scenes at America's Most Exciting Sport.* Guilford, Conn.: Lyons Press, 2004.

Coplon, Jeff. *Gold Buckle: The Grand Obsession of Rodeo Bull Riders.* San Francisco: HarperCollins-West, 1995.

Ehringer, Gavin, and Gary Vorhes. *Rodeo Legends: Twenty Extraordinary Athletes of America's Sport.* Colorado Springs, Colo.: Western Horseman Magazine, 2003.

Fredriksson, Kristine. *American Rodeo from Buffalo Bill to Big Business.* College Station: University of Texas A&M Press, 1985.

Jordan, Bob. *Rodeo History and Legends.* Montrose, Colo.: Rodeo Stuff, 1993.

Porter, Willard H. *Who's Who in Rodeo.* Oklahoma City, Okla.: National Cowboy Hall of Fame, 1982.

St. John, Bob. *On Down the Road: The World of the Rodeo Cowboy.* Austin, Tex.: Eakin Press, 1983.

Woerner, Gail Hughbanks. *Fearless Funnymen: The History of the Rodeo Clown.* Austin, Tex.: Eakin Press, 1993.

_____. *Rope to Win: The History of Steer, Calf, and Team Roping.* Austin, Tex.: Eakin, 2007.

Wooden, Wayne S., and Gavin Ehringer. *Rodeo in America: Wranglers, Roughstock, and Paydirt.* Lawrence: University Press of Kansas, 1996.

## Sailing

Cardwell, Jerry D. *Sailing Big on a Small Sailboat.* 3d ed. Dobbs Ferry, N.Y.: Sheridan House, 2007.

Compton, Nic. *Sailing Solo: The Legendary Sailors and the Great Races.* Camden, Maine: International Marine/McGraw-Hill, 2003.

Conner, Dennis, and Michael Levitt. *The America's Cup: The History of Sailing's Greatest Competition in the Twentieth Century.* New York: St. Martin's Press, 1998.

Deaves, Robert. *Finnatics: The History and Techniques of Finn Sailing.* Newport, Isle of Wight, England: The International Finn Association, 1999.

Dewar, Oliver. *Extreme Sail.* London: Pavilion, 2006.

Elvstrøm, Paul, and Soren Krause. *Paul Elvstrøm Explains the Racing Rules of Sailing, 2005-2008 Rules.* Camden, Maine: International Marine/McGraw-Hill, 2005.

## Skateboarding

Blomquist, Christopher. *Skateboarding in the X Games.* New York: PowerKids, 2003.

Brooke, Michael. *The Concrete Wave: The History of Skateboarding.* Toronto: Warwick House, 1999.

Davis, James. *Skateboarding Is Not a Crime: Fifty Years of Street Culture.* Buffalo, N.Y.: Firefly Books, 2004.

Gutman, Bill, and Shawn Frederick. *Catching Air: The Excitement and Daring of Individual Action Sports—Snowboarding, Skateboarding, BMX Biking, In-line Skating.* New York: Citadel Press, 2004.

Noll, Rhyn. *Skateboarding: Past-Present-Future.* Atglen, Pa.: Schiffer Publishing, 2003.

## Sumo Wrestling

Cuyler, Patricia. *Sumo: From Rite to Sport.* New York: Weatherhill, 1979.

Hall, Mina. *The Big Book of Sumo.* Berkeley, Calif.: Stone Bridge, 1997.

Newton, Clyde, and Gerald Toff. *Dynamic Sumo.* New York: Kodansha, 2000.

## Surfing

Chase, Linda, and Elizabeth Pepin. *Surfing: Women of the Waves.* Layton, Utah: Gibbs Smith, 2007.

Finney, Ben, and James D. Houston. *Surfing: A History of the Ancient Hawaiian Sport.* Rev. ed. San Francisco: Pomegranate Artbooks, 1996.

Gabbard, Andrea. *Girl in the Curl: A Century of Women in Surfing.* Berkeley, Calif.: Seal Press, 2000.

Kampion, Drew. *Stoked! A History of Surf Culture.* Salt Lake City, Utah: G. Smith, 2003.

Slater, Kelly, and Jason Borte. *Pipe Dreams: A Surfer's Journey.* New York: ReganBooks, 2003.

Southerden, Louise, and Layne Beachley. *Surf's Up: The Girl's Guide to Surfing.* New York: Ballantine Books, 2005.

Warshaw, Matt. *The Encyclopedia of Surfing.* Orlando, Fla.: Harcourt, 2005.

_____. *Surfriders: In Search of the Perfect Wave.* New York: Collins, 1997.

Young, Nat. *The History of Surfing.* Salt Lake City, Utah: Gibbs Smith, 2006.

## Triathlon

Allen, Mark, and Bob Babbitt. *Mark Allen's Total Triathlete.* Chicago: Contemporary Books, 1988.

Cook, Jeff. *The Triathletes: A Season in the Lives of Four Women in the Toughest Sport of All.* New York: St. Martin's Press, 1992.

Finch, Michael. *Triathlon Training.* Champaign, Ill.: Human Kinetics, 2004.

Kearns, Brad. *Breakthrough Triathlon Training.* New York: McGraw-Hill, 2005.

Scott, Dave, and Liz Barrett. *Dave Scott's Triathlon Training.* New York: Simon & Schuster, 1986.

Tinley, Scott. *Triathlon: A Personal History.* Boulder, Colo.: VeloPress, 1998.

# Sports Resources on the World Wide Web

Sports sites on the World Wide Web offer rich sources of information on athletes, teams, leagues, and the various sports themselves. Through careful searching, one can find up-to-date news on almost every sport; schedules; detailed statistics; sports; biographies of athletes; histories of teams, leagues, and individual sports; and much more. Since the previous edition of *Great Athletes* was published in 2001, both the numbers and quality of sports Web sites offering unrestricted access have increased significantly, making it easier than ever before to find information. However, while finding information on the Web has grown easier, evaluating the reliability of the information one finds may be growing harder.

The vast majority of sports Web sites are maintained by fans and bloggers whose objectivity and accuracy can be difficult to judge. Even articles on sites such as Wikipedia may present problems. Wikipedia articles are often detailed, up to date, and accurate, but they are not fully vetted and can be altered at any time by any user. Search engines such as Google and Yahoo! are efficient tools for finding information on athletes quickly, but if they are used carelessly, they may direct users to unreliable sites. For this reason, it is generally wise to begin any Web search with a list of Web sites that are proven to be reliable.

The purpose of this list is to help guide readers to the best Web sources for racing and individual sports and to call attention to the variety of sites available online, with particular emphasis on the sports covered in *Great Athletes*. Preference has been given to sites maintained by professional sports organizations, reputable news services, online magazines, halls of fame, and television networks, as well as other sites that provide accurate and unbiased information. As it is neither possible nor necessary to list every possible sports Web site, some of the sites listed here may be regarded as representative types that have many counterparts that are not listed. For example, the California Fish and Game Department is listed under Angling because it is an outstanding example of a state Web site that provides information on fishing. Similar sites are maintained by virtually every U.S. state and Canadian province and can be easily found with online search engines.

Most of the sites listed here can be found quickly by entering their names into an online search engine. If that approach does not work, one can simply type a URL (uniform resource locator) into the address line of a Web browser. Note that it is usually unnecessary to enter "http://" and that many sites can be found through more than a single URL. As still more sites are certain to emerge, it is advisable to use text searches to find new sites. Also, look for links to other sites on the pages that your visit.

Every site listed here was inspected and found to be working in January, 2009. Many of these sites offer links to merchandisers, but every effort has been made to avoid sites that serve primarily as sites for vendors and sports handicappers. URLs often change; if a link fails to work, search the name of the Web site with a standard Web search engine such as Google or Yahoo!

## Contents

# 1. General Sites

**Africa South of the Sahara Sports News**
http://www-sul.stanford.edu/depts/ssrg/africa/
　　sports.html

**AllSports**
http://www.allsports.com

**Ballparks and Racetracks**
http://www.ballparks.com

*Black College Sports Review* (**magazine**)
http://www.black-sports.com

**Broadcast Sports**
http://www.broadcastsports.com

**Cable News Network (CNN)/Sports Illustrated
　　(SI)**
http://sportsillustrated.cnn.com

**Canada's Sports Hall of Fame**
http://www.cshof.ca

**Canadian Broadcasting Corporation (CBC)
　　Sports**
http://cbc.ca/sports

**CBS SportsLine**
http://cbs.sportsline.com

**Click Afrique.com**
http://www.clickafrique.com

**College Sports Information Directors of America
　　(CoSIDA)**
http://www.cosida.com

**ESPN**
http://espn.go.com

**Excite: Sports**
http://sports.excite.com

**Express Sport Live (European Sporting News)**
http://www.sportslive.net

**FOXSports**
http://www.foxsports.com

**History of Women in Sports Timeline**
http://www.northnet.org/stlawrenceaauw/
　　timeline.htm

**Home Box Office (HBO) Sports**
http://www.hbo.com/realsports

**International Association for Sports Information**
http://www.iasi.org/home.html

**Latin American Network Information Center
　　(LANIC): Sports News**
http://lanic.utexas.edu/la/region/sports

**MaxPreps: America's Source for High
　　School Sports**
http://www.maxpreps.com/national/home.aspx

**MSNBC Sports**
http://nbcsports.msnbc.com

**National Collegiate Athletic Association (NCAA)**
http://www.ncaa.org

**New England Sports Network**
http://www.nesn.com

**One on One Sports**
http://www.1on1sports.com

**PioneerPlanet: Sports**
http://www.pioneerplanet.com/sports

**Real Fans Sports Network**
http://www.realfans.com

**Rivals**
http://www.rivals.com

**Sport Science**
http://www.exploratorium.edu/sports

**The Sporting Life**
http://www.sporting-life.com

**SportingNews.com**
http://www.sportingnews.com

*Sports Illustrated* (**magazine**)
http://www.pathfinder.com/si

**Sports Illustrated for Kids**
http://www.sikids.com

**Sports Network**
http://www.sportsnetwork.com/home.asp

**Sports Schedules as You Like 'Em**
http://www.cs.rochester.edu/u/ferguson/
    schedules

**SportsFan Radio Network**
http://www.sportsfanradio.com

**SportsFeed (news)**
http://www.sportsfeed.com

**SportsLine USA**
http://www.sportsline.com

**Turner Network Television (TNT) Sports**
http://tnt.turner.com/sports

**USA Network Sports**
http://www.usanetwork.com/sports

**USA Today-Sports**
http://www.usatoday.com

**Women's Sports Information**
http://www.womenssportsinformation.com

**World Wide Web Virtual Library: Sports**
http://sportsvl.com

**Yahoo! Sports**
http://dir.yahoo.com/recreation/sports

## 2. Angling

*American Angler: The Fly-Fishing Magazine*
http://www.flyfishingmagazines.com

**The Angling Channel**
http://www.theanglingchannel.com

**Angling Masters International**
http://www.anglingmasters.com

**The Angling Report**
http://www.anglingreport.com

**Angling.com**
http://www.angling.com

**Bassdozer: Bass Fishing, Bass Lures, Bass Boats**
http://www.bassdozer.com

**California Department of Fish and Game**
http://www.dfg.ca.gov/fish/fishing

*Cyberangler: Online Fishing Magazine*
http://cyberangler.com

**Fishing.Net/Angler Community**
http://www.fishing.net

*Florida Sport Fishing: The Journal for the
    Saltwater Angler*
http://floridasportfishing.com/magazine

*GAFF Magazine* (**Gulf Atlantic Florida Fishing**)
http://www.gaffmag.net

*Salt Water Sportsman* (magazine)
http://www.saltwatersportsman.com

*Sport Fishing: The Magazine of Saltwater Fishing*
http://www.sportfishingmag.com

## 3. Auto Racing

**AMA Pro Racing**
http://www.amaproracing.com

**Formula One**
http://www.formula1.com

**Go Racing**
http://www.goracing.com

**Indianapolis Motor Speedway**
http://www.indianapolismotorspeedway.com

**Motocross.com**
http://www.motocross.com

**MotoWorld**
http://www.motoworld.com

**NASCAR**
http://www.nascar.com

**Official Site of the Indianapolis 500**
http://www.indy500.com

**RaceWire**
http://www.racewire.com

**SpeedFX**
Http://www.speedfx.com

## Bicycling. *See* Cycling

## 4. Billiards

**American Pool Players Association**
http://www.poolplayers.com

**Billiard Congress of America**
http://home.bca-pool.com

**European Pocket Billiard Federation**
http://www.epbf.com

**North American Pool and Billiard Association**
http://www.napba.com

**Women's Professional Billiards Association (WPBA)**
http://home.bca-pool.com

**World Pool-Billiards Association**
http://www.wpa-pool.com

## 5. Bodybuilding

**BodyBuilding.com**
http://www.bodybuilding.com

**International Federation of Bodybuilding and Fitness (IFBB)**
http://www.ifbb.com

**Mr. Olympia**
http://www.mrolympia.com

## 6. Bowling

**BowlersJournal.com International**
http://www.bowlersjournal.com

**Bowling World**
http://www.bowlingworld.com

**International Bowling Museum and Hall of Fame**
http://www.bowlingmuseum.com

**Professional Bowlers Association (PBA)**
http://www.pbatour.com

**United States Bowling Congress**
http://www.bowl.com

## 7. Chess

**Association of Chess Professionals**
http://www.chess-players.org

**Chessbase News**
http://www.chessbase.com

**International Correspondence Chess Federation (ICCF)**
http://www.iccf.com

**United States Chess Federation (USCF)**
http://www.uschess.org

**The Week in Chess**
http://www.chesscenter.com/twic/twic.html

**World Chess Federation (FIDE)**
http://www.fide.com

## 8. Cycling

*Bicycling* (magazine): Tour de France News
http://www.tourdefrancenews.com

**CyclingNews.com: The World Centre of Cycling**
http://www.cyclingnews.com

**Le Tour de France**
http://www.letour.fr

**RoadCycling.com**
http://www.roadcycling.com

**USA Cycling**
http://www.usacycling.org

*VeloNews: The Journal of Competitive Cycling*
http://www.velonews.com

## 9. Horse Racing

**The Horse Racing Channel**
http://www.horseracing.com

**Horses and Horse Information**
http://www.horses-and-horse-information.com

**National Thoroughbred Racing Association (NTRA)**
http://www.ntraracing.com

**United States Trotting Association (USTA)**
http://www.ustrotting.com

## 10. Hydroplane and Powerboat Racing

**HydroInsider.com**
http://www.kndu.com/Global/
    category.asp?C=78290&nav=menu484_4_4

**Unlimited Light Hydroplane Racing Association (ULHRA)**
http://www.ulhra.org

**Canadian Boating Federation (CBF)**
http://www.cbfnc.ca

**American Boat Racing Association (ABRA)**
http://www.abrahydroplanes.com

*Boat Sport, Speed and Spray, Hydroplane Quarterly*
http://www.boatsport.org

*Powerboat* (magazine)
http://www.powerboatmag.com

**American Power Boat Association (APBA)**
http://www.solarnavigator.net/a_p_b_a.htm

**International Power Boat Association (IPBA)**
http://www.ipbalogracing.org

## 11. In-line Skating

**Inline Skating Resource Center**
http://www.iisa.org

**USA Roller Sports**
http://www.usarollersports.org

## Judo. *See* Martial Arts

## 12. Martial Arts

**AAU Karate**
http://aaukarate.org

**AAU Taekwando**
http://www.aautaekwondo.org

*Black Belt* (magazine)
http://www.blackbeltmag.com

**International TaeKwon-Do Assocaation**
http://www.itatkd.com

**Jiu Jitsu International**
http://www.jiu-jitsu-international.info

**The Martial Arts Network**
http://www.martial-arts-network.com

**The Original Judo Information Site**
http://judoinfo.com

**United States Fight League**
http://www.usfightleague.com

**United States Judo Association**
http://www.usja-judo.org

**USA Jiu-Jitsu**
http://www.usajj.com

**USA Judo**
http://www.usjudo.org

**World Karate Federation**
http://www.karateworld.org

**World Taekwando Federation**
http://www.wtf.org

## 13. Mountaineering

**Alpine Club of Canada**
http://www.alpineclubofcanada.ca

**American Alpine Institute**
http://www.aai.cc

**Association of Mountaineering Instructors (AMI)**
http://www.ami.org.uk

**British Mountaineering Council (BMC)**
http://www.thebmc.co.uk

*Climb Magazine*
http://www.climbmagazine.com

**International Mountaineering and Climbing Federation (UIAA)**
http://www.theuiaa.org

*Rock and Ice* **(magazine)**
http://www.rockandice.com

## Pool. *See* Billiards

## Powerboat Racing. *See* Hydroplane and Powerboat Racing

## 14. Rodeo

**American Professional Rodeo Association (APRA)**
http://www.apra.com

**Canadian Professional Rodeo Association (CPRA)**
http://www.rodeocanada.com

**International Gay Rodeo Association (IGRA)**
http://www.igra.com

**International Professional Rodeo Association (IPRA)**
http://www.iprarodeo.com

**National Cowboy and Western Heritage Museum**
http://www.nationalcowboymuseum.org

**National High School Rodeo Association**
http://www.nhsra.com

**National Intercollegiate Rodeo Association (NIRA)**
http://www.collegerodeo.com

**National Little Britches Rodeo Association**
http://www.nlbra.com

**National Professional Rodeo Association (NPRA)**
http://www.npra.com

**Professional Armed Forces Rodeo Association (PAFRA)**
http://www.pafra2000.com

**Women's Professional Rodeo Association (WPRA)**
http://www.wpra.com

## 15. Sailing and Yachting

**American Model Yachting Association (AMYA)**
http://www.modelyacht.org

**American Sailing Association**
http://www.asa.com

**America's Cup**
http://www.americascup.com/en

**CupInfo: America's Cup News and Information**
http://www.cupinfo.com

**International Sailing Federation (ISAF)**
http://www.sailing.org

**Royal Yachting Association (RYA)**
http://www.rya.org.uk

*Sail Magazine*
http://www.sailmagazine.com

*Sailing Magazine*
http://www.sailingmagazine.net

**US Sailing**
http://ussailing.org

**Yachting Club of America**
http://www.ycaol.com

*Yachting Magazine*
http://www.yachtingmagazine.com

## 16. Skateboarding

**International Skateboarding Federation**
http://www.internationalskateboardingfederation
.org

*Skateboarder Magazine*
http://www.skateboardermag.com

**Transworld Skateboarding**
http://www.skateboarding.transworld.net

**USA Skateboarding**
http://www.usaskateboarding.org

## 17. Sled-Dog Racing

**International Sled Dog Racing Association (ISDRA)**
http://www.isdra.org

*Mushing* (magazine)
http://www.mushing.com

**Sleddoggin.com**
http://sleddoggin.com

## 18. Sumo Wrestling

**Japan Sumo Association (Nihon Sumō Kyōkai)**
http://www.sumo.or.jp/eng

*Sumo Fan Magazine*
http://www.sumofanmag.com

**Sumo Reference (databases)**
http://sumodb.sumogames.com

**Sumo Talk (blogs)**
http://www.sumotalk.com

**United States Sumo Federation**
http://www.ussumofederation.org

## 19. Triathlon

*Inside Triathlon* (magazine)
http://www.insidetriathlon.com

**New York Triathlon**
http://www.nytc.org

*Triathlete* (magazine)
http://www.triathletemag.com

**USA Triathlon**
http://www.usatriathlon.org

## 20. Waterskiing

**International Waterski Federation (IWSF)**
http://www.iwsf.com

**USA Waterski**
http://www.usawaterski.org

*Waterski* (magazine)
http://www.waterskimag.com

**Waterski and Wakeboard Canada**
Http://www.waterski-wakeboard.ca

## Yachting. *See* Sailing and Yachting

# Glossary

**action (bowling):** How the bowling pins are affected by the technique of the bowler.

**aft:** Nautical term for the rear of a vessel.

**aikido:** Japanese martial art based on the central principle of utilizing opponents' weight and momentum against them.

**air:** Rudimentary trick in which a skateboarder lifts all four wheels off the skating surface.

**alley:** Bowling lane.

**America's Cup:** International series of yacht races that is one of the most prestigious events of its kind. Boats in this class must be 75-foot monohulls with 110-foot masts, and they are essentially longer and lighter than the previously used twelve-meter sloops. The races are of two types: match races, which involve only two boats at a time, and fleet races, for all entrants in a round-robin competition. There is no fixed timetable for competitions. The cup is defended about every three to four years, and the winner selects the next race location. The America's Cup originated in 1851, in England. The entry from the United States New York Yacht Club (NYYC) won the race. Sometime thereafter, the owners gave the trophy to the NYYC with the requirement that it be defended whenever challenged, and the trophy was renamed the America's Cup.

**angling:** Colloquial term for sportfishing, which is distinguished from commercial fishing.

**arrows (bowling):** Seven triangular marks set into the lane just beyond the foul line, which bowlers use as target points for releasing the ball.

**Association of Surfing Professionals (ASP):** Governing body for surfing founded in 1976 that oversees professional surfing on an international level and conducts the World Surfing Tour.

**ASP.** *See* Association of Surfing Professionals.

**attack:** Cycling term for a sudden attempt to break away from the peloton, the main group of cyclists, in order to seize the lead.

**auto racing:** General term for various forms of competitions—based on either speed or time—among drivers and their specially modified cars.

**backside:** Generic term to describe a skateboarding trick undertaken with one's back facing away from a ramp or other skating apparatus.

**backstretch:** On a racetrack, the straightaway on the side opposite the homestretch and the finish line.

**balance:** Bodybuilding term describing a well-proportioned physique, in which the various muscle groups are in even and pleasing proportion to one another. Among competitive bodybuilders, this is an especially desirable quality.

**bareback riding:** Rodeo competition that involves riding an unsaddled wild, bucking horse for eight seconds, using only one hand to grip a strap attached to the horse's torso. Riders are judged on their control during the ride and how hard the horse bucks. The event has been compared to riding a jackhammer with one hand.

**bell lap:** Last lap of a cycling race.

**belt:** Martial arts term for a cloth belt of varying colors worn to indicate a particular level of achievement in judo and other forms of martial arts. In judo, the efficiency grades are of two types: kyu (pupil) and dan (master), the highest grade. Starting with the beginner level, the colors won in judo are white, yellow, orange, green, blue, brown, and black, which signifies the dan or master grade and is itself divided into ten degrees. Sixth-, seventh-, and eighth-degree black belts have the option of wearing a red and white belt; ninth- and tenth-degree black belts may choose a solid red belt.

**biceps:** Muscles located at the front of the upper arm, opposite the triceps.

**bicycle motocross (BMX):** Originally a form of closed-circuit bicycle racing on hilly dirt tracks. Also a type of freestyle cycling, better known by its acronym, which incorporates elements of dirt-bike racing and skateboarding. Competitions are conducted in five major categories: dirt, flatland, street, ramp, and vert. *See also* motocross.

**billiards:** Parlor games played on rectangular tables on which competitors use long cue sticks to hit hard, solid balls either into pockets along the edges of the table or into each other depending on the specific game being played. *See also* pool.

**blanket finish:** Situation occurring when the results of a horse race are not immediately clear because of the close finishes of two or more horses.

**BMX.** *See* bicycle motocross.

**bodybuilding:** Form of weight training, often competitive, that incorporates nutrition, weightlifting, and other exercise.

**boom:** Pole used to extend the bottom of a sail on a boat.

**bow:** Front part of a boat. Also known as the prow.

**bowling:** Individual sport in which competitors roll a heavy, solid ball down a lane toward a set of pins.

**box:** One bowling frame.

**breakaway:** Single rider or group of cyclists who have begun an attack by riding away from another, larger group of cyclists.

**bronco:** Untamed horse often used in rodeo competition.

**bronco buster:** Person skilled in taming wild horses.

**bull riding:** Rodeo competition that involves riding a twisting, jumping bull for eight seconds, using only one hand to grip a strap attached to the bull's torso. In major competitions, the biggest and fastest bulls weigh more than a ton.

**CART.** *See* Championship Auto Racing Teams.

**carve:** Situation occurring when a skateboarder moves in a long, curved motion.

**century:** Bicycle race 100 miles in length. A double century is a 200-mile race.

**Championship Auto Racing Teams (CART):** Official governing body of the FedEx Championship Series.

**chassis:** Frame of a car.

**check:** Placing an opposing chess player's king one move away from being captured. When the opponent cannot make a move that takes the king out of check, a checkmate is declared and the opponent wins the game.

**checkered flag:** Flag with black and white squares that is waved to signal the end of an auto race and to indicate the winner.

**checkmate:** Moment in a chess game when a player's king finds itself in a position from which it cannot escape capture and the opposing player is declared the winner.

**chess:** Board game in which two players engage sixteen pieces of varying maneuverability and strategic importance across a checkered space with the goal of checkmating the opponent's king.

**chute:** Narrow holding pen adjacent to the rodeo arena, used to restrain an animal so that the rider can mount it. As the ride begins, a gate opens into the arena, releasing the animal.

**circuit:** In sports such as auto racing or cycling, the race course itself. Can also refer to an organized athletic league or conference or a set of leagues or conferences.

**classics:** Oldest and most important road races of the cycling season. The typical classic race course may be from city to city or point to point and is much shorter in length and duration than the multistage tours.

**clean game:** Bowling game in which a bowler has had a strike or spare in every frame.

**count:** Number of bowling pins knocked over with the first ball of a frame in a game.

**crew chief:** Auto racing term for head mechanic and race manager responsible for in-race decisions.

**criterium:** Cycling race of a specified number of laps over a closed course or around an oval track.

**cue ball:** White ball that is the only ball billiards and pool players are permitted to strike with a cue stick.

**cue stick:** Long leather- or rubber-tipped pole used to put the cue ball in play in billiard and pool games.

**cycling:** General term for bicycle sport.

**deck:** Flat, wooden surface of a skateboard.

**definition:** Bodybuilding term for the distinctness or clarity of outline and detail of the exercised muscles. Well-defined bodybuilders have so little body fat that even the very fine grooves or "striations" of their major muscle groups are clearly visible.

**derailleur:** Bike mechanism used to shift gears by moving the chain.

**deuce:** Colloquial bowling term for a score of 200. Also known as a par.

**distaff:** Horse race in which only female horses run. The most famous American example of this type of race is the Breeders' Cup Ladies' Classic, formerly known as the Breeder's Cup Distaff.

**dog sled racing.** *See* Iditarod Trail Sled Dog Race.

**dojo:** Gymnasium or school in which martial arts are taught and practiced. In Japanese, *dojo* means "place of the way."

**double:** Bowling term for two consecutive strikes.

**drafting:** Tactic of driving or riding just behind and very close to another car or cyclist in order to take advantage of the slipstream—the tunnel or pocket of reduced air resistance and forward suction created by the moving object in front. Slipstreaming allows the second vehicle or rider to maintain a certain speed while expending less energy. *See also* slipstreaming.

**drag:** Effect of wind resistance over a race car during a race.

**drag racing:** Auto sport that pits two cars against each other and the clock in a contest of acceleration on a straightaway that is usually one-eighth or one-quarter mile in length.

**echelon:** Line of cyclists; used as a strategy to race at a higher speed than an individual rider can. *See also* paceline.

**Eclipse Award:** Annual American horse-racing award given in numerous subcategories, including horse, jockey, and trainer of the year.

**ends:** Bowling term for the portion of the lane that houses the pins.

**equine:** General term for anything involving a horse.

**fakie:** Moment when a skateboarder faces forward but skates backward.

**field sprint:** In a cycling road race, a dash for the finish line by the primary group of cyclists.

**fixed-gear cycling:** Track cycling event involving bicycles equipped with only one gear speed that travel only as fast as their riders can pedal.

**forcing the pace:** Cycling term for increasing the pace to a point that other cyclists cannot sustain.

**Formula One:** Highest and fastest level of racing competition on the Grand Prix circuit. Formula One cars are open-wheeled and seat only one driver. They must be built according to "formulas" or specifications that govern details such as engine size, weight, and design which are set by the Fédération Internationale de'l Automobile, the worldwide sanctioning body of auto racing. These cars frequently average speeds well above 100 miles per hour in competition.

**Formula Two:** Racing circuit, renamed Formula 3000 in 1985, that was traditionally a training ground for Formula One.

**frame:** One of the ten periods or units into which bowling games are divided.

**freestyle:** Surfing event that allows individual competitors to select the stunts or maneuvers they perform.

**frontside:** Generic term for skateboard trick undertaken while one faces a ramp or other skating apparatus.

**funny car:** Highly modified top fuel dragster fitted with a late-model production car body usually made of fiberglass. Nearly as fast as the standard top fuel dragsters, funny cars are powered by similar types of engines that are mounted in the front and that run on nitromethane fuel. Funny cars can reach speeds in the range of 290 miles per hour. *See also* top fuel.

**furlong:** On a horse racing track, a measurement of one-eighth of a mile.

**gate (horse racing):** Movable steel contraption the width of the track and fitted with a row of narrow stalls occupied by the horse and jockey at the start of a race. The starting line.

**gear:** Cycling term for the mechanism that alters the rate of motion on a bike.

**goofyfoot:** Situation occurring when a skateboarder or surfer positions the right foot in front of the left foot, the opposite of the tradition style.

**grand master:** Highest international rank for a chess champion.

**Grand Prix (auto racing):** Class of races for formula cars that constitutes the most elite series of races in international auto racing competition. These events are now held almost exclusively on specially mapped-out city streets. Drivers who accumulate the most points on the Grand Prix circuit are awarded the World Championship of Drivers title at the end of the racing season.

**grappling:** Type of martial art in which competitors grab their opponents' arms, legs, or torso to push and pull them to the ground.

**green flag:** Flag used in auto racing to signal drivers that a race has started or has resumed.

**grind:** Skateboarding trick in which the competitor scrapes the trucks along a hard surface.

**grip tape:** Sandpaper with adhesive on one side attached to the upper half of the skateboard deck, providing grip for the skateboarder's feet.

**gutter:** Concave spaces on either side of the bowling lane.

**gutter ball:** Colloquial bowling term for a ball bowled into one of the gutters along the side of a lane.

**half pipe:** Skateboarding ramp shaped like the letter U.

**hamstrings:** Muscles located at the back of the upper legs.

**hapkido:** Korean martial art that employs kicks and principles of aikido.

**harness racing:** Form of horse racing in which jockeys ride two-wheel carts pulled by the horses.

**hill climb:** Auto race up a hill, one car at a time, in a race against the clock.

**homestretch:** On a racetrack, the length of track between the final turn and the finish line. Also an expression that means something is almost completed.

**horse racing:** Sport in which jockeys guide horses around an oval track, usually composed of dirt or grass, at high speeds.

**horsepower:** Unit of power that measures an automotive engine's pulling strength.

**hot rod:** Car used in racing that is modified to increase its speed and acceleration.

**hot-rodder:** Person who drives or builds hot-rod cars.

**hydroplaning:** Racing sport in which lightweight boats skim across bodies of water.

**Iditarod Trail Sled Dog Race:** 1,158-mile sled-dog racing endurance test. The Iditarod is an annual event that starts in Anchorage, Alaska, and ends in Nome. First held in 1973, it commemorates a well-known attempt in the winter of 1925 to rush emergency medicines and other supplies to Nome, which was fighting a diphtheria epidemic. The sport's longest and most prestigious event.

**Indianapolis 500:** Annual car racing event held at Indianapolis, Indiana, on or near Memorial Day. First run in 1911, the 500-mile race is automobile racing's most prestigious event, featuring the fastest cars and most successful drivers.

**Indy car:** Car that outwardly resembles a Formula One car but is several hundred pounds heavier, boosted for greater horsepower, and goes faster. These cars frequently reach speeds well above 200 miles per hour on a straightaway. The only type of race cars allowed on the Championship Auto Racing Teams (CART) circuit, which includes the popular Indianapolis 500.

**Ironman Triathlon, The:** Triathlon world championship, held annually in Hawaii. The competition includes 2.4-mile swim, a 112-mile bicycle ride, and a 26.2-mile run. *See* triathlon.

**jersey:** Uniform shirt worn by a cyclist during a race. *See* yellow jersey.

**jockey:** Professional rider of racehorses.

*juryo:* Japanese term for the second-highest division in sumo wrestling.

**karate:** Japanese martial art that employs punches, kicks, and offensive techniques.

**keirin:** Paced cycling competition in which riders are guided around a track until the final 600 meters, at which point they sprint toward the finish. Keirin became an official Olympic event in 2000.

**kendo:** Japanese martial art equivalent to sword fighting.

**kick:** Quick acceleration near the end of a cycling race.

**kickboxing:** Martial art that combines boxing with kicking techniques.

**kung fu:** General term for Chinese martial arts.

**lane:** Wooden or urethane playing surface on which the bowling ball is rolled toward the pins.

**lap:** One complete trip around any racetrack.

**lariat:** Rope used to catch and subdue livestock that is used in calf-roping events in rodeo competitions.

**lasso:** Specific type of lariat with a noose; used to capture livestock by roping around the animals around their necks.

**line bowling:** Style of bowling that involves rolling the ball along an imaginary line from the point of release to the target point.

**mainsail:** Principal sail on a ship having several sails.

*makuuchi:* Japanese term for Sumo wrestling divisions.

**martial arts:** General term for any person-to-person combat sport, such as tae kwon do and judo.

**mast:** Main pole that supports the sails of a boat.

**master:** Title given to a martial artist who has achieved an advanced ranking after many years of study. *See also* belt.

**match play:** Bowling tournament format in which individual bowlers compete head-to-head.

**match sprint:** 1,000-meter cycling race around a velodrome track. Only the last 200 meters are timed. During the first 800 meters, the cyclists try to position themselves for the final 200-meter rush to the finish line.

**McTwist:** Skateboarding trick named after skater Mike McGill in which the rider makes a 540-degree rotation off a ramp.

**metric century:** Bike race 100 kilometers in length. *See also* century.

**mixed martial arts:** Combat sport that incorporates elements from numerous disciplines, including boxing, wrestling, jujitsu, sambo, and grappling.

**modified stock car:** Standard assembly-line car whose power and efficiency have been boosted for greater performance, such as major improvements in the engine, transmission, suspension, and fuel-injection system.

**motocross:** Motorcycle sport on a closed-circuit track with terrain designed to emulate a natural environment. *See also* bicycle motocross.

**motor-paced cycling:** Cycling time trial in which a car or motorcycle is used to cut wind resistance for the cyclist, who rides just behind and very close to the vehicle in front in order to ride in the slipstream created by the vehicle. The reduced air resistance ensures the possibility of reaching higher speeds with less effort.

**mountain biking:** Sport in which specialized bicycles, usually with thick tires and enhanced suspensions, race through mountainous terrain.

**mountaineering:** Endurance and adventure sport in which climbers test their limits by ascending tall, and often treacherous, mountains.

**Mr./Ms. America:** U.S. amateur title awarded to the male and female champions in the Mr./Ms. America bodybuilding competition. Entrants compete for the title in three divisions, according to their height: tall, medium, and short. Sanctioned by the Amateur Athletic Union.

**Mr./Ms. Olympia:** World professional title awarded to the male and female champions in the Mr. and Ms. Olympia bodybuilding competitions. Entrants compete for the title in a number of weight classifications. Sanctioned by the International Federation of Bodybuilding.

**Mr./Ms. Universe:** World amateur title awarded to the male and female champions in the Mr./Ms. Universe bodybuilding competition. Entrants compete for the title in a number of weight classifications. Sanctioned by the International Federation of Bodybuilding.

**Muay Thai:** Sport similar to kickboxing developed and primarily practiced in Southeast Asian countries, especially Thailand.

**muscle mass:** Relative size of a muscle, a muscle group, or of the physique as a whole. Along with clear definition and well-balanced proportion, muscle mass is a desirable quality among bodybuilders.

**NASCAR.** *See* National Association for Stock Car Auto Racing.

**National Association for Stock Car Auto Racing (NASCAR):** Professional stock car-racing circuit that stages competitions in thirteen separate vehicle divisions at tracks throughout the United States. Its premier circuit is the Sprint Cup (formerly Winston Cup) series, in which vehicles with engines as large as 750 horsepower reach speeds as high as 200 miles per hour.

**National Hotrod Association (NHRA):** Governing body of drag racing in the United States and Canada, founded in 1951.

**National Physique Committee (NPC):** Governing body of American amateur bodybuilding competitions.

**NHRA.** *See* National Hotrod Association.

**900:** Skateboarding trick in which a competitor rotates two and one-half times, or about 900 degrees, while in the air; first accomplished by Tony Hawk at the 1999 Summer X Games.

**nose:** Front end of a skateboard.

**nosegrind:** Grinding on only the front truck of a skateboard.

**noseslide:** Skateboarding trick in which the competitor slides the board's nose against a hard surface.

**NPC.** *See* National Physique Committee.

**oaks:** Race for female horses under the age of four. In England the cutoff age is five.

**ollie:** Skateboarding trick in which riders elevate their entire boards by quickly knocking their tail against the ground.

**omnium:** Track cycling event that involves a series of races, each at distances ranging from one-quarter mile to two miles.

**open wheel:** Race car with wheels on the outside of its body used in Formula One and CART.

**over:** Bowler who has scored above 200.

**pace car:** Car that leads participating race cars around the track prior to the start of a race.

**paceline:** Group of cyclists riding single file who alternate positions in order to expend as little energy as possible.

**par:** Bowling term for a single-game score of 200. Also known as a deuce.

**PBA.** *See* Professional Bowlers Association.

**PBR.** *See* Professional Bull Riders.

**peloton:** French term for pack—the main group of cyclists in a race, typically near the front of the field of competitors. In tour events, all cyclists who cross the finish line in a peloton are given the same finishing time.

**perfect game:** Bowling term for a game with a score of 300, the maximum number of points possible in a single game. A 300 game requires twelve consecutive strikes.

**pin:** One of the ten wooden figures that make up the bowling target.

**pin bowling:** Style of bowling that involves rolling the ball directly toward either a single pin or a specific pocket.

**pit stop:** Moment when an auto racer leaves the raceway for an off-track area to change the vehicle's tires, refuel, or have repairs done.

**pocket (bowling):** For a right-hander, the small space between the headpin (1-pin) and the 3-pin; for a left hander, between the headpin and the 2-pin. The likelihood of rolling a strike is greatest at these target points. The ten bowling pins are assembled in the shape of a triangle. The topmost pin closest to the bowler is the headpin, or 1-pin. The very next row, left to right, includes the 2-pin and the 3-pin, then come the 4-, the 5-, and the 6-pins, and finally pins 7, 8, 9, and 10.

**pole position:** Auto racing term for the innermost front-row position on the starting line. An advantage awarded to the driver with the fastest times in qualifying time trials held prior to the main racing event.

**pool:** Variation of billiards played on tables with six pockets into which balls are shot. Also known as pocket billiards.

**powerboating:** Racing sport in which motorboats race at high speeds across bodies of water.

**PRCA.** *See* Professional Rodeo Cowboys Association.

**Professional Bowlers Association (PBA):** Governing body of ten-pin bowling.

**Professional Bull Riders (PBR):** Organization founded in 1992 that oversees bull-riding competition in several countries, including the United States, Canada, and Mexico.

**Professional Rodeo Cowboys Association (PRCA):** Organization that sanctions and promotes rodeos in the United States.

**Prow.** *See* bow.

**pull:** To ride at the front of a group of cyclists, where the wind resistance is greatest and where the lead cyclist is without the benefit of a slipstream. Instead, the leader creates the drafting effect for the others. Cycling team members are expected to take turns pulling the others during a race in order to allow every member a chance to conserve energy while the team maintains the highest possible overall speed.

**pursuit:** Track cycling event in which individuals or teams of riders start the race at opposite sides of the oval track and try to overtake their opponents.

**quadriceps:** Muscles located at the front of the upper leg.

**qualifying:** For an individual athlete or a team of athletes, the act of becoming eligible for a particular game or tournament by fulfilling certain requirements. Qualifying can arise through a variety of ways, such as through preliminary heats or through individual statistics or through team win-loss records.

**rail:** Outer edge of the bottom half the skateboard deck.

*randori:* Judo sparring sessions designed to develop strength, speed, stamina, and technique. From a Japanese word for free exercise.

**regatta:** Series of races involving rowboats, sailboats, or speedboats.

**reins:** Straps connected to the horse's mouth, allowing the rider to control the horse's movements.

**rigging:** Apparatuses that support the masts and control the sails of a boat.

**rodeo:** Competitive sport modeled on jobs undertaken by cowboys, such as roping calves, riding bulls and unbroken horses, and wrestling steer.

**saddle:** Colloquial cycling term for the bicycle seat.

**saddle bronc riding:** Rodeo competition that involves riding a saddled wild, bucking horse for eight seconds using one hand to grip a strap attached to the saddle. Riders are judged on how well they ride and how hard the horse bucks. Rodeo's classic event has its roots in the Old West, when restless ranch hands would compete to see who was the best at riding wild horses.

**sail:** Large, billowing expanse of fabric, such as cotton or polyester, used on sailboats and ships to harness the wind and propel the vessels forward.

**sailing:** Water sport that involves mastery of numerous aspects related to the sailboat.

**schooner:** Fore-and-aft-rigged ship equipped with two or more masts. *See* rigging.

**seaworthy:** Condition of a boat that is able perform under normal conditions at sea.

**sensei:** Title accorded to instructors in the martial

arts such as judo. From a Japanese word for instructor.

**720:** Skateboarding trick in which skateboarders rotate two times, or 720 degrees, while in the air.

**shoot the tube:** To ride a surfboard into the hollow tunnel of water created by the curl of an ocean wave.

**sit-ski:** Much-wider-than-normal water ski with a seat affixed to the top. Invented especially for disabled athletes who are paralyzed from the waist down.

**skateboarding:** Extreme sport designed to be a type of land surfing in which participants ride on flat boards with wheels over varying terrain and obstacles.

**skatepark:** Designated area filled with ramps and other obstacles where skateboarders can practice techniques and tricks.

**skipper:** Person in charge of any vessel. Also known as captain on large vessels.

**slalom:** Waterskiing event that involves zigzagging through a line of buoys set out lengthwise across the water. One of three basic waterskiing events, the others being jump skiing and trick riding.

**slingshotting:** Maneuver in auto racing and cycling in which the slipstreaming car or cyclist uses the power and energy conserved to shoot past the lead racer.

**slipstreaming:** Riding in the slipstream, the pocket of reduced air resistance and forward suction behind a rapidly moving object, such as a lead race car, a lead cyclist, or a motorcycle, in order to conserve energy while maintaining speed. *See also* drafting.

**spare:** Bowling term for the feat of knocking down all ten pins with two balls in a single frame.

**spot bowling:** Style of bowling that involves rolling the ball across a specific marker—such as one of the seven triangular arrows set into the line just beyond the foul line—as the target point for releasing the ball.

**stage race:** Cycling race divided into a succession of individual stages or segments. Each stage is really only a shorter race. Distances of each race vary, sometimes greatly. Cyclists who win entire races are those with the lowest overall cumulative times. The Tour de France is the world's longest and most famous stage race.

**steeplechase:** Horse-racing event that takes place on a steeplechase course consisting of obstacles such as fences, water jumps, and open ditches.

**stock car:** Technically speaking, an unmodified race car that resembles its standard assembly-line model. In actuality, however, the likeness ends with the visible similarities. For the purposes of competition, stock cars are always modified to some degree to ensure peak performance. Alterations are often made to the engine and other critical components—whatever makes the car go faster.

**street skating:** Type of skateboarding that utilizes fixed objects in public places, such as curbs, handrails, and steps.

**strike:** Knocking down all ten bowling pins on the first roll in a single frame.

**strike out:** To finish a bowling game with consecutive strikes.

**strongman:** Strength competition that involves the lifting of various objects.

**stunt driving:** Activity involving motorcycles or automobiles in which riders or drivers leap over obstacles and perform other various tricks.

**sumo:** Traditional Japanese sport similar to wrestling in which two rikishi try to knock each other out of a circular playing surface.

**sumotori:** Japanese term for practitioner of sumo wrestling.

**superspeedway:** Oval course for auto racing at least two miles in circumference.

**surfing:** Water sport in which participants ride ocean waves standing on boards of varying sizes.

**tail:** Back end of a skateboard.

**thoroughbreds:** Racehorses bred for speed and stamina. Descended from Arabian stallions that were brought over to England between 1690 and 1730 and crossed with English racing mares. These sensitive, spirited animals have delicate heads, slender bodies, and long muscles and legs.

**time trial:** Form of cycling competition in which riders start races at timed intervals. The cyclist with the best time wins.

**top fuel:** Category of professional drag racing called the top fuel eliminators, featuring dragsters that burn a potent blend of methanol and nitromethane fuel. Top fuel vehicles are of two types—funny cars and top fuel dragsters—and are the most powerful piston-driven machines in the world. The driver relies primarily on a hand-activated parachute to stop the car, a process that can take as much as twelve hundred feet. Top fuel competition involves a series of elimination heats, two cars per heat. These cars are built with a lightweight tubular frame, wide rear tires, and a powerful engine placed front (funny cars) or back (top fuel dragsters) of the frame; they often reach speeds in the range of 290 miles per hour over the one-quarter-mile course. *See also* funny car.

**Tour de France:** Three-week-long cycling event held each July in France (and sometimes extending into neighboring countries), widely regarded as the most prestigious cycling race in the world.

**tours:** Most important and usually the longest stage races of the international cycling season. A tour is won by completing all of the stages in the shortest amount of time. The most famous of these is the approximately 2,200-mile-long Tour de France.

**train:** Fast paceline in cycling.

**triathlon:** Rigorous multisport competition that involves long-distance swimming, biking, and running races. *See* Ironman Triathlon.

**triceps:** Muscles located at the back of the upper arm, opposite the biceps.

**trim:** To adjust the sails of a vessel in order to keep it on course as wind conditions change.

**triple crown of U.S. thoroughbred racing:** Unofficial championship title awarded to horses that wins the Kentucky Derby, Preakness Stakes, and Belmont Stakes during the same season. Through 2009, only eleven horses had won the triple crown. Ironically, the last three winners, Seattle Slew (1973), Secretariat (1977), and Affirmed (1978) all won during a single decade.

**triple:** Bowling term for three consecutive strikes.

**trucks:** Axles that connect skateboard decks to their wheels.

**UCI.** *See* Union Cycliste Internationale.

**Union Cycliste Internationale (UCI):** Cycling's international governing body.

**United States Bowling Congress (USBC):** Sanctioning body of ten-pin bowling in the United States. The organization was formed in 2005 through a merger between American Bowling Congress (ABC), USA Bowling (USAB), Women's International Bowling Congress (WIBC), and Young American Bowling Alliance (YABA).

**USA Cycling:** Cycling's governing body in the United States, based in Colorado Springs, Colorado.

**USBC.** *See* United States Bowling Congress.

**velodrome:** Cycling racetrack with banked turns that is usually constructed of wood or concrete. Modern Olympic velodromes are indoor arenas, but most velodromes are built outdoors.

**vert skating:** Type of skateboarding done on ramps and apparatuses specifically designed for skateboarding.

**victory lane:** Place on the infield of a race course where winners celebrate after races.

**victory lap:** Extra lap taken by the winning cyclist or driver after a race is over in a gesture of celebration between athlete and spectator.

**waterskiing:** Sport in which participants ride across a body of water, often performing tricks, with skis attached to both feet while holding on to a rope pulled by a motorboat.

*wing chun:* Chinese martial art that emphasizes close-range fighting.

**WIBC.** *See* Women's International Bowling Congress.

**winner's circle:** Section apart from a racetrack's finish line where winning jockeys and horses are officially recognized after races.

**Women's International Bowling Congress (WIBC):** Organization that oversaw women's bowling from 1919 to 2005, when it became part of the United States Bowling Congress.

**World Surfing Champion:** Annual title given to the surfer with the best combined finishes over the course of the year's competition.

**World's Strongest Man:** Strength competition featuring numerous lifting events, ranging from tradition—Atlas Stones—to the offbeat—Keg Toss. *See also* strongman.

**X Games:** Olympics-style competition for extreme sports, such as skateboarding, BMX, and snowboarding; held in both the summer and the winter seasons.

**yachting:** Water sport in which yachts powered by sails race at high speeds in often treacherous maritime conditions. *See* America's Cup.

**yellow flag:** In auto racing, the caution flag, indicating that an accident has occurred or wreckage is on the track.

**yellow jersey:** Shirt worn by the overall leader during each stage of the Tour de France.

*yokozuna:* Japanese term for grand champion of sumo.

*Christopher Rager*

# Racing and Individual Sport Athletes Time Line

| Birthdate | Athlete | Sport | Nationality |
|---|---|---|---|
| April 2, 1867 | Eugen Sandow | Bodybuilding | Germany |
| January 1, 1878 | Bobby Walthour | Cycling | United States |
| January 29, 1878 | Barney Oldfield | Auto racing | United States |
| November 26, 1878 | Major Taylor | Cycling | United States |
| July 22, 1888 | Floretta Doty McCutcheon | Bowling | United States |
| May 9, 1900 | Bob Askin | Rodeo | United States |
| June 19, 1906 | Earl W. Bascom | Rodeo | United States |
| February 14, 1907 | Johnny Longden | Horse racing | England |
| June 24, 1911 | Juan Manuel Fangio | Auto racing | Argentina |
| June 27, 1913 | Willie Mosconi | Billiards | United States |
| March 14, 1914 | Lee Petty | Auto racing | United States |
| October 30, 1914 | Marion Ladewig | Bowling | United States |
| February 19, 1916 | Eddie Arcaro | Horse racing | United States |
| August 11, 1917 | Abbye Stockton | Bodybuilding | United States |
| July 20, 1919 | Sir Edmund Hillary | Mountaineering | New Zealand |
| August 28, 1921 | Wendell Scott | Auto racing | United States |
| February 8, 1925 | Raimondo D'Inezeo | Equestrian | Italy |
| January 21, 1926 | Steve Reeves | Bodybuilding | United States |
| July 29, 1926 | Don Carter | Bowling | United States |
| February 25, 1928 | Paul Elvstrøm | Yachting | Denmark |
| May 13, 1928 | Jim Shoulders | Rodeo | United States |
| November 12, 1928 | Bill Muncey | Speed boat/hydroplane racing | United States |
| March 5, 1929 | Casey Tibbs | Rodeo | United States |
| December 23, 1929 | Dick Weber | Bowling | United States |
| April 13, 1931 | Dan Gurney | Auto racing | United States |
| August 19, 1931 | Willie Shoemaker | Horse racing | United States |
| January 14, 1932 | Don Garlits | Auto racing | United States |
| December 9, 1932 | Bill Hartack | Horse racing | United States |
| November 23, 1933 | Carmen Salvino | Bowling | United States |
| February 20, 1934 | Bobby Unser | Auto racing | United States |
| December 22, 1934 | David Pearson | Auto racing | United States |
| January 16, 1935 | A. J. Foyt | Auto racing | United States |
| November 5, 1935 | Lester Piggott | Horse racing | England |
| March 4, 1936 | Jim Clark | Auto racing | Scotland |
| March 18, 1937 | Mark Donohue | Auto racing | United States |
| July 2, 1937 | Richard Petty | Auto racing | United States |
| December 3, 1937 | Bobby Allison | Auto racing | United States |
| March 7, 1938 | Janet Guthrie | Auto racing | United States |
| March 12, 1938 | Johnny Rutherford | Auto racing | United States |
| April 27, 1938 | Earl Anthony | Bowling | United States |

| Birthdate | Athlete | Sport | Nationality |
|---|---|---|---|
| August 19, 1938 | Valentin Mankin | Yachting | Soviet Union |
| October 17, 1938 | Evel Knievel | Stunt driving | United States |
| November 19, 1938 | Ted Turner | Yachting | United States |
| March 27, 1939 | Cale Yarborough | Auto racing | United States |
| May 29, 1939 | Al Unser | Auto racing | United States |
| June 11, 1939 | Jackie Stewart | Auto racing | Scotland |
| September 22, 1939 | Junko Tabei | Mountaineering | Japan |
| February 28, 1940 | Mario Andretti | Auto racing | United States |
| March 14, 1940 | Roland Martin | Angling | United States |
| May 29, 1940 | Kōki Taihō | Sumo wrestling | Japan |
| June 19, 1940 | Shirley Muldowney | Auto racing | United States |
| April 6, 1941 | Don Prudhomme | Auto racing | United States |
| November 8, 1942 | Ángel Cordero, Jr. | Horse racing | Puerto Rico |
| February 4, 1943 | Wanda Rutkiewicz | Mountaineering | Poland |
| March 9, 1943 | Bobby Fischer | Chess | United States |
| September 16, 1943 | Dennis Conner | Yachting | United States |
| November 21, 1943 | Larry Mahan | Rodeo | United States |
| September 6, 1944 | Kenny Bernstein | Auto racing | United States |
| September 17, 1944 | Reinhold Messner | Mountaineering | Italy |
| June 17, 1945 | Eddy Merckx | Cycling | Belgium |
| December 12, 1946 | Emerson Fittipaldi | Auto racing | Brazil |
| December 29, 1946 | Laffit Pincay, Jr. | Horse racing | Panama |
| March 13, 1947 | Lyn St. James | Auto racing | United States |
| July 30, 1947 | Arnold Schwarzenegger | Bodybuilding | United States |
| September 9, 1947 | Corky Carroll | Surfing | United States |
| February 22, 1949 | Niki Lauda | Auto racing | Austria |
| May 4, 1949 | John Force | Drag racing | United States |
| 1950 | Gary Fisher | Mountain biking | United States |
| December 20, 1950 | Tom Ferguson | Rodeo | United States |
| April 29, 1951 | Dale Earnhardt | Auto racing | United States |
| May 23, 1951 | Anatoly Karpov | Chess | Soviet Union |
| September 21, 1951 | Eddie Delahoussaye | Horse racing | United States |
| December 3, 1951 | Rick Mears | Auto racing | United States |
| January 10, 1953 | Bobby Rahal | Auto racing | United States |
| August 8, 1953 | Nigel Mansell | Auto racing | England |
| October 13, 1953 | Pat Day | Horse racing | United States |
| January 4, 1954 | Dave Scott | Triathlon | United States |
| February 10, 1954 | Dave Villwock | Hydroplane racing | United States |
| July 1, 1954 | Chip Hanauer | Hydroplane racing | United States |
| November 14, 1954 | Bernard Hinault | Cycling | France |
| December 26, 1954 | Susan Butcher | Sled-dog racing | United States |
| January 3, 1955 | Willy T. Ribbs | Auto racing | United States |
| February 24, 1955 | Alain Prost | Auto racing | France |
| March 27, 1955 | Chris McCarron | Horse racing | United States |
| August 14, 1956 | Rusty Wallace | Auto racing | United States |
| February 26, 1957 | Connie Carpenter | Cycling, speed skating | United States |
| January 12, 1958 | Mark Allen | Triathlon | United States |
| August 7, 1958 | Russell Baze | Horse racing | Canada |

| Birthdate | Athlete | Sport | Nationality |
|---|---|---|---|
| October 1, 1958 | Bill Bowness | Waterskiing | United States |
| October 31, 1958 | Jeannie Longo | Cycling | France |
| October 6, 1959 | Walter Ray Williams, Jr. | Bowling, horseshoes | United States |
| November 11, 1959 | Lee Haney | Bodybuilding | United States |
| March 21, 1960 | Ayrton Senna | Auto racing | Brazil |
| June 2, 1960 | Kyle Petty | Auto racing | United States |
| September 17, 1960 | Damon Hill | Auto racing | England |
| 1961 | Lynn Hill | Mountaineering | United States |
| May 19, 1961 | Lisa Wagner | Bowling | United States |
| June 26, 1961 | Greg LeMond | Cycling | United States |
| July 4, 1961 | Connie Paraskevin-Young | Cycling, speed skating | United States |
| March 1, 1962 | Russell Coutts | Yachting | New Zealand |
| June 2, 1962 | Paula Newby-Fraser | Triathlon | Zimbabwe |
| August 21, 1962 | Pete Weber | Bowling | United States |
| April 13, 1963 | Garry Kasparov | Chess | Soviet Union |
| July 24, 1963 | Julie Krone | Horse racing | United States |
| May 13, 1964 | Ronnie Coleman | Bodybuilding | United States |
| July 3, 1964 | Tom Curren | Surfing | United States |
| July 16, 1964 | Miguel Indurain | Cycling | Spain |
| October 28, 1965 | Martin Potter | Surfing | England |
| December 12, 1966 | Royce Gracie | Martial arts | Brazil |
| June 29, 1967 | Jeff Burton | Auto racing | United States |
| May 12, 1968 | Tony Hawk | Skateboarding | United States |
| September 28, 1968 | Mika Häkkinen | Auto racing | Finland |
| January 3, 1969 | Michael Schumacher | Auto racing | Germany |
| May 8, 1969 | Akebono | Sumo wrestling | United States |
| October 11, 1969 | Ty Murray | Rodeo | United States |
| December 11, 1969 | Viswanathan Anand | Chess | India |
| December 21, 1969 | Magnus Samuelsson | Strongman | Sweden |
| April 9, 1971 | Jacques Villeneuve | Auto racing | Canada |
| May 20, 1971 | Tony Stewart | Auto racing | United States |
| July 9, 1971 | Jeanette Lee | Billiards | United States |
| August 4, 1971 | Jeff Gordon | Auto racing | United States |
| September 18, 1971 | Lance Armstrong | Cycling | United States |
| February 11, 1972 | Kelly Slater | Surfing | United States |
| May 24, 1972 | Layne Beachley | Surfing | Australia |
| December 2, 1973 | Jan Ullrich | Cycling | Germany |
| April 4, 1974 | Dave Mirra | Freestyle bicycle motocross | United States |
| October 10, 1974 | Dale Earnhardt, Jr. | Auto racing | United States |
| May 16, 1975 | Simon Whitfield | Triathlon | Canada |
| June 25, 1975 | Vladimir Kramnik | Chess | Russia |
| March 23, 1976 | Chris Hoy | Cycling | Scotland |
| July 8, 1976 | Ellen MacArthur | Sailing | England |
| November 16, 1976 | Trevor Brazile | Rodeo | United States |
| August 23, 1978 | Kenny Bartram | Motocross | United States |
| February 16, 1979 | Valentino Rossi | Motorcycle racing | Italy |
| March 25, 1982 | Danica Patrick | Auto racing | United States |
| January 7, 1985 | Lewis Hamilton | Auto racing | England |

# All-Time Great Athletes

# Chess Halls of Fame

The U.S. Chess Hall of Fame was launched in Washington, D.C., in 1985, when it made Paul Morphy and Bobby Fischer charter members. Morphy and Fischer were also charter members of the World Chess Hall of Fame, which was established in Miami, Florida, in 2001. Members of both halls, with their dates of induction, are listed below.

## U.S. Chess Hall of Fame

Lev Alburt (2003)
Pal Benko (1993)
Hans Berliner (1990)
Arthur Bisguier (1994)
Walter Shawn Browne (2003)
Donald Byrne (2003)
Robert Byrne (1994)
John Collins (1991)
Arthur Dake (1991)
Arnold Denker (1992)
Ed Edmondson (1995)
Arpad Elo (1988)
Larry Evans (1994)
Reuben Fine (1986)
Bobby Fischer (1985)
Benjamin Franklin (1999)
Gisela Gresser (1992)
Kenneth Harkness (1997)

Hermann Helms (1988)
Al Horowitz (1989)
Isaac Kashdan (1986)
Lubomir Kavalek (2001)
George Koltanowski (1986)
Anatoly Lein (2004)
Sam Loyd (1987)
George Mackenzie (1992)
Frank Marshall (1986)
Edmar Mednis (2000)
Paul Morphy (1985)
Victor Palciauskas (1993)
Harry Pillsbury (1986)
Fred Reinfeld (1996)
Samuel Reshevsky (1986)
Leonid Shamkovitch (2004)
Wilhelm Steinitz (1987)
Milan Vukcevich (1998)

## World Chess Hall of Fame

Alexander Alekhine (2004)
Mikhail Botvinnik (2003)
Jose Raúl Capablanca (2001)
Max Euwe (2004)
Bobby Fischer (2001)
Anatoly Karpov (2004)
Emanuel Lasker (2001)
Paul Morphy (2001)
Tigran Petrosian (2003)
Vasily Smyslov (2003)
Boris Spassky (2003)
Mikhail Tal (2003)
Wilhelm Steinitz (2001)

# Cycling Hall of Fame.com Top 25 Cyclists

1. Eddy Merckx, Belgium
2. Bernard Hinault, France
3. Lance Armstrong, United States
4. Jacques Anquetil, France
5. Fausto Coppi, Italy
6. Miguel Indurain, Spain
7. Gino Bartali, Italy
8. Louison Bobet, France
9. Felice Gimondi, Italy
10. Greg Lemond, United States
11. Joop Zoetemelk, Holland
12. Alfredo Binda, Italy
13. Lucien Van Impe, Belgium
14. Jan Ullrich, Germany
15. Sean Kelly, Ireland
16. Laurent Fignon, France
17. Rik Van Looy, Belgium
18. Francesco Moser, Italy
19. Federico Bahamontes, Spain
20. Jan Janssen, Holland
21. Philippe Thys, France
22. Raymond Poulidor, France
23. Charly Gaul, Luxembourg
24. Erik Zabel, Germany
25. Antonin Magne, France

# Eclipse Award for Outstanding Jockey

Every January since 1971, the National Thoroughbred Racing Association, in conjunction with the *Daily Racing Form* and the National Turf Writers Association, has bestowed its Eclipse Award on the previous year's most outstanding jockey. Other Eclipse Awards are given in several categories of outstanding racehorses, and the award itself is named after a famous eighteenth century racehorse. In 1995, jockey Russell Baze became the first jockey to win at least four hundred races four years in a row and was rewarded with the Eclipse Special Award.

| | | | |
|---|---|---|---|
| 1971 | Laffit Pincay, Jr. | 1990 | Craig Perret |
| 1972 | Braulio Baeza | 1991 | Pat Day |
| 1973 | Laffit Pincay, Jr. | 1992 | Kent Desormeaux |
| 1974 | Laffit Pincay, Jr. | 1993 | Mike Smith |
| 1975 | Braulio Baeza | 1994 | Mike Smith |
| 1976 | Sandy Hawley | 1995 | Jerry Bailey |
| 1977 | Steve Cauthen | 1996 | Jerry Bailey |
| 1978 | Darrel McHargue | 1997 | Jerry Bailey |
| 1979 | Laffit Pincay, Jr. | 1998 | Gary Stevens |
| 1980 | Chris McCarron | 1999 | Jorge Chavez |
| 1981 | William Shoemaker | 2000 | Jerry Bailey |
| 1982 | Angel Cordero, Jr. | 2001 | Jerry Bailey |
| 1983 | Angel Cordero, Jr. | 2002 | Jerry Bailey |
| 1984 | Pat Day | 2003 | Jerry Bailey |
| 1985 | Laffit Pincay, Jr. | 2004 | John Velazquez |
| 1986 | Pat Day | 2005 | John Velazquez |
| 1987 | Pat Day | 2006 | Edgar Prado |
| 1988 | Jose Santos | 2007 | Garrett Gomez |
| 1989 | Kent Desormeaux | 2008 | Garrett Gomez |

# Formula One World Drivers Champions

Every year since 1950, the Fédération Internationale de l'Automobile (FIA) has named a single Formula One driver its world champion. The champions are determined by a point-scoring system based on the year's races.

| | |
|---|---|
| 1950 Nino Farina | 1980 Alan Jones |
| 1951 Juan Manuel Fangio | 1981 Nelson Piquet |
| 1952 Alberto Ascari | 1982 Keke Rosberg |
| 1953 Alberto Ascari | 1983 Nelson Piquet |
| 1954 Juan Manuel Fangio | 1984 Niki Lauda |
| 1955 Juan Manuel Fangio | 1985 Alain Prost |
| 1956 Juan Manuel Fangio | 1986 Alain Prost |
| 1957 Juan Manuel Fangio | 1987 Nelson Piquet |
| 1958 Mike Hawthorn | 1988 Ayrton Senna |
| 1959 Jack Brabham | 1989 Alain Prost |
| 1960 Jack Brabham | 1990 Ayrton Senna |
| 1961 Phil Hill | 1991 Ayrton Senna |
| 1962 Graham Hill | 1992 Nigel Mansell |
| 1963 Jim Clark | 1993 Alain Prost |
| 1964 John Surtees | 1994 Michael Schumacher |
| 1965 Jim Clark | 1995 Michael Schumacher |
| 1966 Jack Brabham | 1996 Damon Hill |
| 1967 Denny Hulme | 1997 Jacques Villeneuve |
| 1968 Graham Hill | 1998 Mika Hakkinen |
| 1969 Jackie Stewart | 1999 Mika Hakkinen |
| 1970 Jochen Rindt | 2000 Michael Schumacher |
| 1971 Jackie Stewart | 2001 Michael Schumacher |
| 1972 Emerson Fittipaldi | 2002 Michael Schumacher |
| 1973 Jackie Stewart | 2003 Michael Schumacher |
| 1974 Emerson Fittipaldi | 2004 Michael Schumacher |
| 1975 Niki Lauda | 2005 Fernando Alonso |
| 1976 James Hunt | 2006 Fernando Alonso |
| 1977 Niki Lauda | 2007 Kimi Räikkönen |
| 1978 Mario Andretti | 2008 Lewis Hamilton |
| 1979 Jody Scheckter | |

# Indianapolis 500 Winners

| | | |
|---|---|---|
| 1911 Ray Harroun | 1946 George Robson | 1979 Rick Mears |
| 1912 Joe Dawson | 1947 Mauri Rose | 1980 Johnny Rutherford |
| 1913 Jules Goux | 1948 Mauri Rose | 1981 Bobby Unser |
| 1914 Rene Thomas | 1949 Bill Holland | 1982 Gordon Johncock |
| 1915 Ralph DePalma | 1950 Johnnie Parsons | 1983 Tom Sneva |
| 1916 Dario Resta | 1951 Lee Wallard | 1984 Rick Mears |
| 1917-1918 (no races) | 1952 Troy Ruttman | 1985 Danny Sullivan |
| 1919 Howdy Wilcox | 1953 Bill Vukovich | 1986 Bobby Rahal |
| 1920 Gaston Chevrolet | 1954 Bill Vukovich | 1987 Al Unser |
| 1921 Tommy Milton | 1955 Bob Sweikert | 1988 Rick Mears |
| 1922 Jimmy Murphy | 1956 Pat Flaherty | 1989 Emerson Fittipaldi |
| 1923 Tommy Milton | 1957 Sam Hanks | 1990 Arie Luyendyk |
| 1924 Joe Boye | 1958 Jimmy Bryan | 1991 Rick Mears |
|      L. L. Corum | 1959 Rodger Ward | 1992 Al Unser, Jr. |
| 1925 Pete DePaolo | 1960 Jim Rathmann | 1993 Emerson Fittipaldi |
| 1926 Frank Lockhart | 1961 A. J. Foyt | 1994 Al Unser, Jr. |
| 1927 George Souders | 1962 Rodger Ward | 1995 Jacques Villeneuve |
| 1928 Louis Meyer | 1963 Parnelli Jones | 1996 Buddy Lazier |
| 1929 Ray Keech | 1964 A. J. Foyt | 1997 Arie Luyendyk |
| 1930 Billy Arnold | 1965 Jim Clark | 1998 Eddie Cheever, Jr. |
| 1931 Louis Schneider | 1966 Graham Hill | 1999 Kenny Brack |
| 1932 Fred Frame | 1967 A. J. Foyt | 2000 Juan Pablo Montoya |
| 1933 Louis Meyer | 1968 Bobby Unser | 2001 Helio Castroneves |
| 1934 Bill Cummings | 1969 Mario Andretti | 2002 Helio Castroneves |
| 1935 Kelly Petillo | 1970 Al Unser | 2003 Gil de Ferran |
| 1936 Louis Meyer | 1971 Al Unser | 2004 Buddy Rice |
| 1937 Wilbur Shaw | 1972 Mark Donohue | 2005 Dan Wheldon |
| 1938 Floyd Roberts | 1973 Gordon Johncock | 2006 Sam Hornish, Jr. |
| 1939 Wilbur Shaw | 1974 Johnny Rutherford | 2007 Dario Franchitti |
| 1940 Wilbur Shaw | 1975 Bobby Unser | 2008 Scott Dixon |
| 1941 Floyd Davis | 1976 Johnny Rutherford | 2009 Helio Castroneves |
|      Mauri Rose | 1977 A. J. Foyt | |
| 1942-1945 (no races) | 1978 Al Unser | |

# Jockeys' Hall of Fame

A branch of the National Museum of Racing and Hall of Fame in Saratoga Springs, New York, the Jockeys' Hall of Fame inducted its first members in 1955. Members are listed below, with their dates of induction.

Frank D. Adams (1970)
John Adams (1965)
Joe Aitcheson, Jr. (1978)
G. Edward Arcaro (1958)
Ted F. Atkinson (1957)
Braulio Baeza (1976)
Jerry Bailey (1995)
George Barbee (1996)
Caroll K. Bassett (1972)
Russell Baze (1999)
Walter Blum (1987)
William N. Boland (2006)
George Bostwick (1968)
Sam Boulmetis, Sr. (1973)
Steve Brooks (1963)
Don Brumfield (1996)
Thomas H. Burns (1983)
James H. Butwell (1984)
J. Dallett Byers (1967)
Steve Cauthen (1994)
Frank Coltiletti (1970)
Angel Cordero, Jr. (1988)
Robert H. Crawford (1973)
Pat Day (1991)
Eddie Delahoussaye (1993)
Kent Desormeaux (2004)
Lavelle Ensor (1962)
Laverne Fator (1955)
Earlie Fires (2001)
Jerry Fishback (1992)

Mack Garner (1969)
Edward Garrison (1955)
Avelino Gomez (1982)
Henry F. Griffin (1956)
O. Eric Guerin (1972)
William J. Hartack (1959)
Sandy Hawley (1992)
Albert Johnson (1971)
William J. Knapp (1969)
Julie Krone (2000)
Clarence Kummer (1972)
Charles Kurtsinger (1967)
John P. Loftus (1959)
John Eric Longden (1958)
J. Linus McAtee (1956)
Chris McCarron (1989)
Conn McCreary (1974)
Rigan McKinney (1968)
James McLaughlin (1955)
Daniel A. Maher (1955)
Walter Miller (1955)
Isaac B. Murphy (1955)
Ralph Neves (1960)
Joe Notter (1963)
Winfield O'Connor (1956)
George M. Odom (1955)
Frank O'Neill (1956)
Ivan H. Parke (1978)
Gilbert W. Patrick (1970)
Laffit Pincay, Jr. (1975)

Samuel Purdy (1970)
John Reiff (1956)
Alfred Robertson (1971)
John L. Rotz (1983)
Earl Sande (1955)
Jose Santos (2007)
John Sellers (2007)
Carroll H. Shilling (1970)
William Shoemaker (1958)
Willie Simms (1977)
Tod Sloan (1955)
Mike Smith (2003)
Alfred P. Smithwick (1973)
Gary Stevens (1997)
James Stout (1968)
Fred Taral (1955)
Bayard Tuckerman, Jr. (1973)
Ron Turcotte (1979)
Nash Turner (1955)
Robert N. Ussery (1980)
Jacinto Vasquez (1998)
Jorge Velasquez (1990)
Thomas Walsh (2005)
Jack Westrope (2002)
Jimmy Winkfield (2004)
George M. Woolf (1955)
Raymond Workman (1956)
Manuel Ycaza (1977)

# Motorsports Hall of Fame

The Motorsports Hall of Fame is operated by the Motorsports Museum and Hall of America Foundation, Inc. in Novi, Michigan. The hall honors drivers, pilots, designers, owners, builders, and maintainers of all forms of motorized vehicles that compete for speed, distance, and other records. Chosen by a panel of historians, journalists, prior inductees, and retired competitors, inductees must either have been retired from competition for at least three years or have been engaged at the top levels of their fields for twenty years to be eligible. Members are inducted in nine fields: air racing, at large, drag racing, historic, motorcycles, open wheel, power boats, sports cars, and stock cars. This list includes all members inducted through 2007. Dates of their induction are given in parentheses.

## Air Racing
Cook Cleland (2000)
Jacqueline Cochran (1993)
Glenn Curtiss (1990)
Jimmy Doolittle (1989)
Amelia Earhart (1992)
Bill Falck (1994)
Darryl Greenamyer (1997)
Tony LeVier (2001)
Paul Mantz (2002)
Lyle Shelton (1999)
Roscoe Turner (1991)
Steve Wittman (1998)

## At Large
J. C. Agajanian (1992)
Art Arfons (1991)
George Bignotti (1993)
Clint Brawner (1998)
Craig Breedlove (1993)
Malcolm Campbell (1994)
Tom Carnegie (2006)
Colin Chapman (1997)
Chris Economaki (1994)
Shav Glick (2004)
Andy Granatelli (2001)
John Holman (2005)
Tony Hulman (1991)
Parnelli Jones (1992)
Frank Kurtis (1999)
Leo Mehl (2007)
Ralph Moody (2005)
Fred Offenhauser (2002)
Barney Oldfield (1989)
Roger Penske (1995)

Bill Simpson (2003)
Mickey Thompson (1990)
A. J. Watson (1996)
Smokey Yunick (2000)

## Drag Racing
Joe Amato (2004)
Keith Black (1995)
Art Chrisman (1997)
Ed Donovan (2003)
Don Garlits (1989)
Bob Glidden (1994)
C. J. Hart (1999)
Eddie Hill (2002)
Tommy Ivo (2005)
Bill Jenkins (1996)
Connie Kalitta (1992)
Chris Karamesines (2006)
Tom McEwen (2001)
Buddy Martin (2007)
Shirley Muldowney (1990)
Don Nicholson (1998)
Danny Ongais (2000)
Wally Parks (1993)
Don Prudhomme (1991)
Ronnie Sox (2007)

## Historic
Wilbur Shaw (1991)
Ralph DePalma (1992)
Louis Meyer (1993)
Eddie Rickenbacker (1994)
Louis Chevrolet (1995)
Rex Mays (1995)
Peter DePaolo (1995)

Henry Ford (1996)
Mauri Rose (1996)
Fred Duesenburg (1997)
Tommy Milton (1998)
Jimmy Murphy (1998)
Frank Lockhart (1999)
Harry Miller (1999)
Ray Harroun (2000)
Earl Cooper (2001)
Gaston Chevrolet (2002)
Tommy Hinnershitz (2003)
Johnnie Parsons (2004)
Troy Ruttman (2005)
Curtis Turner (2006)
Jim Rathmann (2007)

## Motorcycles
Cannon Ball Baker (1989)
Jim Davis (1997)
Roger DeCoster (1994)
Bob Hannah (2000)
Eddie Lawson (2002)
Joe Leonard (1991)
Dick Mann (1993)
Bart Markel (1999)
Gary Nixon (2003)
Joe Petrali (1992)
Carroll Resweber (1998)
Kenny Roberts (1990)
Bubba Shobert (2007)
Malcolm Smith (1996)
Freddie Spencer (2001)
Jay Springsteen (2005)
Don Vesco (2004)
Jeff Ward (2006)

## Open Wheel

Mario Andretti (1990)
Tony Bettenhausen (1997)
Jimmy Bryan (1999)
Jim Clark (1990)
Emerson Fittipaldi (2001)
A. J. Foyt (1989)
Sam Hanks (2000)
Ted Horn (1993)
Gordon Johncock (2002)
Mel Kenyon (2003)
Jim McGee (2007)
Nigel Mansell (2006)
Rick Mears (1998)
Bobby Rahal (2004)
Johnny Rutherford (1996)
Tom Sneva (2005)
Al Unser, Sr. (1991)
Bobby Unser (1994)
Bill Vukovich, Sr. (1992)
Rodger Ward (1995)

## Power Boats

Bill Cantrell (1992)
Dean Chenoweth (1991)
Betty Cook (1996)
Tom D'Eath (2000)

Danny Foster (2005)
Chip Hanauer (1995)
Ted Jones (2003)
Carl Kiekhaefer (1998)
Bernie Little (1994)
Bill Muncey (1989)
Ron Musson (1993)
Bob Nordskog (1997)
Bill Seebold (1999)
Mira Slovak (2001)
Gar Wood (1990)

## Sports Cars

Bob Bondurant (2003)
Geoff Brabham (2004)
Briggs Cunningham (1997)
Mark Donohue (1990)
John Fitch (2007)
George Follmer (1999)
Elliott Forbes-Robinson (2006)
Peter Gregg (2000)
Dan Gurney (1991)
Jim Hall (1994)
Hurley Haywood (2005)
Phil Hill (1989)
Al Holbert (1993)
Denis Hulme (1998)

Bruce McLaren (1995)
Ken Miles (2001)
Brian Redman (2002)
Peter Revson (1996)
Carroll Shelby (1992)

## Stock Cars

Bobby Allison (1992)
Buck Baker (1998)
Wood Brothers (2000)
Dale Earnhardt (2002)
Bill Elliott (2007)
Tim Flock (1999)
Bill France, Jr. (2004)
William France, Sr. (1990)
Ned Jarrett (1997)
Junior Johnson (1991)
Fred Lorenzen (2001)
Hershel McGriff (2006)
Benny Parsons (2005)
David Pearson (1993)
Lee Petty (1996)
Richard Petty (1989)
Glenn Roberts (1995)
Darrell Waltrip (2003)
Cale Yarborough (1994)

# NASCAR's Fifty Greatest Drivers

As NASCAR approached its fiftieth anniversary in 1998, it followed the example of the National Basketball Association by forming a panel to select the fifty greatest drivers in its history. The thirty-six selected drivers who were still living at that time were invited to attend a special ceremony at the Daytona 500 International Speedway in February, 1998.

| | | |
|---|---|---|
| Bobby Allison | Ray Hendrick | David Pearson |
| Davey Allison | Jack Ingram | Lee Petty |
| Buck Baker | Ernee Irvan | Richard Petty |
| Buddy Baker | Bobby Isaac | Tim Richmond |
| Geoffrey Bodine | Dale Jarrett | Edward Glenn "Fireball" Roberts |
| Neil Bonnett | Ned Jarrett | Ricky Rudd |
| Robert "Red" Byron | Robert "Junior" Johnson | Marshall Teague |
| Jerry Cook | Jimmie Johnson | Herb Thomas |
| Dale Earnhardt | Alan Kulwicki | Curtis Turner |
| Ralph Earnhardt | Terry Labonte | Rusty Wallace |
| Bill Elliott | Fred Lorenzen | Darrell Waltrip |
| Richie Evans | DeWayne "Tiny" Lund | Joe Weatherly |
| Charles "Red" Farmer | Hershel McGriff | Bob Welborn |
| Tim Flock | Mark Martin | Rex White |
| A. J. Foyt | Everett "Cotton" Owens | Glen Wood |
| Harry Gant | Marvin Panch | Cale Yarborough |
| Jeff Gordon | Benny Parsons | Lee Roy Yarbrough |

# Professional Bowlers Association Hall of Fame

The Professional Bowlers Association Hall of Fame inducts members under several categories, including performance, meritorious service, and veterans. The members listed here are those who have been inducted based on their competitive bowling performances. Their years of induction are given in parentheses.

Bill Allen (1983)
Earl Anthony (1981)
Mike Aulby (1996)
Joe Berardi (1989)
Bluth Ray (1975)
Parker Bohn III (2000)
Roy Buckley (1992)
Nelson Burton, Jr. (1979)
Don Carter (1975)
Paul Colwell (1991)
Steve Cook (1993)
Dave Davis (1978)
Gary Dickinson (1988)
Mike Durbin (1984)

Buzz Fazio (1976)
David Ferraro (1997)
Jim Godman (1987)
Billy Hardwick (1977)
Marshall Holman (1990)
Tommy Hudson (1989)
Dave Husted (1996)
Don Johnson (1977)
Larry Laub (1985)
Amleto Monacelli (1997)
David Ozio (1995)
George Pappas (1986)
John Petraglia (1982)
Dick Ritger (1978)

Mark Roth (1987)
Carmen Salvino (1975)
Harry Smith (1975)
Dave Soutar (1979)
Jim Stefanich (1980)
Brian Voss (1994)
Wayne Webb (1993)
Dick Weber (1975)
Pete Weber (1998)
Billy Welu (1975)
Mark Williams (1999)
Walter Ray Williams, Jr. (1995)
Wayne Zahn (1981)

# Surfers' Hall of Fame

Headquartered in the iconic surfers' center of Huntington Beach, California, the Surfers' Hall of Fame inducted its first members in 2002. Members with their years of induction are listed below.

Lisa Andersen (2002)
Robert August (2002)
Wayne "Rabbit" Bartholomew (2008)
Layne Beachley (2006)
Corky Carroll (2002)
Tom Carroll (2005)
Sean Collins (2008)
Tom Curren (2003)
Mike Doyle (2003)
Brad Gerlach (2008)
Jack Haley (2004)
Laird Hamilton (2002)

Carl Hayward (2005)
Bob Hurley (2006)
Andy Irons (2003)
Bruce Irons (2007)
Bud Llamas (2003)
Gerry Lopez (2004)
Rob Machado (2006)
Bob McKnight (2005)
Al Merrick (2007)
Sofia Mulanovich (2007)
Greg Noll (2006)
David Nuuhiwa (2004)
Mark Occhilupo (2004)

Jack O'Neill (2003)
Mike Parsons (2008)
Jericho Poppler (2004)
Martin Potter (2007)
Mark Richards (2005)
Kelly Slater (2002)
Paul Strauch (2003)
Shaun Tomson (2003)
Peter Townend (2004)
Joel Tudor (2002)
Robert "Wingnut" Weaver (2002)

# Indexes

# Name Index

# Country Index

# Sport Index